Core 1 & 2

Core 1 & 2

Hugh Neill and Douglas Quadling

Series editor Hugh Neill

CAMBRIDGE
UNIVERSITY PRESS

CAMBRIDGE UNIVERSITY PRESS
Cambridge, New York, Melbourne, Madrid, Cape Town, Singapore,
São Paulo, Delhi, Dubai, Tokyo, Mexico City

Cambridge University Press
The Edinburgh Building, Cambridge CB2 8RU, UK

www.cambridge.org
Information on this title: www.cambridge.org/9780521548960

First published 2004
8th printing 2010

Printed in the United Kingdom at the University Press, Cambridge

A catalogue record for this publication is available from the British Library

ISBN 978-0-521-54896-0 Paperback

Contents

Introduction

Cambridge Advanced Mathematics has been written especially for the OCR modular examinations. Each book or half-book in the series corresponds to one module. This book covers the first two core mathematics modules, C1 and C2.

The books are divided into chapters roughly corresponding to specification headings. Occasionally a section includes an important result that is difficult to prove or outside the specification. These sections are marked with an asterisk (*) in the section heading, and there is usually a sentence early on explaining precisely what it is that the student needs to know.

Occasionally within the text paragraphs appear in a grey box. These paragraphs are usually outside the main stream of the mathematical argument, but may help to give insight, or suggest extra work or different approaches.

The authors have assumed that the students have access to graphic calculators. Although these are not permitted in parts of the examination, it is assumed that students will use them throughout the course to assist their learning of mathematics.

Numerical work is presented in a form intended to discourage premature approximation. In ongoing calculations inexact numbers appear in decimal form like 3.456..., signifying that the number is held in a calculator to more places than are given. Numbers are not rounded at this stage; the full display could be, for example, 3.456 123 or 3.456 789. Final answers are then stated with some indication that they are approximate, for example '3.46 correct to 3 significant figures'.

There are plenty of exercises, and each chapter contains a miscellaneous exercise which includes some questions of examination standard. The authors thank Charles Parker, Lawrence Jarrett and Tim Cross, the OCR examiners who contributed to these exercises. In each module there are also two revision exercises, with many questions taken from OCR examination papers, and two practice examination papers.

The authors also thank Peter Thomas and Val Dixon, who read the book very carefully and made many extremely useful comments, and OCR and Cambridge University Press for their help in producing this book. However, the responsibility for the text, and for any errors, remains with the authors.

Module C1

Core 1

1 Coordinates, points and lines

This chapter uses coordinates to describe points and lines in two dimensions. When you have completed it, you should be able to

- find the distance between two points
- find the mid-point of a line segment, given the coordinates of its end points
- find the gradient of a line segment, given the coordinates of its end points
- find the equation of the line though a given point with a given gradient
- find the equation of the line joining two points
- recognise different forms of the equations of lines
- find the point of intersection of two lines
- tell from their gradients if two lines are parallel or perpendicular.

1.1 The distance between two points

When you choose an origin O, draw an x-axis to the right on the page and a y-axis up the page and choose a scale for the axes, you are setting up a coordinate system. The coordinates of this system are called **cartesian coordinates** after the French mathematician René Descartes, who lived in the 17th century.

In Fig. 1.1, two points A and B have cartesian coordinates (4, 3) and (10, 7). The part of the line AB which lies between A and B is called a **line segment**. The length of the line segment is the distance between the points.

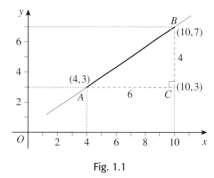

Fig. 1.1

A third point C has been added to Fig. 1.1 to form a right-angled triangle. You can see that C has the same x-coordinate as B and the same y-coordinate as A; that is, C has coordinates (10, 3).

It is easy to see that AC has length $10 - 4 = 6$, and CB has length $7 - 3 = 4$. Using Pythagoras' theorem in triangle ABC shows that the length of the line segment AB is

$$\sqrt{(10-4)^2 + (7-3)^2} = \sqrt{6^2 + 4^2} = \sqrt{36 + 16} = \sqrt{52}.$$

You can give this answer as 7.21..., if you need to, but often it is better to leave the answer as $\sqrt{52}$.

The idea of coordinate geometry is to use algebra so that you can do calculations like this when A and B are any points, and not just the particular points in Fig. 1.1. It often helps to use a notation which shows at a glance which point a coordinate refers to. One way of doing this is with **suffixes**, calling the coordinates of the first point (x_1, y_1), and the coordinates of the second point (x_2, y_2). Thus, for example, x_1 stands for 'the x-coordinate of the first point'.

Fig. 1.2 shows these two general points, and the point C such that ACB is a right-angled triangle. You can see that C now has coordinates (x_2, y_1), and that $AC = x_2 - x_1$ and $CB = y_2 - y_1$. Pythagoras' theorem now gives

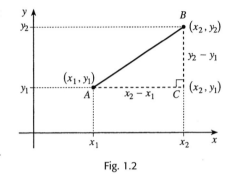

$$AB = \sqrt{(x_2 - x_1)^2 + (y_2 - y_1)^2}.$$

Fig. 1.2

An advantage of using algebra is that this formula works whatever the shape and position of the triangle. In Fig. 1.3, the coordinates of A are negative, and in Fig. 1.4 the line slopes downhill rather than uphill as you move from left to right. Use Figs. 1.3 and 1.4 to work out for yourself the length of AB in each case. You can then use the formula to check your answers.

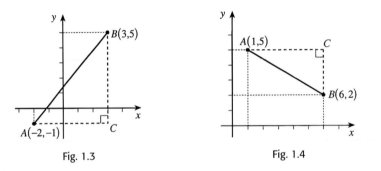

Fig. 1.3   Fig. 1.4

In Fig. 1.3,

$$x_2 - x_1 = 3 - (-2) = 3 + 2 = 5 \quad \text{and} \quad y_2 - y_1 = 5 - (-1) = 5 + 1 = 6,$$

so $$AB = \sqrt{(3 - (-2))^2 + (5 - (-1))^2} = \sqrt{5^2 + 6^2} = \sqrt{25 + 36} = \sqrt{61}.$$

And in Fig. 1.4,

$$x_2 - x_1 = 6 - 1 = 5 \quad \text{and} \quad y_2 - y_1 = 2 - 5 = -3,$$

so $$AB = \sqrt{(6 - 1)^2 + (2 - 5)^2} = \sqrt{5^2 + (-3)^2} = \sqrt{25 + 9} = \sqrt{34}.$$

Also, it doesn't matter which way round you label the points A and B. If you think of B as 'the first point' (x_1, y_1) and A as 'the second point' (x_2, y_2), the formula doesn't change. For Fig. 1.1, it would give

$$BA = \sqrt{(4 - 10)^2 + (3 - 7)^2} = \sqrt{(-6)^2 + (-4)^2} = \sqrt{36 + 16} = \sqrt{52}, \text{ as before.}$$

The distance between the points (x_1, y_1) and (x_2, y_2), which is the length of the line segment joining them, is

$$\sqrt{(x_2 - x_1)^2 + (y_2 - y_1)^2}.$$

Notice that the box above should really talk about 'the distance between the points *with coordinates* (x_1, y_1) and (x_2, y_2)'. This is a common shorthand which will be used frequently. Another shorthand, which you will see in Exercise 1A Question 6, is to use the notation $D(3, -2)$ to mean the point D with coordinates $(3, -2)$.

Example 1.1.1

Find the distance between the points

(a) $(2, 3)$ and $(7, 15)$,   (b) $(2, -8)$ and $(-6, 7)$,   (c) $(p, 0)$ and $(0, 2q)$.

Using the formula $\sqrt{(x_2 - x_1)^2 + (y_2 - y_1)^2}$, the distances are

(a) $\sqrt{(7 - 2)^2 + (15 - 3)^2} = \sqrt{5^2 + 12^2}$
$$= \sqrt{25 + 144}$$
$$= \sqrt{169} = 13.$$

(b) $\sqrt{((-6) - 2)^2 + (7 - (-8)^2)} = \sqrt{(-8)^2 + 15^2}$
$$= \sqrt{64 + 225}$$
$$= \sqrt{289} = 17.$$

(c) $\sqrt{(0 - p)^2 + (2q - 0)^2} = \sqrt{p^2 + 4q^2}.$

Exercise 1A

Do not use a calculator. Where appropriate, leave square roots in your answers.

1 Find the lengths of the line segments joining these pairs of points.

(a) $(2, 5)$ and $(7, 17)$ (b) $(6, 5)$ and $(2, 2)$

(c) $(16, 10)$ and $(1, 2)$ (d) $(10, 9)$ and $(4, 1)$

(e) $(-3, 2)$ and $(1, -1)$ (f) $(3, -2)$ and $(-1, 1)$

(g) $(4, -5)$ and $(-1, 0)$ (h) $(-3, -3)$ and $(-7, 3)$

2 Show that the triangle formed by the points $(-3, -2)$, $(2, -7)$ and $(-2, 5)$ is isosceles.

3 Show that the triangle formed by the points $(3, -2)$, $(4, 7)$ and $(1, -2)$ is not isosceles.

4 Show that the points $(7, 12)$, $(-3, -12)$ and $(14, -5)$ lie on a circle with centre $(2, 0)$.

5 The points A with coordinates $(-6, -3)$ and B with coordinates $(-3, -7)$ lie on a circle. Find the length of the chord AB.

6 The vertices of a quadrilateral *DEFG* are $D(3, -2)$, $E(0, -3)$, $F(-2, 3)$ and $G(4, 1)$.

  (a) Find the length of each side of the quadrilateral.

  (b) What type of quadrilateral is *DEFG*?

1.2   The mid-point of a line segment

You can also use coordinates to find the mid-point of a line segment.

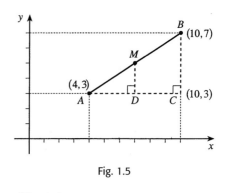

In Fig. 1.5, the **mid-point** M is the point of the line segment such that $AM = MB$, so that $AM = \frac{1}{2}AB$. The lines MD and BC have been drawn parallel to the y-axis, so they are parallel to each other. Then $AD = \frac{1}{2}AC$ and $DM = \frac{1}{2}CB$. So

$$AD = \tfrac{1}{2}AC = \tfrac{1}{2}(10 - 4) = \tfrac{1}{2}(6) = 3$$
$$DM = \tfrac{1}{2}CB = \tfrac{1}{2}(7 - 3) = \tfrac{1}{2}(4) = 2.$$

Fig. 1.5

The x-coordinate of M is the same as the x-coordinate of D, which is

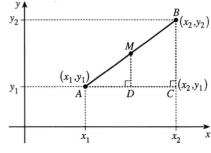

$$4 + AD = 4 + \tfrac{1}{2}(10 - 4) = 4 + 3 = 7.$$

The y-coordinate of M is

$$3 + DM = 3 + \tfrac{1}{2}(7 - 3) = 3 + 2 = 5.$$

So the mid-point M has coordinates $(7, 5)$.

Fig. 1.6

In Fig. 1.6 points M and D have been added in the same way as in Fig. 1.5. Exactly as before,

$$AD = \tfrac{1}{2}AC = \tfrac{1}{2}(x_2 - x_1), \qquad DM = \tfrac{1}{2}CB = \tfrac{1}{2}(y_2 - y_1).$$

So the x-coordinate of M is

$$x_1 + AD = x_1 + \tfrac{1}{2}(x_2 - x_1)$$
$$= x_1 + \tfrac{1}{2}x_2 - \tfrac{1}{2}x_1$$
$$= \tfrac{1}{2}x_1 + \tfrac{1}{2}x_2$$
$$= \tfrac{1}{2}(x_1 + x_2).$$

The y-coordinate of M is

$$y_1 + DM = y_1 + \tfrac{1}{2}(y_2 - y_1)$$
$$= y_1 + \tfrac{1}{2}y_2 - \tfrac{1}{2}y_1$$
$$= \tfrac{1}{2}y_1 + \tfrac{1}{2}y_2$$
$$= \tfrac{1}{2}(y_1 + y_2).$$

So, to find the mid-point of two points you find the average of the x-coordinates and the average of the y-coordinates.

> The mid-point of the line segment joining (x_1, y_1) and (x_2, y_2) has coordinates
>
> $$\left(\frac{x_1 + x_2}{2}, \frac{y_1 + y_2}{2} \right).$$

Now that you have an algebraic form for the coordinates of the mid-point M you can use it for any two points. For example, for Fig. 1.3 the mid-point of AB is

$$\left(\frac{(-2) + 3}{2}, \frac{(-1) + 5}{2} \right) = \left(\frac{1}{2}, \frac{4}{2} \right) = \left(\tfrac{1}{2}, 2 \right).$$

And for Fig. 1.4 it is $\left(\dfrac{1 + 6}{2}, \dfrac{5 + 2}{2} \right) = \left(\dfrac{7}{2}, \dfrac{7}{2} \right) = \left(3\tfrac{1}{2}, 3\tfrac{1}{2} \right).$

Again, it doesn't matter which you call the first point and which the second. In Fig. 1.5, if you take (x_1, y_1) as $(10, 7)$ and (x_2, y_2) as $(4, 3)$, you find that the mid-point is

$$\left(\frac{10 + 4}{2}, \frac{7 + 3}{2} \right) = (7, 5), \text{ as before.}$$

Example 1.2.1
Find the mid-point of the line segment with ends $(-3, 6)$ and $(1, -4)$.

Averaging the x-coordinates and the y-coordinates, the mid-point is

$$\left(\frac{(-3) + 1}{2}, \frac{6 + (-4)}{2} \right) = \left(\frac{-2}{2}, \frac{2}{2} \right) = (-1, 1).$$

Example 1.2.2
The mid-point of the line joining $(-3, 6)$ to another point P is $(2, 1)$. Find the coordinates of P.

Let the coordinates of P be (a, b). Then, using the averages rule,

$$\left(\frac{(-3) + a}{2}, \frac{6 + b}{2} \right) = (2, 1).$$

Looking at the x-coordinate,

$$\frac{(-3) + a}{2} = 2, \text{ giving } -3 + a = 4, \text{ so } a = 7.$$

Similarly, looking at the y-coordinate,

$$\frac{6 + b}{2} = 1, \text{ giving } 6 + b = 2, \text{ so } b = -4.$$

The coordinates of P are $(7, -4)$.

Exercise 1B

1   Find the coordinates of the mid-points of the line segments joining these pairs of points.

(a) $(2, 11), (6, 15)$ (b) $(5, 7), (-3, 9)$

(c) $(-2, -3), (1, -6)$ (d) $(-3, 4), (-8, 5)$

(e) $(a, b), (3a, 5b)$ (f) $(-a, -2b), (3a, -4b)$

2 $A(-2, 1)$ and $B(6, 5)$ are the opposite ends of the diameter of a circle. Find the coordinates of its centre.

3 $M(5, 7)$ is the mid-point of the line segment joining $A(3, 4)$ to B. Find the coordinates of B.

4 The points A with coordinates $(4, 1)$ and B with coordinates $(-6, -7)$ lie on a circle. Find the mid-point of the chord AB.

5 $A(1, -2)$, $B(6, -1)$, $C(9, 3)$ and $D(4, 2)$ are the vertices of a parallelogram. Verify that the mid-points of the diagonals AC and BD coincide.

6 Which one of the points $A(5, 2)$, $B(6, -3)$ and $C(4, 7)$ is the mid-point of the line segment joining the other two? Check your answer by calculating two distances.

7 Show that the points $(3, 1)$, $(-3, -7)$ and $(11, -5)$ form an isosceles triangle. Find the mid-point of the side which is not one of the equal sides.

1.3   The gradient of a line segment

The gradient of a line is a measure of its steepness. A line which goes up as you move from left to right is said to have a positive gradient. The steeper the line, the larger the gradient.

Unlike the distance and the mid-point, the gradient is a property of the whole line, not just of a particular line segment. If you take any two points on the line and find the increases in the x- and y-coordinates as you go from one to the other, as in Fig. 1.7, then the value of the fraction

$$\frac{y\text{-step}}{x\text{-step}}$$

is the same whichever points you choose. This is the **gradient** of the line.

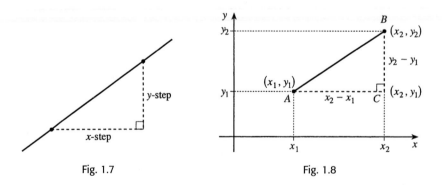

Fig. 1.7   Fig. 1.8

In Fig. 1.8 the x-step and y-step are $x_2 - x_1$ and $y_2 - y_1$, so that:

> The gradient of the line joining (x_1, y_1) to (x_2, y_2) is $\dfrac{y_2 - y_1}{x_2 - x_1}$.

This formula applies whether the coordinates are positive or negative. In Fig. 1.3, for example, the gradient of AB is $\dfrac{5 - (-1)}{3 - (-2)} = \dfrac{5 + 1}{3 + 2} = \frac{6}{5}$.

But notice that in Fig. 1.4 the gradient is $\dfrac{2 - 5}{6 - 1} = \dfrac{-3}{5} = -\frac{3}{5}$; the negative gradient tells you that the line slopes downhill as you move from left to right.

As with the other formulae, it doesn't matter which point has the suffix 1 and which has the suffix 2. In Fig. 1.1, you can calculate the gradient as either $\dfrac{7 - 3}{10 - 4} = \dfrac{4}{6} = \frac{2}{3}$, or $\dfrac{3 - 7}{4 - 10} = \dfrac{-4}{-6} = \frac{2}{3}$.

Two lines are **parallel** if they have the same gradient.

Example 1.3.1

Find the gradient of the line which passes through the points

(a) $(1, 3)$ and $(6, 2)$,   (b) $(-2, -5)$ and $(-6, -10)$.

State which of the lines slopes downwards to the right.

(a) Using the formula $\dfrac{y_2 - y_1}{x_2 - x_1}$, the gradient is

$$\frac{2 - 3}{6 - 1} = \frac{-1}{5} = -\frac{1}{5}.$$

(b) Using the formula $\dfrac{y_2 - y_1}{x_2 - x_1}$, the gradient is

$$\frac{-10 - (-5)}{(-6) - (-2)} = \frac{-10 + 5}{-6 + 2} = \frac{-5}{-4} = \frac{5}{4}.$$

As the gradient of the first line is negative, it slopes downwards to the right.

Example 1.3.2

Show that the points $P(1, 3)$, $Q(2, 6)$, $R(4, -3)$ and $S(1, -12)$ form a trapezium but not a parallelogram.

It is a great help to draw a sketch. The sketch need not be drawn on graph paper, and need not be drawn accurately, but the points should be positioned in roughly the correct place. Fig. 1.9 is an example of a sketch where the points are not accurately placed, but good enough to suggest that the parallel sides are PQ and RS.

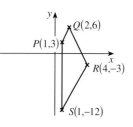

Fig. 1.9

The gradient of PQ is $\dfrac{6 - 3}{2 - 1} = 3.$

The gradient of QR is $\dfrac{(-3) - 6}{4 - 2} = \dfrac{-9}{2} = -4\frac{1}{2}.$

The gradient of RS is $\dfrac{(-12) - (-3)}{1 - 4} = \dfrac{-9}{-3} = 3.$

When you try to find the gradient of SP you get $\dfrac{(-12)-3}{1-1}$ which you cannot calculate because it involves division by 0. Fig. 1.9 shows that SP is parallel to the y-axis.

From the gradients, PQ and RS are parallel and QR and SP are not parallel, so $PQRS$ is a trapezium but not a parallelogram.

Exercise 1C

Start each question by drawing a sketch.

1 Find the gradients of the lines joining the following pairs of points.

   (a) $(3, 8)$, $(5, 12)$ (b) $(1, -3)$, $(-2, 6)$

   (c) $(-4, -3)$, $(0, -1)$ (d) $(-5, -3)$, $(3, -9)$

2 Find the gradients of the lines AB and BC where A is $(3, 4)$, B is $(7, 6)$ and C is $(-3, 1)$. What can you deduce about the points A, B and C?

3 The points A, B, C and D have coordinates $(2, 3)$, $(-3, 11)$, $(4, -2)$ and $(1, 8)$ respectively. Is AB parallel to CD?

4 The points $(3, -7)$ and $(8, 1)$ lie on the circumference of a circle. Find the gradient of the chord formed by the line joining these points.

5 The gradient of the line joining $(1, 3)$ to $(x, 7)$ is $\frac{2}{3}$. Find x.

6 The vertices of a quadrilateral $ABCD$ are $A(1, 1)$, $B(7, 3)$, $C(9, -7)$ and $D(-3, -3)$. The points P, Q, R and S are the mid-points of AB, BC, CD and DA respectively.

   (a) Find the gradient of each side of $PQRS$.

   (b) What type of quadrilateral is $PQRS$?

7 The vertices of a quadrilateral $PQRS$ are $P(1, 2)$, $Q(7, 0)$, $R(6, -4)$ and $S(-3, -1)$.

   (a) Find the gradient of each side of the quadrilateral.

   (b) What type of quadrilateral is $PQRS$?

1.4   Solving problems

In this section the results of the first three sections are brought together. You are expected to use whichever method you find most appropriate. A number of the problems can be done in several ways. Choose the method which suits you.

Example 1.4.1

The ends of a line segment are $(p - 3q, p + 4q)$ and $(p + 3q, p - 4q)$, where q is a positive number. Find the length of the line segment, its gradient and the coordinates of its mid-point.

For the length and gradient you have to calculate

$$x_2 - x_1 = (p + 3q) - (p - 3q) = p + 3q - p + 3q = 6q$$
and $\quad y_2 - y_1 = (p - 4q) - (p + 4q) = p - 4q - p - 4q = -8q.$

The length is $\sqrt{(x_2 - x_1)^2 + (y_2 - y_1)^2} = \sqrt{(6q)^2 + (-8q)^2} = \sqrt{36q^2 + 64q^2}$
$$= \sqrt{100q^2} = 10q,$$

since q is positive.

The gradient is $\dfrac{y_2 - y_1}{x_2 - x_1} = \dfrac{-8q}{6q} = -\frac{4}{3}.$

For the mid-point you have to calculate

$$x_1 + x_2 = (p - 3q) + (p + 3q) = p - 3q + p + 3q = 2p$$
and $\quad y_1 + y_2 = (p + 4q) + (p - 4q) = p + 4q + p - 4q = 2p.$

The mid-point is $\left(\dfrac{2p}{2}, \dfrac{2p}{2}\right)$, that is (p, p).

Try drawing your own figure to illustrate the results in this example.

Example 1.4.2
Prove that the points $A(1, 1)$, $B(5, 3)$, $C(3, 0)$ and $D(-1, -2)$ form a parallelogram.

Start by drawing a sketch, shown in Fig. 1.10.

Method 1 (using distances)   In this method, find the lengths of the opposite sides. If both pairs of opposite sides are equal in length, then $ABCD$ is a parallelogram.

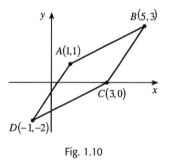

Fig. 1.10

$$AB = \sqrt{(5 - 1)^2 + (3 - 1)^2} = \sqrt{20}$$
$$DC = \sqrt{(3 - (-1))^2 + (0 - (-2))^2} = \sqrt{20}$$
$$CB = \sqrt{(5 - 3)^2 + (3 - 0)^2} = \sqrt{13}$$
$$DA = \sqrt{(1 - (-1))^2 + (1 - (-2))^2} = \sqrt{13}$$

Therefore $AB = DC$ and $CB = DA$, so $ABCD$ is a parallelogram.

Method 2 (using mid-points)   In this method, begin by finding the mid-points of the diagonals AC and BD. If these points are the same, then the diagonals bisect each other, so the quadrilateral is a parallelogram.

The mid-point of AC is $\left(\dfrac{1 + 3}{2}, \dfrac{1 + 0}{2}\right)$, which is $(2, \frac{1}{2})$. The mid-point of BD is $\left(\dfrac{5 + (-1)}{2}, \dfrac{3 + (-2)}{2}\right)$, which is also $(2, \frac{1}{2})$. So $ABCD$ is a parallelogram.

Method 3 (using gradients)   In this method, find the gradients of the opposite sides. If both pairs of opposite sides are parallel, then $ABCD$ is a parallelogram.

The gradients of AB and DC are $\dfrac{3-1}{5-1} = \dfrac{2}{4} = \frac{1}{2}$ and $\dfrac{0-(-2)}{3-(-1)} = \dfrac{2}{4} = \frac{1}{2}$ respectively, so AB is parallel to DC. The gradients of DA and CB are both $\frac{3}{2}$, so DA is parallel to CB. As the opposite sides are parallel, $ABCD$ is a parallelogram.

Exercise 1D

Do not use a calculator. Where appropriate, leave square roots in your answers. Where the question has numerical coordinates, start by drawing a sketch.

1 Find the lengths of the line segments joining these pairs of points. In parts (a) and (d) assume that $a > 0$.

    (a) $(2a, a)$ and $(10a, -14a)$ (b) $(a+1, 2a+3)$ and $(a-1, 2a-1)$

    (c) $(2, 9)$ and $(2, -14)$ (d) $(12a, 5b)$ and $(3a, 5b)$

2 Show that the points $(1, -2)$, $(6, -1)$, $(9, 3)$ and $(4, 2)$ are vertices of a parallelogram.

3 Find the coordinates of the mid-points of the line segments joining these pairs of points.

    (a) $(p+2, 3p-1)$, $(3p+4, p-5)$ (b) $(p+3, q-7)$, $(p+5, 3-q)$

    (c) $(p+2q, 2p+13q)$, $(5p-2q, -2p-7q)$ (d) $(a+3, b-5)$, $(a+3, b+7)$

4 Find the gradients of the lines joining the following pairs of points.

    (a) $(p+3, p-3)$, $(2p+4, -p-5)$ (b) $(p+3, q-5)$, $(q-5, p+3)$

    (c) $(p+q-1, q+p-3)$, $(p-q+1, q-p+3)$ (d) $(7, p)$, $(11, p)$

5 The point $P(x, y)$ lies on the straight line joining $A(3, 0)$ and $B(5, 6)$. Find expressions for the gradients of AP and PB. Hence show that $y = 3x - 9$.

6 A line joining a vertex of a triangle to the mid-point of the opposite side is called a median. Find the length of the median AM in the triangle $A(-1, 1)$, $B(0, 3)$, $C(4, 7)$.

7 A triangle has vertices $A(-2, 1)$, $B(3, -4)$ and $C(5, 7)$.

    (a) Find the coordinates of M, the mid-point of AB, and N, the mid-point of AC.

    (b) Show that MN is parallel to BC.

8 The points $A(2, 1)$, $B(2, 7)$ and $C(-4, -1)$ form a triangle. M is the mid-point of AB and N is the mid-point of AC.

    (a) Find the lengths of MN and BC.   (b) Show that $BC = 2MN$.

9 The origin O and the points $P(4, 1)$, $Q(5, 5)$ and $R(1, 4)$ form a quadrilateral.

    (a) Show that OR is parallel to PQ.   (b) Show that OP is parallel to RQ.

    (c) Show that $OP = OR$.   (d) What shape is $OPQR$?

10 The origin O and the points $L(-2, 3)$, $M(4, 7)$ and $N(6, 4)$ form a quadrilateral.

    (a) Show that $ON = LM$.   (b) Show that ON is parallel to LM.

    (c) Show that $OM = LN$.   (d) What shape is $OLMN$?

11 The vertices of a quadrilateral are $T(3, 2)$, $U(2, 5)$, $V(8, 7)$ and $W(6, 1)$. The mid-points of UV and VW are M and N respectively. Show that the triangle TMN is isosceles.

12 The points $A(2, 1)$, $B(6, 10)$ and $C(10, 1)$ form an isosceles triangle with AB and BC of equal length. The point G is $(6, 4)$.

   (a) Write down the coordinates of M, the mid-point of AC.

   (b) Show that $BG = 2GM$ and that BGM is a straight line.

   (c) Write down the coordinates of N, the mid-point of BC.

   (d) Show that AGN is a straight line and that $AG = 2GN$.

1.5 What is meant by the equation of a straight line or of a curve?

How can you tell whether or not the points $(3, 7)$ and $(1, 5)$ lie on the curve $y = 3x^2 + 2$? The answer is to substitute the coordinates of the points into the equation and see whether they fit; that is, whether the equation is **satisfied** by the coordinates of the point.

For $(3, 7)$: the right side is $3 \times 3^2 + 2 = 29$ and the left side is 7, so the equation is not satisfied. The point $(3, 7)$ does not lie on the curve $y = 3x^2 + 2$.

For $(1, 5)$: the right side is $3 \times 1^2 + 2 = 5$ and the left side is 5, so the equation is satisfied. The point $(1, 5)$ lies on the curve $y = 3x^2 + 2$.

> The equation of a line or curve is a rule for determining whether or not the point with coordinates (x, y) lies on the line or curve.

This is an important way of thinking about the equation of a line or curve.

1.6 The equation of a line

Gradient–intercept form
If you know the gradient of a line and the coordinates of the point where it crosses the y-axis you can find the equation of the line easily.

If the line crosses the y-axis at $A(0, c)$ and its gradient is m, let $P(x, y)$ be another point on the line, shown in Fig. 1.11.

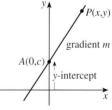

P lies on the line if (and only if) the gradient of AP is m.

The gradient of AP is $\dfrac{y - c}{x - 0}$. Equating this to m gives $\dfrac{y - c}{x - 0} = m$ or $y - c = mx$, which you can write as $y = mx + c$.

Fig. 1.11

> The equation of the line with gradient m through the point $(0, c)$ is
> $$y = mx + c.$$

In the equation $y = mx + c$, c is called the **y-intercept**.

Example 1.6.1
Find the equation of the straight line with gradient 3 through the point $(0, 2)$.

Using the result in the blue box, the equation of the line of gradient 3 through $(0, 2)$ is

$$y = 3x + 2.$$

Unfortunately, you do not always know the y-intercept, so you need another form of the equation.

Line through a given point with a given gradient
You may need to find the equation of the line with gradient m through a point which is not on the y-axis. Let this point be A with coordinates (x_1, y_1). Fig. 1.12 shows this line and another point P with coordinates (x, y) on it.

The gradient of AP is $\dfrac{y - y_1}{x - x_1}$.

Equating to m gives $\dfrac{y - y_1}{x - x_1} = m,$ or $y - y_1 = m(x - x_1).$

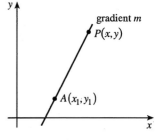

Fig. 1.12

> The equation of the line through (x_1, y_1) with gradient m is
> $y - y_1 = m(x - x_1).$

Notice that the coordinates of $A(x_1, y_1)$ satisfy this equation.

Example 1.6.2
(a) Find the equation of the line with gradient 2 which passes through the point $(3, 1)$.

(b) Find the y-intercept of this line.

(a) Using the equation $y - y_1 = m(x - x_1)$, the equation of the line is

$$y - 1 = 2(x - 3).$$

Multiplying out the bracket and simplifying, you get $y - 1 = 2x - 6$, or

$$y = 2x - 5.$$

(b) The equation $y = 2x - 5$ is in the form $y = mx + c$ with $c = -5$.

So the y-intercept is -5.

Line through two given points
Sometimes you need to find the equation of a straight line which passes through two given points.

Example 1.6.3
Find the equation of the line joining the points $(3, 4)$ and $(-1, 2)$.

To find this equation, first find the gradient of the line joining $(3, 4)$ to $(-1, 2)$. Then you can use the equation $y - y_1 = m(x - x_1)$.

The gradient of the line joining $(3, 4)$ to $(-1, 2)$ is $\dfrac{2 - 4}{(-1) - 3} = \dfrac{-2}{-4} = \dfrac{1}{2}$.

The equation of the line through $(3, 4)$ with gradient $\frac{1}{2}$ is $y - 4 = \frac{1}{2}(x - 3)$. After multiplying out and simplifying you get $2y - 8 = x - 3$, or $2y = x + 5$.

Since you used the point $(3, 4)$ to find the equation, it is a good idea to check your answer by using the point $(-1, 2)$. When $x = -1$ and $y = 2$, the left side is $2 \times 2 = 4$ and the right side is $-1 + 5 = 4$.

The form $y = mx + c$

The answers to Examples 1.6.1–1.6.3 can all be written in the form $y = mx + c$, where m and c are numbers.

But is the reverse true? That is, if you have an equation $y = mx + c$, is it always the equation of a straight line?

To show this, you can write $y = mx + c$ as $y - c = m(x - 0)$, or

$$\frac{y - c}{x - 0} = m \qquad \text{(except when } x = 0\text{)}.$$

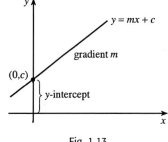

Fig. 1.13

This equation tells you that, for all points (x, y) whose coordinates satisfy the equation, the line joining $(0, c)$ to (x, y) has gradient m. That is, (x, y) lies on the line through $(0, c)$ with gradient m.

The point $(0, c)$ lies on the y-axis. You saw on page 13 that the number c is called the y-intercept of the line. See Fig. 1.13.

To find the x-intercept, put $y = 0$ in the equation, which gives $x = -\dfrac{c}{m}$. But notice that you can't do this division if $m = 0$. In that case the line is parallel to the x-axis, so there is no x-intercept.

To find the y-intercept of a straight line, put $x = 0$ and solve for y.

To find the x-intercept of a straight line, put $y = 0$ and solve for x.

Example 1.6.4
Find the y- and x-intercepts of the line $y = 2x + 4$.

Using the results in the box, to find the y-intercept, put $x = 0$. The y-intercept is 4.

To find the x-intercept of a straight line, put $y = 0$. Then $2x + 4 = 0$, so $x = -2$. Therefore the x-intercept is -2.

Lines parallel to the axes

When $m = 0$ in the equation $y = mx + c$, all the points on the line have coordinates of the form (something, c). Thus the points $(1, 2)$, $(-1, 2)$, $(5, 2)$, ... all lie on the straight line $y = 2$, shown in Fig. 1.14. As a special case, the x-axis has equation $y = 0$.

Similarly, a straight line parallel to the y-axis has an equation of the form $x = k$. All points on it have coordinates $(k, \text{something})$. Thus the points $(3, 0)$, $(3, 2)$, $(3, 4)$, ... all lie on the line $x = 3$, shown in Fig. 1.15. The y-axis itself has equation $x = 0$.

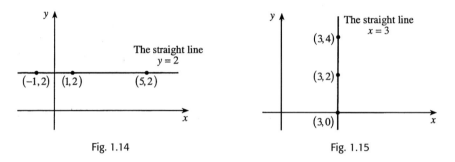

Fig. 1.14   Fig. 1.15

The line $x = k$ does not have a gradient; its gradient is undefined. Its equation cannot be written in the form $y = mx + c$.

Example 1.6.5

Find the equation of the straight line through $(3, 2)$ parallel to
(a) $y = 3x - 2$,   (b) $x = 2$.

(a) The line $y = 3x - 2$ has gradient 3, so the equation of a line parallel to it has the form $y = 3x + c$. If this line passes through $(3, 2)$, then $(3, 2)$ must satisfy the equation, so

$$2 = 3 \times 3 + c$$

giving $c = -7$.

The equation of the line is $y = 3x - 7$.

(b) The line $x = 2$ is parallel to the y-axis (see Fig. 1.15). The equation of a line parallel to this has the form $x = c$.

If this line passes through $(3, 2)$, then $(3, 2)$ must satisfy the equation, so

$$3 = c.$$

The equation of the line is $x = 3$.

1.7   The equation $ax + by + c = 0$

Suppose you have the equation $y = \frac{2}{3}x + \frac{4}{3}$. To eliminate the fractions multiply by 3 to get $3y = 2x + 4$, which can be rearranged to get $2x - 3y + 4 = 0$. This equation is in the form $ax + by + c = 0$ where a, b and c are constants.

It is also important to recognise that there are lines (of the form $x = $ constant) that can't be written in the form $y = mx + c$ but can be written in the form $ax + by + c = 0$ where a, b and c are constants.

Notice that the straight lines $y = mx + c$ and $ax + by + c = 0$ both contain the letter c, but it doesn't have the same meaning. For $y = mx + c$, c is the y-intercept, but there is no similar meaning for the c in $ax + by + c = 0$.

A simple way to find the gradient of $ax + by + c = 0$ is to rearrange it into the form $y = \ldots$. Here are some examples.

Example 1.7.1
Find the gradient of the line $2x + 3y - 4 = 0$.

Write this equation in the form $y = \ldots$, and then use the fact that the straight line $y = mx + c$ has gradient m.

From $2x + 3y - 4 = 0$ you find that $3y = -2x + 4$ and $y = -\frac{2}{3}x + \frac{4}{3}$. Therefore, comparing this equation with $y = mx + c$, the gradient is $-\frac{2}{3}$.

Example 1.7.2
One side of a parallelogram lies along the straight line with equation $3x - 4y - 7 = 0$. The point $(2, 3)$ is a vertex of the parallelogram. Find the equation of one other side giving your answer in the form $ax + by + c = 0$.

The line $3x - 4y - 7 = 0$ can be written in the form $4y = 3x - 7$ which is the same as $y = \frac{3}{4}x - \frac{7}{4}$. Its gradient is therefore $\frac{3}{4}$.

The line through $(2, 3)$ with gradient $\frac{3}{4}$ is $y - 3 = \frac{3}{4}(x - 2)$.

Multiplying by 4 gives $4(y - 3) = 3(x - 2)$ so $4y - 12 = 3x - 6$ or $4y - 6 = 3x$.

Putting this in the required form gives $3x - 4y + 6 = 0$.

1.8 The point of intersection of two lines

Example 1.8.1
Find the coordinates of the point of intersection of the lines $2x - y = 4$ and $3x + 2y = -1$, shown in Fig. 1.16.

You want the point (x, y) which lies on both lines, so the coordinates (x, y) satisfy both equations. Therefore you need to solve the equations simultaneously.

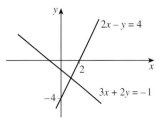

Fig. 1.16

Method 1   This uses the elimination method of solving equations.

Multiplying the first equation by 2 you get

$$\left.\begin{array}{r} 4x - 2y = 8 \\ 3x + 2y = -1 \end{array}\right\}.$$

Adding these equations, you get

$$7x = 7, \quad \text{so} \quad x = 1.$$

Substituting in the equation $2x - y = 4$, you find $y = -2$.

So the point of intersection is $(1, -2)$.

Method 2   This uses the substitution method of solving equations.

From the first equation $y = 2x - 4$.

Substituting for y in the other equation you get

$$\begin{array}{r} 3x + 2(2x - 4) = -1 \\ 3x + 4x - 8 = -1 \\ 7x = -1 + 8 = 7 \\ x = 1. \end{array}$$

Substituting this value of x in the equation $y = 2x - 4$ gives $y = -2$.

So the point of intersection is $(1, -2)$.

Notice how the sketch is helpful in checking this answer.

This argument applies to straight lines with any equations provided they are not parallel. To find points of intersection, solve the equations simultaneously.

Exercise 1E

1 Test whether the given point lies on the straight line (or curve) with the given equation.

(a) $(1, 2)$ on $y = 5x - 3$

(b) $(3, -2)$ on $y = 3x - 7$

(c) $(3, -4)$ on $x^2 + y^2 = 25$

(d) $(2, 2)$ on $3x^2 + y^2 = 40$

(e) $(1, 1\frac{1}{2})$ on $y = \dfrac{x + 2}{3x - 1}$

(f) $\left(5p, \dfrac{5}{p}\right)$ on $y = \dfrac{5}{x}$

(g) $(p, (p - 1)^2 + 1)$ on $y = x^2 - 2x + 2$

(h) $(t^2, 2t)$ on $y^2 = 4x$

2 Find the equations of the straight lines through the given points with the gradients shown. Your final answers should not contain any fractions.

(a) $(2, 3)$, gradient 5

(b) $(1, -2)$, gradient -3

(c) $(0, 4)$, gradient $\frac{1}{2}$

(d) $(-2, 1)$, gradient $-\frac{3}{8}$

(e) $(0, 0)$, gradient -3

(f) $(3, 8)$, gradient 0

(g) $(-5, -1)$, gradient $-\frac{3}{4}$

(h) $(-3, 0)$, gradient $\frac{1}{2}$

(i) $(-3, -1)$, gradient $\frac{3}{8}$

(j) $(3, 4)$, gradient $-\frac{1}{2}$

(k) $(2, -1)$, gradient -2

(l) $(-2, -5)$, gradient 3

(m) $(0, -4)$, gradient 7

(n) $(0, 2)$, gradient -1

(o) $(3, -2)$, gradient $-\frac{5}{8}$

(p) $(3, 0)$, gradient $-\frac{3}{5}$

(q) $(d, 0)$, gradient 7

(r) $(0, 4)$, gradient m

(s) $(0, c)$, gradient 3

(t) $(c, 0)$, gradient m

3 Find the equations of the lines joining the following pairs of points. Leave your final answer without fractions and in one of the forms $y = mx + c$ or $ax + by + c = 0$.

(a) $(1, 4)$ and $(3, 10)$

(b) $(4, 5)$ and $(-2, -7)$

(c) $(3, 2)$ and $(0, 4)$

(d) $(3, 7)$ and $(3, 12)$

(e) $(10, -3)$ and $(-5, -12)$

(f) $(3, -1)$ and $(-4, 20)$

(g) $(2, -3)$ and $(11, -3)$

(h) $(2, 0)$ and $(5, -1)$

(i) $(-4, 2)$ and $(-1, -3)$

(j) $(-2, -1)$ and $(5, -3)$

(k) $(-3, 4)$ and $(-3, 9)$

(l) $(-1, 0)$ and $(0, -1)$

(m) $(2, 7)$ and $(3, 10)$

(n) $(-5, 4)$ and $(-2, -1)$

(o) $(0, 0)$ and $(5, -3)$

(p) $(0, 0)$ and (p, q)

(q) (p, q) and $(p + 3, q - 1)$

(r) $(p, -q)$ and (p, q)

(s) (p, q) and $(p + 2, q + 2)$

(t) $(p, 0)$ and $(0, q)$

4 Find the gradients of the following lines. In part (l) assume $q \neq 0$.

(a) $2x + y = 7$

(b) $3x - 4y = 8$

(c) $5x + 2y = -3$

(d) $y = 5$

(e) $3x - 2y = -4$

(f) $5x = 7$

(g) $x + y = -3$

(h) $y = 3(x + 4)$

(i) $7 - x = 2y$

(j) $3(y - 4) = 7x$

(k) $y = m(x - d)$

(l) $px + qy = pq$

5 Find the equation of the line through $(-2, 1)$ parallel to $y = \frac{1}{2}x - 3$. Give your answer in the form $ax + by = c$.

6 Find the equation of the line through $(4, -3)$ parallel to $y + 2x = 7$. Give your answer in the form $y = mx + c$.

7 Find the equation of the line through $(1, 2)$ parallel to the line joining $(3, -1)$ and $(-5, 2)$. Give your answer in the form $ax + by + c = 0$.

8 Find the equation of the line through $(3, 9)$ parallel to the line joining $(-3, 2)$ and $(2, -3)$. Give your answer in the form $ax + by = c$.

9 Find the equation of the line through $(1, 7)$ parallel to the x-axis. Give your answer in the form $ax + by + c = 0$.

10 Find the equation of the line through $(d, 0)$ parallel to $y = mx + c$.

11 Find the points of intersection of the following pairs of straight lines.

(a) $3x + 4y = 33, 2y = x - 1$ (b) $y = 3x + 1, y = 4x - 1$

(c) $2y = 7x, 3x - 2y = 1$ (d) $y = 3x + 8, y = -2x - 7$

(e) $x + 5y = 22, 3x + 2y = 14$ (f) $2x + 7y = 47, 5x + 4y = 50$

(g) $2x + 3y = 7, 6x + 9y = 11$ (h) $3x + y = 5, x + 3y = -1$

(i) $y = 2x + 3, 4x - 2y = -6$ (j) $ax + by = c, y = 2ax$

(k) $y = mx + c, y = -mx + d$ (l) $ax - by = 1, y = x$

12 There are some values of a, b and c for which the equation $ax + by + c = 0$ does not represent a straight line. Give an example of such values.

1.9 The gradients of perpendicular lines

In Section 1.3 it is stated that two lines are parallel if they have the same gradient. But what can you say about the gradients of two lines which are perpendicular?

First, if a line has a positive gradient, then the perpendicular line has a negative gradient, and vice versa. But you can be more exact than this.

In Fig. 1.17, if the gradient of PB is m, you can draw a 'gradient triangle' PAB in which PA is one unit and AB is m units.

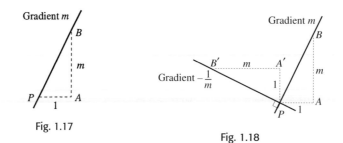

Fig. 1.17

Fig. 1.18

In Fig 1.18, the gradient triangle PAB has been rotated through a right-angle to $PA'B'$, so that PB' is perpendicular to PB. The y-step for $PA'B'$ is 1 and the x-step is $-m$, so

$$\text{gradient of } PB' = \frac{y\text{-step}}{x\text{-step}} = \frac{1}{-m} = -\frac{1}{m}.$$

Therefore the gradient of the line perpendicular to PB is $-\dfrac{1}{m}$.

Thus if the gradients of the two perpendicular lines are m_1 and m_2, then $m_1 m_2 = -1$. It is also true that if two lines have gradients m_1 and m_2, and if $m_1 m_2 = -1$, then the lines are perpendicular.

If a line has gradient m, the gradient of the line perpendicular to it is $-\dfrac{1}{m}$.

Two lines with gradients m_1 and m_2 are perpendicular if $m_1 m_2 = -1$.

Notice that the condition does not work if the lines are parallel to the axes. However, you can see that a line $x = $ constant is perpendicular to one of the form $y = $ constant.

Example 1.9.1

Four lines have gradients 2, $\frac{2}{3}$, -3 and $-\frac{4}{3}$. Find the gradients of lines at right angles to them.

Using the rule $m_1 m_2 = -1$, the gradients of the perpendicular lines are, in turn, $\dfrac{-1}{2}$, $\dfrac{-1}{\frac{2}{3}}$, $\dfrac{-1}{-3}$ and $\dfrac{-1}{-\frac{4}{3}}$. These simplify to $-\frac{1}{2}$, $-\frac{3}{2}$, $\frac{1}{3}$ and $\frac{3}{4}$.

The gradients of the four lines are $-\frac{1}{2}$, $-\frac{3}{2}$, $\frac{1}{3}$ and $\frac{3}{4}$.

Example 1.9.2

A line is perpendicular to $2x - 3y = 4$. Find its gradient.

The line $2x - 3y = 4$ can be written as $3y = 2x - 4$ which is $y = \frac{2}{3}x - \frac{4}{3}$.

The gradient of this line is $\frac{2}{3}$, so the gradient of the line perpendicular to it is $-\frac{3}{2}$.

Example 1.9.3

Find the equation of the line through $(1, 6)$ which is perpendicular to $y = 2x + 3$, giving your answer in the form $ax + by = c$.

The line $y = 2x + 3$ has gradient 2, so the perpendicular line has gradient $-\frac{1}{2}$.

Using $y - y_1 = m(x - x_1)$, the line through $(1, 6)$ with gradient $-\frac{1}{2}$ is $y - 6 = -\frac{1}{2}(x - 1)$.

This simplifies to $2y - 12 = -x + 1$, which is $x + 2y = 13$.

Example 1.9.4

A quadrilateral is formed by the points $(0, -5)$, $(-1, 2)$, $(4, 7)$ and $(5, 0)$. Find the mid-points and gradients of the diagonals. Hence show that the quadrilateral is a rhombus.

> You could tackle this question in several ways. This solution shows that the points form a parallelogram, and then that its diagonals are perpendicular.

Fig. 1.19 is a sketch. The mid-points of the diagonals are $\left(\dfrac{0+4}{2}, \dfrac{-5+7}{2}\right)$, or $(2, 1)$, and $\left(\dfrac{-1+5}{2}, \dfrac{2+0}{2}\right)$, or $(2, 1)$. As these are the same point, the quadrilateral is a parallelogram.

The gradients of the diagonals are $\dfrac{7-(-5)}{4-0} = \dfrac{12}{4} = 3$ and $\dfrac{0-2}{5-(-1)} = \dfrac{-2}{6} = -\frac{1}{3}$. As the product of the gradients is -1, the diagonals are perpendicular. Therefore the parallelogram is a rhombus.

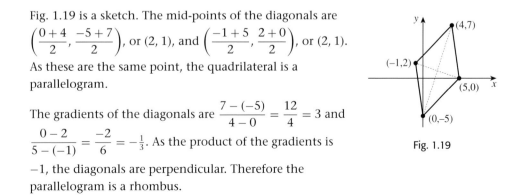

Fig. 1.19

Example 1.9.5

Find the coordinates of the foot of the perpendicular from $A(-2, -4)$ to the line joining $B(0, 2)$ and $C(-1, 4)$.

Fig. 1.20 is a sketch. The foot of the perpendicular is the point of intersection, P, of the line joining B to C and the line through A perpendicular to BC. First find the gradient of BC and its equation.

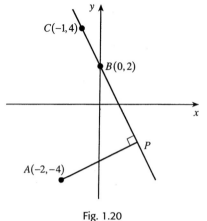

The gradient of BC is $\dfrac{4-2}{-1-0} = \dfrac{2}{-1} = -2.$

As you know the y-intercept is 2, the equation of BC is $y = -2x + 2$.

The gradient of the line through A perpendicular to BC is $-\dfrac{1}{-2} = \tfrac{1}{2}.$

Fig. 1.20

The equation of the line through $(-2, -4)$ with gradient $\tfrac{1}{2}$ is

$$y - (-4) = \tfrac{1}{2}(x - (-2)), \quad \text{or} \quad x - 2y = 6.$$

These lines meet at the point P, whose coordinates satisfy the simultaneous equations $2x + y = 2$ and $x - 2y = 6$. This is the point $(2, -2)$.

Example 1.9.6

Find the equation of the perpendicular bisector of the points $A(3, 6)$ and $B(-1, 4)$. Give your answer in the form $ax + by = c$.

Fig. 1.21 shows the situation. The perpendicular bisector of two points A and B is the line which passes through the mid-point of AB at right angles to AB.

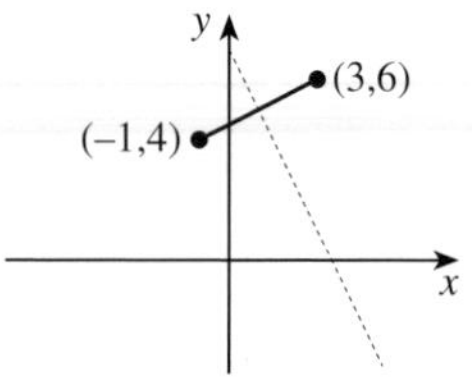

The mid-point of AB is $\left(\dfrac{3 + (-1)}{2}, \dfrac{6 + 4}{2}\right)$, which is $(1, 5)$.

The gradient of AB is $\dfrac{4-6}{-1-3} = \dfrac{-2}{-4} = \tfrac{1}{2}.$

Fig. 1.21

The gradient of the line perpendicular to AB is $\dfrac{-1}{\frac{1}{2}} = -2.$

The equation of the perpendicular bisector is therefore

$$y - 5 = -2(x - 1), \quad \text{or} \quad y - 5 = -2x + 2.$$

Putting this into the required form gives $2x + y = 7$.

Exercise 1F

1 In each part write down the gradient of a line which is perpendicular to one with the given gradient.

(a) 2 (b) -3 (c) $\frac{3}{4}$ (d) $-\frac{5}{6}$ (e) -1 (f) $1\frac{3}{4}$

(g) $-\dfrac{1}{m}$ (h) m (i) $\dfrac{p}{q}$ (j) 0 (k) $-m$ (l) $\dfrac{a}{b-c}$

2 In each part find the equation of the line through the given point which is perpendicular to the given line. Write your final answer so that it doesn't contain fractions.

(a) $(2, 3)$, $y = 4x + 3$ (b) $(-3, 1)$, $y = -\frac{1}{2}x + 3$

(c) $(2, -5)$, $y = -5x - 2$ (d) $(7, -4)$, $y = 2\frac{1}{2}$

(e) $(-1, 4)$, $2x + 3y = 8$ (f) $(4, 3)$, $3x - 5y = 8$

(g) $(5, -3)$, $2x = 3$ (h) $(0, 3)$, $y = 2x - 1$

(i) $(0, 0)$, $y = mx + c$ (j) (a, b), $y = mx + c$

(k) (c, d), $ny - x = p$ (l) $(-1, -2)$, $ax + by = c$

3 Find the equation of the line through the point $(-2, 5)$ which is perpendicular to the line $y = 3x + 1$. Give your answer in the form $ax + by = c$. Find also the point of intersection of the two lines.

4 Find the equation of the line through the point $(1, 1)$ which is perpendicular to the line $2x - 3y = 12$. Find also the point of intersection of the two lines.

5 A line through a vertex of a triangle which is perpendicular to the opposite side is called an altitude. Find the equation of the altitude through the vertex A of the triangle ABC where A is the point $(2, 3)$, B is $(1, -7)$ and C is $(4, -1)$.

6 $P(2, 5)$, $Q(12, 5)$ and $R(8, -7)$ form a triangle.

(a) Find the equations of the altitudes (see Question 5) through (i) R and (ii) Q.

(b) Find the point of intersection of these altitudes.

(c) Show that the altitude through P also passes through this point.

Miscellaneous exercise 1

1 Show that the triangle formed by the points $(-2, 5)$, $(1, 3)$ and $(5, 9)$ is right-angled.

2 Find the coordinates of the point where the lines $2x + y = 3$ and $3x + 5y - 1 = 0$ meet.

3 A triangle is formed by the points $A(-1, 3)$, $B(5, 7)$ and $C(0, 8)$.

(a) Show that the angle ACB is a right angle.

(b) Find the coordinates of the point where the line through B parallel to AC cuts the x-axis.

4 $A(7, 2)$ and $C(1, 4)$ are two vertices of a square $ABCD$.

(a) Find in the form $ax + by = c$ the equation of the diagonal BD.

(b) Find the coordinates of B and of D.

5 A quadrilateral $ABCD$ is formed by the points $A(-3, 2)$, $B(4, 3)$, $C(9, -2)$ and $D(2, -3)$.

   (a) Show that all four sides are equal in length.

   (b) Show that $ABCD$ is not a square.

6 P is the point $(7, 5)$ and l_1 is the line with equation $3x + 4y = 16$.

   (a) Find the equation of the line l_2 which passes through P and is perpendicular to l_1.

   (b) Find the point of intersection of the lines l_1 and l_2.

   (c) Find the perpendicular distance of P from the line l_1.

7 Prove that the triangle with vertices $(-2, 8)$, $(3, 20)$ and $(11, 8)$ is isosceles. Find its area.

8 The three straight lines $y = x$, $7y = 2x$ and $4x + y = 60$ form a triangle. Find the coordinates of its vertices.

9 Find the equation of the line through $(1, 3)$ which is parallel to $2x + 7y = 5$. Give your answer in the form $ax + by = c$.

10 Find the equation of the perpendicular bisector of the line joining $(2, -5)$ and $(-4, 3)$. Give your answer in the form $ax + by + c = 0$.

11 The points $A(1, 2)$, $B(3, 5)$, $C(6, 6)$ and D form a parallelogram. Find the coordinates of the mid-point of AC. Use your answer to find the coordinates of D.

12 The point P is the foot of the perpendicular from the point $A(0, 3)$ to the line $y = 3x$.

   (a) Find the equation of the line AP.

   (b) Find the coordinates of the point P.

   (c) Find the perpendicular distance of A from the line $y = 3x$.

13 Points which lie on the same straight line are called collinear. Show that the points $(-1, 3)$, $(4, 7)$ and $(-11, -5)$ are collinear.

14 Find the equation of the straight line that passes through the points $(3, -1)$ and $(-2, 2)$, giving your answer in the form $ax + by + c = 0$. Hence find the coordinates of the point of intersection of the line and the x-axis. (OCR)

15 The coordinates of the points A and B are $(3, 2)$ and $(4, -5)$ respectively. Find the coordinates of the mid-point of AB, and the gradient of AB.

   Hence find the equation of the perpendicular bisector of AB, giving your answer in the form $ax + by + c = 0$, where a, b and c are integers. (OCR)

16 The curve $y = 1 + \dfrac{1}{2 + x}$ crosses the x-axis at the point A and the y-axis at the point B.

   (a) Calculate the coordinates of A and of B.

   (b) Find the equation of the line AB.

   (c) Calculate the coordinates of the point of intersection of the line AB and the line with equation $3y = 4x$. (OCR)

17 The straight line p passes through the point $(10, 1)$ and is perpendicular to the line r with equation $2x + y = 1$. Find the equation of p.

Find also the coordinates of the point of intersection of p and r, and deduce the perpendicular distance from the point $(10, 1)$ to the line r. (OCR)

18 Show by calculation that the points $P(0, 7)$, $Q(6, 5)$, $R(5, 2)$ and $S(-1, 4)$ are the vertices of a rectangle.

19 The line $3x - 4y = 8$ meets the y-axis at A. The point C has coordinates $(-2, 9)$. The line through C perpendicular to $3x - 4y = 8$ meets it at B. Calculate the area of the triangle ABC.

20 The points $A(-3, -4)$ and $C(5, 4)$ are the ends of the diagonal of a rhombus $ABCD$.

(a) Find the equation of the diagonal BD.

(b) Given that the side BC has gradient $\frac{5}{3}$, find the coordinates of B and hence of D.

21 Find the equations of the medians (see Exercise 1D Question 6) of the triangle with vertices $(0, 2)$, $(6, 0)$ and $(4, 4)$. Show that the medians are concurrent (all pass through the same point).

22 The line l_1 passes through the points $A(4, 8)$ and $B(10, 26)$. Show that an equation for l_1 is $y = 3x - 4$.

The line l_1 intersects the line l_2, which has equation $y = 5x + 4$, at C. Find the coordinates of C.

23 The point A has coordinates $(1, 7)$ and the point B has coordinates $(3, 1)$. The mid-point of AB is P. Find the equation of the straight line which passes through P and which is perpendicular to the line $5y + x = 7$. Give your answer in the form $y = mx + c$. (OCR)

24 (a) The point A has coordinates $(2, 3)$ and the line l_1 has equation $x + 4y = 31$. The line l_2 passes through A and is perpendicular to l_1. Find the equation of l_2 in the form $y = mx + c$.

(b) The lines l_1 and l_2 intersect the point M. Find the coordinates of M.

(c) The point A is a vertex of the square $ABCD$. The diagonals of the square intersect at M. Find the coordinates of C. (OCR)

25 The coordinates of A, B and C are $(-2, 3)$, $(2, 5)$ and $(4, 1)$ respectively.

(a) Find the gradients of the lines AB, BC and CA.

(b) Hence or otherwise show that the triangle ABC is a right-angled triangle. (OCR)

2 Surds

The first part of this chapter is about expressions involving square and cube roots. When you have completed it, you should

- be able to simplify expressions involving square, cube and other roots.

2.1 Different kinds of number

At first numbers were used only for counting, and 1, 2, 3, ... were all that was needed. These are **natural numbers**, or **positive integers**.

Then it was found that numbers could also be useful for measurement and in commerce. For these purposes fractions were also needed. Integers and fractions together make up the **rational numbers**. These are numbers which can be expressed in the form $\frac{p}{q}$ where p and q are integers, and q is not 0.

One of the most remarkable discoveries of the ancient Greek mathematicians was that there are numbers which cannot be expressed in this way. These are called **irrational numbers**. The first such number to be found was $\sqrt{2}$, which is the length of the diagonal of a square with side 1 unit, by Pythagoras' theorem. The argument that the Greeks used to prove this can be adapted to show that the square root, cube root, ... of any positive integer is either an integer or an irrational number. Many other numbers are now known to be irrational, of which the most famous is π.

Rational and irrational numbers together make up the **real numbers**. Integers, rational and irrational numbers and real numbers can all be either positive or negative.

When rational numbers are written as decimals, they either come to a stop after a number of places, or the sequence of decimal digits eventually starts repeating in a regular pattern. For example,

$$\frac{7}{10} = 0.7, \quad \frac{7}{11} = 0.6363..., \quad \frac{7}{12} = 0.5833..., \quad \frac{7}{13} = 0.538\ 461\ 538\ 461\ 53...,$$

$$\frac{7}{14} = 0.5, \quad \frac{7}{15} = 0.466..., \quad \frac{7}{16} = 0.4375, \quad \frac{7}{17} = 0.411\ 764\ 705\ 882\ 352\ 941\ 176....$$

The reverse is also true, that if a decimal number stops or repeats indefinitely then it is a rational number. So if an irrational number is written as a decimal, the pattern of the decimal digits never repeats however long you continue the calculation.

2.2 Surds and their properties

In solving problems about areas or using Pythagoras' theorem, you have often needed to find a square root. Some positive integers like 25, or rational numbers like $\frac{16}{9}$, are the squares of numbers of the same form: $25 = 5^2$ and $\frac{16}{9} = \left(\frac{4}{3}\right)^2$. Numbers like this are called **perfect squares**. Then $\sqrt{25} = 5$ and $\sqrt{\frac{16}{9}} = \frac{4}{3}$.

Similarly, numbers like 27 and 0.008 are cubes of numbers of the same form: $27 = 3^3$ and $0.008 = 0.2^3$. These numbers are perfect cubes. Then $\sqrt[3]{27} = 3$ and $\sqrt[3]{0.008} = 0.2$.

But when you have met expressions such as $\sqrt{2}$, $\sqrt{8}$ and $\sqrt{12}$ before, it is likely that you have used a calculator to express them in decimal form. You might have written

$$\sqrt{2} = 1.414\ldots \quad \text{or} \quad \sqrt{2} = 1.414 \text{ correct to three decimal places} \quad \text{or} \quad \sqrt{2} \approx 1.414.$$

Why is the statement '$\sqrt{2} = 1.414$' incorrect?

Expressions like $\sqrt{2}$ or $\sqrt[3]{9}$ are called **surds**. However, expressions like $\sqrt{4}$ or $\sqrt[3]{27}$, which are whole numbers, are not surds.

This section is about calculating with surds. You need to remember that $\sqrt{x}$ always means the **positive** square root of x, or 0 if x is 0.

The main properties that you will use are:

> If x and y are positive numbers, then
> $$\sqrt{xy} = \sqrt{x} \times \sqrt{y} \quad \text{and} \quad \sqrt{\frac{x}{y}} = \frac{\sqrt{x}}{\sqrt{y}}.$$

To show that this is true, remember that the number $\sqrt{x}$ has two properties:

$$\sqrt{x} \times \sqrt{x} = x, \quad \text{and} \quad \sqrt{x} \text{ is positive.}$$

Similarly

$$\sqrt{y} \times \sqrt{y} = y \quad \text{and} \quad \sqrt{y} \text{ is positive.}$$

So, to prove that $\sqrt{xy} = \sqrt{x} \times \sqrt{y}$, you have to show that

$$\left(\sqrt{x} \times \sqrt{y}\right) \times \left(\sqrt{x} \times \sqrt{y}\right) = xy, \quad \text{and that} \quad \sqrt{x} \times \sqrt{y} \text{ is positive.}$$

The second of these is obvious, since the result of multiplying two positive numbers together is always a positive number. To prove the first, change the order of multiplying the numbers:

$$\left(\sqrt{x} \times \sqrt{y}\right) \times \left(\sqrt{x} \times \sqrt{y}\right) = \left(\sqrt{x} \times \sqrt{x}\right) \times \left(\sqrt{y} \times \sqrt{y}\right)$$
$$= x \times y$$
$$= xy.$$

So $\sqrt{xy} = \sqrt{x} \times \sqrt{y}$.

Similarly, to prove that $\sqrt{\dfrac{x}{y}} = \dfrac{\sqrt{x}}{\sqrt{y}}$, you have to show that

$$\frac{\sqrt{x}}{\sqrt{y}} \times \frac{\sqrt{x}}{\sqrt{y}} = \frac{x}{y}, \quad \text{and that} \quad \frac{\sqrt{x}}{\sqrt{y}} \text{ is positive.}$$

The second of these is obvious, since the result of dividing one positive number by another positive number is always a positive number. To prove the first, use the rule for multiplying fractions, $\dfrac{a}{b} \times \dfrac{c}{d} = \dfrac{ac}{bd}$:

$$\frac{\sqrt{x}}{\sqrt{y}} \times \frac{\sqrt{x}}{\sqrt{y}} = \frac{\sqrt{x} \times \sqrt{x}}{\sqrt{y} \times \sqrt{y}} = \frac{x}{y}.$$

So $\sqrt{\dfrac{x}{y}} = \dfrac{\sqrt{x}}{\sqrt{y}}$.

You can use these properties to express square roots like $\sqrt{8}$ and $\sqrt{12}$ in terms of smaller surds:

$$\sqrt{8} = \sqrt{4 \times 2} = \sqrt{4} \times \sqrt{2} = 2\sqrt{2}; \qquad \sqrt{12} = \sqrt{4 \times 3} = \sqrt{4} \times \sqrt{3} = 2\sqrt{3}.$$

Square roots like $\sqrt{8}$ and $\sqrt{12}$ are surds because they are not whole numbers. But they can be expressed in terms of smaller surds, because 8 and 12 have factors which are perfect squares: $8 = 4 \times 2 = 2^2 \times 2$ and $12 = 4 \times 3 = 2^2 \times 3$. So

$$\sqrt{8} = \sqrt{2^2 \times 2} = \sqrt{2^2} \times \sqrt{2} = 2\sqrt{2}, \quad \text{and} \quad \sqrt{12} = \sqrt{2^2 \times 3} = \sqrt{2^2} \times \sqrt{3} = 2\sqrt{3}.$$

You can also simplify products and quotients of square roots:

$$\sqrt{18} \times \sqrt{2} = \sqrt{18 \times 2} = \sqrt{36} = 6; \qquad \frac{\sqrt{27}}{\sqrt{3}} = \sqrt{\frac{27}{3}} = \sqrt{9} = 3.$$

Use a calculator to check the results of these calculations.

Example 2.2.1
Simplify   (a) $\sqrt{28} + \sqrt{63}$,   (b) $\sqrt{5} \times \sqrt{10}$.

Notice that alternative methods of solution may be possible, as in part (b).

(a) $\sqrt{28} + \sqrt{63} = \sqrt{4 \times 7} + \sqrt{9 \times 7}$
$$= \left(\sqrt{4} \times \sqrt{7}\right) + \left(\sqrt{9} \times \sqrt{7}\right)$$
$$= 2\sqrt{7} + 3\sqrt{7}$$
$$= 5\sqrt{7}.$$

(b) **Method 1** $\sqrt{5} \times \sqrt{10} = \sqrt{5 \times 10}$
$$= \sqrt{50}$$
$$= \sqrt{25 \times 2}$$
$$= 5\sqrt{2}.$$

Method 2 $\sqrt{5} \times \sqrt{10} = \sqrt{5} \times \sqrt{5 \times 2}$
$$= \sqrt{5} \times \left(\sqrt{5} \times \sqrt{2}\right)$$
$$= \left(\sqrt{5} \times \sqrt{5}\right) \times \sqrt{2}$$
$$= 5\sqrt{2}.$$

Example 2.2.2

Simplify (a) $\dfrac{\sqrt{32}}{\sqrt{2}}$,   (b) $\left(\sqrt{8}-\sqrt{3}\right)\left(\sqrt{8}+\sqrt{3}\right)$.

(a) **Method 1** $\dfrac{\sqrt{32}}{\sqrt{2}} = \dfrac{\sqrt{2}\times\sqrt{16}}{\sqrt{2}}$

$$= \dfrac{\sqrt{2}\times 4}{\sqrt{2}}$$
$$= 4.$$

Method 2 $\dfrac{\sqrt{32}}{\sqrt{2}} = \sqrt{\dfrac{32}{2}}$

$$= \sqrt{16}$$
$$= 4.$$

(b) $\left(\sqrt{8}-\sqrt{3}\right)\left(\sqrt{8}+\sqrt{3}\right) = \left(\sqrt{8}\right)^2 - \left(\sqrt{3}\right)^2$
$$= 8 - 3 = 5.$$

Example 2.2.2(b) uses the formula for the difference of two squares:

> **The difference of two squares**
>
> $$p^2 - q^2 = (p-q)(p+q)$$

However, it is written with $p = \sqrt{x}$ and $q = \sqrt{y}$, so it appears as

$$x - y = \left(\sqrt{x}-\sqrt{y}\right)\left(\sqrt{x}+\sqrt{y}\right).$$

Similar rules to those for square roots also apply to cube roots and higher roots.

Example 2.2.3

Simplify   (a) $\sqrt[3]{16}$,   (b) $\sqrt[3]{12}\times\sqrt[3]{18}$.

(a) $\sqrt[3]{16} = \sqrt[3]{8\times 2}$
$$= \sqrt[3]{8}\times\sqrt[3]{2}$$
$$= 2\times\sqrt[3]{2}.$$

(b) $\sqrt[3]{12}\times\sqrt[3]{18} = \sqrt[3]{12\times 18}$
$$= \sqrt[3]{216}$$
$$= 6.$$

Example 2.2.4

Show that if neither x nor y is equal to 0, then $\sqrt{x+y}$ is never equal to $\sqrt{x}+\sqrt{y}$.

If you square $\sqrt{x+y}$, you get $x + y$.

If you square $\sqrt{x}+\sqrt{y}$, you get

$$\left(\sqrt{x}+\sqrt{y}\right)\left(\sqrt{x}+\sqrt{y}\right) = \left(\sqrt{x}\right)^2 + 2\sqrt{x}\sqrt{y} + \left(\sqrt{y}\right)^2$$
$$= x + 2\sqrt{xy} + y.$$

But neither x nor y is equal to 0, so xy is not equal to 0, and $\sqrt{xy}$ is not equal to 0.

Hence the square of $\sqrt{x+y}$ is not equal to the square of $\sqrt{x}+\sqrt{y}$.

Therefore, if neither x nor y is equal to 0, then $\sqrt{x+y}$ is never equal to $\sqrt{x}+\sqrt{y}$.

It is also true that if $x > y$ and y is not equal to 0, then $\sqrt{x-y}$ is never equal to $\sqrt{x}-\sqrt{y}$.

So beware, and do not be tempted!

> If x and y are positive numbers, then
> $$\sqrt{x+y} \neq \sqrt{x}+\sqrt{y} \quad \text{and} \quad \sqrt{x-y} \neq \sqrt{x}-\sqrt{y}.$$

Exercise 2A

Do not use a calculator in this exercise.

1 Simplify the following.

(a) $\sqrt{3} \times \sqrt{3}$ (b) $\sqrt{10} \times \sqrt{10}$ (c) $\sqrt{16} \times \sqrt{16}$ (d) $\sqrt{8} \times \sqrt{2}$

(e) $\sqrt{32} \times \sqrt{2}$ (f) $\sqrt{3} \times \sqrt{12}$ (g) $5\sqrt{3} \times \sqrt{3}$ (h) $2\sqrt{5} \times 3\sqrt{5}$

(i) $3\sqrt{6} \times 4\sqrt{6}$ (j) $2\sqrt{20} \times 3\sqrt{5}$ (k) $(2\sqrt{7})^2$ (l) $(3\sqrt{3})^2$

(m) $\sqrt[3]{5} \times \sqrt[3]{5} \times \sqrt[3]{5}$ (n) $(2\sqrt[4]{3})^4$ (o) $(2\sqrt[3]{2})^6$ (p) $\sqrt[4]{125} \times \sqrt[4]{5}$

2 Simplify the following.

(a) $\sqrt{18}$ (b) $\sqrt{20}$ (c) $\sqrt{24}$ (d) $\sqrt{32}$

(e) $\sqrt{40}$ (f) $\sqrt{45}$ (g) $\sqrt{48}$ (h) $\sqrt{50}$

(i) $\sqrt{54}$ (j) $\sqrt{72}$ (k) $\sqrt{135}$ (l) $\sqrt{675}$

3 Simplify the following.

(a) $\sqrt{8}+\sqrt{18}$ (b) $\sqrt{3}+\sqrt{12}$ (c) $\sqrt{20}-\sqrt{5}$

(d) $\sqrt{32}-\sqrt{8}$ (e) $\sqrt{50}-\sqrt{18}-\sqrt{8}$ (f) $\sqrt{27}+\sqrt{27}$

(g) $\sqrt{99}+\sqrt{44}+\sqrt{11}$ (h) $8\sqrt{2}+2\sqrt{8}$ (i) $2\sqrt{20}+3\sqrt{45}$

(j) $\sqrt{52}-\sqrt{13}$ (k) $20\sqrt{5}+5\sqrt{20}$ (l) $\sqrt{48}+\sqrt{24}-\sqrt{75}+\sqrt{96}$

4 Simplify the following.

(a) $\dfrac{\sqrt{8}}{\sqrt{2}}$ (b) $\dfrac{\sqrt{27}}{\sqrt{3}}$ (c) $\dfrac{\sqrt{40}}{\sqrt{10}}$ (d) $\dfrac{\sqrt{50}}{\sqrt{2}}$

(e) $\dfrac{\sqrt{125}}{\sqrt{5}}$ (f) $\dfrac{\sqrt{54}}{\sqrt{6}}$ (g) $\dfrac{\sqrt{3}}{\sqrt{48}}$ (h) $\dfrac{\sqrt{50}}{\sqrt{200}}$

5 Simplify the following.

(a) $(\sqrt{2}-1)(\sqrt{2}+1)$ (b) $(3-\sqrt{2})(3+\sqrt{2})$

(c) $(\sqrt{7}+\sqrt{3})(\sqrt{7}-\sqrt{3})$ (d) $(2\sqrt{2}+1)(2\sqrt{2}-1)$

(e) $(4\sqrt{3}-\sqrt{2})(4\sqrt{3}+\sqrt{2})$ (f) $(\sqrt{10}+\sqrt{5})(\sqrt{10}-\sqrt{5})$

(g) $(4\sqrt{7}-\sqrt{5})(4\sqrt{7}+\sqrt{5})$ (h) $(2\sqrt{6}-3\sqrt{3})(2\sqrt{6}+3\sqrt{3})$.

6 In Question 5, every answer is an integer. Copy and complete each of the following.

(a) $(\sqrt{3} - 1)($ $) = 2$

(b) $(\sqrt{5} + 1)($ $) = 4$

(c) $(\sqrt{6} - \sqrt{2})($ $) = 4$

(d) $(2 + \sqrt{3})($ $) = 1$

(e) $(3 - \sqrt{2})($ $) = 1$

(f) $(3 - \sqrt{6})($ $) = 3$

2.3 Rationalising denominators

If you are using a calculator, then it is easy to calculate $\dfrac{1}{\sqrt{2}}$ directly. But without a calculator, if you know that $\sqrt{2} = 1.414\ 213\ 562...$, finding $\dfrac{1}{\sqrt{2}}$ as a decimal is a very unpleasant calculation.

Denominators of the form $a\sqrt{b}$

The first example, $\dfrac{1}{\sqrt{2}}$, can be greatly simplified by multiplying top and bottom by $\sqrt{2}$, giving

$$\frac{1}{\sqrt{2}} = \frac{1}{\sqrt{2}} \times \frac{\sqrt{2}}{\sqrt{2}} = \frac{1 \times \sqrt{2}}{\sqrt{2} \times \sqrt{2}} = \frac{\sqrt{2}}{2}.$$

Using this, from $\sqrt{2} = 1.414\ 213\ 562...$ you can find at once that

$$\frac{1}{\sqrt{2}} = 0.717\ 106\ 781....$$

You can see that the result $\dfrac{1}{\sqrt{2}} = \dfrac{\sqrt{2}}{2}$ is just another way of writing $\sqrt{2} \times \sqrt{2} = 2$. Generalising, you can deduce the following:

> To remove the surd $\sqrt{x}$ from the denominator of a fraction, multiply by $\dfrac{\sqrt{x}}{\sqrt{x}}$ to get
>
> $$\frac{1}{\sqrt{x}} \times \frac{\sqrt{x}}{\sqrt{x}} = \frac{\sqrt{x}}{x}.$$

Removing the surd from the denominator is called **rationalising the denominator**.

Example 2.3.1

Rationalise the denominator in the expressions   (a) $\dfrac{6}{\sqrt{2}}$,   (b) $\dfrac{3\sqrt{2}}{\sqrt{10}}$,   (c) $\dfrac{2}{3\sqrt{2}}$.

(a) $\dfrac{6}{\sqrt{2}} = \dfrac{6}{\sqrt{2}} \times \dfrac{\sqrt{2}}{\sqrt{2}} = \dfrac{6 \times \sqrt{2}}{\sqrt{2} \times \sqrt{2}} = \dfrac{6\sqrt{2}}{2} = 3\sqrt{2}.$

(b) **Method 1** $\dfrac{3\sqrt{2}}{\sqrt{10}} = \dfrac{3}{\sqrt{5}} = \dfrac{3}{\sqrt{5}} \times \dfrac{\sqrt{5}}{\sqrt{5}} = \dfrac{3\sqrt{5}}{5}.$

Method 2 $\dfrac{3\sqrt{2}}{\sqrt{10}} = \dfrac{3\sqrt{2}}{\sqrt{10}} \times \dfrac{\sqrt{10}}{\sqrt{10}} = \dfrac{3\sqrt{2} \times \sqrt{10}}{\sqrt{10} \times \sqrt{10}}$

$$= \dfrac{3\sqrt{20}}{10} = \dfrac{3\sqrt{4} \times \sqrt{5}}{10} = \dfrac{6\sqrt{5}}{10} = \dfrac{3\sqrt{5}}{5}.$$

(c) $\dfrac{2}{3\sqrt{2}} = \dfrac{2}{3\sqrt{2}} \times \dfrac{\sqrt{2}}{\sqrt{2}} = \dfrac{2\sqrt{2}}{3\sqrt{2} \times \sqrt{2}} = \dfrac{2\sqrt{2}}{3 \times 2} = \dfrac{\sqrt{2}}{3}.$

Denominators of the form $a + \sqrt{b}$ or $a - \sqrt{b}$

Just as calculating $\dfrac{1}{\sqrt{2}}$ as a decimal without a calculator is unpleasant, calculating $\dfrac{1}{3 + \sqrt{2}}$ as a decimal is also not a pleasant task.

To rationalise the denominator in an expression such as $\dfrac{1}{3 + \sqrt{2}}$ it is useful to look at the results of Exercise 2A Questions 5 and 6. From Question 5(b) you see that if you multiply $(3 + \sqrt{2})$ by $(3 - \sqrt{2})$ the result is an integer.

$$(3 + \sqrt{2})(3 - \sqrt{2}) = 3^2 - (\sqrt{2})^2 = 9 - 2 = 7.$$

This result suggests that to rationalise the denominator in $\dfrac{1}{3 + \sqrt{2}}$, you multiply by $\dfrac{3 - \sqrt{2}}{3 - \sqrt{2}}$, which of course is equal to 1, to get

$$\dfrac{1}{3 + \sqrt{2}} \times \dfrac{3 - \sqrt{2}}{3 - \sqrt{2}} = \dfrac{3 - \sqrt{2}}{(3 + \sqrt{2})(3 - \sqrt{2})} = \dfrac{3 - \sqrt{2}}{9 - 2} = \dfrac{3 - \sqrt{2}}{7}.$$

The calculation of the product $(3 + \sqrt{2})(3 - \sqrt{2})$ in the previous line uses the difference of two squares, $p^2 - q^2 = (p - q)(p + q)$, with $p = a$ and $q = \sqrt{b}$.

> To rationalise the denominator in $\dfrac{1}{a + \sqrt{b}}$ multiply by $\dfrac{a - \sqrt{b}}{a - \sqrt{b}}$.
>
> To rationalise the denominator in $\dfrac{1}{a - \sqrt{b}}$ multiply by $\dfrac{a + \sqrt{b}}{a + \sqrt{b}}$.

Example 2.3.2

Rationalise the denominator in the expressions (a) $\dfrac{2}{2 + \sqrt{3}}$, (b) $\dfrac{1}{3 - \sqrt{5}}$, (c) $\dfrac{2}{\sqrt{5} - 2}$.

(a) Multiplying by $\dfrac{2 - \sqrt{3}}{2 - \sqrt{3}}$,

$$\dfrac{2}{2 + \sqrt{3}} = \dfrac{2}{2 + \sqrt{3}} \times \dfrac{2 - \sqrt{3}}{2 - \sqrt{3}} = \dfrac{2(2 - \sqrt{3})}{2^2 - (\sqrt{3})^2} = \dfrac{4 - 2\sqrt{3}}{4 - 3} = \dfrac{4 - 2\sqrt{3}}{1} = 4 - 2\sqrt{3}.$$

(b) Similarly,

$$\dfrac{1}{3 - \sqrt{5}} = \dfrac{1}{3 - \sqrt{5}} \times \dfrac{3 + \sqrt{5}}{3 + \sqrt{5}} = \dfrac{3 + \sqrt{5}}{(3)^2 - (\sqrt{5})^2} = \dfrac{3 + \sqrt{5}}{9 - 5} = \dfrac{3 + \sqrt{5}}{4}.$$

(c) Similarly,

$$\frac{2}{\sqrt{5}-2} = \frac{2}{\sqrt{5}-2} \times \frac{\sqrt{5}+2}{\sqrt{5}+2} = \frac{2(\sqrt{5}+2)}{(\sqrt{5})^2 - 2^2} = \frac{2\sqrt{5}+4}{5-4} = 2\sqrt{5}+4.$$

Example 2.3.3

In Fig. 2.1, angle $B = 90°$. Find an expression for $\tan\theta°$, giving your answer in the form $\dfrac{a - b\sqrt{c}}{d}$, where a, b, c and d are integers.

Using $\tan\theta° = \dfrac{\text{opposite}}{\text{adjacent}} = \dfrac{BC}{AB}$,

$$\tan\theta° = \frac{2}{3 + \sqrt{2}}.$$

Then, using the result in the box,

$$\tan\theta° = \frac{2}{3 + \sqrt{2}} = \frac{2}{3 + \sqrt{2}} \times \frac{3 - \sqrt{2}}{3 - \sqrt{2}}$$

$$= \frac{6 - 2\sqrt{2}}{3^2 - (\sqrt{2})^2} = \frac{6 - 2\sqrt{2}}{9 - 2} = \frac{6 - 2\sqrt{2}}{7}.$$

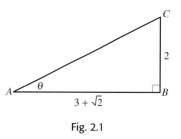

Fig. 2.1

2.4 Applications in geometry

Calculating with surds using these rules is often useful in geometry, especially when Pythagoras' theorem is involved.

Example 2.4.1

Fig. 2.2 shows the vertical cross-section of a roof of a building. It is a right-angled triangle ABC, with $AB = 15$ m. The height of the roof, BD, is 10 m.

Calculate   (a) z,   (b) $\cos\angle DAB$,   (c) x,   (d) y.

(a) Use Pythagoras' theorem in triangle ADB.

$$z^2 + 10^2 = 15^2$$
$$z^2 = 225 - 100 = 125$$
$$z = \sqrt{125} = \sqrt{25 \times 5} = 5\sqrt{5}.$$

(b) In triangle ADB,

$$\cos\angle DAB = \frac{AD}{AB} = \frac{z}{15} = \frac{5\sqrt{5}}{15} = \frac{\sqrt{5}}{3}.$$

(c) Angle BAC in triangle ABC is the same as angle DAB in triangle ADB. So, in triangle ABC,

$$\frac{AB}{AC} = \cos\angle BAC = \cos\angle DAB = \frac{\sqrt{5}}{3}.$$

That is,

$$\frac{15}{x} = \frac{\sqrt{5}}{3}.$$

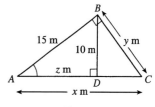

Fig. 2.2

Multiplying both sides of the equation by $3x$,

$$45 = x \times \sqrt{5}$$
$$x = \frac{45}{\sqrt{5}} = \frac{9 \times 5}{\sqrt{5}} = 9 \times \sqrt{5} = 9\sqrt{5}.$$

(d) Use Pythagoras' theorem in triangle ABC.

$$15^2 + y^2 = \left(9\sqrt{5}\right)^2$$
$$y^2 = 81 \times 5 - 15^2 = 405 - 225 = 180.$$

So $y = \sqrt{180} = \sqrt{36 \times 5} = 6\sqrt{5}.$

Exercise 2B

1 Rationalise the denominator in each of the following expressions, and simplify them.

(a) $\dfrac{1}{\sqrt{3}}$ (b) $\dfrac{1}{\sqrt{5}}$ (c) $\dfrac{4}{\sqrt{2}}$ (d) $\dfrac{6}{\sqrt{6}}$

(e) $\dfrac{11}{\sqrt{11}}$ (f) $\dfrac{2}{\sqrt{8}}$ (g) $\dfrac{12}{\sqrt{3}}$ (h) $\dfrac{14}{\sqrt{7}}$

(i) $\dfrac{\sqrt{6}}{\sqrt{2}}$ (j) $\dfrac{\sqrt{2}}{\sqrt{6}}$ (k) $\dfrac{3\sqrt{5}}{\sqrt{3}}$ (l) $\dfrac{4\sqrt{6}}{\sqrt{5}}$

(m) $\dfrac{7\sqrt{2}}{2\sqrt{3}}$ (n) $\dfrac{4\sqrt{2}}{\sqrt{12}}$ (o) $\dfrac{9\sqrt{12}}{2\sqrt{18}}$ (p) $\dfrac{2\sqrt{18}}{9\sqrt{12}}$

2 Simplify the following, giving each answer in the form $k\sqrt{3}$.

(a) $\sqrt{75} + \sqrt{12}$ (b) $6 + \sqrt{3}\left(4 - 2\sqrt{3}\right)$

(c) $\dfrac{12}{\sqrt{3}} - \sqrt{27}$ (d) $\dfrac{2}{\sqrt{3}} + \dfrac{\sqrt{2}}{\sqrt{6}}$

(e) $\sqrt{2} \times \sqrt{8} \times \sqrt{27}$ (f) $\left(3 - \sqrt{3}\right)\left(2 - \sqrt{3}\right) - \sqrt{3} \times \sqrt{27}$

3 $ABCD$ is a rectangle in which $AB = 4\sqrt{5}$ cm and $BC = \sqrt{10}$ cm. Giving each answer in simplified surd form, find

(a) the area of the rectangle, (b) the length of the diagonal AC.

4 Solve the following equations, giving each answer in the form $k\sqrt{2}$.

(a) $x\sqrt{2} = 10$ (b) $2y\sqrt{2} - 3 = \dfrac{5y}{\sqrt{2}} + 1$ (c) $z\sqrt{32} - 16 = z\sqrt{8} - 4$

5 Express in the form $k\sqrt[3]{3}$

(a) $\sqrt[3]{24}$ (b) $\sqrt[3]{81} + \sqrt[3]{3}$ (c) $\left(\sqrt[3]{3}\right)^4$ (d) $\sqrt[3]{3000} - \sqrt[3]{375}.$

6 You are given that, correct to twelve decimal places, $\sqrt{26} = 5.099\,019\,513\,593.$

(a) Find the value of $\sqrt{104}$ correct to ten decimal places.

(b) Find the value of $\sqrt{650}$ correct to ten decimal places.

(c) Find the value of $\dfrac{13}{\sqrt{26}}$ correct to ten decimal places.

7 Find the length of the third side in each of the following right-angled triangles, giving each answer in simplified surd form.

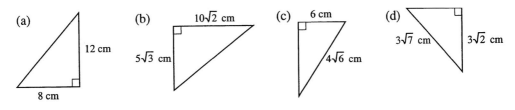

(a) 12 cm, 8 cm

(b) $10\sqrt{2}$ cm, $5\sqrt{3}$ cm

(c) 6 cm, $4\sqrt{6}$ cm

(d) $3\sqrt{7}$ cm, $3\sqrt{2}$ cm

8 Solve the simultaneous equations $7x - (3\sqrt{5})y = 9\sqrt{5}$ and $(2\sqrt{5})x + y = 34$.

9 Rationalise the denominators in the following expressions.

(a) $\dfrac{1}{\sqrt{2}-1}$
(b) $\dfrac{2}{3-\sqrt{3}}$
(c) $\dfrac{2}{4-\sqrt{2}}$
(d) $\dfrac{2}{6-\sqrt{2}}$

(e) $\dfrac{\sqrt{2}-1}{\sqrt{2}+1}$
(f) $\dfrac{3-\sqrt{3}}{2-\sqrt{3}}$
(g) $\dfrac{2+\sqrt{2}}{4-\sqrt{2}}$
(h) $\dfrac{1+2\sqrt{2}}{4-\sqrt{2}}$

10 In triangle ABC, B is a right angle, $AB = 5 - \sqrt{2}$ and $AC = 5 + \sqrt{2}$. Calculate and simplify $\cos \angle BAC$.

11 Solve the simultaneous equations $x\sqrt{5} + 2y = 3$ and $x + y = 1$, giving your answers in as simple a form as possible.

12 A formula for the radius of the circle touching all three sides of a triangle is $r = \dfrac{2\Delta}{p}$, where Δ is the area of the triangle and p is its perimeter. Find, in as simple a form as possible, the radius of this circle for right-angled triangles having sides

(a) 1 cm, 1 cm, $\sqrt{2}$,

(b) 1 cm, $\sqrt{3}$ cm, 2 cm,

(c) 1 cm, 2 cm, $\sqrt{5}$ cm.

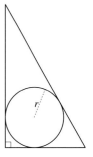

Miscellaneous exercise 2

1 Simplify the following.

(a) $5(\sqrt{2}+1) - \sqrt{2}(4 - 3\sqrt{2})$
(b) $(\sqrt{2})^4 + (\sqrt{3})^4 + (\sqrt{4})^4$
(c) $(\sqrt{5}-2)^2 + (\sqrt{5}-2)(\sqrt{5}+2)$
(d) $(2\sqrt{2})^5$.

2 Simplify the following.

(a) $\sqrt{27} + \sqrt{12} - \sqrt{3}$
(b) $\sqrt{63} - \sqrt{28}$
(c) $\sqrt{100\,000} + \sqrt{1000} + \sqrt{10}$
(d) $\sqrt[3]{2} + \sqrt[3]{16}$.

3 Rationalise the denominators of the following.

(a) $\dfrac{9}{2\sqrt{3}}$
(b) $\dfrac{1}{5\sqrt{5}}$
(c) $\dfrac{2\sqrt{5}}{3\sqrt{10}}$
(d) $\dfrac{\sqrt{8}}{\sqrt{15}}$

4 Simplify the following.

(a) $\dfrac{4}{\sqrt{2}} - \dfrac{4}{\sqrt{8}}$

(b) $\dfrac{10}{\sqrt{5}} + \sqrt{20}$

(c) $\dfrac{1}{\sqrt{2}}(2\sqrt{2} - 1) + \sqrt{2}(1 - \sqrt{8})$

(d) $\dfrac{\sqrt{6}}{\sqrt{2}} + \dfrac{3}{\sqrt{3}} + \dfrac{\sqrt{15}}{\sqrt{5}} + \dfrac{\sqrt{18}}{\sqrt{6}}$.

5 Rationalise the denominators of the following.

(a) $\dfrac{4}{3 - \sqrt{3}}$

(b) $\dfrac{6}{5 + \sqrt{5}}$

(c) $\dfrac{3 - \sqrt{2}}{3 + \sqrt{2}}$

(d) $\dfrac{2\sqrt{7} - 3}{4 + \sqrt{7}}$

6 Express $\dfrac{5}{\sqrt{7}}$ in the form $k\sqrt{7}$ where k is a rational number.   (OCR)

7 Find the gradient of the line joining $(1, 2)$ to $(\sqrt{2}, 3)$.

8 In the diagram, angles ABC and ACD are right angles. Given that $AB = CD = 2\sqrt{6}$ cm and $BC = 7$ cm, show that the length of AD is between $4\sqrt{6}$ cm and $7\sqrt{2}$ cm.

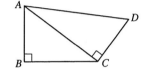

9 In the triangle PQR, Q is a right angle, $PQ = (6 - 2\sqrt{2})$ cm and $QR = (6 + 2\sqrt{2})$ cm.

(a) Find the area of the triangle.

(b) Show that the length of PR is $2\sqrt{22}$ cm.

10 It can be shown that $\tan 75° = \dfrac{\sqrt{3} + 1}{\sqrt{3} - 1}$. Use a calculator to check this, and write an expression for $\tan 75°$ in the form $a + b\sqrt{3}$, where a and b are rational numbers.

11 Solve the simultaneous equations $5x - 3y = 41$ and $(7\sqrt{2})x + (4\sqrt{2})y = 82$.

12 The coordinates of the points A and B are $(2, 3)$ and $(4, -3)$ respectively. Find the length of AB and the coordinates of the mid-point of AB.   (OCR)

13 An isosceles right-angled triangle has its two shorter sides of length a. Write down an expression for its perimeter in terms of a.

A length of rope 10 metres long is to be pegged out to form an isosceles right-angled triangle. Find, in as simple a form as possible, exact expressions for the lengths of the sides.

14 (a) Find the equation of the line l through the point $A(2, 3)$ with gradient $-\frac{1}{2}$.

(b) Show that the point P with coordinates $(2 + 2t, 3 - t)$ will always lie on l whatever the value of t.

(c) Find the values of t such that the length AP is 5 units.

(d) Find the value of t such that OP is perpendicular to l (where O is the origin). Hence find the length of the perpendicular from O to l.

15 You are given that y is not 0, and that $x > y$. Now suppose that $\sqrt{x - y} = \sqrt{x} - \sqrt{y}$.

(a) Show that $\left(\sqrt{x} - \sqrt{y}\right)^2 = x - 2\sqrt{x}\sqrt{y} + y$.

(b) Deduce that $y(x - y) = 0$, and hence that either $y = 0$ or $x = y$.

(c) What can you deduce about $\sqrt{x - y}$ and $\sqrt{x} - \sqrt{y}$?

3 Some important graphs

This chapter introduces the idea of a function and investigates the graphs representing functions of various kinds. When you have completed it, you should

- understand function notation
- know the shapes of the graphs of positive integer powers of x
- know the shapes of graphs of functions of the form $f(x) = ax^2 + bx + c$
- be able to suggest possible equations of such functions from their graphs
- know how to use the factorised form of a function to sketch its graph
- be able to find the point(s) of intersection of two graphs.

To get full value from this chapter you will need either a graphic calculator or a computer with graph-plotting software, so that you can check for yourself the graphs which accompany the text, and carry out further research along similar lines.

3.1 The idea of a function

You are already familiar with formulae which summarise calculations which need to be performed frequently, such as:

the area of a circle with radius x metres is πx^2 square metres;

the volume of a cube of side x metres is x^3 cubic metres;

the time that it takes to travel k kilometres at x kilometres per hour is $\dfrac{k}{x}$ hours.

You will often have used different letters from x in these formulae, such as r for radius or s for speed, but in this chapter x will always be used for the letter in the formula, and y for the quantity you want to calculate. Notice that some formulae also involve other letters, called **constants**; these might be either a number like π, which is irrational and cannot be written out in full, or a quantity like the distance k, which you choose for yourself depending on the distance you intend to travel.

Expressions such as πx^2, x^3 and $\dfrac{k}{x}$ are examples of **functions** of x. The essential feature of a function is that, having chosen x, you can get a *unique* value of y from it.

It is often useful to have a way of writing functions in general, rather than always having to refer to particular functions. The notation which is used for this is $f(x)$ (read 'f of x', or sometimes just 'f x'). The letter f stands for the function itself, and x for the number of which you choose to calculate its value. This is called **evaluating** the function f at x.

If you want to refer to the value of the function when x has a particular value, say $x = 2$, then you write the value as $f(2)$. For example, if $f(x)$ stands for the function x^3, then $f(2) = 2^3 = 8$.

If a problem involves more than one function, you can use different letters for each function. Two functions can, for example, be written as $f(x)$ and $g(x)$.

Functions are not always defined by algebraic formulae. Sometimes it is easier to describe them in words, or to define them using a flow chart or a computer program. All that matters is that each value of x chosen leads to a unique value of $y = f(x)$.

3.2 Graphs

You are familiar with drawing graphs. You set up a coordinate system for cartesian coordinates using x- and y-axes, and choose the scales on each axis.

The axes divide the plane of the paper or screen into four quadrants, numbered as shown in Fig. 3.1.

The first quadrant is in the top right corner, where x and y are both positive. The other quadrants then follow in order going anticlockwise round the origin.

	y	
Second quadrant $(x < 0, y > 0)$		First quadrant $(x > 0, y > 0)$
		x
Third quadrant $(x < 0, y < 0)$		Fourth quadrant $(x > 0, y < 0)$

Fig. 3.1

Example 3.2.1
In which quadrants is $xy > 0$?

If the product of two numbers is positive, either both are positive or both are negative. So either $x > 0$ and $y > 0$, or $x < 0$ and $y < 0$. The point (x, y) therefore lies in either the first or the third quadrant.

The graph of a function $f(x)$ is made up of all the points whose coordinates (x, y) satisfy the equation $y = f(x)$. When you draw such a graph on graph paper, you choose a few values of x and work out $y = f(x)$ for these. You then plot the points with coordinates (x, y), and join up these points by eye, usually with a smooth curve. If you have done this accurately, the coordinates of other points of the curve will also satisfy the equation $y = f(x)$. Calculators and computers make graphs in much the same way, but they can plot many more points much more quickly.

For some functions there is a restriction on the values of x you can choose.

Example 3.2.2
Draw the complete graph of $y = f(x)$, where $f(x) = \sqrt{4 - x^2}$.

You can only calculate the values of the function $f(x) = \sqrt{4 - x^2}$ if x is between -2 and 2 inclusive, since if $x > 2$ or $x < -2$ the value of $4 - x^2$ is negative, and a negative number does not have a square root.

Also $f(x)$ cannot be negative (remember that $\sqrt{a}$ is positive or zero by definition) and it cannot be greater than $\sqrt{4} = 2$. So the graph of $y = \sqrt{4 - x^2}$, shown in Fig. 3.2, lies between -2 and 2 inclusive in the x-direction, and between 0 and 2 inclusive in the y-direction.

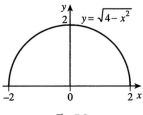

Fig. 3.2

However, many functions have a value when x is any real number, and then it is impossible to show the whole graph. The skill is to choose the values of x between which to draw the graph, so that you include all the important features.

3.3   Positive integer powers of x

This section looks at graphs of functions of the form $y = \mathrm{f}(x)$, where $\mathrm{f}(x) = x^n$, and n is a positive integer. Notice that $(0, 0)$ and $(1, 1)$ satisfy the equation $y = x^n$ for all these values of n, so that all the graphs include the points $(0, 0)$ and $(1, 1)$.

First look at the graphs when x is positive. Then x^n is also positive, so that the graphs lie entirely in the first quadrant. Fig. 3.3 shows the graphs for $n = 1, 2, 3$ and 4 for values of x from 0 to somewhere beyond 1.

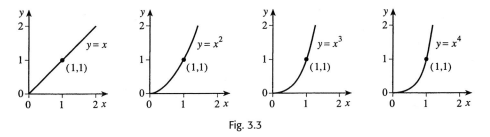

Fig. 3.3

Points to notice are:

* $n = 1$ is a special case: it gives the straight line $y = x$ through the origin, which makes an angle of $45°$ with each axis.

* For $n > 1$, the x-axis is a tangent to the graphs at the origin. This is because, when x is small, x^n is very small. For example, $0.1^2 = 0.01$, $0.1^3 = 0.001$, $0.1^4 = 0.0001$.

* For each increase in the index n, the graph stays closer to the x-axis between $x = 0$ and $x = 1$, but then climbs more steeply beyond $x = 1$. This is because $x^{n+1} = x \times x^n$, so that $x^{n+1} < x^n$ when $0 < x < 1$ and $x^{n+1} > x^n$ when $x > 1$.

What happens when x is negative depends on whether n is odd or even. To see this, suppose $x = -a$, where a is a positive number.

If n is even, notice that $(-a)^n = a^n$. (Think of $n = 2$ or $n = 4$.)

So for the graph of $y = \mathrm{f}(x)$ where $\mathrm{f}(x) = x^n$,

$$\begin{aligned} \mathrm{f}(-a) &= (-a)^n \\ &= a^n \quad \text{(since } n \text{ is even)} \\ &= \mathrm{f}(a). \end{aligned}$$

So the value of y on the graph is the same for $x = -a$ and $x = a$. This means that the graph is symmetrical about the y-axis. This is illustrated in Fig. 3.4 for the graphs of $y = x^2$ and $y = x^4$. Functions with the property that $\mathrm{f}(-a) = \mathrm{f}(a)$ for all values of a are called **even functions**.

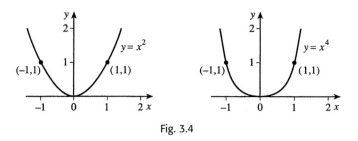

Fig. 3.4

If n is odd, notice that $(-a)^n = -a^n$. (Think of $n = 1$ or $n = 3$.)

So for the graph of $y = f(x) = x^n$,

$$f(-a) = (-a)^n$$
$$= -a^n \quad \text{(since } n \text{ is odd)}$$
$$= -f(a).$$

The value of y for $x = -a$ is minus the value for $x = a$. Note that the points with coordinates (a, a^n) and $(-a, -a^n)$ are symmetrically placed on either side of the origin. This means that the whole graph is symmetrical about the origin. This is illustrated in Fig. 3.5 for the graphs of $y = x$ and $y = x^3$. Functions with the property that $f(-a) = -f(a)$ for all values of a are called **odd functions**.

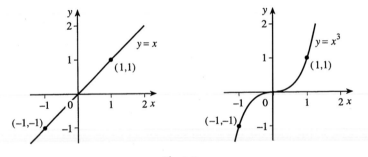

Fig. 3.5

Exercise 3A

1 Given $f(x) = 2x + 5$, find the following values.

(a) $f(3)$ (b) $f(0)$ (c) $f(-4)$ (d) $f\left(-2\tfrac{1}{2}\right)$

2 Given $f(x) = 3x^2 + 2$, find the following values.

(a) $f(4)$ (b) $f(-1)$ (c) $f(-3)$ (d) $f(3)$

3 Given $f(x) = x^2 + 4x + 3$, find the following values.

(a) $f(2)$ (b) $f\left(\tfrac{1}{2}\right)$ (c) $f(-1)$ (d) $f(-3)$

4 Given $g(x) = x^3$ and $h(x) = 4x + 1$, find the following values.

(a) $g(2) + h(2)$ (b) $3g(-1) - 4h(-1)$

(c) Show that $g(5) = h(31)$.   (d) Find the value of $h(g(2))$.

5   Sketch the graphs of the following functions.

(a) $y = x^5$ (b) $y = x^6$ (c) $y = x^{10}$ (d) $y = x^{15}$

6   Given $f(x) = x^n$ and $f(3) = 81$, determine the value of n.

7   Of the following functions, one is even and two are odd. Determine which is which.

(a) $f(x) = x^7$ (b) $g(x) = x^4 + 3x^2$ (c) $h(x) = x(x^2 - 1)$

8   Given that $f(x) = ax + b$ and that $f(2) = 7$ and $f(3) = 12$, find a and b.

3.4   Graphs of the form $y = ax^2 + bx + c$

In Chapter 1, you found out how to sketch graphs of straight lines, and what the constants m and c mean in the equation $y = mx + c$.

Exercise 3B gives you experience of plotting the graphs of functions with equations of the form $y = ax^2 + bx + c$, and examining their properties using a graphic calculator or a computer. A summary of the main points appears after the exercise.

Exercise 3B

1   Display, on the same set of axes, the following graphs.

(a) $y = x^2 - 2x + 5$ (b) $y = x^2 - 2x + 1$ (c) $y = x^2 - 2x$ (d) $y = x^2 - 2x - 6$

2   Display, on the same set of axes, the following graphs.

(a) $y = x^2 + x - 4$ (b) $y = x^2 + x - 1$ (c) $y = x^2 + x + 2$ (d) $y = x^2 + x + 5$

3   The diagram shows the graph of $y = ax^2 - bx$. On a copy of the diagram, sketch the following graphs.

(a) $y = ax^2 - bx + 4$

(b) $y = ax^2 - bx - 6$

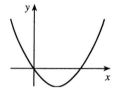

4   What is the effect on the graph of $y = ax^2 + bx + c$ of changing the value of c?

5   Display the following graphs.

(a) $y = x^2 - 4x + 1$ (b) $y = x^2 - 2x + 1$ (c) $y = x^2 + 1$ (d) $y = x^2 + 2x + 1$

6   Display the graph of $y = 2x^2 + bx + 4$ for different values of b. How does changing b affect the curve $y = ax^2 + bx + c$?

7   Display the following graphs.

(a) $y = x^2 + 1$ (b) $y = 3x^2 + 1$ (c) $y = -3x^2 + 1$ (d) $y = -x^2 + 1$

8 Display the following graphs.

(a) $y = -4x^2 + 3x + 1$ (b) $y = -x^2 + 3x + 1$

(c) $y = x^2 + 3x + 1$ (d) $y = 4x^2 + 3x + 1$

9 Display the graph of $y = ax^2 - 2x$ for different values of a.

10 How does changing a affect the shape of the graph of $y = ax^2 + bx + c$?

11 Which of the following could be the equation of the curve
shown in the diagram?

(a) $y = x^2 - 2x + 5$

(b) $y = -x^2 - 2x + 5$

(c) $y = x^2 + 2x + 5$

(d) $y = -x^2 + 2x + 5$

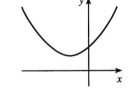

12 Which of the following could be the equation of the curve
shown in the diagram?

(a) $y = -x^2 + 3x + 4$

(b) $y = x^2 - 3x + 4$

(c) $y = x^2 + 3x + 4$

(d) $y = -x^2 - 3x + 4$

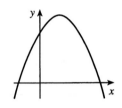

3.5   The shapes of graphs of the form $y = ax^2 + bx + c$

In Exercise 3B, you should have found a number of results, which are summarised below.

All the graphs have the same general shape, which is called a **parabola**. These parabolas have a vertical **axis of symmetry**. The point where a parabola meets its axis of symmetry is called the **vertex**.

Changing c moves the graph up and down in the y-direction.

Changing b moves the axis of symmetry of the graph in the x-direction. If a and b have the same sign the axis of symmetry is to the left of the y-axis; if a and b have opposite signs the axis of symmetry is to the right of the y-axis.

If a is positive the vertex is at the lowest point of the graph; if a is negative the vertex is at the highest point. The larger the size of a the more the graph is elongated.

3.6 The point of intersection of two graphs

The principle for finding the point of intersection of two curves or a line and a curve is the same as that for finding the point of intersection of two graphs which are straight lines.

Suppose that you have two graphs, with equations $y = f(x)$ and $y = g(x)$. You want the point (x, y) which lies on both graphs, so the coordinates (x, y) satisfy both equations. Therefore x must satisfy the equation $f(x) = g(x)$.

Example 3.6.1

Find the point of intersection of the line $y = 2$ with the graph $y = x^2 - 3x + 4$ (see Fig. 3.6).

Solving these equations simultaneously gives $x^2 - 3x + 4 = 2$.

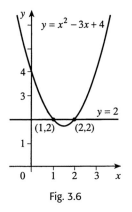

$$x^2 - 3x + 4 = 2$$
$$x^2 - 3x + 2 = 0$$
$$(x - 1)(x - 2) = 0$$

giving $x = 1$ and $x = 2$.

Substituting these values in either equation ($y = 2$ is obviously easier!) to find y, the points of intersection are $(1, 2)$ and $(2, 2)$.

If you do not know how to write $x^2 - 3x + 4$ in the form $(x - 1)(x - 2)$, refer to Section 4.3.

Fig. 3.6

Example 3.6.2

Find the point of intersection of the line $y = 2x - 1$ with the graph $y = x^2$ (see Fig. 3.7).

Solving these equations gives $2x - 1 = x^2$.

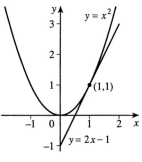

$$2x - 1 = x^2$$
$$x^2 - 2x + 1 = 0$$
$$(x - 1)(x - 1) = 0$$

giving $x = 1$.

Substituting these values in either equation to find y gives the point of intersection as $(1, 1)$.

The fact that there is only one point of intersection shows that this line is a tangent to the graph. You can check this by showing both graphs on your graphic calculator. The point $(1, 1)$ is called the **point of contact** of the tangent and the curve.

Fig. 3.7

Example 3.6.3

Find the point of intersection of the graphs $y = x^2 - 2x - 6$ and $y = 12 + x - 2x^2$.

Solving these equations simultaneously gives $x^2 - 2x - 6 = 12 + x - 2x^2$.

$$x^2 - 2x - 6 = 12 + x - 2x^2$$
$$3x^2 - 3x - 18 = 0$$
$$x^2 - x - 6 = 0$$
$$(x - 3)(x + 2) = 0$$

giving $x = 3$ or $x = -2$.

Substituting these values in either equation to find y gives the points of intersection as $(3, -3)$ and $(-2, 2)$.

Check the solution with your graphic calculator.

Exercise 3C

1 Find the point or points of intersection for the following lines and curves.

(a) $x = 3$ and $y = x^2 + 4x - 7$ (b) $y = 3$ and $y = x^2 - 5x + 7$

(c) $y = 8$ and $y = x^2 + 2x$ (d) $y + 3 = 0$ and $y = 2x^2 + 5x - 6$

2 Find the points of intersection for the following lines and curves. Check your answers in each case by displaying the graphs on a graphic calculator.

(a) $y = x + 1$ and $y = x^2 - 3x + 4$ (b) $y = 2x + 3$ and $y = x^2 + 3x - 9$

(c) $y = 3x + 11$ and $y = 2x^2 + 2x + 5$ (d) $y = 4x + 1$ and $y = 9 + 4x - 2x^2$

(e) $3x + y - 1 = 0$ and $y = 6 + 10x - 6x^2$

3 In both the following, show that the line and curve meet only once, find the point of intersection and use a graphic calculator to check that the line touches the curve.

(a) $y = 2x + 2$ and $y = x^2 - 2x + 6$ (b) $y = -2x - 7$ and $y = x^2 + 4x + 2$

4 Find the points of intersection between the curve $y = x^2 - x$ and the following lines.

(a) $y = x$ (b) $y = x - 1$

Use a graphic calculator to see how the lines are related to the curve.

5 Find the points of intersection between the curve $y = x^2 + 5x + 18$ and the following lines.

(a) $y = -3x + 2$ (b) $y = -3x + 6$

Use a graphic calculator to see how the lines are related to the curve.

6 Find the points of intersection between the line $y = x + 5$ and the following curves.

(a) $y = 2x^2 - 3x - 1$ (b) $y = 2x^2 - 3x + 7$

Use a graphic calculator to see how the line and the curves are related.

7 Find the points of intersection of the following curves.

    (a) $y = x^2 + 5x + 1$ and $y = x^2 + 3x + 11$

    (b) $y = x^2 - 3x - 7$ and $y = x^2 + x + 1$

    (c) $y = 7x^2 + 4x + 1$ and $y = 7x^2 - 4x + 1$

    Use a graphic calculator to see how the curves in each part are related.

8 Find the points of intersection of the following curves. Check your answers by using a graphic calculator.

    (a) $y = \frac{1}{2}x^2$ and $y = 1 - \frac{1}{2}x^2$ (b) $y = 2x^2 + 3x + 4$ and $y = x^2 + 6x + 2$

    (c) $y = x^2 + 7x + 13$ and $y = 1 - 3x - x^2$ (d) $y = 6x^2 + 2x - 9$ and $y = x^2 + 7x + 1$

    (e) $y = (x - 2)(6x + 5)$ and $y = (x - 5)^2 + 1$ (f) $y = 2x(x - 3)$ and $y = x(x + 2)$

3.7 Using factors to sketch graphs

The graphs of some functions of the form $f(x) = ax^2 + bx + c$ which factorise can also be drawn by another method. For example, take the functions

$$f(x) = x^2 - 6x + 5 = (x - 1)(x - 5) \quad \text{and} \quad g(x) = 12x - 4x^2 = -4x(x - 3).$$

In the first case, $f(1) = 0$ and $f(5) = 0$, so that the points $(1, 0)$ and $(5, 0)$ lie on the graph of $f(x)$. The graph crosses the y-axis when $x = 0$. As $f(0) = 5$, the graph crosses the y-axis at $(0, 5)$. This is shown in Fig. 3.8.

Similarly $g(0) = g(3) = 0$, so that $(0, 0)$ and $(3, 0)$ lie on the graph of $g(x)$. Since $g(0) = 0$, the graph crosses the y-axis at $(0, 0)$, that is, it passes through the origin. This is shown in Fig. 3.9.

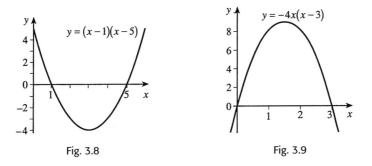

Fig. 3.8   Fig. 3.9

You can draw the graph of any function of this type which can be factorised as

$$a(x - r)(x - s),$$

by first noting that it cuts the x-axis at the points $(r, 0)$ and $(s, 0)$. The sign of the constant a tells you whether it 'bends upwards' (like $y = x^2$) or 'bends downwards'.

> Note that in Figs. 3.8 and 3.9 different scales have been used on the two axes. If you don't do this, the graphs will not fit on a normal-sized page. If equal scales had been used the elongation in both figures would have been more obvious.

Example 3.7.1

Draw a sketch of the graph of $f(x) = 3x^2 - 2x - 1$.

You can factorise the expression as $f(x) = (3x + 1)(x - 1)$, but to apply the method you need to write it as

$$f(x) = 3\left(x + \tfrac{1}{3}\right)(x - 1).$$

So the graph passes through $\left(-\tfrac{1}{3}, 0\right)$ and $(1, 0)$. The constant 3 tells you that the graph faces upwards and is elongated.

This is enough information to give a good idea of the shape of the graph, from which you can draw a sketch like Fig. 3.10. It is also worth noting that $f(0) = -1$, so that the graph cuts the y-axis at the point $(0, -1)$.

Note that the sketch does not have marks against the axes, except to say where the graph cuts them.

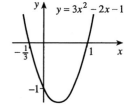

Fig. 3.10

3.8 Predicting functions from their graphs

You can also use the factor form to predict the equation of the graph of a function of the type $f(x) = ax^2 + bx + c$, if you know the points where its graph crosses the x-axis and the coordinates of one other point on the graph.

Example 3.8.1

Find the equation of the graph of the type $y = ax^2 + bx + c$ which crosses the x-axis at the points $(1, 0)$ and $(4, 0)$ and also passes through the point $(3, -4)$. (See Fig. 3.11.)

Since the curve cuts the axes at $(1, 0)$ and $(4, 0)$, the equation has the form

$$y = a(x - 1)(x - 4).$$

Since the point $(3, -4)$ lies on this curve,

$$-4 = a(3 - 1)(3 - 4)$$
$$-4 = a \times 2 \times (-1)$$
$$-4 = -2a$$
$$a = 2.$$

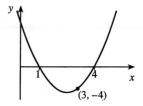

Fig. 3.11

The equation of the curve is therefore

$$y = 2(x - 1)(x - 4), \quad \text{or} \quad y = 2x^2 - 10x + 8.$$

You can extend this method to drawing graphs of functions with more than two factors. For example,

$$f(x) = a(x - r)(x - s)(x - t)$$

defines a function whose equation, when multiplied out, starts with $f(x) = ax^3 - \ldots$

The graph passes through the points $(r, 0)$, $(s, 0)$ and $(t, 0)$. The sign of the constant a tells you whether, for large positive values of x, the graph lies in the first or the fourth quadrant.

Example 3.8.2
Sketch the graphs of (a) $y = 2x(x - 1)(x - 4)$, (b) $y = -(x + 2)(x - 1)^2$.

(a) To find where the graph meets the x-axis, that is to find where the graph meets $y = 0$, put $2x(x - 1)(x - 4) = 0$.

This gives $x = 0$, $x - 1 = 0$ or $x - 4 = 0$ showing that the graph meets the x-axis at $x = 0$, $x = 1$ and $x = 4$.

When x is large (think of $x = 10$ say), the value of y is positive, showing that the graph lies in the first quadrant.

The sketch is shown in Fig. 3.12.

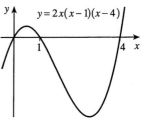

Fig. 3.12

(b) To find where the graph meets the x-axis, that is to find where the graph meets $y = 0$, put $-(x + 2)(x - 1)^2 = 0$.

This gives $x + 2 = 0$ and $x - 1 = 0$ showing that the graph meets the x-axis at $x = -2$ and $x = 1$.

As the factor $(x - 1)$ is squared, there are only two points of the graph on the x-axis. At $x = 1$, that is, at $(1, 0)$ the x-axis is a tangent to the graph.

When $x = 0$, $y = -2 \times (-1)^2 = -2$, so the graph passes through $(0, -2)$.

When x is large (think of $x = 10$ say), the value of y is negative, showing that the graph lies in the fourth quadrant.

The sketch is shown in Fig. 3.13.

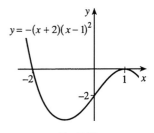

Fig. 3.13

When you think about large values of x it is often useful to substitute a number for x mentally. When you do this, make sure that the number you substitute is greater than any of the values you have already used in the sketch. So in Example 3.8.2(a), use a value bigger than $x = 4$; in Example 3.8.2(b), use a value bigger than $x = 1$.

Exercise 3D

1 Sketch each of the following graphs.

(a) $y = (x - 2)(x - 4)$

(b) $y = (x + 3)(x - 1)$

(c) $y = x(x - 2)$

(d) $y = (x + 5)(x + 1)$

(e) $y = x(x + 3)$

(f) $y = 2(x + 1)(x - 1)$

2 Sketch each of the following graphs.

(a) $y = 3(x + 1)(x - 5)$

(b) $y = -2(x - 1)(x - 3)$

(c) $y = -(x + 3)(x + 5)$

(d) $y = 2\left(x + \frac{1}{2}\right)(x - 3)$

(e) $y = -3(x - 4)^2$

(f) $y = -5(x - 1)\left(x + \frac{4}{5}\right)$

3 By first factorising the function, sketch each of the following graphs.

(a) $y = x^2 - 2x - 8$

(b) $y = x^2 - 2x$

(c) $y = x^2 + 6x + 9$

(d) $y = 2x^2 - 7x + 3$

(e) $y = 4x^2 - 1$

(f) $y = -(x^2 - x - 12)$

(g) $y = -x^2 - 4x - 4$

(h) $y = -(x^2 - 7x + 12)$

(i) $y = 11x - 4x^2 - 6$

4 Find the equation, in the form $y = x^2 + bx + c$, of the parabola which

(a) crosses the x-axis at the points $(2, 0)$ and $(5, 0)$

(b) crosses the x-axis at the points $(-7, 0)$ and $(-10, 0)$

(c) passes through the points $(-5, 0)$ and $(3, 0)$

(d) passes through the points $(-3, 0)$ and $(1, -16)$.

5 Sketch each of the following graphs.

(a) $y = (x + 3)(x - 2)(x - 3)$

(b) $y = x(x - 4)(x - 6)$

(c) $y = x^2(x - 4)$

(d) $y = x(x - 4)^2$

(e) $y = -(x + 6)(x + 4)(x + 2)$

(f) $y = -3(x + 1)(x - 3)^2$

6 Find the equation, in the form $y = ax^2 + bx + c$, of the following parabolas.

(a) Crosses the x-axis at $(1, 0)$ and $(5, 0)$ and crosses the y-axis at $(0, 15)$

(b) Crosses the x-axis at $(-2, 0)$ and $(7, 0)$ and crosses the y-axis at $(0, -56)$

(c) Passes through the points $(-6, 0)$, $(-2, 0)$ and $(0, -6)$

(d) Crosses the x-axis at $(-3, 0)$ and $(2, 0)$ and also passes through $(1, 16)$

(e) Passes through the points $(-10, 0)$, $(7, 0)$ and $(8, 90)$

7 Sketch each of the following graphs.

(a) $y = x^2 - 4x - 5$

(b) $y = 4x^2 - 4x + 1$

(c) $y = -x^2 - 3x + 18$

(d) $y = 2x^2 - 9x + 10$

(e) $y = -(x^2 - 4x - 5)$

(f) $y = 3x^2 + 9x$

8 Here are the equations of nine parabolas.

A $y = (x - 3)(x - 8)$ B $y = 14 + 5x - x^2$ C $y = 6x^2 - x - 70$

D $y = x(3 - x)$ E $y = (x + 2)(x - 7)$ F $y = -3(x + 3)(x + 7)$

G $y = x^2 + 2x + 1$ H $y = x^2 + 8x + 12$ I $y = x^2 - 25$

Answer the following questions without drawing the graphs of these parabolas.

(a) Which of the parabolas cross the y-axis at a positive value of y?

(b) For which of the parabolas is the vertex at the highest point of the graph?

(c) For which of the parabolas is the vertex to the left of the y-axis?

(d) Which of the parabolas pass through the origin?

(e) Which of the parabolas does not cross the x-axis at two separate points?

(f) Which of the parabolas has the y-axis as its axis of symmetry?

(g) Which two of the parabolas have the same axis of symmetry?

(h) Which of the parabolas have the vertex in the fourth quadrant?

9 Suggest a possible equation for each of the graphs shown below.

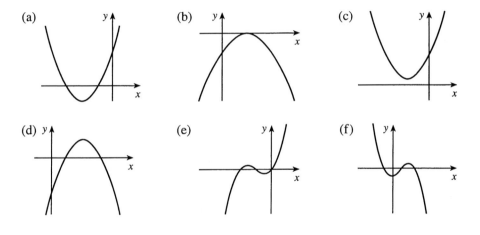

(a)   (b)   (c)

(d)   (e)   (f)

Miscellaneous exercise 3

1 The function f is defined by $f(x) = 7x - 4$.

(a) Find the values of $f(7)$, $f(\frac{1}{2})$ and $f(-5)$.

(b) Find the value of x such that $f(x) = 10$.

(c) Find the value of x such that $f(x) = x$.

(d) Find the value of x such that $f(x) = f(37)$.

2 The function f is defined by $f(x) = x^2 - 3x + 5$. Find the two values of x for which $f(x) = f(4)$.

3 The diagram shows the graph of $y = x^n$, where n is an integer. Given that the curve passes between the points $(2, 200)$ and $(2, 2000)$, determine the value of n.

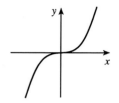

4 Find the points of intersection of the curves $y = x^2 - 7x + 5$ and $y = 1 + 2x - x^2$.

5 Find the points of intersection of the line $y = 2x + 3$ and the curve $y = 2x^2 + 3x - 7$.

6 Show that the line $3x + y - 2 = 0$ is a tangent to the curve $y = (4x - 3)(x - 2)$ and find the point of contact.

7 Find the coordinates of any points of intersection of the curves $y = (x - 2)(x - 4)$ and $y = x(2 - x)$. Sketch the two curves to show the relationship between them.

8 Given that k is a positive constant, sketch the following graphs.

   (a) $y = (x + k)(x - 2k)$ (b) $y = (x + 4k)(x + 2k)$

   (c) $y = x(x - k)(x - 5k)$ (d) $y = (x + k)(x - 2k)^2$

9 The function f is defined by $f(x) = ax^2 + bx + c$. Given that $f(0) = 6$, $f(-1) = 15$ and $f(1) = 1$, find the values of a, b and c.

10 Find the point where the line $y = 3 - 4x$ meets the curve $y = 4(4x^2 + 5x + 3)$.

11 Sketch the following graphs.

   (a) $y = (x + 4)(x + 2) + (x + 4)(x - 5)$ (b) $y = (x + 4)(x + 2) + (x + 4)(5 - x)$

12 A function f is defined by $f(x) = ax + b$. Given that $f(-2) = 27$ and $f(1) = 15$, find the value of x such that $f(x) = -5$.

13 A curve with equation $y = ax^2 + bx + c$ crosses the x-axis at $(-4, 0)$ and $(9, 0)$ and also passes through the point $(1, 120)$. Where does the curve cross the y-axis?

14 Show that the curves $y = 2x^2 + 5x$, $y = x^2 + 4x + 12$ and $y = 3x^2 + 4x - 6$ have one point in common and find its coordinates.

15 Given that the curves $y = x^2 - 3x + c$ and $y = k - x - x^2$ meet at the point $(-2, 12)$, find the values of c and k. Hence find the other point where the two curves meet.

16 Find the value of the constant p if the three curves $y = x^2 + 3x + 14$, $y = x^2 + 2x + 11$ and $y = px^2 + px + p$ have one point in common.

17 The straight line $y = x - 1$ meets the curve $y = x^2 - 5x - 8$ at the points A and B. The curve $y = p + qx - 2x^2$ also passes through the points A and B. Find the values of p and q.

18 Find, in surd form, the points of intersection of the curves $y = x^2 - 5x - 3$ and $y = 3 - 5x - x^2$.

19 Suggest a possible equation for each of the graphs shown below.

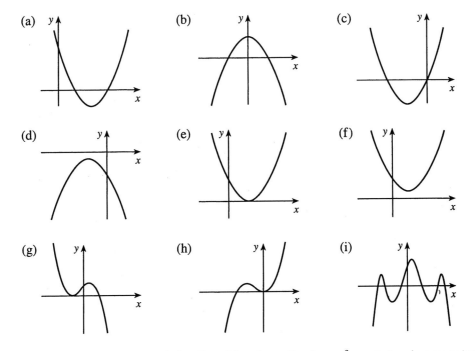

20 Show that the curves $y = 2x^2 - 7x + 14$ and $y = 2 + 5x - x^2$ meet at only one point and use a graphic calculator to confirm the relationship between the curves. Without further calculation or sketching, deduce the number of points of intersection of the following curves.

(a) $y = 2x^2 - 7x + 12$ and $y = 2 + 5x - x^2$

(b) $y = 2x^2 - 7x + 14$ and $y = 1 + 5x - x^2$

(c) $y = 2x^2 - 7x + 34$ and $y = 22 + 5x - x^2$

4 Quadratics

This chapter is about expressions of the form $ax^2 + bx + c$ and their graphs. When you have completed it, you should

- know how, if it is possible, to express a quadratic as a product of factors
- know how to complete the square in a quadratic expression
- know how to locate the vertex and the axis of symmetry of the quadratic graph $y = ax^2 + bx + c$
- be able to solve quadratic equations
- know that the discriminant of the quadratic expression $ax^2 + bx + c$ is the value of $b^2 - 4ac$, and know how to use it
- be able to solve a pair of simultaneous equations involving a quadratic equation and a linear equation
- be able to recognise and solve equations which can be reduced to quadratic equations by a substitution.

4.1 Quadratic expressions

You know that the graph of the equation $y = bx + c$ is a straight line. What happens if you add on a term ax^2, giving $y = ax^2 + bx + c$? The expression $ax^2 + bx + c$, where a, b and c are constants, is called a **quadratic**. Thus x^2, $x^2 - 6x + 8$, $2x^2 - 3x + 4$ and $-3x^2 - 5$ are all examples of quadratics.

When you write a quadratic as $ax^2 + bx + c$, b and c can be any numbers you please, including 0. But a cannot be 0, because the expression would then become just $bx + c$, which is not a quadratic. The numbers a, b and c are called **coefficients**: a is the coefficient of x^2, b is the coefficient of x and c is often called the constant term.

For the quadratic $2x^2 - x + 4$, the coefficient of x^2 is 2, the coefficient of x is -1 and the constant term is 4.

To keep things simple, most of the quadratics in this chapter have coefficients which are integers, but this is not a requirement; a, b and c can be any kind of real number.

For example, you could have $a = \frac{2}{3}$, $b = \sqrt{2}$ and $c = -\pi$, in which case the quadratic would be $\frac{2}{3}x^2 + \sqrt{2}x - \pi$. The theory would still apply, though the arithmetic would be more complicated.

The variable x is also assumed to be a real number. In more advanced mathematics a new kind of number is invented, called a complex number, and then some of the statements in this chapter have to be modified. (On some calculators it is possible for the answer to be given as a complex number.) But for the present you should understand the word 'number' to mean 'real number' unless stated otherwise.

4.2   Alternative forms for quadratics

You can write a quadratic expression such as $x^2 - 6x + 8$ in a number of ways. These include the **factor form** $(x - 4)(x - 2)$, useful for solving the quadratic equation $x^2 - 6x + 8 = 0$; and the **completed square form** $(x - 3)^2 - 1$, useful for locating the vertex of the parabola which is the graph of $y = x^2 - 6x + 8$, shown in Fig. 4.1.

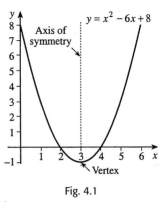

Fig. 4.1

If you write the equation of the graph $y = x^2 - 6x + 8$ in the form $y = (x - 2)(x - 4)$ you can find where the graph meets the x-axis, which has equation $y = 0$. Solving the equations $y = (x - 2)(x - 4)$ and $y = 0$ simultaneously gives $(x - 2)(x - 4) = 0$. You will be familiar with solving this equation by using the argument:

if $(x - 2)(x - 4) = 0$

then either $x - 2 = 0$ or $x - 4 = 0$

so $x = 2$ or $x = 4$.

Thus the graph meets the x-axis at $x = 2$ and $x = 4$, that is, at the points $(2, 0)$ and $(4, 0)$.

Example 4.2.1
Find where the quadratic $y = (2x - 1)(x - 2)$ meets the x-axis.

The graph $y = (2x - 1)(x - 2)$ meets the x-axis, $y = 0$, when $(2x - 1)(x - 2) = 0$.

$$(2x - 1)(x - 2) = 0$$

so $2x - 1 = 0$ or $x - 2 = 0$

giving $x = \frac{1}{2}$ or $x = 2$.

So $y = (2x - 1)(x - 2)$ meets the x-axis at $x = \frac{1}{2}$ and $x = 2$, that is, at the points $\left(\frac{1}{2}, 0\right)$ and $(2, 0)$.

Since $(x - 3)^2$ can be expanded as $x^2 - 6x + 9$, the equation $y = x^2 - 6x + 8$ can be written as $y = (x - 3)^2 - 1$. It is then easy to locate the axis of symmetry and the vertex of the graph.

The value of the perfect square $(x - 3)^2$ is always greater than or equal to 0, and only 0 when $x = 3$. That is, for any real number x,

$$(x - 3)^2 \geqslant 0.$$

Therefore, from $y = (x - 3)^2 - 1$ it follows that $y \geqslant -1$. Also $y = -1$ when $x = 3$. So the vertex is at the point $(3, -1)$. The axis of symmetry is $x = 3$. These properties are shown in Fig. 4.1.

Here are some more examples of using the completed square form.

Example 4.2.2

Locate the vertex and the axis of symmetry of the quadratic graph $y = 3 - 2(x + 2)^2$.

Since $2(x + 2)^2$ is greater than or equal to 0, whatever the value of x, y is less than or equal to 3. It takes the value 3 when $x = -2$, so the point $(-2, 3)$ is the vertex.

As the vertex lies on the axis of symmetry, the axis is a vertical line passing through $(-2, 3)$, and has equation $x = -2$.

Example 4.2.3

Solve the equation $3(x - 2)^2 - 2 = 0$.

As $3(x - 2)^2 - 2 = 0$, $3(x - 2)^2 = 2$ and $(x - 2)^2 = \frac{2}{3}$.

Therefore $(x - 2) = \pm\sqrt{\frac{2}{3}}$, so $x = 2 \pm \sqrt{\frac{2}{3}}$.

4.3   Factorising quadratics

This section is about finding factors of quadratics like $x^2 - 2x - 3$ and $3x^2 - 2x - 5$. However, in this section the factors are restricted to those cases where the coefficients of the quadratic to be factorised, and the linear factors which make it up, are all integers.

In this sense, $x^2 - 3 = (x - \sqrt{3})(x + \sqrt{3})$ will be said *not* to factorise, because the terms in the linear factors contain $\sqrt{3}$.

There are three important special cases to get out of the way quickly.

No constant term

If the constant term is zero, as in $x^2 - 2x$ and $3x^2 - 2x$, the quadratic always factorises by taking out the factor x to get

$$x^2 - 2x = x(x - 2) \quad \text{and} \quad 3x^2 - 2x = x(3x - 2).$$

Difference of two squares

If the coefficient of x is zero, and the other terms have the form of the difference of two squares such as $x^2 - 9$ and $4x^2 - 25$, the quadratic can always be factorised.

Using the result from Section 2.2,

$$p^2 - q^2 = (p - q)(p + q)$$

with $p = x$ and $q = 3$ gives

$$x^2 - 9 = (x - 3)(x + 3).$$

And putting $p = 2x$ and $q = 5$ gives

$$4x^2 - 25 = (2x - 5)(2x + 5).$$

Sum of two squares

Expressions such as $x^2 + 9$ and $4x^2 + 25$ which are the sum of two squares *never* factorise.

It is easy to see why. Since $x^2 \geq 0$, $x^2 + 9$ is always greater than or equal to 9, so it can never be 0. But if $x^2 + 9$ had factors $(x - p)(x - q)$, it would be 0 when $x = p$ and $x = q$. Putting these two statements together, it follows that $x^2 + 9$ doesn't factorise.

> The factors of $ax^2 + bx$ are given by
> $$ax^2 + bx = x(ax + b).$$
> The factors of $x^2 - a^2$ are given by
> $$(x - a)(x + a).$$
> The sum of two squares, $x^2 + a^2$, has no factors.

Example 4.3.1

Find the factors of   (a) $3x^2 + 4x$,   (b) $4x^2 - 1$.

(a) There is no constant term so
$$3x^2 + 4x = x(3x + 4).$$

(b) This has the difference of two squares form, so
$$4x^2 - 1 = (2x - 1)(2x + 1).$$

The general case

Finding the factors of other quadratics can be a hit-and-miss process. It is simple enough to factorise an expression such as $x^2 - 2x - 3$: x^2 can only split as $x \times x$, and 3 as 3×1, so if there are simple factors they must have the form $(x \ldots 3)(x \ldots 1)$ with $+$ or $-$ signs in place of the dots. To get a product of -3 one of these signs must be $+$ and the other $-$, and a quick check produces the answer $(x - 3)(x + 1)$.

Factorising a quadratic such as $6x^2 - 7x - 10$ is a much tougher proposition. The $6x^2$ might split either as $x \times 6x$ or as $2x \times 3x$, the 10 as 1×10 or as 2×5, and in each case there are two ways of pairing the factors. Trying all the possibilities until you get the correct coefficient of x, in this case -7, can take a long time, but if you can see the factors quickly this process is the quickest way.

Example 4.3.2

Find the factors of (a) $x^2 - 8x + 12$,   (b) $6x^2 - x - 2$.

(a) The first term x^2 splits as $x \times x$. The constant term 12 is positive, so the signs inside the brackets must be either both positive or both negative. The middle term $-8x$ then shows that both signs are negative. So the factors have the form $(x - \ldots)(x - \ldots)$.

The factors of 12 are 1×12, 2×6 and 3×4, so the possibilities are $(x - 1)(x - 12)$, $(x - 2)(x - 6)$ and $(x - 3)(x - 4)$. Multiplying each of these out gives $x^2 - 13x + 12$, $x^2 - 8x + 12$ and $x^2 - 7x + 12$ respectively, so

$$x^2 - 8x + 12 = (x - 2)(x - 6).$$

(b) The possible factors of 6 are 1×6 and 2×3, and the factors of 2 are 1×2. The sign of the constant term -6 is negative, so one factor is positive and one is negative. The possible factors of $6x^2 - x - 2$ which need to be tested are

$$(x - 1)(6x + 2), \quad (x + 1)(6x - 2), \quad (x - 2)(6x + 1), \quad (x + 2)(6x - 1),$$
$$(2x + 1)(3x - 2), \quad (2x - 1)(3x + 2), \quad (2x + 2)(3x - 1), \quad (2x - 2)(3x + 1).$$

Notice that every possible combination which gives $6x^2$ as the first term and -2 as the constant term has been taken.

When you test these, you find that the correct combination is $(2x + 1)(3x - 2)$, so $6x^2 - x - 2 = (2x + 1)(3x - 2)$.

There is a way of shortening the work of finding the factors of $6x^2 - x - 2$. When you write out the factors, some of them, in this case, $(x - 1)(6x + 2)$, $(x + 1)(6x - 2)$, $(2x + 2)(3x - 1)$ and $(2x - 2)(3x + 1)$, have a bracket which has a factor of 2. Each of these can be factorised further to give

$$(x - 1)(6x + 2) = 2(x - 1)(3x + 1), \quad (x + 1)(6x - 2) = 2(x + 1)(3x - 1),$$
$$(2x + 2)(3x - 1) = 2(x + 1)(3x - 1), \quad (2x - 2)(3x + 1) = 2(x - 1)(3x + 1).$$

Each of these has a factor of 2, but 2 does not divide $6x^2 - x - 2$. So none of these four cases can possibly work. This leaves just

$$(x - 2)(6x + 1), \quad (x + 2)(6x - 1), \quad (2x + 1)(3x - 2), \quad (2x - 1)(3x + 2)$$

to be tested, which is much quicker than before.

Example 4.3.3
Find the factors of (a) $6x^2 - 5x - 4$, (b) $12x^2 - 10x - 8$.

(a) The possibilities for the factors of $6x^2 - 5x - 4$ are:

$$(x - 1)(6x + 4), \quad (x + 1)(6x - 4), \quad (x - 4)(6x + 1), \quad (x + 4)(6x - 1),$$
$$(x - 2)(6x + 2), \quad (x + 2)(6x - 2), \quad (2x + 1)(3x - 4), \quad (2x - 1)(3x + 4),$$
$$(2x + 4)(3x - 1), \quad (2x - 4)(3x + 1), \quad (2x + 2)(3x - 2), \quad (2x - 2)(3x + 2).$$

Knocking out the cases where one of the factors has a common factor leaves

$$(x - 4)(6x + 1), \quad (x + 4)(6x - 1), \quad (2x + 1)(3x - 4), \quad (2x - 1)(3x + 4),$$

to be tested.

When you test, $(2x + 1)(3x - 4)$ is the possibility that gives $-5x$ as the middle term, so

$$6x^2 - 5x - 4 = (2x + 1)(3x - 4).$$

(b) To factorise $12x^2 - 10x - 8$, first notice that you can take out the factor of 2, to get

$$12x^2 - 10x - 8 = 2(6x^2 - 5x - 4).$$

Concentrating now on $6x^2 - 5x - 4$, and using part (a),

$$12x^2 - 10x - 8 = 2(6x^2 - 5x - 4) = 2(2x + 1)(3x - 4).$$

If you count the number of possibilities for factors of $12x^2 - 10x - 8$ without first taking out the factor 2, you will quickly convince yourself of the benefit of taking out the numerical factor first.

Example 4.3.4
Solve the quadratic equations (a) $x^2 - 8x + 12 = 0$,　(b) $6x^2 - x - 2 = 0$.

(a) Using the factors from Example 4.3.2, $x^2 - 8x + 12 = (x - 2)(x - 6)$.

If　$(x - 2)(x - 6) = 0$
then　either $x - 2 = 0$ or $x - 6 = 0$
so　$x = 2$ or $x = 6$.

(b) From Example 4.3.2, $6x^2 - x - 2 = (2x + 1)(3x - 2)$.

If　$(2x + 1)(3x - 2) = 0$
then　either $2x + 1 = 0$ or $3x - 2 = 0$
so　$x = -\frac{1}{2}$ or $x = \frac{2}{3}$.

Exercise 4A

1 Factorise each of the following quadratics.

  (a) $x^2 + 11x + 24$　　　　(b) $l^2 - 7l + 12$　　　　(c) $q^2 - 12q + 35$

  (d) $x^2 + x - 6$　　　　　　(e) $x^2 + 5x - 24$　　　　(f) $n^2 - 7n - 60$

  (g) $r^2 - 17r + 16$　　　　(h) $x^2 - 14x + 33$　　　　(i) $x^2 + 4x - 21$

2 Factorise each of the following quadratics.

  (a) $3x^2 - 8x + 4$　　　　(b) $4x^2 - 12x + 5$　　　　(c) $12x^2 + x - 1$

  (d) $3x^2 - 4x - 4$　　　　(e) $8x^2 - 15x - 2$　　　　(f) $6x^2 + 5x - 6$

  (g) $4x^2 - 8x - 5$　　　　(h) $9x^2 - 30x + 9$　　　　(i) $12x^2 - 10x - 8$

3 Use the 'difference of two squares' to write down the factors of the following quadratics.

  (a) $x^2 - 1$　　　　　　　(b) $4 - 25d^2$　　　　　　(c) $100 - 4z^2$

  (d) $(x + 1)^2 - 4x^2$　　　(e) $(2x + 1)^2 - x^2$　　　(f) $(2x + 1)^2 - (x - 3)^2$

4 Not all quadratics have factors in which each of the coefficients is an integer. Find, where possible, factors of the following in which all the coefficients are integers.

(a) $x^2 + 2x + 2$ (b) $x^2 - 13x + 40$ (c) $x^2 + 6x - 12$

(d) $4x^2 + 16$ (e) $x^2 + 14x$ (f) $j^2 - 4j - 60$

(g) $x^2 + 16x + 12$ (h) $7 - 8x - 4x^2$ (i) $2x^2 + 5x - 3$

5 Solve the following quadratic equations.

(a) $x^2 - 2x - 35 = 0$ (b) $x^2 - 2x - 3 = 0$ (c) $x^2 + 6x - 27 = 0$

(d) $6x^2 - 5x - 6 = 0$ (e) $6 + 5x - 6x^2 = 0$ (f) $12x^2 + x - 6 = 0$

6 Find the x-coordinates of the points where the following quadratic graphs meet the x-axis.

(a) $y = x^2 + 3x - 4$ (b) $y = 2x^2 - 18$ (c) $y = 2x^2 - x - 1$

(d) $y = 2x^2 - 5x + 2$ (e) $y = x^2 - 6x + 9$ (f) $y = 1 - 9x^2$

4.4   Completing the square

When you try to write the quadratic expression $x^2 + bx + c$ in completed square form, the key point is to note that when you square $(x + \frac{1}{2}b)$ you get

$$\left(x + \tfrac{1}{2}b\right)^2 = x^2 + bx + \tfrac{1}{4}b^2, \quad \text{so} \quad x^2 + bx = \left(x + \tfrac{1}{2}b\right)^2 - \tfrac{1}{4}b^2.$$

Now add c to both sides:

$$x^2 + bx + c = (x^2 + bx) + c$$
$$= \left(x + \tfrac{1}{2}b\right)^2 - \tfrac{1}{4}b^2 + c.$$

Example 4.4.1
Write $x^2 + 10x + 32$ in completed square form.

$$x^2 + 10x + 32 = (x^2 + 10x) + 32$$
$$= \left\{(x + 5)^2 - 25\right\} + 32$$
$$= (x + 5)^2 + 7.$$

Don't try to learn the form $x^2 + bx + c = \left(x + \tfrac{1}{2}b\right)^2 + c - \tfrac{1}{4}b^2$. Learn that you halve the coefficient of x, and write $x^2 + bx = \left(x + \tfrac{1}{2}b\right)^2 - \tfrac{1}{4}b^2$. Then add c to both sides.

If you need to write $ax^2 + bx + c$ in completed square form, but the coefficient a of x^2 is not 1, you can rewrite $ax^2 + bx + c$ by taking out the coefficient of x^2 as a factor from the first two terms:

$$ax^2 + bx + c = a\left(x^2 + \frac{b}{a}x\right) + c.$$

Then complete the square of the quadratic expression $x^2 + \dfrac{b}{a}x$ inside the bracket.

Example 4.4.2

Express $2x^2 + 10x + 7$ in completed square form. Use your result to find the axis of symmetry and the vertex of the graph of $y = 2x^2 + 10x + 7$.

Start by taking out the coefficient of x^2 as a factor from the first two terms:

$$2x^2 + 10x + 7 = 2(x^2 + 5x) + 7.$$

Dealing with the terms inside the bracket,

$$x^2 + 5x = \left(x + \tfrac{5}{2}\right)^2 - \tfrac{25}{4},$$

so
$$
\begin{aligned}
2x^2 + 10x + 7 &= 2(x^2 + 5x) + 7 \\
&= 2\left\{\left(x + \tfrac{5}{2}\right)^2 - \tfrac{25}{4}\right\} + 7 \\
&= 2\left(x + \tfrac{5}{2}\right)^2 - \tfrac{25}{2} + 7 \\
&= 2\left(x + \tfrac{5}{2}\right)^2 - \tfrac{11}{2}.
\end{aligned}
$$

> It's worth checking your result mentally at this stage.

The equation of the graph can be written as $y = 2\left(x + \tfrac{5}{2}\right)^2 - \tfrac{11}{2}$.

The minimum value of this occurs when the square $\left(x + \tfrac{5}{2}\right)^2$ is 0, which is when $x = -\tfrac{5}{2}$. The minimum value is then $y = -\tfrac{11}{2}$.

So the axis of symmetry is $x = -\tfrac{5}{2}$, and the vertex is $\left(-\tfrac{5}{2}, \tfrac{11}{2}\right)$.

If the coefficient of x^2 is negative, the technique is similar to Example 4.4.3.

Example 4.4.3

Express $3 - 4x - 2x^2$ in completed square form. Use your result to find the axis of symmetry and the vertex of the graph of $y = 3 - 4x - 2x^2$.

Start by taking out the coefficient of x^2 as a factor from the terms which involve x:

$$3 - 4x - 2x^2 = 3 - 2(x^2 + 2x).$$

Dealing with the terms inside the bracket, $x^2 + 2x = (x + 1)^2 - 1$,

so
$$
\begin{aligned}
3 - 4x - 2x^2 &= 3 - 2(x^2 + 2x) \\
&= 3 - 2\left\{(x + 1)^2 - 1\right\} \\
&= 3 - 2(x + 1)^2 + 2 \\
&= 5 - 2(x + 1)^2.
\end{aligned}
$$

The equation of the graph can be written as $y = 5 - 2(x + 1)^2$.

This shows that the maximum value, at the vertex, is 5 when $x = -1$.

So the axis of symmetry is $x = -1$, and the vertex is $(-1, 5)$.

Example 4.4.4

Express $3x^2 - 8x - 3$ in completed square form, and use your result to solve the equation $3x^2 - 8x - 3 = 0$.

$$3x^2 - 8x - 3 = 3\left(x^2 - \tfrac{8}{3}x\right) - 3$$
$$= 3\{(x - \tfrac{4}{3})^2 - \tfrac{16}{9}\} - 3$$
$$= 3\{(x - \tfrac{4}{3})^2 - \tfrac{16}{9} - 1\}$$
$$= 3\{(x - \tfrac{4}{3})^2 - \tfrac{25}{9}\}.$$

The equation $3x^2 - 8x - 3 = 0$ is the same as $3\{(x - \tfrac{4}{3})^2 - \tfrac{25}{9}\} = 0$.

$$3\{(x - \tfrac{4}{3})^2 - \tfrac{25}{9}\} = 0$$
$$(x - \tfrac{4}{3})^2 - \tfrac{25}{9} = 0$$
$$(x - \tfrac{4}{3})^2 = \tfrac{25}{9}$$

giving $\quad x - \tfrac{4}{3} = \tfrac{5}{3} \quad$ or $\quad x - \tfrac{4}{3} = -\tfrac{5}{3}.$

So $\qquad x = \tfrac{4}{3} + \tfrac{5}{3} = 3 \quad$ or $\quad x = \tfrac{4}{3} - \tfrac{5}{3} = -\tfrac{1}{3}.$

Exercise 4B

1 Find (i) the vertex and (ii) the equation of the line of symmetry of each of the following quadratic graphs.

(a) $y = (x - 2)^2 + 3$ (b) $y = (x - 5)^2 - 4$ (c) $y = (x + 3)^2 - 7$

(d) $y = (2x - 3)^2 + 1$ (e) $y = (5x + 3)^2 + 2$ (f) $y = (3x + 7)^2 - 4$

(g) $y = (x - 3)^2 + c$ (h) $y = (x - p)^2 + q$ (i) $y = (ax + b)^2 + c$, where $a \neq 0$

2 Find (i) the least (or, if appropriate, the greatest) value of each of the following quadratic expressions and (ii) the value of x for which this occurs.

(a) $(x + 2)^2 - 1$ (b) $(x - 1)^2 + 2$ (c) $5 - (x + 3)^2$

(d) $(2x + 1)^2 - 7$ (e) $3 - 2(x - 4)^2$ (f) $(x + p)^2 + q$

(g) $(x - p)^2 - q$ (h) $r - (x - t)^2$ (i) $c - (ax + b)^2$

3 Solve the following quadratic equations. Leave surds in your answer.

(a) $(x - 3)^2 - 3 = 0$ (b) $(x + 2)^2 - 4 = 0$ (c) $2(x + 3)^2 = 5$

(d) $(3x - 7)^2 = 8$ (e) $(x + p)^2 - q = 0$ (f) $a(x + b)^2 - c = 0$

4 Express the following in completed square form.

(a) $x^2 + 2x + 2$ (b) $x^2 - 8x - 3$ (c) $x^2 + 3x - 7$

(d) $5 - 6x + x^2$ (e) $x^2 + 14x + 49$ (f) $2x^2 + 12x - 5$

(g) $3x^2 - 12x + 3$ (h) $7 - 8x - 4x^2$ (i) $2x^2 + 5x - 3$

5 Use the completed square form to factorise the following expressions.

(a) $x^2 - 2x - 35$ (b) $x^2 - 14x - 176$ (c) $x^2 + 6x - 432$

(d) $6x^2 - 5x - 6$ (e) $14 + 45x - 14x^2$ (f) $12x^2 + x - 6$

6 Use the completed square form to find as appropriate the least or greatest value of each of the following expressions, and the value of x for which this occurs.

(a) $x^2 - 4x + 7$ (b) $x^2 - 3x + 5$ (c) $4 + 6x - x^2$

(d) $2x^2 - 5x + 2$ (e) $3x^2 + 2x - 4$ (f) $3 - 7x - 3x^2$

7 By completing the square find (i) the vertex, and (ii) the equation of the line of symmetry, of each of the following parabolas.

(a) $y = x^2 - 4x + 6$ (b) $y = x^2 + 6x - 2$ (c) $y = 7 - 10x - x^2$

(d) $y = x^2 + 3x + 1$ (e) $y = 2x^2 - 7x + 2$ (f) $y = 3x^2 - 12x + 5$

4.5 Solving quadratic equations

You saw at the beginning of Section 4.2 how to solve a quadratic equation which you can split into factors.

$$x^2 - 6x + 8 = 0$$
$$(x - 2)(x - 4) = 0$$
either $x - 2 = 0$ or $x - 4 = 0$
so $x = 2$ or $x = 4$.

The **solution** of the equation $x^2 - 6x + 8 = 0$ is $x = 2$ or $x = 4$. The numbers 2 and 4 are the **roots** of the equation.

If the quadratic expression has factors which you can find easily, then this is certainly the quickest way to solve it. However, the expression may not have factors, or they may be hard to find: try finding the factors of $30x^2 - 11x - 30$.

If you cannot factorise a quadratic expression easily to solve an equation, then you will have to use the quadratic formula:

> The solution of $ax^2 + bx + c = 0$, where $a \neq 0$, is
> $$x = \frac{-b \pm \sqrt{b^2 - 4ac}}{2a}.$$

It is helpful to know how this formula is derived by expressing $ax^2 + bx + c$ in completed square form. Start by dividing both sides of the equation by a (which cannot be zero, otherwise the equation would not be a quadratic equation):

$$x^2 + \frac{b}{a}x + \frac{c}{a} = 0.$$

Completing the square of the expression on the left side, you find that

$$x^2 + \frac{b}{a}x + \frac{c}{a} = \left(x + \frac{b}{2a}\right)^2 - \frac{b^2}{4a^2} + \frac{c}{a} = \left(x + \frac{b}{2a}\right)^2 - \frac{b^2 - 4ac}{4a^2}.$$

So you can continue with the equation

$$\left(x + \frac{b}{2a}\right)^2 - \frac{b^2 - 4ac}{4a^2} = 0, \quad \text{which is} \quad \left(x + \frac{b}{2a}\right)^2 = \frac{b^2 - 4ac}{4a^2}.$$

There are two possibilities. Either

$$x + \frac{b}{2a} = +\sqrt{\frac{b^2 - 4ac}{4a^2}} = \frac{\sqrt{b^2 - 4ac}}{\sqrt{4a^2}} \quad \left(\text{using } \sqrt{\frac{p}{q}} = \frac{\sqrt{p}}{\sqrt{q}}, \text{ see Section 2.2}\right)$$

or

$$x + \frac{b}{2a} = -\sqrt{\frac{b^2 - 4ac}{4a^2}} = -\frac{\sqrt{b^2 - 4ac}}{\sqrt{4a^2}}.$$

Since $4a^2 = (2a)^2$, $\sqrt{4a^2}$ is either $+2a$ (if a is positive) or $-2a$ (if a is negative). In either case,

$$x + \frac{b}{2a} = \pm\frac{\sqrt{b^2 - 4ac}}{2a},$$

So

$$x = -\frac{b}{2a} \pm \frac{\sqrt{b^2 - 4ac}}{2a} = \frac{-b \pm \sqrt{b^2 - 4ac}}{2a}.$$

This shows that if $ax^2 + bx + c = 0$ and $a \neq 0$, then $x = \dfrac{-b \pm \sqrt{b^2 - 4ac}}{2a}$.

Example 4.5.1

Use the quadratic equation formula to solve the equations

(a) $2x^2 - 3x - 4 = 0$,   (b) $2x^2 - 3x + 4 = 0$,

(c) $30x^2 - 11x - 30 = 0$,   (d) $4x^2 + 4x + 1 = 0$.

(a) Comparing this with $ax^2 + bx + c = 0$, put $a = 2$, $b = -3$ and $c = -4$. Then

$$x = \frac{-(-3) \pm \sqrt{(-3)^2 - 4 \times 2 \times (-4)}}{2 \times 2} = \frac{3 \pm \sqrt{9 + 32}}{4} = \frac{3 \pm \sqrt{41}}{4}.$$

> Sometimes it will be sufficient to leave the roots like this in surd form, but you may need to find the numerical values $\dfrac{3 + \sqrt{41}}{4} \approx 2.35$ and $\dfrac{3 - \sqrt{41}}{4} \approx -0.85$. Try substituting these numbers in the equation and see what happens.

(b) Putting $a = 2$, $b = -3$ and $c = 4$,

$$x = \frac{-(-3) \pm \sqrt{(-3)^2 - 4 \times 2 \times 4}}{2 \times 2} = \frac{3 \pm \sqrt{9 - 32}}{4} = \frac{3 \pm \sqrt{-23}}{4}.$$

But there is no real number whose square is -23. This means that the equation $2x^2 - 3x + 4 = 0$ has no real roots.

Try putting $2x^2 - 3x + 4$ in completed square form; what can you deduce about the graph of $y = 2x^2 - 3x + 4$?

(c) Putting $a = 30$, $b = -11$ and $c = -30$,

$$x = \frac{-(-11) \pm \sqrt{(-11)^2 - 4 \times 30 \times (-30)}}{2 \times 30} = \frac{11 \pm \sqrt{121 + 3600}}{60}$$

$$= \frac{11 \pm \sqrt{3721}}{60} = \frac{11 \pm 61}{60}$$

so $x = \frac{72}{60} = \frac{6}{5}$ or $x = -\frac{50}{60} = -\frac{5}{6}$.

This third example factorises, but the factors are difficult to find. But once you know the roots of the equation you can deduce that

$$30x^2 - 11x - 30 = (6x + 5)(5x - 6).$$

This can be a useful way of finding the factors of a complicated quadratic.

(d) Putting $a = 4$, $b = 4$ and $c = 1$,

$$x = \frac{-4 \pm \sqrt{4^2 - 4 \times 4 \times 1}}{2 \times 4} = \frac{-4 \pm \sqrt{16 - 16}}{8}$$

$$= \frac{-4 \pm \sqrt{0}}{8} = \frac{-4}{8} = -\frac{1}{2}$$

so $x = -\frac{1}{2}$.

4.6 The discriminant $b^2 - 4ac$

If you look back at Example 4.5.1 you will see that in part (a) the roots of the equation involved surds, in part (b) there were no roots, in part (c) the roots were fractions and in part (d) there was only one root.

You can predict which case will arise by calculating the value of the expression under the square root sign, $b^2 - 4ac$, and thinking about the effect that this value has in the quadratic equation formula $x = \dfrac{-b \pm \sqrt{b^2 - 4ac}}{2a}$.

- If $b^2 - 4ac$ is a perfect square, the equation will have roots which are integers or fractions.
- If $b^2 - 4ac > 0$, the equation $ax^2 + bx + c = 0$ will have two roots.
- If $b^2 - 4ac < 0$, there will be no real roots.
- If $b^2 - 4ac = 0$, the root has the form $x = -\dfrac{b \pm 0}{2a} = -\dfrac{b}{2a}$, and there is one root only.

  Sometimes it is said that there are two coincident roots, or a **repeated root**, because the root values $-\dfrac{b + 0}{2a}$ and $-\dfrac{b - 0}{2a}$ are equal.

The expression $b^2 - 4ac$ is called the **discriminant** of the quadratic expression $ax^2 + bx + c$ because, by its value, it discriminates between the types of solution of the equation $ax^2 + bx + c = 0$.

Example 4.6.1

What can you deduce from the values of the discriminants of these quadratic equations?

(a) $2x^2 - 3x - 4 = 0$ (b) $2x^2 - 3x - 5 = 0$

(c) $2x^2 - 4x + 5 = 0$ (d) $2x^2 - 4x + 2 = 0$

(a) As $a = 2$, $b = -3$ and $c = -4$, $b^2 - 4ac = (-3)^2 - 4 \times 2 \times (-4) = 9 + 32 = 41$. The discriminant is positive, so the equation $2x^2 - 3x - 4 = 0$ has two roots. Also, as 41 is not a perfect square, the roots are irrational.

(b) As $a = 2$, $b = -3$, and $c = -5$, $b^2 - 4ac = (-3)^2 - 4 \times 2 \times (-5) = 9 + 40 = 49$. The discriminant is positive, so the equation $2x^2 - 3x - 5 = 0$ has two roots. Also, as 49 is a perfect square, the roots are rational.

(c) $b^2 - 4ac = (-4)^2 - 4 \times 2 \times 5 = 16 - 40 = -24$. As the discriminant is negative, the equation $2x^2 - 4x + 5 = 0$ has no real roots.

(d) $b^2 - 4ac = (-4)^2 - 4 \times 2 \times 2 = 16 - 16 = 0$. As the discriminant is zero, the equation $2x^2 - 4x + 2 = 0$ has only one (repeated) root.

Example 4.6.2

Find any points of intersection of the line $y = x + 2$ and the curve $x^2 + 4y + 2y^2 = 4$. Interpret your answer geometrically.

You need to substitute either $y = x + 2$ or $x = y - 2$ into the equation of the curve.

Substituting $x = y - 2$ is slightly less work (why?) so

$$x^2 + 4y + 2y^2 = 4$$
$$(y - 2)^2 + 4y + 2y^2 = 4$$
$$y^2 - 4y + 4 + 4y + 2y^2 = 4$$
$$3y^2 = 0$$
$$y^2 = 0$$
$$y = 0.$$

$y = 0$ is a repeated root of this equation.

Substituting in $x = y - 2$ to find x shows that there is just one point of intersection, namely $(-2, 0)$.

Fig. 4.2 shows the graph with equation $x^2 + 4y + 2y^2 = 4$. You can see that the only lines which have just one point in common with the curve are tangents. So $y = x + 2$ is the equation of the tangent to the curve at the point $(-2, 0)$.

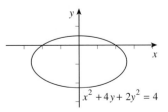

Fig. 4.2

Example 4.6.3

The equation $kx^2 - 2x - 7 = 0$ has two real roots. What can you deduce about the value of the constant k?

The discriminant is $(-2)^2 - 4 \times k \times (-7) = 4 + 28k$. As the equation has two real roots, the value of the discriminant is positive, so $4 + 28k > 0$, and $k > -\frac{1}{7}$.

Example 4.6.4

The equation $3x^2 + 2x + k = 0$ has a repeated root. Find the value of k.

The equation has repeated roots if $b^2 - 4ac = 0$; that is, if $2^2 - 4 \times 3 \times k = 0$. This gives $k = \frac{1}{3}$.

> Notice how, in these examples, there is no need to solve the quadratic equation. You can find all you need to know from the discriminant.

Exercise 4C

1 Use the quadratic formula to solve the following equations. Leave irrational answers in surd form. If there is no solution, say so.

(a) $x^2 + 3x - 5 = 0$ (b) $x^2 - 4x - 7 = 0$ (c) $x^2 + 6x + 9 = 0$

(d) $x^2 + 5x + 2 = 0$ (e) $x^2 + x + 1 = 0$ (f) $3x^2 - 5x - 6 = 0$

(g) $2x^2 + 7x + 3 = 0$ (h) $8 - 3x - x^2 = 0$ (i) $5 + 4x - 6x^2 = 0$

2 Use the value of the discriminant $b^2 - 4ac$ to determine whether the following equations have two roots, one root or no roots. In parts (i) and (j), assume $p > 0$ and $q > 0$.

(a) $x^2 - 3x - 5 = 0$ (b) $x^2 + 2x + 1 = 0$ (c) $x^2 - 3x + 4 = 0$

(d) $3x^2 - 6x + 5 = 0$ (e) $2x^2 - 7x + 3 = 0$ (f) $5x^2 + 9x + 4 = 0$

(g) $3x^2 + 42x + 147 = 0$ (h) $3 - 7x - 4x^2 = 0$ (i) $x^2 + px - q = 0$

(j) $x^2 - px - q = 0$

3 The following equations have repeated roots. Find the value of k in each case. Leave your answers as integers, exact fractions or surds.

(a) $x^2 + 3x - k = 0$ (b) $kx^2 + 5x - 8 = 0$ (c) $x^2 - 18x + k = 0$

(d) $-3 + kx - 2x^2 = 0$ (e) $4x^2 - kx + 6 = 0$ (f) $kx^2 - px + q = 0$

4 The following equations have the number of roots shown in brackets. Deduce as much as you can about the value of k.

(a) $x^2 + 3x + k = 0$ (2)   (b) $x^2 - 7x + k = 0$ (1)   (c) $kx^2 - 3x + 5 = 0$ (0)

(d) $3x^2 + 5x - k = 0$ (2)   (e) $x^2 - 4x + 3k = 0$ (1)   (f) $kx^2 - 5x + 7 = 0$ (0)

(g) $x^2 - kx + 4 = 0$ (2)   (h) $x^2 + kx + 9 = 0$ (0)

5 Use the value of the discriminant to determine the number of points of intersection of the following graphs with the x-axis.

(a) $y = x^2 - 5x - 5$

(b) $y = x^2 + x + 1$

(c) $y = x^2 - 6x + 9$

(d) $y = x^2 + 4$

(e) $y = x^2 - 10$

(f) $y = 3 - 4x - 2x^2$

(g) $y = 3x^2 - 5x + 7$

(h) $y = x^2 + bx + b^2$

(i) $y = x^2 - 2qx + q^2$

6 If a and c are both positive, what can be said about the graph of $y = ax^2 + bx - c$?

7 If a is negative and c is positive, what can be said about the graph of $y = ax^2 + bx + c$?

4.7   Simultaneous equations

This section takes forward the ideas in Section 3.6, and involves solving simultaneous equations such as $y = x^2$ and $5x + 4y = 21$. The method can be used to find the points of intersection of a line and a curve.

Example 4.7.1
Solve the simultaneous equations $y = x^2$, $x + y = 6$.

These equations are usually best solved by finding an expression for x or y from one equation and substituting it into the other. It is usually easier to find x or y from the equation of the straight line, and to substitute it into the equation of the curve.

So substituting $x = 6 - y$ into the equation $y = x^2$ gives

$$y = (6 - y)^2$$
$$y = 36 - 12y + y^2$$
$$y^2 - 13y + 36 = 0$$
$$(y - 4)(y - 9) = 0$$

giving $y = 4$ or $y = 9$.

Substituting to find x gives $x = 2$ or $x = -3$.

The solution is therefore $x = 2$, $y = 4$ or $x = -3$, $y = 9$.

Notice that the answers go together in pairs. It would be wrong to give the answer in the form $x = 2$ or $x = -3$ and $y = 4$ or $y = 9$, because $x = 2$ and $y = 9$ do not satisfy the original equations. You can see this if you interpret the equations as finding the points of intersection of the graphs $y = x^2$ and $x + y = 6$, as in Fig. 4.3.

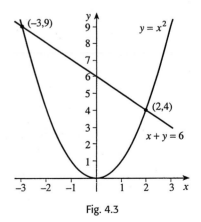

Fig. 4.3

Here is an example with a harder substitution.

Example 4.7.2

Solve the simultaneous equations $x^2 - 2xy + 3y^2 = 6$ and $2x - 3y = 3$.

From the equation of the straight line, $2x = 3 + 3y$. You are less likely to make mistakes if you avoid fractions. So, squaring the equation $2x = 3 + 3y$,

$$4x^2 = (3 + 3y)^2 = 9 + 18y + 9y^2.$$

Before you substitute for $4x^2$ and $2x$, it is helpful to multiply the first equation by 4. Then

$$4x^2 - 8xy + 12y^2 = 24,$$

so $(9 + 18y + 9y^2) - 4y(3 + 3y) + 12y^2 = 24.$

This reduces to $9y^2 + 6y - 15 = 0$, and, dividing by 3, to $3y^2 + 2y - 5 = 0$. Solving this equation gives $(y - 1)(3y + 5) = 0$, so $y = 1$ or $y = -\frac{5}{3}$.

Substituting in the second equation to find x, you obtain $x = 3$ and $x = -1$. Therefore the solution is $x = 3$, $y = 1$ or $x = -1$, $y = -\frac{5}{3}$.

> It is worth checking your answers in the original equations.

Example 4.7.3

At how many points does the line $x + 2y = 3$ meet the curve $2x^2 + y^2 = 4$?

From $x + 2y = 3$, $x = 3 - 2y$. Substituting in $2x^2 + y^2 = 4$, $2(3 - 2y)^2 + y^2 = 4$, so $2(9 - 12y + 4y^2) + y^2 = 4$, which reduces to $9y^2 - 24y + 14 = 0$.

The discriminant d of this equation is $d = 24^2 - 4 \times 9 \times 14 = 576 - 504 = 72$. As $d > 0$, this equation has two solutions, so the line meets the curve in two points.

4.8 Equations which reduce to quadratic equations

Sometimes you will come across equations which are not quadratic, but which can be changed into quadratic equations, usually by making the right substitution.

Example 4.8.1

Solve the equation $t^4 - 13t^2 + 36 = 0$.

This equation in t has degree 4 and is a quartic equation, but if you write t^2 as x you can see that it becomes $x^2 - 13x + 36 = 0$, which is a quadratic equation in x.

Then $(x - 4)(x - 9) = 0$, so $x = 4$ or $x = 9$.

Now recall that $x = t^2$, so $t^2 = 4$ or $t^2 = 9$, giving $t = \pm 2$ or $t = \pm 3$.

Example 4.8.2

Solve the equation $\sqrt{x} = 6 - x$

(a) by writing $\sqrt{x}$ as y,   (b) by squaring both sides of the equation.

(a) Writing $\sqrt{x} = y$, the equation becomes $y = 6 - y^2$ or $y^2 + y - 6 = 0$. Therefore $(y + 3)(y - 2) = 0$, so $y = -3$ or $y = 2$. But, as $y = \sqrt{x}$, and $\sqrt{x}$ is never negative, the only solution is $y = 2$, giving $x = 4$.

(b) Squaring both sides gives $x = (6 - x)^2 = 36 - 12x + x^2$ or $x^2 - 13x + 36 = 0$. Therefore $(x - 4)(x - 9) = 0$, so $x = 4$ or $x = 9$. Checking the answers shows that when $x = 4$, the equation $\sqrt{x} = 6 - x$ is satisfied, but when $x = 9$, $\sqrt{x} = 3$ and $6 - x = -3$, so $x = 9$ is not a root. Therefore $x = 4$ is the only root.

This is important. Squaring is not a reversible step, because it introduces the root or roots of the equation $\sqrt{x} = -(6 - x)$ as well. Notice that $x = 9$ does satisfy this last equation, but $x = 4$ doesn't! The moral is that, when you square an equation in the process of solving it, it is essential to check your answers.

Exercise 4D

1 Solve the following pairs of simultaneous equations.

(a) $y = x + 1$ $x^2 + y^2 = 25$ (b) $x + y = 7$ $x^2 + y^2 = 25$

(c) $y = x - 3$ $y = x^2 - 3x - 8$ (d) $y = 2 - x$ $x^2 - y^2 = 8$

(e) $2x + y = 5$ $x^2 + y^2 = 25$ (f) $y = 1 - x$ $y^2 - xy = 0$

(g) $7y - x = 49$ $x^2 + y^2 - 2x - 49 = 0$ (h) $y = 3x - 11$ $x^2 + 2xy + 3 = 0$

2 Find the coordinates of the points of intersection of the given straight lines with the given curves.

(a) $y = 2x + 1$ $y = x^2 - x + 3$ (b) $y = 3x + 2$ $x^2 + y^2 = 26$

(c) $y = 2x - 2$ $y = x^2 - 5$ (d) $x + 2y = 3$ $x^2 + xy = 2$

(e) $3y + 4x = 25$ $x^2 + y^2 = 25$ (f) $y + 2x = 3$ $2x^2 - 3xy = 14$

(g) $y = 2x - 12$ $x^2 + 4xy - 3y^2 = -27$ (h) $2x - 5y = 6$ $2xy - 4x^2 - 3y = 1$

3 In each case find the number of points of intersection of the straight line with the curve.

(a) $y = 1 - 2x$ $x^2 + y^2 = 1$ (b) $y = \frac{1}{2}x - 1$ $y = 4x^2$

(c) $y = 3x - 1$ $xy = 12$ (d) $4y - x = 16$ $y^2 = 4x$

(e) $3y - x = 15$ $4x^2 + 9y^2 = 36$ (f) $4y = 12 - x$ $xy = 9$

4 Solve the following equations; give irrational answers in terms of surds.

(a) $x^4 - 5x^2 + 4 = 0$ (b) $x^4 - 10x^2 + 9 = 0$ (c) $x^4 - 3x^2 - 4 = 0$

(d) $x^4 - 5x^2 - 6 = 0$ (e) $x^6 - 7x^3 - 8 = 0$ (f) $x^6 + x^3 - 12 = 0$

5 Solve the following equations.

(a) $x - 8 = 2\sqrt{x}$ (b) $x + 15 = 8\sqrt{x}$ (c) $t - 5\sqrt{t} - 14 = 0$

(d) $t = 3\sqrt{t} + 10$ (e) $t - \sqrt{t} - 6 = 0$ (f) $x - 3\sqrt{x} = 4$

6 Solve the following equations. (In most cases, multiplication by an appropriate expression will turn the equation into a form you should recognise.)

(a) $x = 3 + \dfrac{10}{x}$ (b) $x + 5 = \dfrac{6}{x}$ (c) $2t + 5 = \dfrac{3}{t}$

(d) $x = \dfrac{12}{x + 1}$ (e) $\sqrt{t} = 4 + \dfrac{12}{\sqrt{t}}$ (f) $\sqrt{t}(\sqrt{t} - 6) = -9$

Miscellaneous exercise 4

1 Solve the simultaneous equations $x + y = 2$ and $x^2 + 2y^2 = 11$. (OCR)

2 The quadratic polynomial $x^2 - 10x + 17$ is denoted by f(x). Express f(x) in the form $(x - a)^2 + b$ stating the values of a and b.

Hence find the least possible value that f(x) can take and the corresponding value of x. (OCR)

3 Solve the simultaneous equations $2x + y = 3$ and $2x^2 - xy = 10$. (OCR)

4 For what values of k does the equation $2x^2 - kx + 8 = 0$ have a repeated root?

5 (a) Solve the equation $x^2 - (6\sqrt{3})x + 24 = 0$, giving your answer in terms of surds, simplified as far as possible.

(b) Find all four solutions of the equation $x^4 - (6\sqrt{3})x^2 + 24 = 0$ giving your answers correct to 2 decimal places. (OCR)

6 Show that the line $y = 3x - 3$ and the curve $y = (3x + 1)(x + 2)$ do not meet.

7 Express $9x^2 - 36x + 52$ in the form $(Ax - B)^2 + C$, where A, B and C are integers. Hence, or otherwise, find the set of values taken by $9x^2 - 36x + 52$ for real x. (OCR)

8* Find the points of intersection of the curves $y = 6x^2 + 4x - 3$ and $y = x^2 - 3x - 1$, giving the coordinates correct to 2 decimal places.

9 (a) Express $9x^2 + 12x + 7$ in the form $(ax + b)^2 + c$ where a, b, c are constants whose values are to be found.

(b) Find the set of values taken by $\dfrac{1}{9x^2 + 12x + 7}$ for real values of x. (OCR)

10 Find, correct to 3 significant figures, all the roots of the equation $8x^4 - 8x^2 + 1 = \frac{1}{2}\sqrt{3}$. (OCR)

11 Find constants a, b and c such that, for all values of x,

$$3x^2 - 5x + 1 = a(x + b)^2 + c.$$

Hence find the coordinates of the minimum point on the graph of $y = 3x^2 - 5x + 1$. (Note: the minimum point or maximum point is the vertex.) (OCR, adapted)

12 Find the points of intersection of the curve $xy = 6$ and the line $y = 9 - 3x$.   (OCR)

13* The equation of a curve is $y = ax^2 - 2bx + c$, where a, b and c are constants with $a > 0$.

   (a) Find, in terms of a, b and c, the coordinates of the vertex of the curve.

   (b) Given that the vertex of the curve lies on the line $y = x$, find an expression
       for c in terms of a and b. Show that in this case, whatever the value
       of b, $c \geqslant -\dfrac{1}{4a}$.   (OCR, adapted)

14 (a) The diagram shows the graphs of $y = x - 1$ and
        $y = kx^2$, where k is a positive constant. The graphs
        intersect at two distinct points A and B. Write
        down the quadratic equation satisfied by the
        x-coordinates of A and B, and hence show that
        $k < \frac{1}{4}$.

   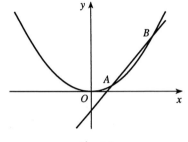
   Fig. 4.4

   (b) Describe briefly the relationship between the
        graphs of $y = x - 1$ and $y = kx^2$ in each of the
        cases   (i) $k = \frac{1}{4}$,   (ii) $k > \frac{1}{4}$.

   (c) Show, by means of a graphical argument or otherwise, that when k is a negative
        constant, the equation $x - 1 = kx^2$ has two real roots, one of which lies between 0
        and 1.

15 Use the following procedure to find the least (perpendicular) distance of the point $(1, 2)$
    from the line $y = 3x + 5$, *without* having to find the equation of a line perpendicular to
    $y = 3x + 5$ (as you did in Chapter 1).

   (a) Let (x, y) be a general point on the line. Show that its distance, d, from $(1, 2)$ is given
        by $d^2 = (x - 1)^2 + (y - 2)^2$.

   (b) Use the equation of the line to show that $d^2 = (x - 1)^2 + (3x + 3)^2$.

   (c) Show that $d^2 = 10x^2 + 16x + 10$.

   (d) By completing the square, show that the minimum distance required is $\frac{3}{5}\sqrt{10}$.

16 Point O is the intersection of two roads which cross at right angles; one road runs from
    north to south, the other from east to west. Car A is 100 metres due west of O and
    travelling east at a speed of 20 m s^{-1}, and Car B is 80 metres due north of O and travelling
    south at 20 m s^{-1}.

   (a) Show that after t seconds their distance apart, d metres, is given by
        $d^2 = (100 - 20t)^2 + (80 - 20t)^2$.

   (b) Show that this simplifies to $d^2 = 400((5 - t)^2 + (4 - t)^2)$.

   (c) Show that the minimum distance apart of the two cars is $10\sqrt{2}$ metres.

17 A mail-order photographic developing company offers a picture-framing service to its customers. It will enlarge and mount any photograph, under glass and in a rectangular frame. Its charge is based on the size of the enlargement. It charges £6 per metre of perimeter for the frame and £15 per square metre for the glass. Write down an expression for the cost of enlarging and mounting a photograph in a frame which is x metres wide and y metres high.

A photograph was enlarged and mounted in a square frame of side z metres at a cost of £12. Formulate and solve a quadratic equation for z.

18 (a) Calculate the discriminant of the quadratic polynomial $2x^2 + 6x + 7$.

   (b) State the number of real roots of the equation $2x^2 + 6x + 7 = 0$, and hence explain why $2x^2 + 6x + 7$ is always positive.

19 Solve the simultaneous equations $y = 2x^2 - 3x + 4$, $y = 4x + 1$. (OCR)

20 (a) Express $4x^2 - 16x + 8$ in the form $a(x + b)^2 + c$.

   (b) Hence find the coordinates of the vertex of the graph of $y = 4x^2 - 16x + 8$.

   (c) Sketch the graph of $y = 4x^2 - 16x + 8$, giving the x-coordinates of the points where the graph meets the x-axis. (OCR)

21 It is given that x and y satisfy the simultaneous equations $y - x = 4$, $2x^2 + xy + y^2 = 8$.

   (a) Show that $x^2 + 3x + 2 = 0$.

   (b) Solve the simultaneous equations. (OCR)

22 (a) Calculate the discriminant of $3x^2 - 4x + 2$.

   (b) Hence state the number of real roots of the equation $3x^2 - 4x + 2 = 0$. (OCR)

23 (a) Express $x^2 + 8x + 18$ in the form $(x + a)^2 + b$.

   (b) Sketch the graph of $y = x^2 + 8x + 18$, stating the coordinates of its vertex. (OCR)

24 (a) Given that $\sqrt{x} = y$, show that the equation $\sqrt{x} + \dfrac{10}{\sqrt{x}} = 7$ may be written as $y^2 - 7y + 10 = 0$.

   (b) Hence solve the equation $\sqrt{x} + \dfrac{10}{\sqrt{x}} = 7$. (OCR)

5 Differentiation

This chapter is about finding the gradient of the tangent at a point on a graph. When you have completed it, you should

- know how to find the gradient at a point on a quadratic curve and certain other curves
- be able to find the equations of the tangent and normal to a curve at a point
- understand how the gradient of the tangent at a point can be obtained from the gradients of chords through the point.

The first part of this chapter includes a number of experimental calculations from which the main results can be inferred. Proofs of some of these results are given at the end of the chapter; these may if you wish be omitted on a first reading.

5.1 The gradient of a curve

The gradient of the line $y = bx + c$ is b. It is easy to show this. Take two points on the line; the simplest are $(0, c)$ and $(1, b + c)$. The gradient of the line joining these is $\dfrac{(b + c) - c}{1 - 0}$, which is $\dfrac{b}{1}$ or just b.

You would get the same answer if you took any other two points on the line, but the algebra would be a bit more complicated.

But how could you find the gradient of a curve? Indeed, what do you mean by the gradient of a curve? A straight line has the same direction everywhere, but a curve keeps changing direction as you move along it. So you have to think about 'the gradient of a curve at a point'. The gradient will be different at different points of the curve.

Fig. 5.1

Draw a curve and choose a particular point on it (see Fig. 5.1). Call the point P. If the curve is reasonably smooth, you can draw a tangent to the curve at P. This is a straight line, so you can find its gradient. The direction of the curve at P is the same as the direction of the tangent. So it seems natural to define the gradient of the curve at P as the gradient of the tangent.

> The **gradient of a curve** at any point is the gradient of the tangent to the curve at that point.

But the problem is, how to calculate the gradient of the tangent. To find the gradient of a straight line you need to know the coordinates of two points on it. But, as Fig. 5.1 shows, the only point you know on the tangent is the point P. There is no obvious way of finding any other point on the tangent.

This difficulty doesn't occur for other lines through *P*. Fig. 5.2 shows several lines through *P*, including the tangent. The other lines meet the curve again, at points labelled *M* and *N* to the left of *P*, and *R* and *S* to the right of *P*. And the gradients of these lines can be calculated, as the gradients of the line segments *PM*, *PN*, *PR* and *PS*; these are called **chords** of the curve. (You are already familiar with chords when the curve is a circle.)

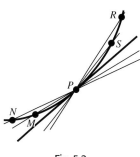

This suggests a first step to finding the gradient of the tangent. In Fig. 5.2 the gradient of the tangent is clearly less than the gradients of *PR* and *PS*, and greater than the gradients of *PN* and *PM*. So although this doesn't give the gradient of the tangent exactly, it does restrict it to a small interval of possible values.

Fig. 5.2

Example 5.1.1 shows how this idea can be applied to a particular curve at a particular point.

Example 5.1.1
On the graph of $y = x^2$ take *P* to be the point $(0.4, 0.16)$, and let *R* and *N* be the points with x-coordinates 0.5 and 0.3 respectively. Calculate the gradients of the chords *PR* and *PN*. What can be deduced about the gradient of the tangent at *P*?

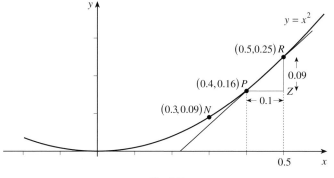

Fig. 5.3

Begin with the chord *PR*, shown in Fig. 5.3. At *R*, with $x = 0.5$, the y-coordinate is $0.5^2 = 0.25$. To find the gradient from $P(0.4, 0.16)$ to $R(0.5, 0.25)$ calculate the x-step $0.5 - 0.4 = 0.1$ and the y-step $0.25 - 0.16 = 0.09$. These are shown in Fig. 5.3 by *PZ* and *ZR*. Then

$$\text{gradient of } PR = \frac{y\text{-step}}{x\text{-step}} = \frac{0.09}{0.1} = 0.9.$$

For the chord *PN* to the left of *P*, where *N* has coordinates $(0.3, 0.09)$, the x-step from *P* to *N* is $0.3 - 0.4 = -0.1$, and the y-step is $0.09 - 0.16 = -0.07$; both are negative. The gradient is then

$$\frac{-0.07}{-0.1} = 0.7.$$

(You could of course take the *x*-step and *y*-step from *N* to *P* rather than from *P* to *N*, in which case both would be positive. But you will see as the chapter develops why it is a good idea to take the steps from *P* to the point at the other end of the chord.)

The gradient of the tangent at *P* is less than the gradient of *PR* and greater than the gradient of *PN*. So the gradient of the tangent at *P* is between 0.7 and 0.9.

Example 5.1.1 already gives you a useful approximation to the gradient of the curve $y = x^2$ at *P*, but it would be better to get a more accurate estimate. Fig. 5.2 suggests that if you take points *S* and *M* on the curve closer to *P* than *R* and *N*, the gradients of *PS* and *PM* will be closer to the gradient of the tangent.

Before embarking on any more calculation it is useful to introduce some new notation. The greek letter δ (delta) is used as an abbreviation for 'the increase in'. Thus 'the increase in *x*' is written as δx, and 'the increase in *y*' as δy. These are the quantities called the '*x*-step' and '*y*-step' in Chapter 1. Thus in the calculations for the chord *PR* in Example 5.1.1 you can write

$$\delta x = 0.5 - 0.4 = 0.1 \quad \text{and} \quad \delta y = 0.25 - 0.16 = 0.09.$$

With this notation, you can write the gradient of the chord as $\dfrac{\delta y}{\delta x}$.

Some people use the capital letter Δ rather than δ. Either is acceptable.

Notice that, in the fraction $\dfrac{\delta y}{\delta x}$, you cannot 'cancel out' the deltas. While you are getting used to the notation it is a good idea to read δ as 'the increase in', so that you are not tempted to read it as an ordinary algebraic symbol. Remember also that δx or δy could be negative, making the *x*-step or *y*-step a decrease.

Example 5.1.2
In the context of Example 5.1.1, find a better estimate for the gradient of the tangent at *P* by taking points *S* and *M* on the curve with *x*-coordinates 0.41 and 0.39.

First you need to calculate the *y*-coordinates of *S* and *M*. These are $0.41^2 = 0.1681$ and $0.39^2 = 0.1521$. So *S* is the point $(0.41, 0.1681)$, and *M* is $(0.39, 0.1521)$.

For the chord *PS*,

$$\delta x = 0.41 - 0.4 = 0.01 \quad \text{and} \quad \delta y = 0.1681 - 0.16 = 0.0081,$$

so the gradient is $\dfrac{\delta y}{\delta x} = \dfrac{0.0081}{0.01} = 0.81.$

Fig. 5.4 is the figure corresponding to Fig. 5.3 for the chord *PS*.

Fig. 5.4 is not very useful as an illustration, because *P* and *S* are so close together. There is a small triangle there, like the triangle in Fig. 5.3, but you could be excused for missing it. In Fig. 5.4 it has become difficult to distinguish between the chord *PS* and the tangent at *P*.

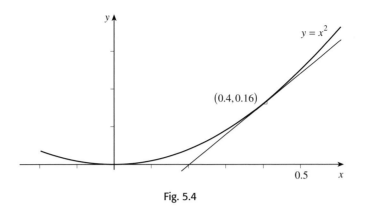

Fig. 5.4

For the chord PM,

$$\delta x = 0.39 - 0.4 = -0.01 \quad \text{and} \quad \delta y = 0.1521 - 0.16 = -0.0079,$$

so the gradient is $\dfrac{\delta y}{\delta x} = \dfrac{-0.0079}{-0.01} = 0.79.$

The gradient of the tangent at P is less than the gradient of PS and greater than the gradient of PM. It is therefore between 0.79 and 0.81.

By now you are probably beginning to suspect that the gradient of the tangent at P is 0.8. But if you still have doubts, try calculating the gradients of the chords PT and PL, where T is $(0.4001, 0.4001^2)$ and L is $(0.3999, 0.3999^2)$. What does this tell you about the gradient of the tangent at P?

The next example uses the method for a curve with a more complicated equation.

Example 5.1.3
Make an estimate of the gradient of the curve $y = 1 + 5x - 2x^2$ at the point P with coordinates $(1, 4)$.

There is an important difference between this example and the previous ones. Because $1 + 5x - 2x^2$ is a quadratic with the coefficient of x^2 negative, the graph is a parabola with its vertex at the top. So if you take a point N to the left of P, the gradient of the chord PN will be greater than the gradient of the tangent at P; and if R is to the right of P, the gradient of PR will be less than the gradient of the tangent at P. This is illustrated in Fig. 5.5.

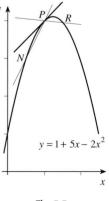

Fig. 5.5

Now that you know how the argument is going to proceed, you can take a shortcut from the start by choosing points R and N very close to P. Suppose that the x-coordinates of R and N are taken to be 1.001 and 0.999. Then the y-coordinates are

$$1 + 5 \times 1.001 - 2 \times 1.001^2 = 4.000\,998$$

and $\quad 1 + 5 \times 0.999 - 2 \times 0.999^2 = 3.998\,998.$

So, for the chord *PR*,

$$\delta x = 1.001 - 1 = 0.001 \quad \text{and} \quad \delta y = 4.000\,998 - 4 = 0.000\,998,$$

giving a gradient of $\dfrac{\delta y}{\delta x} = \dfrac{0.000\,998}{0.001} = 0.998.$

And for the chord *PN*,

$$\delta x = 0.999 - 1 = -0.001 \quad \text{and} \quad \delta y = 3.998\,998 - 4 = -0.001\,002,$$

giving a gradient of $\dfrac{\delta y}{\delta x} = \dfrac{-0.001\,002}{-0.001} = 1.002.$

So the gradient of the curve at *P* is greater than 0.998 and less than 1.002. It is a reasonable guess that the gradient of the curve at *P* is 1.

This is still only a 'reasonable guess', not a proof. But it is best for the time being to work on the assumption that it is correct, and to defer the proof until you have seen how these calculations can be used.

Exercise 5A

You should keep a record of your answers to this exercise. You will need to refer to them in the next section. If you are working with other students in a group, you can save time by splitting the work and pooling your results.

1 Carry out calculations similar to those in Examples 5.1.1 and 5.1.2 to find intervals within which the gradient of $y = x^2$ lies at the points

   (a) $(2, 4)$ (b) $(0.6, 0.36)$ (c) $(-1, 1)$.

   Use your answers to guess the gradient of the curve at these points.

2 Carry out calculations similar to those in Example 5.1.3 to find intervals within which the gradient of $y = 1 + 5x - 2x^2$ lies at the points

   (a) $(0, 1)$ (b) $(-1, -6)$ (c) $(2, 3)$.

   Use your answers to guess the gradient of the curve at these points.

3 For the given curves find intervals within which the gradient lies at the given points. Use your answers to guess the gradient of the curves at these points.

   (a) $y = 10x^2$ at   (i) $(0.5, 2.5)$ (ii) $(1.2, 14.4)$ (iii) $(-2, 40)$

   (b) $y = x^2 + 3$ at   (i) $(0.4, 3.16)$ (ii) $(1.5, 5.25)$ (iii) $(-1, 4)$

   (c) $y = 3x^2 - 4x + 2$ at   (i) $(1, 1)$ (ii) $(0, 2)$ (iii) $(2, 6)$

5.2 Gradient formulae

If you collect together the results of Example 5.1.2 and Exercise 5A Question 1 for the curve $y = x^2$, you can set out the gradients at various points as in Table 5.6.

x-coordinate of P	-1	0.4	0.6	2
gradient at P	-2	0.8	1.2	4

Table 5.6

It is not difficult to see a pattern! At each of the four points the gradient is twice the x-coordinate. This is unlikely to be a coincidence. If you try to find the gradient at any other point on the curve you will find that the same thing happens.

You can express this algebraically by saying that the 'gradient formula' for the curve $y = x^2$ is $2x$.

Try doing the same thing for the results of Example 5.1.3 and Exercise 5A Question 2 for the curve $y = 1 + 5x - 2x^2$. You then get the values set out in Table 5.7.

x-coordinate of P	-1	0	1	2
gradient at P	9	5	1	-3

Table 5.7

The pattern is not quite so obvious this time, but you will notice that as you move across the table the values of x go up by 1 each time, and the values of y go down by 4. And since the gradient is 5 when $x = 0$, it is $5 - 4 \times 1$ when $x = 1$, $5 - 4 \times 2$ when $x = 2$, and so on. This suggests that the gradient formula for the curve $y = 1 + 5x - x^2$ is $5 - 4x$.

The process of finding the gradient formula for a curve is called **differentiation**. When you find the gradient formula, you are **differentiating**.

If the curve you are differentiating is written as $y = f(x)$, then the gradient formula for the curve is called the **derivative** of $f(x)$. It is denoted by $f'(x)$. This is pronounced 'f dashed x'.

So you can write

$$\text{if } f(x) = x^2, \quad \text{then} \quad f'(x) = 2x;$$

and $\quad$ if $f(x) = 1 + 5x - x^2$, $\quad$ then $\quad f'(x) = 5 - 4x$.

Remember that so far these formulae are just suggestions based on a few numerical experiments. They will be proved later in the chapter.

Exercise 5B

1 Use your answers to Exercise 5A Question 3 to suggest gradient formulae for the curves with equations

(a) $y = 10x^2$, (b) $y = x^2 + 3$, (c) $y = 3x^2 - 4x + 2$.

Write your conclusions using $f(x)$, $f'(x)$ notation.

5.3   Some rules for differentiation

Now that you have several examples of gradient formulae, the next step is to look to see if you can find a pattern in the results. In Table 5.8 the examples are numbered according to their appearance in Exercise 5A.

	Equation of curve	Gradient formula
1	$y = x^2$	$2x$
2	$y = 1 + 5x - 2x^2$	$5 - 4x$
3(a)	$y = 10x^2$	$20x$
3(b)	$y = x^2 + 3$	$2x$
3(c)	$y = 3x^2 - 4x + 2$	$6x - 4$

Table 5.8

Remember also that, for the straight line with equation $y = bx + c$, the gradient formula is the constant b.

You will notice at once that

- if x^2 appears in the equation (1, 3(b)), it becomes $2x$ in the gradient formula
- if a multiple of x^2 appears in the equation (2, 3(a), 3(c)), it becomes the same multiple of $2x$ in the gradient formula
- if a multiple of x appears in the equation (2, 3(c) and the straight line), the multiplier appears as a constant term in the gradient formula
- if a constant term appears in the equation (2, 3(b), 3(c) and the straight line), it disappears in the gradient formula.

These rules can be summed up for any quadratic curve.

$$\text{If } f(x) = ax^2 + bx + c, \quad \text{then} \quad f'(x) = 2ax + b.$$

Example 5.3.1

For the curve with equation $y = 3x^2 - 8x - 2$, find the gradient at $(3, 1)$.

Begin by finding the gradient formula from the result in the box with $a = 3$, $b = -8$ and $c = -2$. The gradient formula is then $6x - 8$.

To find the gradient at $(3, 1)$ substitute $x = 3$ in the gradient formula to get $6 \times 3 - 8 = 10$.

You have already used the notation $f(x)$ with a particular value substituted for x. For instance, if in Example 5.3.1 $f(x)$ is used to denote $3x^2 - 8x - 2$, then $f(3)$ gives the y-coordinate of the point on the curve where $x = 3$. This idea can be extended to the expression for the derivative. When you differentiate you get $f'(x) = 6x - 8$. You can now substitute $x = 3$ and write $f'(3) = 6 \times 3 - 8 = 10$, which gives the gradient of the curve at the point where $x = 3$.

Example 5.3.2

If $f(x) = 5 - 2x - 4x^2$, find $f(-1)$ and $f'(-1)$.

$$f(-1) = 5 - 2 \times (-1) - 4 \times (-1)^2 = 5 + 2 - 4 = 3.$$

Differentiating, $f'(x) = -2 - 8x.$

So $f'(-1) = -2 - 8 \times (-1) = -2 + 8 = 6.$

5.4 Extending the differentiation rule

So far differentiation has been used only for quadratic curves, but exactly the same methods can be used to find the gradients of curves whose equations contain x^3, x^4 and higher powers of x. The question is how to extend the rule for differentiating x^2 to higher powers.

Begin by noticing that the gradient formula $2x$ for the curve $y = x^2$ could be written as $2 \times x^1$.

The numerical multiplier 2 in this expression is the power of x in the equation of the curve, and the new power of x is 1 less than that power, since $2 - 1 = 1$.

Try applying the same rule to the curve $y = x^3$. The power of x is now 3, so in the gradient formula you would expect the numerical multiplier to be 3, and the new power of x to be $3 - 1$, that is 2. That is, the gradient formula would be $3x^2$.

This is a very optimistic generalisation, but there are several ways of testing it out. Look back to Chapter 3 at the graph of $y = x^3$, in Fig. 3.5. You will see that at the origin the x-axis is a tangent to the curve, so the gradient when $x = 0$ is 0. At every other point on the curve the gradient is positive. This is just what you would expect if the gradient formula is $3x^2$.

Another way of testing the formula would be to choose a particular point and estimate the gradient by the numerical method used in Section 5.1, as in Example 5.4.1.

Example 5.4.1

Make a numerical estimate of the gradient of $y = x^3$ at the point P with coordinates $(0.4, 0.064)$. Test whether this is the answer that you would get by using the suggested gradient formula $3x^2$.

Take points R to the right of P and N to the left of P with x-coordinates 0.401 and 0.399.

The y-coordinate of R is $0.401^3 = 0.064\,481...$, so for the chord PR

$$\delta x = 0.401 - 0.4 = 0.001 \quad \text{and} \quad \delta y = 0.064\,481... - 0.064 = 0.000\,481...,$$

giving

$$\frac{\delta y}{\delta x} = \frac{0.000\,481...}{0.001} = 0.481.....$$

The y-coordinate of N is $0.399^3 = 0.063\,521...$, so for the chord PN

$$\delta x = 0.399 - 0.4 = -0.001 \quad \text{and} \quad \delta y = 0.063\,521... - 0.064 = -0.000\,478...,$$

giving

$$\frac{\delta y}{\delta x} = \frac{-0.000\,478...}{-0.001} = 0.478... \,.$$

The gradient of the tangent at P is between 0.478... and 0.481... . It is a reasonable guess that the gradient is 0.48.

Substituting $x = 0.4$ in the suggested gradient formula $3x^2$ gives $3 \times 0.4^2 = 3 \times 0.16 = 0.48$.

With this encouragement, you could try extending the rule to $y = x^4$. The multiplier for the gradient formula would be 4, and the new power of x would be $4 - 1 = 3$. So you might expect the gradient formula to be $4x^3$.

You can test this out in the same way as for $y = x^3$. In fact it is also quite easy to prove. A proof is given in Section 5.8.

All these formulae can be summed up in a single statement by replacing the numerical powers 2, 3, 4, ... in the equations $y = x^2$, $y = x^3$, $y = x^4$, ... by the letter n.

> If $f(x) = x^n$, where n is a positive integer, then $f'(x) = nx^{n-1}$.

There is one other rule for differentiation which you have probably hardly noticed, but which needs to be stated for completeness. Look back at the rule for differentiating $ax^2 + bx + c$ in Section 5.3. This is stated for a single function with three coefficients, but it could be broken down into three separate and simpler statements:

If $f(x) = x^2$,   then $f'(x) = 2x$.
If $g(x) = x$,   then $g'(x) = 1$.
If $h(x) = 1$,   then $h'(x) = 0$.

You could then put these together and say:

The derivative of $ax^2 + bx + c$ is $a \times (2x) + b \times 1 + c \times 0$, which is $2ax + b$.

When you do this you are using a rule for combining derivatives. It is sufficient to state it for two functions $f(x)$ and $g(x)$. If there are more than two functions, you can reach the obvious extension by using the rule more than once.

> The derivative of $af(x) + bg(x)$, where a and b are constants, is $af'(x) + bg'(x)$.

Example 5.4.2
Differentiate   (a) $x^5 - 4x^3 + 7x^2$,   (b) $(x + 2)(2x - 3)$.

(a) The derivatives of x^5, x^3 and x^2 are $5x^4$, $3x^2$ and $2x$. So the derivative of
$x^5 - 4x^3 + 7x^2$ is $5x^4 - 4(3x^2) + 7(2x)$,   which is $5x^4 - 12x^2 + 14x$.

(b) None of the rules for differentiation apply directly to an expression like this. But you can multiply out the brackets to get a quadratic which you can differentiate.

Since $(x + 2)(2x - 3) = 2x^2 + x - 6$, the derivative is $2(2x) + 1 = 4x + 1$.

> If you cannot immediately differentiate a given function using the rules you know, see if you can write the function in a different form which enables you to apply one of the rules.

5.5 An alternative notation

The advantage of the f(x), f′(x) notation is that you can use it in two ways. With x inside the bracket it refers to the function and its derivative as a whole. But if you replace x by a particular number p, then f(p), f′(p) stand for the value of the function and the gradient at a single point where $x = p$.

But there are occasions when this notation becomes a bit unwieldy. For example, look back to Example 3.2.2, which was worded

'Draw the complete graph of $y = $ f(x),   where f(x) $= \sqrt{4 - x^2}$'.

You may have wondered, why not simply say

'Draw the complete graph of $y = \sqrt{4 - x^2}$'?

The answer is that it was very convenient to have the f(x) notation available for use in the solution.

However, if you just want to use x and y and don't need f(x) notation, it is useful to have a way of writing the derivative in terms of x and y.

There is already a symbol $\dfrac{\delta y}{\delta x}$ which does this for the gradient of a chord. This suggests using a similar symbol for the gradient of the tangent, writing the letter 'd' instead of the greek δ.

> If y is a function of x, $\dfrac{dy}{dx}$ denotes the derivative.

There is, though, an important difference between $\dfrac{\delta y}{\delta x}$ and $\dfrac{dy}{dx}$. The symbol $\dfrac{\delta y}{\delta x}$ stands for a genuine fraction, the result of dividing δy by δx. But $\dfrac{dy}{dx}$ is not a fraction, but a single symbol; no meaning is given to the separate elements dy and dx. In speech it is pronounced (rather rapidly!) 'd y d x' with no hint that there is a fraction bar present.

Example 5.5.1

If $y = 4x^3 - 3x^4$, find $\dfrac{dy}{dx}$.

This is exactly the same question as 'If $f(x) = 4x^3 - 3x^4$, find $f'(x)$', or 'Differentiate $4x^3 - 3x^4$'. The answer is $\dfrac{dy}{dx} = 4(3x^2) - 3(4x^3) = 12x^2(1 - x)$.

The main advantages of $\dfrac{dy}{dx}$ notation will be seen in Chapter 12 when you come to apply differentiation to mathematical models in various real-world situations. However, there may be occasions before then when you will find it convenient, so it is worth getting used to it at this stage.

Exercise 5C

1 Write down the gradient formula for each of the following functions.

(a) x^2 (b) $x^2 - x$ (c) $4x^2$ (d) $3x^2 - 2x$

(e) $2 - 3x$ (f) $x - 2 - 2x^2$ (g) $2 + 4x - 3x^2$ (h) $\sqrt{2}x - \sqrt{3}x^2$

2 For each of the following functions $f(x)$, write down $f'(x)$. You may need to rearrange some of the functions before differentiating them.

(a) $3x - 1$ (b) $2 - 3x^2$ (c) 4 (d) $1 + 2x + 3x^2$

(e) $x^2 - 2x^2$ (f) $3(1 + 2x - x^2)$ (g) $2x(1 - x)$ (h) $x(2x + 1) - 1$

3 Find the derivative of each of the following functions $f(x)$ at $x = -3$.

(a) $-x^2$ (b) $3x$ (c) $x^2 + 3x$ (d) $2x - x^2$

(e) $2x^2 + 4x - 1$ (f) $-(3 - x^2)$ (g) $-x(2 + x)$ (h) $(x - 2)(2x - 1)$

4 For each of the following functions $f(x)$, find x such that $f'(x)$ has the given value.

(a) $2x^2$ value 3   (b) $x - 2x^2$ value -1

(c) $2 + 3x + x^2$ value 0   (d) $x^2 + 4x - 1$ value 2

(e) $(x - 2)(x - 1)$ value 0   (f) $2x(3x + 2)$ value 10

5 Repeat the numerical test in Example 5.4.1 by estimating the gradient of $y = x^3$ at the points

(a) $(1, 1)$,   (b) $(-0.5, -0.125)$.

6 Make numerical estimates of the gradient of $y = x^4$ at two points of your choice, and use them to check the differentiation rule $\dfrac{dy}{dx} = 4x^3$.

7 Find $\dfrac{dy}{dx}$ for the following equations.

(a) $y = x^3 + 2x^2$ (b) $y = 1 - 2x^3 + 3x^2$ (c) $y = x^3 - 6x^2 + 11x - 6$

(d) $y = 2x^3 - 3x^2 + x$ (e) $y = x(1 + x^2)$ (f) $y = (2 - x^2)(2 + x^2)$

8 Find f$'(-2)$ for each of the following functions f(x).

(a) $2x - x^3$ (b) $2x - x^2$ (c) $1 - 2x - 3x^2 + 4x^3$

(d) $2 - x$ (e) $x^2(1 + x)$ (f) $y = (3 - x^2)^2$

9 For each of the following functions f(x), find the value(s) of x such that f$'(x)$ is equal to the given number.

(a) x^3 12   (b) $x^3 - x^2$ 8   (c) $3x - 3x^2 + x^3$ 108

(d) $x^3 - 3x^2 + 2x$ -1 (e) $x(1 + x)^2$ 0   (f) $x(1 - x)(1 + x)$ 2

5.6 Finding equations of tangents

Now that you know how to find the gradient of the tangent at a point on a curve, it is easy to find the equation of the tangent.

Example 5.6.1
Find the equation of the tangent at the point $(2, 6)$ on the curve $y = $ f(x), where f$(x) = 2x^2 - 3x + 4$.

To find the gradient, differentiate to get f$'(x) = 4x - 3$. The gradient of the tangent at $(2, 6)$ is f$'(2) = 4 \times 2 - 3 = 5$.

The tangent is the line through $(2, 6)$ with gradient 5. Using the equation of a line in the form $y - y_1 = m(x - x_1)$ (see Section 1.6), the equation of the tangent is

$$y - 6 = 5(x - 2), \quad \text{which is} \quad y = 5x - 4.$$

The important thing to remember is that, in the equation of a line, m has to be a number. You have to substitute the x-coordinate of the point into the gradient formula before you can find the equation of the line.

Example 5.6.2
Find the equation of the tangent to the graph of $y = x^2 - 4x + 2$ which is parallel to the x-axis.

From Section 1.6, a line parallel to the x-axis has gradient 0.

Let f$(x) = x^2 - 4x + 2$. Then f$'(x) = 2x - 4$.

To find when the gradient is 0 you need to solve $2x - 4 = 0$, which gives $x = 2$.

When $x = 2$, $y = 2^2 - 4 \times 2 + 2 = -2$.

From Section 1.6, the equation of a line parallel to the x-axis has the form $y = c$. So the equation of the tangent is $y = -2$.

Example 5.6.3

Show that there are two points on $y = x^2(x - 2)$ at which the gradient is equal to 4. Find the equations of the tangents at these points.

Before you can differentiate, you must multiply out the brackets to get the equation in the form $y = x^3 - 2x^2$. The gradient formula is then $\dfrac{dy}{dx} = 3x^2 - 4x$. This is equal to 4 if $3x^2 - 4x = 4$, that is if x is a root of the quadratic equation

$$3x^2 - 4x - 4 = 0.$$

This can be factorised as

$$(x - 2)(3x + 2) = 0,$$

so the gradient is equal to 4 if $x = 2$ or $x = -\frac{2}{3}$.

You know the gradient of the tangents, but you do not yet know the y-coordinates of the points on the curve that they have to pass through. To find these you have to substitute the values of x already found into the equation $y = x^2(x - 2)$.

When $x = 2$, $y = 2^2 \times (2 - 2) = 0$. The line through $(2, 0)$ with gradient 4 has equation

$$y - 0 = 4(x - 2), \quad \text{which is} \quad y = 4x - 8.$$

When $x = -\frac{2}{3}$, $y = \left(-\frac{2}{3}\right)^2 \times \left(-\frac{2}{3} - 2\right) = \frac{4}{9} \times \left(-\frac{8}{3}\right) = -\frac{32}{27}$. The equation of the line through $\left(-\frac{2}{3}, -\frac{32}{27}\right)$ with gradient 4 has equation

$$y - \left(-\frac{32}{27}\right) = 4\left(x - \left(-\frac{2}{3}\right)\right)$$
$$y + \frac{32}{27} = 4x + \frac{8}{3}$$
$$y = 4x + \frac{40}{27}.$$

The equations of the tangents with gradient 4 are $y = 4x - 8$ and $y = 4x + \frac{40}{27}$.

Check this by displaying the curve and the two lines on a graphic calculator.

5.7 The normal to a curve at a point

Another line which you sometimes need to find is the line through a point of a curve at right angles to the tangent at that point. This is called the **normal** to the curve at the point.

Fig. 5.9 shows a curve with equation $y = f(x)$. The tangent and normal at the point A have been drawn.

If you know the gradient of the tangent at A, you can find the gradient of the normal by using the result in Section 1.9 for perpendicular lines. If the gradient of the tangent is m, the gradient of the normal is $-\dfrac{1}{m}$ provided that $m \neq 0$.

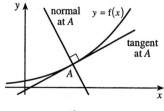

Fig. 5.9

Example 5.7.1

Find the equations of the normal to the curve at the given point in

(a) Example 5.6.1, (b) Example 5.6.2.

(a) For the curve with equation $y = 2x^2 - 3x + 4$ at the point $(2, 6)$, the gradient of the tangent is 5. The gradient of the normal is therefore $-\frac{1}{5}$.

The equation of the normal is

$$y - 6 = -\tfrac{1}{5}(x - 2) \quad \text{which is} \quad y = -0.2x + 6.4.$$

(b) Since the tangent at $(2, -2)$ is parallel to the x-axis, the normal is parallel to the y-axis. It therefore has equation $x = 2$.

For the curve in Examples 5.6.1 and 5.7.1(a), try plotting the curve $y = 2x^2 - 3x + 4$, the tangent $y = 5x - 4$ and the normal $y = -0.2x + 6.4$ on your graphic calculator. You may be surprised by the results.

> If you draw a curve together with its tangent and normal at a point, the normal will only appear perpendicular in your diagram if the scales are the same on both the x- and y-axes. However, no matter what the scales are, the tangent will always appear as a tangent.

Exercise 5D

1 Find the equation of the tangent to the curve at the point with the given x-coordinate.

(a) $y = x^2$ where $x = -1$
(b) $y = 2x^2 - x$ where $x = 0$

(c) $y = x^2 - 2x + 3$ where $x = 2$
(d) $y = 1 - x^2$ where $x = -3$

(e) $y = x(2 - x)$ where $x = 1$
(f) $y = (x - 1)^2$ where $x = 1$

2 Find the equation of the normal to the curve at the point with the given x-coordinate.

(a) $y = -x^2$ where $x = 1$
(b) $y = 3x^2 - 2x - 1$ where $x = 1$

(c) $y = 1 - 2x^2$ where $x = -2$
(d) $y = 1 - x^2$ where $x = 0$

(e) $y = 2(2 + x + x^2)$ where $x = -1$
(f) $y = (2x - 1)^2$ where $x = \frac{1}{2}$

3 Find the equation of the tangent to the curve $y = x^2$ which is parallel to the line $y = x$.

4 Find the equation of the tangent to the curve $y = x^2$ which is parallel to the x-axis.

5 Find the equation of the tangent to the curve $y = x^2 - 2x$ which is perpendicular to the line $2y = x - 1$.

6 Find the equation of the normal to the curve $y = 3x^2 - 2x - 1$ which is parallel to the line $y = x - 3$.

7 Find the equation of the normal to the curve $y = (x - 1)^2$ which is parallel to the y-axis.

8 Find the equation of the normal to the curve $y = 2x^2 + 3x + 4$ which is perpendicular to the line $y = 7x - 5$.

9 Find the equation of the tangent to the curve $y = x^3 + x$ at the point for which $x = -1$.

10 One of the tangents to the curve with equation $y = 4x - x^3$ is the line with equation $y = x - 2$. Find the equation of the other tangent parallel to $y = x - 2$.

11 The graphs of $y = x^2 - 2x$ and $y = x^3 - 3x^2 - 2x$ both pass through the origin. Show that they share the same tangent at the origin.

12 Find the equation of the tangent to the curve with equation $y = x^3 - 3x^2 - 2x - 6$ at the point where it crosses the y-axis.

13 Find the coordinates of the point of intersection of the tangents to the graph of $y = x^2$ at the points at which it meets the line with equation $y = x + 2$.

5.8*   Proving the gradient formulae

The rest of this chapter shows how some of the gradient formulae found in Sections 5.1–5.4 can be proved. You may if you wish omit this section and go straight on to Miscellaneous exercise 5.

In Examples 5.1.1 and 5.1.2 the gradient of $y = x^2$ at the point P with coordinates $(0.4, 0.16)$ was guessed from the gradients of chords joining this point to points on the curve with x-coordinates 0.5, 0.3, 0.41 and 0.39. By using some simple algebra all these calculations (and many similar ones) could have been done at the same time.

The x-coordinates of the points R, S, N and M were all chosen to be close to 0.4, the x-coordinate of P. So to save time you could take a point Q with x-coordinate $0.4 + h$, work out the gradient of the chord PQ and then substitute various values for h such as 0.1, -0.1, 0.01 and -0.01 in this to find the gradients of the chords PR, PN, and so on.

Example 5.8.1
Find the gradient of the chord joining $P(0.4, 0.16)$ to $Q(0.4 + h, (0.4 + h)^2)$

Using the delta notation,

$$\delta x = (0.4 + h) - 0.4 = h,$$

and $$\delta y = (0.4 + h)^2 - 0.16 = (0.16 + 0.8h + h^2) - 0.16 = 0.8h + h^2,$$

so $$\frac{\delta y}{\delta x} = \frac{0.8h + h^2}{h} = \frac{h(0.8 + h)}{h} = 0.8 + h.$$

This confirms what appeared to be happening in Examples 5.1.1 and 5.1.2. For any chord to the right of P, for which $h > 0$, the gradient is greater than 0.8; and for any chord to the left, with $h < 0$, the gradient is less than 0.8.

In fact, by taking h close enough to 0, you can make the gradient of the chord as close to 0.8 as you choose. From Example 5.8.1, the gradient of the chord is $0.8 + h$. So if you want to find a chord through $(0.4, 0.16)$ with a gradient between, say, $0.799\,999$ and $0.800\,001$, you can do it by taking h somewhere between $-0.000\,001$ and $+0.000\,001$.

The only value that you cannot take for h is 0 itself. But you can say that 'in the limit, as h tends to 0, the gradient of the chord tends to 0.8'.

The conventional way of writing this is

$$\lim_{h \to 0} \text{(gradient of chord)} = \lim_{h \to 0} (0.8 + h) = 0.8.$$

The symbol $h \to 0$ is read 'as h tends to 0', or sometimes simply 'h tends to 0'.

This is fine as far as it goes, but that is not very far. Taking P to be the point with $x = 0.4$ was a special numerical example. In Exercise 5A Question 1 you then carried out similar calculations for points with $x = 2$, $x = 0.6$ and $x = -1$. All these calculations could have been done together by taking a more algebraic approach and taking P to be the point at which $x = p$.

Example 5.8.2
Find the gradient of the chord of $y = x^2$ joining $P(p, p^2)$ to $Q(p + h, (p + h)^2)$.

The argument is exactly the same as in Example 5.8.1.

$$\delta x = (p + h) - p = h,$$

and
$$\delta y = (p + h)^2 - p^2 = (p^2 + 2ph + h^2) - p^2 = 2ph + h^2,$$

so
$$\frac{\delta y}{\delta x} = \frac{2ph + h^2}{h} = \frac{h(2p + h)}{h} = 2p + h.$$

You can see that Example 5.8.1 is just a special case of this with $p = 0.4$

Now in any particular application the value of p remains constant, but h can be varied to bring Q as close to P as you choose. Then, by the same argument as before,

$$\lim_{h \to 0} \text{(gradient of chord)} = \lim_{h \to 0} (2p + h) = 2p.$$

This shows that, as we guessed from the special cases in Section 5.2, the gradient of $y = x^2$ at any point P is double the x-coordinate of P. That is, the gradient formula for the curve $y = x^2$ is $2x$.

Example 5.8.3 uses the same method to find the derivative of the quadratic curve in Example 5.1.3.

Example 5.8.3
For the curve with equation $y = 1 + 5x - 2x^2$, prove that $\dfrac{dy}{dx} = 5 - 4x$.

Take any point P on the curve with coordinates $(p, 1 + 5p - 2p^2)$. Let Q be another point on the curve with x-coordinate $p + h$.

The y-coordinate of Q is

$$1 + 5(p + h) - 2(p + h)^2 = 1 + 5(p + h) - 2(p^2 + 2ph + h^2)$$
$$= 1 + 5p + 5h - 2p^2 - 4ph - 2h^2.$$

So, for the chord PQ,

$$\delta x = (p + h) - p = h,$$

and $\delta y = (1 + 5p + 5h - 2p^2 - 4ph - 2h^2) - (1 + 5p - 2p^2) = 5h - 4ph - 2h^2,$

and $\dfrac{\delta y}{\delta x} = \dfrac{5h - 4ph - 2h^2}{h} = \dfrac{h(5 - 4p - 2h)}{h} = 5 - 4p - 2h.$

Now for a fixed value of p, $\dfrac{\delta y}{\delta x}$ can be made as close to $5 - 4p$ as you like by making h small enough. That is,

$$\lim_{h \to 0} \frac{\delta y}{\delta x} = \lim_{h \to 0} (5 - 4p - 2h) = 5 - 4p.$$

This shows that the gradient of the curve at the point where $x = p$ is $5 - 4p$, for any value of p. The gradient formula for the curve is therefore

$$\frac{dy}{dx} = 5 - 4x.$$

A similar approach can be used for any curve if you know its equation.

Fig. 5.10 shows a curve which has an equation of the form $y = f(x)$. Suppose that you want the gradient of the tangent at the point P, with coordinates $(p, f(p))$. The chord joining this point to any other point Q on the curve with coordinates $(p+h, f(p + h))$ has

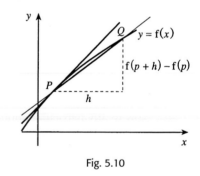

$$\delta x = h, \quad \delta y = f(p + h) - f(p)$$

so that its gradient is

$$\frac{\delta y}{\delta x} = \frac{f(p + h) - f(p)}{h}.$$

Fig. 5.10

Now let the value of h change so that the point Q takes different positions on the curve. Then, if Q is close to P, so that h is close to 0, the gradient of the chord is close to the gradient of the tangent at p. In the limit, as h tends to 0, this expression tends to $f'(p)$.

If the curve $y = f(x)$ has a tangent at $(p, f(p))$, then its gradient is

$$\lim_{h \to 0} \frac{f(p + h) - f(p)}{h}.$$

This quantity is called the derivative of $f(x)$ at $x = p$; it is denoted by $f'(p)$.

In general the derivative is $f'(x)$, where $f'(x) = \lim_{h \to 0} \dfrac{f(x + h) - f(x)}{h}.$

Example 5.8.4 uses the definition in the last line of the box to prove the result for the derivative of the general quadratic function given in Section 5.3.

Example 5.8.4
Prove that, if $f(x) = ax^2 + bx + c$, then $f'(x) = 2ax + b$.

First
$$\begin{aligned} f(x+h) - f(x) &= (a(x+h)^2 + b(x+h) + c) - (ax^2 + bx + c) \\ &= a((x+h)^2 - x^2) + b((x+h) - x) \\ &= a(2xh + h^2) + bh \\ &= h(a(2x+h) + b). \end{aligned}$$

Then
$$f'(x) = \lim_{h \to 0} \frac{h(a(2x+h) + b)}{h} = \lim_{h \to 0} (2ax + ah + b) = 2ax + b.$$

There are functions for which this method lands you in some tricky algebra, and it is sometimes easier to use a different notation. Instead of finding the gradient of the chord joining the points with x-coordinates p and $p + h$ (or x and $x + h$), you can take the points to have coordinates $(p, f(p))$ and $(q, f(q))$, so that

$$\delta x = q - p \quad \text{and} \quad \delta y = f(q) - f(p).$$

Then the gradient is $\dfrac{\delta y}{\delta x} = \dfrac{f(q) - f(p)}{q - p}$.

To see how this works, here is a quadratic example worked in this notation.

Example 5.8.5
Find the derivative at $x = p$ for the function $f(x) = 3x^2$.

For this function, $f(q) - f(p) = 3q^2 - 3p^2 = 3(q^2 - p^2) = 3(q - p)(q + p)$.

So
$$\frac{\delta y}{\delta x} = \frac{f(q) - f(p)}{q - p} = \frac{3(q - p)(q + p)}{q - p} = 3(q + p).$$

Now, in this method, q has taken the place of $p + h$, so that instead of taking the limit 'as h tends to 0' you take it 'as q tends to p'. It is easy to see that, as q tends to p, $3(q + p)$ tends to $3(p + p) = 3(2p) = 6p$.

Therefore, if $f(x) = 3x^2$, $f'(p) = 6p$. Since this holds for any value of p, you can write $f'(x) = 6x$.

With this notation, the definition of the derivative takes the form:

The derivative of $f(x)$ at $x = p$ is $\quad f'(p) = \lim_{q \to p} \dfrac{f(q) - f(p)}{q - p}$.

Example 5.8.6
Use an algebraic method to find the derivative of the function $f(x) = x^4$ at $x = p$.

At $x = p$, $f(p) = p^4$ and at $x = q$, $f(q) = q^4$. The chord joining (p, p^4) and (q, q^4) has $\delta x = q - p$, $\delta y = q^4 - p^4$.

Writing δy as $(q^2)^2 - (p^2)^2$, you can use the difference of two squares twice to get

$$\delta y = (q^2 - p^2)(q^2 + p^2) = (q - p)(q + p)(q^2 + p^2).$$

Then $\quad \dfrac{\delta y}{\delta x} = \dfrac{(q - p)(q + p)(q^2 + p^2)}{q - p} = (q + p)(q^2 + p^2).$

Then in the limit, as q tends to p,

$$f'(p) = \lim_{q \to p} \frac{f(q) - f(p)}{q - p} = \lim_{q \to p} ((q + p)(q^2 + p^2)) = 2p(2p^2) = 4p^3.$$

This confirms the guess in Section 5.4 that the derivative of x^4 is $4x^3$.

Exercise 5E*

1 Use an algebraic method to find the derivative of the function $f(x) = x^3$ at $x = p$. (You will need to use either the expansion $(p + h)^3 = p^3 + 3p^2h + 3ph^2 + h^3$ or the product of factors $(q - p)(q^2 + qp + p^2) = q^3 - p^3$.)

2 Use an algebraic method to find the derivative of the function $f(x) = x^8$ at $x = p$. (Let $p + h = q$ and use the difference of two squares formula on $q^8 - p^8$ as often as you can.)

Miscellaneous exercise 5

1 Find the equation of the tangent to $y = 5x^2 - 7x + 4$ at the point $(2, 10)$.

2 Given the function $f(x) = x^3 + 5x^2 - x - 4$, find
   (a) $f'(-2)$ (b) the values of a such that $f'(a) = 56$.

3 Find the equation of the normal to $y = x^4 - 4x^3$ at the point for which $x = \frac{1}{2}$.

4 Find the equation of the tangent at $x = 3$ to the curve with equation $y = 2x^2 - 3x + 2$.

5 Find the point on the curve $y = 2x^2 - 3x + 1$ where the tangent has gradient 1.

6 Find the two points on the curve $y = 2x^3 - 5x^2 + 9x - 1$ at which the gradient is 13.

7 Find the equation of the normal to $y = (2x - 1)(3x + 5)$ at the point $(1, 8)$. Give your answer in the form $ax + by + c = 0$, where a, b and c are integers.

8 The curve $y = x^2 - 3x - 4$ crosses the x-axis at P and Q. The tangents to the curve at P and Q meet at R. The normals to the curve at P and Q meet at S. Find the distance RS.

9 The equation of a curve is $y = 2x^2 - 5x + 14$. The normal to the curve at the point $(1, 11)$ meets the curve again at the point P. Find the coordinates of P.

10 The line $y = 6x - 7$ is a tangent to the curve $y = x^2 + k$. Find k.

11 At a particular point of the curve $y = 5x^2 - 12x + 1$ the equation of the normal is $x + 18y + c = 0$. Find the value of the constant c.

12 A normal to the curve $y = x^2$ has gradient 2. Find where it meets the curve.

6 Inequalities

This chapter is about inequality relationships, and how to solve inequalities. When you have completed it, you should

- know the rules for working with inequality symbols
- be able to solve linear inequalities
- be able to solve quadratic inequalities.

6.1 Notation for inequalities

You often want to compare one number with another and say which is the bigger. This comparison is expressed by using the inequality symbols $>$, $<$, $\leqslant$ and $\geqslant$. You have already met inequalities in Chapters 3 and 4.

The symbol $a > b$ means that a is greater than b. You can visualise this geometrically as in Fig. 6.1, which shows three number lines, with a to the right of b.

Notice that it does not matter whether a and b are positive or negative. The position of a and b in relation to zero on the number line is irrelevant. In all three lines, $a > b$. As an example, in the bottom line, $-4 > -7$.

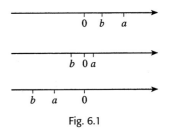

Fig. 6.1

Similarly, the symbol $a < b$ means that a is less than b. You can visualise this geometrically on a number line, with a to the left of b.

> These four expressions are equivalent.
>
> $a > b$ a is greater than b
> $b < a$ b is less than a

The symbol $a \geqslant b$ means 'either $a > b$ or $a = b$'; that is, a is greater than or equal to, but not less than, b. Similarly, the symbol $a \leqslant b$ means 'either $a < b$ or $a = b$'; that is, a is less than or equal to, but not greater than, b.

> These expressions are equivalent.
>
> $a \geqslant b$ a is greater than or equal to b
> $b \leqslant a$ b is less than or equal to a

Since, for any two numbers a and b, a must be either greater than, equal to, or less than b, it follows that another way of writing

    a is greater than or equal to b

is to say that

> a is not less than b.

Similarly,

> b is less than or equal to a

is equivalent to

> b is not greater than a,

The symbols $<$ and $>$ are called **strict** inequalities, and the symbols $\leqslant$ and $\geqslant$ are called **weak** inequalities.

6.2   Solving linear inequalities

When you solve an inequality such as $3x + 10 > 10x - 11$, you have to write a simpler statement with precisely the same meaning. In this case the simpler statement turns out to be $x < 3$. But how do you get from the complicated statement to the simple one?

Adding or subtracting the same number on both sides

You can add or subtract the same number on both sides of an inequality. For instance you can add the number 11 to both sides. In the example you would get

$$(3x + 10) + 11 > (10x - 11) + 11,$$
$$3x + 21 > 10x.$$

Justifying such a step involves showing that, for any number c, 'if $a > b$ then $a + c > b + c$'.

This is saying that if a is to the right of b on the number line, then $a + c$ is to the right of $b + c$. Fig. 6.2 shows that this is true whether c is positive or negative.

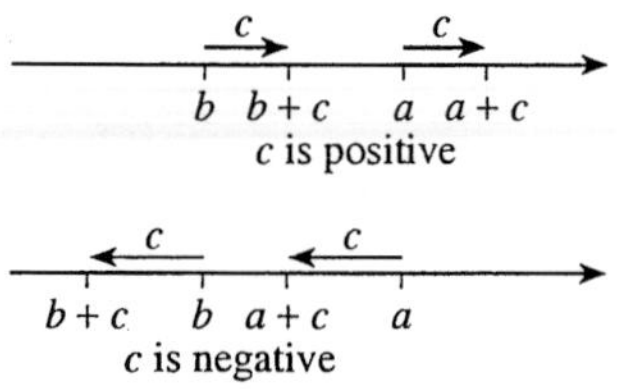

c is positive

Since subtracting c is the same as adding $-c$, you can also subtract the same number from both sides.

c is negative

Fig. 6.2

In the example, if you subtract $3x$ from both sides you get

$$(3x + 21) - 3x > 10x - 3x,$$
$$21 > 7x.$$

Multiplying both sides by a positive number

You can multiply (or divide) both sides of an inequality by a positive number. In the example above, you can divide both sides by the positive number 7 (or multiply both sides by $\frac{1}{7}$), and get:

$$21 \times \tfrac{1}{7} > 7x \times \tfrac{1}{7},$$
$$3 > x.$$

Here is a justification of the step, 'if $c > 0$ and $a > b$, then $ca > cb$'.

As $a > b$, a is to the right of b on the number line.

As $c > 0$, ca and cb are enlargements of the positions of a and b relative to the number 0.

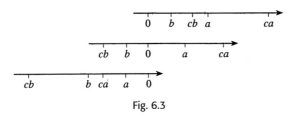

Fig. 6.3

Fig. 6.3 shows that, whether a and b are positive or negative, ca is to the right of cb, so $ca > cb$.

Multiplying both sides by a negative number
If $a > b$, and you subtract $a + b$ from both sides, then you get $-b > -a$, which is the same as $-a < -b$. This shows that if you multiply both sides of an inequality by -1, then you change the direction of the inequality. Suppose that you wish to multiply the inequality $a > b$ by -2. This is the same as multiplying $-a < -b$ by 2, so $-2a < -2b$.

You can also think of multiplying by -2 as reflecting the points corresponding to a and b in the origin, and then multiplying by 2 as an enlargement.

You can summarise this by saying that if you multiply (or divide) both sides of an inequality by a negative number, you must change the direction of the inequality. Thus if $c < 0$ and $a > b$, then $ca < cb$ (see Fig. 6.4).

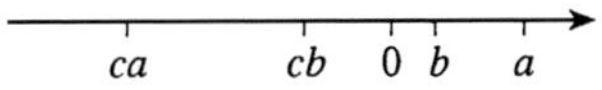

Fig. 6.4

> **Summary of operations on inequalities**
> - You can add or subtract a number on both sides of an inequality.
> - You can multiply or divide an inequality by a positive number.
> - You can multiply or divide an inequality by a negative number, but you must change the direction of the inequality.

Solving inequalities is simply a matter of exploiting these three rules.

> You can link the inequality operation involving multiplication with the rule '$+ \times + = +$'. For if $a > b$ and $c > 0$, both $a - b$ and c are positive numbers, so $c(a - b)$ is also positive. So $ca - cb$ is positive, $ca - cb > 0$ and $ca > cb$.

Example 6.2.1
Solve the inequality $-3x < 21$.

In this example you need to divide both sides by -3. Remembering to change the direction of the inequality, $-3x < 21$ becomes $x > -7$.

Example 6.2.2

Solve the inequality $\frac{1}{3}(4x + 3) - 3(2x - 4) \geq 20$.

Use the rule about multiplying by a positive number to multiply both sides by 3, in order to clear the fractions. In the solution, a reason is given only when an operation is carried out which affects the inequality.

$$\frac{1}{3}(4x + 3) - 3(2x - 4) \geq 20,$$
$$(4x + 3) - 9(2x - 4) \geq 60, \qquad \text{multiply both sides by 3}$$
$$4x + 3 - 18x + 36 \geq 60,$$
$$-14x + 39 \geq 60,$$
$$-14x \geq 21, \qquad \text{subtract 39 from both sides}$$
$$x \leq -\tfrac{3}{2}. \qquad \text{divide both sides by } -14, \text{ change} \geq \text{to} \leq$$

Solving inequalities of this type is similar to solving equations. However, when you multiply or divide by a number, remember to reverse the inequality if that number is negative.

Exercise 6A

Solve the following inequalities.

1 (a) $x - 3 > 11$ (b) $x + 7 < 11$ (c) $2x + 3 \leq 8$ (d) $3x - 5 \geq 16$

   (e) $3x + 7 > -5$ (f) $5x + 6 \leq -10$ (g) $2x + 3 < -4$ (h) $3x - 1 \leq -13$

2 (a) $\dfrac{x + 3}{2} > 5$ (b) $\dfrac{x - 4}{6} \leq 3$ (c) $\dfrac{2x + 3}{4} < -5$ (d) $\dfrac{3x + 2}{5} \leq 4$

   (e) $\dfrac{4x - 3}{2} \geq -7$ (f) $\dfrac{5x + 1}{3} > -3$ (g) $\dfrac{3x - 2}{8} < 1$ (h) $\dfrac{4x - 2}{3} \geq -6$

3 (a) $-5x \leq 20$ (b) $-3x \geq -12$ (c) $5 - x < -4$ (d) $4 - 3x \leq 10$

   (e) $2 - 6x \leq 0$ (f) $6 - 5x > 1$ (g) $6 - 5x > -1$ (h) $3 - 7x < -11$

4 (a) $\dfrac{3 - x}{5} < 2$ (b) $\dfrac{5 - x}{3} \geq 1$ (c) $\dfrac{3 - 2x}{5} > 3$ (d) $\dfrac{7 - 3x}{2} < -1$

   (e) $\dfrac{5 - 4x}{2} \leq -3$ (f) $\dfrac{3 - 2x}{5} > -7$ (g) $\dfrac{3 + 2x}{4} < 5$ (h) $\dfrac{7 - 3x}{4} \leq -5$

5 (a) $x - 4 \leq 5 + 2x$ (b) $x - 3 \geq 5 - x$ (c) $2x + 5 < 4x - 7$

   (d) $3x - 4 > 5 - x$ (e) $4x \leq 3(2 - x)$ (f) $3x \geq 5 - 2(3 - x)$

   (g) $6x < 8 - 2(7 + x)$ (h) $5x - 3 > x - 3(2 - x)$ (i) $6 - 2(x + 1) \leq 3(1 - 2x)$

6 (a) $\frac{1}{3}(8x + 1) - 2(x - 3) > 10$ (b) $\frac{5}{2}(x + 1) - 2(x - 3) < 7$ (c) $\dfrac{2x + 1}{3} - \dfrac{4x + 5}{2} \leq 0$

   (d) $\dfrac{3x - 2}{2} - \dfrac{x - 4}{3} < x$ (e) $\dfrac{x + 1}{4} + \dfrac{1}{6} \geq \dfrac{2x - 5}{3}$ (f) $\dfrac{x}{2} - \dfrac{3 - 2x}{5} \leq 1$

   (g) $\dfrac{x - 1}{3} - \dfrac{x + 1}{4} > \dfrac{x}{2}$ (h) $\dfrac{x}{3} \geq 5 - \dfrac{3x}{4}$

6.3 Quadratic inequalities

In Chapter 4, you saw that a quadratic function might take one of three forms:

$$f(x) = ax^2 + bx + c \qquad \text{the expanded form}$$
$$f(x) = a(x - p)(x - q) \qquad \text{the factor form}$$
$$f(x) = a(x - r)^2 + s \qquad \text{the completed square form.}$$

If you need to solve a quadratic inequality of the form $f(x) < 0$, $f(x) > 0$, $f(x) \leqslant 0$ or $f(x) \geqslant 0$, by far the easiest form to use is the factor form.

Here are some examples which show ways of solving quadratic inequalities. But before the examples, here is a useful definition.

> For inequalities of the form $f(x) > 0$, $f(x) < 0$, $f(x) \geqslant 0$ and $f(x) \leqslant 0$ the points at which $f(x) = 0$ are called the **critical values**.

Example 6.3.1
Solve the inequality $(x - 2)(x - 4) < 0$.

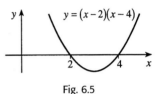
Fig. 6.5

Method 1   Sketch the graph of $y = (x - 2)(x - 4)$. The graph cuts the x-axis at $x = 2$ and $x = 4$. As the coefficient of x^2 is positive, the parabola bends upwards, as shown in Fig. 6.5.

You need to find the values of x such that $y < 0$.

From the graph you can see that this happens when x lies between 2 and 4, that is $x > 2$ and $x < 4$.

Remembering that $x > 2$ is the same as $2 < x$, you can write this as $2 < x < 4$, meaning that x is greater than 2 and less than 4.

> When you write an inequality of the kind $r < x$ and $x < s$ in the form $r < x < s$, it is essential that $r < s$. It makes no sense to write $7 < x < 3$; x cannot be both greater than 7 and less than 3.

An inequality of the type $r < x < s$ (or $r < x \leqslant s$ or $r \leqslant x < s$ or $r \leqslant x \leqslant s$) is called an **interval** consisting of all the numbers between r and s (including r or s where the sign adjacent to them is $\leqslant$).

Method 2   Find the critical values for the inequality $(x - 2)(x - 4) < 0$. These values are $x = 2$ and $x = 4$.

Make a table showing the signs of the factors in the product $(x - 2)(x - 4)$ between, at and outside the critical values. Then use the property that the product of two positive or two negative numbers is positive, but the product of a positive and a negative number is negative.

	$x < 2$	$x = 2$	$2 < x < 4$	$x = 4$	$x > 4$
$x - 2$	$-$	0	$+$	$+$	$+$
$x - 4$	$-$	$-$	$-$	0	$+$
$(x - 2)(x - 4)$	$+$	0	$-$	0	$+$

Table 6.6

From Table 6.6 you can see that $(x - 2)(x - 4) < 0$ when $2 < x < 4$.

Example 6.3.2
Solve the inequality $(x + 1)(5 - x) \leqslant 0$.

Fig. 6.7 shows the graph of $y = (x + 1)(5 - x)$, which cuts the x-axis at $x = -1$ and $x = 5$. As the coefficient of x^2 is negative, the parabola has its vertex at the top. So $y \leqslant 0$ when either $x \leqslant -1$ or $x \geqslant 5$.

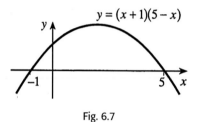

$y = (x + 1)(5 - x)$

Fig. 6.7

Note that in this case the inequality is also satisfied by the critical values -1 and 5.

Note also that you must not write '$x \leqslant -1$ or $x \geqslant 5$' as '$5 \leqslant x \leqslant -1$'.

Example 6.3.3
Solve the inequality $x^2 \leqslant a^2$, where a is a positive number.

This is the same as $x^2 - a^2 \leqslant 0$ or $(x + a)(x - a) \leqslant 0$. The critical values are $x = -a$ and $x = a$.

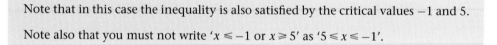

	$x < -a$	$x = -a$	$-a < x < a$	$x = a$	$x > a$
$x + a$	$-$	0	$+$	$+$	$+$
$x - a$	$-$	$-$	$-$	0	$+$
$(x + a)(x - a)$	$+$	0	$-$	0	$+$

Table 6.8

Table 6.8 shows that, if $x^2 \leqslant a^2$, then $-a \leqslant x \leqslant a$. It also shows the converse that, if $-a \leqslant x \leqslant a$, then $x^2 \leqslant a^2$.

The result of Example 6.3.3 is important. You can write it more concisely as:

> If $a > 0$, then these statements are equivalent.
> $$x^2 \leqslant a^2 \qquad -a \leqslant x \leqslant a$$

Using similar arguments, you can also get the following equivalence.

> If $a > 0$, then these statements are equivalent.
> $$x^2 \geqslant a^2 \qquad x \leqslant -a \text{ or } x \geqslant a$$

It is usually easiest to solve inequalities by graphical or tabular methods using the critical values. If you have access to a graphic calculator, you can use it to obtain the sketch, which makes the whole process even easier.

Example 6.3.4 shows how inequality arguments can be expressed in a more algebraic form.

Example 6.3.4
Solve the inequalities   (a) $(2x + 1)(x - 3) < 0$,   (b) $(2x + 1)(x - 3) > 0$.

(a) If the product of two factors is negative, one of them must be negative, and the other positive. So there are two possibilities to consider.

If $2x + 1$ is negative and $x - 3$ is positive, then $x < -\frac{1}{2}$ and $x > 3$. This is obviously impossible.

But if $2x + 1$ is positive and $x - 3$ is negative, then $x > -\frac{1}{2}$ and $x < 3$, which happens if $-\frac{1}{2} < x < 3$.

(b) If the product of two factors is positive, either both are positive or both are negative.

If both $2x + 1$ and $x - 3$ are positive, then $x > -\frac{1}{2}$ and $x > 3$, which happens if $x > 3$.

If both $2x + 1$ and $x - 3$ are negative, then $x < -\frac{1}{2}$ and $x < 3$, which happens if $x < -\frac{1}{2}$.

So $(2x + 1)(x - 3) > 0$ if $x > 3$ or $x < -\frac{1}{2}$.

> You could solve both parts at once by constructing a table as in Example 6.3.3, and reading off the sign from the last line.

There may be times when you don't have access to a graphic calculator, or when factorising the given expression is difficult or impossible. In those cases, start by finding the critical values.

Example 6.3.5

Solve algebraically the inequalities   (a) $2x^2 - 8x + 11 \leqslant 0$,   (b) $2x^2 - 8x + 5 \leqslant 0$.

(a) The critical values of the inequality $2x^2 - 8x + 11 \leqslant 0$ are the solutions of $2x^2 - 8x + 11 = 0$. These are

$$x = \frac{-(-8) \pm \sqrt{(-8)^2 - 4 \times 2 \times 11}}{2 \times 2} = \frac{8 \pm \sqrt{-24}}{4},$$

and since the discriminant is –24, there are no critical values.

The graph of $y = 2x^2 - 8x + 11$ must therefore be one of the shapes in Fig. 6.9.

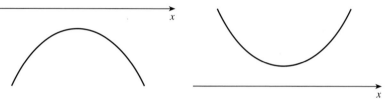

Fig. 6.9

You can quickly tell that the correct graph is the one on the right, either because the coefficient of x^2 is positive, or because when $x = 0$, $y = 11$, which is positive.

So there are no values of x for which $2x^2 - 8x + 11 \leqslant 0$.

(b) Completing the square,

$$2x^2 - 8x + 5 = 2(x - 2)^2 - 3,$$

so $\quad 2(x - 2)^2 - 3 \leqslant 0$

$\qquad (x - 2)^2 - \frac{3}{2} \leqslant 0$

$\qquad (x - 2)^2 \leqslant \frac{3}{2}.$

Using the result in the blue box at the top of page 97 with $x - 2$ in place of x, this is equivalent to

$$-\sqrt{\tfrac{3}{2}} \leqslant x - 2 \leqslant \sqrt{\tfrac{3}{2}}.$$

Adding 2 to all these expressions,

$$2 - \sqrt{\tfrac{3}{2}} \leqslant x \leqslant 2 + \sqrt{\tfrac{3}{2}}.$$

Inequalities sometimes appear when you use the discriminant of a quadratic to decide whether or not it has roots.

Example 6.3.6

Find the values of k for which the quadratic equation $kx^2 + 3kx + 5 = 0$ has two distinct roots.

For the quadratic equation to have distinct roots, the discriminant '$b^2 - 4ac$' must be greater than 0. In this case $a = k$, $b = 3k$, and $c = 5$, so $(3k)^2 - 4 \times k \times 5 > 0$. That is,

$$9k^2 - 20k > 0.$$

The critical values are the roots of $9k^2 - 20k = 0$, that is

$$k(9k - 20) = 0$$

giving $k = 0$ or $k = \frac{20}{9}$.

	$k < 0$	$k = 0$	$0 < k < \frac{20}{9}$	$k = \frac{20}{9}$	$k > \frac{20}{9}$
k	$-$	0	$+$	$+$	$+$
$9k - 20$	$-$	$-$	$-$	0	$+$
$k(9k - 20)$	$+$	0	$-$	0	$+$

Reading from the table, the required values of k which make $9k^2 - 20k > 0$ are $k < 0$ and $k > \frac{20}{9}$.

Example 6.3.7

Find the values of k for which the quadratic equation $x^2 + (k - 1)x + k + 2 = 0$ has no roots.

If the quadratic equation has no roots, then the discriminant '$b^2 - 4ac$' is less than 0. In this case $a = 1$, $b = k - 1$ and $c = k + 2$, so $(k - 1)^2 - 4 \times 1 \times (k + 2) < 0$. That is,

$$k^2 - 2k + 1 - 4(k + 2) < 0$$
$$k^2 - 6k - 7 < 0$$
$$(k + 1)(k - 7) < 0.$$

The critical values are the roots of $(k + 1)(k - 7) = 0$, which are –1 and 7.

	$k < -1$	$k = -1$	$-1 < k < 7$	$k = 7$	$k > 7$
$k + 1$	$-$	0	$+$	$+$	$+$
$k - 7$	$-$	$-$	$-$	0	$+$
$(k + 1)(k - 7)$	$+$	0	$-$	0	$+$

Reading from the table, the required values of k which make $(k + 1)(k - 7) < 0$ are $-1 < k < 7$.

Exercise 6B

1 Use sketch graphs to solve the following inequalities.

(a) $(x - 2)(x - 3) < 0$ (b) $(x - 4)(x - 7) > 0$ (c) $(x - 1)(x - 3) < 0$

(d) $(x - 4)(x + 1) \geqslant 0$ (e) $(2x - 1)(x + 3) > 0$ (f) $(3x - 2)(2x + 5) \leqslant 0$

(g) $(x + 2)(4x + 5) \geqslant 0$ (h) $(1 - x)(3 + x) < 0$ (i) $(3 - 2x)(5 - x) > 0$

(j) $(x - 5)(x + 5) < 0$ (k) $(3 - 4x)(3x + 4) > 0$ (l) $(2 + 3x)(2 - 3x) \leqslant 0$

2 Use a table based on critical values to solve the following inequalities.

(a) $(x-3)(x-6) < 0$ (b) $(x-2)(x-8) > 0$ (c) $(x-2)(x+5) \leqslant 0$

(d) $(x-3)(x+1) \geqslant 0$ (e) $(2x+3)(x-2) > 0$ (f) $(3x-2)(x+5) \leqslant 0$

(g) $(x+3)(5x+4) \geqslant 0$ (h) $(2-x)(5+x) < 0$ (i) $(5-2x)(3-x) > 0$

(j) $(3x+1)(3x-1) \geqslant 0$ (k) $(2-7x)(3x+4) < 0$ (l) $(5+3x)(1-3x) \leqslant 0$

3 Use any method you like to solve the following inequalities. Leave irrational numbers in terms of surds. Some inequalities may be true for all values of x, others for no values of x.

(a) $x^2 + 5x + 6 > 0$ (b) $x^2 - 7x + 12 < 0$ (c) $x^2 - 2x - 15 \leqslant 0$

(d) $2x^2 - 18 \geqslant 0$ (e) $2x^2 - 5x + 3 \geqslant 0$ (f) $6x^2 - 5x - 6 < 0$

(g) $x^2 + 5x + 2 > 0$ (h) $7 - 3x^2 < 0$ (i) $x^2 + x + 1 < 0$

(j) $2x^2 - 5x + 5 > 0$ (k) $12x^2 + 5x - 3 > 0$ (l) $3x^2 - 7x + 1 \leqslant 0$

Miscellaneous exercise 6

1 Solve the inequality $x^2 - x - 42 \leqslant 0$.

2 Solve the inequality $(x+1)^2 < 9$.

3 Solve the inequality $x(x+1) < 12$.   (OCR)

4* Solve the inequality $x - x^3 < 0$.

5* Solve the inequality $x^3 \geqslant 6x - x^2$.

Use the discriminant '$b^2 - 4ac$' in answering Questions 6 to 8. You may need to check the value $k = 0$ separately.

6 Find the values of k for which the following equations have two distinct roots.

(a) $kx^2 + kx + 2 = 0$ (b) $kx^2 + 3x + k = 0$ (c) $x^2 - 2kx + 4 = 0$

7 Find the values of k for which the following equations have no roots.

(a) $kx^2 - 2kx + 5 = 0$ (b) $k^2x^2 + 2kx + 1 = 0$ (c) $x^2 - 5kx - 2k = 0$

8 Find the range of values of k for which the equation $x^2 + 3kx + k = 0$ has any roots.

9 Find the set of values of x for which $9x^2 + 12x + 7 > 19$.   (OCR)

10 Sketch, on the same diagram, the graphs of $y = \dfrac{1}{x}$ and $y = x - \frac{3}{2}$. Find the solution set of the inequality $x - \frac{3}{2} > \dfrac{1}{x}$.   (OCR)

Revision exercise 1

1 (a) Find the constants a and b such that, for all values of x, $x^2 + 6x + 20 = (x + a)^2 + b$.

  (b) Hence state the least value of $x^2 + 6x + 20$, and state also the value of x for which this least value occurs.

  (c) Write down the greatest value of $\dfrac{1}{x^2 + 6x + 20}$.

2 Prove that the triangle with vertices at the points $(1, 2)$, $(9, 8)$ and $(12, 4)$ is right-angled, and calculate its area.

3 Simplify   (a) $3\sqrt{3} + 3\sqrt{27}$,   (b) $3\sqrt{2} \times 4\sqrt{8}$.

4 The diagram shows a sketch of part of the curve $y = x^3 + 3$. The points A, B and C lie on the curve and have x-coordinates 2, 2.01 and 2.1 respectively.

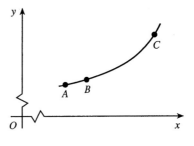

  (a) Find the exact value of the gradient of the chord AC.

  (b) Find the exact value of the gradient of the chord AB.

  (c) Explain how your answers to parts (a) and (b) relate to the gradient of the curve $y = x^3 + 3$ at A.   (OCR)

5 Write $x^2 + 10x + 38$ in the form $(x + b)^2 + c$ where the values of b and c are to be found.

  (a) State the minimum value of $x^2 + 10x + 38$ and the value of x for which this occurs.

  (b) Determine the values of x for which $x^2 + 10x + 38 \geqslant 22$.

6 Find where the line $y = 5 - 2x$ meets the curve $y = (3 - x)^2$. What can you deduce from your answer?

7 (a) Solve the simultaneous equations $y = 2x + 2$, $y = x^2 + 3x - 18$.

  (b) Show that the simultaneous equations $y = 2x - 20$, $y = x^2 + 3x - 18$ have no real solutions.

  (c) The graph of $y = 2x + k$ meets the graph of $y = x^2 + 3x - 18$ at only one point. Find the value of the constant k.   (OCR)

8 (a) Find the equation of the line which is parallel to the line $2x + y = 5$ and which passes through the point $(2, 5)$.

  (b) Find the equation of the line l which is perpendicular to the line $2x + y = 5$ and which passes through the point $(1, k)$, where k is constant.

  (c) Hence find the value of k for which the line l passes through the origin.   (OCR)

9 Find the coordinates of the point where the normal to the curve with equation $y = x^2$ at the point for which $x = 2$ meets the curve again.

10 Solve the inequality $x^2 - x - 2 > 0$.

11 (a) Find the gradient of the straight line l with equation $4y - 3x + 2 = 0$.

    (b) Find an equation of the straight line which passes through the origin and which is perpendicular to l. (OCR)

12 Simplify   (a) $\sqrt{75} - \sqrt{27}$,   (b) $\dfrac{\sqrt{18}}{2\sqrt{2}}$,   (c) $\left(\dfrac{4}{2\sqrt{2}}\right)^3$.

13 Solve the simultaneous equations
$$2x + 3y = 5,$$
$$x^2 + 3xy = 4.$$

14 Find the coordinates of the vertex of the parabola with equation $y = 3x^2 + 6x + 10$

    (a) by using the completed square form,

    (b) by using differentiation.

15 (a) Express the quadratic polynomial $x^2 - (2\sqrt{2})x + 4$ in the form $(x + a)^2 + b$, stating the exact values of the constants a and b.

    (b) Hence write down the equation of the line of symmetry of the curve
$$y = x^2 - (2\sqrt{2})x + 4.$$ (OCR)

16 Solve the equation $x\sqrt{8} - 11 = \dfrac{3x}{\sqrt{2}}$, giving your answer in the form $k\sqrt{2}$, where k is an integer. (OCR)

17 A rhombus has opposite vertices at $(-1, 3)$ and $(5, -1)$.

    (a) Find the equations of its diagonals.

    One of the other vertices is $(0, -2)$.

    (b) Find the fourth vertex.

18 Solve the inequalities
    (a) $2(3 - x) < 4 - (2 - x)$,   (b) $(x - 3)^2 < x^2$,   (c) $(x - 2)(x - 3) \geqslant 6$.

19 Find, correct to 3 significant figures, all the roots of the equation $x^4 - 4x^2 + 1 = 0$. (OCR)

20 Find the equation of the tangent to the curve with equation $y = 2x^2 - x - 2$ which is perpendicular to the straight line with equation $2x - 3y + 4 = 0$.

21 Find the equation of the straight line through $A(1, 4)$ which is perpendicular to the line passing through the points $B(2, -2)$ and $C(4, 0)$. Hence find the area of the triangle ABC, giving your answer in the simplest possible form.

22 In triangle ABC shown in the diagram, $AB = 7$ cm, $BC = 1$ cm, angle $ABC = 90°$ and angle $BAC = \alpha°$. Find the value of $\cos \alpha$, giving your answer in simplified surd form with a rational denominator. (OCR)

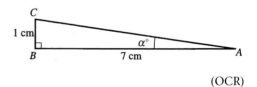

23 The quadratic equation $(p - 1)x^2 + 4x + (p - 4) = 0$ has a repeated root. Find the possible values of p.

24 The quadratic equation $x^2 + (k+1)x + 16 = 0$ has two distinct real roots. Find the set of possible values of the constant k.   (OCR)

25 Points A and B have coordinates $(-1, 2)$ and $(7, -4)$ respectively.
  (a) Write down the coordinates of M, the mid-point of AB.

  (b) Calculate the distance MB.

  (c) The point P lies on the circle with AB as diameter and has coordinates $(2, y)$ where y is positive. Calculate the value of y, giving your answer in surd form.

26 The equation $x^2 + 4kx + 3k = 0$, where k is a constant, has distinct real roots.
  (a) Prove that $k(4k - 3) > 0$.

  (b) Hence find the set of possible values of k.

  It is given instead that the x-axis is a tangent to the graph of $y = x^2 + 4kx + 3k$.

  (c) Write down the possible values of k.   (OCR)

27 Solve the inequalities   (a) $2x^2 - 5x + 2 \leqslant 0$,   (b) $(2x - 3)^2 < 16$,   (c) $\frac{1}{3}x - \frac{1}{4}(2x - 5) \leqslant \frac{1}{5}$.

28 A tangent to the curve $y = 3 - 5x - 2x^2$ has gradient -1. Find the coordinates of the point of contact, and the equation of the tangent.

29 Show that any root of the equation $5 + x - \sqrt{3 + 4x} = 0$ is also a root of the equation $x^2 + 6x + 22 = 0$. Hence show that the equation $5 + x - \sqrt{3 + 4x} = 0$ has no solutions.

7 Index notation

You have already used index notation in the form of squares, cubes and other integer powers. In this chapter the notation is extended to powers which are zero, negative numbers and fractions. When you have completed it, you should

- know the rules of indices
- know the meaning of negative, zero and fractional indices
- be able to simplify expressions involving indices.

7.1 Working with indices

In the 16th century, when mathematics books began to be printed, mathematicians were finding how to solve cubic and quartic equations. They found it was more economical to write and to print the products *xxx* and *xxxx* as x^3 and x^4.

This is how index notation started. But it turned out to be much more than a convenient shorthand. The new notation led to important mathematical discoveries, and mathematics as it is today would be inconceivable without index notation.

You will already have used simple examples of this notation. In general, the symbol a^m stands for the result of multiplying *m a* s together:

$$a^m = \overbrace{a \times a \times a \times \cdots \times a}^{m \text{ of these}}.$$

The number a is called the **base**, and the number m is the **index** (plural 'indices'). Notice that, although a can be any kind of number, m must be a positive integer. Another way of describing this is 'a raised to the mth power', or more shortly 'a to the power m'. When this notation is used, expressions can often be simplified by using a few simple rules.

One of these is the **multiplication rule**,

$$a^m \times a^n = \overbrace{a \times a \times \cdots \times a}^{m \text{ of these}} \overbrace{a \times a \times \cdots \times a}^{n \text{ of these}} = \overbrace{a \times a \times \cdots \times a}^{m+n \text{ of these}} = a^{m+n}.$$

This is used, for example, in finding the volume of a cube of side a:

$$\text{volume} = \text{base area} \times \text{height} = a^2 \times a = a^2 \times a^1 = a^{2+1} = a^3.$$

Closely linked with this is the **division rule**,

$$a^m \div a^n = (\overbrace{a \times a \times \cdots \times a}^{m \text{ of these}}) \div (\overbrace{a \times a \times \cdots \times a}^{n \text{ of these}})$$

$$= \overbrace{a \times a \times \cdots \times a}^{m-n \text{ of these}} \quad \text{(since } n \text{ of the } a \text{ s cancel out)}$$

$$= a^{m-n}, \quad \text{provided that } m > n.$$

Example 7.1.1

Simplify   (a) $10^3 \times 10^4 \div 10^2$,   (b) $\dfrac{p^4 q^5}{p q^3}$.

(a) $10^3 \times 10^4 \div 10^2 = 10^{3+4} \div 10^2 = 10^7 \div 10^2 = 10^{7-2} = 10^5$.

(b) $\dfrac{p^4 q^5}{p q^3} = \dfrac{p^4}{p} \times \dfrac{q^5}{q^3} = (p^4 \div p) \times (q^5 \div q^3) = p^{4-1} \times q^{5-3} = p^3 q^2$.

Another rule is the **power-on-power rule**,

$$(a^m)^n = \overbrace{\overbrace{a \times a \times \cdots \times a}^{m \text{ of these}} \times \overbrace{a \times a \times \cdots \times a}^{m \text{ of these}} \times \cdots \times \overbrace{a \times a \times \cdots \times a}^{m \text{ of these}}}^{n \text{ of these brackets}} = \overbrace{a \times a \times \cdots \times a}^{m \times n \text{ of these}} = a^{m \times n}.$$

Example 7.1.2

Express 8^4 as a power of 2.

Since $8 = 2^3$, $8^4 = (2^3)^4 = 2^{3 \times 4} = 2^{12}$.

One further rule, the **factor rule**, has two bases but just one index:

$$(a \times b)^m = \overbrace{(a \times b) \times (a \times b) \times \cdots \times (a \times b)}^{m \text{ of these brackets}} = \overbrace{a \times a \times \cdots \times a}^{m \text{ of these}} \times \overbrace{b \times b \times \cdots \times b}^{m \text{ of these}} = a^m \times b^m.$$

In explaining these rules multiplication signs have been used. But, as in other parts of algebra, they are usually omitted if there is no ambiguity. For completeness, here are the rules again.

The multiplication rule:	$a^m \times a^n = a^{m+n}$
The division rule:	$a^m \div a^n = a^{m-n}$, provided that $m > n$
The power-on-power rule:	$(a^m)^n = a^{m \times n}$
The factor rule:	$(a \times b)^m = a^m \times b^m$

Example 7.1.3

Given that $zx^4 = (x^3 y)^2$, express z as simply as possible in terms of x and y.

Begin by using the factor rule to separate the powers of x and y.

$$zx^4 = (x^3)^2 \times y^2.$$

Using the power-on-power rule,

$$zx^4 = x^{3 \times 2} \times y^2 = x^6 y^2.$$

Divide both sides by x^4 and rearrange the factors to get the powers of x together.

$$z = x^6 y^2 \div x^4 = (x^6 \div x^4) \times y^2.$$

Using the division rule,

$$z = x^{6-4} \times y^2 = x^2 y^2.$$

If $zx^4 = (x^3 y)^2$, then $z = x^2 y^2$.

Example 7.1.4

Simplify $(2a^2b)^3 \div (4a^4b)$.

$$
\begin{aligned}
(2a^2b)^3 \div (4a^4b) &= (2^3(a^2)^3b^3) \div (4a^4b) && \text{factor rule} \\
&= (8a^{2\times3}b^3) \div (4a^4b) && \text{power-on-power rule} \\
&= (8 \div 4) \times (a^6 \div a^4) \times (b^3 \div b^1) && \text{rearranging} \\
&= 2a^{6-4}b^{3-1} && \text{division rule} \\
&= 2a^2b^2.
\end{aligned}
$$

Exercise 7A

1 Simplify the following expressions.

(a) $a^2 \times a^3 \times a^7$ (b) $(b^4)^2$ (c) $c^7 \div c^3$

(d) $d^5 \times d^4$ (e) $(e^5)^4$ (f) $(x^3y^2)^2$

(g) $5g^5 \times 3g^3$ (h) $12h^{12} \div 4h^4$ (i) $(2a^2)^3 \times (3a)^2$

(j) $(p^2q^3)^2 \times (pq^3)^3$ (k) $(4x^2y)^2 \times (2xy^3)^3$ (l) $(6ac^3)^2 \div (9a^2c^5)$

(m) $(3m^4n^2)^3 \times (2mn^2)^2$ (n) $(49r^3s^2)^2 \div (7rs)^3$ (o) $(2xy^2z^3)^2 \div (2xy^2z^3)$

2 Simplify the following, giving each answer in the form 2^n.

(a) $2^{11} \times (2^5)^3$ (b) $(2^3)^2 \times (2^2)^3$ (c) 4^3 (d) 8^2

(e) $\dfrac{2^7 \times 2^8}{2^{13}}$ (f) $\dfrac{2^2 \times 2^3}{(2^2)^2}$ (g) $4^2 \div 2^4$ (h) $2 \times 4^4 \div 8^3$

7.2   Zero and negative indices

The definition of a^m in Section 7.1, as the result of multiplying m a s together, makes no sense if m is zero or a negative integer. You can't multiply -3 a s or 0 a s together. But extending the meaning of a^m when the index is zero or negative is possible, and useful, since it turns out that the rules still work with such index values.

Look at this sequence: $2^5 = 32,\ \ 2^4 = 16,\ \ 2^3 = 8,\ \ 2^2 = 4,\ \ \dots$

On the left sides, the base is always 2, and the indices go down by 1 at each step. On the right, the numbers are halved at each step. So you might continue the process

$$\dots,\ 2^2 = 4,\ 2^1 = 2,\ 2^0 = 1,\ 2^{-1} = \tfrac{1}{2},\ 2^{-2} = \tfrac{1}{4},\ 2^{-3} = \tfrac{1}{8},\ \dots$$

and you can go on like this indefinitely. Now compare

$$2^1 = 2 \text{ with } 2^{-1} = \tfrac{1}{2}, \quad 2^2 = 4 \text{ with } 2^{-2} = \tfrac{1}{4}, \quad 2^3 = 8 \text{ with } 2^{-3} = \tfrac{1}{8}.$$

It looks as if 2^{-n} should be defined as $\dfrac{1}{2^n}$, with the special value in the middle $2^0 = 1$.

This can be standardised, for any base a (except 0), and any positive integer n, as the **negative power rule**.

$$a^{-n} = \frac{1}{a^n} \quad \text{and} \quad a^0 = 1.$$

Example 7.2.1
Write as a simple fraction (a) 2^{-5}, (b) $\left(\frac{3}{5}\right)^{-2}$, (c) $\left(1\frac{1}{2}\right)^{-1}$.

(a) $2^{-5} = \dfrac{1}{2^5} = \frac{1}{32}$.

(b) $\left(\frac{3}{5}\right)^{-2} = \dfrac{1}{\left(\frac{3}{5}\right)^2} = \dfrac{1}{\frac{9}{25}} = \frac{25}{9}$.

(c) $\left(1\frac{1}{2}\right)^{-1} = \left(\frac{3}{2}\right)^{-1} = \dfrac{1}{\frac{3}{2}} = \frac{2}{3}$.

Note that in handwritten work it is safer, though not strictly necessary, to insert brackets in the two-tier fraction $\dfrac{1}{\left(\frac{3}{2}\right)}$ to avoid confusing it with $\dfrac{\left(\frac{1}{3}\right)}{2}$.

Notice that in Example 7.2.1 parts (b) and (c) use the rule that $\dfrac{1}{a/b} = \dfrac{b}{a}$. This is because

$$\frac{b}{a} \times \frac{a}{b} = 1, \quad \text{so} \quad \frac{b}{a} = 1 \div \frac{a}{b} = \frac{1}{a/b}.$$

Before going on to use the negative power rule, you need to be sure that the rules which were established in Section 7.1 for positive indices still work when some of the indices are negative. Here are three examples.

The multiplication rule: $\quad a^3 \times a^{-7} = a^3 \times \dfrac{1}{a^7} = \dfrac{1}{a^7 \div a^3}$

$$= \frac{1}{a^{7-3}} \qquad \text{using the division rule for positive indices}$$

$$= \frac{1}{a^4} = a^{-4} = a^{3+(-7)}.$$

The power-on-power rule: $\quad (a^{-2})^{-3} = \left(\dfrac{1}{a^2}\right)^{-3} = \dfrac{1}{(1/a^2)^3} = \dfrac{1}{1/(a^2)^3}$

$$= \frac{1}{1/a^6} \qquad \text{using the power-on-power rule for positive indices}$$

$$= a^6 = a^{(-2)\times(-3)}.$$

The factor rule: $\quad (ab)^{-3} = \dfrac{1}{(ab)^3} = \dfrac{1}{a^3 b^3} \qquad$ using the factor rule for positive indices

$$= \frac{1}{a^3} \times \frac{1}{b^3} = a^{-3} b^{-3}.$$

Try making up some more examples like these for yourself.

Example 7.2.2

Simplify   (a) $2^{-3} \div 3^{-2}$,   (b) $x^{-1} \times x^{-2}$,   (c) $(x^{-1})^{-2}$,   (d) $(p^3 q^{-1})^2$.

(a) $2^{-3} \div 3^{-2} = \dfrac{1}{2^3} \div \dfrac{1}{3^2} = \frac{1}{8} \div \frac{1}{9} = \frac{1}{8} \times 9 = \frac{9}{8}$.

(b) Using the multiplication rule,

$$x^{-1} \times x^{-2} = x^{(-1)+(-2)} = x^{-3} = \frac{1}{x^3}.$$

(c) Using the power-on-power rule,

$$(x^{-1})^{-2} = x^{(-1)\times(-2)} = x^2.$$

(d) First use the factor rule, then the power-on-power rule.

$$(p^3 q^{-1})^2 = (p^3)^2 \times (q^{-1})^2 = p^{3\times 2} \times q^{(-1)\times 2} = p^6 \times q^{-2} = p^6 \times \frac{1}{q^2} = \frac{p^6}{q^2}.$$

Example 7.2.3

If $a = 5$, find the value of $4a^{-2}$.

The important thing to notice is that the index -2 goes only with the a and not with the 4. So $4a^{-2}$ means $4 \times \dfrac{1}{a^2}$. When $a = 5$, $4a^{-2} = 4 \times \dfrac{1}{25} = 0.16$.

Example 7.2.4

Simplify   (a) $4a^2 b \times (3ab^{-1})^{-2}$,   (b) $\left(\dfrac{MLT^{-2}}{L^2}\right) \div \left(\dfrac{LT^{-1}}{L}\right)$.

(a) **Method 1**   Change the expression into a form where all the indices are positive.

$$4a^2 b \times (3ab^{-1})^{-2} = 4a^2 b \times \frac{1}{(3a \times 1/b)^2} = 4a^2 b \times \frac{1}{9a^2 \times 1/b^2} = 4a^2 b \times \frac{b^2}{9a^2}$$

$$= \tfrac{4}{9} b^{1+2} = \tfrac{4}{9} b^3.$$

Method 2   Use the index rules directly with positive and negative indices.

$$
\begin{aligned}
4a^2 b \times (3ab^{-1})^{-2} &= 4a^2 b \times (3^{-2} a^{-2} (b^{-1})^{-2}) && \text{factor rule} \\
&= 4a^2 b \times (3^{-2} a^{-2} b^2) && \text{power-on-power rule} \\
&= \left(4 \times \frac{1}{3^2}\right) \times (a^2 a^{-2}) \times (bb^2) = \tfrac{4}{9} a^0 b^3 = \tfrac{4}{9} b^3.
\end{aligned}
$$

(b) This is an application in mechanics: M, L, T stand for dimensions of mass, length and time in the measurement of viscosity. Taking the brackets separately,

$$\left(\frac{MLT^{-2}}{L^2}\right) = ML^{1-2}T^{-2} = ML^{-1}T^{-2}$$

and $\left(\dfrac{LT^{-1}}{L}\right) = L^{1-1}T^{-1} = L^0 T^{-1} = T^{-1}$,

so $\left(\dfrac{MLT^{-2}}{L^2}\right) \div \left(\dfrac{LT^{-1}}{L}\right) = (ML^{-1}T^{-2}) \div T^{-1} = ML^{-1}T^{-2-(-1)} = ML^{-1}T^{-1}$.

Example 7.2.5

Find the number x such that $2^{x+1} \div 4^{x+2} = 8^{x+3}$.

Since 4 and 8 are powers of 2, the whole equation can be written in terms of powers of 2. Using the power-on-power rule followed by the division rule,

$$2^{x+1} \div (2^2)^{x+2} = (2^3)^{x+3}$$
$$2^{x+1} \div 2^{2x+4} = 2^{3x+9}$$
$$2^{(x+1)-(2x+4)} = 2^{3x+9}$$
$$2^{-x-3} = 2^{3x+9}.$$

You can now equate the indices on the two sides of the equation to get

$$-x - 3 = 3x + 9,$$

so $4x + 12 = 0$, giving $x = -3$.

Since there are several steps in the solution, it is a good idea to check the answer. If $x = -3$, $2^{x+1} = 2^{-2} = \dfrac{1}{2^2} = \frac{1}{4}$, $4^{x+2} = 4^{-1} = \frac{1}{4}$ and $8^{x+3} = 8^0 = 1$. So the left side is equal to $\frac{1}{4} \div \frac{1}{4} = 1$, which agrees with the right side.

One application of negative indices is in writing down very small numbers. You probably know how to write very large numbers in standard form, or scientific notation. For example, it is easier to write the speed of light as $3.00 \times 10^8\,\mathrm{m\,s^{-1}}$ than as $300\,000\,000\,\mathrm{m\,s^{-1}}$. Similarly, the wavelength of red light, about $0.000\,000\,75$ metres, is more easily appreciated written as 7.5×10^{-7} metres.

Computers and calculators often give users the option to work in scientific notation, and if numbers become too large (or too small) to be displayed in ordinary numerical form they will switch into standard form, for example 3.00E8 or 7.5E−7. The symbol E stands for 'exponent', yet another word for 'index'. You can write this in scientific notation by simply replacing the symbol E m by $\times\ 10^m$, for any integer m.

When you do calculations with numbers in standard form, the technique is to separate the powers of 10 from the rest of the expression to be evaluated, and to combine these using the rules for indices listed in Section 7.1.

At the end it may be necessary to make an adjustment to get the final answer in standard form. For example, if the calculation comes to 38.4×10^{-5}, you would write this as $(3.84 \times 10^1) \times 10^{-5}$, which is $3.84 \times (10^1 \times 10^{-5}) = 3.84 \times 10^{-4}$. If it comes to 0.093×10^{-3}, you would write it as $(9.3 \times 10^{-2}) \times 10^{-3}$, which is $9.3 \times (10^{-2} \times 10^{-3}) = 9.3 \times 10^{-5}$.

Example 7.2.6

Calculate the universal constant of gravitation, G, from $G = \dfrac{gR^2}{M}$ where, in SI units, $g \approx 9.81$, $R \approx 6.37 \times 10^6$ and $M \approx 5.97 \times 10^{24}$. ($R$ and M are the Earth's radius and mass, and g is the acceleration due to gravity at the Earth's surface.)

$$G \approx \frac{9.81 \times (6.37 \times 10^6)^2}{5.97 \times 10^{24}} = \frac{9.81 \times (6.37)^2}{5.97} \times \frac{(10^6)^2}{10^{24}}$$

$$\approx 66.7 \times \frac{10^{12}}{10^{24}} = 6.67 \times 10^1 \times 10^{-12} = 6.67 \times 10^{1-12} = 6.67 \times 10^{-11}.$$

Exercise 7B

1 Express each of the following as an integer or a fraction.

(a) 2^{-3} (b) 4^{-2} (c) 5^{-1} (d) 3^{-2}

(e) 10^{-4} (f) 1^{-7} (g) $\left(\frac{1}{2}\right)^{-1}$ (h) $\left(\frac{1}{3}\right)^{-3}$

(i) $\left(2\frac{1}{2}\right)^{-1}$ (j) 2^{-7} (k) 6^{-3} (l) $\left(1\frac{1}{3}\right)^{-3}$

2 If $x = 2$, find the value of each of the following.

(a) $4x^{-3}$ (b) $(4x)^{-3}$ (c) $\frac{1}{4}x^{-3}$ (d) $\left(\frac{1}{4}x\right)^{-3}$ (e) $(4 \div x)^{-3}$ (f) $(x \div 4)^{-3}$

3 If $y = 5$, find the value of each of the following.

(a) $(2y)^{-1}$ (b) $2y^{-1}$ (c) $\left(\frac{1}{2}y\right)^{-1}$ (d) $\frac{1}{2}y^{-1}$ (e) $\dfrac{1}{(2y)^{-1}}$ (f) $\dfrac{2}{(y^{-1})^{-1}}$

4 Express each of the following in as simple a form as possible.

(a) $a^4 \times a^{-3}$

(b) $\dfrac{1}{b^{-1}}$

(c) $(c^{-2})^3$

(d) $d^{-1} \times 2d$

(e) $e^{-4} \times e^{-5}$

(f) $\dfrac{f^{-2}}{f^3}$

(g) $12g^3 \times (2g^2)^{-2}$

(h) $(3h^2)^{-2}$

(i) $(3i^{-2})^{-2}$

(j) $\left(\frac{1}{2}j^{-2}\right)^{-3}$

(k) $(2x^3y^{-1})^3$

(l) $(p^2q^4r^3)^{-4}$

(m) $(4m^2)^{-1} \times 8m^3$

(n) $(3n^{-2})^4 \times (9n)^{-1}$

(o) $(2xy^2)^{-1} \times (4xy)^2$

(p) $(5a^3c^{-1})^2 \div (2a^{-1}c^2)$

(q) $(2q^{-2})^{-2} \div (4/q)^2$

(r) $(3x^{-2}y)^2 \div (4xy)^{-2}$

5 Solve the following equations.

(a) $3^x = \frac{1}{9}$

(b) $5^y = 1$

(c) $2^z \times 2^{z-3} = 32$

(d) $7^{3x} \div 7^{x-2} = \frac{1}{49}$

(e) $4^y \times 2^y = 8^{120}$

(f) $3^t \times 9^{t+3} = 27^2$

6 The length of each edge of a cube is 3×10^{-2} metres.

(a) Find the volume of the cube.

(b) Find the total surface area of the cube.

7 An athlete runs 2×10^{-1} km in 7.5×10^{-3} hours. Find her average speed in km h^{-1}.

8 The volume, $V\,\text{m}^3$, of l metres of wire is given by $V = \pi r^2 l$, where r metres is the radius of the circular cross-section.

(a) Find the volume of 80 m of wire with radius of cross-section $2 \times 10^{-3}\,\text{m}$.

(b) Another type of wire has radius of cross-section $5 \times 10^{-3}\,\text{m}$. What length of this wire has a volume of $8 \times 10^{-3}\,\text{m}^3$?

(c) Another type of wire is such that a length of 61 m has a volume of $6 \times 10^{-3}\,\text{m}^3$. Find the radius of the cross-section.

9 An equation which occurs in the study of waves is $y = \dfrac{\lambda d}{a}$.

(a) Calculate y when $\lambda = 7 \times 10^{-7}$, $d = 5 \times 10^{-1}$ and $a = 8 \times 10^{-4}$.

(b) Calculate λ when $y = 10^{-3}$, $d = 0.6$ and $a = 2.7 \times 10^{-4}$.

10 Solve the equation $\dfrac{3^{5x+2}}{9^{1-x}} = \dfrac{27^{4+3x}}{729}$.

7.3 Fractional indices

Section 7.2 gave a meaning for the power a^m when m is any negative integer. It is possible to go further, and to find a meaning for a^m when m is any rational number.

Remember from Section 2.1 that a rational number is a number of the form $\dfrac{p}{q}$, where p and q are integers and q is not 0. For example, $\frac{3}{4}, \frac{8}{5}$ and $-\frac{7}{2}$ are rational numbers. The problem is to find a meaning for powers such as $a^{\frac{3}{4}}, a^{\frac{8}{5}}$ and $a^{-\frac{7}{2}}$.

To do this, suppose that the power-on-power rule can still be used if m is not an integer. For example, take $m = \frac{1}{2}$ and $n = 2$. Then the rule would give

$$\left(a^{\frac{1}{2}}\right)^2 = a^{\frac{1}{2} \times 2} = a^1, \quad \text{which is just } a.$$

So $a^{\frac{1}{2}}$ would be a number whose square is a.

There are only two numbers with this property, $+\sqrt{a}$ and $-\sqrt{a}$. Since in mathematics every symbol needs to have a definite meaning, a choice has to be made between these. So $\sqrt{a}$ is defined to be the positive square root of a.

$$a^{\frac{1}{2}} = \sqrt{a}.$$

Now take $m = \frac{1}{3}$ and $n = 3$. The power-on-power rule then gives

$$\left(a^{\frac{1}{3}}\right)^3 = a^{\frac{1}{3} \times 3} = a^1 = a.$$

By the same reasoning as before, $a^{\frac{1}{3}}$ is the cube root of a. This time there is no ambiguity; each number has only one real cube root.

$$a^{\frac{1}{3}} = \sqrt[3]{a}.$$

Notice that, for $a^{\frac{1}{2}} = \sqrt{a}$, the number a has to be positive or zero; $a^{\frac{1}{2}}$ has no meaning if a is negative. But for $a^{\frac{1}{3}} = \sqrt[3]{a}$, a can be positive, negative or zero; every number has a cube root. This is looked at in more detail in Section 7.5.

Obviously the argument could be generalised to any rational number of the form $\dfrac{1}{q}$, using the power-on-power rule as

$$\left(a^{\frac{1}{q}}\right)^q = a^{\frac{1}{q} \times q} = a^1 = a.$$

So $a^{\frac{1}{q}}$ is the qth root of a. If q is even, $a^{\frac{1}{q}}$ is defined to be the positive qth root.

$$a^{\frac{1}{q}} = \sqrt[q]{a}.$$

Example 7.3.1

Express as simply as possible   (a) $36^{\frac{1}{2}}$,   (b) $\left(\frac{1}{8}\right)^{\frac{1}{3}}$,   (c) $64^{-\frac{1}{2}}$.

(a) $36^{\frac{1}{2}} = \sqrt{36} = 6$.

(b) $\left(\frac{1}{8}\right)^{\frac{1}{3}} = \sqrt[3]{\frac{1}{8}} = \frac{1}{2}$.

(c) $64^{-\frac{1}{2}} = \dfrac{1}{64^{\frac{1}{2}}} = \frac{1}{8}$.

What about a power like $a^{\frac{2}{3}}$? You could find this by writing $\frac{2}{3}$ either as $\frac{1}{3} \times 2$ or as $2 \times \frac{1}{3}$ and using the power-on-power rule directly. This would give either

$$a^{\frac{2}{3}} = a^{\frac{1}{3} \times 2} = \left(a^{\frac{1}{3}}\right)^2 = \left(\sqrt[3]{a}\right)^2, \quad \text{or} \quad a^{\frac{2}{3}} = a^{2 \times \frac{1}{3}} = \left(a^2\right)^{\frac{1}{3}} = \sqrt[3]{a^2}.$$

Both forms are equally valid. It makes no difference to the final answer whether you take the cube root first and then square, or square first and then take the cube root.

For practical calculation, the first form is the best to use if a has an exact cube root, and the second is best if it hasn't. For example, if you want to find $8^{\frac{2}{3}}$, it is slightly simpler to work out

$$8^{\frac{2}{3}} = \left(\sqrt[3]{8}\right)^2 = 2^2 = 4$$

than $8^{\frac{2}{3}} = \sqrt[3]{8^2} = \sqrt[3]{64} = 4$.

But if you want $7^{\frac{2}{3}}$,

$$7^{\frac{2}{3}} = \sqrt[3]{7^2} = \sqrt[3]{49} = 3.6593...$$

has the edge over

$$7^{\frac{2}{3}} = \left(\sqrt[3]{7}\right)^2 = (1.9129...)^2 = 3.6593....$$

By exactly the same reasoning, $a^{\frac{p}{q}}$ can be found either as

$$a^{\frac{p}{q}} = a^{\frac{1}{q} \times p} = \left(a^{\frac{1}{q}}\right)^p = \left(\sqrt[q]{a}\right)^p, \quad \text{or as} \quad a^{\frac{p}{q}} = a^{p \times \frac{1}{q}} = \left(a^p\right)^{\frac{1}{q}} = \sqrt[q]{a^p}.$$

This is the general form of the **fractional power rule**.

$$a^{\frac{p}{q}} = \left(\sqrt[q]{a}\right)^p = \sqrt[q]{a^p}.$$

Example 7.3.2

Simplify   (a) $9^{\frac{5}{2}}$,   (b) $3^{\frac{1}{2}} \times 3^{\frac{3}{2}}$,   (c) $16^{-\frac{3}{4}}$.

(a) $9^{\frac{5}{2}} = \left(\sqrt{9}\right)^5 = 3^5 = 243$.

(b) $3^{\frac{1}{2}} \times 3^{\frac{3}{2}} = 3^{\frac{1}{2} + \frac{3}{2}} = 3^2 = 9$.

(c) **Method 1** $16^{-\frac{3}{4}} = (2^4)^{-\frac{3}{4}} = 2^{-3} = \frac{1}{8}$.

   Method 2 $16^{-\frac{3}{4}} = \dfrac{1}{16^{\frac{3}{4}}} = \dfrac{1}{(\sqrt[4]{16})^3} = \dfrac{1}{2^3} = \frac{1}{8}$.

There are often good alternative ways for solving problems involving indices, and you should try experimenting with them. Many people prefer to think with positive indices rather than negative ones; if you are one of them, writing $16^{-\frac{3}{4}} = \dfrac{1}{16^{\frac{3}{4}}}$, as in Method 2 of Example 7.3.2(c), makes good sense as a first step.

Example 7.3.3
Simplify   (a) $\left(2\frac{1}{4}\right)^{-\frac{1}{2}}$,   (b) $2x^{\frac{1}{2}} \times 3x^{-\frac{5}{2}}$,   (c) $(2x^2 y^{-4})^{\frac{1}{2}}$.

(a) $\left(2\frac{1}{4}\right)^{-\frac{1}{2}} = \left(\frac{9}{4}\right)^{-\frac{1}{2}} = \dfrac{1}{\left(\frac{9}{4}\right)^{\frac{1}{2}}} = \left(\frac{4}{9}\right)^{\frac{1}{2}} = \sqrt{\frac{4}{9}} = \frac{2}{3}.$

(b) $2x^{\frac{1}{2}} \times 3x^{-\frac{5}{2}} = 6x^{\frac{1}{2}-\frac{5}{2}} = 6x^{-2} = \dfrac{6}{x^2}.$

(c) Using the factor rule and then the power-on-power rule,

$$(2x^2 y^{-4})^{\frac{1}{2}} = 2^{\frac{1}{2}} \times (x^2)^{\frac{1}{2}} \times (y^{-4})^{\frac{1}{2}}$$
$$= 2^{\frac{1}{2}} \times x^{2\times\frac{1}{2}} \times y^{-4\times\frac{1}{2}}$$
$$= 2^{\frac{1}{2}} \times x \times y^{-2}$$
$$= \dfrac{x\sqrt{2}}{y^2}.$$

In Example 7.3.3, the answer given to part (c) breaks the convention of writing numbers before letters. It is sometimes safer to write $x\sqrt{2}$ rather than $\sqrt{2}x$ to avoid possible confusion with $\sqrt{2x}$.

You will quite often need to use the fractional power rule in reverse, to convert expressions involving roots into index notation. This is illustrated by the next example.

Example 7.3.4
Write in index notation   (a) $2x\sqrt{x}$,   (b) $\dfrac{6}{\sqrt[3]{x}}$,   (c) $\dfrac{1}{x^2\sqrt{x}}$.

(a) $2x\sqrt{x} = 2x^1 \times x^{\frac{1}{2}} = 2x^{1+\frac{1}{2}} = 2x^{\frac{3}{2}}.$

(b) $\dfrac{6}{\sqrt[3]{x}} = 6 \times \dfrac{1}{x^{\frac{1}{3}}} = 6x^{-\frac{1}{3}}.$

(c) $\dfrac{1}{x^2\sqrt{x}} = \dfrac{1}{x^2 \times x^{\frac{1}{2}}} = \dfrac{1}{x^{2+\frac{1}{2}}} = \dfrac{1}{x^{\frac{5}{2}}} = x^{-\frac{5}{2}}.$

7.4   Equations with rational indices

You have often solved equations such as $x^3 = 27$, $\sqrt{x} = 5$ and $\dfrac{1}{x} = 20$. But you probably have not realised that these are all equations of the same type, since they can all be written as $x^n = A$, with n equal to 3, $\frac{1}{2}$ and -1 respectively.

Here is a rather more complicated equation of the same type.

Example 7.4.1

Find x if $x^{\frac{3}{4}} = 27$.

If $x^{\frac{3}{4}}$ is raised to the power $\frac{4}{3}$, the power-on-power rule gives

$$\left(x^{\frac{3}{4}}\right)^{\frac{4}{3}} = x^{\frac{3}{4} \times \frac{4}{3}} = x^1 = x.$$

So the given equation can be solved by raising both sides to the power $\frac{4}{3}$. This gives

$$x = 27^{\frac{4}{3}} = \left(\sqrt[3]{27}\right)^4 = 3^4 = 81.$$

As a check, if $x = 81$, then $x^{\frac{3}{4}} = 81^{\frac{3}{4}} = \left(\sqrt[4]{81}\right)^3 = 3^3 = 27$.

The method used in this example can be used to solve any equation of the form $x^n = A$. Raising both sides to the power $\frac{1}{n}$ gives

$$(x^n)^{\frac{1}{n}} = A^{\frac{1}{n}}.$$

Since $(x^n)^{\frac{1}{n}} = x^{n \times \frac{1}{n}} = x^1 = x$, the solution of the equation is $x = A^{\frac{1}{n}}$.

Applying this to the three equations at the beginning of this section gives the solutions $27^{\frac{1}{3}} = 3$, $5^2 = 25$ and $20^{-1} = \frac{1}{20}$.

But you may have noticed a snag. If n is equal to 2, then $A^{\frac{1}{2}} = \sqrt{A}$ is only one of the roots of the equation $x^2 = A$; assuming that A is positive, there are two roots of the equation, $A^{\frac{1}{2}}$ and $-A^{\frac{1}{2}}$. The same happens if n is any even integer, or if it is a fraction with an even numerator such as $\frac{2}{3}$ or $\frac{4}{5}$. So to make this into a general rule it would be safer to restrict it to positive values of x and A.

> If n is a rational number and $A > 0$, the positive solution of the equation $x^n = A$ is $x = A^{\frac{1}{n}}$.

Example 7.4.2

Solve the equation $x^{\frac{3}{2}} = 10$, giving your answer correct to 3 significant figures.

If $n = \frac{3}{2}$, then $\dfrac{1}{n} = \frac{2}{3}$. The solution of the equation is therefore

$$x = 10^{\frac{2}{3}} = \sqrt[3]{10^2} = \sqrt[3]{100} = 4.64, \text{ correct to 3 significant figures.}$$

You may sometimes want to solve an equation with rational indices which is a quadratic equation in disguise.

Example 7.4.3

Solve the equation $5x^{\frac{1}{3}} = x^{\frac{2}{3}} + 4$.

The key is to notice that $x^{\frac{2}{3}} = \left(x^{\frac{1}{3}}\right)^2$. So if you write $x^{\frac{1}{3}}$ as u, the equation is

$$5u = u^2 + 4,$$

a quadratic equation for u. Writing this as

$$u^2 - 5u + 4 = 0,$$
$$(u - 1)(u - 4) = 0,$$

the roots for u are 1 and 4.

Since the values of x are required, it is now necessary to solve for x the equations

$$x^{\frac{1}{3}} = 1 \quad \text{and} \quad x^{\frac{1}{3}} = 4.$$

This gives two roots for x:

$$x = 1^3 = 1 \quad \text{and} \quad x = 4^3 = 64.$$

7.5 Powers of negative bases

So far in this chapter it has been assumed that the base a is a positive number. This section investigates whether the negative and fractional power rules still apply if the base is a negative number. You may if you wish omit this section on a first reading and go straight on to Exercise 7C.

You have often used positive integer powers with negative bases. For example,

$$(-5)^2 = (-5) \times (-5) = +5^2, \quad (-5)^3 = (-5) \times (-5) \times (-5) = -5^3, \quad \text{and so on.}$$

There is no problem in extending this to negative integer indices. For example,

$$(-5)^{-2} = \frac{1}{(-5)^2} = \frac{1}{5^2} = +5^{-2}, \quad (-5)^{-3} = \frac{1}{(-5)^3} = \frac{1}{-5^3} = -\frac{1}{5^3} = -5^{-3}, \quad \text{and so on.}$$

You can sum up these results in a single rule.

> If m is an integer (positive, negative or zero), and a is a positive number, then
> $$(-a)^m = \begin{cases} +a^m & \text{if } m \text{ is an even integer or zero,} \\ -a^m & \text{if } m \text{ is an odd integer.} \end{cases}$$

The situation is different when m is a fractional index. For example, taking a to be -64, you can write $(-64)^{\frac{1}{3}} = -4$. This is because $a^{\frac{1}{3}} = \sqrt[3]{a}$, and $(-4)^3 = -64$, so that $\sqrt[3]{-64} = -4$. But $(-64)^{\frac{1}{2}}$ has no meaning, because $a^{\frac{1}{2}} = \sqrt{a}$, and a negative number doesn't have a real square root.

You can reason similarly for any index of the form $\dfrac{1}{q}$, and sum the results up in another rule.

> If q is an integer, either positive or negative but not zero, and a is a positive number, then
> $$(-a)^{\frac{1}{q}} \begin{cases} \text{has no meaning if } q \text{ is even,} \\ = -a^{\frac{1}{q}} \text{ if } q \text{ is odd.} \end{cases}$$

Example 7.5.1

Find, where possible, (a) $(-8)^{\frac{1}{3}}$,   (b) $(-32)^{-\frac{1}{5}}$,   (c) $(-81)^{\frac{1}{4}}$.

(a) $(-8)^{\frac{1}{3}} = \sqrt[3]{-8} = -2$, because $(-2)^3 = -8$.

(b) $(-32)^{-\frac{1}{5}} = \dfrac{1}{(-32)^{\frac{1}{5}}} = \dfrac{1}{-32^{\frac{1}{5}}} = -\frac{1}{2}$,

(c) $(-81)^{\frac{1}{4}}$ has no meaning; $\sqrt[4]{-81}$ doesn't exist, because there is no number x such that $x^4 = -81$.

What about other fractional powers? Here the situation is a bit more complicated, but a few numerical examples will illustrate the possibilities.

Example 7.5.2

Find, where possible,

(a) $(-27)^{\frac{2}{3}}$,   (b) $(-16)^{\frac{3}{4}}$,   (c) $(-8)^{\frac{5}{3}}$,   (d) $(-32)^{-\frac{3}{5}}$,   (e) $(-125)^{-\frac{2}{3}}$.

(a) $(-27)^{\frac{2}{3}}$ is $\left(\sqrt[3]{-27}\right)^2 = (-3)^2 = 9$.

(b) $(-16)^{\frac{3}{4}}$ would be $\left(\sqrt[4]{-16}\right)^3$; but since $\sqrt[4]{-16}$ does not exist, neither does $(-16)^{\frac{3}{4}}$.

(c) $(-8)^{\frac{5}{3}}$ is $\left(\sqrt[3]{-8}\right)^5 = (-2)^5 = -32$.

(d) $(-32)^{-\frac{3}{5}} = \dfrac{1}{(-32)^{\frac{3}{5}}}$,   which is $\dfrac{1}{(\sqrt[5]{-32})^3} = \dfrac{1}{(-2)^3} = \dfrac{1}{-8} = -\frac{1}{8}$.

(e) $(-125)^{-\frac{2}{3}} = \dfrac{1}{(-125)^{\frac{2}{3}}}$,   which is $\dfrac{1}{(\sqrt[3]{-125})^2} = \dfrac{1}{(-5)^2} = \frac{1}{25}$.

You can see from this example that, when the expression has a meaning, the answer is sometimes positive and sometimes negative.

To see why, write $(-a)^{\frac{p}{q}}$ as $\left(\sqrt[q]{-a}\right)^p$. If q is even, the root inside the bracket has no meaning, and nothing more can be done. But if q is odd, $\sqrt[q]{-a}$ is itself a negative number. When this is raised to the power p, the answer will be positive if p is even, and negative if p is odd.

Don't try to remember this as a rule. You won't very often come across powers like this, and when you do it is better to reason out what happens from scratch.

One last question remains: what happens if the base is 0? Here there is no problem if the index is positive. For example, $0^5 = 0$, $0^{\frac{1}{2}} = \sqrt{0} = 0$, and so on. But 0^{-5} would be $\dfrac{1}{0^5}$, or $\dfrac{1}{0}$, which is meaningless; and similarly for any negative power. And there is no sensible way of giving a meaning to the power 0^0.

> If $m > 0$, $0^m = 0$. If $m \le 0$, 0^m has no meaning.

Exercise 7C

1 Evaluate the following without using a calculator.

(a) $25^{\frac{1}{2}}$ (b) $8^{\frac{1}{3}}$ (c) $36^{\frac{1}{2}}$ (d) $32^{\frac{1}{5}}$

(e) $81^{\frac{1}{4}}$ (f) $9^{-\frac{1}{2}}$ (g) $16^{-\frac{1}{4}}$ (h) $49^{-\frac{1}{2}}$

(i) $1000^{-\frac{1}{3}}$ (j) $(-27)^{\frac{1}{3}}$ (k) $64^{\frac{2}{3}}$ (l) $(-125)^{-\frac{4}{3}}$

2 Evaluate the following without using a calculator.

(a) $4^{\frac{1}{2}}$ (b) $\left(\frac{1}{4}\right)^{2}$ (c) $\left(\frac{1}{4}\right)^{-2}$ (d) $4^{-\frac{1}{2}}$

(e) $\left(\frac{1}{4}\right)^{-\frac{1}{2}}$ (f) $\left(\frac{1}{4}\right)^{\frac{1}{2}}$ (g) $(4^{4})^{\frac{1}{2}}$ (h) $\left(\left(\frac{1}{4}\right)^{\frac{1}{4}}\right)^{2}$

3 Evaluate the following without using a calculator.

(a) $8^{\frac{2}{3}}$ (b) $4^{\frac{3}{2}}$ (c) $9^{-\frac{3}{2}}$ (d) $27^{\frac{4}{3}}$

(e) $32^{\frac{2}{5}}$ (f) $32^{\frac{3}{5}}$ (g) $64^{-\frac{5}{6}}$ (h) $4^{2\frac{1}{2}}$

(i) $10\,000^{-\frac{3}{4}}$ (j) $\left(\frac{1}{125}\right)^{-\frac{4}{3}}$ (k) $\left(3\frac{3}{8}\right)^{\frac{2}{3}}$ (l) $\left(2\frac{1}{4}\right)^{-\frac{1}{2}}$

4 Simplify the following expressions, assuming that the letters stand for positive numbers.

(a) $a^{\frac{1}{3}} \times a^{\frac{5}{3}}$ (b) $3b^{\frac{1}{2}} \times 4b^{-\frac{3}{2}}$ (c) $\left(6c^{\frac{1}{4}}\right) \times (4c)^{\frac{1}{2}}$

(d) $(d^{2})^{\frac{1}{3}} \div \left(d^{\frac{1}{3}}\right)^{2}$ (e) $(24e)^{\frac{1}{3}} \div (3e)^{\frac{1}{3}}$ (f) $(25p^{2}q^{4})^{\frac{1}{2}}$

5 Solve the following equations, given that $x > 0$.

(a) $x^{\frac{1}{2}} = 8$ (b) $x^{\frac{1}{3}} = 3$ (c) $x^{\frac{2}{3}} = 4$ (d) $x^{\frac{3}{2}} = 27$

(e) $x^{-\frac{3}{2}} = 8$ (f) $x^{-\frac{2}{3}} = 9$ (g) $x^{\frac{3}{2}} = x\sqrt{2}$ (h) $x^{\frac{3}{2}} = 2\sqrt{x}$

6 The time, T seconds, taken by a pendulum of length l metres to complete one swing is given by $T = 2\pi l^{\frac{1}{2}} g^{-\frac{1}{2}}$ where $g \approx 9.81$ m s^{-2}.

(a) Find the value of T for a pendulum of length 0.9 metres.

(b) Find the length of a pendulum which takes 3 seconds for a complete swing.

7 The radius, r cm, of a sphere of volume V cm^3 is given by $r = \left(\dfrac{3V}{4\pi}\right)^{\frac{1}{3}}$. Find the radius of a sphere of volume 1150 cm^3.

8 Solve the following equations.

(a) $4^{x} = 32$ (b) $9^{y} = \frac{1}{27}$ (c) $16^{z} = 2$ (d) $100^{x} = 1000$

(e) $8^{y} = 16$ (f) $8^{z} = \frac{1}{128}$ (g) $(2^{t})^{3} \times 4^{t-1} = 16$ (h) $\dfrac{9^{y}}{27^{2y+1}} = 81$

9 Solve the following equations.

(a) $x^{\frac{1}{2}} + 2x^{-\frac{1}{2}} = 3$ (b) $x + x^{\frac{1}{2}} = 12$ (c) $1 + x = 2x^{\frac{1}{2}}$

(d) $x^{\frac{2}{3}} = 2x^{\frac{1}{3}}$ (e) $x^{\frac{2}{3}} = 2x^{-\frac{1}{3}}$ (f) $2x^{\frac{1}{3}} + x^{\frac{2}{3}} = 3$

10 Rewrite the following expressions using index notation.

(a) $\dfrac{1}{\sqrt{x}}$ (b) $4\sqrt{x}$ (c) $\sqrt{4x}$

(d) $3x^{2}\sqrt{x}$ (e) $\dfrac{1}{\sqrt[3]{x^{2}}}$ (f) $\dfrac{6}{x\sqrt[3]{x}}$

11 Simplify the following expressions by using index notation. Give your final answers in surd form.

(a) $\sqrt[3]{4} \times \sqrt[3]{6}$
(b) $\dfrac{\sqrt{50}}{\sqrt[3]{250}}$
(c) $\sqrt[6]{\tfrac{2}{3}} \times \sqrt[3]{18}$

12 (a) Without using a calculator, state which of these expressions has a value when $x = -64$. Find this value when it exists.

(i) $x^{\frac{2}{3}}$
(ii) $x^{\frac{3}{2}}$
(iii) $x^{-\frac{1}{3}}$

(iv) $\left(\tfrac{1}{2}x\right)^{\frac{4}{5}}$
(v) $x^{\frac{1}{6}}$
(vi) $(4x)^{\frac{3}{4}}$

(b) Investigate whether your calculator gives the answers you obtained in part (a).

(c) What can you say about p or q if $x^{\frac{p}{q}}$ has a value when x is negative?

Miscellaneous exercise 7

1 Evaluate the following without using a calculator.

(a) $\left(\tfrac{1}{2}\right)^{-1} + \left(\tfrac{1}{2}\right)^{-2}$
(b) $32^{-\frac{4}{5}}$
(c) $\left(4\tfrac{1}{2}\right)^{-\frac{1}{3}}$
(d) $\left(1\tfrac{7}{9}\right)^{1\frac{1}{2}}$

2 Simplify the following expressions.

(a) $\left(4p^{\frac{1}{4}}q^{-3}\right)^{\frac{1}{2}}$
(b) $\dfrac{(5b)^{-1}}{(8b^6)^{\frac{1}{3}}}$

(c) $(2x^6y^8)^{\frac{1}{4}} \times (8x^{-2})^{\frac{1}{4}}$
(d) $\left(m^{\frac{1}{3}}n^{\frac{1}{2}}\right)^2 \times \left(m^{\frac{1}{6}}n^{\frac{1}{3}}\right)^4 \times (mn)^{-2}$

3 Express $(9a^4)^{-\frac{1}{2}}$ as an algebraic fraction in simplified form.   (OCR)

4 Express $\dfrac{1}{\left(\sqrt{a}\right)^{\frac{4}{3}}}$ in the form a^n, stating the value of n.   (OCR)

5 By letting $y = x^{\frac{1}{3}}$, or otherwise, find the values of x for which $x^{\frac{1}{3}} - 2x^{-\frac{1}{3}} = 1$.   (OCR)

6 Solve the equation $4^{2x} \times 8^{x-1} = 32$.

7 Given that, in standard form, $3^{236} \approx 4 \times 10^{112}$, and $3^{-376} \approx 4 \times 10^{-180}$, find approximations, also in standard form, for the following.

(a) 3^{376}
(b) 3^{612}
(c) $\left(\sqrt{3}\right)^{236}$
(d) $(3^{-376})^{\frac{5}{2}}$

8 The table below shows, for three of the planets in the solar system, details of their mean distance from the Sun and the time taken for one orbit round the Sun.

Planet	Mean radius of orbit r metres	Period of revolution T seconds
Mercury	5.8×10^{10}	7.6×10^6
Jupiter	7.8×10^{11}	3.7×10^8
Pluto	5.9×10^{12}	7.8×10^9

(a) Show that $r^3 T^{-2}$ has approximately the same value for each planet in the table.

(b) The Earth takes one year for one orbit of the Sun. Find the mean radius of the Earth's orbit around the Sun.

9 Simplify

(a) $2^{-\frac{3}{2}} + 2^{-\frac{1}{2}} + 2^{\frac{1}{2}} + 2^{\frac{3}{2}}$, giving your answer in the form $k\sqrt{2}$,

(b) $\left(\sqrt{3}\right)^{-3} + \left(\sqrt{3}\right)^{-2} + \left(\sqrt{3}\right)^{-1} + \left(\sqrt{3}\right)^{0} + \left(\sqrt{3}\right)^{1} + \left(\sqrt{3}\right)^{2} + \left(\sqrt{3}\right)^{3}$, giving your answer in the form $a + b\sqrt{3}$.

10 Express each of the following in the form 2^n.

(a) $2^{70} + 2^{70}$ (b) $2^{-400} + 2^{-400}$ (c) $2^{\frac{1}{3}} + 2^{\frac{1}{3}} + 2^{\frac{1}{3}} + 2^{\frac{1}{3}}$

(d) $2^{100} - 2^{99}$ (e) $8^{0.1} + 8^{0.1} + 8^{0.1} + 8^{0.1} + 8^{0.1} + 8^{0.1} + 8^{0.1} + 8^{0.1}$

11 Solve the equation $\dfrac{125^{3x}}{5^{x+4}} = \dfrac{25^{x-2}}{3125}$.

12 The formulae for the volume V and the surface area S of a cube are $V = x^3$ and $S = 6x^2$, where x is the length of an edge. Find expressions for

(a) S in terms of V,   (b) V in terms of S,

giving each answer in the form $(S \text{ or } V) = 2^m \times 3^n \times (V \text{ or } S)^p$.

13 Einstein's law $E = mc^2$ gives the energy of the radiation created by the destruction of a particle of mass m, where c is the velocity of light. The units for m, c and E are respectively kilograms, metres per second and joules. Given that the speed of light is 3.0×10^8 metres per second, find the energy created by a neutron of mass 1.7×10^{-27} kilograms.

8 Graphs of nth power functions

In this chapter the work of Chapters 3 and 5 is extended to include graphs with equations $y = x^n$ where n is any rational number. When you have completed it, you should

- be familiar with the shapes of these graphs, particularly when n is either a negative integer or $\frac{1}{2}$
- know that the rule for differentiating x^n is valid when n is any rational number.

8.1 Graphs of negative integer powers

In Section 3.3 you investigated the shapes of graphs with equations $y = x^n$ for positive integer values of n. You can now extend the investigation to negative values of n.

A negative integer n can be written as $-m$, where m is a positive integer. Then x^n becomes x^{-m}, or $\frac{1}{x^m}$.

It is simplest to begin with the part of the graph for which x is positive, then to use this to extend the graph for negative x.

Fig. 3.3 showed the graphs of $y = x^n$ for $x \geqslant 0$ when n is 1, 2, 3 and 4. These graphs are reproduced here as Fig. 8.1.

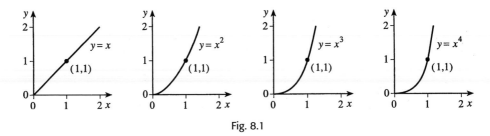

Fig. 8.1

All these graphs are in the first quadrant when $x > 0$, and they all include the origin and the point $(1, 1)$.

When x is positive, $\frac{1}{x^m}$ is also positive, so the graphs of $y = x^{-m}$ are also in the first quadrant when $x > 0$. Also, just as when n is positive, the graphs include the point $(1, 1)$.

But there is an important difference when $x = 0$, since then $x^m = 0$ and $\frac{1}{x^m}$ is not defined. So there is no point on these graphs for which $x = 0$.

To look at this more closely, take a value of x close to 0, say 0.01. Then for $n = -1$ the corresponding value of y is $0.01^{-1} = \frac{1}{0.01^1} = \frac{1}{0.01} = 100$; and for $n = -2$ it is $0.01^{-2} = \frac{1}{0.01^2} = \frac{1}{0.0001} = 10\,000$. Even if you use a very small scale, the graphs will disappear off the top of the page or screen as x is reduced towards zero.

What happens if x is large? For example, take $x = 100$. Then for $n = -1$ the corresponding value of y is $100^{-1} = \dfrac{1}{100^1} = \dfrac{1}{100} = 0.01$; and for $n = -2$ it is $100^{-2} = \dfrac{1}{100^2} = \dfrac{1}{10\,000} = 0.0001$. So x^n becomes very small, and the graphs come very close to the x-axis.

These are the main things you need to know to draw the graphs for positive values of x. They are shown in Fig. 8.2 for $n = -1, -2, -3$ and -4.

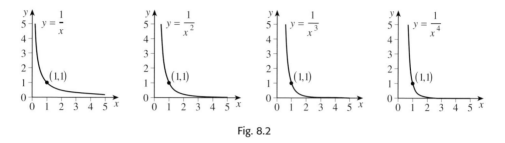

Fig. 8.2

Now consider the part of the graphs for which x is negative. You found in Chapter 3 that, for positive n, this depends on whether n is odd or even. The same is true when n is negative, and for the same reason. If n is even, x^n is an even function and its graph is symmetrical about the y-axis. If n is odd, x^n is an odd function and its graph is symmetrical about the origin.

Fig. 8.3 shows the graphs of $y = x^{-1}$ and $y = x^{-2}$ extended in this way, for all values of x except 0.

Try sketching for yourself the corresponding graphs of $y = x^{-3}$ and $y = x^{-4}$.

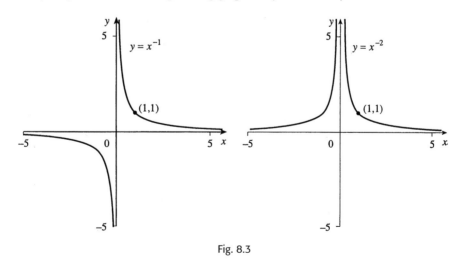

Fig. 8.3

8.2 Differentiation with negative integer indices

In Chapter 5 you found that, for positive integer powers of x, the derivative of $f(x) = x^n$ is $f'(x) = nx^{n-1}$. An obvious question to ask is whether this is still true when n is a negative integer.

You could investigate this in a number of ways:

- using the evidence of the graphs
- with a numerical check
- by algebraic proof of particular cases.

The three examples which follow illustrate each of these in turn, for the cases $n = -1$ and $n = -2$. If the rule still holds when n is negative, the derivatives would be as follows.

$$n = -1: \text{if } y = x^{-1} = \frac{1}{x}, \text{ then } \frac{dy}{dx} = -1 \times x^{-2} = -\frac{1}{x^2}.$$

$$n = -2: \text{if } y = x^{-2} = \frac{1}{x^2}, \text{ then } \frac{dy}{dx} = -2 \times x^{-3} = -\frac{2}{x^3}.$$

Example 8.2.1
Find whether the suggested differentiation rules are consistent with the graphs
(a) when $n = -1$,   (b) when $n = -2$.

Note first that, for both graphs in Fig. 8.3, the gradient is very steep when x is close to 0, and very gentle when x is a long way from 0. This is in line with the expressions suggested for $\frac{dy}{dx}$ for both $n = -1$ and $n = -2$.

(a) If $y = x^{-1}$, Fig. 8.3 shows that the gradient of the graph is negative both when x is positive and when x is negative. This is consistent with the suggested derivative $\frac{dy}{dx} = -\frac{1}{x^2}$, which is negative both when $x > 0$ and when $x < 0$.

(b) If $y = x^{-2}$, Fig. 8.3 shows that the gradient of the graph is negative when x is positive, and positive when x is negative. This is consistent with the suggested derivative $\frac{dy}{dx} = -\frac{2}{x^3}$, which is negative when $x > 0$ but positive when $x < 0$.

Example 8.2.2
Make a numerical estimate of the gradient of the tangent to $y = \frac{1}{x^2}$ at the point $(2, 0.25)$, and check that this agrees with the value given by the rule $\frac{dy}{dx} = -\frac{2}{x^3}$.

From Fig. 8.3, you would expect the gradient of the tangent to be less than the gradient of a chord to the right of $(2, 0.25)$, and greater than the gradient of a chord to the left. (Note that all these gradients are negative.)

Take first the chord joining $(2, 0.25)$ to $(2.01, 0.247\,51...)$. For this chord,

$$\delta x = 2.01 - 2 = 0.01, \quad \delta y = 0.247\,51... - 0.25 = -0.002\,48...,$$

and $\quad \dfrac{\delta y}{\delta x} = \dfrac{-0.002\,48...}{0.01} = -0.248....$

Now take the chord joining $(2, 0.25)$ to $(1.99, 0.252\,51...)$. For this chord,

$$\delta x = 1.99 - 2 = -0.01, \quad \delta y = 0.252\,51... - 0.25 = 0.002\,51...,$$

and $\quad \dfrac{\delta y}{\delta x} = \dfrac{0.002\,51...}{-0.01} = -0.251....$

So the gradient of the tangent is less than $-0.248\ldots$ and greater than $-0.251\ldots$. A reasonable guess is that the gradient is -0.25.

When $x = 2$, the suggested derivative $-\dfrac{2}{x^3} = -\dfrac{2}{2^3} = -0.25$. So the numerical estimate supports the value given by the differentiation rule.

Example 8.2.3*

Find the derivative of the function $f(x) = \dfrac{1}{x}$ at $x = p$.

It is simplest to work with the notation used in Examples 5.8.5 and 5.8.6. Begin by finding the gradient of the chord joining points on the graph with $x = p$ and $x = q$.

At $x = p$, $f(p) = \dfrac{1}{p}$, and at $x = q$, $f(q) = \dfrac{1}{q}$. The chord joining $\left(p, \dfrac{1}{p}\right)$ and $\left(q, \dfrac{1}{q}\right)$ has

$$\delta x = q - p, \quad \delta y = \frac{1}{q} - \frac{1}{p} = \frac{p}{pq} - \frac{q}{pq} = \frac{p - q}{pq} = -\frac{q - p}{pq},$$

and

$$\frac{\delta y}{\delta x} = \frac{-\left(\dfrac{q - p}{qp}\right)}{q - p} = -\frac{1}{qp}.$$

Then, in the limit as q tends to p,

$$f'(p) = \lim_{q \to p} \frac{f(q) - f(p)}{q - p} = \lim_{q \to p} \left(-\frac{1}{qp}\right) = -\frac{1}{p^2}.$$

Since the result in Example 8.2.3 is true for any value of p except 0, you can write $f'(x) = -\dfrac{1}{x^2}$.

The results of these examples don't add up to a proof that the differentiation rule works with all negative integer indices, but the evidence is encouraging. It is in fact correct, but it is not possible to give a proof at this stage.

If you write $n = -m$, so that $f(x) = x^{-m} = \dfrac{1}{x^m}$, the rule gives $f'(x) = -mx^{-m-1} = -\dfrac{m}{x^{m+1}}$.

> If $f(x) = \dfrac{1}{x^m}$, where m is a positive integer, then $f'(x) = -\dfrac{m}{x^{m+1}}$.

There is no need to learn this as a separate rule. In any particular case you can just use $f'(x) = nx^{n-1}$ with a negative value for n. But after some practice you will probably find yourself using it without thinking.

Example 8.2.4

Find $\dfrac{dy}{dx}$ if   (a) $y = \dfrac{2}{x^4}$,   (b) $y = \dfrac{1}{5x^5}$,   (c) $y = \dfrac{x - 3}{x^2}$.

(a) Write y as $2 \times \dfrac{1}{x^4} = 2x^{-4}$. Then $\dfrac{dy}{dx} = 2 \times (-4x^{-5}) = -8x^{-5} = -\dfrac{8}{x^5}$.

(b) Write y as $\dfrac{1}{5} \times \dfrac{1}{x^5} = \dfrac{1}{5}x^{-5}$. Then $\dfrac{dy}{dx} = \dfrac{1}{5} \times (-5x^{-6}) = -x^{-6} = -\dfrac{1}{x^6}$.

(c) Split the function as $y = \dfrac{x}{x^2} - \dfrac{3}{x^2} = \dfrac{1}{x} - \dfrac{3}{x^2} = x^{-1} - 3x^{-2}$.

Then $\dfrac{dy}{dx} = -x^{-2} + 6x^{-3} = -\dfrac{1}{x^2} + \dfrac{6}{x^3}$.

You may sometimes want to write this as a single fraction, as in the original equation.

$$\frac{dy}{dx} = -\frac{x}{x^3} + \frac{6}{x^3} = \frac{-x+6}{x^3} = \frac{6-x}{x^3}.$$

Example 8.2.5

(a) Find the equation of the normal to $y = \dfrac{1}{x}$ at the point $\left(\tfrac{1}{2}, 2\right)$.

(b) Find where this normal cuts the curve again.

(a) It helps to accompany the solution with a sketch (Fig. 8.4), and to use it to check the accuracy of the calculations as you go on.

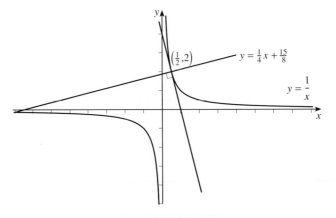

Fig. 8.4

Since $\dfrac{dy}{dx} = -\dfrac{1}{x^2}$, the gradient of the tangent at $\left(\tfrac{1}{2}, 2\right)$ is $-\dfrac{1}{\left(\tfrac{1}{2}\right)^2} = -4$.

The gradient of the normal is therefore, by the rule in Section 1.9, $-\dfrac{1}{-4} = \tfrac{1}{4}$.

The equation of the normal is

$$y - 2 = \tfrac{1}{4}\left(x - \tfrac{1}{2}\right), \quad \text{or more simply} \quad y = \tfrac{1}{4}x + \tfrac{15}{8}.$$

(b) To find where the normal meets the curve again, solve its equation simultaneously with $y = \dfrac{1}{x}$ to get the equation

$$\frac{1}{x} = \tfrac{1}{4}x + \tfrac{15}{8}.$$

Multiplying this by $8x$ and rearranging the terms produces the quadratic equation

$$2x^2 + 15x - 8 = 0.$$

The factors of the left side may not be immediately obvious. But remember that you already know one root, $x = \tfrac{1}{2}$, because the normal certainly cuts the curve at

$\left(\frac{1}{2}, 2\right)$. So $2x - 1$ must be one factor. It is then easy to see that the left side factorises to give

$$(2x - 1)(x + 8) = 0.$$

The other intersection is therefore where $x = -8$. Substituting this in $y = \dfrac{1}{x}$ gives the y-coordinate of the point of intersection as $y = \dfrac{1}{-8} = -\frac{1}{8}$. (You could equally well substitute in $y = \frac{1}{4}x + \frac{15}{8}$, but the arithmetic is harder.)

The normal meets the curve again at $\left(-8, -\frac{1}{8}\right)$.

Exercise 8A

1 Differentiate each of the following functions. For each part, give your answer in two forms: the first using a negative index, and the second with a positive index.

   (a) x^{-2}
   (b) x^{-5}
   (c) $3x^{-3}$
   (d) $-2x^{-2}$
   (e) $\frac{1}{4}x^{-4}$
   (f) $-\frac{1}{3}x^{-6}$

2 Differentiate each of these functions $f(x)$. Give your answers $f'(x)$ in a similar form, without negative or fractional indices.

   (a) $\dfrac{1}{4x}$
   (b) $\dfrac{3}{x^2}$
   (c) x^0
   (d) $\dfrac{3}{x} + \dfrac{1}{3x^3}$
   (e) $\dfrac{x - 2}{x^2}$

3 Find the equation of the tangent to the curve at the given point.

   (a) $y = \dfrac{4}{x}$ at $(1, 4)$
   (b) $y = \dfrac{1}{x^2}$ at $(1, 1)$
   (c) $y = \dfrac{1}{3x^2}$ at $\left(\frac{1}{3}, 3\right)$

   (d) $y = x + \dfrac{9}{x}$ at $(3, 6)$
   (e) $y = \dfrac{1 - x}{x^3}$ at $(1, 0)$
   (f) $y = \dfrac{x^2 - 4}{x^3}$ at $(-2, 0)$

4 Find the equation of the normal to the curve at the given point.

   (a) $y = \dfrac{4}{x^2}$ at $(2, 1)$
   (b) $y = \dfrac{1}{2x^4}$ at $\left(1, \frac{1}{2}\right)$

   (c) $y = x^2 + \dfrac{16}{x^2}$ at $(2, 8)$
   (d) $y = \dfrac{x + 2}{x^3}$ at $(-1, -1)$

5 Find the point(s) of intersection of these pairs of graphs. Illustrate your answers with sketch graphs.

   (a) $y = x^2$, $y = 8x^{-1}$
   (b) $y = x^{-1}$, $y = 3x^{-2}$
   (c) $y = x$, $y = 4x^{-3}$

   (d) $y = 8x^{-2}$, $y = 2x^{-4}$
   (e) $y = 9x^{-3}$, $y = x^{-5}$
   (f) $y = \frac{1}{4}x^4$, $y = 16x^{-2}$

6 Three graphs have equations   (p) $y = x^{-2}$, (q) $y = x^{-3}$, (r) $y = x^{-4}$.

   A line $x = k$ meets the three graphs at points P, Q and R, respectively. Give the order of the points P, Q and R on the line (from the bottom up) when k takes the following values.

   (a) 2
   (b) $\frac{1}{2}$
   (c) $-\frac{1}{2}$
   (d) -2

7 For what values of x are these inequalities satisfied? Sketch graphs illustrating your answers.

   (a) $0 < x^{-3} < 0.001$
   (b) $x^{-2} < 0.0004$
   (c) $x^{-4} \geqslant 100$
   (d) $8x^{-4} < 0.00005$

8.3   Graphs of $y = x^n$ for fractional n

When fractional values of n are included, the graphs of $y = x^n$ have many different possible shapes. One new feature is that, when n is a fraction, the function x^n may or may not be defined for negative values of x. For example, $x^{\frac{1}{3}}$ (the cube root of x) and $x^{-\frac{4}{5}}$ have values when $x < 0$, but $x^{\frac{1}{2}}$ (the square root of x) and $x^{-\frac{3}{4}}$ do not. (See Section 7.5.) Even when x^n is defined for negative x, some calculators and computers are not programmed to do the calculation. So it is simplest to concentrate on values of $x \geqslant 0$.

Much the most important of these graphs is that of $y = x^{\frac{1}{2}}$, or $y = \sqrt{x}$. The clue to finding the shape of this graph is to note that if $y = x^{\frac{1}{2}}$, then $x = y^2$. The graph can therefore be obtained from that of $y = x^2$ by swapping the x- and y-axes. This has the effect of tipping the graph on its side, so that instead of facing upwards it faces to the right.

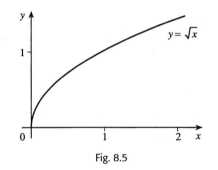

Fig. 8.5

But this is not quite the whole story. If $x = y^2$, then either $y = +\sqrt{x}$ or $y = -\sqrt{x}$. Since you want only the first of these possibilities, you must remove the part of the graph of $x = y^2$ below the x-axis, leaving only the part shown in Fig. 8.5 as the graph of $y = x^{\frac{1}{2}}$, or $y = \sqrt{x}$.

Notice that the graph exists only for $x \geqslant 0$, as you would expect. The tangent to the graph at the origin is the y-axis.

It is worth experimenting for yourself with various other fractional powers, using a calculator or a computer. You will find that:

- it is still true that the graph of $y = x^n$ contains the point $(1, 1)$;

- if n is positive it also contains the point $(0, 0)$;

- if $n > 1$ the x-axis is a tangent to the graph; if $0 < n < 1$ the y-axis is a tangent. (To show this convincingly you may need to zoom in to display an enlarged version of the graph close to the origin.)

To illustrate the variety of shapes which are possible when both positive and negative values of x are included, Fig. 8.6 shows six graphs with equation $y = x^n$ where n is a positive fraction.

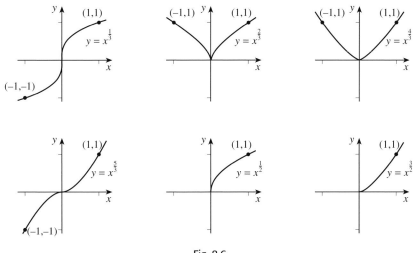

Fig. 8.6

8.4   The differentiation rule with fractional indices

You will probably not be surprised that the differentiation rule for $y = x^n$ still holds when the index n is a fraction.

Example 8.4.1

Assuming the usual differentiation rule, find $\dfrac{\mathrm{d}y}{\mathrm{d}x}$ when

(a) $y = \sqrt{x}$,   (b) $y = x\sqrt{x}$,   (c) $y = \dfrac{1}{\sqrt{x}}$.

(a) Since $\sqrt{x} = x^{\frac{1}{2}}$, the rule $\dfrac{\mathrm{d}y}{\mathrm{d}x} = nx^{n-1}$ gives $\dfrac{\mathrm{d}y}{\mathrm{d}x} = \frac{1}{2}x^{-\frac{1}{2}}$.

In surd notation, $x^{-\frac{1}{2}} = \dfrac{1}{x^{\frac{1}{2}}} = \dfrac{1}{\sqrt{x}}$. So $\dfrac{\mathrm{d}y}{\mathrm{d}x} = \frac{1}{2} \times \dfrac{1}{\sqrt{x}} = \dfrac{1}{2\sqrt{x}}$.

(b) In index notation, $x\sqrt{x} = x^1 \times x^{\frac{1}{2}} = x^{\frac{3}{2}}$.

So $\dfrac{\mathrm{d}y}{\mathrm{d}x} = \frac{3}{2}x^{\frac{1}{2}} = \frac{3}{2}\sqrt{x}$.

(c) In index notation, $\dfrac{1}{\sqrt{x}} = x^{-\frac{1}{2}}$.

So $\dfrac{\mathrm{d}y}{\mathrm{d}x} = -\frac{1}{2}x^{-\frac{3}{2}} = -\frac{1}{2} \times \dfrac{1}{x\sqrt{x}} = -\dfrac{1}{2x\sqrt{x}}$.

The proof of the differentiation rule with fractional indices is too difficult to give at this stage. You can, of course, check it numerically for any particular function and a particular value of x. It can also be proved quite simply for some functions by the usual algebraic method. The next example illustrates this for the function $x^{\frac{1}{2}}$. You may skip this if you wish.

Example 8.4.2*

Use an algebraic method to find the derivative of the function $f(x) = \sqrt{x}$ at $x = p$.

It is simplest to use the same notation as was used in Example 8.2.3.

At $x = p$, $f(p) = \sqrt{p}$ and at $x = q$, $f(q) = \sqrt{q}$. The chord joining $(p, \sqrt{p})$ and $(q, \sqrt{q})$ has
$\delta x = q - p$, $\delta y = \sqrt{q} - \sqrt{p}$.

Notice that you can write δx as the difference of two squares in the form

$$\delta x = q - p = \left(\sqrt{q}\right)^2 - \left(\sqrt{p}\right)^2 = \left(\sqrt{q} - \sqrt{p}\right)\left(\sqrt{q} + \sqrt{p}\right),$$

so
$$\frac{\delta y}{\delta x} = \frac{\sqrt{q} - \sqrt{p}}{\left(\sqrt{q} - \sqrt{p}\right)\left(\sqrt{q} + \sqrt{p}\right)} = \frac{1}{\sqrt{q} + \sqrt{p}}.$$

Then in the limit, as q tends to p,

$$f'(p) = \lim_{q \to p} \frac{f(q) - f(p)}{q - p}$$

$$= \lim_{q \to p} \frac{1}{\sqrt{q} + \sqrt{p}}$$

$$= \frac{1}{\sqrt{p} + \sqrt{p}} = \frac{1}{2\sqrt{p}}.$$

Notice that this does not work when $p = 0$. In this case $\dfrac{\delta y}{\delta x} = \dfrac{1}{\sqrt{q}}$, which does not have any limit as $q \to 0$. You can see from the graph of $y = \sqrt{x}$ in Fig. 8.5 that the tangent at $x = 0$ is the y-axis, which does not have a gradient.

Since the result in Example 8.4.2 is true for any value of p greater than 0, you can write the derivative of $f(x) = \sqrt{x}$ as $f'(x) = \dfrac{1}{2\sqrt{x}}$. This is the just the same as the expression obtained for the derivative in Example 8.4.1(a) by assuming the usual differentiation rule for $f(x) = x^n$.

You could go on accumulating more evidence by using the method in Example 8.4.2 to differentiate other similar functions, but the algebra would be more complicated. You should by now have seen enough examples to justify using the general rule for any rational power of x, positive or negative.

> If $f(x) = x^n$, where n is a rational number, then $f'(x) = nx^{n-1}$.

Compare this with the similar statement in the first box in Section 5.4, which was restricted to positive integer values of n.

Example 8.4.3
Find the equation of the tangent to $y = \sqrt[3]{x}$ at the point $(8, 2)$.

In index notation $\sqrt[3]{x} = x^{\frac{1}{3}}$. So the rule gives $\dfrac{dy}{dx} = \frac{1}{3}x^{\left(\frac{1}{3}-1\right)} = \frac{1}{3}x^{-\frac{2}{3}}$.

In surd notation this is $\dfrac{1}{3\left(\sqrt[3]{x}\right)^2}$.

The gradient of the tangent at $(8, 2)$ is therefore $\dfrac{1}{3\left(\sqrt[3]{8}\right)^2} = \dfrac{1}{3 \times 2^2} = \dfrac{1}{12}$.

Thus the equation of the tangent is

$$y - 2 = \tfrac{1}{12}(x - 8), \text{ which is } x - 12y + 16 = 0.$$

Exercise 8B

1 Differentiate each of the following functions. Give your answer with a fractional index.

(a) $x^{\frac{1}{3}}$

(b) $x^{\frac{5}{2}}$

(c) $5x^{\frac{2}{5}}$

(d) $-5x^{-\frac{3}{5}}$

(e) $4x^{-\frac{1}{2}}$

(f) $-2x^{-\frac{3}{2}}$

2 Differentiate each of these functions f(x). Give your answers f$'(x)$ in a similar form, without negative or fractional indices.

(a) $\sqrt[4]{x^3}$

(b) $6\sqrt[3]{x}$

(c) $\dfrac{4}{\sqrt{x}}$

(d) $\sqrt{16x^5}$

(e) $\dfrac{1}{\sqrt[3]{8x}}$

(f) $\dfrac{1+x}{\sqrt[4]{x}}$

3 On each of the graphs   (a) $y = x^{\frac{1}{3}}$,   (b) $y = x^{\frac{2}{3}}$,   (c) $y = x^{-\frac{2}{3}}$,   (d) $y = x^{-\frac{4}{3}}$, P is the point where $x = 8$ and Q is the point where $x = 8.1$. Find

(i) the y-coordinates of P and Q,

(ii) the gradient of the chord PQ,

(iii) the value of $\dfrac{dy}{dx}$ at P (assuming the differentiation rule),

(iv) the equation of the tangent at P.

4 Find the equation of the tangent to the curve at the given point.

(a) $y = \sqrt{x}$ at $(9, 3)$

(b) $y = \dfrac{6}{\sqrt[3]{x}}$ at $(8, 3)$

(c) $y = 2x\sqrt{x}$ at $(1, 2)$

(d) $y = 4x + \dfrac{1}{\sqrt{x}}$ at $\left(\tfrac{1}{4}, 3\right)$

5 Find the coordinates of the point(s) at which the curve has the given gradient.

(a) $y = \sqrt[3]{x^2}$, gradient $\tfrac{1}{3}$

(b) $y = \sqrt[3]{x}$, gradient $\tfrac{1}{3}$

(c) $y = \dfrac{3}{\sqrt[3]{x^2}}$, gradient $\tfrac{1}{16}$

(d) $y = \dfrac{x^2 + 3}{\sqrt{x}}$, gradient 0

6 Find the equation of the tangent to $y = \sqrt[4]{x}$ with gradient 2.

7 If $n > 0$ the graph of $y = x^n$ passes through the origin. Show that the x-axis is a tangent if $n > 1$, and that the y-axis is a tangent if $0 < n < 1$. What happens if $n = 1$?

Miscellaneous exercise 8

1 Find the equation of the normal to the curve with equation $y = \sqrt{x}$ at the point $(1, 1)$. Calculate the coordinates of the point at which this normal meets the graph of $y = -\sqrt{x}$.

2 For the curve $y = \dfrac{4}{x^2}$, find

(a) the equation of the tangent at $(-2\sqrt{2}, \frac{1}{2})$,

(b) the equation of the normal at $(\sqrt{2}, 2)$.

Show that the lines in parts (a) and (b) are the same. Illustrate this with a sketch.

3 On the curve $y = \dfrac{1}{x}$, P is the point at which $x = p$. Find the following, in terms of p.

(a) The y-coordinate of P.

(b) The value of $\dfrac{dy}{dx}$ at P.

(c) The equation of the tangent at P.

(d) The coordinates of the points Q and R where the tangent meets the x- and y-axes.

(e) The area of the triangle OQR.

4 Find the equations of the tangent and the normal to the graph with equation $y = \dfrac{1}{x} - \dfrac{4}{x^2}$ at the points where $x = 1$ and $x = 8$.

5 (a) Show that $\sqrt{2x} = \sqrt{2}\sqrt{x}$. Hence differentiate $\sqrt{2x}$, giving your answer in surd form.

(b) Differentiate $\sqrt{4x^3}$ and $\sqrt[3]{4x^4}$, giving your answers in surd form.

6 Differentiate the following, giving your answers in index form.

(a) $\dfrac{\sqrt{x} - 1}{x^2}$ (b) $\dfrac{x\sqrt{x} - 1}{x\sqrt{x}}$ (c) $\left(\dfrac{\sqrt{x} - 1}{x^2}\right)^2$ (d) $\left(\dfrac{x\sqrt{x} - 1}{x\sqrt{x}}\right)^2$

7 The tangents at $x = \frac{1}{4}$ to $y = \sqrt{x}$ and $y = \dfrac{1}{\sqrt{x}}$ meet at P. Find the coordinates of P.

8 The normals at $x = 2$ to $y = \dfrac{1}{x^2}$ and $y = \dfrac{1}{x^3}$ meet at Q. Find the coordinates of Q.

9 (a) Draw a sketch to show the graphs of $y = \dfrac{1}{x^2}$ and $y = \sqrt{x}$ and their point of intersection at the point $P(1, 1)$. Find the gradient of each curve at P, and show that the tangent at P to each curve is the normal to the other curve.

(b) The graphs of $y = x^m$ and $y = x^n$ intersect at the point $P(1, 1)$. Find the connection between m and n if the tangent to each curve at P is the normal to the other curve.

9 Polynomials

This chapter is about polynomials, which include linear and quadratic expressions. When you have completed it, you should

- be able to add, subtract and multiply polynomials.

9.1 Polynomials

You already know a good deal about polynomials from your work on quadratics in Chapter 4, because a quadratic is a special case of a polynomial. Here are some examples of polynomials.

$$3x^3 - 2x^2 + 1 \qquad 3 \qquad 4 - 2x \qquad x^2 \qquad 1$$
$$2x^4 \qquad 1 - 2x + 3x^5 \qquad \sqrt{2}x^2 \qquad \tfrac{1}{2}x^{17} \qquad x$$

> An expression consisting of a sum of multiples of non-negative integer powers of x is called a **polynomial** in x.
>
> Thus $ax + b$, $ax^2 + bx + c$, $ax^3 + bx^2 + cx + d$, $ax^4 + bx^3 + cx^2 + dx + e$, where a, b, etc. are numbers, are polynomials in x.

The highest power of x is called the **degree** of the polynomial. The expressions ax^4, bx^3, cx^2, dx and e which make up the polynomial are called **terms**. The numbers a, b, etc. are called **coefficients**; a is the **leading coefficient**. The coefficient of the term without x is the **constant term**.

Thus, in the quadratic polynomial $4x^2 - 3x + 1$, the degree is 2; the coefficients of x^2 and x, and the constant term, are 4, -3 and 1 respectively.

Polynomials with low degree have special names: if the polynomial has

- degree 0, it is called a **constant polynomial**, or a **constant**
- degree 1, it is called a **linear polynomial**
- degree 2, it is called a **quadratic polynomial**, or a **quadratic**
- degree 3, it is called a **cubic polynomial**, or a **cubic**
- degree 4, it is called a **quartic polynomial**, or a **quartic**.

> There are names for some polynomials of higher degree, but it isn't worth learning them.

The general polynomial of degree 4 in the box, $ax^4 + bx^3 + cx^2 + dx + e$, is only a quartic if the leading coefficient, a, is not zero. If $a = 0$, the polynomial becomes $bx^3 + cx^2 + dx + e$, and is no longer a quartic. Similarly, if you say that $ax^2 + bx + c$ is a quadratic, then that carries with it the condition that $a \neq 0$.

When a polynomial such as $3x^4 + x^2 - 7x + 5$ is written with the term of highest degree first and the other terms in descending degree order finishing with the constant term, the terms are said to be in **descending order**. If the terms are written in the reverse order, that is, $5 - 7x + x^2 + 3x^4$, they are said to be in **ascending order** (or ascending powers of x). They are of course the same polynomial; it doesn't matter what order the terms are written in.

The functions $\dfrac{1}{x} = x^{-1}$ and $\sqrt{x} = x^{\frac{1}{2}}$ are not polynomials, because the powers of x are not positive integers or zero.

Polynomials have much in common with integers. You can add them, subtract them and multiply them together and the result is another polynomial.

9.2 Addition, subtraction and multiplication of polynomials

To add or subtract two polynomials, you simply add or subtract the coefficients of corresponding powers; in other words, you collect like terms. Suppose that you want to add $2x^3 + 3x^2 - 4$ to $x^2 - x - 2$. Then you can set out the working like this:

$$
\begin{array}{rrrr}
2x^3 & + \ 3x^2 & & - \ 4 \\
& x^2 & - \ x & - \ 2 \\
\hline
2x^3 & + \ 4x^2 & - \ x & - \ 6 \\
\end{array}
$$

Notice that you must leave gaps in places where the coefficient is zero. You need to do addition so often that it is worth getting used to setting out the work in a line, thus:

$$(2x^3 + 3x^2 - 4) + (x^2 - x - 2) = (2 + 0)x^3 + (3 + 1)x^2 + (0 + (-1))x + ((-4) + (-2))$$
$$= 2x^3 + 4x^2 - x - 6.$$

You will soon find that you can miss out the middle step and go straight to the answer.

The result of the polynomial calculation $(2x^3 + 3x^2 - 4) - (2x^3 + 3x^2 - 4)$ is 0. This is a special case, and it is called the **zero polynomial**. It has no degree.

> Look back at the definition of a polynomial, and see why the zero polynomial was not included there.

Multiplying polynomials is harder. It relies on the rules for multiplying out brackets,

$$a(b + c + \cdots + k) = ab + ac + \cdots + ak \quad \text{and} \quad (b + c + \cdots + k)a = ba + ca + \cdots + ka.$$

These rules enable you to multiply brackets such as $(a + b)(c + d)$.

Replace $c + d$ for the time being by z. Then

$$(a + b)(c + d) = (a + b)z$$
$$= az + bz.$$

Now replace z by $c + d$.

$$az + bz = a(c + d) + b(c + d)$$
$$= ac + ad + bc + bd.$$

So:

$$(a + b)(c + d) = ac + ad + bc + bd.$$

Don't learn this. Just remember that every term in the left bracket must multiply every term in the right bracket.

For example, when you multiply out $(3x - 2)(4x + 5)$ you get an expression with four terms,

$$(3x)(4x), \quad (3x)(5), \quad (-2)(4x), \quad (-2)(5),$$

that is

$$12x^2, \qquad 15x, \qquad -8x, \qquad -10.$$

But you can then combine $15x$ and $-8x$ to get $7x$. The expression then becomes

$$12x^2 + 7x - 10.$$

Similarly, if you want to multiply out $(5x + 3)(2x^2 - 5x + 1)$, you get the six terms

$$(5x)(2x^2), \quad (5x)(-5x), \quad (5x)(1), \quad (3)(2x^2), \quad (3)(-5x) \text{ and } (3)(1),$$

that is,

$$10x^3, \qquad -25x^2, \qquad 5x, \qquad 6x^2, \qquad -15x \quad \text{and} \quad 3.$$

You can then combine $-25x^2$ and $6x^2$ to give $-19x^2$, and $5x$ and $-15x$ to get $-10x$. The expression then becomes

$$10x^3 - 19x^2 - 10x + 3.$$

Example 9.2.1
Find the coefficients of x and x^2 in the product $(2x + 3)(3x^2 - 2x + 4)$.

The terms in x come from the products of the arrowed terms below.

$$(2x + 3)(3x^2 - 2x + 4\,)$$

So the terms in x are $2x \times 4 + 3 \times (-2x) = 8x - 6x = 2x$. The coefficient of x is 2.

The terms in x^2 come from the products of the arrowed terms below.

$$(2x + 3)(3x^2 - 2x + 4)$$

The terms in x^2 are $-4x^2 + 9x^2 = 5x^2$. The coefficient of x^2 is 5.

If you can, try to carry out this process mentally without the arrow diagrams.

In practice, it is sometimes easier to set out the steps of a multiplication in the following way. This way has the advantage that terms which can be combined because they have the same degree are vertically aligned. For the product $(5x + 3)(2x^2 - 5x + 1)$,

		$2x^2$	$-$		$5x$	$+$	1	$\times$
$10x^3$	$-$		$25x^2$	$+$	$5x$			$5x$
	$+$		$6x^2$	$-$	$15x$	$+$	3	$+3$
$10x^3$	$+$	$(-25 + 6)x^2$		$+$	$(5 - 15)x$	$+$	3	

giving the result $10x^3 - 19x^2 - 10x + 3$.

However, it is worth learning to work horizontally. The arrows below show the term $5x$ from the first bracket multiplied by $-5x$ from the second bracket to get $-25x^2$.

$$(5x + 3)(2x^2 - 5x + 1) = 5x(2x^2 - 5x + 1) + 3(2x^2 - 5x + 1)$$
$$= (10x^3 - 25x^2 + 5x) + (6x^2 - 15x + 3)$$
$$= 10x^3 - 19x^2 - 10x + 3.$$

You could shorten the process and write

$$(5x + 3)(2x^2 - 5x + 1) = 10x^3 - 25x^2 + 5x + 6x^2 - 15x + 3$$
$$= 10x^3 - 19x^2 - 10x + 3.$$

If you multiply a polynomial of degree m by a polynomial of degree n, you have a calculation of the type

$$(ax^m + bx^{m-1} + \ldots)(Ax^n + Bx^{n-1} + \ldots) = aAx^{m+n} + \ldots$$

in which the largest power of the product is $m + n$. Also the coefficient aA is not zero because neither of a and A is zero. This shows that:

> When you multiply two polynomials, the degree of the product polynomial is the sum of the degrees of the two polynomials.

Example 9.2.2
The product $(Ax + B)(2x - 9) = 6x^2 - 19x - 36$ where A and B are constants. Find the values of A and B.

The coefficient of x^2 on the left side is $2A$ and on the right is 6.

So $2A = 6$,   giving $A = 3$.

The constant term on the left side is $-9B$ and on the right is -36, so $B = 4$.

As a check look at the term in x.

On the left the x term is $-9A + 2B$, which is $-9 \times 3 + 2 \times 4 = -27 + 8 = -19$.

So $A = 3$ and $B = 4$.

Exercise 9

1 State the degree of each of the following polynomials.

(a) $x^3 - 3x^2 + 2x - 7$ (b) $5x + 1$ (c) $8 + 5x - 3x^2 + 7x + 6x^4$

(d) 3 (e) $3 - 5x$ (f) x^0

2 In each part find $p(x) + q(x)$, and give your answer in descending order.

(a) $p(x) = 3x^2 + 4x - 1$, $q(x) = x^2 + 3x + 7$

(b) $p(x) = 4x^3 + 5x^2 - 7x + 3$, $q(x) = x^3 - 2x^2 + x - 6$

(c) $p(x) = 3x^4 - 2x^3 + 7x^2 - 1$, $q(x) = -3x - x^3 + 5x^4 + 2$

(d) $p(x) = 2 - 3x^3 + 2x^5$, $q(x) = 2x^4 + 3x^3 - 5x^2 + 1$

(e) $p(x) = 3 + 2x - 4x^2 - x^3$, $q(x) = 1 - 7x + 2x^2$

3 For each of the pairs of polynomials given in Question 2 find $p(x) - q(x)$.

4 Note that $p(x) + p(x)$ may be shortened to $2p(x)$. Let $p(x) = x^3 - 2x^2 + 5x - 3$ and $q(x) = x^2 - x + 4$. Express each of the following as a single polynomial.

(a) $2p(x) + q(x)$ (b) $3p(x) - q(x)$ (c) $p(x) - 2q(x)$ (d) $3p(x) - 2q(x)$

5 Find the following polynomial products.

(a) $(2x - 3)(3x + 1)$ (b) $(x^2 + 3x - 1)(x - 2)$

(c) $(x^2 + x - 3)(2x + 3)$ (d) $(3x - 1)(4x^2 - 3x + 2)$

(e) $(x^2 + 2x - 3)(x^2 + 1)$ (f) $(2x^2 - 3x + 1)(4x^2 + 3x - 5)$

(g) $(x^3 + 2x^2 - x + 6)(x + 3)$ (h) $(x^3 - 3x^2 + 2x - 1)(x^2 - 2x - 5)$

(i) $(2x + 1)(3x - 2)(x + 5)$ (j) $(3x + 4)(x + 1)(2x - 3)$

6 In each of the following products, find the coefficient of x and the coefficient of x^2.

(a) $(x + 2)(x^2 - 3x + 6)$ (b) $(x - 3)(x^2 + 2x - 5)$

(c) $(2x + 1)(x^2 - 5x + 1)$ (d) $(3x - 2)(x^2 - 2x + 7)$

(e) $(2x - 3)(3x^2 - 6x + 1)$ (f) $(2x - 5)(3x^3 - x^2 + 4x + 2)$

(g) $(3x - 4)(2x - 5)(3x - 2)$ (h) $(3x^2 + 1)(2x^2 - 5x + 3)$

7 In each of the following, the product of $Ax + B$ with another polynomial is given. Using the fact that A and B are constants, find A and B.

(a) $(Ax + B)(x - 3) = 4x^2 - 11x - 3$ (b) $(Ax + B)(x + 5) = 2x^2 + 7x - 15$

(c) $(Ax + B)(3x - 2) = 6x^2 - x - 2$ (d) $(Ax + B)(2x + 5) = 6x^2 + 11x - 10$

(e) $(Ax + B)(x^2 - 1) = x^3 + 2x^2 - x - 2$ (f) $(Ax + B)(x^2 + 4) = 2x^3 - 3x^2 + 8x - 12$

Miscellaneous exercise 9

1 Let $p(x) = 3x^2 + 2x - 1$ and $q(x) = x^2 - 2x + 3$. Find $p(x) + q(x)$, $p(x) - q(x)$ and $p(x)q(x)$.

2 The polynomials $f(x)$ and $g(x)$ are $2x^2 + ax - 3$ and $3x^2 - bx - 2$ respectively, where a and b are constants. In the product $f(x)g(x)$, the coefficient of x^3 is 6 and the coefficient of x is 1. Find the coefficient of x^2.

3 Let $p(x) = x^2 - 6x - 3$ and $q(x) = x^2 - 2x + 4$.

(a) Calculate $p(x) - q(x)$ and $p(x)q(x)$.

The polynomial $p(x) + aq(x)$, where a is a constant, is a perfect square.

(b)* Calculate the two possible values of a.

4 In the product of $8x^3 + 3x^2 - 8x - 4$ and $3x - 4$, find the coefficients of

(a) x,   (b) x^3.

5 Calculate the polynomial $(3x^2 + 4x - 3)^2 - (3x^2 - x + 2)^2$.

10 Transforming graphs

You now know about a lot of particular functions and their graphs. This chapter is about functions in general. When you have completed it, you should

- be able to modify equations of the form $y = f(x)$ so as to translate, stretch or reflect their graphs.

You should have a graphic calculator available as you work through this chapter.

10.1 Translating graphs

Use a graphic calculator with a window going from $x = -9$ to $x = 9$ and $y = -6$ to $y = 6$ to display the graphs of $y = x^2$ and $y = x^2 + 3$. What do you notice about the graphs?

You should see that the second graph has the same shape as the first but is moved by 3 units in the y-direction.

Fig. 10.1 shows a graph whose equation is $y = f(x)$. What is the graph whose equation is $y = f(x) + k$?

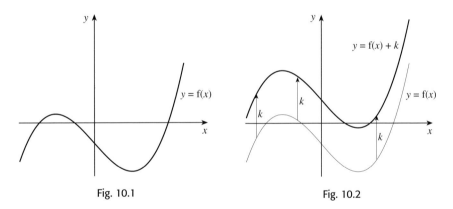

Fig. 10.1   Fig. 10.2

The answer is shown in Fig. 10.2. For each particular value of x, the y-coordinate on the second graph is k more than the y-coordinate on the first. So the whole of the second graph must lie k units higher than the first graph.

Of course, if k is negative, the second graph will be lower than the first by an amount $(-k)$ units

The transformation which converts the first graph into the second is called a **translation**. A translation is defined by its magnitude and direction; this one is a translation of k units in the y-direction.

Example 10.1.1

Without using a calculator,

(a) use the graph of $y = \frac{1}{2}x$ to sketch the graph of $y = \frac{1}{2}x + 3$,

(b) use the graph of $y = x^3$ to sketch the graph $y = x^3 - 4$.

(a) The graph of $y = \frac{1}{2}x$ is a straight line through the origin with gradient $\frac{1}{2}$. So $y = \frac{1}{2}x + 3$ is a line parallel to this, 3 units higher, as in Fig. 10.3.

(b) The graph of $y = x^3 - 4$ is lower than $y = x^3$, by an amount $-(-4)$ units, that is by 4 units, as in Fig. 10.4.

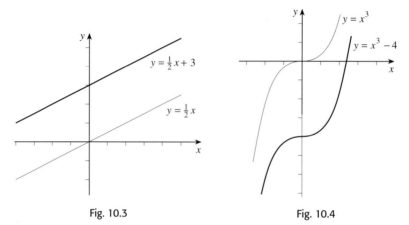

Fig. 10.3   Fig. 10.4

Notice that you can write the equation $y = f(x) + k$ as $y - k = f(x)$. This shows that:

> Replacing y by $y - k$ in the equation of a graph produces a translation of k units in the y-direction.

But what happens if you replace x by $x - k$?

Example 10.1.2

Use your calculator to display the graphs of

(a) $y = x^2$ and $y = (x - 3)^2$,   (b) $y = x^3$ and $y = (x - 3)^3$,

(c) $y = x^2$ and $y = (x + 3)^2$,   (d) $y = \frac{1}{2}x$ and $y = \frac{1}{2}(x - 3)$.

In parts (a) and (b) you should see that the curve has been translated by 3 units to the right.

In part (c) you should see that the curve has been translated by 3 units to the left. It is helpful in this case to think of $x + 3$ as $x - (-3)$.

Part (d) is complicated by the fact that the graph is a straight line, but you should see that if you translate the original graph by 3 units to the right you get the new graph. The complication is that you can also write the equation as $y = \frac{1}{2}x - \frac{3}{2}$ and think of the graph as having been translated by $\frac{3}{2}$ in the negative y-direction.

Example 10.1.2 shows that, if you want to translate the graph of $y = f(x)$ in the x-direction, the rule is similar with y replaced by x:

> Replacing x by $x - k$ in the equation of a graph produces a translation of k units in the x-direction.

This result is illustrated in Fig. 10.5. The graph of $y = f(x - k)$ is obtained from that of $y = f(x)$ by a shift to the right of k units.

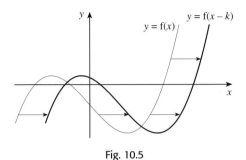

Fig. 10.5

Example 10.1.3

Without using a calculator, sketch the graphs of (a) $y = 3(x - 2)$, (b) $y = (x + 2)^2$.

(a) The graph of $y = 3x$ is a straight line through the origin with gradient 3. So $y = 3(x - 2)$ is a line parallel to this, 2 units to the right, as in Fig. 10.6.

(b) You can write $(x + 2)^2$ as $(x - (-2))^2$. The graph of $y = (x + 2)^2$ is to the left of $y = x^2$ by an amount $-(-2)$ units, that is by 2 units, as in Fig. 10.7.

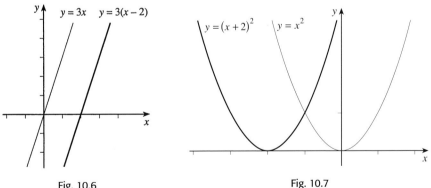

Fig. 10.6   Fig. 10.7

You may be surprised by the minus sign in the equation $y = f(x - k)$, but it can easily be justified by expressing the result in the second box in different words:

> If the point with coordinates (r, s) lies on the graph $y = f(x)$, then the point $(r + k, s)$ lies on the graph $y = f(x - k)$.

So you have to show that, if $s = f(r)$, then $s = f((r + k) - k)$. The two equations are clearly the same, since $(r + k) - k = r$.

In the next example the graph of $y = x^2$ is modified by two translations performed one after the other, first in the x-direction and then in the y-direction.

Example 10.1.4

Without using a calculator, describe the graph of $y = x^2 - 6x + 4$.

In completed square form, $x^2 - 6x + 4 = (x - 3)^2 - 5$. You can get from $y = x^2$ to $y = (x - 3)^2 - 5$ via the graph of $y = (x - 3)^2$.

Replacing x by $x - 3$ in the equation $y = x^2$ produces a translation of 3 units parallel to the x-axis. Then you obtain $y = (x - 3)^2 - 5$ from $y = (x - 3)^2$ by a translation of -5 parallel to the y-axis. The combination of the two translations is shown in Fig. 10.8.

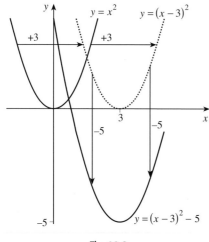

Fig. 10.8

This example takes you a stage further than Chapter 4, where the completed square form was used to find the vertex of a quadratic. Now you can see that, as the graph is obtained from $y = x^2$ by a pair of translations, the two graphs have the same shape and size.

Exercise 10A

Do not use a calculator in this exercise.

1 Use translations to sketch the following pairs of graphs. Label which is which.

(a) $y = -\frac{1}{2}x$ and $y = -\frac{1}{2}x + 4$ (b) $y = 2x$ and $y = 2(x + 3)$

(c) $y = x^2$ and $y = x^2 - 2$ (d) $y = x^2$ and $y = (x - 3)^2$

(e) $y = x^3$ and $y = (x + 2)^3$ (f) $y = \dfrac{1}{x}$ and $y = \dfrac{1}{x - 1}$

(g) $y = \dfrac{1}{x}$ and $y = \dfrac{1}{x + 3}$ (h) $y = \sqrt{x}$ and $y = \sqrt{x + 2}$

(i) $y = \sqrt{x}$ and $y = \sqrt{x} + 2$

2 (a) Show that the point $(9, 3)$ lies on $y = \sqrt{x}$.

(b) The point $(9, 3)$ is translated a distance 2 in the x-direction. Where does it move to?

(c) The graph $y = \sqrt{x}$ is translated a distance 2 in the x-direction. What is the equation of the new graph?

(d) Check that the point in your answer to part (b) lies on the graph in your answer to part (c).

3 The following translations are each applied to the graph of $y = x^2 + 3x$. Find the equation of each of the transformed graphs, giving your answer in as simple a form as possible.

(a) A translation of 3 units in the positive x-direction.

(b) A translation of 4 units in the positive y-direction.

(c) A translation of 3 units in the positive x-direction followed by a translation of 4 units in the positive y-direction.

4 The following translations are each applied to the graph of $y = x^2 - 5x + 7$. Find the equation of each of the transformed graphs, giving your answer in as simple a form as possible.

(a) A translation of -2 units in the positive x-direction.

(b) A translation of -5 units in the positive y-direction.

(c) A translation of -5 units in the positive y-direction followed by a translation of -2 units in the positive x-direction.

5 Give details of

(a) the translation which will convert the graph with equation $y = (x + 3)^2$ into the graph with equation $y = x^2$,

(b) the translations which will convert the graph of $y = (x - 5)^2$ into the graph with equation $y = (x - 8)^2$, and then into the graph with equation $y = (x - 8)^2 - 3$.

6 Describe the relationship of the graph of $y = x^2 + 8x + 14$ with that of the graph of $y = x^2$. Illustrate by means of a sketch graph.

7 The graph of $y = \dfrac{1}{x}$ is translated 2 units downwards, and the new graph is translated 1 unit to the left. Find the equations of the graph after the first translation, and of the graph in its final position.

As a check, find the coordinates of the points where the final graph cuts the x- and y-axes. From which points on the original graph did they come?

10.2 Stretching graphs

What happens if you multiply a function by a constant?

Use your calculator to sketch the graphs of

(a) $y = x^2$ and $y = 3x^2$,   (b) $y = x^3$ and $y = 2x^3$,   (c) $y = x$ and $y = 4x$.

In each part the original graph has been subjected to a kind of stretching.

In each part of the question, imagine that the graph is drawn on an elastic sheet. If the sheet is then held along the top and bottom edges and pulled so that the position of the new x-axis lies immediately above the old one the y-coordinate of each point on the sheet will be increased in the same ratio.

In part (a) this ratio is 3. For parts (b) and (c) the ratios are 2 and 4 respectively.

These transformations are all examples of stretches in the y-direction.

In general, if you multiply a function by a constant c, then for each particular value of x the y-coordinate is c times as large as before. What this means geometrically depends on whether c is positive or negative. First suppose that $c > 0$.

This transformation is called a **stretch** by a factor of c in the y-direction. This is illustrated in Fig. 10.9, with a value of $c = 3$.

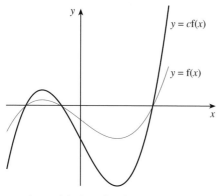

A stretch in the y-direction with $c = 3$

Fig. 10.9

The word 'stretch' is rather misleading, since if c is less than 1 the y-coordinates are reduced. But there is no mathematical advantage in separating the cases $c < 1$ and $c > 1$, so even if 'stretch' appears misleading, it is always used.

Notice that you can write the equation $y = cf(x)$ as $\dfrac{y}{c} = f(x)$. This shows that:

> Replacing y by $\dfrac{y}{c}$ in the equation of a graph produces a stretch of factor c in the y-direction.

But what happens if you replace x by $\dfrac{x}{c}$?

Example 10.2.1
Use your calculator to display the graphs of

(a) $y = x^2$ and $y = \left(\dfrac{x}{2}\right)^2$,   (b) $y = x^3$ and $y = \left(\dfrac{x}{2}\right)^3$,

(c) $y = x^2$ and $y = (2x)^2$,   (d) $y = x$ and $y = 2x$.

In parts (a) and (b) you should see that the curve has been stretched by a factor of 2 in the x-direction.

In part (c) you might think correctly that the curve has been stretched in the y-direction by a factor of 4, but you should also see that you can get the same result by stretching it in the x-direction by a factor of $\frac{1}{2}$. It is helpful in this case to think of $2x$ as $\dfrac{x}{\frac{1}{2}}$.

Part (d) is again complicated by the fact that the graph is a straight line, but you should see that if you stretch the original graph by a factor of $\frac{1}{2}$ in the x-direction you get the graph of $y = 2x$.

Example 10.2.1 shows that, if you want to stretch a graph in the x-direction, keeping the y-axis fixed:

> Replacing x by $\dfrac{x}{c}$ in the equation of a graph produces a stretch of factor c in the x-direction.

For example, to get from the graph of $y = f(x)$ to that of $y = f(2x)$, you need to write $2x$ as $\dfrac{x}{\frac{1}{2}}$.

So this is a stretch of factor $\frac{1}{2}$ in the x-direction; the x-coordinate of each point of the graph is halved. This is illustrated in Fig. 10.10.

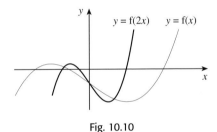

Fig. 10.10

Example 10.2.2
Without using a calculator, find the effect of applying to the graph of $y = x$ a stretch of
(a) factor $\frac{1}{3}$ in the y-direction,   (b) factor 3 in the x-direction.

(a) Replacing y by $\dfrac{y}{\frac{1}{3}}$ gives the equation $\dfrac{y}{\frac{1}{3}}$, or $y = \frac{1}{3}x$.

(b) Replacing x by $\dfrac{x}{3}$ gives the equation $y = \dfrac{x}{3}$, or $y = \frac{1}{3}x$.

> In this example the answers to parts (a) and (b) are the same! They are illustrated in Fig. 10.11. Try to visualise from the figure how the transformation can be achieved by either a stretch in the y-direction or a stretch in the x-direction.

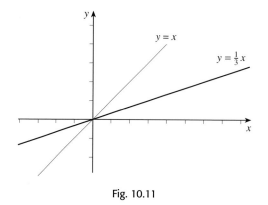

Fig. 10.11

Example 10.2.3

Without using a calculator, find the effect of applying the stretches in Example 10.2.1 to the graph of $y = x - 3$.

Using the same methods as in Example 10.2.1, the equations are

(a) $\dfrac{y}{\frac{1}{3}} = x - 3$,   or $y = \frac{1}{3}x - 1$;

(b) $y = \dfrac{x}{3} - 3$,   or $y = \frac{1}{3}x - 3$.

These are illustrated in Fig. 10.12.

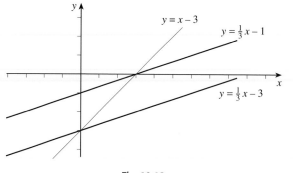

Fig. 10.12

In this example the answers to the two parts are different. Notice that a stretch in the y-direction leaves points on the x-axis unchanged, so both the original and transformed graphs pass through $(3, 0)$. A stretch in the x-direction leaves points on the y-axis unchanged, so both graphs pass through $(0, -3)$

Example 10.2.4

The graph $y = x^2$ is stretched by a factor of 4 in the y-direction, then by a factor of 4 in the x-direction. How else could you achieve the final result?

The double stretch is equivalent to an all-round enlargement of factor 4, like a photographic enlargement, which doesn't distort the shape of the graph. It is achieved by replacing y by $\frac{1}{4}y$ and x by $\frac{1}{4}x$. So the equation of the final graph is

$$\tfrac{1}{4}y = \left(\tfrac{1}{4}x\right)^2$$

which you can write more simply as $y = \frac{1}{4}x^2$.

But you could also get $y = \frac{1}{4}x^2$ from $y = x^2$ by a stretch in the y-direction alone, in which the y-coordinate of each point on the graph is multiplied by $\frac{1}{4}$.

Also $y = \frac{1}{4}x^2$ can be written as $y = \left(\frac{1}{2}x\right)^2$. This is what you would get from $y = x^2$ by a stretch of factor 2 in the x-direction alone.

> Try drawing with the same axes, the graphs of $y = x^2$ and $y = \frac{1}{4}x^2$, and think how the first can be transformed into the second by each of the three transformations described in Example 10.2.4.

Finally, what happens if $c < 0$? The simplest way of dealing with this is to regard multiplication by c as a combination of multiplication by $(-c)$ and a change of sign. Since $(-c) > 0$, you already know how to deal with the first transformation. Now it is necessary to interpret the effect of changing the sign of the x- or y-coordinate. This is explained in the next section.

10.3 Reflecting graphs

If you draw with the same axes the graphs of $y = f(x)$ and $y = -f(x)$, then for each value of x the values of y on the two graphs differ only in having opposite signs, so that the corresponding points are mirror images in the x-axis. The complete graphs are therefore mirror images of each other as in Fig. 10.13.

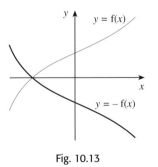

Fig. 10.13

> You have to imagine a 'mathematical' mirror, capable of reflection in both directions. If $f(x)$ takes both positive and negative values, then the reflection converts positive to negative and negative to positive. A more practical way of doing this is to rotate the graph about the x-axis through $180°$.

Since you can write $y = -f(x)$ as $-y = f(x)$, another way of expressing this is:

> Replacing y by $-y$ in the equation of a graph produces a reflection in the x-axis.

But what happens if you replace x by $-x$?

Example 10.3.1
Use your calculator to display the graphs of
(a) $y = 2x$ and $y = 2(-x)$,   (b) $y = x^3$ and $y = (-x)^3$.   (c) $y = x^2$ and $y = (-x)^2$.

> In parts (a) and (b) you should see that the curve has been reflected in the y-axis.
>
> In part (c) you might think correctly that the curve has not been altered, but as the curve is symmetrical about the y-axis, you could also say that the curve has been reflected in the y-axis.

Example 10.3.1 shows that, if you want to reflect a graph in the y-axis the rule is:

> Replacing x by $-x$ in the equation of a graph produces a reflection in the y-axis.

Fig. 10.14 shows the graph of $y = f(x)$ and its reflection in the y-axis, $y = f(-x)$.

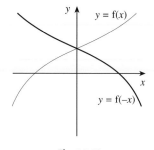

Fig. 10.14

With these results it is possible to make precise the ideas of even functions (such as x^2 or x^4) and odd functions (such as x^3) introduced in Section 3.3.

The graph of an even function is symmetrical about the y-axis, so reflection in the y-axis leaves it unchanged. This means that $y = f(x)$ and $y = f(-x)$ are the same equation, so that $f(-x) = f(x)$.

The graph of an odd function is symmetrical about the origin, so a combination of reflections in the x- and y-axes leaves it unchanged. This means that $y = f(x)$ and $-y = f(-x)$ are the same equation, so that $f(-x) = -f(x)$.

However, in using the terms 'odd' and 'even', you mustn't think that every function is either odd or even. There are many functions, such as $x^2 + x$, which are neither odd nor even.

Example 10.3.2

Without using a calculator, show that the graph of

(a) $y = -x^2$ is symmetrical about the y-axis,

(b) $y = x^3 - 3x$ is symmetrical about the origin,

(c) $y = x^2 + 4x - 12$ is neither symmetrical about the y-axis nor symmetrical about the origin.

    (a) The reflection of $y = -x^2$ in the y-axis is $y = -(-x)^2$. Since $(-x)^2 = x^2$, this equation can be written as $y = -x^2$.

       This is the same as the original equation, so reflection in the y-axis leaves the graph unchanged. That is, the graph is symmetrical about the y-axis.

    (b) If a graph is symmetrical about the origin, it is the graph of an odd function, so then $y = f(x)$ and $y = -f(-x)$ are the same equation.

       If $f(x) = x^3 - 3x$, then $f(-x) = (-x)^3 - 3(-x) = -x^3 + 3x$, which is $-(x^3 - 3x)$.

       So $f(x) = -f(-x)$. This means that the graph of $y = f(x)$ is symmetrical about the origin.

    (c) If $f(x) = x^2 + 4x - 12$, then

$$f(-x) = (-x)^2 + 4(-x) - 12$$
$$= x^2 - 4x - 12.$$

       As $x^2 + 4x - 12$ and $x^2 - 4x - 12$ are not the same function, $f(x)$ is not symmetrical about the y-axis.

       As $-f(-x) = -(x^2 - 4x - 12)$
$$= -x^2 + 4x + 12,$$

       and $x^2 + 4x - 12$ and $-x^2 + 4x + 12$ are not the same function, $f(x)$ is not symmetrical about the origin.

       So $y = x^2 + 4x - 12$ is neither symmetrical about the y-axis nor symmetrical about the origin.

Example 10.3.3

A water engineer, who is studying the motion of a wave travelling at 2 metres per second along a narrow channel without change of shape, starts measurements when the wave has equation $y = f(x)$, as shown in Fig. 10.15.

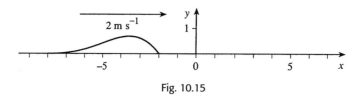

Fig. 10.15

(a) Find the equation of the wave 4 seconds later.

(b) Find the equation of the wave *t* seconds later.

(c) The engineer has placed a sensor on the *y*-axis to plot the height of the wave at this position against the time. Find the shape of the graph.

> (a) The wave travels 8 metres in 4 seconds, so the graph is translated 8 metres in the *x*-direction (see Fig. 10.16). Its equation is then $y = f(x - 8)$.

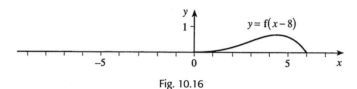

Fig. 10.16

> (b) The wave travels 2*t* metres in *t* seconds, so its equation is then $y = f(x - 2t)$.

> (c) Substituting $x = 0$ in the equation in (b) gives the equation of the height on the *y*-axis as $y = f(-2t)$.

> Now Fig. 10.15 is shown as a graph of *y* against *x* with equation $y = f(x)$, but changing the letter *x* to *t*, and the *x*-axis to a *t*-axis, would not change the shape of the graph. To convert $y = f(t)$ into $y = f(-2t)$ you need a stretch of factor $\frac{1}{2}$ combined with a reflection in the *y*-axis.

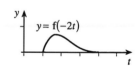

Fig. 10.17

> This produces the graph shown in Fig. 10.17.

Exercise 10B

Do not use a calculator in this exercise.

1 Use stretches and reflections to sketch the following pairs of graphs. Label which is which.

(a) $y = x$ and $y = 2x$ (b) $y = x$ and $y = -x$

(c) $y = x^2$ and $y = 3x^2$ (d) $y = x^2$ and $y = -x^2$

(e) $y = \sqrt{x}$ and $y = 2\sqrt{x}$ (f) $y = 2\sqrt{x}$ and $y = 2\sqrt{-x}$

(g) $y = x + 3$ and $y = 2x + 3$ (h) $y = x + 3$ and $y = 2(x + 3)$

(i) $y = x^3$ and $y = (-x)^3$ (j) $y = x - 2$ and $y = -x - 2$

(k) $y = x^2 + 1$ and $y = (-x)^2 + 1$ (l) $y = \dfrac{1}{x^2}$ and $y = -\dfrac{1}{2x^2}$

2 (a) Show that the point (16, 4) lies on $y = \sqrt{x}$.

(b) The point (16, 4) is transformed by a stretch of factor $\frac{1}{2}$ in the x-direction. Where does it move to?

(c) The graph $y = \sqrt{x}$ is transformed by a stretch of factor $\frac{1}{2}$ in the x-direction. What is the equation of the new graph?

(d) Check that the point in your answer to part (b) lies on the graph in your answer to part (c).

3 The graph of $y = (2x + 1)^2$ is stretched by a factor of 2 in the x-direction. What is the equation of the new graph?

4 The graph of $y = \dfrac{1}{x^2}$ is stretched by a factor of 3 in the x-direction. Show that the same result could be achieved by a stretch in the y-direction, and find the factor of the stretch.

5 The graph $y = 2x^2$ is stretched by a factor of 2 in the y-direction. Find the equation of the new graph. The graph is then stretched by a factor of 3 in the x-direction. Find the equation of the final graph and state clearly how you could achieve the same final result with

(a) just one stretch in the x-direction,   (b) just one stretch in the y-direction.

6 In which axis is the graph of $y = x^2 - 7x + 6$ reflected if its new equation is

(a) $y = x^2 + 7x + 6$,   (b) $y = -x^2 + 7x - 6$?

7 The graph of $y = (x - 2)^2$ is transformed into the graph of $y = (x + 2)^2$ when it is reflected in one of the coordinate axes. Which axis is it?

8 Prove that if (r, s) lies on $y = f(x)$, then (cr, s) lies on $y = f\left(\dfrac{x}{c}\right)$. What property of transformations does this establish?

9* Determine if the following functions are 'even', 'odd' or 'neither even nor odd'.

(a) $f(x) = x^3 + 3x$ (b) $f(x) = 7x^2 - 8$

(c) $f(x) = (x - 1)(x - 3)$ (d) $f(x) = x^5 + 3x^3 + 1$

Find $f'(x)$ for each of the four functions and determine if it is even, odd or neither even nor odd. What does this suggest about derivatives of even and odd functions?

Miscellaneous exercise 10

Do not use a calculator in this exercise.

1 Starting with the graph of $y = \dfrac{1}{x}$, use a translation to sketch the graph of $y = \dfrac{1}{1 + x}$. Hence sketch the graph of $y = \dfrac{1}{1 + \frac{1}{3}x}$.

2 The diagram shows the graph of $y = f(x)$. The curve passes through the origin O and the point A with coordinates $(a, 0)$, where a is a positive constant. Sketch, on separate diagrams, the graphs of

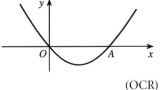

(a) $y = f(x + a)$ (b) $y = f(-x)$ (OCR)

3 The graph of $y = \dfrac{1}{x}$ is first stretched by a factor of 3 in the x-direction and then stretched by a factor of $\frac{1}{3}$ in the y-direction. What is the effect on the original curve?

4 The straight line $y = ax + b$ is transformed by two translations. One translation is by 4 units in the positive x-direction and the other is by 7 units in the positive y-direction. Given that the equation of the transformed line is $y = 6x - 27$, find the values of a and b.

5 The graph of the straight line $y = x$ is transformed as follows:

translation by 4 units in the positive x-direction,

followed by stretch in the y-direction with scale factor 2,

followed by reflection in the x-axis.

Find the equations of the graphs which result after each transformation.

6 If the graph of $y = f(x)$ is reflected in the x-axis and then in the y-axis, what is its new equation? If the graph is the same as the original, what type of function is $f(x)$?

7 The diagram shows the graph of $y = f(x)$ for $-2 \leqslant x \leqslant 1$. Outside this interval $f(x)$ is zero.

Sketch, on separate diagrams, the graphs of

(a) $y = f(x + 1)$,

(b) $y = -f(3x)$.   (OCR)

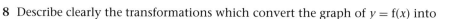

8 Describe clearly the transformations which convert the graph of $y = f(x)$ into

(a) $y = af(x)$,   (b) $y = f(x) + a$,

(c) $y = f(x + a)$,   (d) $y = f(ax)$,

where a is a positive constant.

9* Draw a sketch of the graph of an even function $f(x)$ which has a derivative at every point. Let P be the point on the graph for which $x = p$ (where $p > 0$) and draw the tangent at P on your sketch. Also draw the tangent at the point P' for which $x = -p$.

(a) What is the relationship between the gradient at P' and the gradient at P? What can you deduce about the relationship between $f'(p)$ and $f'(-p)$? What does this tell you about the derivative of an even function?

(b) Show that the derivative of an odd function is even.

11 Investigating shapes of graphs

This chapter explains how you can use differentiation to find the shape of a graph from its equation. When you have finished it, you should

- understand the terms 'stationary point', 'maximum point', 'minimum point' and 'turning point'
- appreciate the significance of zero, positive and negative derivatives
- be able to locate maximum and minimum points on a graph
- recognise that the derivative of a function is itself a function
- understand the significance of the second derivative for the shapes of graphs
- be able to use second derivatives where appropriate to distinguish maximum and minimum points.

11.1 Stationary points

In Chapter 4 you found the coordinates of the vertex of a quadratic graph by writing its equation in completed square form. You used the property that the vertex of the graph is either its highest or lowest point. This is where the $(x + \ldots)^2$ part of the completed square expression is 0.

Another way of finding the vertex is to use differentiation. At the vertex the tangent is parallel to the x-axis, so that the gradient is 0. (See Fig. 11.1.)

Differentiation gives you the formula for the gradient. Putting this equal to zero gives an equation for the x-coordinate of the vertex. Example 11.1.1 uses the method to find the vertex of a graph which you looked at before in Section 4.2; Fig. 4.1 is reproduced here as Fig. 11.2.

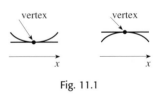

Fig. 11.1

Example 11.1.1

Locate the vertex of the parabola with equation $y = x^2 - 6x + 8$.

The gradient formula is $\dfrac{dy}{dx} = 2x - 6$. The gradient is zero when $2x - 6 = 0$, which gives $x = 3$. This is the x-coordinate of the vertex.

To find the y-coordinate of the vertex, substitute $x = 3$ in the equation, giving $y = 3^2 - 6 \times 3 + 8 = -1$. So the vertex has coordinates $(3, -1)$.

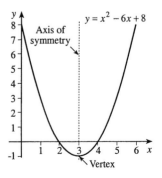

Fig. 11.2

An advantage of the gradient method is that it is not restricted to quadratic graphs. Graphs with other equations do not have a 'vertex', but they may have 'peaks' or 'troughs' which occur at points where the gradient is zero.

The next two examples apply the gradient method to graphs for which f(x) is a cubic and a quartic polynomial.

Example 11.1.2

Fig. 11.3 shows part of the graph with equation $y = x^3 - 6x^2 + 9x - 1$. Find the coordinates of the peak at P and the trough at T.

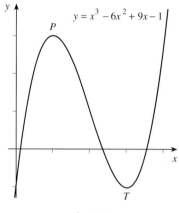

Fig. 11.3

The gradient of the curve is 0 at both P and T. Differentiating its equation gives the gradient formula

$$\frac{dy}{dx} = 3x^2 - 12x + 9.$$

So the x-coordinates of P and T satisfy the quadratic equation

$$3x^2 - 12x + 9 = 0.$$

Dividing by the common factor 3 and factorising,

$$x^2 - 4x + 3 = 0$$
$$(x - 1)(x - 3) = 0.$$

So the x-coordinates of P and T are 1 and 3.

To find the y-coordinates of P and T, substitute 1 and 3 for x in the equation $y = x^3 - 6x^2 + 9x - 1$. This gives $y = 1 - 6 + 9 - 1 = 3$ for P, and $y = 27 - 54 + 27 - 1 = -1$ for T. So the coordinates of P are $(1, 3)$, and the coordinates of T are $(3, -1)$.

Points of a graph at which the gradient is 0 are called **stationary points**. The standard method of locating stationary points is to write down the gradient formula for the graph, and to solve the equation obtained by putting this equal to 0.

Example 11.1.3
Find the stationary points on the graph with equation $y = x^4 - 4x^3 + 4x^2$.

The gradient formula is

$$\frac{dy}{dx} = 4x^3 - 12x^2 + 8x.$$

So the x-coordinates of the stationary points satisfy the equation

$$4x^3 - 12x^2 + 8x = 0.$$

Notice that $4x$ is a factor of the left side, and you can check that the other factor $x^2 - 3x + 2$ can be split into two linear factors $(x - 1)(x - 2)$. So the equation can be written as

$$4x(x - 1)(x - 2) = 0$$

giving $x = 0$, $x = 1$ or $x = 2$.

Substituting these values of x in the equation $y = x^4 - 4x^3 + 4x^2$ gives $y = 0$, $y = 1 - 4 + 4 = 1$ and $y = 16 - 32 + 16 = 0$ respectively. The stationary points are therefore $(0, 0)$, $(1, 1)$ and $(2, 0)$.

Finding stationary points is often an important step in finding the shape of a graph. For Example 11.1.3, Fig. 11.4 shows the three stationary points with short lines indicating the horizontal tangents at these points. From this you can be sure that between $x = 0$ and $x = 2$ the curve has the form shown by the solid line in Fig. 11.5, with a peak at $(1, 1)$. You would probably guess that there are also troughs at $(0, 0)$ and $(2, 0)$, so that the graph continues as indicated by the dotted lines. You would in fact be right, but it is not so obvious. This part of the investigation is dealt with in the next section.

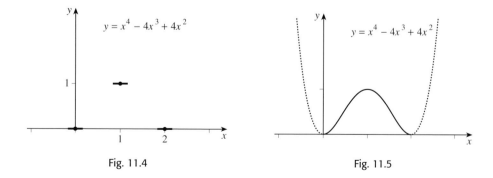

Fig. 11.4   Fig. 11.5

Exercise 11A

1 Find the stationary points on the graphs with the following equations.

(a) $y = 2x^2 + 4x - 5$ (b) $y = 1 + 6x - x^2$ (c) $y = x^3 + 3x^2 - 9x$

(d) $y = x^3 - 12x$ (e) $y = x^3 - 12x^2$ (f) $y = x^5 - 5x + 4$

(g) $y = (x^2 - 4)^2$ (h) $y = x(x + 1)^2$ (i) $y = x^3 - 3x^2 + 3x$

2 Find and plot the stationary points on the graphs with the following equations. Use these, and anything else you notice about the equations, to make guesses about the shape of the graphs. Then use a graphic calculator to check your guesses.

(a) $y = 3 + 2x - x^2$ (b) $y = x^2 + x - 8$ (c) $y = (x + 5)(1 - x)$

(d) $y = (x - 2)^2$ (e) $y = 3 + x^3$ (f) $y = x^3 + 3x^2 - 2$

(g) $y = x^2(x + 1)$ (h) $y = x^3(x + 1)$ (i) $y = x^4 - 4x^3 - 20x^2$

11.2   Maximum and minimum points

The mathematical terms for the peaks and troughs of graphs are 'maximum points' and 'minimum points'. At a maximum point the value of a function f(x) is higher than anywhere else on the graph in its immediate neighbourhood; it is called the 'maximum value' of the function.

But just as you can stand on top of one hill and see higher peaks across a valley, a graph may have several maximum points, each with a different maximum value. A maximum value of a function is not necessarily the greatest value it can take, but only the greatest value amongst the points on the graph in an interval around the maximum point. This is illustrated in Fig. 11.6, in which both Q and S are maximum points.

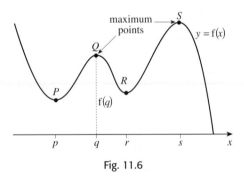

Fig. 11.6

This idea can be expressed as a precise definition:

> On the graph of $y = f(x)$ a point Q, with coordinates $(q, f(q))$, is a **maximum point** if $f(q)$ is greater than the value of $f(x)$ at all the other points in an interval of values of x around q. Then $f(q)$ is called a **maximum value** of $f(x)$.

The most obvious way of knowing that you have reached a peak is that you stop climbing uphill and start to walk downhill. You can use this idea to show that you are at a maximum point of a graph.

In Fig. 11.6, as you move along the curve from P to Q, the gradient $\dfrac{dy}{dx}$ is positive and you are gaining height the whole time. The mathematical term for this is that f(x) is an **increasing function** between $x - p$ and $x - q$.

Once you are past Q the gradient is negative and you are losing height. Between $x = q$ and $x = r$, f(x) is a **decreasing function**.

> If f$'(x)$ is positive in an interval of values of x, then f(x) is an increasing function in that interval.
>
> If f$'(x)$ is negative in an interval, then f(x) is a decreasing function in that interval.

You can use this idea to show that Q is a maximum point on a graph with equation $y = $ f(x). Begin by finding $\dfrac{dy}{dx} = $ f$'(x)$. If $\dfrac{dy}{dx}$ is positive in an interval to the left of $x = q$, and negative in an interval to the right, then Q is higher than any other point on the curve in an interval around it. That is, Q is a maximum point. This is illustrated in Fig. 11.7.

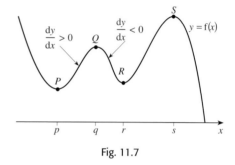

Fig. 11.7

Example 11.2.1

Find the maximum point on the graph of $y = 8 + 6x - x^2$.

> The gradient formula for the graph is
>
> $$\frac{dy}{dx} = 6 - 2x = 2(3 - x).$$
>
> There is a stationary point where $x = 3$.
>
> When $x < 3$, $\dfrac{dy}{dx}$ is positive; and when $x > 3$, $\dfrac{dy}{dx}$ is negative.
>
> The stationary point at $x = 3$ is therefore a maximum point.
>
> When $x = 3$, $y = 8 + 6 \times 3 - 3^2 = 8 + 18 - 9 = 17$.
>
> So the maximum point has coordinates $(3, 17)$.

Example 11.2.2

For the graph of $y = x^3 - 6x^2 + 9x - 1$ in Example 11.1.2, show that $(1, 3)$ is a maximum point.

> From Example 11.1.2,
>
> $$\frac{dy}{dx} = 3x^2 - 12x + 9 = 3(x - 1)(x - 3).$$
>
> You can now use the critical values method from Section 6.3 to investigate the sign of f$'(x)$ for different values of x. The critical values are those for which $(x - 1)(x - 3) = 0$, which are 1 and 3. So the table of signs is:

	$x < 1$	$x = 1$	$1 < x < 3$	$x = 3$	$x > 3$
$x - 1$	$-$	0	$+$	$+$	$+$
$x - 3$	$-$	$-$	$-$	0	$+$
$\dfrac{dy}{dx}$	$+$	0	$-$	0	$+$

The question asked is about the point with $x = 1$. The table shows that in the interval $x < 1$ to the left of this point the gradient is positive, so that y is increasing. In the interval $1 < x < 3$ to the right the gradient is negative, so y is decreasing. This shows that $(1, 3)$ is a maximum point.

It is useful to express this method in the form of a precise rule:

> On the graph of $y = f(x)$, if $\dfrac{dy}{dx} > 0$ in an interval to the left of q, and $\dfrac{dy}{dx} < 0$ in an interval to the right of q, then $(q, f(q))$ is a maximum point.

To get the corresponding conditions for a minimum point, you have to change the direction of some of the inequalities:

> On the graph of $y = f(x)$ a point Q, with coordinates $(q, f(q))$, is a **minimum point** if $f(q)$ is less than the value of $f(x)$ at all the other points in an interval of values of x around q. Then $f(q)$ is called a **minimum value** of $f(x)$.
>
> If $\dfrac{dy}{dx} < 0$ in an interval to the left of q, and $\dfrac{dy}{dx} > 0$ in an interval to the right of q, then $(q, f(q))$ is a minimum point.

As an example, look back to the point R in Fig. 11.6. The gradient $\dfrac{dy}{dx}$ is negative when x is between q and r, and positive between r and s. So R is a minimum point on the graph.

Example 11.2.3
Find the minimum value of $f(x) = x^2 - 8x + 12$.

Differentiating,

$$f'(x) = 2x - 8 = 2(x - 4).$$

Since $f'(x)$ is negative when $x < 4$, and positive when $x > 4$, the graph of $y = f(x)$ has a minimum point where $x = 4$.

The minimum value of $f(x)$ is $f(4) = 4^2 - 8 \times 4 + 12 = 16 - 32 + 12 = -4$.

Example 11.2.4

In Example 11.1.3, show that the graph of $y = x^4 - 4x^3 + 4x^2$ has the shape predicted in Fig. 11.5.

It was shown in Example 11.1.3 that the gradient formula is $4x(x-1)(x-2)$. The critical values are $x = 0$, $x = 1$ and $x = 2$, and the table of signs is shown below.

	$x < 0$	$x = 0$	$0 < x < 1$	$x = 1$	$1 < x < 2$	$x = 2$	$x > 2$
$4x$	$-$	0	$+$	$+$	$+$	$+$	$+$
$x - 1$	$-$	$-$	$-$	0	$+$	$+$	$+$
$x - 2$	$-$	$-$	$-$	$-$	$-$	0	$+$
$\dfrac{dy}{dx}$	$-$	0	$+$	0	$-$	0	$+$

This shows that, as you pass through $x = 0$ and $x = 2$ the gradient changes from negative to positive, so $(0, 0)$ and $(2, 0)$ are minimum points. But as you pass through $x = 1$ the gradient changes from positive to negative, so $(1, 1)$ is a maximum point. These results agree with the graph in Fig. 11.5.

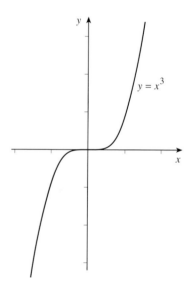

In all the examples so far the stationary points have been either maximum or minimum points. You may be tempted to think that this is always so, but in fact you have already met exceptions.

The simplest is the graph of $y = x^3$, shown in Fig. 11.8. Since $\dfrac{dy}{dx} = 3x^2$, the gradient is 0 when $x = 0$. That is, the origin is a stationary point. But it is neither a maximum nor a minimum point. Since $\dfrac{dy}{dx}$ is positive both to the left and to the right of $x = 0$, x^3 is an increasing function for all values of x.

Fig. 11.8

Example 11.2.5

Find (a) the stationary points,   (b) the maximum or minimum point on the graph with equation $y = x^3(x - 4)$.

(a) Before differentiating you must multiply out the brackets to get $y = x^4 - 4x^3$. Then

$$\frac{dy}{dx} = 4x^3 - 12x^2 = 4x^2(x - 3).$$

It follows that $\dfrac{dy}{dx} = 0$ when $x = 0$ and when $x = 3$, where $y = 0$ and $y = 27 \times (-1) = -27$ respectively. So the stationary points are $(0, 0)$ and $(3, -27)$.

(b) The critical values of x are 0 and 3, giving the table of signs:

	$x < 0$	$x = 0$	$0 < x < 3$	$x = 3$	$x > 3$
$4x^2$	$+$	0	$+$	$+$	$+$
$x - 3$	$-$	$-$	$-$	0	$+$
$f'(x)$	$-$	0	$-$	0	$+$

This shows a sign change from $-$ to $+$ at $x = 3$, so $(3, -27)$ is a minimum point. But there is no sign change at $x = 0$; the gradient is negative on both sides. So this stationary point is neither a maximum nor a minimum point. This is illustrated in Fig. 11.9.

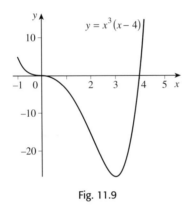

Fig. 11.9

Maximum and minimum points are sometimes also called **turning points**. A complete procedure for locating turning points, and deciding for each whether it is a maximum or a minimum, can then be summed up as follows:

To find the minimum and maximum points on the graph of $y = f(x)$:

Step 1 Find an expression for $\dfrac{dy}{dx} = f'(x)$.

Step 2 List the values of x for which $\dfrac{dy}{dx}$ is 0.

Step 3 Taking each of these values of x in turn, find the sign of $\dfrac{dy}{dx}$ in intervals to the left and to the right of that value.

Step 4 If these signs are $-$ and $+$ respectively, the graph has a minimum point. If they are $+$ and $-$ it has a maximum point. If the signs are the same, it has neither.

Step 5 For each value of x which gives a minimum or maximum, calculate $y = f(x)$.

Example 11.2.6

Find the turning points on the graph of $y = x^2(6 - x)$, and determine whether they are maximum or minimum points.

Step 1 $y = x^2(6 - x) = 6x^2 - x^3$, which gives $\dfrac{dy}{dx} = 12x - 3x^2 = 3x(4 - x)$.

Step 2 $\dfrac{dy}{dx} = 0$ when $x = 0$ or $x = 4$.

Step 3   Using the values of x in Step 2 as critical values, make a table of signs.

	$x < 0$	$x = 0$	$0 < x < 4$	$x = 4$	$x > 4$
$3x$	$-$	0	$+$	$+$	$+$
$4 - x$	$+$	$+$	$+$	0	$-$
$\dfrac{dy}{dx}$	$-$	0	$+$	0	$-$

Step 4   There is a minimum where $x = 0$ and a maximum where $x = 4$.

Step 5   When $x = 0$, $y = 0$, so $(0, 0)$ is a minimum point on the graph.

When $x = 4$, $y = 32$, so $(4, 32)$ is a maximum point on the graph.

Exercise 11B

1 For each of the following graphs in the given interval, find whether $\dfrac{dy}{dx}$ is positive or negative, and state whether y is an increasing or decreasing function of x in the interval.

(a) $y = x^2 - 4x + 7$, $x > 2$

(b) $y = 5x^2 + 7x - 3$, $x < -0.7$

(c) $y = 3 + 8x - 2x^2$, $x > 2$

(d) $y = 4 - 6x - 4x^2$, $x < -\frac{3}{4}$

(e) $y = x^3 - 3x$, $x > 1$

(f) $y = 5 - x^4$, $x < 0$

(g) $y = 3x - 4x^2 - x^3$, $x < -3$

(h) $y = x^3 - 3x^2$, $0 < x < 2$

2 For each of the following functions $f(x)$, find $f'(x)$ and the interval in which $f(x)$ is increasing.

(a) $x^2 - 5x + 6$

(b) $x^2 + 6x - 4$

(c) $7 - 3x - x^2$

(d) $3x^2 - 5x + 7$

(e) $5x^2 + 3x - 2$

(f) $7 - 4x - 3x^2$

3 For each of the following functions $f(x)$, find $f'(x)$ and the interval in which $f(x)$ is decreasing.

(a) $x^2 + 4x - 9$

(b) $x^2 - 3x - 5$

(c) $5 - 3x + x^2$

(d) $2x^2 - 8x + 7$

(e) $4 + 7x - 2x^2$

(f) $3 - 5x - 7x^2$

4 For each of the following functions f(x), find f'(x) and any intervals in which f(x) is increasing.

(a) $x^3 - 12x$

(b) $2x^3 - 18x + 5$

(c) $2x^3 - 9x^2 - 24x + 7$

(d) $x^3 - 3x^2 + 3x + 4$

(e) $x^4 - 2x^2$

(f) $x^4 + 4x^3$

(g) $3x - x^3$

(h) $2x^5 - 5x^4 + 10$

(i) $3x + x^3$

5 For each of the following functions f(x), find f'(x) and any intervals in which f(x) is decreasing. In part (i), n is an integer.

(a) $x^3 - 27x$

(b) $x^4 + 4x^2 - 5$

(c) $x^3 - 3x^2 + 3x - 1$

(d) $12x - 2x^3$

(e) $2x^3 + 3x^2 - 36x - 7$

(f) $3x^4 - 20x^3 + 12$

(g) $36x^2 - 2x^4$

(h) $x^5 - 5x$

(i) $x^n - nx$ ($n > 1$)

6 For the graphs of each of the following functions:

(i) find the coordinates of the stationary point;

(ii) say, with reasoning, whether this is a maximum or a minimum point;

(iii) check your answer by using the method of 'completing the square' to find the vertex;

(iv) state the range of possible values of y.

(a) $y = x^2 - 8x + 4$

(b) $y = 3x^2 + 12x + 5$

(c) $y = 5x^2 + 6x + 2$

(d) $y = 4 - 6x - x^2$

(e) $y = x^2 + 6x + 9$

(f) $y = 1 - 4x - 4x^2$

7 Find the turning points on the following graphs, and say whether they are maximum or minimum points.

(a) $x^3 - 12x + 5$

(b) $y = 1 - 6x^2 - x^3$

(c) $y = 2x^3 - 3x^2 - 12x$

(d) $y = x^3 - 4x^2 + 5x$

(e) $y = x^4 - 2x^2 + 3$

(f) $y = 5 + 4x - x^4$

8 Find the coordinates of the stationary points on the following graphs, and find whether these points are maxima or minima or neither.

(a) $y = 2x^3 + 3x^2 - 72x + 5$

(b) $y = x^3 - 3x^2 - 45x + 7$

(c) $y = 3x^4 - 8x^3 + 6x^2$

(d) $y = 3x^5 - 20x^3 + 1$

(e) $y = 2x + x^2 - 4x^3$

(f) $y = x^3 + 3x^2 + 3x + 1$

11.3 An application to roots of equations

In Section 3.6 you saw how the points of intersection of a graph $y = f(x)$ and a line $y = k$ can be found by solving the equation f(x) = k.

Often you want to reverse this process. Starting with an equation f(x) = k, drawing the graphs of $y = f(x)$ and $y = k$ will tell you something about the roots. The x-coordinates of the points of intersection are the roots of the equation. So if you know the shape of the graph $y = f(x)$, you can find how many roots there are and their approximate values. This is illustrated in Fig. 11.10.

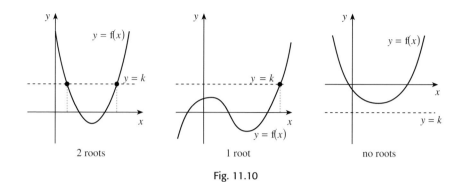

Fig. 11.10

Example 11.3.1

What can you say about the roots of the equation $x^3(x - 4) = k$ if k is equal to

(a) 10, (b) −10, (c) −30?

Show that the equation can never have more than two roots.

The shape of the graph of $y = x^3(x - 4)$ was found in Example 11.2.5, and the graph is reproduced in Fig. 11.11.

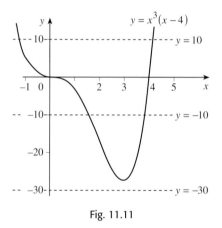

Fig. 11.11

The roots of the equation are the x-coordinates of the points of intersection of the graph with $y = k$, a line parallel to the x-axis. You can see that the largest number of points in which such a line could cut the curve is two. So the equation can never have more than two roots.

(a) If $k = 10$, the line $y = k$ is above the x-axis. One of the roots is negative and the other is greater than 4.

(b) If $k = -10$, $y = k$ is below the x-axis. Both roots are between 0 and 4.

(c) The minimum point on the graph has y-coordinate −27, so the line $y = -30$ never meets the graph. The equation with $k = -30$ has no roots.

Example 11.3.2
(a) Sketch the graph of $y = x^2(6 - x)$. Verify that the point $(-2, 32)$ is on the graph.
(b) For what values of k does the equation $x^3 - 6x^2 + k = 0$ have three real roots? What can you then say about the values of the roots?
(c) What can you say about the roots of the equations
     (i) $6x^2 - x^3 = 0$,   (ii) $x^3 - 6x^2 + 32 = 0$?

(a) You often don't want to draw a graph accurately, but you need a rough idea of its general features: for example, maximum and minimum points, where the graph cuts the axes, and perhaps one or two other particular points. You can then put this information together to make a sketch of the graph.

For the graph of $y = x^2(6 - x)$ you already know from Example 11.2.6 that $(0, 0)$ is a minimum point and that $(4, 32)$ is a maximum point.

To find where the graph cuts the y-axis, put $x = 0$ in the equation, which gives $y = 0$. To find where it cuts the x-axis put $y = 0$, which gives $x = 0$ or $x = 6$. So the points of the graph on the axes are $(0, 0)$ and $(6, 0)$.

When $x = -2$, $y = (-2)^2 \times (6 - (-2)) = 4 \times 8 = 32$. This verifies that $(-2, 32)$ is on the graph.

Before doing any of these calculations, it is a good idea to have drawn a pair of axes on the paper. Then, as you collect each piece of information, you can add it to the diagram. Notice that in this example it would be very awkward to get the points $(4, 32)$ and $(-2, 32)$ on the graph if you use equal scales on the two axes; so this is the time to decide to have a smaller scale on the y-axis than the x-axis. You will then have drawn something like Fig. 11.12; this should be enough to be able to sketch in the graph in Fig. 11.13.

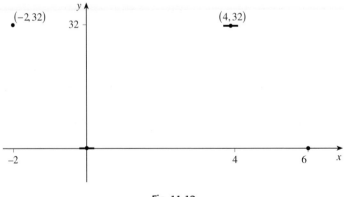

Fig. 11.12

(b) The equation $x^3 - 6x^2 + k = 0$ can be rearranged as $6x^2 - x^3 = k$, which is $x^2(6 - x) = k$. For this equation to have three real roots, the line $y = k$ must cut the graph of $y = x^2(6 - x)$ at three points. Fig. 11.13 shows that for this to happen

k must be between the minimum and maximum values of the function, that is between 0 and 32. So the equation has three real roots if $0 < k < 32$.

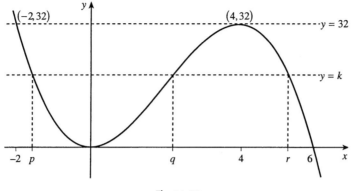

Fig. 11.13

The values of these roots are the x-coordinates of the points of intersection, which are labelled p, q and r in Fig. 11.13. The graph shows that p is between -2 and 0, q is between 0 and 4, and r is between 4 and 6.

(c) (i) The equation $6x^2 - x^3 = 0$ is $x^2(6 - x) = 0$, which is satisfied by $x = 0$ and $x = 6$.

These are just the x-coordinates of the points where the graph cuts the x-axis.

The interesting thing to notice about this equation is that the root $x = 0$ comes from a factor x^2 in the equation, and this corresponds to the point where the line $y = 0$ is a tangent to the graph. The root $x = 0$ is called a repeated root. (You will remember that in Section 4.6 a quadratic equation with only one root was said to have a repeated root. This is a similar situation for a cubic equation.)

(ii) The roots of $x^3 - 6x^2 + 32 = 0$ are the x-coordinates of the points where the graph meets the line $y = 32$. Fig. 11.13 shows that these roots are -2 and 4; and since the line touches the graph at $(4, 32)$, you would expect 4 to be a repeated root. And taking a hint from what happened in part (i), this suggests that the cubic equation might be written in factor form as $(x + 2)(x - 4)^2 = 0$.

You can use the method of multiplying polynomials in Section 9.2 to check this.

$$\begin{aligned}
(x + 2)(x - 4)^2 &= (x + 2)(x^2 - 8x + 16) \\
&= x(x^2 - 8x + 16) + 2(x^2 - 8x + 16) \\
&= (x^3 - 8x^2 + 16x) + (2x^2 - 16x + 32) \\
&= x^3 - 6x^2 + 32,
\end{aligned}$$

which is just as expected.

Exercise 11C

1 Find the minimum point on the graph of $y = x^2 - 5x$. Use your answer to find the value of k for which the equation $x^2 - 5x = k$ has two real roots.

   Check your answer using the discriminant of the quadratic $x^2 - 5x - k$.

2 Use the graph of $y = 4x - 3x^2$ to find the values of k for which the equation $3x^2 - 4x + k = 0$ has no real roots.

3 Use the graph of $y = x^4 - 4x^3 + 4x^2$ (Fig. 11.5) to find the number of roots of the following equations.

   (a) $x^4 - 4x^3 + 4x^2 = 2$ (b) $x^4 - 4x^3 + 4x^2 = 1$

   (c) $2x^4 - 8x^3 + 8x^2 = 1$ (d) $x^4 - 4x^3 + 4x^2 + 1 = 0$

4 Sketch the graph of $y = x^3 - 3x$. Use it to find the number of roots of the following equations and their approximate values.

   (a) $x^3 - 3x = 1$ (b) $x^3 - 3x + 2 = 0$ (c) $x^3 = 3(x + 1)$

5 Use the graph of $y = x^3 + 4x$ to show that the equation $x^3 + 4x = k$ has exactly one root for any value of k.

6 The graph of $y = x^3 + 12x^2 + 36x$ is used to find solutions of the equation $x^3 + 12x^2 + 36x = k$ for various values of k.

   (a) Find the coordinates of the maximum and minimum points, and use these to sketch the graph.

   (b) Verify that the point $(-8, -32)$ is on the graph.

   (c) Find the number of real roots of the equation when k is
       (i) 0,   (ii) 20,   (iii) −20,   (iv) −40.

   (d) For what values of k does the equation have three real roots? What can you say about these roots?

7 The graph of $y = x^4 - 2x^3 - 2x^2$ is used to find solutions of the equation $x^4 - 2x^3 - 2x^2 = k$ for various values of k.

   (a) Find the coordinates of the maximum and minimum points, and sketch the graph.

   (b) Find the coordinates of the points where the graph meets the x-axis.

   (c) Find the number of roots of the equation when k is
       (i) 4,   (ii) −4,   (iii) −8.

   (d) For what values of k does the equation have
       (i) 0,   (ii) 1,   (iii) 2,   (iv) 3,   (v) 4 real roots?

   (e) In case (v) of part (d), what can you say about the values of these roots?

11.4   Second derivatives

You know that all quadratic graphs have one of the two shapes in Fig. 11.14. The parabola (a) on the left is said to 'bend upwards'; (b) on the right is said to 'bend downwards'.

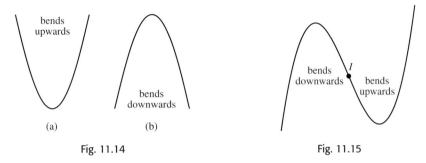

Fig. 11.14   Fig. 11.15

Most of the curves in this chapter are more complicated than this. Fig. 11.15, for example can be thought of as having two parts. In the left part, as far as the point marked I, the curve bends downwards; then, after I, it bends upwards.

Some curves have three parts. For example, in Fig. 11.9, if you go from left to right along the curve, it bends upwards as far as the origin; then it bends downwards as far as $x = 2$, after which it bends upwards again.

Knowing whether a graph bends upwards or downwards is often useful in investigating its shape. The question is, how to tell from the equation which way it bends.

Fig. 11.16 shows the graph of a function which is bending upwards, with the tangents at several points along the curve. The gradients of the tangents at P and Q are negative; at R the gradient is 0; then at S and T the gradient is positive. All the way, as you move from left to right, the gradient increases.

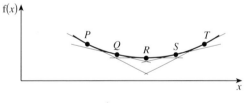

Fig. 11.16

The word 'increases' is the clue. You know that the gradient of the graph $y = f(x)$ is itself a function. It is called the 'gradient function', and denoted by $f'(x)$. But temporarily it will help to give it a function name of its own, and to use the symbol $g(x)$ to stand for the gradient function of $f(x)$. For example, if $f(x) = x^2$, then $g(x) = 2x$.

Then Fig. 11.17 shows that $g(x)$ is an increasing function. And it was shown at the beginning of Section 11.2 that, if $g'(x) > 0$ in an interval, then $g(x)$ is an increasing function in that interval. And in that case the graph $y = f(x)$ bends upwards.

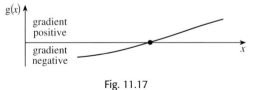

Fig. 11.17

So the way to show that the graph $y = f(x)$ bends upwards is to differentiate to get the gradient function $g(x) = f'(x)$. You then differentiate $g(x)$ to get $g'(x)$. If $g'(x)$ is positive, then the gradient function is increasing, so $y = f(x)$ bends upwards.

You will see that g'(x) is what you get if you differentiate f(x), and then differentiate the result a second time. This produces the 'second derivative' of f(x) (sometimes called the 'second order derivative'). It is denoted by f''(x) This is pronounced 'f two-dashed x', or 'f double-dashed x'.

Example 11.4.1

If $f(x) = 2x^3 + 3x^2 + 4x + 5$, find $f''(x)$.

The derivative of f(x) is $f'(x) = 6x^2 + 6x + 4$.

The derivative of f'(x) is $f''(x) = 12x + 6$.

Just as there are two ways of writing the derivative, either as $f'(x)$ or $\dfrac{dy}{dx}$, there are two ways of writing the second derivative. The derivative of $\dfrac{dy}{dx}$ is written as $\dfrac{d^2y}{dx^2}$. This is pronounced 'd squared y d x squared', or sometimes 'd two y d x squared'. The reason for this rather curious notation is explained in Chapter 12.

Example 11.4.2

Show that the graph of $y = 3x^2 + 7x - 2$ bends upwards for all values of x.

Two successive differentiations give $\dfrac{dy}{dx} = 6x + 7$ and $\dfrac{d^2y}{dx^2} = 6$.

Since $\dfrac{d^2y}{dx^2}$ is positive and independent of x, the graph bends upwards for all values of x.

Now draw for yourself a curve which bends downwards and draw tangents at a number of points. You will see that the gradient is decreasing as you move from left to right along the curve. If the equation is $y = f(x)$, $g(x) = f'(x)$ is a decreasing function, so that $g'(x) = f''(x)$ is negative.

> If $y = f(x)$, the derivative of $\dfrac{dy}{dx} = f'(x)$ is called the **second derivative** of f(x) with respect to x, and is denoted by $\dfrac{d^2y}{dx^2}$ or $f''(x)$.
>
> If $\dfrac{d^2y}{dx^2} = f''(x)$ is positive in an interval of values of x, the graph of $y = f(x)$ bends upwards in that interval.
>
> If $\dfrac{d^2y}{dx^2} = f''(x)$ is negative in an interval of values of x, the graph of $y = f(x)$ bends downwards in that interval.

Example 11.4.3

Find the interval in which the graph of $y = x^3 + 9x^2 - 2x$ bends downwards.

Differentiating twice gives $\dfrac{dy}{dx} = 3x^2 + 18x - 2$ and $\dfrac{d^2y}{dx^2} = 6x + 18 = 6(x + 3)$.

The graph bends downwards where $x + 3 < 0$, that is $x < -3$.

11.5   Maxima and minima revisited

One of the most important uses of the second derivative is to decide whether a stationary point on a graph is a maximum or a minimum.

Look back at Figs. 11.14 and 11.15. These show graphs with maximum or minimum points. Which is which depends on whether the graph is bending upwards or downwards. Where the graph bends upwards, the stationary point is a minimum; where it bends downwards, the stationary point is a maximum. So whether the graph has a maximum or minimum depends on the sign of the second derivative at the stationary point.

It is often simpler to use this instead of considering the change in sign of $f'(x)$ to decide whether a point on a graph is a minimum or a maximum. The procedure described in Section 11.2 can then be amended as follows.

> To find the minimum and maximum points on the graph of $y = f(x)$:
>
> **Step 1**   Find an expression for $\dfrac{dy}{dx} = f'(x)$.
>
> **Step 2**   List the values of x for which $\dfrac{dy}{dx}$ is 0.
>
> **Step 3**   Find an expression for $\dfrac{d^2y}{dx^2} = f''(x)$.
>
> **Step 4**   For each value of x in Step 2, find the sign of $\dfrac{d^2y}{dx^2}$. If the sign is +, the graph has a minimum point; if −, a maximum.
>
> [If the value of $\dfrac{d^2y}{dx^2}$ is 0, follow the old procedure.]
>
> **Step 5**   For each value of x giving a minimum or maximum, calculate $y = f(x)$.

Example 11.5.1

Find the turning points on the graph of $y = x^2(6 - x)$, and determine whether they are maximum or minimum points.

Step 1 $y = x^2(6 - x) = 6x^2 - x^3$, which gives $\dfrac{dy}{dx} = 12x - 3x^2 = 3x(4 - x)$.

Step 2 $\dfrac{dy}{dx} = 0$ when $x = 0$ or $x = 4$.

Step 3 $\dfrac{d^2y}{dx^2} = 12 - 6x$.

Step 4   When $x = 0$, $\dfrac{d^2y}{dx^2} = 12 - 6 \times 0 = 12$.

When $x = 4$, $\dfrac{d^2y}{dx^2} = 12 - 6 \times 4 = -12$.

So there is a minimum point where $x = 0$ and a maximum point where $x = 4$.

Step 5   When $x = 0$, $y = 0$, so $(0, 0)$ is a minimum point on the graph.

When $x = 4$, $y = 32$, so $(4, 32)$ is a maximum point on the graph.

Example 11.5.1 is the same as Example 11.2.6, but solved by the new procedure. Steps 1, 2 and 5 are the same, but there is a different way of deciding between maximum and minimum points. You can use whichever method you prefer.

The reason for having two methods is that, although the second method is often easier, it doesn't always work. This is illustrated by the next example.

Example 11.5.2

Find the nature of the stationary points on the graphs of $y = x^3$, $y = x^4$ and $y = -x^4$.

The derivatives are $\dfrac{dy}{dx} = 3x^2$, $\dfrac{dy}{dx} = 4x^3$ and $\dfrac{dy}{dx} = -4x^3$. All the graphs have stationary values where $x = 0$ and nowhere else.

The second derivatives are $\dfrac{d^2y}{dx^2} = 6x$, $\dfrac{d^2y}{dx^2} = 12x^2$ and $\dfrac{d^2y}{dx^2} = -12x^2$. For each graph the value of $\dfrac{d^2y}{dx^2}$ where $x = 0$ is 0.

Sketches of all three graphs in the neighbourhood of the origin are shown in Fig. 11.18. One has a minimum, one has a maximum and one has neither.

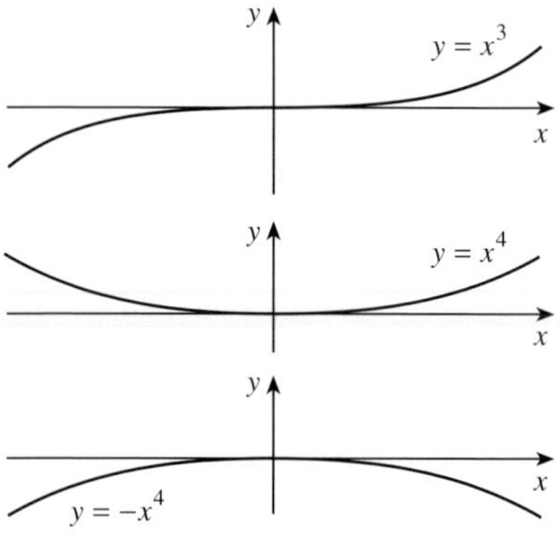

Fig. 11.18

What this example shows is that if the second derivative at a stationary point is 0, you can't use this method to decide whether it is a maximum, a minimum or neither. In that case you have to go back to the earlier method.

You will also find later on that for some functions it can be very laborious to find the second derivative. In that case, it is more efficient to use the old procedure. But this will not apply to any of the functions you have met so far.

Example 11.5.3
Find the minimum and maximum points on the graph of $f(x) = x^4 + x^5$.

Step 1 $f'(x) = 4x^3 + 5x^4 = x^3(4 + 5x)$.

Step 2 $f'(x) = 0$ when $x = 0$ or $x = -0.8$.

Step 3 $f''(x) = 12x^2 + 20x^3 = 4x^2(3 + 5x)$.

Step 4 $f''(-0.8) = 4 \times (-0.8)^2 \times (3 - 4) < 0$, so $x = -0.8$ gives a maximum.
$f''(0) = 0$, so you have to use the old procedure.

	$-0.8 < x < 0$	$x = 0$	$x > 0$
x^3	$-$	0	$+$
$4 + 5x$	$+$	$+$	$+$
$f'(x)$	$-$	0	$+$

The table shows that $x = 0$ gives a minimum.

Step 5   The maximum point is $(-0.8, 0.081\,92)$; the minimum point is $(0, 0)$.

Exercise 11D

1 Draw and compare the graphs of $y = f(x)$ and $y = f'(x)$ in each of the following cases. Check that $y = f(x)$ bends upwards when $y = f'(x)$ is decreasing, and downwards when $y = f'(x)$ is increasing.

(a) $f(x) = x^2$ (b) $f(x) = 5 - x^2$ (c) $f(x) = x^2 + 4x$

(d) $f(x) = 3x^2 - 6x$ (e) $f(x) = (2 + x)(4 - x)$ (f) $f(x) = (x + 3)^2$

(g) $f(x) = x^4$ (h) $f(x) = x^2(x - 2)$ (i) $f(x) = 3 - 2x$

2 In each part of the question, the diagram shows the graph of $y = f(x)$. Draw a graph of the gradient function $y = f'(x)$.

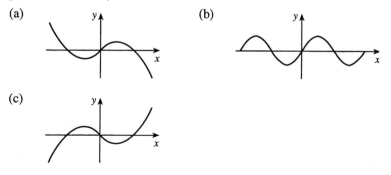

3 Write down the signs of f'(x) and f''(x) for the following graphs $y = f(x)$.

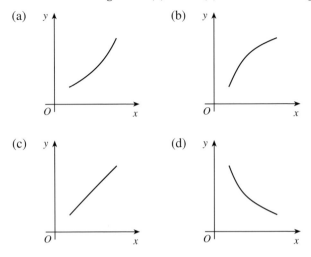

(a)

(b)

(c)

(d)

4 Find $\dfrac{d^2y}{dx^2}$ for the following equations.

(a) $y = 3x - 4$

(b) $y = 5 + 3x - 2x^2$

(c) $y = x^3 + 5x^2 - 2x + 13$

(d) $y = x^6$

5 Use first and second derivatives to locate and describe the stationary points on the graphs of the following functions. If this method fails then you should use the change of sign of the first derivative to distinguish stationary points which are maxima, minima or neither.

(a) $f(x) = 3x - x^3$

(b) $f(x) = x^3 - 3x^2$

(c) $f(x) = 3x^4 + 1$

(d) $f(x) = 2x^3 - 3x^2 - 12x + 4$

(e) $f(x) = 2x^3 - 12x^2 + 24x + 6$

6 Find the maximum and minimum points (if any) on the following graphs.

(a) $y = 3x^4 - 4x^3 - 12x^2 - 3$

(b) $y = x^3 - 3x^2 + 3x + 5$

(c) $y = 16x - 3x^3$

(d) $y = 2x^5 - 7$

(e) $y = 3x^4 - 8x^3 + 6x^2 + 1$

7 Consider the graph of $y = f(x)$ where $f(x) = x^3 - x$.

(a) Use the fact that $f(x) = x(x^2 - 1) = x(x - 1)(x + 1)$ to find where the graph cuts the x-axis and hence sketch the graph.

(b) Find f'(x) and sketch the graph of $y = f'(x)$.

(c) Find f''(x) and sketch the graph of $y = f''(x)$.

(d) Check the consistency of your sketches: for example, check that the graph of $y = f(x)$ is bending upwards where $f''(x) \geq 0$.

8 For the graph of $y = f(x)$ where $f(x) = x^3 + x$

   (a) use factors to show that the graph crosses the x-axis once only;

   (b) find $f'(x)$ and $f''(x)$;

   (c) find the interval in which the graph is bending upwards;

   (d) use the information gained to sketch the graph of $y = x^3 + x$;

   (e) check your work using a graphic calculator or a computer.

11.6 Graphs of other functions

So far all the functions in this chapter have been polynomials. Although their graphs can take many different forms, they have some features in common. For example, there are no breaks in the graphs, so that they are just a succession of peaks and troughs.

When you introduce into the equations powers of x which are not positive integers, there are some new complications. Fig. 11.19 shows three graphs which you have already met in Chapter 8. None of these could possibly be graphs of polynomials.

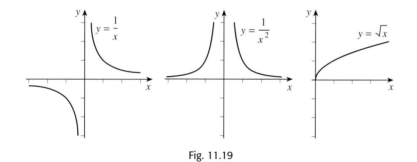

Fig. 11.19

Here are some of the new features that may appear when you draw the graph of $y = f(x)$ for functions like this.

- There may be some values of x for which $f(x)$ does not exist. For example, $\dfrac{1}{x}$ has no meaning if $x = 0$, and $\sqrt{x}$ has no meaning if $x < 0$. So the first thing to do in investigating the shape of the graph is to discard any values of x for which $f(x)$ has no meaning.

- When there is a break in the graph, the sign of the gradient may be different on either side of the break. For example, in the graph of $y = \dfrac{1}{x^2}$, $\dfrac{dy}{dx}$ is positive when $x < 0$ and negative when $x > 0$. So when you make a table of signs, it should be split into two parts, for values of x on either side of the break.

- There may be points on the graph at which the tangent is vertical. For example, the tangent to $y = \sqrt{x}$ at the origin is the y-axis. For this curve, $\dfrac{dy}{dx} = \dfrac{1}{2\sqrt{x}}$, and this has no meaning when $x = 0$.

• It is even possible for the graph to have a shape like Fig. 11.20.

  This is the graph of $y = \sqrt[3]{x^2} = x^{\frac{2}{3}}$, for which $\dfrac{dy}{dx} = \frac{2}{3}x^{-\frac{1}{3}} = \dfrac{2}{3\sqrt[3]{x}}$.

  This has the origin as a minimum point. But when $x = 0$, $\dfrac{dy}{dx}$ is not equal to 0; in fact, $\dfrac{dy}{dx}$ does not even exist for this value of x.

  So when you use the procedure for finding turning points, you need to consider values of x for which $f'(x)$ doesn't exist as well as those for which $f'(x)$ is equal to 0.

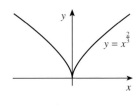

Fig. 11.20

None of these things can happen with polynomials. However, with these differences, all the results given for polynomials earlier in the chapter still apply. For example, it is still true that, if $f'(x)$ is positive in an interval of values of x, then $f(x)$ is an increasing function in that interval; you just have to be sure that the interval does not include a point where there is a break in the graph.

The similarities and differences are illustrated by the following examples.

Example 11.6.1
Find the maximum value of $f(x) = x(1 - \sqrt{x})$.

Since the function involves $\sqrt{x}$, it only exists if $x \geqslant 0$.

To differentiate, $f(x)$ can be expressed in terms of powers of x, as

$$f(x) = x(1 - \sqrt{x}) = x - x^{\frac{3}{2}}.$$

Then $f'(x) = 1 - \frac{3}{2}x^{\frac{1}{2}} = 1 - \frac{3}{2}\sqrt{x}.$

To find where $f(x)$ takes its maximum value, put $f'(x)$ equal to 0 to get

$$\tfrac{3}{2}\sqrt{x} = 1, \quad \text{so} \quad \sqrt{x} = \tfrac{2}{3} \quad \text{and} \quad x = \tfrac{4}{9}.$$

To check that the stationary value is a maximum,

$$f''(x) = -\tfrac{3}{4}x^{-\frac{1}{2}} = -\frac{3}{4\sqrt{x}}$$

so $f''\left(\tfrac{4}{9}\right) = -\dfrac{3}{4\sqrt{\tfrac{4}{9}}}.$

There is no need to work this out. It is obviously negative, so the stationary value is a maximum.

The maximum value of $f(x)$ is therefore

$$f\left(\tfrac{4}{9}\right) = \tfrac{4}{9}\left(1 - \sqrt{\tfrac{4}{9}}\right) = \tfrac{4}{9} \times \left(1 - \tfrac{2}{3}\right) = \tfrac{4}{9} \times \tfrac{1}{3} = \tfrac{4}{27}.$$

This completes the solution, but it is interesting to check it by considering the shape of the graph of $f(x) = x(1 - \sqrt{x})$. Obviously $f(0) = f(1) = 0$, and the expression in the bracket is positive if $0 < x < 1$ and negative if $x > 1$. So the value of the function starts at 0 when $x = 0$, rises to a maximum value of $\frac{4}{27}$, when $x = \frac{4}{9}$, then falls to 0 again when $x = 1$. After that it becomes negative.

Example 11.6.2

Find the turning points on the graph of $y = x^2 + \dfrac{1}{x^2}$, and decide whether they are maximum or minimum points.

The expression has no meaning when $x = 0$, so there is a break in the graph.

Differentiating, write the equation as $y = x^2 + x^{-2}$ so that

$$\frac{dy}{dx} = 2x - 2x^{-3} = 2x - \frac{2}{x^3}.$$

There are stationary points where

$$2x - \frac{2}{x^3} = 0$$

which is where $x = \dfrac{1}{x^3}$, that is, $x^4 = 1$, so $x = -1$ or $x = 1$.

To decide whether these give maximum or minimum points, differentiate again to get

$$\frac{d^2y}{dx^2} = 2 - (-6x^{-4}) = 2 + \frac{6}{x^4}.$$

This expression is clearly positive for all values of x (except 0, where it has no meaning), so the graph bends upwards everywhere. Therefore both stationary points are minimum points.

Display this graph on your graphic calculator to see how this can happen.

Finally, you have to find the values of y at these points, which are

$$(-1)^2 + \frac{1}{(-1)^2} = 2 \text{ and } 1^2 + \frac{1}{1^2} = 2.$$

The graph has two minimum points, at $(-1, 2)$ and $(1, 2)$.

The next example is of a graph which has a minimum point at which $\dfrac{dy}{dx}$ is not 0. You may leave it out if you wish, and go straight to Exercise 11E.

Example 11.6.3*

Find the turning points on the graph of $y = x^{\frac{2}{3}}(1 - x)$, and determine whether they are maxima or minima.

Begin by noticing that $x^{\frac{2}{3}} = \sqrt[3]{x^2}$ has a value whether x is positive or negative, because x^2 is positive in either case. Also, this value is positive, because the cube root of a positive number is positive. So there are no values of x for which the graph doesn't exist.

The expression for y when multiplied out is $y = x^{\frac{2}{3}} - x^{\frac{5}{3}}$, which gives

$$\frac{dy}{dx} = \tfrac{2}{3}x^{-\frac{1}{3}} - \tfrac{5}{3}x^{\frac{2}{3}}.$$

This can be written as

$$\frac{dy}{dx} = \tfrac{1}{3}x^{-\frac{1}{3}}(2 - 5x).$$

The only value of x for which $\dfrac{dy}{dx} = 0$ is where $2 - 5x = 0$, that is $x = 0.4$. But you also have to consider $x = 0$, where $\dfrac{dy}{dx}$ does not exist, as a possible turning point.

Since $\dfrac{dy}{dx}$ doesn't exist at $x = 0$, $\dfrac{d^2y}{dx^2}$ certainly doesn't exist. So for $x = 0$, at least, you have to use a table of signs. In fact, since the arithmetic is quite complicated, it is just as easy to use a table of signs for both values of x.

Note that $x^{-\frac{1}{3}}$, that is $\dfrac{1}{\sqrt[3]{x}}$, is positive when x is positive, and negative when x is negative.

	$x < 0$	$x = 0$	$0 < x < 0.4$	$x = 0.4$	$x > 0.4$
$\tfrac{1}{3}x^{-\frac{1}{3}}$	$-$	no value	$+$	$+$	$+$
$2 - 5x$	$+$	$+$	$+$	0	$-$
$\dfrac{dy}{dx}$	$-$	no value	$+$	0	$-$

Now notice that, although $\dfrac{dy}{dx}$ does not have a value when $x = 0$, the table shows that $\dfrac{dy}{dx} < 0$ in an interval to the left of 0, and $\dfrac{dy}{dx} > 0$ in an interval to the right of 0. This was the condition given in Section 11.2 for the graph to have a minimum point at $x = 0$. At $x = 0.4$ the graph has an ordinary maximum point.

The values of y at the two points are 0 and $\sqrt[3]{0.4^2} \times 0.6 = 0.3257\ldots$.

Fig. 11.21 shows the graph, with a minimum at $(0, 0)$ and a maximum at $(0.4, 0.326)$ correct to 3 decimal places.

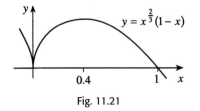

Fig. 11.21

Exercise 11E

1 Find the stationary points on the following curves, and whether they are maximum or minimum points. Check your answers with a graphic calculator.

(a) $y = x + \dfrac{1}{x}$

(b) $y = x + \dfrac{4}{x^2}$

(c) $y = 2\sqrt{x} - x$

(d) $y = x^2 - 4\sqrt{x}$

(e) $y = \dfrac{1}{x} - \dfrac{1}{x^2}$

(f) $y = 4x^2 - \dfrac{1}{x}$

(g) $y = \sqrt{x} + \dfrac{4}{x}$

(h) $y = \dfrac{1}{x} - \dfrac{3}{x^3}$

(i) $y = x - 12\sqrt[3]{x}$

2 Find the interval(s) of values of x for which the following functions are increasing.

(a) $y = \sqrt{x} + \dfrac{2}{\sqrt{x}}$

(b) $y = x^3 + \dfrac{3}{x}$

(c) $y = x - \dfrac{1}{x}$

3* Find the turning points on the following curves, and whether they are maximum or minimum points.

(a) $y = \dfrac{2}{x^4} - \dfrac{1}{x}$

(b) $y = \dfrac{x - 3}{x^4}$

(c) $y = \dfrac{(x + 1)^2}{x}$

(d) $y = \dfrac{x^4 + 16}{x^2}$

(e) $y = x^{\frac{4}{3}}(7 - x)$

(f) $y = x^{\frac{1}{3}}(4 - x)$

Miscellaneous exercise 11

1 Use differentiation to find the coordinates of the stationary points on the curve

$$y = x + \frac{4}{x}$$

and determine whether each stationary point is a maximum point or a minimum point.

Find the set of values of x for which y increases as x increases. (OCR)

2 (a) Find the stationary points on the graph of $y = 12x + 3x^2 - 2x^3$ and sketch the graph.

   (b) How does your sketch show that the equation $12x + 3x^2 - 2x^3 = 0$ has exactly three real roots?

   (c) Use your graph to show that the equation $12x + 3x^2 - 2x^3 = -5$ also has exactly three real roots.

   (d) For what range of values of k does the equation $12x + 3x^2 - 2x^3 = k$ have
       (i) exactly three real roots,   (ii) only one real root?

3 Find the coordinates of the stationary points on the graph of

$$y = x^3 - 12x - 12$$

and sketch the graph.

Find the set of values of k for which the equation

$$x^3 - 12x - 12 = k$$

has more than one real root. (OCR)

4 Find the coordinates of the stationary points on the graph of $y = x^3 + x^2$. Sketch the graph and hence write down the set of values of the constant k for which the equation $x^3 + x^2 = k$ has three distinct real roots.

5 Find the coordinates of the stationary points on the curve with equation $y = x(x - 1)^2$. Sketch the curve.

   Find the set of real values of k such that the equation $x(x - 1)^2 = k^2$ has exactly one real root.   (OCR, adapted)

6 It is given that $f(x) = 5x^3 - 15x^2$.

   (a) Find $f'(x)$.

   (b) Find $f''(x)$.

   (c) Find the x-coordinates of the stationary points on the curve $y = 5x^3 - 15x^2$.

   (d) Determine whether each stationary point is a maximum point or a minimum point.   (OCR)

7 (a) Find the coordinates of the stationary points on the curve $y = 2x^3 - 3x^2 - 12x - 7$.

   (b) Determine whether each stationary point is a maximum point or a minimum point.

   (c) It is given that $2x^3 - 3x^2 - 12x - 7$ can be written as $(x + 1)^2(2x - 7)$. Sketch the curve $y = (x + 1)^2(2x - 7)$.

   (d) Write down the set of values of the constant k for which the equation $2x^3 - 3x^2 - 12x - 7 = k$ has exactly one real solution.   (OCR)

8* Find the coordinates of the stationary points on the graph of $y = 3x^4 - 4x^3 - 12x^2 + 10$, and sketch the graph. For what values of k does the equation $3x^4 - 4x^3 - 12x^2 + 10 = k$ have

   (a) exactly four roots,   (b) exactly two roots?

9* Show that the stationary point on $y = ax^2 + bx + c$ has coordinates $\left(-\dfrac{b}{2a}, \dfrac{4ac - b^2}{4a}\right)$.

   Hence show that the condition for $ax^2 + bx + c = 0$ to have no roots is $b^2 - 4ac < 0$. (You should consider the cases $a > 0$ and $a < 0$ separately.)

12 Applications of differentiation

In the last few chapters you have learnt what differentiation means and how to differentiate a lot of functions. This chapter shows how you can apply these ideas to real-world problems. When you have completed it, you should

- know that you can interpret a derivative as a rate of change of one variable with respect to another
- be able to apply these techniques to real-world problems.

12.1 Derivatives as rates of change

The quantities x and y in a relationship $y = f(x)$ are often called **variables**, because x can stand for any number for which $f(x)$ has a meaning, and y for any value of the function. When you draw the graph you have a free choice of the values of x, and then work out y. So x is called the **independent variable** and y the **dependent variable**.

These variables often stand for physical or economic quantities, and then it is convenient to use other letters which suggest what these quantities are: for example t for time, V for volume, C for cost, P for population, and so on.

To illustrate this consider a situation familiar to deep sea divers, that pressure increases with depth below sea level. The independent variable is the depth, z metres, below the surface.

> It will soon be clear why the letter d was avoided for the depth. The letter z is often used for distances in the vertical direction.

The dependent variable is the pressure, p, measured in bars. At the surface the diver experiences only atmospheric pressure, about 1 bar, but the pressure increases as the diver descends. At offshore (coastal) depths the variables are connected approximately by the equation

$$p = 1 + 0.1z.$$

The (z, p) graph is a straight line, shown in Fig. 12.1.

The constant 0.1 in the equation is the amount that the pressure goes up for each extra metre of depth. This is the 'rate of change of pressure with respect to depth'.

This can be expressed algebraically using the 'delta' notation introduced in Section 5.1. If the diver descends a further distance of δz metres, the pressure goes up by δp bars; this rate of change is $\dfrac{\delta p}{\delta z}$. It is represented by the gradient of the graph.

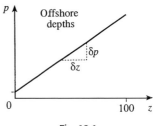

Fig. 12.1

But at ocean depths the (z, p) graph is no longer a straight line: it has the form of a curve which bends upwards, as in Fig. 12.2.

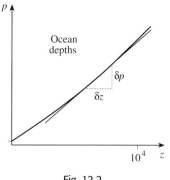

Fig. 12.2

The quantity $\dfrac{\delta p}{\delta z}$ now represents the average rate of change over the extra depth δz. It is represented by the gradient of the chord in Fig. 12.2.

You have already met this idea, and used this notation, in finding the gradient of the graph of $y = f(x)$. It is especially useful when you want to use different letters as variables to describe particular quantities.

In Section 5.5 the symbol $\dfrac{dy}{dx}$ was used to denote the gradient of the tangent, so that

$$\frac{dy}{dx} = \lim_{\delta x \to 0} \frac{\delta y}{\delta x}.$$

In just the same way you can use the symbol $\dfrac{dp}{dz}$, defined as

$$\frac{dp}{dz} = \lim_{\delta z \to 0} \frac{\delta p}{\delta z}.$$

It is important to understand the difference between $\dfrac{\delta p}{\delta z}$ and $\dfrac{dp}{dz}$. The symbol $\dfrac{\delta p}{\delta z}$ means the average rate of change of pressure with depth between one depth and another. For example, if the pressure is 125 bars at a depth of 1000 metres and 138 bars at a depth of 1100 metres, then $\delta p = 138 - 125 = 13$, $\delta z = 1100 - 1000 = 100$, so that $\dfrac{\delta p}{\delta z} = 0.13$. That is, the average rate of increase of pressure with depth between 1000 metres and 1100 metres is 0.13 bars per metre.

But if, for example, $\dfrac{dp}{dz} = 0.14$ when $z = 1100$, this means that at the particular depth of 1100 metres the pressure is increasing at a rate of 0.14 bars per metre. On a graph showing p against z, $\dfrac{\delta p}{\delta z}$ is the gradient of a chord and $\dfrac{dp}{dz}$ is the gradient of a tangent.

> If x and y are the independent and dependent variables respectively in a functional relationship, then
>
> $\dfrac{\delta y}{\delta x}$ represents the average rate of change of y with respect to x over an interval of values of x,
>
> $\dfrac{dy}{dx}$ represents the instantaneous rate of change of y with respect to x for a particular value of x.

This notation can be used in a wide variety of contexts. For example, if the area of burnt grass, t minutes after a fire has started, is A square metres, then $\dfrac{dA}{dt}$ measures the rate at which the fire is spreading in square metres per minute. If, at a certain point on the Earth's surface, distances of x metres on the ground are represented by distances of y metres on a map, then $\dfrac{dy}{dx}$ represents the scale of the map at that point.

Example 12.1.1
Research into the growth of juvenile herrings suggests that after t years their mean length, l cm, is given approximately by the equation $l = 8t - \frac{1}{2}t^2$. According to this formula,

(a) find the rate of growth after 3 years,

(b) find how many years it will take the herrings to become fully grown.

The rate at which the herrings are growing is given by the derivative $\dfrac{dl}{dt} = 8 - t$.

Since the units of length and time are centimetres and years, this equation gives the rate of growth in centimetres per year.

(a) When $t = 3$, $\dfrac{dl}{dt} = 8 - 3 = 5$. So after 3 years the herrings are growing at a rate of 5 centimetres per year.

(b) When the herrings are fully grown the rate of growth is zero, so $\dfrac{dl}{dt} = 0$. This occurs when $t = 8$. So the herrings will be fully grown after 8 years.

Notice in this example that, according to the given equation, the rate of growth becomes negative when $t > 8$. This suggests that the herrings would become shorter, which is unlikely! It is far more probable that, since the research was based on measuring juvenile herrings up to 6 years old, the formula is valid only for a certain interval of values of t. This interval will certainly not extend beyond $t = 8$.

Example 12.1.2
A boy is exactly 4 years older than his sister. Write an expression for the ratio of the boy's age to his sister's age when the sister is x years old. Find the rate at which this ratio is changing when the sister is 20 years old.

When the sister's age is x, her brother's age is $x + 4$. So, denoting the ratio by r,

$r = \dfrac{x+4}{x}$, which can be written as $r = 1 + \dfrac{4}{x} = 1 + 4x^{-1}$.

The rate at which the ratio is changing is measured by the derivative $\dfrac{dr}{dx}$.

Differentiating,

$$\frac{dr}{dx} = -4x^{-2} = -\frac{4}{x^2}.$$

When $x = 20$, $\dfrac{dr}{dx} = -\dfrac{4}{20^2} = -0.01$. The ratio is going down at a rate of 0.01 per year.

You can check the answer to this example by calculating the actual ratios when $x = 19$, 20 and 21; thus $\dfrac{23}{19} = 1.2105...$, $\dfrac{24}{20} = 1.2$ and $\dfrac{25}{21} = 1.1904...$.

Between $x = 20$ and $x = 21$, $\delta x = 21 - 20 = 1$ and $\delta r = 1.1904... - 1.2 = -0.0095...$ so the average rate of change is $\dfrac{\delta r}{\delta x} = -0.0095...$.

Between $x = 20$ and $x = 19$, $\delta x = 19 - 20 = -1$ and $\delta r = 1.2105... - 1.2 = 0.0105...$ so the average rate of change is $\dfrac{\delta r}{\delta x} = -0.0105...$.

These average rates are approximately equal to the rate $\dfrac{dr}{dx} = -0.01$ when $x = 20$.

> Draw a sketch of the (x, r) graph in the neighbourhood of $x = 20$ to illustrate these results.

Example 12.1.3

A sprinter in a women's 100-metre race reaches her top speed of 12 metres per second after she has run 36 metres. Up to that distance her speed is proportional to the square root of the distance she has run. Show that until she reaches full speed the rate of change of her speed with respect to distance is inversely proportional to her speed.

Suppose that after she has run x metres her speed is S metres per second. You are told that, up to $x = 36$, $S = k\sqrt{x}$, and also that $S = 12$ when $x = 36$. So

$$12 = k\sqrt{36}, \quad \text{giving} \quad k = \tfrac{12}{6} = 2.$$

The (x, S) relationship is therefore

$$S = 2\sqrt{x} \quad \text{for} \quad 0 < x < 36.$$

The rate of change of speed with respect to distance is the derivative $\dfrac{dS}{dx}$.

Since $S = 2x^{\frac{1}{2}}$,

$$\frac{dS}{dx} = 2 \times \tfrac{1}{2}x^{-\frac{1}{2}} = \frac{1}{\sqrt{x}}.$$

Since $\sqrt{x} = \dfrac{S}{2}$, $\dfrac{dS}{dx}$ can be written as $\dfrac{2}{S}$.

The rate of change is therefore inversely proportional to her speed.

If she maintains her top speed for the rest of the race, the rate of change of speed with respect to distance drops to 0 for $x > 36$. Fig. 12.3 shows that the gradient, which represents the rate of change, gets smaller as her speed increases, and then becomes zero once she reaches her top speed.

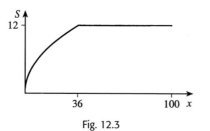

Fig. 12.3

Exercise 12A

1 In each part of this question express each derivative as 'the rate of change of ... with respect to ...', and state its physical significance.

(a) $\dfrac{dh}{dx}$, where h is the height above sea level, and x is the distance travelled (measured horizontally), along a straight road

(b) $\dfrac{dN}{dt}$, where N is the number of people in a stadium at time t after the gates open

(c) $\dfrac{dM}{dr}$, where M is the magnetic force at a distance r from a magnet

(d) $\dfrac{dv}{dt}$, where v is the velocity of a train moving on a straight track at time t

(e) $\dfrac{dq}{dS}$, where q is the rate at which petrol is used in a car in litres per km, and S is the speed of the car in km per hour

2 Defining suitable notation and units, express each of the following as a derivative.

(a) the rate of change of atmospheric pressure with respect to height above sea level

(b) the rate of change of temperature with respect to the time of day

(c) the rate at which the tide is rising

(d) the rate at which a baby's weight increases in the first weeks of life

3 (a) Find $\dfrac{dz}{dt}$ where $z = 3t^2 + 7t - 5$.   (b) Find $\dfrac{d\theta}{dx}$ where $\theta = x - \sqrt{x}$.

(c) Find $\dfrac{dx}{dy}$ where $x = y + \dfrac{3}{y^2}$.   (d) Find $\dfrac{dr}{dt}$ where $r = t^2 + \dfrac{1}{\sqrt{t}}$.

(e) Find $\dfrac{dm}{dt}$ where $m = (t+3)^2$.   (f) Find $\dfrac{df}{ds}$ where $f = 2s^6 - 3s^2$.

(g) Find $\dfrac{dw}{dt}$ where $w = 5t$.   (h) Find $\dfrac{dR}{dr}$ where $R = \dfrac{1 - r^3}{r^2}$.

4 Devise suitable notation to express each of the following in mathematical form.

(a) The distance travelled along the motorway is increasing at a constant rate.

(b) The rate at which a savings bank deposit grows is proportional to the amount of money deposited.

(c) The rate at which the diameter of a tree increases is a function of the air temperature.

5 A hot air balloon is h metres above the ground t minutes after it is released. While it is ascending, the equation connecting h with t is $h = 100t - 2t^2$.

(a) Find the average rate at which the balloon gains height during

(i) the first minute,   (ii) the 20th minute.

(b) Find the rate at which the balloon is gaining height after 10 minutes.

(c) Find how long the balloon takes to reach its greatest height.

6 The index of pollution, I, at a distance of x kilometres from a city centre is given by $I = (x - 15)^2$. The formula is valid for values of x between 0 and 10.

(a) Find the average rate of decrease of the index with respect to distance in moving from the centre of the city to a point 5 kilometres from the centre.

(b) Find the average rate of decrease of the index with respect to distance in moving from a point 5 kilometres from the centre to a point 10 kilometres from the centre.

(c) Find the rate of decrease of the index with respect to distance at a point 5 kilometres from the city centre.

7 The number of people who have completed a city marathon t hours after the start is modelled by the formula $N = 19\,200 - 21\,600t + 7200t^2 - 600t^3$ for values of t between 2 and 6. The organisers use this equation to plan how many stewards they will need to have on duty at the finishing line.

(a) How many runners are expected to have completed the course after 6 hours?

(b) What is the expected average rate per minute of arrival of runners at the finish

(i) between 2 and 3 hours after the start,

(ii) between 3 and $3\frac{1}{2}$ hours after the start?

(c) At what rate per minute are runners expected to be arriving at the finish 3 hours after the start?

8 (a) A circle of radius r has area $A = \pi r^2$. Find $\dfrac{dA}{dr}$.

(b) A sphere of radius r has volume $V = \frac{4}{3}\pi r^3$. Find $\dfrac{dV}{dr}$.

What do you notice about the answers?

9 The quantity of light received by a telescope from a star x light-years away is denoted by Q. It is known that, for stars with a given luminosity, $Q = \dfrac{C}{x^2}$, where C is a constant. Find $\dfrac{dQ}{dx}$, and deduce that $\dfrac{dQ}{dx} = -\dfrac{2Q}{x}$.

10 The pressure and volume of a quantity of air are denoted by P and V. As the air expands adiabatically, the values of P and V are related by the equation $PV^{1.4} = k$, where k is constant. Find $\dfrac{dP}{dV}$ in terms of V and k. Hence show that $\dfrac{dP}{dV} = -\dfrac{1.4P}{V}$.

11 (a) A simple pendulum consists of a small metal ball attached to a fixed point by a cord of length l centimetres. It takes T seconds to make one swing, where $T = 0.2\sqrt{l}$. Find $\dfrac{dT}{dl}$.

(b) The cord originally has length 2.5 metres. If it is lengthened by 2 millimetres, calculate what effect this will have on the time of swing

(i) by using your answer to part (a),   (ii) by direct evaluation of T.

12.2   Second derivatives in practice

A local newspaper reports that 'house prices are increasing, but not as fast as they were'. This is a typical instance of a second derivative in everyday life. If p denotes the mean price of houses in the town, and t the time, then a (t, p) graph would look like Fig. 12.4.

The gradient $\dfrac{\mathrm{d}p}{\mathrm{d}t}$ represents the rate at which house prices are going up. The report says that this rate is going down, so the gradient is decreasing. The graph bends downwards, so the second derivative is negative. This second derivative is written as $\dfrac{\mathrm{d}^2 p}{\mathrm{d}t^2}$.

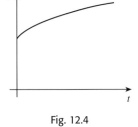

Fig. 12.4

Second derivatives are important in many applications. For example, the number of UK households possessing a computer has been increasing for a long time. Manufacturers will estimate the number of such households, H, in year t, and note that the graph of H against t has a positive gradient $\dfrac{\mathrm{d}H}{\mathrm{d}t}$. But to plan ahead they need to know whether this rate of increase is itself increasing (so that they should increase production of models for first-time users) or decreasing (in which case they might target existing customers to update to more sophisticated equipment). So it is the value of $\dfrac{\mathrm{d}^2 H}{\mathrm{d}t^2}$ which affects strategic planning decisions.

Similarly, a weather forecaster observing the atmospheric pressure p at time t may not be too concerned if $\dfrac{\mathrm{d}p}{\mathrm{d}t}$ is negative; pressure goes up and down all the time. But if she also notices that $\dfrac{\mathrm{d}^2 p}{\mathrm{d}t^2}$ is negative, it may be time to issue a warning of severe weather.

An important application is to motion in a straight line, such as a car travelling along a road. If x is the distance it has travelled in a time t (in appropriate units), then $\dfrac{\mathrm{d}x}{\mathrm{d}t}$ is the rate at which the distance is increasing; this is the speed, or velocity, of the car. So $\dfrac{\mathrm{d}^2 x}{\mathrm{d}t^2}$ is the rate at which the speed is increasing; this is the acceleration of the car.

Example 12.2.1
A government plans the economy on the assumption that the population, P millions, for the next 15 years can be modelled by the equation $P = 60 + 0.02t^3 - 0.001t^4$.

(a) How large is the population expected to be in 10 years time?

(b) At what annual rate is the population expected to be increasing in 10 years time?

(c) During what period does the government expect the annual rate of increase of the population to be increasing?

(a) Substituting $t = 10$ in the equation for P gives

$$P = 60 + 0.02 \times 1000 - 0.001 \times 10\,000 = 60 + 20 - 10 = 70.$$

Since P is the population in millions, the population in 10 years time is expected to be 70 million.

(b) The rate of increase of the population is given by

$$\frac{\mathrm{d}P}{\mathrm{d}t} = 0.02 \times (3t^2) - 0.001 \times (4t^3) = 0.06t^2 - 0.004t^3.$$

When $t = 10$, the value of $\dfrac{\mathrm{d}P}{\mathrm{d}t}$ is

$$0.06 \times 100 - 0.004 \times 1000 = 6 - 4 = 2.$$

In 10 years time it is expected that the population will be increasing at a rate of 2 million per year.

(c) This question asks about the rate of increase of $\dfrac{\mathrm{d}P}{\mathrm{d}t}$, which is

$$\frac{\mathrm{d}^2 P}{\mathrm{d}t^2} = 0.06 \times (2t) - 0.004 \times (3t^2) = 0.12t - 0.012t^2 = 0.012t(10 - t).$$

This is positive when $t(10 - t) > 0$, that is when $0 < t < 10$.

The rate of increase of the population is expected to increase for the next 10 years.

This is illustrated by the graph in Fig. 12.5. Between $t = 0$ and $t = 10$ the graph bends upwards, which shows that the rate of increase of the population is increasing. After that, until $t = 15$, the graph bends downwards; the rate of increase of the population decreases, although the population is still increasing.

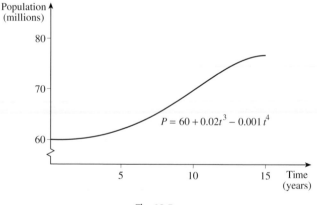

Fig. 12.5

12.3   Maximum and minimum problems

In many real-world situations the aim is to find a strategy which will make some quantity as large or as small as possible. For example, a manufacturer may want to price goods so as to maximise the firm's profits, or to design a component so as to minimise the amount of raw material used. The techniques described in the last chapter can often be useful in reaching such decisions.

The procedures are essentially similar to those for finding maximum and minimum points on graphs. But there are some differences.

One is that in practical applications you will only want to consider values of the independent variable for which the problem makes sense. For example, if the independent variable is a length x metres, you will be interested only in values of the function when $x > 0$.

Another difference is that in a practical situation it will sometimes be obvious from the nature of the problem whether the quantity has a maximum or a minimum value. Steps 3 and 4 in the procedure (in Section 11.5), which are used to distinguish maximum points from minimum points, then simply serve as a check that the technique has been correctly applied.

Example 12.3.1
Fig. 12.6 shows the corner of a garden, bordered by two walls at right angles. A gardener has 30 metres of rabbit fencing. What is the largest rectangular area she can fence off?

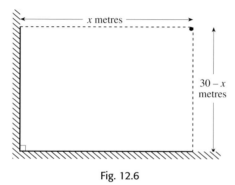

Fig. 12.6

If she makes her rectangle x metres long, she has $(30 - x)$ metres left for the other side of the rectangle. In this way she can fence off an area of $A\,\text{m}^2$, where

$$A = x(30 - x) = 30x - x^2.$$

Notice that this equation only applies if $0 < x < 30$.

The area takes its maximum value when $\dfrac{\mathrm{d}A}{\mathrm{d}x} = 0$, where

$$\frac{\mathrm{d}A}{\mathrm{d}x} = 30 - 2x.$$

So $\dfrac{\mathrm{d}A}{\mathrm{d}x} = 0$ when $x = 15$.

To check that this gives a maximum value of A, find

$$\frac{\mathrm{d}^2A}{\mathrm{d}x^2} = -2.$$

Since this is negative, $x = 15$ gives a maximum value.

To find the maximum area, substitute $x = 15$ in $A = x(30 - x)$ to get

$$A = 15 \times (30 - 15) = 15 \times 15 = 225.$$

The largest area the gardener can fence off is $225\,\text{m}^2$.

Example 12.3.2

Towards the end of the day a market trader has 20 boxes of peaches left unsold. By tomorrow they will be useless. He reckons that if he offers them for sale at x pence a box, he will be able to dispose of $(20 - \frac{1}{5}x)$ boxes. At what price should he offer them to make the most money?

The trader will not sell any boxes if he sets the price at 100 pence. The only values of x which are of interest are between 0 and 100.

If he sells $(20 - \frac{1}{5}x)$ boxes at x pence a box, he will make $x(20 - \frac{1}{5}x)$ pence. He wants to maximise this function.

Let $\quad f(x) = x(20 - \frac{1}{5}x) = 20x - \frac{1}{5}x^2$.

Then $\quad f'(x) = 20 - \frac{2}{5}x$.

The value of x which makes $f'(x) = 0$ is given by

$$\tfrac{2}{5}x = 20, \quad \text{that is } x = 50.$$

This obviously gives a maximum rather than a minimum, but you can check this by finding $f''(x) = -\frac{2}{5}$. Since this is negative, $x = 50$ gives a maximum value of the function.

He should offer the peaches at 50 pence a box.

Example 12.3.3

A pioneer wants to build a storage shed in the shape of a cuboid with a square base, with a capacity of 32 cubic metres. To conserve materials, he wants to make the total area of the roof and the four sides as small as possible. What are the best dimensions for the shed, and what is the total area with these dimensions?

The shed is illustrated in Fig. 12.7. Suppose that the base is a square of side x metres. Then, since the volume is to be 32 cubic metres, the height must be $\dfrac{32}{x^2}$ metres.

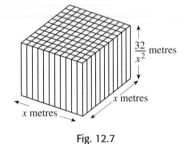

Fig. 12.7

The roof is square with area x^2 square metres. Each side is a rectangle with area $x \times \dfrac{32}{x^2}$ square metres, which is $\dfrac{32}{x}$ square metres. So, if the total area of the roof and the four sides is A square metres,

$$A = x^2 + 4 \times \frac{32}{x} = x^2 + \frac{128}{x}.$$

The problem is to choose x so that A is as small as possible. To do this, follow the procedure for finding a minimum point. Note that only positive values of x are relevant in the problem.

Step 1 $\dfrac{\mathrm{d}A}{\mathrm{d}x} = 2x - \dfrac{128}{x^2}.$

Step 2 $\dfrac{\mathrm{d}A}{\mathrm{d}x} = 0$ when $2x - \dfrac{128}{x^2} = 0$, which gives $x^3 = 64$, $x = 4$.

Step 3 $\dfrac{\mathrm{d}^2 A}{\mathrm{d}x^2} = 2 + \dfrac{256}{x^3}.$

Step 4 When $x = 4$, $\dfrac{\mathrm{d}^2 A}{\mathrm{d}x^2}$ has value $2 + \dfrac{256}{4^3} = 2 + 4 = 6$, which is positive, so the stationary value is a minimum.

Step 5 When $x = 4$, $A = 4^2 + \dfrac{128}{4} = 16 + 32 = 48.$

This shows that the best dimensions for the shed are to make the base 4 metres square and the height 2 metres. This gives a total area for the roof and the sides of 48 square metres.

Notice that, in solving this problem, it was necessary to begin by choosing a suitable independent variable (in this case the length of a side of the square base). Then an equation was found for the quantity to be minimised (the area of the shed) in terms of this independent variable. Only then can you begin to use the procedure for finding the minimum point of the graph. Finally, once the procedure has been completed, the result has to be interpreted in terms of the original problem.

In each of the following examples the argument has a similar pattern.

Example 12.3.4
A wire of length 4 metres is cut into two pieces, and each piece is bent into a square. How should this be done so that the two squares together have
(a) the smallest area,   (b) the largest area?

Let the two pieces have lengths x metres and $(4 - x)$ metres. The areas of the squares are then $\left(\frac{1}{4}x\right)^2$ and $\left(\frac{1}{4}(4 - x)\right)^2$ square metres; see Fig. 12.8. So the total area, $y\,\mathrm{m}^2$, is given by

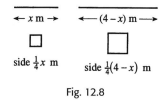

Fig. 12.8

$$y = \tfrac{1}{16}(x^2 + (16 - 8x + x^2))$$
$$= \tfrac{1}{8}(x^2 - 4x + 8).$$

You can evaluate this expression for any real number x, but the problem only has meaning if $0 < x < 4$. Fig. 12.9 shows the graph of the area function for this interval.

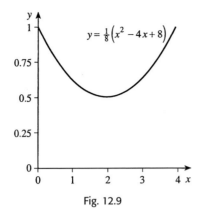

Fig. 12.9

(a) The smallest area is represented by the minimum point on the graph. Since $\frac{dy}{dx} = \frac{1}{8}(2x - 4) = \frac{1}{4}(x - 2)$, this is where $x = 2$. Also $\frac{d^2y}{dx^2} = \frac{1}{4} > 0$, which confirms that the stationary point is a minimum.

So the area is smallest when the wire is cut into two equal parts, each of length 2 metres. The area is then $\frac{1}{8}(2^2 - 4 \times 2 + 8)\,\text{m}^2$, that is, $\frac{1}{2}\,\text{m}^2$.

Since y is a quadratic function of x, this answer could also be found by writing y in completed square form, as $y = \frac{1}{8}\{(x - 2)^2 + 4\}$. As $(x - 2)^2 \geqslant 0$, y is least when $x = 2$, and the least value of y is $\frac{1}{2}$.

(b) From the graph it looks as if the largest value of y is 1, when $x = 0$ and $x = 4$. But these values of x are excluded, since they do not produce two pieces of wire. You can get areas as near to 1 square metre as you like, but you cannot achieve this target. Strictly speaking, there is no largest area.

It is important to notice in this example that the 'largest value' is not associated with a maximum point on the graph, as defined in Section 11.2. Although largest and smallest values can often be found by using the procedure for locating maximum and minimum points, there are exceptional cases when this does not happen.

Example 12.3.5

It is found that the flow of traffic on congested roads can be improved by lowering the speed at which it travels. This is because at higher speeds vehicles travel further apart. A traffic researcher models the distance between vehicles at a speed of S metres per second as D metres, given by the equation $D = \frac{1}{10}S^2 + \frac{1}{2}S + 10$. At this speed the time interval between successive vehicles passing a checkpoint is T seconds, where $T = \frac{D}{S}$. Use this model to find the speed which minimises this time, and the number of vehicles expected to pass the checkpoint in a minute at this speed.

Note that in this situation you are only interested in positive values of S.

You want to find where $\frac{dT}{dS} = 0$, so write the equation for T in the form

$$T = \frac{D}{S} = \frac{\frac{1}{10}S^2 + \frac{1}{2}S + 10}{S} = \frac{\frac{1}{10}S^2}{S} + \frac{\frac{1}{2}S}{S} + \frac{10}{S} = \frac{1}{10}S + \frac{1}{2} + 10S^{-1}.$$

Then $\dfrac{dT}{dS} = \dfrac{1}{10} - 10S^{-2} = \dfrac{1}{10} - \dfrac{10}{S^2}$.

The minimum time interval will occur when

$$\dfrac{1}{10} - \dfrac{10}{S^2} = 0,$$

that is when $S^2 = 100$. Since only positive values of S are of interest, $S = 10$.

To check that this is a minimum, find

$$\dfrac{d^2 T}{dS^2} = -10(-2S^{-3}) = \dfrac{20}{S^3},$$

which is certainly positive. So $S = 10$ gives a minimum value for T.

Substituting $S = 10$ in the expression for T gives the minimum value

$$T = \tfrac{1}{10} \times 10 + \tfrac{1}{2} + \dfrac{10}{10} = 1 + \tfrac{1}{2} + 1 = 2\tfrac{1}{2}.$$

So at 10 metres per second a vehicle passes the checkpoint every $2\tfrac{1}{2}$ seconds. The number of cars passing the checkpoint in a minute is $60 \div 2\tfrac{1}{2}$, which is 24.

In some problems of this kind the quantity you want to maximise or minimise is given by a complicated formula, perhaps including some algebraic constants, and you need to begin by disentangling the formula to simplify the mathematics.

Example 12.3.6

A hole is drilled in a metal plate, and the plate is suspended from a fixed horizontal pin which passes through the hole. If the plate is set swinging as a pendulum, the time T that it takes to make one swing is given by the formula $T = 2\pi \sqrt{\dfrac{x^2 + k^2}{gx}}$, where k and g are positive constants and x is the distance of the centre of mass of the plate from the hole. Find the value of x which makes the time for a swing as short as possible.

You don't know how to differentiate the formula for T. But notice that it can be written as

$$T = \dfrac{2\pi}{\sqrt{g}} \times \sqrt{y}, \quad \text{where} \quad y = \dfrac{x^2 + k^2}{x}.$$

Since $\dfrac{2\pi}{\sqrt{g}}$ is constant, you only need to find the value of x which makes y as small as possible. And you can put the expression for y into a form which can be differentiated by writing

$$y = \dfrac{x^2 + k^2}{x} = \dfrac{x^2}{x} + \dfrac{k^2}{x} = x + k^2 x^{-1}.$$

This formula still includes the letter k, but since this is constant you can treat it just as if it was a number.

So $\dfrac{dy}{dx} = 1 + k^2 \times (-1x^{-2}) = 1 - \dfrac{k^2}{x^2}.$

To find where y is least, the equation $\dfrac{dy}{dx} = 0$ gives

$1 = \dfrac{k^2}{x^2},$ that is $x^2 = k^2.$

In this problem only positive values of x are relevant, so $x = k$.

You can check that this is in fact a minimum rather than a maximum by finding

$\dfrac{d^2 y}{dx^2} = k^2 \times (2x^{-3}) = \dfrac{2k^2}{x^3}.$

When $x = k$, this is equal to $\dfrac{2}{k}$, which is positive.

The time that the pendulum takes to swing is least when x is equal to k.

Example 12.3.7
A hollow cone with base radius a cm and height b cm is placed on a table. What is the volume of the largest cylinder that can be hidden underneath it?

The volume of a cylinder of radius r cm and height h cm is V cm^3, where

$V = \pi r^2 h.$

You can obviously make this as large as you like by choosing r and h large enough. But in this problem the variables are restricted by the requirement that the cylinder has to fit under the cone. Before you can follow the procedure for finding a maximum, you need to find how this restriction affects the values of r and h.

Fig. 12.10 shows the three-dimensional set-up, and Fig. 12.11 is a vertical section through the top of the cone.

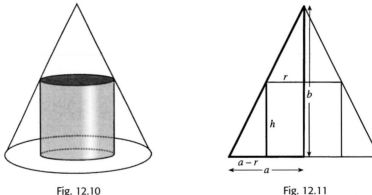

Fig. 12.10   Fig. 12.11

The similar triangles picked out with heavy lines in Fig. 12.11 show that r and h are connected by the equation

$$\frac{h}{a-r} = \frac{b}{a}, \quad \text{so that} \quad h = \frac{b(a-r)}{a}.$$

Substituting this expression for h in the formula for V then gives

$$V = \frac{\pi r^2 b(a-r)}{a} = \left(\frac{\pi b}{a}\right)(ar^2 - r^3).$$

Notice that the original expression for V contains two independent variables r and h. The effect of the substitution is to reduce the number of independent variables to one; h has disappeared, and only r remains. This makes it possible to apply the procedure for finding a maximum.

The physical problem only has meaning if $0 < r < a$. Differentiating by the usual rule (remembering that π, a and b are constants) gives

$$\frac{dV}{dr} = \left(\frac{\pi b}{a}\right)(2ar - 3r^2) = \left(\frac{\pi b}{a}\right)r(2a - 3r).$$

The only value of r in the interval $0 < r < a$ for which $\dfrac{dV}{dr} = 0$ is $\frac{2}{3}a$. It is easy to check that the sign of $\dfrac{dV}{dr}$ is $+$ for $0 < r < \frac{2}{3}a$ and $-$ for $\frac{2}{3}a < r < a$.

Substituting $r = \frac{2}{3}a$ in the expressions for h and V gives

$$h = \frac{b\left(a - \frac{2}{3}a\right)}{a} = \frac{b\left(\frac{1}{3}a\right)}{a} = \frac{1}{3}b,$$

and $\quad V = \pi r^2 h = \pi \left(\frac{2}{3}a\right)^2 \frac{1}{3}b = \frac{4}{27}\pi a^2 b.$

So the cylinder of maximum volume has radius $\frac{2}{3}a$, height $\frac{1}{3}b$, and volume $\frac{4}{27}\pi a^2 b$. Since the volume of the cone is $\frac{1}{3}\pi a^2 b$, the cylinder of maximum volume occupies $\frac{4}{9}$ of the space under the cone.

12.4 Extending $\dfrac{dy}{dx}$ notation

Although $\dfrac{dy}{dx}$ is a symbol which should not be split into smaller bits, it can usefully be adapted by separating off the y, as

$$\frac{d}{dx}y$$

so that if $y = f(x)$, you can write

$$f'(x) = \frac{d}{dx}f(x).$$

This can be used as a convenient shorthand. For example, instead of having to write

$$\text{if } y = x^4 \quad \text{then} \quad \frac{dy}{dx} = 4x^3$$

you can abbreviate this to

$$\frac{d}{dx}x^4 = 4x^3.$$

In this equation $\frac{d}{dx}$ can be thought of as an instruction to differentiate whatever comes after it.

You may have seen calculators which do algebra as well as arithmetic. With these, you can input a function such as x^4, key in 'differentiate', and the output $4x^3$ appears in the display. The symbol $\frac{d}{dx}$, sometimes called the **differential operator**, is the equivalent of pressing the 'differentiate' key.

This explains the notation used for the second derivative, which is what you get by differentiating $\frac{dy}{dx}$; that is,

$$\frac{d}{dx}\frac{dy}{dx}.$$

If you collect the elements of this expression into a single symbol, the top line becomes d^2y, and the bottom line $(dx)^2$. Dropping the brackets, this takes the form

$$\frac{d^2y}{dx^2}.$$

Exercise 12B

1 (a) This graph shows prices, P, plotted against time, t. The rate of inflation, measured by $\frac{dP}{dt}$, is increasing. What does $\frac{d^2P}{dt^2}$ represent and what can be said about its value?

(b) Sketch a graph showing that prices are increasing but that the rate of inflation is slowing down with an overall increase tending to 20%.

2 The graph shows the price, S, of shares in a certain company.

(a) For each stage of the graph comment on $\frac{dS}{dt}$ and $\frac{d^2S}{dt^2}$.

(b) Describe what happened in non-technical language.

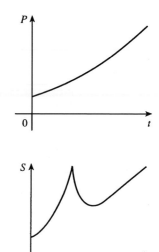

3 Colin sets off for school, which is 800 m from home. His speed is proportional to the distance he still has to go. Let x metres be the distance he has gone, and y metres be the distance that he still has to go.

(a) Sketch graphs of x against t and y against t.

(b) What are the signs of $\frac{dx}{dt}$, $\frac{d^2x}{dt^2}$, $\frac{dy}{dt}$ and $\frac{d^2y}{dt^2}$?

4 The rate of decay of a radioactive substance is proportional to the number, N, of radioactive atoms present at time t.

(a) Write an equation representing this information.

(b) Sketch a graph of N against t.

(c) What is the sign of $\dfrac{d^2 N}{dt^2}$?

5 At a speed of S km per hour my car will travel y kilometres on each litre of petrol, where

$$y = 5 + \tfrac{1}{5}S - \tfrac{1}{800}S^2.$$

Calculate the speed at which the car should be driven for maximum economy.

6 A cricket ball is thrown vertically upwards. At time t seconds its height h metres is given by $h = 20t - 5t^2$. Calculate the ball's maximum height above the ground.

7 The sum of two real numbers x and y is 12. Find the maximum value of their product xy.

8 The product of two positive real numbers x and y is 20. Find the minimum possible value of their sum.

9 The volume of a cylinder is given by the formula $V = \pi r^2 h$. Find the greatest and least values of V if $r + h = 6$.

10 A loop of string of length 1 metre is formed into a rectangle with one pair of opposite sides each x cm. Calculate the value of x which will maximise the area enclosed by the string.

11 One side of a rectangular sheep pen is formed by a hedge. The other three sides are made using fencing. The length of the rectangle is x metres; 120 metres of fencing is available.

(a) Show that the area of the rectangle is $\tfrac{1}{2}x(120 - x)\,\text{m}^2$.

(b) Calculate the maximum possible area of the sheep pen.

12 A rectangular sheet of metal measures 50 cm by 40 cm. Equal squares of side x cm are cut from each corner and discarded. The sheet is then folded up to make a tray of depth x cm. What are the possible values of x? Find the value of x which maximises the capacity of the tray.

13 An open rectangular box is to be made with a square base, and its capacity is to be 4000 cm^3. Find the length of the side of the base when the amount of material used to make the box is as small as possible. (Ignore 'flaps'.)

14 An open cylindrical wastepaper bin, of radius r cm and capacity V cm^3, is to have a surface area of 5000 cm^2.

(a) Show that $V = \tfrac{1}{2}r(5000 - \pi r^2)$.

(b) Calculate the maximum possible capacity of the bin.

15* A circular cylinder is cut out of a sphere of radius 10 cm. Calculate the maximum possible volume of the cylinder. (It is probably best to take as your independent variable the height, or half the height, of the cylinder.)

Miscellaneous exercise 12

1 A particle moves along the x-axis. Its displacement at time t is $x = 6t - t^2$.

   (a) What does $\dfrac{dx}{dt}$ represent?

   (b) Is x increasing or decreasing when   (i) $t = 1$,   (ii) $t = 4$?

   (c) Find the greatest (positive) displacement of the particle. How is this connected to your answer to part (a)?

2 The rate at which a radioactive mass decays is known to be proportional to the mass remaining at that time. If, at time t, the mass remaining is m, this means that m and t satisfy the equation

   $$\frac{dm}{dt} = -km$$

   where k is a positive constant. (The negative sign ensures that $\dfrac{dm}{dt}$ is negative, which indicates that m is decreasing.)

   Write down similar equations which represent the following statements.

   (a) The rate of growth of a population of bacteria is proportional to the number, n, of bacteria present.

   (b) When a bowl of hot soup is put in the freezer, the rate at which its temperature, $\theta°C$, decreases as it cools is proportional to its current temperature.

3 The rate at which Nasreen's coffee cools is proportional to the difference between its temperature, $\theta°$, and room temperature, $\alpha°$. Sketch a graph of θ against t given that $\alpha = 20$ and that $\theta = 95$ when $t = 0$. State the signs of θ, $\dfrac{d\theta}{dt}$ and $\dfrac{d^2\theta}{dt^2}$ for $t > 0$.

4 A car accelerates to overtake a truck. Its initial speed is u, and in a time t after it starts to accelerate it covers a distance x, where $x = ut + kt^2$ and k is a constant.

   Use differentiation to show that its speed is then $u + 2kt$, and show that its acceleration is constant.

5 A car is travelling at $20\,\text{m}\,\text{s}^{-1}$ when the driver applies the brakes. At a time t seconds later the car has travelled a further distance x metres, where $x = 20t - 2t^2$. Use differentiation to find expressions for the speed and the acceleration of the car at this time. For how long do these formulae apply?

6 Find the least possible value of $x^2 + y^2$ given that $x + y = 10$.

7 The sum of the two shorter sides of a right-angled triangle is $18\,\text{cm}$. Calculate

   (a) the least possible length of the hypotenuse,

   (b) the greatest possible area of the triangle.

8 The cross-section of an object has the shape of a quarter-circle of radius r adjoining a rectangle of width x and height r, as shown in the diagram.

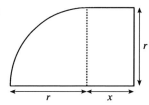

(a) The perimeter and area of the cross-section are P and A respectively. Express each of P and A in terms of r and x, and hence show that $A = \frac{1}{2}Pr - r^2$.

(b) Taking the perimeter P of the cross-section as fixed, find x in terms of r for the case when the area A of the cross-section is a maximum, and show that, for this value of x, A is a maximum and not a minimum.   (OCR)

9 The costs of a firm which makes climbing boots are of two kinds:
Fixed costs (plant, rates, office expenses): £2000 per week;
Production costs (materials, labour): £20 for each pair of boots made.

Market research suggests that, if they price the boots at £30 a pair they will sell 500 pairs a week, but that at £55 a pair they will sell none at all; and between these values the graph of sales against price is a straight line.

If they price boots at £x a pair ($30 \leqslant x \leqslant 55$) find expressions for

(a) the weekly sales,

(b) the weekly receipts,

(c) the weekly costs (assuming that just enough boots are made).

Hence show that the weekly profit, £P, is given by

$$P = -20x^2 + 1500x - 24\,000.$$

Find the price at which the boots should be sold to maximise the profit.   (OCR)

10* The manager of a supermarket usually adds a mark-up of 20% to the wholesale prices of all the goods he sells. He reckons that he has a loyal core of F customers and that, if he lowers his mark-up to x% he will attract an extra $k(20 - x)$ customers from his rivals. Each week the average shopper buys goods whose wholesale value is £A. Show that with a mark-up of x% the supermarket will have an anticipated weekly profit of

$$£\tfrac{1}{100}Ax((F + 20k) - kx).$$

Show that the manager can increase his profit by reducing his mark-up below 20% provided that $20k > F$.   (OCR)

13 Circles

This chapter is about circles and their equations. When you have completed it, you should

- be able to write down the equation of a circle with centre (a, b) and radius r
- be able to use the equation of a circle in the form $x^2 + y^2 + 2gx + 2fy + c = 0$
- be able to use algebraic methods to solve problems involving lines and circles.

13.1 The equation of a circle

This chapter shows how you can explore the geometry of the circle using coordinate methods.

Example 13.1.1
A point with coordinates (x, y) lies on a circle with centre $(3, 2)$ and radius 5. Find an equation satisfied by x and y.

If the point is to lie on a circle of radius 5, then the distance of the point (x, y) from the point $(3, 2)$ must be 5. See Fig. 13.1.

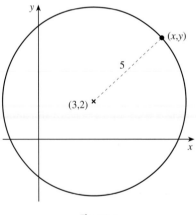

Fig. 13.1

Using the distance formula in Section 1.1,
$$\sqrt{(x-3)^2 + (y-2)^2} = 5.$$

Squaring both sides you get
$$(x-3)^2 + (y-2)^2 = 25.$$

In Section 1.5 it was stated that the equation of a curve is a rule satisfied by the coordinates (x, y) of any point which lies on it, and not by any points which do not lie on it. So $(x-3)^2 + (y-2)^2 = 25$ is actually the equation of the circle with centre $(3, 2)$ and radius 5.

In general, let P with coordinates (x, y) be a point on the circumference of a circle with centre $C(a, b)$ and radius r, where, of course, $r > 0$. Then, for all possible positions of P on the circle, the distance $CP = r$. See Fig. 13.2.

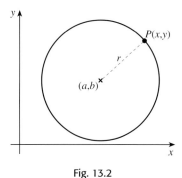

Fig. 13.2

But, from the distance formula in Section 1.1, the distance CP is $\sqrt{(x - a)^2 + (y - b)^2}$, so the equation of the circle is

$$\sqrt{(x - a)^2 + (y - b)^2} = r, \quad \text{or} \quad (x - a)^2 + (y - b)^2 = r^2.$$

> The equation of a circle with centre (a, b) and radius r is
> $$(x - a)^2 + (y - b)^2 = r^2.$$
> When the centre is $(0, 0)$, the equation is $x^2 + y^2 = r^2$.

Example 13.1.2
Write down the coordinates of the centre and the radius of the following circles.
(a) $(x - 2)^2 + (y - 5)^2 = 25$,   (b) $(x - 1)^2 + (y + 3)^2 = 18$,   (c) $(x + 4)^2 + y^2 = 50$.

(a) Comparing $(x - 2)^2 + (y - 5)^2 = 25$ with $(x - a)^2 + (y - b)^2 = r^2$ shows that the centre is $(2, 5)$, and the radius is 5.

(b) Writing $(x - 1)^2 + (y + 3)^2 = 18$ as $(x - 1)^2 + (y - (-3))^2 = \left(\sqrt{18}\right)^2$, and then comparing it with $(x - a)^2 + (y - b)^2 = r^2$ shows that the centre is $(1, -3)$, and the radius is $\sqrt{18}$, which is $3\sqrt{2}$.

(c) Writing $(x + 4)^2 + y^2 = 50$ as $(x - (-4))^2 + (y - 0)^2 = \left(\sqrt{50}\right)^2$ shows that the centre is $(-4, 0)$, and the radius is $\sqrt{50}$, which is $5\sqrt{2}$.

Example 13.1.3
Find the equation of the circle with centre $(1, 2)$ and radius 3.

Using the formula in the box, the equation is $(x - 1)^2 + (y - 2)^2 = 9$.

You can also multiply out the brackets to get

$$x^2 - 2x + 1 + y^2 - 4y + 4 = 9, \quad \text{or} \quad x^2 + y^2 - 2x - 4y - 4 = 0.$$

> Either of the forms $(x - 1)^2 + (y - 2)^2 = 9$ and $x^2 + y^2 - 2x - 4y - 4 = 0$ is usually acceptable.

Notice that if you multiply out the brackets in the equation $(x - a)^2 + (y - b)^2 = r^2$ you get the equation

$$x^2 + y^2 - 2ax - 2by + (a^2 + b^2 - r^2) = 0.$$

Look at the left side of this equation. It starts with $x^2 + y^2$, and the rest consists of terms in x, y and a constant.

For example, $x^2 + y^2 - 4x + 6y - 36 = 0$ is an equation with these properties. You can rewrite it in the form

$$x^2 - 4x + \qquad y^2 + 6y \qquad = 36,$$

where the x-terms and the y-terms have been separated on the left, and temporary gaps have been left. These gaps will be filled by completing the square (see Section 4.4) and making the right side of the equation fit. Thus

$$(x^2 - 4x + 4) + (y^2 + 6y + 9) = 36 + 4 + 9,$$

where, as 4 and 9 were added to the left side of the equation, they are also added to the right side. Thus

$$(x - 2)^2 + (y + 3)^2 = 49.$$

Comparing with the equation in the box, this is the equation of a circle with centre $(2, -3)$ and radius 7.

Example 13.1.4
Find the centre and radius of the circle $x^2 + y^2 - 2x + 4y - 7 = 0$.

Writing the equation as $(x^2 - 2x) + (y^2 + 4y) = 7$, completing the squares inside the brackets and compensating the right side gives

$$(x^2 - 2x + 1) + (y^2 + 4y + 4) = 7 + 1 + 4,$$

that is, $(x - 1)^2 + (y + 2)^2 = 12$.

The circle has centre $(1, -2)$ and radius $\sqrt{12} = 2\sqrt{3}$.

The multiples of x or y or the constant can be 0, and the equation is still a circle.

Example 13.1.5
Sketch the circle $x^2 + y^2 + 6x = 0$.

To sketch the circle you have to find its centre and radius.

Write the equation as $(x^2 + 6x + \quad) + y^2 = 0$.

Completing the square inside the brackets and compensating the right side then gives

$$(x^2 + 6x + 9) + y^2 = 9,$$

that is, $(x + 3)^2 + y^2 = 9$.

The circle has centre $(-3, 0)$ and radius 3.

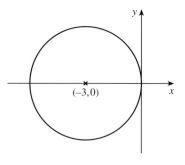

Fig. 13.3 shows a sketch of the circle, which passes through the origin.

Fig. 13.3

In the equation $(x + 3)^2 + y^2 = 9$, the term y^2 is $(y - 0)^2$.

More generally, consider the equation $x^2 + y^2 + 2gx + 2fy + c = 0$, which has the properties outlined above. Then, carrying through the same process,

$$x^2 + 2gx + y^2 + 2fy = -c,$$
$$x^2 + 2gx + g^2 + y^2 + 2fy + f^2 = g^2 + f^2 - c,$$
$$(x + g)^2 + (y + f)^2 = g^2 + f^2 - c.$$

Comparing with the equation in the blue box at the start of the section, it follows that:

> The equation $x^2 + y^2 + 2gx + 2fy + c = 0$ represents a circle, centre $(-g, -f)$ and radius $\sqrt{g^2 + f^2 - c}$, provided that $g^2 + f^2 - c > 0$.

If $g^2 + f^2 - c = 0$, the equation $(x + g)^2 + (y + f)^2 = g^2 + f^2 - c$ becomes

$$(x + g)^2 + (y + f)^2 = 0.$$

Since the sum of two squares is only 0 if both the squares are themselves 0, both $x + g = 0$ and $y + f = 0$, so $x = -g$ and $y = -f$. Thus the point $(-g, -f)$ is the only point satisfying the equation $x^2 + y^2 + 2gx + 2fy + c = 0$. This is sometimes called a 'point circle'.

If $g^2 + f^2 - c < 0$, the equation is not satisfied by any values of x and y, so there is no curve corresponding to the equation $x^2 + y^2 + 2gx + 2fy + c = 0$.

Sometimes, to avoid fractions, it is more convenient to choose the coefficients of x^2 and y^2 to be equal, but not equal to 1. You can always get back to the standard form of the equation by dividing through by the coefficient. This is illustrated in the next example.

Example 13.1.6
Find the centre and radius of the circle $2x^2 + 2y^2 - 6x + 2y - 3 = 0$.

Dividing by 2, you find $x^2 + y^2 - 3x + y - \frac{3}{2} = 0$.

For this equation $g = -\frac{3}{2}$, $f = \frac{1}{2}$ and $c = -\frac{3}{2}$, so the centre is $\left(\frac{3}{2}, -\frac{1}{2}\right)$ and the radius is

$$\sqrt{\left(-\frac{3}{2}\right)^2 + \left(\frac{1}{2}\right)^2 - \left(-\frac{3}{2}\right)} = \sqrt{\frac{9}{4} + \frac{1}{4} + \frac{3}{2}} = 2.$$

Exercise 13A

1 Write down the equation of the following circles.

(a) centre $(0, 0)$ and radius 3   (b) centre $(2, 0)$ and radius 5

(c) centre $(1, 4)$ and radius 2   (d) centre $(-5, 7)$ and radius 1

(e) centre $(6, -2)$ and radius 10   (f) centre $(-7, -3)$ and radius 10

2 Determine the centre and radius of the following circles.

(a) $(x-3)^2 + (y-2)^2 = 25$ (b) $(x+4)^2 + (y+1)^2 = 9$

(c) $(x-6)^2 + y^2 = 20$ (d) $x^2 + y^2 - 4x - 10y - 20 = 0$

(e) $x^2 + y^2 + 8x - 2y - 1 = 0$ (f) $x^2 + y^2 - 2x + y + 1 = 0$

3 Sketch the following circles.

(a) $x^2 + y^2 - 16 = 0$ (b) $x^2 + y^2 + 6x + 6y = 0$

(c) $x^2 + y^2 + 4x - 6y + 9 = 0$ (d) $2x^2 + 2y^2 - 8x - 12y + 24 = 0$

(e) $x^2 + y^2 - 3x - 10y = 0$ (f) $x^2 + y^2 - 3x - 5y = 0$

4 A circle has centre $(2, 5)$ and passes through the point $(4, 1)$. Find its equation.

5 A circle has centre $(5, 5)$ and passes through the origin. Find its equation.

6 Of the following equations, three represent circles and three do not. Determine which represent circles and, for each of these, find the centre and radius.

(a) $(x+7)^2 + (y-4)^2 + 25 = 0$ (b) $x^2 + y^2 + 5x - 3y - 16 = 0$

(c) $9x^2 + 12x + 9y^2 - 24y + 4 = 0$ (d) $x^2 + 2xy + 3y^2 + 4x + 5y + 6 = 0$

(e) $x^2 + y^2 + 14x - 10y + 78 = 0$ (f) $(x+y)^2 + (x-y)^2 + 4(x+y) = 2044$

7 The equation $x^2 + y^2 - 4\sqrt{2}x + 8\sqrt{3}y + c = 0$ represents a circle. Show that $c < 56$.

13.2 Some background knowledge

You may need to know some of the following properties of circles in order to answer some of the questions in the remainder of this chapter. If you know them already, skip this section and go on to Section 13.3.

Properties 1, 2 and 3 all depend on one idea, that a circle is symmetrical about any one of its diameters. This means that if you fold a circle along a diameter, one of the two semicircles into which the diameter cuts the circle will fit exactly on the other.

Before giving the properties, there is one result which will be necessary.

Preliminary result 1   If A and B are symmetrical about a line l, the line AB is at right angles to l.

Draw lines AM and BN at right angles to l. Then fold the part of the paper above l over, so that MA becomes MA'. Then MA' and NB are parallel, so A' can coincide with B only if M and N are the same point. That is, the line AB is at right angles to l.

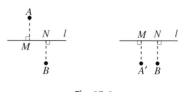

Fig. 13.4

Property 1 The tangent is perpendicular to the diameter at the point of contact. See the first part of Fig. 13.5.

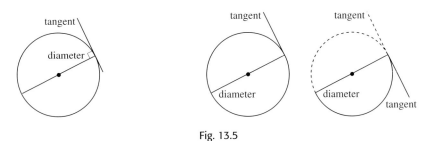

Fig. 13.5

The second part of Fig. 13.5 shows first the circle and the tangent (or rather part of the tangent), and then the same circle after it has been folded over. The dotted line shows where the circle and the tangent were before they were folded. Both the dotted part and the ordinary parts of the lines are tangents, and they are therefore part of the same full straight line which is a tangent. The angle between the two parts of the line is 180°, so each of the angles between the diameter and the tangent is a right angle.

Property 2 If a diameter of a circle is drawn perpendicular to a chord AB, then the point M where it meets AB is the mid-point of AB. See the first part of Fig. 13.6.

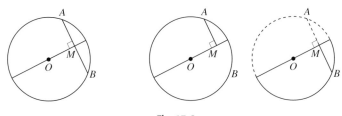

Fig. 13.6

The second part of Fig. 13.6 shows first the circle and the chord (or rather part of the chord), and then the same circle after it has been folded over. The dotted line shows where the circle and the chord were before they were folded. As the angle between the diameter and the chord is a right angle, the dotted part of the chord fits precisely on to the other part of the chord. The two parts are therefore equal.

Preliminary result 2 If two circles, with centres O and M, meet at A and B, the common chord AB is at right angles to OM. See Fig. 13.7.

The line OM contains diameters of both circles, so both circles are symmetrical about OM. Therefore their points of intersection, A and B, are symmetrical about OM. So, by preliminary result 1, AB is at right angles to OM.

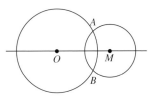

Fig. 13.7

Property 3   If a diameter of a circle (with centre *O*) is drawn passing through the mid-point *M* of a chord *AB*, then the diameter is at right angles to *AB*. See the first part of Fig. 13.8.

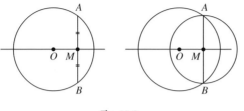

Fig. 13.8

Since *M* is the mid-point of *AB*, *MA* = *MB*. So a circle with centre *M* and radius *MA* also passes through *B*, as shown in the second part of Fig. 13.8. Therefore, by preliminary result 2, the common chord *AB* of the two circles is at right angles to *OM*. That is, the diameter is at right angles to *AB*.

Property 4   The angle in a semicircle is a right angle. This means that, if *AOB* is a diameter of a circle and if *M* is a point on the circumference, then angle *AMB* is a right angle. See the first part of Fig. 13.9.

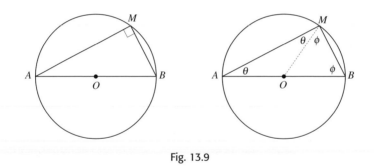

Fig. 13.9

In the second part the radius is drawn to *M*. As triangle *AOM* is isosceles (the radii are equal) it has two equal angles marked θ. Similarly, triangle *MOB* is isosceles and has two equal angles marked ϕ. The angle at *M* is $\theta + \phi$. But, focusing on the whole triangle, *AMB*, $2\theta + 2\phi = 180°$. Dividing this equation by 2 gives $\theta + \phi = 90°$, so *AMB* is a right angle.

13.3   Lines and circles

To find the equation of a tangent to a circle, you need to know its gradient. You can't find this by differentiating in the usual way, because its equation is not of the form $y = f(x)$, but you can use the fact that the tangent to a circle is perpendicular to the radius at the point of contact.

Example 13.3.1

Find the equation of the tangent to $x^2 + y^2 - 8x - 2y + 12 = 0$ at the point $(6, 2)$.

Writing the equation of the circle in the form

$$(x^2 - 8x + 16) + (y^2 - 2y + 1) = 16 + 1 - 12 = 5$$
$$(x - 4)^2 + (y - 1)^2 = 5,$$

shows that the curve is a circle, centre $(4, 1)$. See Fig. 13.10.

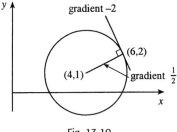

Fig. 13.10

The gradient of the radius joining $(4, 1)$ to $(6, 2)$ is $\dfrac{2 - 1}{6 - 4} = \dfrac{1}{2}$. The tangent is perpendicular to this radius, so the gradient of the tangent is $-\dfrac{1}{\frac{1}{2}} = -2$. The equation of the tangent is therefore $y - 2 = -2(x - 6)$, that is $y + 2x = 14$.

> Notice that in this last example, the magnitude of the radius is never used. In fact, it has been taken for granted that $(6, 2)$ is a point on the circle, and this really ought to be checked. If in place of $(6, 2)$ you took a point on the radius inside the circle, then the method would give you the equation of a line perpendicular to the radius; that is, the line segment (or chord) having that point as its mid-point. Draw a figure for yourself to illustrate this.

Example 13.3.2

A map shows a circular lake and a road which passes close to it. On the ground the road has equation $4x + 3y = 12$, and the lake occupies the interior of the circle with equation $x^2 + y^2 - 10x - 8y + 32 = 0$, the units being kilometres. What is the distance of the lake from the road at its closest point?

The centre of the circle is $(5, 4)$, and its radius is $\sqrt{25 + 16 - 32} = 3$. See Fig. 13.11.

You can find the nearest point of the road from the centre of the lake, by finding where the line from the centre of the lake perpendicular to the road meets the road.

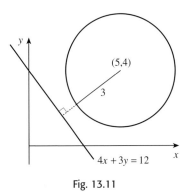

Fig. 13.11

The gradient of the road is $-\frac{4}{3}$, so the gradient of the line perpendicular to it is $\frac{3}{4}$. The equation of the perpendicular to the road through $(5, 4)$ is $y - 4 = \frac{3}{4}(x - 5)$, which simplifies to $3x - 4y = -1$.

Solving this equation simultaneously with $4x + 3y = 12$ gives the point $\left(\frac{9}{5}, \frac{8}{5}\right)$.

The distance of this point from $(5, 4)$ is $\sqrt{\left(5 - \frac{9}{5}\right)^2 + \left(4 - \frac{8}{5}\right)^2} = \sqrt{\left(\frac{16}{5}\right)^2 + \left(\frac{12}{5}\right)^2} = 4$.

So the nearest point of the lake is $(4 - 3)$ km from the road, that is 1 km.

Example 13.3.3

The line with equation $x + y = k$ is a tangent to the circle $x^2 + y^2 + 4x - 6y + 11 = 0$. Find the possible values of k.

> Two methods are given. Method 2 is more general than Method 1 and can be used with curves other than circles.

Method 1   The circle has centre $(-2, 3)$. The tangent line has gradient -1, so the radius perpendicular to the tangent has gradient 1, and, as it passes through the centre $(-2, 3)$, its equation is $y = x + 5$. To find where this line meets the circle, solve $y = x + 5$ simultaneously with $x^2 + y^2 + 4x - 6y + 11 = 0$.

$$x^2 + (x + 5)^2 + 4x - 6(x + 5) + 11 = 0$$
$$x^2 + (x^2 + 10x + 25) + 4x - 6x - 30 + 11 = 0$$
$$2x^2 + 8x + 6 = 0$$
$$x^2 + 4x + 3 = 0$$
$$(x + 1)(x + 3) = 0$$
$$x = -1 \text{ or } -3.$$

Since $y = x + 5$, the y-coordinates are 4 and 2, so the points where the radius meets the circle are $(-1, 4)$ and $(-3, 2)$. The line $x + y = k$ must pass through one or other of these points, so the value of k is either $-1 + 4 = 3$ or $-3 + 2 = -1$. Therefore $k = 3$ or -1.

Method 2   Start by apparently finding the points of intersection of the line with the circle, by substituting $y = k - x$ into the equation of the circle.

$$x^2 + (k - x)^2 + 4x - 6(k - x) + 11 = 0$$
$$x^2 + (k^2 - 2kx + x^2) + 4x - 6k + 6x + 11 = 0$$
$$2x^2 + (-2k + 10)x + (k^2 - 6k + 11) = 0.$$

If the line is a tangent to the circle, this equation has a repeated root, so the discriminant '$b^2 - 4ac$' of the equation must be 0. Therefore

$$(-2k + 10)^2 - 4 \times 2 \times (k^2 - 6k + 11) = 0$$
$$(4k^2 - 40k + 100) - 8k^2 + 48k - 88 = 0$$
$$-4k^2 + 8k + 12 = 0$$
$$k^2 - 2k - 3 = 0$$
$$(k - 3)(k + 1) = 0$$
$$k = 3 \text{ or } -1.$$

Example 13.3.4

Find the equation of the circle which has the line joining $(1, 3)$ to $(-2, 5)$ as its diameter.

Method 1   The centre of the circle is the mid-point of the diameter, and the radius is half the distance between the points. So the centre is $(-\frac{1}{2}, 4)$, and the radius is $\frac{1}{2}\sqrt{(-3)^2 + 2^2} = \frac{1}{2}\sqrt{13}$.

So the equation of the circle is $\left(x - \left(-\frac{1}{2}\right)\right)^2 + (y - 4)^2 = \frac{13}{4}$.

After multiplying out the brackets, this reduces to $x^2 + y^2 + x - 8y + 13 = 0$.

Method 2 Let A and B be the two points at opposite ends of the diameter, and let P, with coordinates (x, y), be a point on the circle, as shown in Fig. 13.12.

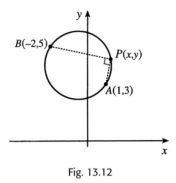

Fig. 13.12

This method relies on the fact that P lies on the circle if, and only if, AP is perpendicular to BP.

> This is the 'angle in a semicircle is a right angle' property of a circle.

The gradients of AP and BP are respectively $\dfrac{y - 3}{x - 1}$ and $\dfrac{y - 5}{x - (-2)}$, and these are perpendicular if, and only if, $\dfrac{y - 3}{x - 1} \times \dfrac{y - 5}{x - (-2)} = -1$.

This is the same as $(x - 1)(x + 2) + (y - 3)(y - 5) = 0$.

On multiplying out the brackets, you get $x^2 + y^2 + x - 8y + 13 = 0$, as before.

This result generalises to:

> The circle which has (a, b) and (c, d) as the ends of a diameter is
> $(x - a)(x - c) + (y - b)(y - d) = 0$.

Exercise 13B

1 Find the equation of the normal to the circle $x^2 + y^2 = 40$ at the point $(6, 2)$.

2 Find the equation of the normal to the circle $x^2 + y^2 - 4x - 30 = 0$ at the point $(7, 3)$.

3 Find the equation of the tangent to the circle $x^2 + y^2 = 10$ at the point $(-3, 1)$.

4 Find the equation of the tangent to the circle $x^2 + (y + 3)^2 = 18$ at the point $(3, 0)$.

5 Find the equation of the tangent to the circle $x^2 + y^2 - 8x + 2y = 0$ at the origin.

6 Find the equation of the tangent to the circle $x^2 + y^2 + 10x + 2y + 13 = 0$ at the point $(-3, 2)$.

7 Find the coordinates of the points where the straight line $y = 1$ meets the circle
   $x^2 + y^2 - 14x + 2y + 45 = 0$.

8 Find the coordinates of the points where the straight line $x + 10 = 0$ meets the circle
   $(x + 3)^2 + (y + 8)^2 = 625$.

9 Find the coordinates of the points where the straight line $y = 3x + 6$ meets the circle
   $x^2 + y^2 - 8x + 4y - 30 = 0$.

10 Find the coordinates of the points where the straight line $y = 4 - x$ meets the circle
    $(x - 1)^2 + (y + 3)^2 = 20$.

11 Show that the straight line $x + 2y - 3 = 0$ does not meet the circle
    $x^2 + y^2 + 3x + 2y - 5 = 0$.

12 Show that the straight line $y = x - 8$ is a tangent to the circle $x^2 + y^2 - 6x + 2y + 2 = 0$
    and find the coordinates of the point of contact.

13 Find the length of the chord formed when the line $x - 2y + 4 = 0$ intersects the circle
    $(x - 2)^2 + (y + 7)^2 = 85$, giving your answer in the form $k\sqrt{5}$ where k is a constant.

14 The equation of a circle is $x^2 + y^2 - 8ax + 6ay + 21a^2 = 0$, where a is a positive constant.
    Find, in terms of a,

    (a) the shortest distance between the circle and the origin,

    (b) the shortest distance between the circle and the y-axis,

    (c) the equation of the tangent to the circle at the point $(4a, -a)$.

15 The straight line with equation $y = -3x + c$ is a tangent to the circle
    $x^2 + y^2 - 4x - 2y - 5 = 0$. Find the possible values of c.

16 The straight line with equation $y = kx$ is a tangent to the circle $x^2 + y^2 - 4x - 4y + 7 = 0$.
    Find the possible values of k, giving your answers in the form $a + b\sqrt{7}$.

Miscellaneous exercise 13

1 Find the centre and radius of the circle with equation $x^2 + y^2 - 7x + y + 8 = 0$.

2 The circle with equation $x^2 + y^2 + 8x - 22y + c = 0$ has radius 7. Find the value of c.

3 The circle C has equation $x^2 + y^2 + 12x - 4y + 11 = 0$. Determine whether the following
   points lie inside, on or outside C.

   $P(-4, 7)$ $Q(-5, -3)$ $R(-2, 6)$ $S(-1, 4)$ $T(-9, 6)$

4 Find the centre and radius of the circle with equation $3x^2 + 3y^2 - 9x + 15y + 23 = 0$.

5 Points A and B have coordinates $(-3, -6)$ and $(9, 2)$ respectively. Find the equation of the
   circle which has AB as diameter.

6 Find the centre and radius of the circle with equation $x^2 + y^2 - 6y = 0$. Find also the
   coordinates of the points of intersection of the line $x - 2y + 3 = 0$ and this circle.   (OCR)

7 Find the equation of the tangent to the circle $x^2 + y^2 + 8x + 4y + 7 = 0$ at the point $(-1, 0)$.

8 Three points are $P(-2, 7)$, $Q(2, 3)$ and $R(4, 5)$. Show that PQ is perpendicular to QR. Find the equation of the circle which passes through the points P, Q and R.

9 The straight line $y = 20 - 3x$ meets the circle $x^2 + y^2 - 2x - 14y = 0$ at the points A and B. Calculate the exact length of the chord AB.   (OCR)

10 The line $y = -3x + k$ is a tangent to the circle $x^2 + y^2 = 10$. Find the possible values of k.

11 The straight line $y = 2x + k$ meets the circle $x^2 + y^2 - 2x + 4y = 0$ at two points. Find the set of possible values of k.

12 (a) Determine the translation which transforms the circle with equation
       $x^2 + y^2 + 4x - 8y = 0$ to the circle with equation $x^2 + y^2 + 10x - 10y + 30 = 0$.

   (b) The circle with equation $x^2 + y^2 - 7x - y - 3 = 0$ is translated 5 units in the positive x-direction and 2 units in the negative y-direction. Find the equation of the resulting circle.

   (c) The circle with equation $x^2 + y^2 + 10x - 2y + 10 = 0$ is reflected in the x-axis and then translated by 4 units in the positive x-direction. Find the equation of the resulting circle.

13 Verify that the circle with equation $x^2 + y^2 - 2rx - 2ry + r^2 = 0$ touches both the coordinate axes. Find the radii of the two circles which pass through the point $(16, 2)$ and touch both the coordinate axes.   (OCR)

14 It is given that the circle $x^2 + y^2 - 14x - 10y + c = 0$ lies wholly in the first quadrant. Show that $49 < c < 74$.

15 Prove that each of the circles $x^2 + y^2 - 4x = 0$ and $x^2 + y^2 - 12x - 8y + 43 = 0$ lies completely outside the other.   (OCR)

16 Prove that the equation $x^2 + y^2 - 8x + 4ky + 3k^2 = 0$ represents a circle for all values of k.

17 Circle C_1 has equation $x^2 + y^2 + 4x - 6y - 12 = 0$ and circle C_2 has equation $x^2 + y^2 - 20x + 12y + 100 = 0$. Point P lies on C_1 and point Q lies on C_2. The distance between P and Q is denoted by d. Show that $4 \leqslant d \leqslant 26$.

18 A circle passes through the point $(9, -1)$ and is such that the straight lines $x = -7$ and $x = 13$ are tangents to the circle. Find the equation of each of the circles which satisfy these conditions.

19 The circles C_1, C_2 and C_3 touch as shown and have centres which lie on a straight line parallel to the x-axis. The radii are in the ratio $4 : 2 : 1$. Given that the equation of C_1 is $x^2 + y^2 + 10x - 8y - 23 = 0$, find the equation of C_3.

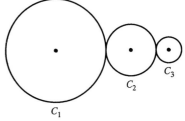

Revision exercise 2

1 Simplify $\left(4x^{\frac{1}{2}}y\right)^2 \div (2x^{-1}y^2)$.

2 (a) Calculate the gradient of the graph of $y = 12\sqrt[3]{x}$ at the point where $x = 8$ and hence find the equation of the tangent to the graph of $y = 12\sqrt[3]{x}$ at the point where $x = 8$.

   (b) Find the equation of the line passing through the points with coordinates $(15, 30)$ and $(-31, -14)$.

   (c) Hence find the coordinates of the point where the tangent in part (a) meets the line in part (b).

3 A sketch of part of the graph of $y = f(x)$ for $-2 \leqslant x \leqslant 2$ is shown in the diagram.

   Sketch, on separate axes, the graphs of

   (a) $y = f(x - 2)$ for $0 \leqslant x \leqslant 4$,

   (b) $y = -f(2x)$ for $-1 \leqslant x \leqslant 1$,

   (c) $y = 3f\left(\frac{1}{2}x\right)$ for $-4 \leqslant x \leqslant 4$.

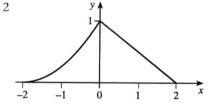

4 Show that the equation $2^{x+1} + 2^{x-1} = 160$ can be written in the form $2.5 \times 2^x = 160$. Hence find the value of x which satisfies the equation.

5 The equations of three circles are $x^2 + y^2 - 2x - 4y - 4 = 0$, $x^2 + y^2 - 8x + 4y + 16 = 0$ and $4x^2 + 4y^2 - 48x - 16y + 135 = 0$. Find the number of points common to at least two of the circles.

6 Differentiate $x + \dfrac{1}{x}$, $2\sqrt{x}$, $\dfrac{3}{\sqrt{x}}$ and $\dfrac{\left(\sqrt{x} + 1\right)^2}{x}$ with respect to x.

7 Without using a calculator, draw a sketch of $y = x^4 - x^5$, indicating those points for which $\dfrac{d^2y}{dx^2}$ is positive and those for which $\dfrac{d^2y}{dx^2}$ is negative.

8 (a) Given that $t^{\frac{1}{4}} = y$, show that the equation $t^{\frac{1}{4}} + 2t^{-\frac{1}{4}} = 3$ may be written as $y^2 - 3y + 2 = 0$.

   (b) Hence solve the equation $t^{\frac{1}{4}} + 2t^{-\frac{1}{4}} = 3$. (OCR)

9 (a) Given that $y = x^3 - 6x^2 + 9x + 2$, find $\dfrac{dy}{dx}$.

   (b) Hence find the coordinates of the stationary points on the curve $y = x^3 - 6x^2 + 9x + 2$ and determine whether each stationary point is a maximum or a minimum.

   (c) The tangent to the curve at (a, b) is parallel to the tangent at $(-1, -14)$. Show that the distance between (a, b) and $(-1, -14)$ is $6\sqrt{37}$. (OCR)

10 (a) Express $\left(\frac{3}{4}\right)^{-2}$ as an exact fraction in its simplest form.

   (b) Simplify $\dfrac{\left(2\sqrt{x}\right)^4}{8x}$. (OCR)

11 Differentiate $x^3 + x^{\frac{1}{2}}$ with respect to x.

12 The graph of $y = f(x)$ is shown in the diagram; $f(x)$ is zero for $x \geqslant 3$ and $x \leqslant -2$.

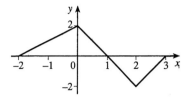

On separate diagrams, sketch the graphs of

(a) $y = f(x - 1)$,

(b) $y = f(2x)$.

13 A curve has equation $y = 2x^3 - 9x^2 + 12x - 5$. Show that one of the stationary points lies on the x-axis, and determine whether this point is a maximum or a minimum.

14 Solve the inequality $x^2 + x - 6 \geqslant 0$.

15 Show that the circles with equations $x^2 + y^2 - 6x + 4y - 23 = 0$ and $x^2 + y^2 - 22x - 8y + 121 = 0$ touch one another, and find the coordinates of their common point.

16 Differentiate $\sqrt{x} + \dfrac{1}{\sqrt{x}}$ and $\left(\sqrt{x} + \dfrac{1}{\sqrt{x}} \right)^2$ with respect to x.

17 The diagram shows a circle which passes through the points $A(2, 9)$ and $B(10, 3)$. AB is a diameter of the circle.

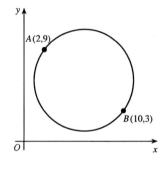

(a) Calculate the radius of the circle.

(b) Find an equation of the straight line through A and B. Give your answer in the form $ax + by = c$.

(c) Show that the tangent to the circle at B has equation $4x - 3y - 31 = 0$.   (OCR)

18 Simplify $\dfrac{x^{\frac{2}{3}} x^{\frac{1}{2}}}{x^{\frac{1}{6}}}$.   (OCR)

19 It is given that $f(x) = 2x^3 - x^2 + x^{\frac{3}{2}} + 5$.

(a) Find $f'(x)$.

(b) Find the gradient of the curve $y = f(x)$ at the point where $x = 4$.   (OCR)

20 The diagram shows the graph of $y = f(x)$. The point $P(2, 1)$ lies on the curve.

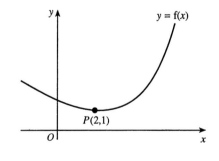

(a) Sketch, on separate diagrams, the following graphs.
(i) $y = -f(x)$ (ii) $y = 2f(x + 3)$

(b) The graph of $y = 2f(x + 3)$ is obtained from the graph of $y = f(x)$ by a sequence of two geometrical transformations. Describe each of these transformations fully.   (OCR)

21 (a) Sketch the graph of $y = 3\sqrt{x}$, for $x \geqslant 0$.

(b) The graph of $y = 3\sqrt{x}$ is stretched by a factor of 2 parallel to the y-axis. State the equation of the transformed graph.

(c) Describe the single transformation that transforms the graph of $y = 3\sqrt{x}$ to the graph of $y = 3\sqrt{x - k}$.   (OCR)

22 The equation of a circle is $x^2 + y^2 - 2x + 6y - 15 = 0$.

    (a) Find the centre and radius of the circle.

    (b) The line $y = x + 1$ intersects the circle at A and B. Find the exact length of AB.   (OCR)

23 The ends of a diameter of a circle are $(-1, 2)$ and $(5, 4)$.

    (a) Find the centre and radius of the circle.

    (b) Find the equation of the circle, giving your answer in expanded form (i.e. not involving brackets).   (OCR)

24 A curve has equation $y = \dfrac{1}{x} - \dfrac{1}{x^2}$. Use differentiation to find the coordinates of the stationary point and determine whether the stationary point is a maximum point or a minimum point. Deduce, or obtain otherwise, the coordinates of the stationary point of each of the following curves.

    (a) $y = \dfrac{1}{x} - \dfrac{1}{x^2} + 5$ (b) $y = \dfrac{2}{x-1} - \dfrac{2}{(x-1)^2}$

25 Display on the same axes the curves with equations $y = x^3$ and $y = \sqrt[3]{x}$, and give the coordinates of their points of intersection.

Practice examination 1 for C1

Time 1 hour 30 minutes

Answer all the questions.

You are **not** permitted to use a calculator in this paper.

1 Express $(2 - \sqrt{3})^2$ in the form $a - b\sqrt{3}$, where a and b are integers.　　[3]

2 Solve the inequality $2x^2 + 3x > 0$.　　[4]

3 (i) (a) Multiply out $x(x + 4)(x - 4)$.　　[2]
　　　(b) Hence differentiate $x(x + 4)(x - 4)$ with respect to x.　　[2]

　(ii) Differentiate $\dfrac{1}{x^2}$ with respect to x.　　[2]

4 (i) Express the quadratic polynomial $x^2 - 4x + 9$ in completed square form.　　[3]

　(ii) Hence, or otherwise,
　　　(a) write down the coordinates of the vertex of the graph of $y = x^2 - 4x + 9$,　　[2]
　　　(b) solve the equation $x^2 - 4x + 9 = 11$, leaving your answers in surd form.　　[3]

5 Three points have coordinates $A(1, 7)$, $B(-3, -1)$ and $C(2, 4)$, with respect to the origin O.
　(i) Show that OC is parallel to BA, and that OA is the same length as BC.　　[4]

　(ii) The mid-point of AB is M. Calculate the coordinates of the point of intersection of the lines OA and CM.　　[5]

6 (i) Sketch, on the same diagram, the curves with equations
　　(a) $y = \sqrt{x}$,
　　(b) $y = \sqrt{x + 4}$.
　　State the coordinates of any points at which the curves meet the axes.　　[5]

　(ii) Find the coordinates of the point on the curve $y = \sqrt{x}$ at which the gradient is $\frac{1}{4}$.　　[5]

7 (i) Solve the simultaneous equations
$$2x^2 + xy = 10,$$
$$x + y = 3.$$
　　　　[6]

　(ii) Show that the simultaneous equations
$$2x^2 + xy = 10,$$
$$x + y = a,$$
always have two distinct solutions, for all possible values of the constant a.　　[4]

8 A window consists of two rectangles, one above the other. The width of each rectangle is $2x$ metres and the height of the upper rectangle is half its width (see diagram). The total perimeter of the window (**not** including the dotted line between the two parts of the window) is 6 metres.

(i) Show that the height of the lower part of the window is $(3 - 3x)$ metres.   [2]

The lower part of the window is tinted, and the glass for this part costs £4 per m². The glass for the untinted part of the window costs £2 per m².

(ii) The total cost of the glass for the window is £y. Show that $y = 24x - 20x^2$.   [3]

(iii) Use differentiation to show that this total cost is a maximum (and not a minimum) when the window is 1.8 metres high.   [5]

9 Let C be the circle with equation $x^2 + y^2 - 2x + 4y - 11 = 0$.
   (i) Find the centre and radius of C.   [4]

   (ii) Determine whether the origin lies inside or outside C, explaining your reasoning carefully.   [3]

   (iii) The point A has coordinates $(2, -1)$. Find the equation of the chord of the circle which has A as its mid-point.   [5]

Practice examination 2 for C1

Time 1 hour 30 minutes

Answer all the questions.

You are **not** permitted to use a calculator in this paper.

1 Evaluate
   (i) $(3^2 + 4^2)^{\frac{1}{2}}$, [1]

   (ii) 2^{-3}, [1]

   (iii) $8^{\frac{2}{3}}$, [1]

   (iv) $(\sqrt[3]{2})^6$. [1]

2 Given that $y = 2x + \dfrac{1}{x}$, find

   (i) $\dfrac{dy}{dx}$, [3]

   (ii) $\dfrac{d^2 y}{dx^2}$. [2]

3 (i) Express $2x^2 + 8x + 19$ in the form $a(x + b)^2 + c$. [4]

   (ii) Hence state the least value of $2x^2 + 8x + 19$ as x varies, and the corresponding value of x. [2]

4 The point $A(3, 9)$ lies on the curve with equation $y = x^2$. The point B also lies on the curve, and is close to A. The table shows the coordinates of B for two possible positions.

x	y
3.1	9.61
3.05	9.3025

   (i) Calculate the gradient of the chord AB for each of these two cases. [3]

   (ii) Explain briefly (without carrying out any further detailed calculations) how the gradient of the chord AB changes as B moves closer to A. [3]

5 (i) By letting $y = \sqrt{x}$, show that the equation $(1 - 2\sqrt{x})^2 = 3x - 2$ simplifies to

   $y^2 - 4y + 3 = 0$. [3]

   (ii) Hence solve for x the equation $(1 - 2\sqrt{x})^2 = 3x - 2$. [4]

6 The diagram shows a sketch of the graph with equation $y = \dfrac{1}{x^2}$.

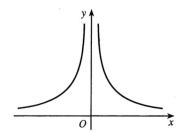

(i)   On separate diagrams, sketch the graphs with equations

(a) $y = \dfrac{1}{x^2} - 1$,

(b) $y = \dfrac{1}{(x - 1)^2}$,

and state the coordinates of any points of intersection with the axes in each case.   [5]

(ii) The graph with equation $y = \dfrac{4}{x^2}$ can be obtained by transforming the graph with

equation $y = \dfrac{1}{x^2}$ **either** by a stretch in the y-direction **or** by a stretch in the

x-direction. State the scale factor for each of these two possibilities.   [3]

7 The point A has coordinates $(7, 7)$ and the line l has equation $x + 3y = 8$.

(i)   Find the equation of the line that passes through A and is perpendicular to l.   [4]

(ii) Hence find the coordinates of the foot of the perpendicular from A to l.   [3]

Two points on the line l are $B(2, 2)$ and $C(11, -1)$.

(iii) Calculate the area of triangle ABC.   [4]

8 The equation of a curve is $y = x^2(3 - x)$.

(i)   Find the equation of the tangent to the curve at the point where $x = 3$.   [6]

(ii) Find the coordinates of the maximum point, M, on the curve.   [4]

(iii) The point O is the origin. Verify that the mid-point of OM lies on the curve.   [2]

9 (i)   Find the equation of the circle with centre $(4, 0)$ and radius 3, giving your answer
         in multiplied-out form.   [3]

The straight line $y = kx$, where k is a constant, meets the circle in part (i).

(ii) Show that the x-coordinates of the points of intersection are given by the equation

$$(k^2 + 1)x^2 - 8x + 7 = 0.$$ [2]

(iii) Hence find the values of k for which the line is a tangent to the circle.   [4]

(iv) For the case $k = 1$, show that the values of x at the points of intersection are
       $2 \pm \tfrac{1}{2}\sqrt{2}$. Hence find the length of the part of the line $y = x$ that lies inside
       the circle.   [4]

Module C2

Core 2

1 Trigonometry

This chapter develops work on sines, cosines and tangents. When you have completed it, you should

- know the shapes of the graphs of sine, cosine and tangent for all angles
- know, or be able to find, exact values of the sine, cosine and tangent of certain special angles
- be able to solve simple trigonometric equations
- know and be able to use identities involving $\sin\theta$, $\cos\theta$ and $\tan\theta$.

Letters of the Greek alphabet are often used to denote angles. In this chapter, θ (theta) and ϕ (phi) will usually be used.

1.1 The graph of $\cos\theta$

You probably first used $\cos\theta$ in calculations with right-angled triangles, so that θ lies between $0°$ and $90°$. However, if you use a calculator, you will find that it gives a value of $\cos\theta$ for any value of θ. This section extends the definition of $\cos\theta$ to angles of any size, positive or negative.

Fig. 1.1 shows a circle of radius 1 unit with centre O; the circle meets the x-axis at A. Draw a line OP at an angle θ to the x-axis, to meet the circle at P. Draw a perpendicular from P to meet OA at N. Let $ON = x$ units and $NP = y$ units, so that the coordinates of P are (x, y).

Look at triangle ONP. Using the definition $\cos\theta = \dfrac{ON}{OP}$, you find that $\cos\theta = \dfrac{x}{1} = x$.

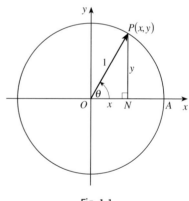

This result, $\cos\theta = x$, is used to extend the definition of $\cos\theta$ for all values of θ.

Example 1.1.1 investigates the consequences of this definition whenever θ is a multiple of $90°$.

Fig. 1.1

Example 1.1.1
Find the value of $\cos\theta$ when   (a) $\theta = 180°$,   (b) $\theta = 270°$.

(a) When $\theta = 180°$, P is the point $(-1, 0)$. As the x-coordinate of P is -1, $\cos 180° = -1$. See Fig. 1.2.

(b) When $\theta = 270°$, P is the point $(0, -1)$, so $\cos 270° = 0$. See Fig. 1.3.

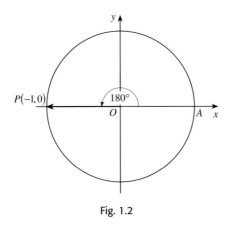

Fig. 1.2

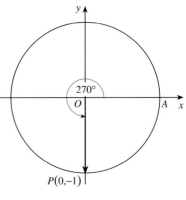

Fig. 1.3

As θ increases, the point P moves round the circle. When $\theta = 360°$, P is once again at A, and as θ becomes greater than 360°, the point P moves round the circle again.

For example, when OP has turned through 400°, P is in the same position as when $\theta = 40°$; it follows that $\cos 400° = \cos 40°$. See Fig. 1.4.

This is a special case of a general rule that the values of $\cos\theta$ repeat themselves every time θ increases by 360°. Written as an equation,

$$\cos\theta = \cos(\theta - 360°).$$

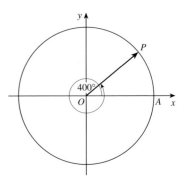

Fig. 1.4

If θ is negative, P moves round the circle in the opposite (clockwise) sense, starting from A as before. Fig. 1.5 shows this with $\theta = -150°$, so that P is in the third quadrant. Since the x-coordinate of P is negative, this shows that $\cos(-150°)$ is negative.

In Fig. 1.5, as angle $NOP = 30°$, the length ON is $1 \times \cos 30° = 0.866....$ Therefore $\cos 150° = -0.866....$.

Calculators use this definition to give values of $\cos\theta$ for all angles. Use a graphic calculator to display the graph of $\cos\theta$, shown in Fig. 1.6.

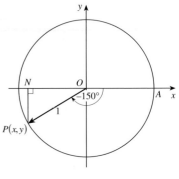

Fig. 1.5

> You will have to input the equation of the graph of $\cos\theta$ as $y = \cos x$ into the calculator, and make sure that it is in degree mode.

Note that the values taken by the cosine function are always between -1 and $+1$ (inclusive). The maximum value of 1 is taken at $\theta = \ldots, -720°, -360°, 0°, 360°, 720°, \ldots$, and the minimum of -1 at $\theta = \ldots, -540°, -180°, 180°, 540°, \ldots$.

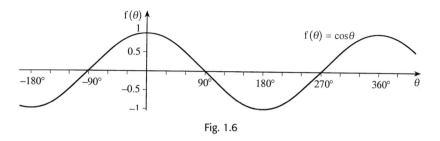

Fig. 1.6

The graph of the cosine function keeps repeating itself. Functions with this property are called **periodic**; the **period** of such a function is the smallest interval for which the function repeats itself. The period of the cosine function is therefore 360°. The property that $\cos(\theta - 360°) = \cos\theta$ is called the **periodic property**. Many natural phenomena have periodic properties, and cosines are often used in applications involving them.

Example 1.1.2
Find the maximum and minimum values of the following functions, and in each case give the smallest positive value of x for which it occurs. (a) $2 + \cos x$, (b) $3\cos 2x$

The maximum and minimum values of the cosine function are $+1$ and -1.

(a) The maximum value of $2 + \cos x$ is $2 + 1 = 3$, and the minimum value is $2 + (-1) = 1$.

The values of x which give the value 1 are $-720°, -360°, 0°, 360°, 720°$, etc. The smallest positive value of these is 360°.

The values of x which give the value -1 are $-540°, -180°, 180°, 540°, 900°$, etc. The smallest positive value of these is 180°.

(b) The maximum value of $3\cos 2x$ is $3 \times 1 = 3$, and the minimum value of $3\cos 2x$ is $3 \times (-1) = -3$.

The values of $2x$ which give the value 1 for $\cos 2x$ are $-720°, -360°, 0°, 360°, 720°$, etc. The smallest positive value of x is when $2x = 360°$, that is, $x = 180°$.

The values of $2x$ which give the value -1 for $\cos 2x$ are $-540°, -180°, 180°, 540°, 900°$, etc. The smallest positive value of x is when $2x = 180°$, that is, $x = 90°$.

Use a graphic calculator to display $2 + \cos x$ and $3\cos 2x$, and verify your solution.

Example 1.1.3
The height in metres of the water in a harbour is given approximately by the formula $d = 6 + 3\cos 30t$ where t is the time in hours from noon. Find (a) the height of the water at 9.45 p.m., and (b) the highest and lowest water levels, and when they occur.

(a) At 9.45 p.m., $t = 9.75$, so $d = 6 + 3\cos(30 \times 9.75) = 6 + 3\cos 292.5 = 7.148...$. Therefore the height of the water is 7.15 metres, correct to 3 significant figures.

(b) The maximum value of d occurs when the value of the cosine function is 1, and is therefore $6 + 3 \times 1 = 9$. Similarly, the minimum value is $6 + 3 \times (-1) = 3$. The highest and lowest water levels are 9 metres and 3 metres. The first times that they occur after noon are when $30t = 360$ and $30t = 180$; that is, at midnight and 6.00 p.m.

Check your answer using a graphic calculator.

1.2 The graphs of $\sin \theta$ and $\tan \theta$

Using the same construction as for the cosine (see Fig. 1.7, which is Fig. 1.1 again), the sine function is defined by

$$\sin \theta = \frac{NP}{OP} = \frac{y}{1} = y.$$

Like the cosine graph, the sine graph (shown in Fig. 1.8, on the facing page) is periodic, with period 360°. It also lies between -1 and 1 inclusive.

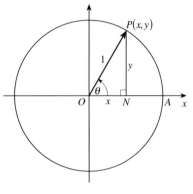

In Fig. 1.7, you will see that $\tan \theta = \dfrac{NP}{ON} = \dfrac{y}{x}$; this is taken as the definition of $\tan \theta$.

The function $\tan \theta$ is not defined for those angles for which x is zero, namely $\theta = \pm 90°, \pm 270°, \ldots$. Fig. 1.9 shows the graph of $\tan \theta$.

Fig. 1.7

Like the graphs of $\cos \theta$ and $\sin \theta$, the graph of $\tan \theta$ is periodic, but its period is 180°. Thus $\tan(\theta - 180°) = \tan \theta$.

As $\cos \theta = x$, $\sin \theta = y$ and $\tan \theta = \dfrac{y}{x}$, it follows that $\tan \theta = \dfrac{\sin \theta}{\cos \theta}$. You could use this as an alternative definition of $\tan \theta$.

Example 1.2.1
Find the maximum and minimum values of the following functions, and in each case give the least positive value of x for which it occurs.

(a) $2 \sin x - 1$, (b) $\dfrac{1}{2 + \sin x}$.

The maximum and minimum values of $\sin x$ are 1 and -1.

(a) So the maximum value of $2 \sin x - 1$ is $2 \times 1 - 1 = 1$, and the minimum value is $2 \times (-1) - 1 = -3$.

The maximum occurs when $x = 90°$, and the minimum when $x = 270°$.

(b) As $\sin x$ lies between -1 and 1, $2 + \sin x$ lies between 1 and 3.

The maximum value of $\dfrac{1}{2 + \sin x}$ occurs when the denominator is 1, giving a maximum of 1. This occurs when $x = 270°$.

Similarly, the minimum value of $\dfrac{1}{2 + \sin x}$ occurs when the denominator is 3, giving a minimum of $\frac{1}{3}$. This occurs when $x = 90°$.

You might find it interesting to display the functions in Example 1.2.1 on a
graphic calculator.

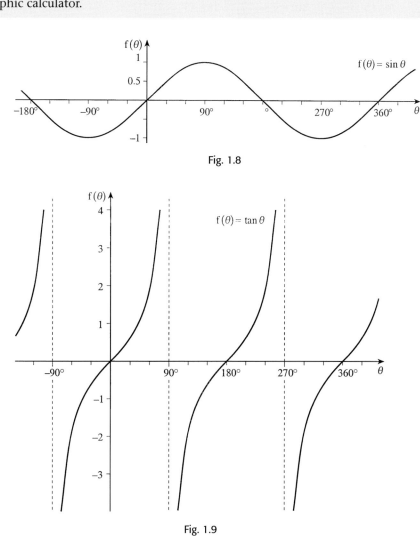

Fig. 1.8

Fig. 1.9

1.3   Exact values of some trigonometric functions

There are a few angles which are a whole number of degrees and whose sines, cosines and
tangents you can find exactly. The most important of these are 45°, 60° and 30°.

To find the cosine, sine and tangent of 45°, draw a right-angled isosceles triangle in which the
equal sides are 1 unit, as in Fig. 1.10.

The length of the hypotenuse is then $\sqrt{2}$ units. Then

$$\cos 45° = \frac{1}{\sqrt{2}}, \quad \sin 45° = \frac{1}{\sqrt{2}}, \quad \tan 45° = 1.$$

If you rationalise the denominators you get

$$\cos 45° = \frac{\sqrt{2}}{2}, \quad \sin 45° = \frac{\sqrt{2}}{2}, \quad \tan 45° = 1.$$

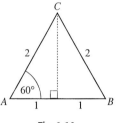

Fig. 1.10

To find the cosine, sine and tangent of 60° and 30°, draw an equilateral triangle of side 2 units, as in Fig. 1.11.

Draw a perpendicular from one vertex, bisecting the opposite side. This perpendicular has length $\sqrt{3}$ units, and it makes an angle of 30° with AC. Then

$$\cos 60° = \frac{1}{2}, \quad \sin 60° = \frac{\sqrt{3}}{2}, \quad \tan 60° = \sqrt{3};$$

$$\cos 30° = \frac{\sqrt{3}}{2}, \quad \sin 30° = \frac{1}{2}, \quad \tan 30° = \frac{1}{\sqrt{3}} = \frac{\sqrt{3}}{3}.$$

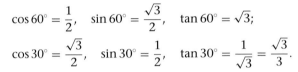

Fig. 1.11

You should be able to recall or reconstruct these results quickly.

Here is a summary of them.

θ	$\sin\theta$	$\cos\theta$	$\tan\theta$
0°	0	1	0
30°	$\frac{1}{2}$	$\frac{\sqrt{3}}{2}$	$\frac{1}{\sqrt{3}} = \frac{\sqrt{3}}{3}$
45°	$\frac{1}{\sqrt{2}} = \frac{\sqrt{2}}{2}$	$\frac{1}{\sqrt{2}} = \frac{\sqrt{2}}{2}$	1
60°	$\frac{\sqrt{3}}{2}$	$\frac{1}{2}$	$\sqrt{3}$
90°	1	0	undefined

Example 1.3.1

Write down the exact values of   (a) $\cos 120°$,   (b) $\sin 240°$,   (c) $\tan 495°$.

(a) **Method 1**   From the graph of $\cos\theta$ in Fig. 1.12, the value of $\cos 120°$ is negative.

Also from Fig. 1.12, the piece of curve between 0° and 60° is exactly the same shape as that between 120° and 180°, so the numerical value (ignoring the sign) of $\cos 120°$ is the same as $\cos 60°$, which is $\frac{1}{2}$.

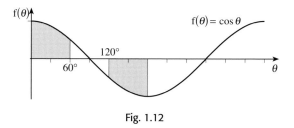

Fig. 1.12

So $\cos 120° = -\cos 60° = -\frac{1}{2}$.

Method 2 From Fig. 1.13, 120° is a second quadrant angle, so the x-coordinate of P is negative and hence $\cos 120°$ is negative.

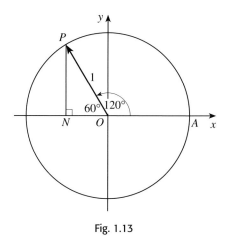

Fig. 1.13

In Fig. 1.13, as angle $NOP = 60°$, the length ON is $1 \times \cos 60° = \frac{1}{2}$.

So $\cos 120° = -\cos 60° = -\frac{1}{2}$.

(b) Using either Method 1 or Method 2, you first find that $\sin 240°$ is negative.

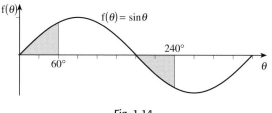

Fig. 1.14

If you use the graph (Fig. 1.14) you see that $\sin 240° = -\sin 60°$, and as $\sin 60° = \frac{1}{2}\sqrt{3}$, $\sin 240° = -\sin 60° = -\frac{1}{2}\sqrt{3}$.

If you use Fig. 1.15, then the length PN is $1 \times \sin 60° = \frac{1}{2}\sqrt{3}$, so $\sin 240° = -\frac{1}{2}\sqrt{3}$.

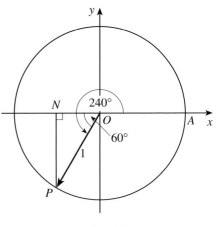

Fig. 1.15

(c) Using either Method 1 or Method 2, you first find that $\tan 495°$ is negative.

Using the graph (Fig. 1.16) you see that $\tan 495° = -\tan 45°$, and as $\tan 45° = 1$, $\tan 495° = -1$.

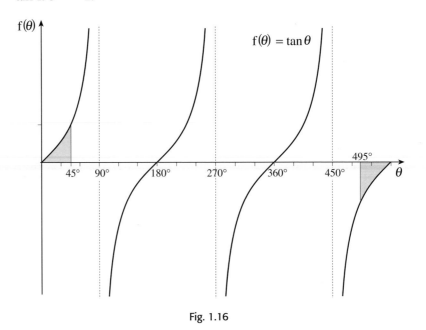

Fig. 1.16

If you use Fig. 1.17, then $\dfrac{PN}{ON} = \tan 45° = 1$. So $\tan 495° = -\tan 45° = -1$.

Use either Method 1 or Method 2, whichever you prefer. However, do not attempt to draw an accurate figure: a rough sketch is all that is needed.

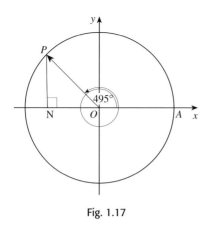

Fig. 1.17

Exercise 1A

1 For each of the following values of θ find, correct to 4 decimal places, the values of
   (i) $\cos\theta$, (ii) $\sin\theta$, (iii) $\tan\theta$.

   (a) $25°$ (b) $125°$ (c) $225°$ (d) $325°$

   (e) $-250°$ (f) $67.4°$ (g) $124.9°$ (h) $554°$

2 Find the maximum value and the minimum value of each of the following functions. In
   each case, give the least positive values of x at which they occur.

   (a) $2 + \sin x$ (b) $7 - 4\cos x$ (c) $5 + 8\cos 2x$

   (d) $\dfrac{8}{3 - \sin x}$ (e) $9 + \sin(4x - 20°)$ (f) $\dfrac{30}{2 + \cos x}$

3 (Do not use a calculator for this question.) In each part of the question a trigonometric
   function of a number is given. Find all the other numbers x, $0° \leqslant x \leqslant 360°$, such that the
   same function of x is equal to the given trigonometric ratio. For example, if you are given
   $\sin 80°$, then $x = 100°$, since $\sin 100° = \sin 80°$.

   (a) $\sin 20°$ (b) $\cos 40°$ (c) $\tan 60°$ (d) $\sin 130°$

   (e) $\cos 140°$ (f) $\tan 160°$ (g) $\sin 400°$ (h) $\cos(-30°)$

   (i) $\tan 430°$ (j) $\sin(-260°)$ (k) $\cos(-200°)$ (l) $\tan 1000°$

4 Without using a calculator, write down the exact values of the following.

   (a) $\sin 135°$ (b) $\cos 120°$ (c) $\sin(-30°)$ (d) $\tan 240°$

   (e) $\cos 225°$ (f) $\tan(-330°)$ (g) $\cos 900°$ (h) $\tan 510°$

   (i) $\sin 225°$ (j) $\cos 630°$ (k) $\tan 405°$ (l) $\sin(-315°)$

   (m) $\sin 210°$ (n) $\tan 675°$ (o) $\cos(-120°)$ (p) $\sin 1260°$

5 Without using a calculator, write down the smallest positive angle which satisfies the
   following equations.

   (a) $\cos\theta = \tfrac{1}{2}$ (b) $\sin\phi = -\tfrac{1}{2}\sqrt{3}$ (c) $\tan\theta = -\sqrt{3}$ (d) $\cos\phi = \tfrac{1}{2}\sqrt{3}$

   (e) $\tan\theta = \tfrac{1}{3}\sqrt{3}$ (f) $\tan\phi = -1$ (g) $\sin\theta = -\tfrac{1}{2}$ (h) $\cos\phi = 0$

(i) $\cos\theta = -\frac{1}{2}$ (j) $\tan\phi = \sqrt{3}$ (k) $\sin\theta = -1$ (l) $\cos\theta = -1$

(m) $\sin\phi = \frac{1}{2}\sqrt{3}$ (n) $\tan\theta = -\frac{1}{3}\sqrt{3}$ (o) $\sin\phi = -\frac{1}{2}\sqrt{2}$ (p) $\tan\phi = 0$

6 Without using a calculator show that

(a) $\tan 45° + \sin 30° = 1\frac{1}{2}$,

(b) $\sin^2 60° = \frac{3}{4}$,

(c) $\sin 60° \cos 30° + \cos 60° \sin 30° = 1$,

(d) $\sin^2 30° + \sin^2 45 = \sin^2 60°$,

(e) $\dfrac{\cos 30°}{\sin 30°} = \tan 60°$,

(f) $(1 + \tan 60°)^2 = 4 + 2\sqrt{3}$.

7 The water levels in a dock follow (approximately) a twelve-hour cycle, and are modelled by the equation $D = A + B \sin 30t$, where D metres is the depth of water in the dock, A and B are positive constants, and t is the time in hours after 8 a.m.

Given that the greatest and least depths of water in the dock are 7.80 m and 2.20 m respectively, find the value of A and the value of B.

Find the depth of water in the dock at noon, giving your answer correct to the nearest cm.

1.4 Symmetry properties of the graphs of $\cos\theta$, $\sin\theta$ and $\tan\theta$

If you examine the graphs of $\cos\theta$, $\sin\theta$ and $\tan\theta$, you can see that they have many symmetry properties. The graph of $\cos\theta$ is shown in Fig. 1.18 (which is a reduced copy of Fig. 1.6 and reproduced here for convenience).

The graph of $\cos\theta$ is symmetrical about the vertical axis. This means that if you replace θ by $-\theta$ the graph is unchanged. Therefore

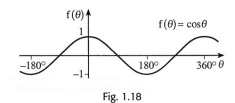

Fig. 1.18

$$\cos(-\theta) = \cos\theta.$$

This shows that $\cos\theta$ is an even function of θ (as defined in C1 Section 3.3).

There are other symmetry properties. For example, if in Fig. 1.18 you translate the graph of $\cos\theta$ by $180°$ in the θ-direction, you get the graph of $\cos(\theta - 180°)$ in Fig. 1.19.

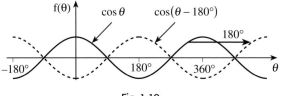

Fig. 1.19

You will notice that the result is the reflection of the $\cos\theta$ graph in the θ-axis, which is the graph of $-\cos\theta$. So

$$\cos(\theta - 180°) = -\cos\theta.$$

This is called the **translation property**.

There is one more useful symmetry property. Using the even and translation properties,

$$\cos(180° - \theta) = \cos(-(\theta - 180°)) = \cos(\theta - 180°) = -\cos\theta.$$

This is called the **supplementary property**. Angles, like θ and $(180° - \theta)$, which add to $180°$ are called supplementary angles.

There are similar properties for the graph of $\sin\theta$, which is shown in Fig. 1.20, which is a reduced copy of Fig. 1.8.

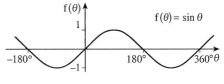

Fig. 1.20

You are asked to prove them as part of Exercise 1B. Their proofs are similar to those for the cosine.

> The functions $\cos\theta$ and $\sin\theta$ have the following properties.
>
> Periodic property: $\cos(\theta - 360°) = \cos\theta$ $\sin(\theta - 360°) = \sin\theta$
>
> Even/odd property: $\cos(-\theta) = \cos\theta$ $\sin(-\theta) = -\sin\theta$
>
> Translation property: $\cos(\theta - 180°) = -\cos\theta$ $\sin(\theta - 180°) = -\sin\theta$
>
> Supplementary property: $\cos(180° - \theta) = -\cos\theta$ $\sin(180° - \theta) = \sin\theta$

If you refer back to the graph of $\tan\theta$ in Fig. 1.9, and think in the same way as with the cosine and sine graphs, you can obtain similar results:

> The function $\tan\theta$ has the following properties.
>
> Periodic property: $\tan(\theta - 180°) = \tan\theta$
>
> Odd property: $\tan(-\theta) = -\tan\theta$
>
> Supplementary property: $\tan(180° - \theta) = -\tan\theta$

Note that the period of the graph of $\tan\theta$ is $180°$, and that the translation property of $\tan\theta$ is the same as the periodic property.

There are also relations between $\cos\theta$ and $\sin\theta$. One is shown in Example 1.4.1.

Example 1.4.1

Establish the property that $\cos(90° - \theta) = \sin\theta$.

> This is easy if $0° < \theta < 90°$: consider a right-angled triangle. But it can be shown for any value of θ.

> If you translate the graph of $\cos\theta$ by $90°$ in the direction of the positive θ-axis, you obtain the graph of $\sin\theta$, so $\cos(\theta - 90°) = \sin\theta$. And since the cosine is an even function, $\cos(90° - \theta) = \cos(-(90° - \theta)) = \cos(\theta - 90°)$. Therefore $\cos(90° - \theta) = \sin\theta$.

Another property, which you are asked to prove in Exercise 1B, is $\sin(90° − \theta) = \cos\theta$.

Exercise 1B

1 Use the various symmetry properties of the sine, cosine and tangent functions to establish the following results. Illustrate the results on a graphic calculator.

(a) $\sin(90° − \theta) = \cos\theta$ (b) $\sin(270° + \theta) = −\cos\theta$

(c) $\sin(90° + \theta) = \cos\theta$ (d) $\cos(90° + \theta) = −\sin\theta$

(e) $\tan(\theta − 180°) = \tan\theta$ (f) $\cos(180° − \theta) = \cos(180° + \theta)$

(g) $\tan(360° − \theta) = −\tan(180° + \theta)$ (h) $\sin(−\theta − 90°) = −\cos\theta$

2 Sketch the graphs of $y = \tan\theta$ and $y = \dfrac{1}{\tan\theta}$ on the same set of axes. Show that the graph of $y = \tan(\theta − 90°)$ can be transformed to the graph of $y = \tan(90° − \theta)$ by a simple transformation, which you should write down.

Hence show that $\tan(90° − \theta) = \dfrac{1}{\tan\theta}$.

1.5 Solving equations involving the trigonometric functions

This section is about solving simple trigonometric equations. You can solve all the equations using appropriate functions on your graphic calculator, but you will understand cosine, sine and tangent better if you can solve the equations algebraically as well.

Solving the equation $\cos\theta = k$

The equation $\cos\theta = k$ only has a solution if k lies between −1 and 1 (inclusive). In general, there are two roots in every interval of 360°; but if $k = \pm 1$ there is only one root.

Fig. 1.21 illustrates this using the graph of $\cos\theta$ with a negative value of k.

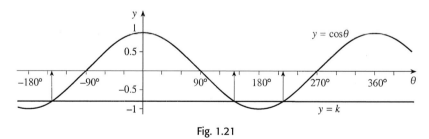

Fig. 1.21

To find an angle θ which satisfies the equation you can use the $[\cos^{-1}]$ key on your calculator (or, on some calculators, the [ARCCOS] key). Make sure that the calculator is in degree mode. It then gives the simplest value of θ such that $\cos\theta = k$.

The calculator will only give you one answer. Usually you want to find all the roots of $\cos\theta = k$ in a given interval (probably one of width $360°$). The problem then is how to find all the other roots in your required interval.

There are three steps in solving the equation of $\cos\theta = k$.

> **Step 1** Find $\cos^{-1} k$.
>
> **Step 2** Use the symmetry property $\cos(-\theta) = \cos\theta$ to find another root.
>
> **Step 3** Add or subtract multiples of $360°$ to find the roots in the required interval.

Example 1.5.1
Solve the equation $\cos\theta = \frac{1}{3}$, giving all roots in the interval $0° \leqslant \theta \leqslant 360°$ correct to 1 decimal place.

Fig. 1.22 shows the graphs of $y = \cos\theta$ and $y = \frac{1}{3}$. You can see that there are two solutions, one between $0°$ and $90°$, and one between $270°$ and $360°$.

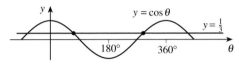

Fig. 1.22

> Note that the sketch does not have to be accurate to get quite a good idea of where the roots are. It can be a useful check on algebraic working.

> **Step 1** The calculator gives $\cos^{-1}\frac{1}{3}$ as $70.52...°$. This is one root in the interval $0° \leqslant \theta \leqslant 360°$.
>
> **Step 2** Use the symmetry property $\cos(-\theta) = \cos\theta$ to show that $-70.52...°$ is another root. Note that $-70.52...°$ is not in the required interval.
>
> **Step 3** Add $360°$ to obtain $-70.52...° + 360° = 289.47...°$, which is in the required interval.

Therefore the roots in the interval $0° \leqslant \theta \leqslant 360°$ are $70.5°$ and $289.5°$, correct to 1 decimal place.

Example 1.5.2
Solve the equation $\cos 3\theta = -\frac{1}{2}$, giving all the roots in the interval $-180° \leqslant \theta \leqslant 180°$.

> This example is similar to the previous example, except for an important extra step at the beginning, and another at the end.

Let $3\theta = \phi$. Then you have to solve the equation $\cos\phi = -\frac{1}{2}$.

But, as $3\theta = \phi$,

$$\text{if } -180° \leqslant \theta \leqslant 180°,$$
$$\text{then } 3 \times (-180°) \leqslant 3\theta \leqslant 3 \times 180°,$$
$$\text{so } -540° \leqslant \phi \leqslant 540°.$$

So the original problem has become: solve the equation $\cos\phi = -\frac{1}{2}$ giving all the roots in the interval $-540° \leqslant \phi \leqslant 540°$. (You should expect six roots of the equation in this interval.)

Step 1   The calculator gives $\cos^{-1}\left(-\frac{1}{2}\right)$ as $120°$.

Step 2   Another root is $-120°$.

Step 3   Adding and subtracting multiples of $360°$ shows that $-120° - 360° = -480°$, $-120° + 360° = 240°$, $120° - 360° = -240°$ and $120° + 360° = 480°$ are also roots.

Therefore the roots of $\cos\phi = -\frac{1}{2}$ in $-540° \leqslant \phi \leqslant 540°$ are $-480°, -240°, -120°$, $120°, 240°$ and $480°$.

Returning to the original equation, and using the fact that $\theta = \frac{1}{3}\phi$, the roots are $-160°, -80°, -40°, 40°, 80°$ and $160°$.

Fig. 1.23 shows the graph of $y = \cos 3\theta$, which is the same as $y = \cos\theta$ but stretched in the x-direction by a factor of $\frac{1}{3}$, and $y = -\frac{1}{2}$. The six roots are shown.

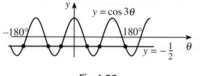

Fig. 1.23

Solving the equation $\sin\theta = k$

The equation $\sin\theta = k$, where $-1 \leqslant k \leqslant 1$, is solved in a similar way. The only difference is that the symmetry property for $\sin\theta$ is $\sin(180° - \theta) = \sin\theta$.

Step 1   Find $\sin^{-1} k$.

Step 2   Use the symmetry property $\sin(180° - \theta) = \sin\theta$ to find another root.

Step 3   Add or subtract multiples of $360°$ to find the roots in the required interval.

Example 1.5.3
Solve the equation $\sin\theta = -0.7$, giving all the roots in the interval $-180° \leqslant \theta \leqslant 180°$ correct to 1 decimal place.

Step 1 The calculator gives $\sin^{-1}(-0.7)$ as $-44.42...°$. This is one root in the interval $-180° \leqslant \theta \leqslant 180°$.

Step 2 Use the symmetry property $\sin(180° - \theta) = \sin\theta$ to show that $180° - (-44.42...°) = 224.42...°$ is another root. Unfortunately it is not in the required interval.

Step 3 Subtract $360°$ to obtain $224.42...° - 360° = -135.57...°$, which is in the required interval.

Therefore the roots in the interval $-180° \leqslant \theta \leqslant 180°$ are $-44.4°$ and $-135.6°$, correct to 1 decimal place.

Fig. 1.24 shows the graphs of $y = \sin\theta$ and $y = -0.7$. As you can see, there are two roots in the interval $-180° \leqslant \theta \leqslant 180°$, both negative.

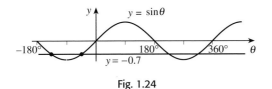

Fig. 1.24

Example 1.5.4
Solve the equation $\sin\frac{1}{3}\theta = \frac{1}{2}\sqrt{3}$, giving all the roots in the interval $0° \leqslant \theta \leqslant 360°$.

Let $\frac{1}{3}\theta = \phi$, so that the equation becomes $\sin\phi = \frac{1}{2}\sqrt{3}$, with roots required in the interval $0° \leqslant \phi \leqslant 120°$.

Step 1 The calculator gives $\sin^{-1}\left(\frac{1}{2}\sqrt{3}\right)$ as $60°$. This is one root in the interval $0° \leqslant \phi \leqslant 120°$.

Step 2 Another root is $180° - 60° = 120°$, which is still in the required interval.

Step 3 Adding and subtracting multiples of $360°$ will not give any more roots in the interval $0° \leqslant \phi \leqslant 120°$.

Therefore the roots of $\sin\phi = \frac{1}{2}\sqrt{3}$ in $0° \leqslant \phi \leqslant 120°$ are $60°$ and $120°$.

Returning to the original equation, since $\theta = 3\phi$, the roots are $\theta = 180°$ and $360°$.

Fig. 1.25 shows the graphs of $y = \sin \frac{1}{3}\theta$, which is the graph of $\sin \theta$ stretched by a factor of 3, and $y = \frac{1}{3}\sqrt{3}$. As you can see, this diagram confirms that the roots are 180° and 360°.

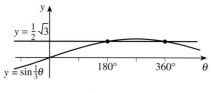

Fig. 1.25

Solving the equation $\tan \theta = k$

The equation $\tan \theta = k$ is also solved in a similar way. Note that there is generally one root for every interval of 180°. Other roots can be found from the periodic property, $\tan(180° + \theta) = \tan \theta$.

> **Step 1** Find $\tan^{-1} k$.
>
> **Step 2** Add or subtract multiples of 180° to find the roots in the required interval.

Example 1.5.5

Solve the equation $\tan \theta = -2$, giving all the roots correct to 1 decimal place in the interval $0° \leq \theta \leq 360°$.

> **Step 1** The calculator gives $\tan^{-1}(-2)$ as $-63.43...°$. Unfortunately, this root is not in the required interval.
>
> **Step 2** Add multiples of 180° to get roots in the required interval. This gives $116.56...°$ and $296.56...°$.

Therefore the roots of $\tan \theta = -2$ in $0° \leq \theta \leq 360°$ are 116.6° and 296.6°, correct to 1 decimal place.

Fig. 1.26 shows the graphs of $y = \tan \theta$ and $y = -2$. Once again the graphs confirm the answers given algebraically.

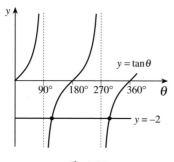

Fig. 1.26

Example 1.5.6

Solve the equation $\cos(\theta - 25°) = -0.95$, giving all the roots correct to 1 decimal place in the interval $-180° \leqslant \theta \leqslant 180°$.

Let $\phi = \theta - 25°$, so that the equation becomes $\cos\phi = -0.95$, with roots required in the interval $-180° \leqslant \phi + 25° \leqslant 180°$, which is $-205° \leqslant \phi \leqslant 155°$.

Step 1   The calculator gives $\cos^{-1}(-0.95)$ as $161.8...°$. This root is not in the required interval for ϕ.

Step 2   Using the symmetry property $\cos(-\theta) = \cos\theta$ another root is $-161.8...°$, which is in the required interval for ϕ.

Step 3   Subtracting from the first root gives $-161.8...° - 360° = -198.1...°$, which is in the required interval for ϕ.

The roots for ϕ are therefore $-198.1...°$ and $-161.8...°$, so the roots for θ, which is $\phi + 25°$, are $-173.1...°$ and $-136.8...°$.

Therefore the roots of $\cos(\theta - 25°) = -0.95$ in $-180° \leqslant \theta \leqslant 180°$ are $-173.2°$ and $-136.8°$, correct to 1 decimal place.

Fig. 1.27 shows the graphs of $y = \cos(\theta - 25°)$, which is the graph of $y = \cos\theta$ translated in the positive x-direction by $25°$, and $y = -0.95$. Both roots are negative, and quite close to $-180°$.

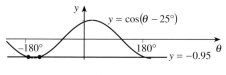

Fig. 1.27

Revisiting Example 1.1.3, here is an application of solving equations of this type.

Example 1.5.7

The height in metres of the water in a harbour is given approximately by the formula $d = 6 + 3\cos 30t$ where t is the time measured in hours from noon. Find the time after noon when the height of the water is 7.5 metres for the second time.

To find when the height is 7.5 metres, solve $6 + 3\cos 30t = 7.5$. This gives $3\cos 30t = 7.5 - 6 = 1.5$, or $\cos 30t = 0.5$. After substituting $\phi = 30t$, the equation reduces to $\cos\phi = 0.5$.

Now $\cos 60° = 0.5$, but $60°$ gives only the first root, $t = 2$. So, using the symmetry property of the cos function, another root of $\cos\phi = 0.5$ is $-60°$. Adding $360°$ gives $\phi = 300°$ as the second root of $\cos\phi = 0.5$. Thus $30t = 300$, and $t = 10$.

The water is at height 7.5 metres for the second time at 10.00 p.m.

Exercise 1C

1 Find, correct to 1 decimal place, the two smallest positive values of θ which satisfy each of the following equations.

(a) $\sin\theta = 0.1$ 　　　　(b) $\sin\theta = -0.84$ 　　　　(c) $\sin\theta = 0.951$

(d) $\cos\theta = 0.8$ 　　　　(e) $\cos\theta = -0.84$ 　　　　(f) $\cos\theta = \sqrt{\frac{2}{3}}$

(g) $\tan\theta = 4$ 　　　　(h) $\tan\theta = -0.32$ 　　　　(i) $\tan\theta = 0.11$

(j) $\sin 2\theta = 0.4$ 　　　　(k) $\cos 3\theta = -0.571$ 　　　　(l) $\tan\frac{1}{2}\theta = -3$

(m) $\sin\frac{3}{2}\theta = 0.3584$ 　　　　(n) $\cos 3\theta = 0.5$ 　　　　(o) $\tan 2\theta = 1$

2 Find all values of θ in the interval $-180° \leqslant \theta \leqslant 180°$ which satisfy each of the following equations, giving your answers correct to 1 decimal place where appropriate.

(a) $\sin\theta = 0.8$ 　　　　(b) $\cos\theta = 0.25$ 　　　　(c) $\tan\theta = 2$

(d) $\sin\theta = -0.67$ 　　　　(e) $\cos\theta = -0.12$ 　　　　(f) $4\tan\theta + 3 = 0$

(g) $4\sin\theta = 5\cos\theta$ 　　　　(h) $2\sin\theta = \dfrac{1}{\sin\theta}$ 　　　　(i) $2\sin\theta = \tan\theta$

3 Find all the solutions in the interval $0° < \theta \leqslant 360°$ of each of the following equations.

(a) $\cos 2\theta = \frac{1}{3}$ 　　　　(b) $\tan 3\theta = 2$ 　　　　(c) $\sin 2\theta = -0.6$

(d) $\cos 4\theta = -\frac{1}{4}$ 　　　　(e) $\tan 2\theta = 0.4$ 　　　　(f) $\sin 3\theta = -0.42$

4 Find the roots in the interval $-180° \leqslant x \leqslant 180°$ of each of the following equations.

(a) $\cos 3x = \frac{2}{3}$ 　　　　(b) $\tan 2x = -3$ 　　　　(c) $\sin 3x = -0.2$

(d) $\cos 2x = 0.246$ 　　　　(e) $\tan 5x = 0.8$ 　　　　(f) $\sin 2x = -0.39$

5 Find the roots (if there are any) in the interval $-180° \leqslant \theta \leqslant 180°$ of the following equations.

(a) $\cos\frac{1}{2}\theta = \frac{2}{3}$ 　　　　(b) $\tan\frac{2}{3}\theta = -3$ 　　　　(c) $\sin\frac{1}{4}\theta = -\frac{1}{4}$

(d) $\cos\frac{1}{3}\theta = \frac{1}{3}$ 　　　　(e) $\tan\frac{3}{4}\theta = 0.5$ 　　　　(f) $\sin\frac{2}{5}\theta = -0.3$

6 Without using a calculator, find the exact roots of the following equations, if there are any, giving your answers in the interval $0° < t \leqslant 360°$.

(a) $\sin 2t = \frac{1}{2}$ 　　　　(b) $\tan 2t = 0$ 　　　　(c) $\cos 3t = \frac{1}{2}\sqrt{3}$

(d) $\tan\frac{3}{2}t = -\sqrt{3}$ 　　　　(e) $\cos 2t = -\frac{1}{2}$ 　　　　(f) $\sin\frac{1}{2}t = 1$

(g) $\cos\frac{1}{5}t = 0$ 　　　　(h) $\tan 3t = -1$ 　　　　(i) $\sin\frac{1}{4}t = 0$

7 Find, to 1 decimal place, all values of z in the interval $-180° \leqslant z \leqslant 180°$ satisfying the following equations.

(a) $\sin z = -0.16$ 　　　　(b) $\cos z(1 + \sin z) = 0$ 　　　　(c) $(1 - \tan z)\sin z = 0$

(d) $\sin 2z = 0.23$ 　　　　(e) $(\cos z)^2 = 0.832$ 　　　　(f) $\sin z(2\sin z + 1) = 0$

8 Without using a calculator, find the exact roots of the following equations, if there are any, giving your answers in the interval $0° < \phi \leq 360°$.

(a) $\sin(\phi - 30°) = \frac{1}{2}$ (b) $\tan(\phi - 45°) = 0$ (c) $\cos(\phi + 135°) = \frac{1}{2}\sqrt{3}$

(d) $\tan(\phi - 45°) = -\sqrt{3}$ (e) $\cos(\phi - 50°) = -\frac{1}{2}$ (f) $\sin(\phi + 50°) = 1$

(g) $\cos(\phi - 50°) = 0$ (h) $\tan(\phi - 180°) = -1$ (i) $\sin(\phi - 20°) = 0$

9 Find, to 1 decimal place, all values of t in the interval $0° \leq t \leq 360°$ satisfying the following equations.

(a) $\cos(t - 25°) = 0.9$ (b) $\sin(t + 32°) = -0.3$ (c) $\tan(t - 110°) = 3$

(d) $\cos(t + 55°) = 0.8$ (e) $\sin(t - 131°) = -0.7$ (f) $\tan(t + 241°) = -0.5$

10 Find all values of θ in the interval $0° \leq \theta \leq 360°$ for which

(a) $\sin 2\theta = \cos 36°$,   (b) $\cos 5\theta = \sin 70°$,   (c) $\tan 3\theta = \tan 60°$.

11 Find all values of θ in the interval $0° \leq \theta \leq 180°$ for which $2 \sin \theta \cos \theta = \frac{1}{2} \tan \theta$.

12 For each of the following angles, give an example of a trigonometric function involving (i) sine, (ii) cosine and (iii) tangent, with that angles as period.

(a) $90°$ (b) $20°$ (c) $48°$

(d) $120°$ (e) $720°$ (f) $600°$

13 Sketch the graphs of each of the following in the interval $0° \leq \phi \leq 360°$. In each case, state the period of the function.

(a) $y = \sin 3\phi$ (b) $y = \cos 2\phi$ (c) $y = \sin 4\phi$

(d) $y = \tan \frac{1}{3}\phi$ (e) $y = \cos \frac{1}{2}\phi$ (f) $y = \sin \left(\frac{1}{2}\phi + 30°\right)$

(g) $y = \sin(3\phi - 20°)$ (h) $y = \tan 2\phi$ (i) $y = \tan \left(\frac{1}{2}\phi + 90°\right)$

14 At a certain latitude in the northern hemisphere, the number d of hours of daylight in each day of the year is taken to be $d = A + B \sin kt$, where A, B, k are positive constants and t is the time in days after the spring equinox.

(a) Assuming that the number of hours of daylight follows an annual cycle of 365 days, find the value of k, giving your answer correct to 3 decimal places.

(b) Given also that the shortest and longest days have 6 and 18 hours of daylight respectively, state the values of A and B. Find, in hours and minutes, the amount of daylight on New Year's Day, which is 80 days before the spring equinox.

(c) A town at this latitude holds a fair twice a year on those days having exactly 10 hours of daylight. Find, in relation to the spring equinox, which two days these are.

1.6 Relations between the trigonometric functions

In algebra you are used to solving equations, which involves finding a value of the unknown, often called x, in an equation such as $2x + 3 - x - 6 = 7$. You are also used to simplifying algebraic expressions like $2x + 3 - x - 6$, which becomes $x - 3$. You may not have realised, however, that these are quite different processes.

When you solve the equation $2x + 3 - x - 6 = 7$, you find that there is one root, $x = 10$. But the expression $x - 3$ is identical to $2x + 3 - x - 6$ for *all* values of x. Sometimes it is important to distinguish between these two situations.

If two expressions take the same values for every value of x, they are said to be **identically equal**. This is written with the symbol $\equiv$, read as 'is identically equal to'. The statement

$$2x + 3 - x - 6 \equiv x - 3$$

is called an **identity**. Thus an identity in x is a statement which is true for all values of x.

Similar ideas occur in trigonometry. In Section 1.2, it was observed that $\tan \theta = \dfrac{\sin \theta}{\cos \theta}$, provided that $\cos \theta \neq 0$. Thus

$$\tan \theta \equiv \frac{\sin \theta}{\cos \theta}.$$

The identity symbol is used even when there are some exceptional values for which neither side is defined. In the example given, neither side is defined when θ is an odd multiple of $90°$, but the identity sign is still used.

There is another relationship which comes immediately from the definitions of $\cos \theta = x$ and $\sin \theta = y$ in Sections 1.1 and 1.2.

In Fig. 1.28, which is a copy of Fig. 1.1, as P lies on the circumference of a circle with radius 1 unit, Pythagoras' theorem gives $x^2 + y^2 = 1$, or $(\cos \theta)^2 + (\sin \theta)^2 \equiv 1$.

Conventionally, $(\cos \theta)^2$ is written as $\cos^2 \theta$ and $(\sin \theta)^2$ as $\sin^2 \theta$, so for all values of θ, $\cos^2 \theta + \sin^2 \theta \equiv 1$.

This is sometimes called Pythagoras' theorem in trigonometry.

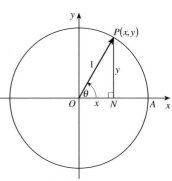

Fig. 1.28

For all values of θ:

$$\tan \theta \equiv \frac{\sin \theta}{\cos \theta}, \quad \text{provided that } \cos \theta \neq 0;$$

$$\cos^2 \theta + \sin^2 \theta \equiv 1.$$

The convention of using $\cos^n \theta$ to stand for $(\cos \theta)^n$ is best restricted to positive powers. In any case, it should *never* be used with $n = -1$, because of the danger of confusion with $\cos^{-1} x$, which is used to find an angle whose cosine is x. If in doubt, you should write $(\cos \theta)^n$ or $(\cos \theta)^{-n}$, which could only mean one thing.

Example 1.6.1

Simplify   (a) $1 - \cos^2 \theta$,   (b) $\dfrac{\sin \theta}{\cos \theta} + \dfrac{\cos \theta}{\sin \theta}$.

(a) As $\cos^2 \theta + \sin^2 \theta \equiv 1$, subtracting $\cos^2 \theta$ from both sides gives

$$\sin^2 \theta \equiv 1 - \cos^2 \theta, \quad \text{so } 1 - \cos^2 \theta \equiv \sin^2 \theta.$$

(b) Combining the fractions gives

$$\frac{\sin \theta}{\cos \theta} + \frac{\cos \theta}{\sin \theta} \equiv \frac{\sin \theta \times \sin \theta + \cos \theta \times \cos \theta}{\cos \theta \sin \theta}$$
$$\equiv \frac{\sin^2 \theta + \cos^2 \theta}{\cos \theta \sin \theta}$$
$$\equiv \frac{1}{\cos \theta \sin \theta} \quad (\text{using } \sin^2 \theta + \cos^2 \theta \equiv 1).$$

Example 1.6.2

Show that   (a) $1 - 2\sin^2 \theta \equiv 2\cos^2 \theta - 1$,   (b) $\dfrac{1}{1 + \cos \theta} + \dfrac{1}{1 - \cos \theta} \equiv \dfrac{2}{\sin^2 \theta}$.

To show that an identity is true, it is usually a good idea to start with one side, the more complicated one, and proceed to show that it is equal to the other side.

In part (a) both sides are equally complicated, so it doesn't really matter which side you start with: in part (b) the left side is clearly more complicated.

(a) $1 - 2\sin^2 \theta \equiv 1 - 2(1 - \cos^2 \theta)$ $(\text{using } \sin^2 \theta \equiv 1 - \cos^2 \theta)$
$ \equiv 1 - 2 + 2\cos^2 \theta$
$ \equiv 2\cos^2 \theta - 1.$

(b) $\dfrac{1}{1 + \cos \theta} + \dfrac{1}{1 - \cos \theta} \equiv \dfrac{1 \times (1 - \cos \theta) + 1 \times (1 + \cos \theta)}{(1 + \cos \theta)(1 - \cos \theta)}$
$\phantom{\dfrac{1}{1 + \cos \theta} + \dfrac{1}{1 - \cos \theta}} \equiv \dfrac{1 - \cos \theta + 1 + \cos \theta}{1 - \cos^2 \theta}$
$\phantom{\dfrac{1}{1 + \cos \theta} + \dfrac{1}{1 - \cos \theta}} \equiv \dfrac{2}{\sin^2 \theta} \quad (\text{using } 1 - \cos^2 \theta \equiv \sin^2 \theta).$

If you can't decide which side is the more complicated, or you can't see what to do, it is often productive to subtract the right side from the left side and attempt to get the result to be identically equal to zero. The next example is Example 1.6.2 part (a) again, using this technique.

Example 1.6.3

Show that $1 - 2\sin^2\theta \equiv 2\cos^2\theta - 1$.

Subtracting the right side from the left gives

$$\text{left side} - \text{right side} = 1 - 2\sin^2\theta - (2\cos^2\theta - 1)$$
$$= 1 - 2\sin^2\theta - 2\cos^2\theta + 1$$
$$= 2 - 2\sin^2\theta - 2\cos^2\theta$$
$$= 0. \quad (\text{using } \sin^2\theta + \cos^2\theta \equiv 1)$$

Hence left side $\equiv$ right side, and $1 - 2\sin^2\theta \equiv 2\cos^2\theta - 1$.

Example 1.6.4

Given that $\sin\theta = \frac{3}{5}$, and that the angle θ is obtuse, find, without using a calculator, the values of $\cos\theta$ and $\tan\theta$.

Since $\cos^2\theta + \sin^2\theta = 1$, $\cos^2\theta = 1 - \left(\frac{3}{5}\right)^2 = \frac{16}{25}$ giving $\cos\theta = \pm\frac{4}{5}$.

As the angle θ is obtuse, $90° < \theta < 180°$, so $\cos\theta$ is negative.

Therefore $\cos\theta = -\frac{4}{5}$.

As $\sin\theta = \frac{3}{5}$ and $\cos\theta = -\frac{4}{5}$,

$$\tan\theta = \frac{\sin\theta}{\cos\theta} = \frac{\frac{3}{5}}{\frac{-4}{5}} = -\frac{3}{4}.$$

Example 1.6.5

Solve the equation $3\cos^2\theta + 4\sin\theta = 4$, giving all the roots in the interval $-180° < \theta \leqslant 180°$ correct to 1 decimal place.

As it stands you cannot solve this equation, but if you replace $\cos^2\theta$ by $1 - \sin^2\theta$ you will obtain the equation

$$3(1 - \sin^2\theta) + 4\sin\theta = 4,$$

which reduces to

$$3\sin^2\theta - 4\sin\theta + 1 = 0.$$

This is a quadratic equation in $\sin\theta$, which you can solve using factors:

$$(3\sin\theta - 1)(\sin\theta - 1) = 0, \text{ giving } \sin\theta = \tfrac{1}{3} \text{ or } \sin\theta = 1.$$

If $\sin\theta = \frac{1}{3}$, there are two roots. The calculator gives $\sin^{-1}\frac{1}{3}$ as $19.47...°$, so this is one root. The other root, obtained from the symmetry of $\sin\theta$, is $180 - 19.47...° = 160.52...°$.

If $\sin\theta = 1$, there is only one root, $\theta = 90°$.

So the roots are $19.5°$, $90°$ and $160.5°$, correct to 1 decimal place.

Exercise 1D

1 For each triangle sketched below,

    (i) use Pythagoras' theorem to find the length of the third side in an exact form,

    (ii) write down the exact values of $\sin\theta$, $\cos\theta$ and $\tan\theta$.

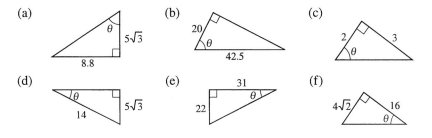

(a)   (b)   (c)

(d)   (e)   (f)

2 Simplify the following expressions, giving your answer in terms of a single trigonometric function.

    (a) $\dfrac{1-\cos^2 x}{\tan^2 x}$
               (b) $\dfrac{\sin^2 x}{1-\sin^2 x}$
               (c) $\dfrac{1-\cos^2 x}{1-\sin^2 x}$

3 (a) Given that angle A is obtuse and that $\sin A = \frac{5}{14}\sqrt{3}$, find the exact value of $\cos A$.

    (b) Given that $180 < B < 360$ and that $\tan B = -\frac{21}{20}$, find the exact value of $\cos B$.

    (c) Find all possible values of $\sin C$ for which $\cos C = \frac{1}{2}$.

    (d) Find the values of D for which $-180° < D < 180°$ and $\tan D = 5\sin D$.

4 Use $\tan\theta \equiv \dfrac{\sin\theta}{\cos\theta}$, $\cos\theta \neq 0$, and $\cos^2\theta + \sin^2\theta \equiv 1$ to establish the following.

    (a) $\dfrac{1}{\sin\theta} - \tan\theta\cos\theta \equiv \dfrac{\cos^2\theta}{\sin\theta}$
                (b) $\dfrac{\sin\theta}{\tan\theta} \equiv \cos\theta$

    (c) $(\cos\theta + \sin\theta)^2 + (\cos\theta - \sin\theta)^2 \equiv 2$
        (d) $\sin\theta\tan\theta + \cos\theta \equiv \dfrac{1}{\cos\theta}$

    (e) $\dfrac{1}{\sin\theta} - \dfrac{1}{\tan\theta} \equiv \dfrac{1-\cos\theta}{\sin\theta}$
           (f) $\dfrac{\sin^2\theta}{1-\cos\theta} \equiv 1+\cos\theta$

    (g) $\dfrac{1}{\cos\theta} + \tan\theta \equiv \dfrac{\cos\theta}{1-\sin\theta}$
           (h) $\dfrac{\tan\theta\sin\theta}{1-\cos\theta} \equiv 1+\dfrac{1}{\cos\theta}$

5 Solve the following equations for θ, giving all the roots in the interval $0° \leqslant \theta \leqslant 360°$ correct to the nearest 0.1.

    (a) $4\sin^2\theta - 1 = 0$
                          (b) $\sin^2\theta + 2\cos^2\theta = 2$

    (c) $4\cos^2\theta + 3\sin\theta = 4$
                     (d) $\cos^2\theta + \sin\theta + 1 = 0$

    (e) $3 - 3\cos\theta = 2\sin^2\theta$
                     (f) $\cos^2\theta + \cos\theta = \sin^2\theta$

    (g) $10\sin^2\theta - 5\cos^2\theta + 2 = 4\sin\theta$
       (h) $4\sin^2\theta\cos\theta = \tan^2\theta$

6 Find all values of θ, $-180° < \theta < 180°$, for which $2\tan\theta - 3 = \dfrac{2}{\tan\theta}$.

Miscellaneous exercise 1

1 Write down the period of each of the following.

  (a) $\sin x$ (b) $\tan 2x$ (OCR)

2 By considering the graph of $y = \cos x$, or otherwise, express the following in terms of $\cos x$.

  (a) $\cos(360° - x)$ (b) $\cos(x + 180°)$ (OCR)

3 Draw the graph of $y = \cos \frac{1}{2}\theta$ for θ in the interval $-360° \leqslant \theta \leqslant 360°$. Mark clearly the coordinates of the points where the graph crosses the θ and y-axes.

4 Solve the following equations for θ, giving your answers in the interval $0° \leqslant \theta \leqslant 360°$.

  (a) $\tan \theta = 0.4$ (b) $\sin 2\theta = 0.4$ (OCR)

5 Solve the equation $3 \cos 2x = 2$, giving all the solutions in the interval $0° \leqslant x \leqslant 180°$ correct to the nearest 0.1.   (OCR)

6 (a) Give an example of a trigonometric function which has a period of $180°$.

  (b) Solve for x the equation $\sin 3x = 0.5$, giving all solutions in the interval $0° < x < 180°$.   (OCR)

7 Find all values of θ, $0° \leqslant \theta \leqslant 360°$, for which $2 \cos(\theta + 30°) = 1$.   (OCR)

8 (a) Express $\sin 2x + \cos(90° - 2x)$ in terms of a single trigonometric function.

  (b) Hence, or otherwise, find all values of x in the interval $0° \leqslant x \leqslant 360°$ for which $\sin 2x + \cos(90° - 2x) = -1$.   (OCR)

9 Find the least positive value of the angle A for which

  (a) $\sin A = 0.2$ and $\cos A$ is negative,   (b) $\tan A = -0.5$ and $\sin A$ is negative,

  (c) $\cos A = \sin A$ and both are negative,   (d) $\sin A = -0.2275$ and $A > 360°$.

10 Prove the following identities.

  (a) $\dfrac{1}{\sin \theta} - \sin \theta \equiv \dfrac{\cos \theta}{\tan \theta}$ (b) $\dfrac{1 - \sin \theta}{\cos \theta} \equiv \dfrac{\cos \theta}{1 + \sin \theta}$

  (c) $\dfrac{1}{\tan \theta} + \tan \theta \equiv \dfrac{1}{\sin \theta \cos \theta}$ (d) $\dfrac{1 - 2 \sin^2 \theta}{\cos \theta + \sin \theta} \equiv \cos \theta - \sin \theta$

11 For each of the following functions, determine the maximum and minimum values of y and the least positive values of x at which these occur.

  (a) $y = 1 + \cos 2x$ (b) $y = 5 - 4 \sin(x + 30°)$

  (c) $y = 29 - 20 \sin(3x - 45°)$ (d) $y = 8 - 3 \cos^2 x$

  (e) $y = \dfrac{12}{3 + \cos x}$ (f) $y = \dfrac{60}{1 + \sin^2(2x - 15°)}$

12 Solve the following equations for θ, giving solutions in the interval $0° \leqslant \theta \leqslant 360°$.

  (a) $\sin \theta = \tan \theta$ (b) $2 - 2 \cos^2 \theta = \sin \theta$

  (c) $\tan^2 \theta - 2 \tan \theta = 1$ (d) $\sin 2\theta - \sqrt{3} \cos 2\theta = 0$

13 The function t is defined by $t(x) = \tan 3x$.

    (a) State the period of $t(x)$.

    (b) Solve the equation $t(x) = \frac{1}{2}$ for $0° \leqslant x \leqslant 180°$.

    (c) Deduce the smallest positive solution of each of the following equations.
        (i) $t(x) = -\frac{1}{2}$
        (ii) $t(x) = 2$ (OCR)

14 In each of the following, construct a formula involving a trigonometric function which could be used to model the situations described.

    (a) Water depths in a canal vary between a minimum of 3.6 metres and a maximum of 6 metres over 24-hour periods.

    (b) Petroleum refining at a chemical plant is run on a 10-day cycle, with a minimum production of 15 000 barrels per day and a maximum of 28 000 barrels per day.

    (c) At a certain town just south of the Arctic circle, the number of hours of daylight varies between 2 and 22 hours during a 360-day year.

15 A tuning fork is vibrating. The displacement, y centimetres, of the tip of one of the prongs from its rest position after t seconds is given by

$$y = 0.1\sin(100\,000t).$$

Find

    (a) the greatest displacement and the first time at which it occurs,

    (b) the time taken for one complete oscillation of the prong,

    (c) the number of complete oscillations per second of the tip of the prong,

    (d) the total time during the first complete oscillation for which the tip of the prong is more than 0.06 centimetres from its rest position.

16 One end of a piece of elastic is attached to a point at the top of a door frame and the other end hangs freely. A small ball is attached to the free end of the elastic. When the ball is hanging freely it is pulled down a small distance and then released, so that the ball oscillates up and down on the elastic. The depth d centimetres of the ball from the top of the door frame after t seconds is given by

$$d = 100 + 10\cos 500t.$$

Find

    (a) the greatest and least depths of the ball,

    (b) the time at which the ball first reaches its highest position,

    (c) the time taken for a complete oscillation,

    (d) the proportion of the time during a complete oscillation for which the depth of the ball is less than 99 centimetres.

17* An oscillating particle has displacement y metres, where y is given by $y = a\sin(kt + \alpha)$, where a is measured in metres, t is measured in seconds and k and α are constants. The time for a complete oscillation is T seconds. Find

(a) k in terms of T,

(b) the number, in terms of k, of complete oscillations per second.

18* The population, P, of a certain type of bird on a remote island varies during the course of a year according to feeding, breeding, migratory seasons and predator interactions. An ornithologist doing research into bird numbers for this species attempts to model the population on the island with the annually periodic equation

$$P = N - C\cos\omega t,$$

where N, C and ω are constants, and t is the time in weeks, with $t = 0$ representing midnight on the first of January.

(a) Taking the period of this function to be 50 weeks, find the value of ω.

(b) Use the equation to describe, in terms of N and C,
   (i) the number of birds of this species on the island at the start of each year;
   (ii) the maximum number of these birds, and the time of year when this occurs.

19* The road to an island close to the shore is sometimes covered by the tide. When the water rises to the level of the road, the road is closed. On a particular day, the water at high tide is a height 4.6 metres above mean sea level. The height, h metres, of the tide is modelled by using the equation $h = 4.6\cos kt$, where t is the time in hours from high tide; it is also assumed that high tides occur every 12 hours.

(a) Determine the value of k.

(b) On the same day, a notice says that the road will be closed for 3 hours. Assuming that this notice is correct, find the height of the road above sea level, giving your answer correct to two decimal places.

(c) In fact, a road repair has raised its level, and it is impassable for only 2 hours 40 minutes. By how many centimetres has the road level been raised?　　　　(OCR)

20* A simple model of the tides in a harbour on the south coast of Cornwall assumes that they are caused by the attractions of the Sun and the Moon. The magnitude of the attraction of the Moon is assumed to be nine times the magnitude of the attraction of the Sun. The period of the Sun's effect is taken to be 360 days and that of the Moon is 30 days. A model for the height, h metres, of the tide (relative to a mark fixed on the harbour wall), at t days, is

$$h = A\cos\alpha t + B\cos\beta t,$$

where the term $A\cos\alpha t$ is the effect due to the Sun, and the term $B\cos\beta t$ is the effect due to the Moon. Given that $h = 5$ when $t = 0$, determine the values of A, B, α and β.　　　　(OCR, adapted)

2 Sequences

This chapter is about sequences of numbers. When you have completed it, you should

- know that a sequence can be constructed from a formula or a recursive definition
- be familiar with triangle, factorial, Pascal and arithmetic sequences
- know how to find the sum of an arithmetic series
- be able to use sigma notation.

2.1 Constructing sequences

Here are six rows of numbers, each forming a pattern of some kind. What are the next three numbers in each row?

(a) $1, \quad 4, \quad 9, \quad 16, \quad 25, \quad \ldots$

(b) $\frac{1}{2}, \quad \frac{2}{3}, \quad \frac{3}{4}, \quad \frac{4}{5}, \quad \frac{5}{6}, \quad \ldots$

(c) $99, \quad 97, \quad 95, \quad 93, \quad 91, \quad \ldots$

(d) $1, \quad 1.1, \quad 1.21, \quad 1.331, \quad 1.4641, \quad \ldots$

(e) $2, \quad 4, \quad 8, \quad 14, \quad 22, \quad \ldots$

(f) $3, \quad 1, \quad 4, \quad 1, \quad 5, \quad \ldots$

Rows of this kind are called **sequences**, and the separate numbers are called **terms**.

The usual notation for the first, second, third, ... terms of a sequence is u_1, u_2, u_3, and so on. There is nothing special about the choice of the letter u, and other letters such as v, x, t and I are often used instead, especially if the sequence appears in some application. If r is a natural number, then the rth term will be u_r, v_r, x_r, t_r or I_r.

> Sometimes it is convenient to number the terms $u_0, u_1, u_2, \ldots$, starting with $r = 0$, but you then have to be careful in referring to 'the first term': do you mean u_0 or u_1?

In (a) and (b) you would have no difficulty in writing a formula for the rth term of the sequence. The numbers in (a) could be rewritten as $1^2, 2^2, 3^2, 4^2, 5^2$, and the pattern could be summed up by writing

$$u_r = r^2.$$

The terms of (b) are $\dfrac{1}{1+1}, \dfrac{2}{2+1}, \dfrac{3}{3+1}, \dfrac{4}{4+1}, \dfrac{5}{5+1}$, so $u_r = \dfrac{r}{r+1}$.

In (c), (d) and (e) you probably expect that there is a formula, but it is not so easy to find it. What is more obvious is how to get each term from the one before. For example, in (c) the terms go down by 2 at each step, so that $u_2 = u_1 - 2$, $u_3 = u_2 - 2$, $u_4 = u_3 - 2$, and so on. These steps can be summarised by the single equation

$$u_{r+1} = u_r - 2.$$

The terms in (d) are multiplied by 1.1 at each step, so the rule is

$$u_{r+1} = 1.1u_r.$$

Unfortunately, there are many other sequences which satisfy the equation $u_{r+1} = u_r - 2$. Other examples are $10, 8, 6, 4, 2, \ldots$ and $-2, -4, -6, -8, -10, \ldots$

The definition is not complete until you know the first term. So to complete the definitions of the sequences (c) and (d) you have to write

(c) $u_1 = 99$ and $u_{r+1} = u_r - 2$,

(d) $u_1 = 1$ and $u_{r+1} = 1.1u_r$.

Definitions like these are called **recursive definitions**, or sometimes 'inductive definitions'.

Sequence (e) originates from geometry. It gives the greatest number of regions into which a plane can be split by different numbers of circles. (Try drawing your own diagrams with 1, 2, 3, 4, ... circles.) This sequence is developed as $u_2 = u_1 + 2$, $u_3 = u_2 + 4$, $u_4 = u_3 + 6$, and so on. Since the increments 2, 4, 6, ... are themselves given by the formula $2r$, this can be summarised by the recursive definition

$$u_1 = 2 \text{ and } u_{r+1} = u_r + 2r.$$

For (f) you may have given the next three terms as 1, 6, 1 (expecting the even-placed terms all to be 1, and the odd-placed terms to go up by 1 at each step). In fact this sequence had a quite different origin, as the first five digits of π in decimal form! With this meaning, the next three terms would be 9, 2, 6.

This illustrates an important point, that a sequence can never be uniquely defined by giving just the first few terms. Try, for example, working out the first eight terms of the sequence defined by

$$u_r = r^2 + (r-1)(r-2)(r-3)(r-4)(r-5).$$

You will find that the first five terms are the same as those given in (a), but the next three are probably very different from your original guess.

A sequence can only be described unambiguously by giving a formula, a recursive definition in terms of a general natural number r, or some other general rule.

Exercise 2A

1 Write down the first five terms of the sequences with the following definitions.

(a) $u_1 = 7$, $u_{r+1} = u_r + 7$

(b) $u_1 = 13$, $u_{r+1} = u_r - 5$

(c) $u_1 = 4$, $u_{r+1} = 3u_r$

(d) $u_1 = 6$, $u_{r+1} = \frac{1}{2}u_r$

(e) $u_1 = 2$, $u_{r+1} = 3u_r + 1$

(f) $u_1 = 1$, $u_{r+1} = u_r^2 + 3$

2 Suggest recursive definitions which would produce the following sequences.

(a) 2, 4, 6, 8, 10, ...

(b) 11, 9, 7, 5, 3, ...

(c) 2, 6, 10, 14, 18, ...

(d) 2, 6, 18, 54, 162, ...

(e) $\frac{1}{3}$, $\frac{1}{9}$, $\frac{1}{27}$, $\frac{1}{81}$, ...

(f) $\frac{1}{2}a$, $\frac{1}{4}a$, $\frac{1}{8}a$, $\frac{1}{16}a$, ...

(g) $b - 2c$, $b - c$, b, $b + c$, ...

(h) 1, -1, 1, -1, 1, ...

(i) $\dfrac{p}{q^3}$, $\dfrac{p}{q^2}$, $\dfrac{p}{q}$, ...

(j) $\dfrac{a^3}{b^2}$, $\dfrac{a^2}{b}$, a, b, ...

(k) x^3, $5x^2$, $25x$, ...

(l) 1, $1 + x$, $(1 + x)^2$, $(1 + x)^3$, ...

3 Write down the first five terms of each sequence and give a recursive definition for it.

(a) $u_r = 2r + 3$

(b) $u_r = r^2$

(c) $u_r = \frac{1}{2}r(r + 1)$

(d) $u_r = \frac{1}{6}r(r + 1)(2r + 1)$

(e) $u_r = 2 \times 3^r$

(f) $u_r = 3 \times 5^{r-1}$

4 For each of the following sequences give a possible formula for the rth term.

(a) 9, 8, 7, 6, ...

(b) 6, 18, 54, 162, ...

(c) 4, 7, 12, 19, ...

(d) 4, 12, 24, 40, 60, ...

(e) $\frac{1}{4}$, $\frac{3}{5}$, $\frac{5}{6}$, $\frac{7}{7}$, ...

(f) $\frac{2}{2}$, $\frac{5}{4}$, $\frac{10}{8}$, $\frac{17}{16}$, ...

2.2   The triangle number sequence

The numbers of crosses in the triangular patterns in Fig. 2.1 are called triangle numbers. If t_r denotes the rth triangle number, you can see by counting the numbers of crosses in successive rows that

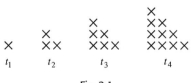

Fig. 2.1

$$t_1 = 1, \quad t_2 = 1 + 2 = 3, \quad t_3 = 1 + 2 + 3 = 6,$$

and in general $t_r = 1 + 2 + 3 + \cdots + r$, where the dots indicate that all the natural numbers between 3 and r have to be included in the addition.

Fig. 2.2 shows a typical pattern of crosses forming a triangle number t_r. (It is in fact drawn for $r = 9$, but any other value of r could have been chosen.) An easy way of finding a formula for t_r is to make a similar pattern of 'noughts', and then to turn it upside down and place it alongside the pattern of crosses, as in Fig. 2.3. The noughts and crosses together then make a

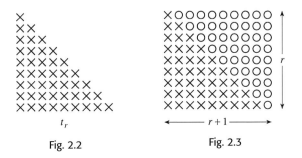

Fig. 2.2

Fig. 2.3

rectangular pattern, $r + 1$ objects wide and r objects high. So the total number of objects is $r(r + 1)$, half of them crosses and half noughts. The number of crosses alone is therefore

$$t_r = \tfrac{1}{2}r(r + 1).$$

This shows that:

> The sum of all the natural numbers from 1 to r is $\tfrac{1}{2}r(r + 1)$.

Example 2.2.1
Find   (a) the sum of the first 50 natural numbers,
(b) the sum of the natural numbers from 31 to 50 inclusive,
(c) the sum of the first 30 even numbers.

(a) Using the formula $\tfrac{1}{2}r(r + 1)$ in the box with $r = 50$, the sum of the first 50 natural numbers is

$$1 + 2 + \cdots + 50 = \tfrac{1}{2} \times 50 \times (50 + 1) = 25 \times 51 = 1275.$$

(b) Using an 'add and subtract method',

$$\begin{aligned} 31 + 32 + \cdots + 50 &= (1 + 2 + \cdots + 50) - (1 + 2 + \cdots + 30) \\ &= 1275 - \tfrac{1}{2} \times 30 \times (30 + 1) \\ &= 1275 - 15 \times 31 = 810. \end{aligned}$$

(c) The 30th even number is 60, so

$$\begin{aligned} 2 + 4 + \cdots + 60 &= 2(1 + 2 + \cdots + 30) \\ &= 2 \times \tfrac{1}{2} \times 30 \times (30 + 1) \\ &= 30 \times 31 = 930. \end{aligned}$$

You can put the geometric argument which gives the result in the box into algebraic form. If you count the crosses from the top downwards you get

$$t_r = \quad 1 \quad + \quad 2 \quad + \quad 3 \quad + \cdots + (r - 2) + (r - 1) + \quad r,$$

but if you count the noughts from the top downwards you get

$$t_r = \quad r \quad + (r - 1) + (r - 2) + \cdots + \quad 3 \quad + \quad 2 \quad + \quad 1.$$

Counting all the objects in the rectangle is equivalent to adding these two equations:

$$2t_r = (r + 1) + (r + 1) + (r + 1) + \cdots + (r + 1) + (r + 1) + (r + 1)$$

with one $(r + 1)$ bracket for each of the r rows. It follows that $2t_r = r(r + 1)$, so that

$$t_r = \tfrac{1}{2}r(r + 1).$$

It is also possible to give a recursive definition for the sequence t_r. Fig. 2.1 shows that to get from any triangle number to the next you simply add an extra row of crosses underneath.

Thus $t_2 = t_1 + 2$, $t_3 = t_2 + 3$, $t_4 = t_3 + 4$, and in general

$$t_{r+1} = t_r + (r + 1).$$

You can complete this definition by specifying either $t_1 = 1$ or $t_0 = 0$. If you choose $t_0 = 0$, then you can find t_1 by putting $r = 0$ in the general equation, as $t_1 = t_0 + 1 = 0 + 1 = 1$. So you may as well define the triangle number sequence by

$$t_0 = 0 \quad \text{and} \quad t_{r+1} = t_r + (r + 1), \quad \text{where } r = 0, 1, 2, 3, \ldots .$$

2.3 The factorial sequence

If, in the definition of t_r, you go from one term to the next by multiplication rather than addition, you get the factorial sequence

$$f_{r+1} = f_r \times (r + 1), \quad \text{where } r = 0, 1, 2, 3, \ldots$$

There would be little point in defining f_0 to be 0 (think about why this is); instead take f_0 to be 1. (This may seem strange, but you will see the reason in the next chapter.) You then get

$$f_1 = f_0 \times 1 = 1 \times 1 = 1, \quad f_2 = f_1 \times 2 = 1 \times 2 = 2, \quad f_3 = f_2 \times 3 = 2 \times 3 = 6,$$

and if you go on in this way you find that, for any $r \geqslant 1$,

$$f_r = 1 \times 2 \times 3 \times \cdots \times r$$

or (sometimes more conveniently)

$$f_r = r \times (r - 1) \times \cdots \times 3 \times 2 \times 1.$$

This sequence is so important that it has its own special notation, $r!$, read as 'factorial r' or 'r factorial' (or often, colloquially, as 'r shriek' or 'r bang').

> **Factorial r** is defined by $0! = 1$ and $(r + 1)! = r! \times (r + 1)$, where $r = 0, 1, 2, 3, \ldots$
>
> For $r \geqslant 1$, $r!$ is the product of all the natural numbers from 1 to r.

Many calculators have a special key labelled [$n!$]. For small values of n the display gives the exact value, but the numbers in the sequence increase so rapidly that from about $n = 14$ onwards only an approximate value in standard form can be displayed.

Example 2.3.1

Calculate (a) $4!$, (b) $6!$, (c) $\dfrac{10!}{7!}$.

(a) $4! = 4 \times 3 \times 2 \times 1 = 24$.

(b) $6! = 6 \times 5 \times 4 \times 3 \times 2 \times 1 = 720$.

(c) $\dfrac{10!}{7!} = \dfrac{10 \times 9 \times 8 \times 7 \times 6 \times 5 \times 4 \times 3 \times 2 \times 1}{7 \times 6 \times 5 \times 4 \times 3 \times 2 \times 1} = \dfrac{10 \times 9 \times 8}{1} = 720$.

This last example is typical. Don't be tempted to multiply out $10!$ and $7!$ and then divide the results. That would be a very long-winded method. Give yourself a chance to cancel.

Here is another example where cancelling is helpful.

Example 2.3.2

Calculate $\dfrac{12!}{8!\,4!}$.

$$\frac{12!}{8!\,4!} = \frac{12 \times 11 \times 10 \times 9 \times 8 \times 7 \times 6 \times 5 \times 4 \times 3 \times 2 \times 1}{(8 \times 7 \times 6 \times 5 \times 4 \times 3 \times 2 \times 1) \times (4 \times 3 \times 2 \times 1)} = \frac{12 \times 11 \times 10 \times 9}{4 \times 3 \times 2 \times 1} = 495.$$

2.4 Pascal sequences

You have almost certainly met **Pascal's triangle** at some time.

The earliest recorded use of Pascal's triangle was in China, but Blaise Pascal (a French mathematician of the 17th century, one of the originators of probability theory) was one of the first people in Europe to publish it. It is usually presented in isosceles form (Fig. 2.4), drawing attention to the symmetry of the sequence.

```
              1       1
          1       2       1
      1       3       6       3       1
  1       4       6       4       1
1     5    10       10    5    1
1   6   15     20     15   6    1
```

Fig. 2.4

You may be surprised to notice that every number in the pattern in Fig. 2.4 except for the 1s is the sum of the two numbers most closely above it.

You will find in the next chapter that these numbers feature in the expansion of expressions like $(x + y)^n$.

For algebraic applications of Pascal's triangle the format of Fig. 2.5 is often more convenient. What now appears is a set of sequences, called Pascal sequences.

```
1,  1
1,  2,   1
1,  3,   3,    1
1,  4,   6,    4,    1
1,  5,  10,   10,    5,   1
1,  6,  15,   20,   15,   6,   1
```

Fig. 2.5

These Pascal sequences are based on a multiplication rule. A typical example, for the 4th row, has a recursive definition

$$p_0 = 1 \quad \text{and} \quad p_{r+1} = \frac{4 - r}{r + 1}p_r, \quad \text{where } r = 0, 1, 2, 3, \ldots$$

Using the recursive definition for $r = 0, 1, 2, \ldots$ in turn produces the terms

$$p_1 = \tfrac{4}{1}p_0 = 4, \quad p_2 = \tfrac{3}{2}p_1 = 6, \quad p_3 = \tfrac{2}{3}p_2 = 4,$$

$$p_4 = \tfrac{1}{4}p_3 = 1, \quad p_5 = \tfrac{0}{5}p_4 = 0, \quad p_6 = \tfrac{(-1)}{6}p_5 = 0, \quad \text{and so on.}$$

You will see that at a certain stage the sequence has a zero term, and because it is formed by multiplication all the terms after that will be zero. So the complete sequence is

$$1, 4, 6, 4, 1, 0, 0, 0, 0, 0, \ldots .$$

Note that in Fig. 2.5, the zeros have been removed.

This is only one of a family of Pascal sequences, and its terms also have a special notation, $\binom{4}{r}$. For example, $\binom{4}{0} = 1$, $\binom{4}{1} = 4$, $\binom{4}{2} = 6$, and so on. Other Pascal sequences have numbers different from 4 in the multiplying factor.

The general definition of a Pascal sequence, whose terms are denoted by $\binom{n}{r}$, is

$$\binom{n}{0} = 1 \quad \text{and} \quad \binom{n}{r+1} = \frac{n-r}{r+1}\binom{n}{r}, \quad \text{where } r = 0, 1, 2, 3, \ldots$$

Check for yourself that the Pascal sequences for $n = 1, 2, 3$ are as follows.

$$
\begin{array}{llllllll}
n = 1: & 1, & 1, & 0, & 0, & 0, & \ldots \\
n = 2: & 1, & 2, & 1, & 0, & 0, & \ldots \\
n = 3: & 1, & 3, & 3, & 1, & 0, & \ldots
\end{array}
$$

You have seen these numbers before: look back at sequence (d) in Section 2.1.

Exercise 2B

1 Calculate the following sums.

(a) $1 + 2 + (\text{all the integers up to}) + 40$ (b) $21 + 22 + (\text{all the integers up to}) + 40$

(c) $2 + 4 + (\text{all the even integers up to}) + 40$ (d) $1 + 3 + (\text{all the odd integers up to}) + 39$

2 Without using a calculator, evaluate the following.

(a) $7!$ (b) $\dfrac{8!}{3!}$ (c) $\dfrac{7!}{4! \times 3!}$

3 Write the following in terms of factorials.

(a) $8 \times 7 \times 6 \times 5$ (b) $9 \times 10 \times 11 \times 12$ (c) $n(n-1)(n-2)$

(d) $n(n^2 - 1)$ (e) $n(n+1)(n+2)(n+3)$ (f) $(n+6)(n+5)(n+4)$

(g) $8 \times 7!$ (h) $n \times (n-1)!$

4 Simplify the following.

(a) $\dfrac{12!}{11!}$ (b) $23! - 22!$ (c) $\dfrac{(n+1)!}{n!}$ (d) $(n+1)! - n!$

5 Use the recursive definition in Section 2.4 to find the Pascal sequences for

(a) $n = 8$,   (b) $n = 9$.

6 Use the recursive definition for $\binom{n}{r}$ to show that $\binom{9}{6} = \dfrac{9 \times 8 \times 7}{1 \times 2 \times 3}$, and show that this can be written as $\dfrac{9!}{6! \times 3!}$.

Use a similar method to write the following in terms of factorials.

(a) $\binom{11}{4}$ (b) $\binom{11}{7}$ (c) $\binom{10}{5}$ (d) $\binom{12}{3}$ (e) $\binom{12}{9}$

7 The answers to Question 6 suggest a general result, that $\binom{n}{r} = \dfrac{n!}{r! \times (n-r)!}$. Assuming this to be true, show that $\binom{n}{r} = \binom{n}{n-r}$.

8 Show by direct calculation that

(a) $\binom{6}{3} + \binom{6}{4} = \binom{7}{4}$, (b) $\binom{8}{5} + \binom{8}{6} = \binom{9}{6}$.

Write a general statement, involving n and r, suggested by these results.

9 Using Fig. 2.3 as an example,

(a) draw a pattern of crosses to represent the rth triangle number t_r;

(b) draw another pattern of noughts to represent t_{r-1};

(c) combine these two patterns to show that $t_r + t_{r-1} = r^2$.

(d) Use the fact that $t_r = \frac{1}{2}r(r+1)$ to show the result in part (c) algebraically.

10 (a) Find an expression in terms of r for $t_r - t_{r-1}$ for all $r \geqslant 1$.

(b) Use this result and that in Question 9(c) to show that $t_r^2 - t_{r-1}^2 = r^3$.

(c) Use part (b) to write expressions in terms of triangle numbers for $1^3, 2^3, 3^3, \ldots, n^3$.

Hence show that $1^3 + 2^3 + 3^3 + \cdots + n^3 = t_n^2 - t_0^2 = \frac{1}{4}n^2(n+1)^2$.

11 The Pascal sequence for $n = 2$ is   1   2   1.

The sum of the terms in this sequence is $1 + 2 + 1 = 4$.

Investigate the sum of the terms in Pascal sequences for other values of n.

12 Show that $\dfrac{(2n)!}{n!} = 2^n(1 \times 3 \times 5 \times \cdots \times (2n-1))$.

2.5 Arithmetic sequences

An **arithmetic sequence**, or **arithmetic progression**, is a sequence whose terms go up or down by constant steps.

Here are some examples.

(a)   1,   3,   5,   7,   9,   ...

(b)   2,   5,   8,   11,   14,   ...

(c)   99,   97,   95,   93,   91,   ...

(d)   3,   1.5,   0,   −1.5,   −3,   ...

It is easy to write down recursive definitions for these sequences. In sequence (a), for example, the step from each term to the next is $+2$. You can write this as an equation, $u_{r+1} = u_r + 2$. You also need to state that the first term, u_1, is 1. The complete definition is then

$$u_1 = 1, \quad u_{r+1} = u_r + 2.$$

Check for yourself that the other three sequences have recursive definitions

(b) $u_1 = 2, \quad u_{r+1} = u_r + 3;$

(c) $u_1 = 99, \quad u_{r+1} = u_r - 2;$

(d) $u_1 = 3, \quad u_{r+1} = u_r - 1.5.$

You will see that these definitions all have the form

$$u_1 = a, \quad u_{r+1} = u_r + d$$

for different values of a and d. The letter a is usually chosen for the first term of the sequence. The step d is called the **common difference**.

Example 2.5.1
An arithmetic sequence is defined by

$$u_1 = 5, \quad u_{r+1} = u_r + 7.$$

Find (a) the fifth term, (b) the fiftieth term.

(a) It is simple to count up

$$u_2 = u_1 + 7 = 5 + 7 = 12, \quad u_3 = u_2 + 7 = 12 + 7 = 19,$$
$$u_4 = u_3 + 7 = 19 + 7 = 26, \quad u_5 = u_4 + 7 = 26 + 7 = 33.$$

The fifth term of the sequence is 33.

(b) You certainly wouldn't want to carry on as in part (a) until you reach u_{50}. It is simpler to note that, in going from the first term to the fiftieth, you have to add 7 on 49 times. So

$$u_{50} = u_1 + 49 \times 7 = 5 + 343 = 348.$$

The fiftieth term of the sequence is 348.

The method used in part (b) of Example 2.5.1 can be applied to any sequence with first term a and common difference d to find a formula for u_r, the rth term. In going from the first term to the rth term you have to add the step d on $(r - 1)$ times. Since the first term is a, the rth term is

$$u_r = a + (r - 1)d.$$

An arithmetic sequence with first term a and common difference d is defined recursively by

$$u_1 = a, \quad u_{r+1} = u_r + d.$$

The rth term of the sequence is given by

$$u_r = a + (r - 1)d.$$

Example 2.5.2

The 10th term of the sequence (b) above is also a term of the sequence (c). Which term is it?

For the sequence (b), $a = 2$ and $d = 3$, so the 10th term is

$$2 + (10 - 1) \times 3 = 2 + 27 = 29.$$

For the sequence (c), $a = 99$ and $d = -2$, so the rth term is

$$99 + (r - 1) \times (-2) = 99 - 2r + 2 = 101 - 2r.$$

This has to equal 29, so

$$101 - 2r = 29,$$

giving

$$r = 36.$$

The 10th term of sequence (b) is the 36th term of sequence (c).

Example 2.5.3

The 12th term of an arithmetic sequence is 23 and the 19th term is 65. Find the first term and the common difference.

You can either reason this out arithmetically or use algebra, whichever you prefer.

Method 1   In getting from the 12th term to the 19th you take 7 steps of the common difference. In doing this the terms increase by $65 - 23$, which is 42. So each step is of amount $42 \div 7$, which is 6.

Therefore, in getting from the first term to the 12th the terms increase by 11 steps of 6, a total increase of 66. So the first term is $23 - 66 = -43$.

Method 2   Let the first term be a and the common difference d. Then, using the formula for the rth term,

$$a + (12 - 1)d = 23 \quad \text{and} \quad a + (19 - 1)d = 65.$$

So a and d can be found from the simultaneous equations

$$a + 11d = 23,$$
$$a + 18d = 65.$$

Subtracting the first equation from the second,

$$7d = 42,$$

which gives $d = 6$. Substituting this in the first equation gives

$$a + 11 \times 6 = 23,$$

so $a = -43$.

The first term is -43 and the common difference is 6.

Example 2.5.4

A person who usually eats 600 grams of bread a day tries to lose weight by reducing his consumption by 15 grams each day. After how many days will his consumption be less than 200 grams?

After $1, 2, 3, \ldots$ days his consumption (in grams) will be $585, 570, 555, \ldots$. This is an arithmetic sequence with first term $a = 585$ and common difference $d = -15$. Using the formula, his consumption on the rth day will be

$$585 + (r - 1) \times (-15) = 585 - 15(r - 1)$$
$$= 600 - 15r.$$

The question asks for the smallest value of r for which this is less than 200. This is found by solving the inequality

$$600 - 15r < 200,$$

which gives

$$15r > 600 - 200 = 400,$$
$$r > \frac{400}{15} = 26\tfrac{2}{3}.$$

The smallest integer value of r for which this is true is 27.

He will get his consumption down below 200 grams after 27 days.

2.6   Finding the sum of arithmetic series

Example 2.6.1

Sarah would like to give a sum of money to a charity each year for 10 years. She decides to give £100 in the first year, and to increase her contribution by £20 each year. How much does she give in the last year, and how much does the charity receive from her altogether?

Although she makes 10 contributions, there are only 9 increases. So in the last year she gives £$(100 + 9 \times 20) =$ £280.

If the total amount the charity receives is £S, then

$$S = 100 + 120 + 140 + \cdots + 240 + 260 + 280.$$

With only 10 numbers it is easy enough to add these up, but you can also find the sum by a method similar to that used in Section 2.2 to find a formula for t_n. If you add up the numbers in reverse order, you get

$$S = 280 + 260 + 240 + \cdots + 140 + 120 + 100.$$

Adding the two equations then gives

$$2S = 380 + 380 + 380 + \cdots + 380 + 380 + 380,$$

where the number 380 occurs 10 times. So

$$2S = 380 \times 10 = 3800, \text{ giving } S = 1900.$$

Over the 10 years the charity receives £1900.

This calculation can be illustrated with diagrams similar to Figs. 2.2 and 2.3. Sarah's contributions are shown by Fig. 2.6, with the first year in the top row. (Each cross is worth £20.) In Fig. 2.7 a second copy, with noughts instead of crosses, is put alongside it, but turned upside down. There are then 10 rows, each with 19 crosses or noughts and worth £380.

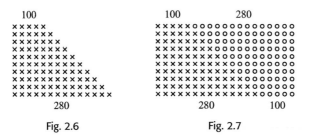

Fig. 2.6   Fig. 2.7

Two features of Example 2.6.1 are typical of arithmetic progressions.

- They usually only continue for a finite number of terms.
- It is often interesting to know the sum of all the terms. In this case, it is usual to describe the sequence as a **series**.

In Example 2.6.1, the annual contributions

$$100, 120, 140, \ldots, 240, 260, 280$$

form an arithmetic sequence, but if they are added as

$$100 + 120 + 140 + \cdots + 240 + 260 + 280$$

they become an **arithmetic series**.

If the general arithmetic sequence

$$a, a + d, a + 2d, a + 3d, \ldots$$

has n terms in all, then from the first term to the last there are $n - 1$ steps of the common difference d. Denote the last term, u_n, by l. Then

$$l = a + (n - 1)d.$$

From this equation you can calculate any one of the four quantities a, l, n, d if you know the other three.

Let S be the sum of the arithmetic series formed by adding these terms. Then it is possible to find a formula for S in terms of a, n and either d or l.

Method 1   This generalises the argument used in Example 2.6.1.

The series can be written as

$$S = \quad a \quad + (a + d) + (a + 2d) + \cdots + (l - 2d) + (l - d) + l.$$

Turning this back to front,

$$S = \quad l \quad + (l - d) + (l - 2d) + \cdots + (a + 2d) + (a + d) + a.$$

Adding these,

$$2S = (a + l) + (a + l) + (a + l) \quad + \cdots + (a + l) \quad + (a + l) + (a + l),$$

where the bracket $(a + l)$ occurs n times. So

$$2S = n(a + l), \quad \text{which gives } S = \tfrac{1}{2}n(a + l).$$

Method 2   This uses the formula for triangle numbers found in Section 2.2.

In the series

$$S = a + (a + d) + (a + 2d) + \cdots + (a + (n - 1)d)$$

you can collect separately the terms involving a and those involving d:

$$S = (a + a + \cdots + a) + (1 + 2 + 3 + \cdots + (n - 1))d.$$

In the first bracket a occurs n times. The second bracket is the sum of the natural numbers from 1 to $n - 1$, or t_{n-1}; using the formula $t_r = \tfrac{1}{2}r(r + 1)$ with $r = n - 1$ gives this sum as

$$t_{n-1} = \tfrac{1}{2}(n - 1)((n - 1) + 1) = \tfrac{1}{2}(n - 1)n.$$

Therefore

$$S = na + \tfrac{1}{2}(n - 1)nd = \tfrac{1}{2}n(2a + (n - 1)d).$$

Since $l = a + (n - 1)d$, this is the same answer as that given by method 1.

Here is a summary of the results about arithmetic series.

> An arithmetic series of n terms with first term a and common difference d has nth term
>
> $$l = a + (n-1)d$$
>
> and sum
>
> $$S = \tfrac{1}{2}n(a+l) = \tfrac{1}{2}n(2a + (n-1)d).$$

Example 2.6.2

Find a formula for the nth term and the sum of n terms for the arithmetic sequence

$$1, \quad 4, \quad 7, \quad 10, \quad 13, \quad \ldots$$

In this sequence $a = 1$ and $d = 3$.

Using the formulae in the blue box,

the nth term is $1 + (n-1) \times 3 = 3n - 2$,

the sum of n terms is $\tfrac{1}{2}n(2 \times 1 + (n-1) \times 3) = \tfrac{1}{2}n(2 + 3n - 3) = \tfrac{1}{2}n(3n - 1)$.

> It is worth checking the sum by putting n equal to a small number, say 3. In that case you can check whether the answer gives $1 + 4 + 7 = 12$.

Example 2.6.3

The first two terms of an arithmetic sequence are 4 and 2. The nth term is -36. Find the number of terms.

For this sequence, $a = 4$ and $d = -2$.

Using the formula for the nth term, $l = a + (n-1)d$,

$$-36 = 4 + (n-1) \times (-2) = 4 - 2n + 2$$
$$-36 = 6 - 2n$$
$$n = 21.$$

The sequence has 21 terms.

Example 2.6.4

Find the sum of the first n odd natural numbers.

Method 1   The odd numbers $1, 3, 5, \ldots$ form an arithmetic series with first term $a = 1$ and common difference $d = 2$. So

$$S = \tfrac{1}{2}n(2a + (n-1)d) = \tfrac{1}{2}n(2 + (n-1)2) = \tfrac{1}{2}n(2n) = n^2.$$

Method 2   Take the natural numbers from 1 to $2n$, and remove the n even numbers $2, 4, 6, \ldots, 2n$. You are left with the first n odd numbers.

The sum of the numbers from 1 to $2n$ is t_r where $r = 2n$, that is

$$t_{2n} = \tfrac{1}{2}(2n)(2n + 1) = n(2n + 1).$$

The sum of the n even numbers is

$$2 + 4 + 6 + \cdots + 2n = 2(1 + 2 + 3 + \cdots + n) = 2t_n = n(n + 1).$$

So the sum of the first n odd numbers is

$$n(2n + 1) - n(n + 1) = n((2n + 1) - (n + 1)) = n(n) = n^2.$$

Method 3   Fig. 2.8 shows a square of n rows with n crosses in each row (drawn for $n = 7$). You can count the crosses in the square by adding the numbers in the 'channels' between the dotted L-shaped lines, which gives

$$n^2 = 1 + 3 + 5 + \cdots (\text{to } n \text{ terms}).$$

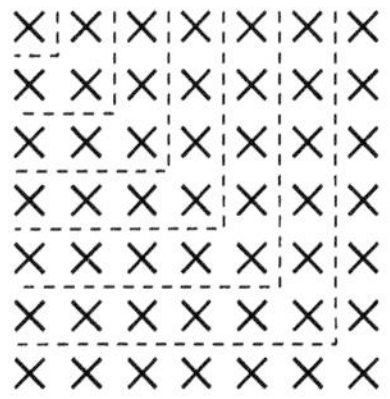

Fig. 2.8

Example 2.6.5

A student reading a 426-page book finds that he reads faster as he gets into the subject. He reads 19 pages on the first day, and his rate of reading then goes up by 3 pages each day. How long does he take to finish the book?

You are given that $a = 19$, $d = 3$ and $S = 426$. Since $S = \tfrac{1}{2}n(2a + (n - 1)d)$,

$$426 = \tfrac{1}{2}n(38 + (n - 1)3)$$
$$852 = n(3n + 35)$$
$$3n^2 + 35n - 852 = 0.$$

Using the quadratic formula,

$$n = \frac{-35 \pm \sqrt{35^2 - 4 \times 3 \times (-852)}}{2 \times 3} = \frac{-35 \pm 107}{6}.$$

Since n must be positive, $n = \dfrac{-35 + 107}{6} = \dfrac{72}{6} = 12$. He will finish the book in 12 days.

Exercise 2C

1   Which of the following sequences are the first four terms of an arithmetic sequence? For those that are, write down the value of the common difference.

(a) 7   10   13   16   ...   (b) 3   5   9   15   ...   (c) 1   0.1   0.01   0.001   ...

(d) 4   2   0 -2 ...   (e) 2 -3 4 -5 ...   (f) $p - 2q$ $p - q$ p $p + q$ ...

(g) $\tfrac{1}{2}a$ $\tfrac{1}{3}a$ $\tfrac{1}{4}a$ $\tfrac{1}{5}a$ ...   (h) x $2x$ $3x$ $4x$ ...

2 Write down the sixth term, and an expression for the rth term, of the arithmetic sequences which begin as follows.

(a) 2   4   6   ...

(b) 17   20   23   ...

(c) 5   2   −1   ...

(d) 1.3   1.7   2.1   ...

(e) 1 $1\frac{1}{2}$ 2   ...

(f) 73   67   61   ...

(g) x $x+2$ $x+4$ ...

(h) $1-x$ 1 $1+x$ ...

3 In the following arithmetic progressions, the first three terms and the last term are given. Find the number of terms.

(a) 4   5   6   ...   17

(b) 3   9   15   ...   525

(c) 8   2   −4   ...   −202

(d) $2\frac{1}{8}$ $3\frac{1}{4}$ $4\frac{3}{8}$ ... $13\frac{3}{8}$

(e) $3x$ $7x$ $11x$ ... $43x$

(f) −3 $-1\frac{1}{2}$ 0   ...   12

(g) $\frac{1}{6}$ $\frac{1}{3}$ $\frac{1}{2}$ ... $2\frac{2}{3}$

(h) $1-2x$ $1-x$ 1   ... $1+25x$

4 Find the sum of the given number of terms of the following arithmetic series.

(a) $2+5+8+\dots$ (20 terms)

(b) $4+11+18+\dots$ (15 terms)

(c) $8+5+2+\dots$ (12 terms)

(d) $\frac{1}{2}+1+1\frac{1}{2}+\dots$ (58 terms)

(e) $7+3+(-1)+\dots$ (25 terms)

(f) $1+3+5+\dots$ (999 terms)

(g) $a+5a+9a+\dots$ (40 terms)

(h) $-3p-6p-9p-\dots$ (100 terms)

5 Find the number of terms and the sum of each of the following arithmetic series.

(a) $5+7+9+\dots+111$

(b) $8+12+16+\dots+84$

(c) $7+13+19+\dots+277$

(d) $8+5+2+\dots+(-73)$

(e) $-14-10-6-\dots+94$

(f) $157+160+163+\dots+529$

(g) $10+20+30+\dots+10\,000$

(h) $1.8+1.2+0.6+\dots+(-34.2)$

6 In each of the following arithmetic sequences you are given two terms. Find the first term and the common difference.

(a) 4th term = 15,   9th term = 35

(b) 3rd term = 12,   10th term = 47

(c) 8th term = 3.5,   13th term = 5.0

(d) 5th term = 2,   11th term = −13

(e) 12th term = −8,   20th term = −32

(f) 3rd term = −3,   7th term = 5

(g) 2nd term = $2x$,   11th term = $-7x$

(h) 3rd term = $2p+7$,   7th term = $4p+19$

7 Find how many terms of the given arithmetic series must be taken to reach the given sum.

(a) $3+7+11+\dots$,   sum = 820

(b) $8+9+10+\dots$,   sum = 162

(c) $20+23+26+\dots$,   sum = 680

(d) $27+23+19+\dots$,   sum = −2040

(e) $1.1+1.3+1.5+\dots$,   sum = 1017.6

(f) $-11-4+3+\dots$,   sum = 2338

8 A squirrel is collecting nuts. It collects 5 nuts on the first day of the month, 8 nuts on the second, 11 on the third and so on in arithmetic progression.

(a) How many nuts will it collect on the 20th day?

(b) After how many days will it have collected more than 1000 nuts?

9 Kulsum is given an interest-free loan to buy a car. She repays the loan in unequal monthly instalments; these start at £30 in the first month and increase by £2 each month after that. She makes 24 payments.

(a) Find the amount of her final payment.   (b) Find the amount of her loan.

10 (a) Find the sum of the natural numbers from 1 to 100 inclusive.

(b) Find the sum of the natural numbers from 101 to 200 inclusive.

(c) Find and simplify an expression for the sum of the natural numbers from $n + 1$ to $2n$ inclusive.

11 An employee starts work on 1 January 2005 on an annual salary of £30,000. His pay scale will give him an increase of £800 per annum on the first of January until 1 January 2020 inclusive. He remains on this salary until he retires on 31 December 2045. How much will he earn during his working life?

2.7   Sigma notation

This section is all about a notation for sums of sequences. You know that $u_1, u_2, \ldots$ is called a sequence, and if you need to add the terms to get $u_1 + u_2 + \cdots + u_n$, the sequence changes its name and is called a series.

A series is completely determined if you know a formula for u_r, the general term, and where the series starts and finishes.

The sum $u_1 + u_2 + \cdots + u_n$ is often abbreviated to

$$\sum_{r=1}^{n} u_n,$$

which means 'the sum of the terms of the sequence u_r from $r = 1$ to $r = n$'.

This notation is called **sigma notation**, and is illustrated in more detail in Fig. 2.9. The letter $\sum$ is the Greek capital letter S.

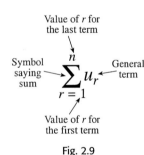

Value of r for the last term

Symbol saying sum → $\sum_{r=1}^{n} u_r$ ← General term

Value of r for the first term

Fig. 2.9

- The symbol $\sum$ is an instruction to add.
- Following the $\sum$ symbol is an expression for the general term of a series.
- Below the $\sum$ symbol is the value of r corresponding to the starting term.
- Above the $\sum$ symbol is the value of r corresponding to the last term.

The expression $\sum_{r=1}^{n} u_r$ is read as 'sum (or sigma) from 1 to n of u_r'.

Example 2.7.1

Express as addition sums (a) $\sum_{r=1}^{3} r$,   (b) $\sum_{r=4}^{7} (2r - 1)$,   (c) $\sum_{r=0}^{4} 1$,   (d) $\sum_{r=3}^{8} r^2$.

(a) The rth term is r and, as the first term has $r = 1$, the first term is 1. For the second term, put $r = 2$, so the second term is 2. The last term is the term for which $r = 3$, so the last term is 3. The $\sum$ symbol means add, so

$$\sum_{r=1}^{3} r = 1 + 2 + 3.$$

(b) The first term is $(2 \times 4 - 1) = 7$, corresponding to $r = 4$. The second term, corresponding to $r = 5$, is $(2 \times 5 - 1) = 9$. Continuing in this way,

$$\sum_{r=4}^{7} (2r - 1) = 7 + 9 + 11 + 13.$$

(c) In this case, the rth term is 1, independent of the value of r, so

$$\sum_{r=0}^{4} 1 = 1 + 1 + 1 + 1 + 1.$$

(d) The first term is 3^2, corresponding to $r = 3$. The second term, corresponding to $r = 4$, is 4^2. Continuing in this way,

$$\sum_{r=3}^{8} r^2 = 3^2 + 4^2 + 5^2 + 6^2 + 7^2 + 8^2.$$

Notice that, in part (c), there are 5 terms and in part (d) there are 6 terms. In general the number of terms in the series $\sum_{r=n}^{N} u_r$ is $N - n + 1$.

There is more than one way to describe a series using sigma notation. For example,

$$\sum_{r=0}^{2} (r + 1) = (0 + 1) + (1 + 1) + (2 + 1) = 1 + 2 + 3,$$

which is the same as $\sum_{r=1}^{3} r$ in Example 2.7.1(a).

Example 2.7.2

Express each of the following sums in $\sum$ notation.

(a) $2 + 4 + 6 + 8 + 10$ (b) $\dfrac{1}{2} + \dfrac{1}{3} + \dfrac{1}{4} + \dfrac{1}{5}$ (c) $6^3 + 7^3 + 8^3$

(a) The general term of this sequence is $(2r)$. The first term corresponds to $r = 1$, and the last to $r = 5$. So the sum can be written as $\sum_{r=1}^{5} 2r$.

(b) The general term of this sequence is $\dfrac{1}{r+1}$. The first term corresponds to $r = 1$, and the last to $r = 4$. So the sum can be written as $\displaystyle\sum_{r=1}^{4} \dfrac{1}{r+1}$.

(c) The general term of this sequence is r^3. The first term corresponds to $r = 6$, and the last to $r = 8$. So the sum can be written as $\displaystyle\sum_{r=6}^{8} r^3$.

These answers are not unique; they are not the only answers possible. In part (b), for example, you could easily argue that the general term is $\dfrac{1}{r}$, with the first term corresponding to $r = 2$ and the last to $r = 5$. So the sum can be written $\displaystyle\sum_{r=2}^{5} \dfrac{1}{r}$.

Sometimes you can break up a complicated series into simpler series. For example, you can write the sum $\displaystyle\sum_{r=1}^{200} (2r + 1)$ in the form

$$\sum_{r=1}^{200} (2r + 1) = (2 \times 1 + 1) + (2 \times 2 + 1) + (2 \times 3 + 1) + \cdots + (2 \times 200 + 1)$$

$$= (2 \times 1 + 2 \times 2 + 2 \times 3 + \cdots + 2 \times 200) + \overbrace{1 + 1 + 1 + \cdots + 1}^{200 \text{ of these}}$$

$$= 2 \times (1 + 2 + 3 + \cdots + 200) + \overbrace{1 + 1 + 1 + \cdots + 1}^{200 \text{ of these}}$$

$$= 2 \sum_{r=1}^{200} r + \sum_{r=1}^{200} 1.$$

You can now go on and sum the series, using the formula for the nth triangle number in Section 2.2, since the sum $\displaystyle\sum_{r=1}^{200} r$ is the same as t_{200}, which is given by

$t_{200} = \frac{1}{2} \times 200 \times 201 = 20\,100.$

Therefore

$$\sum_{r=1}^{200} (2r + 1) = 2 \sum_{r=1}^{200} r + \sum_{r=1}^{200} 1 = 2 \times 20\,100 + 200 = 40\,400.$$

In this example, two important rules about sigma notation were used.

The first rule is called the addition rule for sums:

$$\sum_{r=1}^{n} (u_r + v_r) = (u_1 + v_1) + (u_2 + v_2) + \cdots + (u_n + v_n)$$

$$= (u_1 + u_2 + \cdots + u_n) + (v_1 + v_2 + \cdots + v_n)$$

$$= \sum_{r=1}^{n} u_r + \sum_{r=1}^{n} v_r.$$

The second rule deals with the effect of multiplying each term by a constant k. It is called the multiple rule for sums:

$$\sum_{r=1}^{n} (ku_r) = (ku_1 + ku_2 + \cdots + ku_n) = k(u_1 + u_2 + \cdots + u_n) = k\sum_{r=1}^{n} u_r.$$

> **Addition rule** $\displaystyle\sum_{r=1}^{n} (u_r + v_r) = \sum_{r=1}^{n} u_r + \sum_{r=1}^{n} v_r.$
>
> **Multiple rule** For any number k, $\displaystyle\sum_{r=1}^{n} (ku_r) = k\sum_{r=1}^{n} u_r.$

Example 2.7.3

Find $\displaystyle\sum_{r=1}^{4} (2r + 2^r)$.

Using the addition rule,

$$\sum_{r=1}^{4} (2r + 2^r) = \sum_{r=1}^{4} 2r + \sum_{r=1}^{4} 2^r$$
$$= (2 + 4 + 6 + 8) + (2 + 4 + 8 + 16) = 20 + 30 = 50.$$

Another important fact to notice about sigma notation is that the final result is nothing to do with r. For example,

$$\sum_{r=0}^{2} (3 + 2r + r^2) = 3 + (3 + 2 \times 1 + 1^2) + (3 + 2 \times 2 + 2^2) = 3 + 6 + 11 = 20.$$

So it doesn't matter what letter you use. Thus $\displaystyle\sum_{r=0}^{2} (3 + 2r + r^2)$ is precisely the same sum as $\displaystyle\sum_{i=0}^{2} (3 + 2i + i^2)$. For this reason r is called a **dummy variable**.

When there is no possibility of confusion, you can omit the '$r =$' below the sigma symbol. Thus $\displaystyle\sum_{r=0}^{2} (3 + 2r + r^2)$ can be written as $\displaystyle\sum_{0}^{2} (3 + 2r + r^2)$. However, the '$r =$' will not be omitted in the Core and the Further Pure modules of this course.

2.8   Sequences with alternating signs

The general term of a sequence such as

$$-1, \quad 2, \quad -3, \quad 4, \quad \ldots$$

can be awkward to write down.

It is clear that the rth term involves r, but how do you deal with the alternating sign?

The method is to use $(-1)^r$ or $(-1)^{r+1}$.

The sequence $(-1)^r$ for $r = 1, 2, 3, 4, \ldots$ is

$$-1, \quad 1, \quad -1, \quad 1, \quad \ldots$$

while the sequence $(-1)^{r+1}$ for $r = 1, 2, 3, 4, \ldots$ is

$$1, \quad -1, \quad 1, \quad -1, \quad \ldots .$$

This suggests that the general term of the sequence $\quad -1, \quad 2, \quad -3, \quad 4, \quad \ldots \quad$ is $(-1)^r r$.

The general term of the sequence $\quad 1, \quad -2, \quad 3, \quad -4, \quad \ldots \quad$ is $(-1)^{r+1} r$.

> It is important to make a mental check that you have the correct alternating sign term $(-1)^r$ or $(-1)^{r+1}$.

Example 2.8.1

Write down the first four terms of the sequences with general terms
(a) $(-1)^r 2^r$, (b) $(-1)^{r+1}(3r + 2)$.

(a) The first four terms are $(-1)^1 2^1 = -2, (-1)^2 2^2 = 4, (-1)^3 2^3 = -8$ and $(-1)^4 2^4 = 16$.

(b) The first four terms are $(-1)^{1+1}(3 \times 1 + 2) = 5, (-1)^{2+1}(3 \times 2 + 2) = -8,$
$(-1)^{3+1}(3 \times 3 + 2) = 11$ and $(-1)^{4+1}(3 \times 4 + 2) = -14.$

Example 2.8.2

Write down the general terms of the sequences
(a) $\dfrac{1}{1}, \quad -\dfrac{1}{2}, \quad \dfrac{1}{3}, \quad -\dfrac{1}{4}, \quad \ldots$ (b) $-1, \quad 4, \quad -9, \quad 16, \quad \ldots$

(a) The fact that the first term is positive should alert you to the need to use $(-1)^{r+1}$ rather than $(-1)^r$.

The general term is $(-1)^{r+1}\dfrac{1}{r}$.

(b) The general term is $(-1)^r r^2$.

Exercise 2D

1 Express each of the following as addition sums.

(a) $\displaystyle\sum_{r=2}^{3} r$ (b) $\displaystyle\sum_{r=3}^{5} 2$ (c) $\displaystyle\sum_{r=1}^{4} \dfrac{1}{r}$ (d) $\displaystyle\sum_{r=1}^{4} r^2$ (e) $\displaystyle\sum_{r=2}^{5} (2r + 1)$ (f) $\displaystyle\sum_{r=0}^{2} u_r$

2 Write each of the following sums using sigma notation. (Note that your answers could differ from those given.)

(a) $2 + 3 + 4$ (b) $1 + 4 + 9 + 16$ (c) $3^3 + 4^3 + 5^3 + 6^3 + 7^3$

(d) $\frac{1}{2} + \frac{1}{4} + \frac{1}{6}$ (e) $3 + 5 + 7 + 9$ (f) $2 + 5 + 8 + 11 + 14$

3 Write each of the following expressions as a sum, giving the first three terms and the last term of each of them. For example, $\sum\limits_{r=2}^{n} 2r = 4 + 6 + 8 + \cdots + 2n$.

(a) $\sum\limits_{r=0}^{n} r$ (b) $\sum\limits_{r=2}^{n-1} r^2$ (c) $\sum\limits_{r=4}^{n-4} 3$ (d) $\sum\limits_{r=1}^{2n} \dfrac{1}{r}$ (e) $\sum\limits_{r=0}^{2n-1} r^3$ (f) $\sum\limits_{r=0}^{n-2} u_{r+1}$

4 Say which of the following statements are true and which are false. Be prepared to justify your answer. For the false statements, give the correct right side.

(a) $\sum\limits_{r=1}^{2n} r^3 = \sum\limits_{r=0}^{2n-1} (r+1)^3$ (b) $\sum\limits_{r=1}^{n} 1 = \frac{1}{2}n(n+1)$

(c) $\sum\limits_{r=1}^{2n} r^3 = \sum\limits_{r=0}^{2n} r^3$ (d) $\sum\limits_{r=1}^{n} (2 + r^2) = 2 + \sum\limits_{r=1}^{n} r^2$

5 Calculate the value of each of the following sums.

(a) $\sum\limits_{r=0}^{2} (-1)^r r$ (b) $\sum\limits_{r=0}^{2} (-1)^{r-1} r$ (c) $\sum\limits_{r=0}^{2} (-1)^{r+1} r$

(d) $\sum\limits_{r=1}^{6} (-1)^r r^2$ (e) $\sum\limits_{r=3}^{5} (-1)^{r+1} r^{-1}$ (f) $\sum\limits_{r=3}^{5} (-1)^r$

6 Write each of the following in sigma notation.

(a) $1 - 2 + 3 - 4 + \cdots + 101$ (b) $-2^2 + 4^2 - 6^2 + \cdots - 50^2$ (c) $1 - \frac{1}{2} + \frac{1}{3} - \cdots + \frac{1}{49}$

7 Write each of the following in sigma notation.

(a) $\left(1 + \frac{1}{1}\right) + \left(2 + \frac{1}{2}\right) + \left(3 + \frac{1}{3}\right) + \cdots + \left(100 + \frac{1}{100}\right)$ (b) $1 + \dbinom{n}{1} x + \dbinom{n}{2} x^2 + \cdots + \dbinom{n}{n} x^n$

(c) $1 + 2x + 3x^2 + 4x^3 + \cdots + (n+1)x^n$ (d) $1 - 2x + 3x^2 - 4x^3 + \cdots - 2nx^{2n-1}$

8 It is shown in Section 2.6 that the sum of the arithmetic series

$a + (a + d) + (a + 2d) + \cdots + (a + (n-1)d)$ is

$\frac{1}{2}n(2a + (n-1)d)$.

Use sigma notation to write this statement more concisely.

Miscellaneous exercise 2

1 The sequence $u_1, u_2, u_3, \ldots$ is defined by

$u_1 = 0, \quad u_{r+1} = (2 + u_r)^2.$

Find the value of u_4.

2 A sequence is defined recursively by $u_{r+1} = 3u_r - 1$ and $u_0 = c$.

(a) Find the first five terms of the sequence if (i) $c = 1$, (ii) $c = 2$, (iii) $c = 0$, (iv) $c = \frac{1}{2}$.

(b) Show that, for each of the values of c in part (a), the terms of the sequence are given by the formula $u_r = \frac{1}{2} + b \times 3^r$ for some value of b.

(c) Show that, if $u_r = \frac{1}{2} + b \times 3^r$ for some value of r, then $u_{r+1} = \frac{1}{2} + b \times 3^{r+1}$.

3 The sequence $u_1, u_2, u_3, \ldots$, where u_1 is a given real number, is defined by

$u_{n+1} = \sqrt{(4 - u_n)^2}.$

(a) Given that $u_1 = 1$, evaluate u_2, u_3 and u_4, and describe the behaviour of the sequence.

(b) Given alternatively that $u_1 = 6$, describe the behaviour of the sequence.

(c) For what value of u_1 will all the terms of the sequence be equal to each other? (OCR, adapted)

4 The sequence $u_1, u_2, u_3, \ldots$, where u_1 is a given real number, is defined by $u_{n+1} = u_n^2 - 1$.

(a) Describe the behaviour of the sequence for each of the cases $u_1 = 0$, $u_1 = 1$ and $u_1 = 2$.

(b) Given that $u_2 = u_1$, find exactly the two possible values of u_1.

(c) Given that $u_3 = u_1$, show that $u_1^4 - 2u_1^2 - u_1 = 0$. (OCR)

5 The rth term of an arithmetic progression is $1 + 4r$. Find, in terms of n, the sum of the first n terms of the progression. (OCR)

6 The sum of the first two terms of an arithmetic progression is 18 and the sum of the first four terms is 52. Find the sum of the first eight terms. (OCR)

7 The sum of the first twenty terms of an arithmetic progression is 50, and the sum of the next twenty terms is -50. Find the sum of the first hundred terms of the progression. (OCR)

8 An arithmetic progression has first term a and common difference -1. The sum of the first n terms is equal to the sum of the first $3n$ terms. Express a in terms of n. (OCR)

9 Find the sum of the arithmetic progression $1, 4, 7, 10, 13, 16, \ldots, 1000$.

Every third term of the above progression is removed, i.e. $7, 16$, etc. Find the sum of the remaining terms. (OCR)

10 The sum of the first hundred terms of an arithmetic progression with first term a and common difference d is T. The sum of the first 50 odd-numbered terms, i.e. the first, third, fifth, $\ldots$, ninety-ninth, is $\frac{1}{2}T - 1000$. Find the value of d. (OCR)

11 In the sequence $1.0, 1.1, 1.2, \ldots, 99.9, 100.0$, each number after the first is 0.1 greater than the preceding number. Find

(a) how many numbers there are in the sequence,

(b) the sum of all the numbers in the sequence. (OCR)

12 The sequence $u_1, u_2, u_3, \ldots$ is defined by $u_n = 2n^2$.

(a) Write down the value of u_3.

(b) Express $u_{n+1} - u_n$ in terms of n, simplifying your answer.

(c) The differences between successive terms of the sequence form an arithmetic progression. For this arithmetic progression, state its first term and its common difference, and find the sum of its first 1000 terms. (OCR)

13 Find formulae for the sums of the following arithmetic progressions.

(a) $\displaystyle\sum_{r=1}^{n} (2 + (r - 1)3)$ (b) $\displaystyle\sum_{r=1}^{n} (3 + 2r)$ (c) $\displaystyle\sum_{r=1}^{n} (4 - r)$

14 A small company producing children's toys plans an increase in output. The number of toys produced is to be increased by 8 each week until the weekly number produced reaches 1000. In week 1, the number to be produced is 280; in week 2, the number is 288; etc. Show that the weekly number produced will be 1000 in week 91.

From week 91 onwards, the number produced each week is to remain at 1000. Find the total number of toys to be produced over the first 104 weeks of the plan.   (OCR)

15 In 1971 a newly-built flat was sold with a 999-year lease. The terms of the sale included a requirement to pay 'ground rent' yearly. The ground rent was set at £28 per year for the first 21 years of the lease, increasing by £14 to £42 per year for the next 21 years, and then increasing again by £14 at the end of each subsequent period of 21 years.

(a) Find how many complete 21-year periods there would be if the lease ran for the full 999 years, and how many years there would be left over.

(b) Find the total amount of ground rent that would be paid in all of the complete 21-year periods of the lease.   (OCR)

16 An arithmetic progression has first term a and common difference 10. The sum of the first n terms of the progression is 10 000. Express a in terms of n, and show that the nth term of the progression is

$$\frac{10\,000}{n} + 5(n-1).$$

Given that the nth term is less than 500, show that $n^2 - 101n + 2000 < 0$ and hence find the largest possible value of n.   (OCR)

17 Three sequences are defined recursively by

(a) $u_0 = 0$ and $u_{r+1} = u_r + (2r+1)$,

(b) $u_0 = 0$, $u_1 = 1$ and $u_{r+1} = 2u_r - u_{r-1}$ for $r \geqslant 1$,

(c) $u_0 = 1$, $u_1 = 2$ and $u_{r+1} = 3u_r - 2u_{r-1}$ for $r \geqslant 1$.

For each sequence calculate the first few terms, and suggest a formula for u_r. Check that the formula you have suggested does in fact satisfy all parts of the definition.

18* A sequence F_n is constructed from terms of Pascal sequences as follows:

$$F_0 = \binom{0}{0}, \ F_1 = \binom{1}{0} + \binom{0}{1}, \ F_2 = \binom{2}{0} + \binom{1}{1} + \binom{0}{2},$$
$$\text{and in general } F_n = \sum_{r=0}^{n} \binom{n-r}{r}.$$

Show that terms of the sequence F_n can be calculated by adding up numbers in Fig. 2.5 (see page 248) along diagonal lines. Verify by calculation that, for small values of n, $F_{n+1} = F_n + F_{n-1}$. (This is called the *Fibonacci sequence*, after the man who introduced algebra from the Arabic world to Italy in about the year 1200.)

Use the Pascal sequence property $\binom{n}{r} + \binom{n}{r+1} = \binom{n+1}{r+1}$ (see Exercise 2B Question 8) to explain why $F_3 + F_4 = F_5$ and $F_4 + F_5 = F_6$.

3 The binomial theorem

This chapter is about the expansion of $(x + y)^n$, where n is a positive integer (or zero). When you have completed it, you should

- be able to use Pascal's triangle to find the expansion of $(x + y)^n$ when n is small
- know how to calculate the coefficients in the expansion of $(x + y)^n$ when n is large
- be able to use the notation $\binom{n}{r}$ in the context of the binomial theorem.

3.1 Expanding $(x + y)^n$

The binomial theorem is about calculating $(x + y)^n$ quickly and easily. It is useful to start by looking at $(x + y)^n$ for $n = 2, 3$ and 4.

The expansions are:

$$(x + y)^2 = x(x + y) + y(x + y) = x^2 + 2xy + y^2,$$

$$(x + y)^3 = (x + y)(x + y)^2 = (x + y)(x^2 + 2xy + y^2)$$
$$= x(x^2 + 2xy + y^2) + y(x^2 + 2xy + y^2)$$
$$= x^3 + 2x^2y + \quad xy^2$$
$$\quad\quad + \quad x^2y + 2xy^2 + y^3$$
$$= x^3 + 3x^2y + 3xy^2 + y^3,$$

$$(x + y)^4 = (x + y)(x + y)^3 = (x + y)(x^3 + 3x^2y + 3xy^2 + y^3)$$
$$= x(x^3 + 3x^2y + 3xy^2 + y^3) + y(x^3 + 3x^2y + 3xy^2 + y^3)$$
$$= x^4 + 3x^3y + 3x^2y^2 + \quad xy^3$$
$$\quad\quad + \quad x^3y + 3x^2y^2 + 3xy^3 + y^4$$
$$= x^4 + 4x^3y + 6x^2y^2 + 4xy^3 + y^4.$$

You can summarise these results, including $(x + y)^1$, as follows. The coefficients are in bold type.

$$(x + y)^1 = \mathbf{1}x + \mathbf{1}y$$
$$(x + y)^2 = \mathbf{1}x^2 + \mathbf{2}xy + \mathbf{1}y^2$$
$$(x + y)^3 = \mathbf{1}x^3 + \mathbf{3}x^2y + \mathbf{3}xy^2 + \mathbf{1}y^3$$
$$(x + y)^4 = \mathbf{1}x^4 + \mathbf{4}x^3y + \mathbf{6}x^2y^2 + \mathbf{4}xy^3 + \mathbf{1}y^4$$

Study these expansions carefully. Notice how the powers start from the left with x^n. The powers of x then successively reduce by 1, and the powers of y increase by 1 until reaching the term y^n.

Notice also that the coefficients form the pattern of Pascal's triangle, which you saw in Section 2.4 and which is shown again in Fig. 3.1.

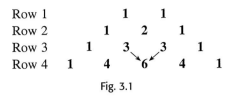

Row 1   1   1
Row 2   1   2   1
Row 3   1   3   3   1
Row 4 1   4   6   4   1

Fig. 3.1

A simple way of building up Pascal's triangle is as follows:

- start each row with 1, placed to the left of the 1 in the row above;
- then add pairs of elements in the row above to get the entry positioned below and between them (as the arrows in Fig. 3.1 show);
- complete the row with a 1.

This is identical to the way in which the two rows of algebra are added to give the final result in the expansions of $(x + y)^3$ and $(x + y)^4$ on the previous page.

You should now be able to predict that the coefficients in the fifth row are

$$\mathbf{1} \quad \mathbf{5} \quad \mathbf{10} \quad \mathbf{10} \quad \mathbf{5} \quad \mathbf{1}$$

and that

$$(x + y)^5 = x^5 + 5x^4 y + 10x^3 y^2 + 10x^2 y^3 + 5xy^4 + y^5.$$

> In Examples 3.1.1 to 3.1.4 the coefficients from Pascal's triangle are shown in bold-faced type to help you to keep track of them.

Example 3.1.1
Write down the expansion of $(1 + y)^6$.

Use the next row of Pascal's triangle, continuing the pattern of powers and replacing x by 1:

$$(1 + y)^6 = \mathbf{1}(1)^6 + \mathbf{6}(1)^5 y + \mathbf{15}(1)^4 y^2 + \mathbf{20}(1)^3 y^3 + \mathbf{15}(1)^2 y^4 + \mathbf{6}(1)y^5 + \mathbf{1}y^6$$
$$= 1 + 6y + 15y^2 + 20y^3 + 15y^4 + 6y^5 + y^6.$$

Example 3.1.2
Multiply out the brackets in the expression $(2x + 3)^4$.

Use the expansion of $(x + y)^4$, replacing x by $(2x)$ and replacing y by 3:

$$(2x + 3)^4 = \mathbf{1} \times (2x)^4 + \mathbf{4} \times (2x)^3 \times 3 + \mathbf{6} \times (2x)^2 \times 3^2 + \mathbf{4} \times (2x) \times 3^3 + \mathbf{1} \times 3^4$$
$$= 16x^4 + 96x^3 + 216x^2 + 216x + 81.$$

Example 3.1.3
Expand $(x^2 + 2)^3$.

$$(x^2 + 2)^3 = \mathbf{1} \times (x^2)^3 + \mathbf{3} \times (x^2)^2 \times 2 + \mathbf{3} \times x^2 \times 2^2 + \mathbf{1} \times 2^3 = x^6 + 6x^4 + 12x^2 + 8.$$

In Example 3.1.4, one of the signs is negative, and it is important to keep track of everything.

Example 3.1.4

Expand $(2x - 3)^6$.

$$(2x - 3)^6 = \mathbf{1} \times (2x)^6 + \mathbf{6} \times (2x)^5 \times (-3) + \mathbf{15} \times (2x)^4 \times (-3)^2 + \mathbf{20} \times (2x)^3 \times (-3)^3$$
$$+ \mathbf{15} \times (2x)^2 \times (-3)^4 + \mathbf{6} \times (2x) \times (-3)^5 + \mathbf{1} \times (-3)^6$$
$$= 64x^6 + 6 \times 32x^5 \times (-3) + 15 \times 16x^4 \times 9 + 20 \times 8x^3 \times (-27)$$
$$+ 15 \times 4x^2 \times 81 + 6 \times 2x \times (-243) + 729$$
$$= 64x^6 - 576x^5 + 2160x^4 - 4320x^3 + 4860x^2 - 2916x + 729.$$

Example 3.1.5

Find the coefficient of x^3 in the expansion of $(3x - 4)^5$.

The term in x^3 comes third in the row with coefficients $1, 5, 10, \ldots$. So the term is

$$10 \times (3x)^3 \times (-4)^2 = 10 \times 27 \times 16x^3 = 4320x^3.$$

The required coefficient is therefore 4320.

Example 3.1.6

Expand $(1 + 2x + 3x^2)^3$.

To use the binomial expansion, you need to write $1 + 2x + 3x^2$ in a form with two terms rather than three. One way to do this is to consider $(1 + (2x + 3x^2))^3$. Then

$$(1 + (2x + 3x^2))^3 = 1^3 + 3 \times 1^2 \times (2x + 3x^2) + 3 \times 1 \times (2x + 3x^2)^2 + (2x + 3x^2)^3.$$

Now you can use the binomial theorem to expand the bracketed terms:

$$(1 + 2x + 3x^2)^3 = 1 + 3(2x + 3x^2) + 3((2x)^2 + 2 \times (2x) \times (3x^2) + (3x^2)^2)$$
$$+ ((2x)^3 + 3 \times (2x)^2 \times (3x^2) + 3 \times (2x) \times (3x^2)^2 + (3x^2)^3)$$
$$= 1 + (6x + 9x^2) + (12x^2 + 36x^3 + 27x^4)$$
$$+ (8x^3 + 36x^4 + 54x^5 + 27x^6)$$
$$= 1 + 6x + 21x^2 + 44x^3 + 63x^4 + 54x^5 + 27x^6.$$

In this kind of detailed work, it is useful to check your answers.

You could do this by expanding $(1 + 2x + 3x^2)^3$ in the form $((1 + 2x) + 3x^2)^3$ to see if you get the same answer. Rather quicker is to give x a particular value, $x = 1$ for example. Then the left side is $(1 + 2 + 3)^3 = 6^3 = 216$; the right is $1 + 6 + 21 + 44 + 63 + 54 + 27 = 216$. It is important to note that if the results are the same, it does not guarantee that the expansion is correct; but if they are different, it is certain that there is a mistake.

Exercise 3A

1 Write down the expansion of each of the following.
   (a) $(x + 1)^3$ (b) $(2x + 1)^3$ (c) $(4 + p)^3$ (d) $(x - 1)^3$
   (e) $(x^2 + 2)^3$ (f) $(1 - 5x^2)^3$ (g) $(x^2 + y^3)^3$ (h) $(3x^2 + 2y^3)^3$
   (i) $(x + 2)^3$ (j) $(2p + 3q)^3$ (k) $(1 - 4x)^3$ (l) $(1 - x^3)^3$

2 Find the coefficient of x in the expansion of
   (a) $(3x + 1)^4$,   (b) $(2x + 5)^3$.

3 Find the coefficient of x^2 in the expansion of
   (a) $(4x + 5)^3$,   (b) $(1 - 3x)^4$.

4 Expand each of the following expressions.
   (a) $(1 + 2x)^5$ (b) $(p + 2q)^6$ (c) $(2m - 3n)^4$ (d) $\left(1 + \frac{1}{2}x\right)^4$

5 Find the coefficient of x^3 in the expansion of
   (a) $(1 + 3x)^5$,   (b) $(2 - 5x)^4$.

6 Expand $(1 + x + 2x^2)^3$. Check your answer with a numerical substitution.

7 Write down the expansion of $(x + 4)^3$ and hence expand $(x + 1)(x + 4)^3$.

8 Expand $(3x + 2)(2x + 3)^3$.

9 In the expansion of $(1 + ax)^4$, the coefficient of x^3 is 1372. Find the constant a.

10 Expand $(x + y)^{11}$.

11 Find the coefficient of $x^6 y^6$ in the expansion of $(2x + y)^{12}$.

3.2   The binomial theorem

The treatment given in Section 3.1 is fine for calculating the coefficients in the expansion of $(x + y)^n$ where n is small, but it is hopelessly inefficient for finding the coefficient of $x^{11} y^4$ in the expansion of $(x + y)^{15}$. Just think of all the rows of Pascal's triangle which you would have to write out! What you need is a formula in terms of n and r for the coefficient of $x^{n-r} y^r$ in the expansion of $(x + y)^n$.

Fortunately, the nth row of Pascal's triangle is the nth Pascal sequence given in Section 2.4. It was shown there that

$$\binom{n}{0} = 1 \quad \text{and} \quad \binom{n}{r + 1} = \frac{n - r}{r + 1} \binom{n}{r}, \quad \text{where } r = 0, 1, 2, \ldots .$$

In fact, you can write Pascal's triangle as

Row 1 $\qquad\qquad\qquad \binom{1}{0} \qquad\quad \binom{1}{1}$

Row 2 $\qquad\qquad \binom{2}{0} \qquad\quad \binom{2}{1} \qquad\quad \binom{2}{2}$

Row 3 $\qquad\quad \binom{3}{0} \qquad\quad \binom{3}{1} \qquad\quad \binom{3}{2} \qquad\quad \binom{3}{3}$

Row 4 $\quad \binom{4}{0} \qquad\quad \binom{4}{1} \qquad\quad \binom{4}{2} \qquad\quad \binom{4}{3} \qquad\quad \binom{4}{4}$

and so on.

This enables you to write down a neater form of the expansion of $(x + y)^n$.

> The **binomial theorem** states that, if n is a natural number,
>
> $$(x + y)^n = \binom{n}{0}x^n + \binom{n}{1}x^{n-1}y + \binom{n}{2}x^{n-2}y^2 + \cdots + \binom{n}{n}y^n.$$

> Many calculators give you values of $\binom{n}{r}$, usually with a key labelled $[_nC_r]$. To find $\binom{10}{4}$, you would normally key in the sequence $[10, _nC_r, 4]$, but you may need to check your calculator manual for details.

Otherwise, to calculate the coefficients, you can use the recursive formula given at the beginning of this section to generate a formula for $\binom{n}{r}$. For example, to calculate $\binom{4}{2}$, start by putting $n = 4$. Then

$$\binom{4}{0} = 1, \text{ so } \binom{4}{1} = \frac{4-0}{0+1}\binom{4}{0} = \frac{4}{1} \times 1 = \frac{4}{1}, \text{ and } \binom{4}{2} = \frac{4-1}{1+1}\binom{4}{1} = \frac{3}{2} \times \frac{4}{1} = \frac{4 \times 3}{1 \times 2}.$$

In the general case,

$$\binom{n}{0} = 1, \quad \binom{n}{1} = \frac{n-0}{0+1} \times 1 = \frac{n}{1}, \quad \binom{n}{2} = \frac{n-1}{1+1}\binom{n}{1} = \frac{n-1}{2} \times \frac{n}{1} = \frac{n(n-1)}{1 \times 2}, \cdots$$

Continuing in this way, you find that

$$\binom{n}{r} = \frac{n(n-1)\cdots(n-(r-1))}{1 \times 2 \times \cdots \times r}.$$

You can also write $\binom{n}{r}$ in the form

$$\binom{n}{r} = \frac{n(n-1)\cdots(n-(r-1))}{1 \times 2 \times \cdots \times r} \times \frac{(n-r) \times (n-r-1) \times \cdots \times 2 \times 1}{(n-r) \times (n-r-1) \times \cdots \times 2 \times 1} = \frac{n!}{r!(n-r)!}.$$

> Notice that this formula works for $r = 0$ and $r = n$ as well as the values in between, since (from Section 2.3) $0! = 1$.

The **binomial coefficients** are given by

$$\binom{n}{r} = \frac{n(n-1)\ldots(n-(r-1))}{1 \times 2 \times \cdots \times r}, \quad \text{or} \quad \binom{n}{r} = \frac{n!}{r!(n-r)!}.$$

When you use the first formula to calculate any particular value of $\binom{n}{r}$, such as $\binom{10}{4}$ or $\binom{12}{7}$, it is helpful to remember that there are as many factors in the top line as there are in the bottom. So you can start by putting in the denominators, and then count down from 10 and 12 respectively, making sure that you have the same number of factors in the numerator as in the denominator.

$$\binom{10}{4} = \frac{10 \times 9 \times 8 \times 7}{1 \times 2 \times 3 \times 4} = 210,$$

$$\binom{12}{7} = \frac{12 \times 11 \times 10 \times 9 \times 8 \times 7 \times 6}{1 \times 2 \times 3 \times 4 \times 5 \times 6 \times 7} = 792.$$

Example 3.2.1

Find the expansion of $(3 - 4x)^5$.

$$(3 - 4x)^5 = (3 + (-4x))^5$$

$$= \binom{5}{0} 3^5 + \binom{5}{1} \times 3^4 \times (-4x) + \binom{5}{2} \times 3^3 \times (-4x)^2$$

$$+ \binom{5}{3} \times 3^2 \times (-4x)^3 + \binom{5}{4} \times 3 \times (-4x)^4 + \binom{5}{5}(-4x)^5$$

$$= 1 \times 243 - \frac{5}{1} \times 81 \times 4x + \frac{5 \times 4}{1 \times 2} \times 27 \times 16x^2$$

$$- \frac{5 \times 4 \times 3}{1 \times 2 \times 3} \times 9 \times 64x^3 + \frac{5 \times 4 \times 3 \times 2}{1 \times 2 \times 3 \times 4} \times 3 \times 256x^4$$

$$- \frac{5 \times 4 \times 3 \times 2 \times 1}{1 \times 2 \times 3 \times 4 \times 5} \times 1024x^5$$

$$= 243 - 1620x + 4320x^2 - 5760x^3 + 3840x^4 - 1024x^5.$$

Example 3.2.2

Find the coefficient of x^3 in   (a) $(1 + x)^7$,   (b) $(x + 2)^5$,   (c) $(2 - 3x)^8$.

(a) The expansion of $(1 + x)^7$ starts with

$$\binom{7}{0} \times 1^7 + \binom{7}{1} \times 1^6 \times x + \binom{7}{2} \times 1^5 \times x^2 + \binom{7}{3} \times 1^4 \times x^3$$

The term in x^3 is

$$\binom{7}{3} \times 1^4 \times x^3 = \frac{7 \times 6 \times 5}{1 \times 2 \times 3} x^3 = 35x^3,$$

so the coefficient of x^3 is 35.

(b) The term in x^3 in $(x + 2)^5$ is

$$\binom{5}{2} \times x^3 \times 2^2 = \frac{5 \times 4}{1 \times 2} \times 4 \times x^3 = 40x^3,$$

so the coefficient of x^3 is 40.

(c) The term in x^3 in $(2 - 3x)^8$ is

$$\binom{8}{3} \times 2^5 \times (-3x)^3 = \frac{8 \times 7 \times 6}{1 \times 2 \times 3} \times 32 \times (-27)x^3,$$
$$= -56 \times 32 \times 27x^3 = -48\,384x^3,$$

so the coefficient of x^3 is $-48\,384$.

From here on, a calculator is used and the detailed calculation of binomial coefficients is omitted.

Example 3.2.3
Calculate the coefficient of $x^{11}y^4$ in the expansion of $(x + y)^{15}$.

The coefficient is $\binom{15}{4}$. Using a calculator, $\binom{15}{4} = 1365$.

Example 3.2.4
Find the first three terms in the expansion of   (a) $(2 + x)^8$,   (b) $(3 - 5x)^7$.

(a) The first three terms of the expansion are

$$\binom{8}{0} \times 2^8 + \binom{8}{1} \times 2^7 \times x + \binom{8}{2} \times 2^6 \times x^2$$
$$= 256 + 8 \times 128 \times x + 28 \times 64 \times x^2$$
$$= 256 + 1024x + 1792x^2.$$

(b) The first three terms of the expansion are

$$\binom{7}{0} \times 3^7 + \binom{7}{1} \times 3^6 \times (-5x) + \binom{7}{2} \times 3^5 \times (-5x)^2$$
$$= 2187 - 7 \times 729 \times 5x + 21 \times 243 \times 25x^2$$
$$= 2187 - 25\,515x + 127\,575x^2.$$

The following example is one in which the value of x is assumed to be small. When this is the case, say for $x = 0.1$, the successive powers of x decrease by a factor of 10 each time and become very small indeed, so higher powers can be neglected in approximations.

In Example 3.2.5 you are asked to put the terms of a binomial expansion in order of **ascending powers** of x. This means that you start with the term with the smallest power of x, then move to the next smallest, and so on.

Example 3.2.5

Find the first four terms in the expansion of $(2 - 3x)^{10}$ in ascending powers of x. By putting $x = \frac{1}{100}$, find an approximation to 1.97^{10} correct to the nearest whole number.

$$(2 - 3x)^{10} = \binom{10}{0} \times 2^{10} + \binom{10}{1} \times 2^9 \times (-3x) + \binom{10}{2} \times 2^8 \times (-3x)^2$$
$$+ \binom{10}{3} \times 2^7 \times (-3x)^3 + \ldots$$
$$= 1024 - 10 \times 512 \times 3x + 45 \times 256 \times 9x^2 - 120 \times 128 \times 27x^3 + \ldots$$
$$= 1024 - 15\,360x + 103\,680x^2 - 414\,720x^3 + \ldots$$

The first four terms are therefore $1024 - 15\,360x + 103\,680x^2 - 414\,720x^3$.

Putting $x = \frac{1}{100}$ gives

$$1.97^{10} \approx 1024 - 15\,360 \times \tfrac{1}{100} + 103\,680 \times \left(\tfrac{1}{100}\right)^2 - 414\,720 \times \left(\tfrac{1}{100}\right)^3$$
$$= 880.353\,28.$$

Therefore $1.97^{10} \approx 880$.

The next term is actually $\binom{10}{4} \times 2^6 \times (3x)^4 = 1\,088\,640x^4 = 0.010\,886\,4$ and the rest are very small indeed.

Example 3.2.6

Find the first three terms in ascending powers of x of the expansion of $(1 + x + 2x^2)^{10}$.

Start by bracketing $(1 + x + 2x^2)^{10}$ in the form $(1 + (x + 2x^2))^{10}$ and use the expansion of $(1 + y)^{10}$ with $y = x + 2x^2$.

The first three terms include the terms in x^2, so the expansion must go as far as the terms in y^2.

$$(1 + (x + 2x^2))^{10} = (1 + y)^{10}$$
$$= \binom{10}{0} \times 1 + \binom{10}{1} y + \binom{10}{2} y^2 + \ldots$$
$$= 1 + 10y + 45y^2 + \ldots$$
$$= 1 + 10(x + 2x^2) + 45(x + 2x^2)^2 + \ldots$$
$$= 1 + 10x + 20x^2 + 45x^2 + \ldots$$
$$= 1 + 10x + 65x^2 + \ldots$$

Note that there is no need to complete the expansion of $45(x + 2x^2)^2$ because it contains terms x^3 and x^4, which are not required.

The first three terms are $1 + 10x + 65x^2$.

3.3* Proving the binomial theorem

If you wish you may skip this section and go straight to Exercise 3B.

One other step is required before you can be sure that the values of $\binom{n}{r}$ are the values that you need for the binomial theorem. In Fig. 3.1 you saw that each term of Pascal's triangle, except for the 1s at the end of each row, is obtained by adding the two terms immediately above it. So it should be true that

$$\binom{n+1}{r+1} = \binom{n}{r} + \binom{n}{r+1}.$$

For example, it should be true that $\binom{6}{3} + \binom{6}{4} = \binom{7}{4}$.

Example 3.3.1

Show that $\binom{6}{3} + \binom{6}{4} = \binom{7}{4}$.

Method 1 Using the recursive definition, $\binom{n}{r+1} = \dfrac{n-r}{r+1}\binom{n}{r}$ with $n = 6$ and $r = 3$,

$$\binom{6}{4} = \frac{6-3}{3+1} \times \binom{6}{3} = \frac{3}{4} \times \binom{6}{3},$$

so

$$\binom{6}{3} + \binom{6}{4} = \binom{6}{3} + \frac{3}{4} \times \binom{6}{3} = \frac{7}{4} \times \binom{6}{3}$$

$$= \frac{7}{4} \times \frac{6 \times 5 \times 4}{1 \times 2 \times 3} = \frac{7 \times 6 \times 5 \times 4}{1 \times 2 \times 3 \times 4} = \binom{7}{4}.$$

Method 2 By manipulating the numbers,

$$\binom{6}{3} + \binom{6}{4} = \frac{6 \times 5 \times 4}{1 \times 2 \times 3} + \frac{6 \times 5 \times 4 \times 3}{1 \times 2 \times 3 \times 4}$$

$$= \frac{6 \times 5 \times 4 \times 4}{1 \times 2 \times 3 \times 4} + \frac{6 \times 5 \times 4 \times 3}{1 \times 2 \times 3 \times 4}$$

$$= \frac{6 \times 5 \times 4 \times 4 + 6 \times 5 \times 4 \times 3}{1 \times 2 \times 3 \times 4}$$

$$= \frac{6 \times 5 \times 4 \times (4+3)}{1 \times 2 \times 3 \times 4}$$

$$= \frac{6 \times 5 \times 4 \times 7}{1 \times 2 \times 3 \times 4}$$

$$= \frac{7 \times 6 \times 5 \times 4}{1 \times 2 \times 3 \times 4}$$

$$= \binom{7}{4}.$$

To show that $\binom{n+1}{r+1} = \binom{n}{r} + \binom{n}{r+1}$, starting from the right side using the recursive definition,

$$\binom{n}{r} + \binom{n}{r+1} = \binom{n}{r} + \frac{n-r}{r+1}\binom{n}{r}$$

$$= \left(1 + \frac{n-r}{r+1}\right) \times \binom{n}{r}$$

$$= \frac{r+1+n-r}{r+1} \times \binom{n}{r}$$

$$= \frac{1+n}{r+1} \times \binom{n}{r}$$

$$= \frac{n+1}{r+1} \times \frac{n \times (n-1) \times \cdots \times (n-r+1)}{1 \times 2 \times \cdots \times r}$$

$$= \frac{(n+1) \times n \times (n-1) \times \cdots \times (n-r+1)}{1 \times 2 \times \cdots \times r \times (r+1)}$$

$$= \binom{n+1}{r+1}.$$

This completes the chain of reasoning which connects Pascal's triangle with the binomial coefficients.

Exercise 3B

1 Find the value of each of the following.

(a) $\binom{7}{3}$ (b) $\binom{8}{6}$ (c) $\binom{9}{5}$ (d) $\binom{13}{4}$

(e) $\binom{6}{4}$ (f) $\binom{10}{2}$ (g) $\binom{11}{10}$ (h) $\binom{50}{2}$

2 Find the coefficient of x^3 in the expansion of each of the following.

(a) $(1+x)^5$ (b) $(1-x)^8$ (c) $(1+x)^{11}$ (d) $(1-x)^{16}$

3 Find the coefficient of x^5 in the expansion of each of the following.

(a) $(2+x)^7$ (b) $(3-x)^8$ (c) $(1+2x)^9$ (d) $\left(1 - \frac{1}{2}x\right)^{12}$

4 Find the coefficient of $x^6 y^8$ in the expansion of each of the following.

(a) $(x+y)^{14}$ (b) $(2x+y)^{14}$ (c) $(3x-2y)^{14}$ (d) $\left(4x + \frac{1}{2}y\right)^{14}$

5 Find the first four terms in the expansion in ascending powers of x of the following.

(a) $(1+x)^{13}$ (b) $(1-x)^{15}$ (c) $(1+3x)^{10}$ (d) $(2-5x)^7$

6 Find the first three terms in the expansion in ascending powers of x of the following.

(a) $(1+x)^{22}$ (b) $(1-x)^{30}$ (c) $(1-4x)^{18}$ (d) $(1+6x)^{19}$

7 Find the first three terms in the expansion, in ascending powers of x, of $(1+2x)^8$. By substituting $x = 0.01$, find an approximation to 1.02^8.

8 Find the first three terms in the expansion, in ascending powers of x, of $(2 + 5x)^{12}$. By substituting a suitable value for x, find an approximation to 2.005^{12} to 2 decimal places.

9 Expand $(1 + 2x)^{16}$ up to and including the term in x^3. Deduce the coefficient of x^3 in the expansion of $(1 + 3x)(1 + 2x)^{16}$.

10 Expand $(1 - 3x)^{10}$ up to and including the term in x^2. Deduce the coefficient of x^2 in the expansion of $(1 + 3x)^2(1 - 3x)^{10}$.

11 Given that the coefficient of x in the expansion of $(1 + ax)(1 + 5x)^{40}$ is 207, determine the value of a.

12 Simplify $(1 - x)^8 + (1 + x)^8$. Substitute a suitable value of x to find the exact value of $0.99^8 + 1.01^8$.

13 Given that the expansion of $(1 + ax)^n$ begins $1 + 36x + 576x^2$, find the values of a and n.

Miscellaneous exercise 3

1 Expand $(3 + 4x)^3$.

2 Find the first three terms in the expansions, in ascending powers of x, of
   (a) $(1 + 4x)^{10}$,   (b) $(1 - 2x)^{16}$.

3 Find the coefficient of a^3b^5 in the expansions of
   (a) $(3a - 2b)^8$,   (b) $\left(5a + \frac{1}{2}b\right)^8$.

4 Expand $(3 + 5x)^7$ in ascending powers of x up to and including the term in x^2. By putting $x = 0.01$, find an approximation, correct to the nearest whole number, to 3.05^7.

5 Obtain the first four terms in the expansion of $\left(2 + \frac{1}{4}x\right)^8$ in ascending powers of x. By substituting an appropriate value of x into this expansion, find the value of 2.0025^8 correct to three decimal places.   (OCR)

6 Find, in ascending powers of x, the first three terms in the expansion of $(2 - 3x)^8$. Use the expansion to find the value of 1.997^8 to the nearest whole number.   (OCR)

7 Expand $\left(x^2 + \frac{1}{x}\right)^3$, simplifying each of the terms.

8 Expand $\left(2x - \frac{3}{x^2}\right)^4$.

9 Expand and simplify $\left(x + \frac{1}{2x}\right)^6 + \left(x - \frac{1}{2x}\right)^6$.   (OCR)

10 Find the coefficient of x^2 in the expansion of $\left(x^4 + \frac{4}{x}\right)^3$.

11 Find the term independent of x in the expansion of $\left(2x + \frac{5}{x}\right)^6$.

12 Find the coefficient of y^4 in the expansion of $(1+y)^{12}$. Deduce the coefficient of

(a) y^4 in the expansion of $(1+3y)^{12}$,

(b) y^8 in the expansion of $(1-2y^2)^{12}$,

(c) $x^8 y^4$ in the expansion of $(x+\frac{1}{2}y)^{12}$.

13 Determine the coefficient of $p^4 q^7$ in the expansion of $(2p-q)(p+q)^{10}$.

14 Find the first three terms in the expansion of $(1+2x)^{20}$. By substitution of a suitable value of x in each case, find approximations to

(a) 1.002^{20},   (b) 0.996^{20}.

15 Write down the first three terms in the binomial expansion of $\left(2-\dfrac{1}{2x^2}\right)^{10}$ in ascending powers of $\dfrac{1}{x}$. Hence find the value of 1.995^{10} correct to three significant figures.   (OCR)

16 Two of the following expansions are correct and two are incorrect. Find the two expansions which are incorrect.

A: $(3+4x)^5 = 243 + 1620x + 4320x^2 + 5760x^3 + 3840x^4 + 1024x^5$

B: $(1-2x+3x^2)^3 = 1 + 6x - 3x^2 + 28x^3 - 9x^4 + 54x^5 - 27x^6$

C: $(1-x)(1+4x)^4 = 1 + 15x + 80x^2 + 160x^3 - 256x^5$

D: $(2x+y)^2(3x+y)^3 = 108x^5 + 216x^4 y + 171x^3 y^2 + 67x^2 y^3 + 13xy^4 + y^6$

17 Find and simplify the term independent of x in the expansion of $\left(\dfrac{1}{2x}+x^3\right)^8$.   (OCR)

18 Find the term independent of x in the expansion of $\left(2x+\dfrac{1}{x^2}\right)^9$.

19 Evaluate the term which is independent of x in the expansion of $\left(x^2-\dfrac{1}{2x^2}\right)^{16}$.   (OCR)

20 Find the coefficient of x^{-12} in the expansion of $\left(x^3-\dfrac{1}{x}\right)^{24}$.   (OCR)

21 Expand $(1+3x+4x^2)^4$ in ascending powers of x as far as the term in x^2. By substituting a suitable value of x, find an approximation to 1.0304^4.

22 Expand and simplify $(3x+5)^3 - (3x-5)^3$.
Hence solve the equation $(3x+5)^3 - (3x-5)^3 = 730$.

23 Solve the equation $(7-6x)^3 + (7+6x)^3 = 1736$.

24 (a) Show that

  (i) $\dbinom{6}{4} = \dbinom{6}{2}$,   (ii) $\dbinom{10}{3} = \dbinom{10}{7}$,   (iii) $\dbinom{15}{12} = \dbinom{15}{3}$,   (iv) $\dbinom{13}{6} = \dbinom{13}{7}$.

(b) State the possible values of x in each of the following.

  (i) $\dbinom{11}{4} = \dbinom{11}{x}$ (ii) $\dbinom{16}{3} = \dbinom{16}{x}$ (iii) $\dbinom{20}{7} = \dbinom{20}{x}$ (iv) $\dbinom{45}{17} = \dbinom{45}{x}$

(c) Use the definition $\dbinom{n}{r} = \dfrac{n!}{r!(n-r)!}$ to prove that $\dbinom{n}{r} = \dbinom{n}{n-r}$.

25 Find the value of 1.0003^{18} correct to 15 decimal places.

26 (a) Expand $(2\sqrt{2} + \sqrt{3})^4$. Give your answer in the form $a + b\sqrt{6}$, where a and b are integers.

   (b) Find the exact value of $(2\sqrt{2} + \sqrt{3})^5$.

27 (a) Expand and simplify $(\sqrt{7} + \sqrt{5})^4 + (\sqrt{7} - \sqrt{5})^4$. By using the fact that $0 < \sqrt{7} - \sqrt{5} < 1$, state the consecutive integers between which $(\sqrt{7} + \sqrt{5})^4$ lies.

   (b) Without using a calculator, find the consecutive integers between which the value of $(\sqrt{3} + \sqrt{2})^6$ lies.

28* Find, in ascending powers of t, the first three terms in the expansions of

   (a) $(1 + \alpha t)^5$,   (b) $(1 - \beta t)^8$.

   Hence find, in terms of α and β, the coefficient of t^2 in the expansion of $(1 + \alpha t)^5 (1 - \beta t)^8$.   (OCR)

29* (a) Show that

   (i) $4 \times \dbinom{6}{2} = 3 \times \dbinom{6}{3} = 6 \times \dbinom{5}{2}$,   (ii) $3 \times \dbinom{7}{4} = 5 \times \dbinom{7}{5} = 7 \times \dbinom{6}{4}$.

   (b) State numbers a, b and c such that

   (i) $a \times \dbinom{8}{5} = b \times \dbinom{8}{6} = c \times \dbinom{7}{5}$,   (ii) $a \times \dbinom{9}{3} = b \times \dbinom{9}{4} = c \times \dbinom{8}{3}$.

   (c) Prove that $(n - r) \times \dbinom{n}{r} = (r + 1) \times \dbinom{n}{r+1} = n \times \dbinom{n-1}{r}$.

30* Prove that $\dbinom{n}{r-1} + 2\dbinom{n}{r} + \dbinom{n}{r+1} = \dbinom{n+2}{r+1}$.

31* Find an expression, in terms of n, for the coefficient of x in the expansion

   $$(1 + 4x) + (1 + 4x)^2 + (1 + 4x)^3 + \cdots + (1 + 4x)^n.$$

32* Given that

   $$a + b(1 + x)^3 + c(1 + 2x)^3 + d(1 + 3x)^3 = x^3$$

   for all values of x, find the values of the constants a, b, c and d.

4 The sine and cosine rules

This chapter shows you how to use trigonometry in triangles which are not right-angled. When you have completed it, you should

- know and be able to use the formula $\Delta = \frac{1}{2}ab\sin C$ for the area of a triangle
- know and be able to use the sine and cosine rules to find unknown sides and angles in triangles which are not right-angled.

4.1 Some notation

You have already used trigonometry to calculate lengths and angles in right-angled triangles. This chapter develops rules which you can use to calculate lengths, angles and areas in triangles which are not right-angled. To state these rules, it helps to have a standard notation.

Fig. 4.1 shows a triangle ABC. In this triangle, the length of the side BC, which is opposite the vertex A, is denoted by a units. Similarly the lengths of CA and AB, which are opposite B and C respectively, are denoted by b units and c units. These units could be centimetres, miles or anything else you like. However, all the sides must be measured in the same units. That is, the units must be consistent.

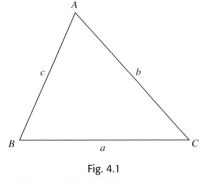

Fig. 4.1

In a practical problem, where particular units are specified, you would usually include the units when you label the sides. (See, for example, Fig. 4.4.) But where a figure might represent any triangle, such as Fig. 4.1, it is usual just to label the sides 'a, b, c' rather than 'a units, b units, c units'. You are already used to doing this when you use coordinates and write (x, y) rather than $(x$ units, y units).

You are probably used to naming the angle at the vertex A as 'angle BAC', or perhaps '$\angle BAC$'. This gets rather clumsy, so when there is no ambiguity the letter A is used as an abbreviation for the size of this angle. Similarly, B and C stand for the size of the angles at the corresponding vertices. These angles will usually be measured in degrees. For example, you might write $A = 60°$, $B = 75°$ and $C = 45°$. However, there is no reason why the angles could not be measured in some other units such as right angles if that were convenient. In that case $A = \frac{2}{3}$ right angle, $B = \frac{5}{6}$ right angle and $C = \frac{1}{2}$ right angle.

Some triangles in this chapter will also be labelled DEF, LMN, PQR, XYZ, etc. The same convention is used for these triangles, but with the letters changed. For example, the triangle PQR would have sides of length p units, q units and r units, and angles of size P, Q and R, where p is opposite the vertex P, and so on.

4.2   The area of an acute-angled triangle

You know the formula

$$\text{area of a triangle} = \tfrac{1}{2} \times \text{base} \times \text{height}$$

for the area of any triangle.

There are no units in this formula; however, the units of the lengths of the base and height must be the same and the unit of area must be consistent with these.

You can use trigonometry to write this formula in a different way.

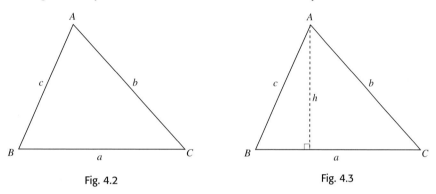

Fig. 4.2   Fig. 4.3

Suppose that you want a formula for the area of the acute-angled triangle ABC in Fig. 4.2. Then, to use the formula area $= \tfrac{1}{2} \times$ base $\times$ height, you need to find the height, which is shown as h in Fig. 4.3.

In the triangle on the right of Fig. 4.3, $\sin C = \dfrac{h}{b}$, so $h = b \sin C$.

The base of the triangle is a, so the area is given by

$$\text{area} = \tfrac{1}{2} \times \text{base} \times \text{height} = \tfrac{1}{2} \times a \times b \sin C = \tfrac{1}{2}ab \sin C.$$

The area of a triangle is denoted by Δ where Δ is the Greek capital 'd', called 'delta'. Then, for an acute-angled triangle,

$$\Delta = \tfrac{1}{2}ab \sin C.$$

The units for Δ would correspond to the units for the sides of the triangle. So if the lengths were a cm and b cm, the area would be Δ cm^2.

Example 4.2.1
Calculate the area of the triangle ABC in Fig. 4.4 in which $BC = 5$ cm, $AC = 7$ cm and angle $C = 20°$.

For this triangle, $a = 5$ and $b = 7$. Substituting these into $\Delta = \tfrac{1}{2}ab \sin C$ gives

$$\Delta = \tfrac{1}{2} \times 5 \times 7 \sin 20° = 5.985\dots.$$

The area of triangle ABC is 5.99 cm^2, correct to 3 significant figures.

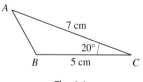

Fig. 4.4

If, in Fig. 4.3, you had calculated the height h from the triangle on the left instead of the triangle on the right, you would have obtained $h = c \sin B$ instead of $h = b \sin C$.

Using this new expression for h gives

$$\Delta = \tfrac{1}{2} \times a \times c \sin B = \tfrac{1}{2}ac \sin B.$$

And, if you had drawn the perpendicular from B to the side AC, and used AC as the base of the triangle you could have obtained the formula

$$\Delta = \tfrac{1}{2}bc \sin A.$$

Therefore you have three ways of expressing the area of an acute-angled triangle,

$$\Delta = \tfrac{1}{2}bc \sin A = \tfrac{1}{2}ca \sin B = \tfrac{1}{2}ab \sin C.$$

4.3   Area of an obtuse-angled triangle

Now suppose that the triangle ABC is obtuse-angled, with an obtuse angle at C, as shown in Fig. 4.5.

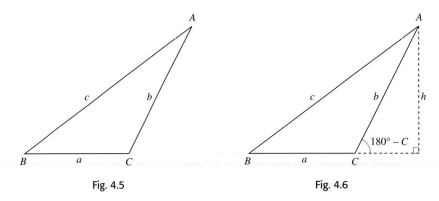

Fig. 4.5   Fig. 4.6

In Fig. 4.6, the height of the triangle ABC is shown as h; using the right-angled triangle with hypotenuse AC shows that $h = b \sin(180° - C)$, giving

$$\Delta = \tfrac{1}{2} \times a \times b \sin(180° - C) = \tfrac{1}{2}ab \sin(180° - C).$$

But you know from the supplementary property of the sine function (Section 1.4) that for any value of θ, $\sin(180° - \theta) = \sin \theta°$.

So in this case $\sin(180° - C) = \sin C$, giving

$$\Delta = \tfrac{1}{2}ab \sin C.$$

The formula $\tfrac{1}{2}ab \sin C$ can therefore be used for the area of any triangle, whether the angle at C is acute or obtuse.

What happens if the angle at C is a right angle?

> The area Δ of a triangle ABC is given by
> $$\Delta = \tfrac{1}{2}bc\sin A = \tfrac{1}{2}ca\sin B = \tfrac{1}{2}ab\sin C,$$
> where the unit of area corresponds to the units for the sides.

A good way to remember this formula is to think of it as

$$\Delta = \tfrac{1}{2} \times \text{one side} \times \text{another side} \times \text{the sine of the angle between them.}$$

This enables you to use the formula for a triangle XYZ without having to re-label it as ABC, or do mental gymnastics with the letters concerned.

Example 4.3.1
Find the areas of the triangles shown in Fig. 4.7.

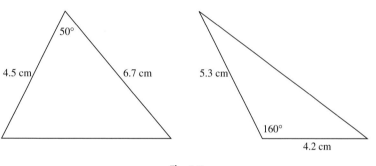

Fig. 4.7

Fig. 4.7 is only a rough sketch of the two triangles.

For the left triangle, the area is given by

$$\Delta = \tfrac{1}{2} \times 4.5 \times 6.7 \times \sin 50° = 11.54\dots .$$

The area is 11.5 cm^2, correct to 3 significant figures.

For the right triangle, the area is given by

$$\Delta = \tfrac{1}{2} \times 5.3 \times 4.2 \times \sin 160° = 3.806\dots .$$

The area is 3.81 cm^2, correct to 3 significant figures.

Example 4.3.2
A triangle ABC with the length $BC = 3.4$ cm and $B = 130°$ has an area of 5.72 cm^2. Find the length of the side AB.

In Fig. 4.8, denoting the side AB by c cm,

$$5.72 = \tfrac{1}{2} \times 3.4 \times c \times \sin 130°$$

giving

$$c = \frac{5.72}{\tfrac{1}{2} \times 3.4 \times \sin 130°} = 4.392....$$

The length of the side AB is 4.39 cm, correct to 3 significant figures.

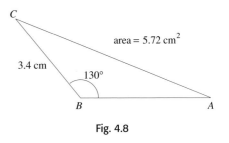

Fig. 4.8

Example 4.3.3

An obtuse-angled triangle ABC with $BC = 4.2$ m and $CA = 15$ m has an area of 7.12 m^2. Find the size of the obtuse angle at C.

In Fig. 4.9, as $7.12 = \tfrac{1}{2} \times 4.2 \times 15 \times \sin C$, $\sin C = 0.2260...$.

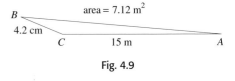

Fig. 4.9

The calculator gives the acute angle whose sine is 0.2260... as 13.06...°. Using the supplementary rule from Section 1.4, the obtuse angle whose sine is 0.2260... is $(180 - 13.06...)°$.

Therefore $C = 166.9°$, correct to 1 decimal place.

Exercise 4A

1 In each part, the lengths of two sides of a triangle and the angle between them are given. Find the area of each triangle, giving your answer in appropriate units.

   (a) 3 cm, 4 cm, 90°   (b) 5 cm, 7 cm, 40°   (c) 3 m, 2 m, 140°

   (d) 5 cm, 3 cm, 30°   (e) 4 cm, 3 cm, 123°   (f) 88 cm, 1 m, 45°

2 In each part, the area of a triangle, the length of one side and an angle which is not opposite to that side are given. Find the length of the other side of the triangle which is not opposite to the given angle.

   (a) 5 cm^2, 3 cm, 40°   (b) 8 cm^2, 4 cm, 90°   (c) 3 m^2, 4 m, 110°

   (d) 23.2 cm^2, 7.1 cm, 43.3° (e) 15.1 cm^2, 1 cm, 136°   (f) 1.40 m^2, 25 m, 85°

3 In each part, the length of two sides of an acute-angled triangle and its area are given. Find the angle between the given sides.

   (a) 3 cm, 6 cm, 5 cm^2 (b) 4 cm, 5 cm, 8 cm^2 (c) 5 m, 8 m, 7 m^2

   (d) 7.5 cm, 8.3 cm, 25.9 cm^2 (e) 10 cm, 15 cm, 15.1 cm^2 (f) 3 m, 5 m, 1.40 m^2

4 In each part, the data of Question 3 now refers to an obtuse-angled triangle. Find the angle between the given sides.

4.4   The sine rule for a triangle

In the formula $\Delta = \frac{1}{2}bc \sin A = \frac{1}{2}ca \sin B = \frac{1}{2}ab \sin C$ for the area of a triangle, if you ignore the Δ and multiply all through by 2 you obtain

$$bc \sin A = ca \sin B = ab \sin C.$$

If you now divide each part of this equation by abc you get

$$\frac{\sin A}{a} = \frac{\sin B}{b} = \frac{\sin C}{c}.$$

This is one form of the sine rule for a triangle. If you know two sides of a triangle and the angle opposite one of them, you can use it to find the angle opposite the other.

Example 4.4.1

In a triangle ABC, $BC = 11$ cm, $CA = 15$ cm and angle $ABC = 73°$. Find the angle BAC.

Begin by drawing a rough sketch like Fig. 4.10.

You are given that $a = 11$, $b = 15$ and $B = 73°$. So you know $\dfrac{\sin B}{b}$ completely, and you want to find A. Neither c nor C is involved, so use $\dfrac{\sin A}{a} = \dfrac{\sin B}{b}.$

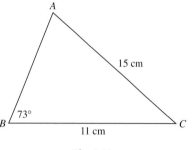

Fig. 4.10

Substituting the known values,

$$\frac{\sin A}{11} = \frac{\sin 73°}{15},$$

so $\sin A = \dfrac{11 \times \sin 73°}{15} = 0.701...$, $A = 44.53...°$.

The angle BAC is $44.5°$ to the nearest $0.1°$.

> Notice that there is another angle, $(180 - 44.53...)°$, whose sine is also $0.701...$.
> But you can't have a triangle with one angle of $73°$ and another of $135.46...°$,
> since the sum of these is greater than $180°$.

You can also use the sine rule if you know two angles of a triangle and the side opposite to one of them, and want to find the side opposite to the other. In that case the algebra is simpler if you replace each fraction by its reciprocal (that is, turn it upside down), and give the rule as

$$\frac{a}{\sin A} = \frac{b}{\sin B} = \frac{c}{\sin C}.$$

Example 4.4.2

In the triangle XYZ, angle $X = 40°$, angle $Z = 85°$ and the length of $XY = 8$ cm. Calculate the length of YZ.

The triangle is sketched in Fig. 4.11. You know that
$X = 40°$, $Z = 85°$ and $z = 8$, and want to find x. So,
adapting the rule with the new letters,

$$\frac{x}{\sin 40°} = \frac{8}{\sin 85°}.$$

This gives $x = \dfrac{8 \sin 40°}{\sin 85°} = 5.161\ldots$

Thus $YZ = 5.16$ cm, correct to 3 significant figures.

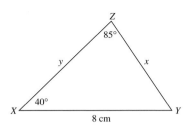

Fig. 4.11

> The **sine rule** for a triangle ABC is
>
> $$\frac{a}{\sin A} = \frac{b}{\sin B} = \frac{c}{\sin C}.$$

Use this formula to calculate a side if you know the length of another side and two of the angles of a triangle.

Use the upside-down form of the formula to calculate the sine of an angle if you know the lengths of two sides and one other angle, which must not be the angle between the two known sides.

Example 4.4.3

In the triangle sketched in Fig. 4.12, calculate   (a) the angle Q,   (b) the length of PQ.

(a) You know that $p = 5$, $q = 4$ and $P = 140°$,

so use $\dfrac{\sin P}{p} = \dfrac{\sin Q}{q}$.

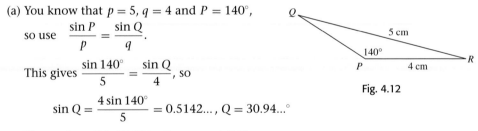

Fig. 4.12

This gives $\dfrac{\sin 140°}{5} = \dfrac{\sin Q}{4}$, so

$\sin Q = \dfrac{4 \sin 140°}{5} = 0.5142\ldots,\ Q = 30.94\ldots°$

The angle at Q is $30.9°$ to the nearest $0.1°$.

Another angle, $(180 - 30.9)°$, also has the property that its sine is $0.5142\ldots$, but it should be clear that this could not be an angle of a triangle in which one of the other angles is $140°$.

(b) To find r you need to know the angle R. This is easy, since $P + Q + R = 180°$, so
$R = 180° - 140° - 30.94\ldots° = 9.05\ldots°$.

Now use the sine rule in the form $\dfrac{p}{\sin P} = \dfrac{r}{\sin R}$, to give $\dfrac{5}{\sin 140°} = \dfrac{r}{\sin 9.05\ldots°}$,

$r = \dfrac{5 \times \sin 9.05\ldots°}{\sin 140°} = 1.224\ldots.$

The length of PQ is 1.22 cm, correct to 3 significant figures.

4.5 The longest and shortest sides of a triangle

Try drawing some sketches of triangles *ABC* (both acute- and obtuse-angled) with the angle at *A* greater than the angle at *B*. Is it always true that the side opposite *A* is longer than the side opposite *B*?

The answer to the question is yes:

> In any triangle *ABC*,
>
> > if $A > B$, then $a > b$,
>
> and   if $a > b$, then $A > B$.

You can use the sine rule to prove this. To see how, try Miscellaneous exercise 4, Questions 17 and 18.

It follows from this that the longest side of a triangle is the side opposite the largest angle, and the shortest side is opposite the smallest angle; it is also true that the largest angle of a triangle is opposite the longest side and the smallest angle is opposite the shortest side.

Exercise 4B

1 In each part of this question, use the sine rule to find the length of the unknown side.

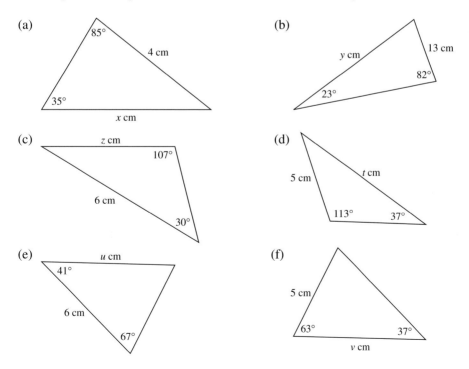

(a) 85° 4 cm 35° *x* cm

(b) *y* cm 13 cm 82° 23°

(c) *z* cm 107° 6 cm 30°

(d) 5 cm *t* cm 113° 37°

(e) *u* cm 41° 6 cm 67°

(f) 5 cm 63° 37° *v* cm

2 In each part, find the lengths of the other two sides, and the area of the triangle.

   (a) In triangle ABC, $A = 58°$, $B = 63°$, $AC = 13$ cm

   (b) In triangle PQR, $Q = 118°$, $R = 30°$, $PR = 14$ cm

   (c) In triangle XYZ, $X = 71°$, $Z = 59°$, $XZ = 12$ cm

   (d) In triangle LMN, $M = 125°$, $N = 15°$, $LN = 13.2$ cm

3 Find the remaining angles of the triangles ABC and XYZ.

   (a) $B = 91°$, $BC = 11.1$ cm, $AC = 12.3$ cm   (b) $X = 71°$, $YZ = 10.1$ cm, $XZ = 9.2$ cm

4 The triangles LMN and DEF are both obtuse-angled. Find the remaining angles.

   (a) $M = 13°$, $MN = 23.1$ cm, $LN = 5.2$ cm   (b) $E = 40°$, $DF = 9$ cm, $DE = 13$ cm

5 The following method is used to find the position of an object that you can see, but not get to, such as a tower across a river.

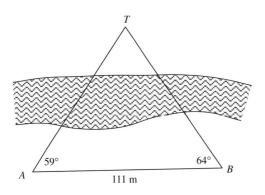

Let the tower be at T. Measure accurately a base line AB on your side of the river, and measure the angles TAB and TBA. Calculate

   (a) the distance AT,

   (b) the perpendicular distance of the tower from the line AB.

6 $ABCD$ is a quadrilateral. The lengths of CB and CD are 4 cm and 3 cm respectively, and the length of the diagonal CA is 5 cm. The angles B and D are 70° and 120° respectively.

   (a) Calculate angle BAD.   (b) Calculate angle BCD.

7 If you try to find the angle A in a triangle with $B = 120°$, $a = 15$ cm and $b = 10$ cm you get an error message. Why?

8 $ABCD$ is a quadrilateral. Angle $BAC = 80°$, angle $BCA = 30°$, angle $ACD = 50°$ and angle $ADC = 60°$. The length of AB is 3 cm. Calculate

   (a) the length AC,   (b) the length CD,   (c) the area of $ABCD$.

4.6 The cosine rule for a triangle

You have seen that, if you know one side of a triangle and the angle opposite to it, together with one other fact, you can use the sine rule to find the other sides and angles. The extra fact can either be another side (as in Example 4.4.1) or another angle (as in Example 4.4.2).

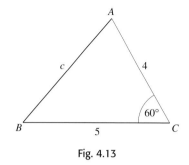

Fig. 4.13

But if you know two sides and the angle between them, the sine rule is no help. For example, suppose that $a = 5$, $b = 4$ and $C = 60°$ and you need to find c. This is shown in Fig. 4.13.

If you try to use the sine rule, you get

$$\frac{5}{\sin A} = \frac{4}{\sin B} = \frac{c}{\sin 60°}.$$

There is something unknown in each of the three fractions. To find c, you would need to know either $\sin A$ or $\sin B$, but you don't know either. You need another method.

In general, the problem is that you know both the lengths a units and b units and the size of the angle C, and you need to find the length c units. The angle C may be either acute (as in Fig. 4.14) or obtuse (as in Fig. 4.15).

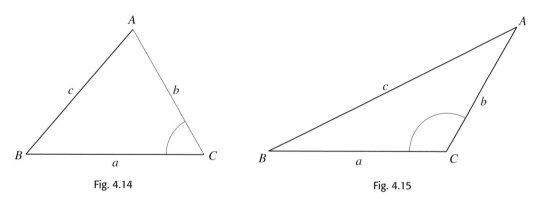

Fig. 4.14   Fig. 4.15

In Sections 1.1 and 1.2 the cosine and sine of an angle were defined using coordinates. It is convenient to go back to these definitions to derive a method for solving this problem.

In Fig. 4.16 and 4.17 the triangles in Fig. 4.14 and 4.15 have been picked up and put down on a set of coordinate axes.

The vertex C is placed on the origin, and the triangle is rotated so that the vertex A is placed on the positive x-axis. The coordinates of A are therefore $(b, 0)$.

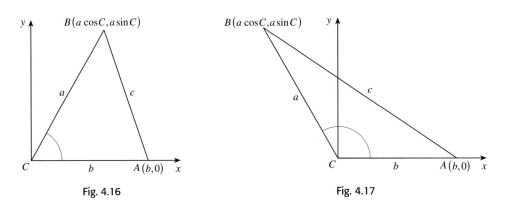

Fig. 4.16   Fig. 4.17

The coordinates of the vertex B are $(a \cos C, a \sin C)$. This is true whether the angle ACB is acute (as in Fig. 4.16) or obtuse (as in Fig. 4.17).

The formula in C1 Section 1.1 for the distance AB in terms of coordinates gives

$$c^2 = (a \cos C - b)^2 + (a \sin C - 0)^2$$
$$= a^2 \cos^2 C - 2(a \cos C)b + b^2 + a^2 \sin^2 C$$
$$= a^2(\cos^2 C + \sin^2 C) + b^2 - 2ab \cos C.$$

Using the identity in Section 1.6, $\cos^2 C + \sin^2 C \equiv 1$. So

$$c^2 = a^2 + b^2 - 2ab \cos C.$$

This is the cosine rule for the triangle ABC.

Example 4.6.1 uses the cosine rule to solve the problem at the beginning of this section.

Example 4.6.1
In the triangle ABC, suppose that $BC = 5$ cm, $CA = 4$ cm and $C = 60°$. Find the length of the side AB (see Fig. 4.18).

Using the cosine rule with $a = 5$, $b = 4$ and $C = 60°$,

$$c^2 = 5^2 + 4^2 - 2 \times 5 \times 4 \times \cos 60°$$
$$= 25 + 16 - 40 \times \tfrac{1}{2}$$
$$= 21,$$

so $c = \sqrt{21} = 4.582....$

The side AB has length 4.58 cm, correct to 3 significant figures.

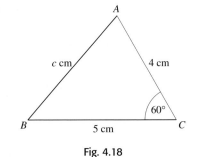

Fig. 4.18

Of course, it may happen that you are given one of the other angles of the triangle, and the lengths of the two sides which border it. In that case you will need the rule in a different form, just as with the area formula in Section 4.3.

For a triangle *ABC* there are three forms of the equation.

The **cosine rule** for a triangle *ABC* has one of the three forms:

$$a^2 = b^2 + c^2 - 2bc \cos A$$
$$b^2 = c^2 + a^2 - 2ca \cos B$$
$$c^2 = a^2 + b^2 - 2ab \cos C$$

The cosine formula in one of these forms can be used to calculate the length of a side of a triangle when you know the lengths of the other two sides and the angle between them.

Don't try to learn these three forms separately. Think of the formula as being like Pythagoras' theorem but with an adjustment, and remember the form of the adjustment.

Example 4.6.2

Find the length of the third side of a triangle given that two of the sides have lengths 4.58 cm and 3.51 cm, and that the angle between them is $130°$.

Fig. 4.19 shows a sketch which is not precisely to scale.

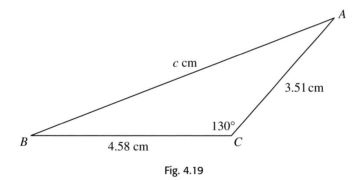

Fig. 4.19

In this case you know that $a = 4.58$, $b = 3.51$ and $C = 130°$, so, using the cosine rule,

$$c^2 = 4.58^2 + 3.51^2 - 2 \times 4.58 \times 3.51 \times \cos 130°$$
$$= 53.963...$$

giving $c = 7.345....$.

The length of the third side is 7.35 cm, correct to 3 significant figures.

You can also use the cosine rule when you know the lengths of all three sides of a triangle and want to find one of the angles. This is illustrated in the next example.

Example 4.6.3
Nottingham is 35 km north of Leicester. Melton Mowbray is 22 km from Leicester on the east side and 27 km from Nottingham. Find the bearing of Melton Mowbray from Leicester, giving your answer to the nearest degree.

Denoting the towns by L, M and N in Fig. 4.20, you are given that $l = 27$, $m = 35$, $n = 22$ and you want to find the angle NLM.

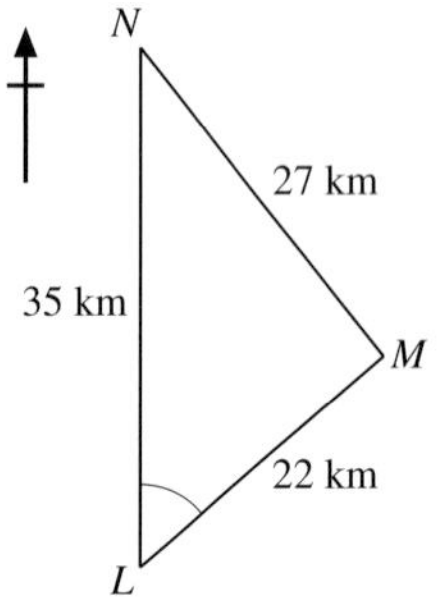

Substituting in the equation $l^2 = m^2 + n^2 - 2mn \cos L$,

$$729 = 1225 + 484 - 1540 \cos L,$$

so $$1540 \cos L = 1225 + 484 - 729 = 980,$$

$$\cos L = \frac{980}{1540} = 0.6363\ldots.$$

This gives $L = 50.47\ldots°$.

The bearing of Melton Mowbray from Leicester is $050°$, to the nearest degree.

Fig. 4.20

If you put the known values of the a, b and c into the formulae in the box on page 291, you get equations for the unknowns $\cos A$, $\cos B$ and $\cos C$. You can then solve these equations to find A, B and C.

For example, if you start with $c^2 = a^2 + b^2 - 2ab \cos C$, you can rewrite it in the form

$$2ab \cos C = a^2 + b^2 - c^2$$

which leads to

$$\cos C = \frac{a^2 + b^2 - c^2}{2ab}.$$

You then have three equivalent formulae for finding angles.

The three forms of the cosine rule used for finding angles are

$$\cos A = \frac{b^2 + c^2 - a^2}{2bc}, \quad \cos B = \frac{c^2 + a^2 - b^2}{2ca} \quad \text{and}$$

$$\cos C = \frac{a^2 + b^2 - c^2}{2ab}.$$

Of course, you do not need to learn the three formulae in the box because you could go back to the box on page 291 and use the original form of the cosine rule. It doesn't matter which you do, as long as you are confident about it and use whichever form you choose accurately.

Example 4.6.4

Calculate the largest angle of the triangle with sides 2 cm, 3 cm and 4 cm.

The largest angle is at the vertex opposite the longest side. In Fig. 4.21, this is the angle A.

Putting the values $a = 4$, $b = 3$ and $c = 2$ into the equation $\cos A = \dfrac{b^2 + c^2 - a^2}{2bc}$ gives

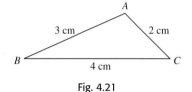

Fig. 4.21

$$\cos A = \frac{3^2 + 2^2 - 4^2}{2 \times 3 \times 2}$$

$$= \frac{9 + 4 - 16}{12}$$

$$= \frac{-3}{12} = -\frac{1}{4} = -0.25.$$

Thus $A = 104.47...^\circ$.

The largest angle is 104.5°, correct to 1 decimal place.

Exercise 4C

1   In each part of this question, find the length of the remaining side.

  (a) $BC = 10$ cm, $AC = 11$ cm, $C = 58^\circ$

  (b) $QR = 13$ cm, $PQ = 5$ cm, $Q = 123^\circ$

  (c) $XY = 15.1$ cm, $XZ = 14.2$ cm, $X = 23^\circ$

  (d) $LN = 14.8$ cm, $LM = 13.2$ cm, $L = 179^\circ$

2   Find the largest angle in each of the following triangles.

  (a) $a = 10$, $b = 11$, $c = 12$ (b) $l = 8$, $m = 19$, $n = 13$

  (c) $x = 14.1$, $y = 20.0$, $z = 15.3$ (d) $d = 9$, $e = 40$, $f = 41$

3   Find the smallest angle in each of the following triangles.

  (a) $a = 10$, $b = 8$, $c = 7$ (b) $x = 9$, $y = 9$, $z = 13$

  (c) $p = 8$, $q = 4$, $r = 5$ (d) $d = 4$, $e = 3$, $f = 5$

4   Find the area of the triangle with sides 8 cm, 9 cm and 10 cm.

4.7 Solving triangles

If you are given information about a triangle and are asked to find all the remaining sides and angles, you are said to be **solving the triangle**.

Precisely how you do this will depend on the information you are given.

> - If you know one side, the opposite angle and one other fact (a side or an angle) then begin by using the sine rule.
> - If you know two sides and the angle between them, or three sides, begin by using the cosine rule.
> - Once you know two angles, you can find the third by using the fact that sum of the three angles is 180°.
> - Once you know three sides and an angle, you can find another angle either by using the cosine rule or by using the sine rule. If you use the sine rule, it is better to use it to find the smaller angle.
> - Don't approximate prematurely, or you will lose accuracy; keep the full values in a calculator memory until the end of the calculation.

Example 4.7.1

In triangle ABC, $a = 9$, $b = 10$ and $B = 20°$. Solve the triangle.

In the sketch (Fig. 4.22) side AB is labelled c.

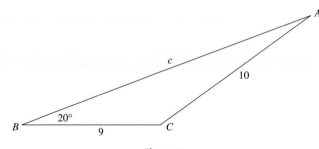

Fig. 4.22

You are given the angle B and the side b, so use the sine rule. As the other piece of information is a, use it in the form $\dfrac{\sin A}{a} = \dfrac{\sin B}{b}$ to get

$$\frac{\sin A}{9} = \frac{\sin 20°}{10}$$

giving $\sin A = \dfrac{9 \times \sin 20°}{10} = 0.307...$,

so $A = 17.92...°$ or $162.07...°$.

But the obtuse angle is impossible because the angle sum would be greater than 180°, so $A = 17.92...°$.

You can now find the third angle from $C = 180° - 20° - 17.92...° = 142.07...°$.

To find c, use the sine formula.

$$\frac{10}{\sin 20°} = \frac{c}{\sin 142.07...°} \quad \text{gives} \quad c = \frac{10 \times \sin 142.07...°}{\sin 20°} = 17.97...$$

The other two angles are $17.9°$ and $\sin 142.1°$, correct to 1 decimal place, and $c = 18.0$, correct to 3 significant figures.

Example 4.7.2

Solve the triangle shown in Fig. 4.23.

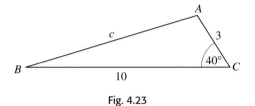

Fig. 4.23

You have no choice about how to start; use the cosine formula to find the side c.

$$c^2 = 10^2 + 3^2 - 2 \times 10 \times 3 \times \cos 40° = 63.03... \quad \text{giving} \quad c = 7.939...$$

> Record this number in the calculator. You are going to need it again later.

You now have a choice: you could either use the sine rule or the cosine rule.

Method 1   Using the sine rule

Find either A or B; choose the smaller angle, B, because the angle at A might be obtuse.

$$\frac{\sin B}{3} = \frac{\sin 40°}{7.939...} \quad \text{giving} \quad \sin B = \frac{3 \times \sin 40°}{7.939...} = 0.2428..., \quad \text{and}$$

$B = 14.05...°$. This leaves angle A to be found by subtraction, giving

$$A = 180° - 40° - 14.05...° = 125.94...°.$$

(Note that if you used $\dfrac{\sin A}{10} = \dfrac{\sin 40°}{7.939...}$, you would get $\sin A = 0.809...$, but you want $A = 180° - 54.05...°$, *not* $54.05...°$.)

Method 2   Using the cosine rule

Find either A or B by the cosine rule.

$$\cos A = \frac{3^2 + 7.939...^2 - 10^2}{2 \times 3 \times 7.939...} = -0.586..., \quad \text{giving} \quad A = 125.94...°$$

Then $B = 180° - 40° - 125.94...° = 14.05...°$.

By either method, the angle at A is $125.9°$, the angle at B is $14.1°$, both correct to 1 decimal place, and the length of side c is 7.94 units, correct to 3 significant figures.

Exercise 4D

In each question solve the given triangle.

1 In triangle ABC, $BC = 5$ cm, $A = 50°$ and $B = 60°$.

2 In triangle XYZ, $XY = 6$ cm, $YZ = 7$ cm and $X = 80°$.

3 In triangle PQR, $PQ = 3$ cm, $QR = 5$ cm and $RP = 7$ cm.

4 In triangle LMN, $MN = 10$ cm, $NL = 11$ cm and $N = 110°$.

5 In triangle DEF, $FD = 7$ cm, $DE = 7$ cm and $D = 40°$.

Miscellaneous exercise 4

1 The shortest side of a triangle is 4.3 m long. Two of the angles are 45.1° and 51.2°. Find the length of the longest side.

2 In triangle ABC the length $BC = 15.1$ cm, angle $BAC = 56°$, angle $ABC = 73°$. Calculate the lengths of the sides AB and AC.

3 The length of the longest side of a triangle is 15 cm. Two of the angles are 39° and 48°. Find the length of the shortest side.

4 In a triangle XYZ find angle Z when $YZ = 4.7$ cm, $XZ = 10.5$ cm and $XY = 8.9$ cm.

5 The sides of a triangle are 7 cm, 9 cm and 12 cm. Find its angles and its area.

6 In triangle LMN, $LN = 8.6$ cm, $LM = 9.9$ cm, $L = 75°$, find the length MN, and the angles M and N.

7 In a quadrilateral $ABCD$, $AB = 4$ cm, $BC = 5$ cm, $CD = 7$ cm, $DA = 5$ cm and angle ABC is 87°. Find angle ADC.

8 In a quadrilateral $PQRS$, $PQ = 4$ cm, $QR = 3$ cm and $RS = 4$ cm. Angle $PQR = 92°$ and angle $QRS = 110°$. Find the lengths of the diagonals and the length PS.

9 In a quadrilateral $ABCD$, $AB = 3$ cm, $BC = 4$ cm, $CD = 7$ cm, $DA = 8$ cm and the diagonal $AC = 6$ cm. Find the area of the quadrilateral.

10 A small weight W is supported by two strings of lengths 1 metre and 1.2 metres from two points 1.4 metres apart on a horizontal ceiling. How far below the ceiling is W?

11 Two ships leave a harbour at the same time. The first steams on a bearing 045° at 16 km h^{-1} and the second on a bearing 305° at 18 km h^{-1}. How far apart will they be after 2 hours?

12 The diagram, which is not drawn to scale, shows a triangular flower bed ABC of which the sides BC, CA and AB are 4 metres, 6 metres and 8 metres long respectively.

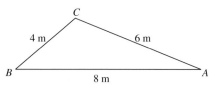

(a) Calculate the size, in degrees, of the angle at *A*.

(b) Calculate the area of the flower bed *ABC*.   (OCR)

13 The first diagram shows a sketch of the Great Pyramid at Giza in Egypt. It can be modelled as a square-based pyramid, where *ABCD* is a horizontal square of side 230 metres. The faces *ABE*, *BCE*, *CDE* and *ADE* can be considered as isosceles triangles, in which the sides of equal length are 214 metres.

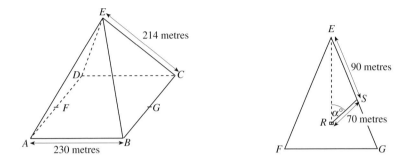

(a) Calculate the vertical height of the pyramid; that is, the height of *E* above the square base *ABCD*.

The second diagram shows a sketch of a vertical cross section through the pyramid. The vertical plane of the cross section passes through the mid-points of the sides *AD* and *BC* of the base of the pyramid. These mid-points are labelled *F* and *G* in both diagrams. A burial chamber is at *R* vertically below the apex of the pyramid. A ventilation shaft slopes upwards from the burial chamber to meet the face *BCE* of the pyramid, as shown on the second diagram. This shaft meets the sloping face of the pyramid at a point *S* on the line *EG*.

The ventilation shaft, *RS* is 70 metres long and it meets the face of the pyramid at *S* so that *ES* is 90 metres.

(b) Calculate the angle, α, that the ventilation shaft makes with the vertical.

(c) Calculate the depth of the burial chamber, *R*, below the vertex, *E*, of the pyramid.   (OCR)

14 The diagram, which is not drawn to scale, shows an obtuse-angled triangle *ABC* in which *AC* = 12 cm, angle *A* = 50° and *BC* = 10 cm.

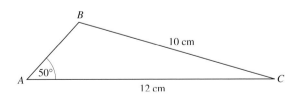

(a) Calculate the size of angle *C*.

(b) Calculate the area of triangle *ABC*.   (OCR, adapted)

15 (a) A triangle ABC has sides BC, CA and AB of lengths 6 cm, 5 cm and 4 cm respectively. Calculate the area of the triangle.

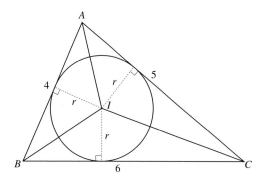

(b) The diagram shows the triangle ABC together with a circle, centre I, drawn inside the triangle ABC and touching the sides BC, CA and AB.

By considering the sum of the areas of triangles IBC, ICA and IAB, or otherwise, calculate the radius, r cm, of the circle.   (OCR, adapted)

16* Two points P and Q are visible from point A but are inaccessible from A. The bearings of P and Q from A are 015° and 034° respectively, and their bearings from B, which is 100 m east of A, are 305° and 325°. Calculate the length PQ.

17* In a triangle ABC, suppose that $A > B$ and consider two cases.

(a) If both angles are acute, use the definition of $\sin\theta°$, or the graph of $\sin\theta°$, to explain why $\sin A > \sin B$.

(b) If the angle at A is obtuse, explain why $(180° - A) > B$, and deduce again that $\sin A > \sin B$.

Hence use the sine rule to show that, in either case, $a > b$.

18* In a triangle ABC, suppose that $a > b$. Use the sine rule to show that $\sin A > \sin B$, and consider three cases.

(a) If the angles at A and B are both acute, explain why $A > B$.

(b) If the angle at A is obtuse and the angle at B is acute, explain why $A > B$.

(c) If the angle at A is acute and the angle at B is obtuse, show that $A > (180° - B)$, and explain why this is impossible.

Use your results to show that, if $a > b$, then $A > B$.

5 Integration

Integration is the reverse process of differentiation. When you have completed this chapter, you should

- understand the term 'indefinite integral' and the need to add an arbitrary constant
- be able to integrate functions which can be expressed as sums of powers of x, and be aware of any exceptions
- know how to find the equation of a graph given its derivative and a point on the graph
- know how to evaluate definite integrals, including infinite and improper integrals
- be able to use definite integrals to find areas.

5.1 Finding a function from its derivative

Example 5.1.1
Fig. 5.1 shows the graph of $y = f(x)$, where $f(x) = x - \frac{1}{2}x^2 + 1$. Draw the graph of $f'(x)$, and give a geometrical description of the connection between the two graphs.

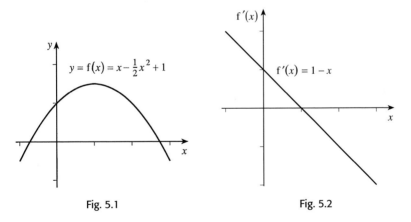

| Fig. 5.1 | Fig. 5.2 |

Since $f'(x) = 1 - \frac{1}{2}(2x) = 1 - x$, its graph is the straight line in Fig. 5.2.

For values of x to the left of 1, $f(x)$ is increasing. So the gradient $f'(x)$ is positive for $x < 1$. In Fig. 5.2, the graph of $f'(x)$ lies above the x-axis.

At $x = 1$, $f(x)$ takes its maximum value, and $f'(x) = 0$. In Fig. 5.2, the graph of $f'(x)$ crosses the x-axis.

For values of x to the right of 1, $f(x)$ is decreasing. So the gradient $f'(x)$ is negative for $x > 1$. In Fig. 5.2, the graph of $f'(x)$ lies below the x-axis.

You can add more detail to the comparison of the two graphs by noting that the graph of f(x) bends downwards. That is, as you move from left to right along the curve the gradient gets smaller. This is shown in Fig. 5.2 by the fact that f'(x) is a decreasing function of x.

You could make a similar comparison between the graphs of f(x) and f'(x) for any function you care to choose. If you know the graph of f(x), then this determines the graph of f'(x).

Is the reverse true? That is, if you know the graph of f'(x), could you use this to draw the graph of f(x)?

Example 5.1.2 examines this geometrically for a graph of f'(x) which is not a straight line.

Example 5.1.2
Fig. 5.3 shows the graph of the gradient function f'(x) of some function f(x). Use this to draw a sketch of the graph of f(x).

Scanning Fig. 5.3 from left to right, you can see that:

For $x < 0$ the graph of f'(x) lies below the x-axis; the gradient is negative, so f(x) is decreasing.

At $x = 0$ the gradient changes from $-$ to $+$, so f(x) has a minimum.

For $0 < x < 2$ the graph of f'(x) lies above the x-axis; the gradient is positive, so f(x) is increasing. Notice that the gradient is greatest when $x = 1$, so that is where the graph of f(x) climbs most steeply.

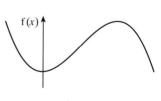

Fig. 5.3

At $x = 2$ the gradient changes from $+$ to $-$, so f(x) has a maximum.

For $x > 2$ the gradient is negative, so f(x) is again decreasing.

Using this information you can make a sketch like Fig. 5.4, which gives an idea of the shape of the graph of f(x). But there is no way of deciding precisely where the graph is located. You could translate it in the y-direction by any amount, and it would still have the same gradient f'(x). So there is no unique answer to the problem; there are many functions f(x) with the given derived function.

Fig. 5.4

This suggests that the answer to the question posed above is 'yes and no'. If you know the graph of f'(x), this tells you the shape of the graph of f(x) but not precisely where it is.

Example 5.1.3 shows this algebraically for the graphs of f'(x) in Examples 5.1.1 and 5.1.2.

Example 5.1.3

What can you say about $f(x)$ if   (a) $f'(x) = 1 - x$,   (b) $f'(x) = 2x - x^2$?

(a) In Example 5.1.1, the derivative $f'(x) = 1 - x$ was obtained from the equation $f(x) = x - \frac{1}{2}x^2 + 1$. Working backwards, the term 1 in $f'(x)$ could have come from a term x in $f(x)$; and the term $-x$ in $f'(x)$ could have come from a term $-\frac{1}{2}x^2$ in $f(x)$. So if $f'(x) = 1 - x$, you can be certain that

$$f(x) = x - \tfrac{1}{2}x^2 + \text{something.}$$

But there is no reason why that 'something' has to be 1, as it was in Example 5.1.1. The equation could equally well be $f(x) = x - \frac{1}{2}x^2$, or $f(x) = x - \frac{1}{2}x^2 + 5$; both these equations give $f'(x) = 1 - x$. The best that you can say about $f(x)$ is that

$$f(x) = x - \tfrac{1}{2}x^2 + k,$$

where k is some number.

Geometrically, the graph in Fig. 5.1 could be translated by any amount in the y-direction without altering the graph of the gradient function in Fig. 5.2.

(b) This is in fact the equation of the graph in Fig. 5.3, so the question is to find the equation of the graph in Fig. 5.4.

Again there are two terms in the expression for $f'(x)$. The first term, $2x$, is easy; you will recognise this at once as the derivative of x^2. The term $-x^2$ in $f'(x)$ is a bit more tricky. You would expect it to come from an expression of the form ax^3 for some number a, which has to be found. If you differentiate ax^3 the result is $3ax^2$, so you need $3a$ to equal -1; that is, $a = -\frac{1}{3}$.

So, by the same argument as in part (a), the best that you can say is that

$$f(x) = x^2 - \tfrac{1}{3}x^3 + k,$$

where k is some number.

The process of getting from $f'(x)$ to $f(x)$ is called **integration**, and the general expression for $f(x)$ is called the **indefinite integral** of $f'(x)$. Integration is the reverse process of differentiation.

The indefinite integral always includes an added constant k, which is called an **arbitrary constant**. The word 'arbitrary' means that, in any application, you can choose its value to fit some extra condition; for example, you can make the graph of $y = f(x)$ go through some given point.

It is easy to find a rule for integrating functions which are powers of x. Because differentiation reduces the index by 1, integration must increase it by 1. So the function x^n must be derived from some multiple of x^{n+1}. But the derivative of x^{n+1} is $(n+1)x^n$; so to reduce the coefficient in the derivative to 1 you have to multiply x^{n+1} by $\dfrac{1}{n+1}$.

The rule is therefore that one integral of x^n is $\dfrac{1}{n+1}x^{n+1}$.

The extension to functions which are sums of multiples of powers of x then follows from the equivalent rules for differentiation.

Example 5.1.4

Find the indefinite integral of   (a) x^4,   (b) $6x - 2x^3$,   (c) $\dfrac{4}{x^3}$.

(a) Putting $n = 4$, the indefinite integral of x^4 is $\dfrac{1}{4+1}x^{4+1} + k = \frac{1}{5}x^5 + k$, where k is an arbitrary constant.

(b) The term $6x$ is the derivative of $6\left(\frac{1}{2}x^2\right)$, and $-2x^3$ is the derivative of $-2\left(\frac{1}{4}x^4\right)$. So the indefinite integral of $6x - 2x^3$ is $3x^2 - \frac{1}{2}x^4 + k$.

(c) Write $\dfrac{4}{x^3}$ as $4x^{-3}$. If $n = -3$, $n + 1 = -3 + 1 = -2$, so the indefinite integral of $4x^{-3}$ is $4\left(\frac{1}{-2}x^{-2}\right) + k = -2x^{-2} + k = -\dfrac{2}{x^2} + k$.

But notice an important exception to this rule. The formula $\dfrac{1}{n+1}x^{n+1}$ has no meaning if $n + 1$ is 0, so it does not give the integral of x^{-1}, or $\dfrac{1}{x}$. It will be shown in C3 that the integral of $\dfrac{1}{x}$ is not a power of x, but a quite different kind of function.

> The indefinite integral of a function made up of the sum of multiples of x^n, where $n \neq -1$, is the corresponding sum of multiples of $\dfrac{1}{n+1}x^{n+1}$, together with an added arbitrary constant.

Example 5.1.5

The graph of $y = f(x)$ passes through $(2, 3)$, and $f'(x) = 6x^2 - 5x$. Find its equation.

The indefinite integral is $6\left(\frac{1}{3}x^3\right) - 5\left(\frac{1}{2}x^2\right) + k$, so the graph has equation

$$y = 2x^3 - \tfrac{5}{2}x^2 + k$$

for some constant k. The coordinates $x = 2$, $y = 3$ have to satisfy this equation, so

$$3 = 2 \times 8 - \tfrac{5}{2} \times 4 + k, \text{ giving } k = 3 - 16 + 10 = -3.$$

The equation of the graph is therefore $y = 2x^3 - \tfrac{5}{2}x^2 - 3$.

Example 5.1.6

A gardener is digging a plot of land. As he gets tired he works more slowly; after t minutes he is digging at a rate of $\dfrac{2}{\sqrt{t}}$ square metres per minute. How long will it take him to dig an area of 40 square metres?

Let A square metres be the area he has dug after t minutes. Then his rate of digging is measured by the derivative $\dfrac{\mathrm{d}A}{\mathrm{d}t}$. So you know that $\dfrac{\mathrm{d}A}{\mathrm{d}t} = 2t^{-\frac{1}{2}}$; in this case $n = -\frac{1}{2}$, so $n + 1 = \frac{1}{2}$ and the indefinite integral is

$$A = 2\left(\frac{1}{\frac{1}{2}}t^{\frac{1}{2}}\right) + k = 4\sqrt{t} + k.$$

To find k, you need to know a pair of values of A and t. Since $A = 0$ when he starts to dig, which is when $t = 0$, $0 = 4\sqrt{0} + k$ and so $k = 0$.

The equation connecting A with t is therefore $A = 4\sqrt{t}$.

To find how long it takes to dig 40 square metres, substitute $A = 40$:

$$40 = 4\sqrt{t}, \text{ so that } \sqrt{t} = 10, \text{ and hence } t = 100.$$

It will take him 100 minutes to dig an area of 40 square metres.

5.2 Notation for indefinite integrals

You already have a short notation for differentiation, so that instead of writing

'the derivative of $3x^2 - \frac{1}{2}x^4$ is $6x - 2x^3$,

or   'if $y = 3x^2 - \frac{1}{2}x^4$, then $\dfrac{\mathrm{d}y}{\mathrm{d}x} = 6x - 2x^3$,

you can simply write without any words

$$\frac{\mathrm{d}}{\mathrm{d}x}\left(3x^2 - \tfrac{1}{2}x^4\right) = 6x - 2x^3.$$

The symbol $\dfrac{\mathrm{d}}{\mathrm{d}x}$ is an instruction to differentiate whatever follows it.

There is a corresponding notation for indefinite integrals, to avoid having to write

'the indefinite integral of $6x - 2x^3$ is $3x^2 - \frac{1}{2}x^4 + k$'

or   'if $\dfrac{\mathrm{d}y}{\mathrm{d}x} = 6x - 2x^3$, then $y = 3x^2 - \frac{1}{2}x^4 + k$'.

The notation used to write this without words is

$$\int (6x - 2x^3)\,\mathrm{d}x = 3x^2 - \tfrac{1}{2}x^4 + k.$$

The symbol $\displaystyle\int$ is called the 'integral sign', and '$\mathrm{d}x$' tells you the letter being used as the variable. The expression $\displaystyle\int (\ldots)\,\mathrm{d}x$ is then read

'the indefinite integral of $(\ldots)$ with respect to x'.

The reason for this rather odd notation will become clearer when you reach Section 5.5.

If the function you are integrating is very simple, then you can leave out the brackets. For example, it would be usual to write $\displaystyle\int x^2\mathrm{d}x$ rather than $\displaystyle\int (x^2)\,\mathrm{d}x$. But if the expression has more than one term, you should put it in brackets.

Example 5.2.1

Find $\int (5x^4 + 9x^2 - 2)\, dx$.

$$\int (5x^4 + 9x^2 - 2)\, dx = 5\left(\tfrac{1}{5}x^5\right) + 9\left(\tfrac{1}{3}x^3\right) - 2x + k$$
$$= x^5 + 3x^3 - 2x + k.$$

This is all you need to write. But don't forget to put in the arbitrary constant!

The notation is often used with other letters for the variable, especially when integration is used in real-world problems. If you see $\int (\ldots)\, dt$, for example, then t is the independent variable and you have to integrate with respect to t.

Example 5.2.2

Find   (a) $\int 8t^3\, dt$,   (b) $\int \dfrac{1}{p^2}\, dp$,   (c) $\int \sqrt{u}\, du$,   (d) $\int (2x+1)(2x-1)\, dx$,   (e) $\int \dfrac{y^4 - 4}{y^2}\, dy$.

(a) $\int 8t^3\, dt = 8\left(\tfrac{1}{4}t^4\right) + k = 2t^4 + k.$

(b) $\int \dfrac{1}{p^2}\, dp = \int p^{-2}\, dp = \dfrac{1}{-2+1}p^{-2+1} + k = -p^{-1} + k = -\dfrac{1}{p} + k.$

(c) $\int \sqrt{u}\, du = \int u^{\frac{1}{2}}\, du = \dfrac{1}{\frac{1}{2}+1}u^{\frac{1}{2}+1} + k = \dfrac{1}{\frac{3}{2}}u^{\frac{3}{2}} + k = \tfrac{2}{3}u\sqrt{u} + k.$

(d) You must multiply out the brackets before you can integrate.

$$\int (2x+1)(2x-1)\, dx = \int (4x^2 - 1)\, dx = 4\left(\tfrac{1}{3}x^3\right) - x + k = \tfrac{4}{3}x^3 - x + k.$$

(e) Begin by splitting the expression to be integrated into two separate fractions.

$$\int \dfrac{y^4 - 4}{y^2}\, dy = \int \left(\dfrac{y^4}{y^2} - \dfrac{4}{y^2}\right) dy$$
$$= \int (y^2 - 4y^{-2})\, dy = \tfrac{1}{3}y^3 - 4\left(\dfrac{y^{-1}}{-1}\right) + k = \tfrac{1}{3}y^3 + \dfrac{4}{y} + k.$$

Exercise 5A

1 Find a general expression for the function f(x) in each of the following cases.

(a) $f'(x) = 4x^3$

(b) $f'(x) = 6x^5$

(c) $f'(x) = 2x$

(d) $f'(x) = 3x^2 + 5x^4$

(e) $f'(x) = 10x^9 - 8x^7 - 1$

(f) $f'(x) = -7x^6 + 3x^2 + 1$

2 Find the following indefinite integrals.

(a) $\int (9x^2 - 4x - 5)\, dx$

(b) $\int (12x^2 + 6x + 4)\, dx$

(c) $\int 7\, dx$

(d) $\int (16x^3 - 6x^2 + 10x - 3)\, dx$

(e) $\int (2x^3 + 5x)\,dx$ (f) $\int (x + 2x^2)\,dx$

(g) $\int (2x^2 - 3x - 4)\,dx$ (h) $\int (1 - 2x - 3x^2)\,dx$

3 Find y in terms of x in each of the following cases.

(a) $\dfrac{dy}{dx} = x^4 + x^2 + 1$ (b) $\dfrac{dy}{dx} = 7x - 3$

(c) $\dfrac{dy}{dx} = 2x^2 + x - 8$ (d) $\dfrac{dy}{dx} = 6x^3 - 5x^2 + 3x + 2$

(e) $\dfrac{dy}{dx} = \frac{2}{3}x^3 + \frac{1}{2}x^2 + \frac{1}{3}x + \frac{1}{6}$ (f) $\dfrac{dy}{dx} = \frac{1}{2}x^3 - \frac{1}{3}x^2 + x - \frac{1}{3}$

(g) $\dfrac{dy}{dx} = x - 3x^2 + 1$ (h) $\dfrac{dy}{dx} = x^3 + x^2 + x + 1$

4 The graph of $y = f(x)$ passes through the origin and $f'(x) = 8x - 5$. Find $f(x)$.

5 A curve passes through the point $(2, -5)$ and satisfies $\dfrac{dy}{dx} = 6x^2 - 1$. Find y in terms of x.

6 A curve passes through $(-4, 9)$ and is such that $\dfrac{dy}{dx} = \frac{1}{2}x^3 + \frac{1}{4}x + 1$. Find y in terms of x.

7 Given that $f'(x) = 15x^2 - 6x + 4$ and $f(1) = 0$, find $f(x)$.

8 Each of the following diagrams shows the graph of a gradient function $f'(x)$. In each case, sketch the graph of a possible function $f(x)$.

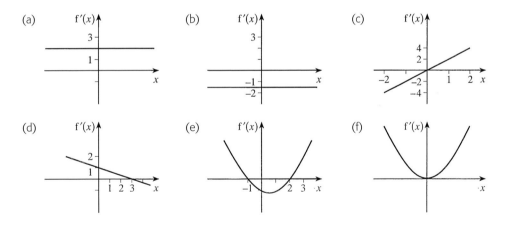

9 The graph of $y = f(x)$ passes through $(4, 25)$ and $f'(x) = 6\sqrt{x}$. Find its equation.

10 Find y in terms of x in each of the following cases.

(a) $\dfrac{dy}{dx} = x^{\frac{1}{2}}$ (b) $\dfrac{dy}{dx} = 4x^{-\frac{2}{3}}$ (c) $\dfrac{dy}{dx} = \sqrt[3]{x}$

(d) $\dfrac{dy}{dx} = 2\sqrt{x} - \dfrac{2}{\sqrt{x}}$ (e) $\dfrac{dy}{dx} = \dfrac{5}{\sqrt[3]{x}}$ (f) $\dfrac{dy}{dx} = \dfrac{-2}{\sqrt[3]{x^2}}$

11 Find a general expression for the function f(x) in each of the following cases.

(a) $f'(x) = x^{-2}$ (b) $f'(x) = 3x^{-4}$ (c) $f'(x) = \dfrac{6}{x^3}$

(d) $f'(x) = 4x - \dfrac{3}{x^2}$ (e) $f'(x) = \dfrac{1}{x^3} - \dfrac{1}{x^4}$ (f) $f'(x) = \dfrac{2}{x^2} - 2x^2$

12 The graph of $y = f(x)$ passes through $(\frac{1}{2}, 5)$ and $f'(x) = \dfrac{4}{x^2}$. Find the equation of the graph.

13 A curve passes through the point $(25, 3)$ and is such that $\dfrac{dy}{dx} = \dfrac{1}{2\sqrt{x}}$. Find the equation of the curve.

14 A curve passes through the point $(1, 5)$ and is such that $\dfrac{dy}{dx} = \sqrt[3]{x} - \dfrac{6}{x^3}$. Find the equation of the curve.

15 In each of the following cases, find y in terms of x.

(a) $\dfrac{dy}{dx} = 3x(x + 2)$ (b) $\dfrac{dy}{dx} = (2x - 1)(6x + 5)$ (c) $\dfrac{dy}{dx} = \dfrac{4x^3 + 1}{x^2}$

(d) $\dfrac{dy}{dx} = \dfrac{x + 4}{\sqrt{x}}$ (e) $\dfrac{dy}{dx} = (\sqrt{x} + 5)^2$ (f) $\dfrac{dy}{dx} = \dfrac{\sqrt{x} + 5}{\sqrt{x}}$

16 Find the following indefinite integrals.

(a) $\displaystyle\int \left(u^2 + \dfrac{1}{u^2} \right) du$ (b) $\displaystyle\int t^5 (3 - t)\, dt$ (c) $\displaystyle\int 4(p + 1)^3\, dp$

(d) $\displaystyle\int \dfrac{1}{y\sqrt{y}}\, dy$ (e) $\displaystyle\int \left(\sqrt[3]{z} + \dfrac{1}{\sqrt[3]{z}} \right)^4 dz$ (f) $\displaystyle\int v(1 + \sqrt{v})\, dv$

17 A tree is growing so that, after t years, its height is increasing at a rate of $\dfrac{30}{\sqrt[3]{t}}$ cm per year. Assume that, when $t = 0$, the height is 5 cm.

(a) Find the height of the tree after 4 years.

(b) After how many years will the height be 4.1 metres?

18 A pond, with surface area 48 square metres, is being invaded by a weed. At a time t months after the weed first appeared, the area of the weed on the surface is increasing at a rate of $\frac{1}{3}t$ square metres per month. How long will it be before the weed covers the whole surface of the pond?

19 The function $f(x)$ is such that $f'(x) = 9x^2 + 4x + c$, where c is a particular constant. Given that $f(2) = 14$ and $f(3) = 74$, find the value of $f(4)$.

5.3 Calculating areas

An important application of integration is to calculate areas and volumes. Many of the formulae you have learnt, such as those for the volume of a sphere or a cone, can be proved by using integration. This chapter deals only with areas.

The particular kind of area to be investigated is illustrated in Fig. 5.5. For any function, the problem is to calculate the area bounded by the x-axis, the graph of $y = \mathrm{f}(x)$, and the lines $x = a$ and $x = b$. This is described as **the area under the graph** from a to b.

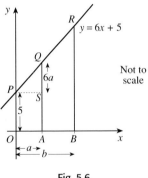

As a start, Example 5.3.1 finds such an area for a very special case when the graph is a straight line.

Fig. 5.5

Example 5.3.1
Find the area under the graph of $y = \mathrm{f}(x)$, where $\mathrm{f}(x) = 6x + 5$,
(a) from 0 to a,   (b) from a to b,
where $b > a > 0$.

(a) In Fig. 5.6, the area under the graph from 0 to a is the area of the trapezium $OAQP$. This can be split into a triangle PSQ and a rectangle $OASP$ by a line PS parallel to the x-axis. The length of the y-intercept is 5; and, since the gradient of PQ is 6, the length SQ is $6a$. So the area of the trapezium is

$$\tfrac{1}{2} \times a \times 6a + a \times 5, \text{ or more simply } 3a^2 + 5a.$$

Fig. 5.6

(b) You want the area of the trapezium $ABRQ$, which can be found as

area $OBRP$ – area $OAQP$.

Area $OAQP$ has already been found in part (a). The trapezium $OBRP$ is of the same kind as $OAQP$, but with b in place of a, so area $OBRP$ is $3b^2 + 5b$.

It follows that the area under the graph from a to b is

$$(3b^2 + 5b) - (3a^2 + 5a).$$

Look at the form of the answer to this example. You can think of this as the difference between the values of the function $3x^2 + 5x$ when $x = b$ and $x = a$. If $\mathrm{I}(x)$ is used to denote this function, then the area is $\mathrm{I}(b) - \mathrm{I}(a)$.

What is the connection between $\mathrm{I}(x) = 3x^2 + 5x$ and $\mathrm{f}(x) = 6x + 5$?

Obviously, in this case, $\mathrm{f}(x)$ is the derivative of $\mathrm{I}(x)$. Or, put another way, $\mathrm{I}(x)$ is an integral of $\mathrm{f}(x)$.

It has to be 'an' integral, rather than 'the' integral, because f(x) has any number of integrals, as explained in Section 5.1. But I(x) is the simplest of these; that is, it is the one for which the arbitrary constant is 0.

So this example suggests a procedure for finding the area under a graph.

To find the area under the graph $y = $ f(x) from $x = a$ to $x = b$:

Step 1   Find the 'simplest' integral of f(x); call it I(x).

Step 2   Work out I(a) and I(b).

Step 3   The area is I(b) − I(a).

At present this is just a guess. You can't base a general theory on the result of just one example. But in fact it is true for any function f(x) with a continuous graph. This is proved in Section 5.4.

Example 5.3.2

Find the area between the graph of $y = 2x - x^2$ and the x-axis.

This is the graph in Fig. 5.3. It is reproduced here as Fig. 5.7. The curve cuts the x-axis when $x = 0$ and $x = 2$, so you want the shaded area under the graph between these values of x.

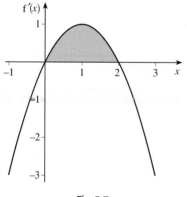

Fig. 5.7

It was shown in Example 5.1.3 that the indefinite integral of $2x - x^2$ is $x^2 - \frac{1}{3}x^3 + k$. The simplest integral has $k = 0$, so I(x) $= x^2 - \frac{1}{3}x^3$. The area is then I(2) − I(0).

So calculate

$$\text{I}(2) = 4 - \tfrac{1}{3} \times 8 = \tfrac{4}{3} \quad \text{and} \quad \text{I}(0) = 0 - 0 = 0,$$

giving an area of $\frac{4}{3} - 0 = \frac{4}{3}$.

Example 5.3.3

Find the area under $y = \dfrac{1}{x^2}$ from $x = 2$ to $x = 5$.

> **Step 1** Let $f(x) = y$. You can write $f(x)$ as x^{-2}, so $I(x)$ is $\frac{1}{-1}x^{-1}$, or $-\dfrac{1}{x}$.
>
> **Step 2** $I(2) = -\frac{1}{2} = -0.5$, $I(5) = -\frac{1}{5} = -0.2$.
>
> **Step 3** The area is $I(5) - I(2) = (-0.2) - (-0.5) = -0.2 + 0.5 = 0.3$.

> The answers to these examples have been given without a unit, because it is not usual to attach a unit to the variables x and y when graphs are drawn. But if in a particular application x and y each denote numbers of units, then when stating the answer a corresponding unit (the x-unit $\times$ the y-unit) should be attached to it.

5.4 Proof of the area procedure

The problem is now to show that the procedure described in Section 5.3 works for a general function $y = f(x)$, whose graph has a form like Fig. 5.5.

Since the procedure involves integration, which is the reverse of differentiation, begin by recalling how results about differentiation were proved in C1 Section 5.8.

To find the derivative, which is the gradient of the tangent, you started by finding the gradient of a chord. This is defined by the values of x at its end-points, which can be denoted by x and $x + \delta x$. You then found the corresponding difference in y, denoted by δy, and considered the limit of $\dfrac{\delta y}{\delta x}$ as δx tends to 0.

It is not obvious how a method like this can be applied to the area in Fig. 5.5, because this involves only the fixed values of x at a and b.

The key is to begin by asking a more general question, which involves a variable x: what is the area, A, under the graph from $x = a$ as far as *any* value of x? This is illustrated by the region with dark shading in Fig. 5.8. Notice that A is also a variable; x is the independent variable, and A is the dependent variable (see C1 Section 12.1).

The point of doing this is that x can now be varied. Suppose that x is increased by δx. Since both y and A are functions of x, you can write the corresponding increases in y and A as δy and δA. This is represented in Fig. 5.9 by the region with light shading.

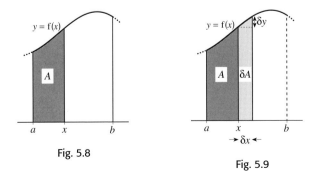

Fig. 5.8

Fig. 5.9

This region is drawn by itself in Fig. 5.10. Dotted lines have been added to show that the area δA of the region is between the areas of two rectangles, each with width δx and having heights of y and $y + \delta y$. So

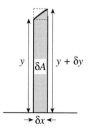

$$\delta A \text{ is between } y\delta x \text{ and } (y + \delta y)\delta x.$$

It follows from this that

$$\frac{\delta A}{\delta x} \text{ is between } y \text{ and } y + \delta y.$$

Fig. 5.10

Now consider the effect of making δx tend to 0. From the definition, $\dfrac{\delta A}{\delta x}$ tends to the derivative $\dfrac{\mathrm{d}A}{\mathrm{d}x}$. Also δy tends to 0, so that $y + \delta y$ tends to y. It follows that

$$\frac{\mathrm{d}A}{\mathrm{d}x} = y.$$

And since $y = f(x)$, it follows that A is an integral of $f(x)$.

There are many such integrals, but if the 'simplest' one is denoted by $I(x)$, then you know that

$$A = I(x) + k$$

for some number k. How do you find k?

In Examples 5.1.5 and 5.1.6 the arbitrary constant could be found because you knew one pair of values taken by the variables. In this case it is clear from Fig. 5.8 that $A = 0$ when $x = a$, so

$$0 = I(a) + k, \text{ which gives } k = -I(a).$$

Therefore

$$A = I(x) - I(a).$$

You find the required area by putting $x = b$ in this expression. That is, the area from $x = a$ to $x = b$ is $I(b) - I(a)$.

This shows that the procedure described in the box in Section 5.3 works for any function, not just the special case $f(x) = 6x + 5$.

5.5   Integration notation

You will carry out the procedure in Section 5.3 so often that it is worth having a special notation to describe it. This notation is an extension of that used for indefinite integrals in Section 5.2.

The 'area under $y = f(x)$ from $x = a$ to $x = b$' is denoted by

$$\int_a^b f(x)\,\mathrm{d}x.$$

This is called a **definite integral**. Notice that a definite integral has a specific value. Unlike an indefinite integral, it is not a function of x, and it involves no arbitrary constant. For example, the result of Example 5.3.2 would be written

$$\int_0^2 (2x - x^2)\, dx = \tfrac{4}{3}.$$

The numbers a and b are often called the **limits**, or the bounds, of integration. (But notice that they are not 'limits' in the sense in which the word has been used in relation to differentiation.) The function $f(x)$ is called the **integrand**.

The symbol $\int$ was originally a letter S, standing for 'sum'. Before the link with differentiation was discovered in the 17th century, attempts were made to calculate areas as the sums of areas of rectangles of height $f(x)$ and width denoted by δx, or dx. (Look at Fig. 5.10, where the lower rectangle has area $f(x)\delta x$.) The notation is based on this idea.

There is also an abbreviation for $I(b) - I(a)$: it is written

$$\left[I(x)\right]_a^b.$$

So, if $I(x)$ is the simplest integral of $f(x)$, $\displaystyle\int_a^b f(x)\, dx = \left[I(x)\right]_a^b.$

Using this notation, you would write the calculation of the area in Example 5.3.3 as

$$\text{Area} = \int_2^5 \frac{1}{x^2}\, dx = \left[-\frac{1}{x}\right]_2^5$$
$$= \left(-\frac{1}{5}\right) - \left(-\frac{1}{2}\right)$$
$$= -0.2 + 0.5 = 0.3.$$

Example 5.5.1
Find $\displaystyle\int_1^3 (3x - 2)(4 - x)\, dx.$

$$\int_1^3 (3x - 2)(4 - x)\, dx = \int_1^3 (-3x^2 + 14x - 8)\, dx$$
$$= \left[-x^3 + 7x^2 - 8x\right]_1^3$$
$$= (-27 + 63 - 24) - (-1 + 7 - 8)$$
$$= 12 - (-2) = 14$$

Example 5.5.2
Find $\displaystyle\int_{-4}^{-1} \left(x^2 - \frac{1}{x^2}\right) dx.$

$$\int_{-4}^{-1} \left(x^2 - \frac{1}{x^2} \right) dx = \int_{-4}^{-1} (x^2 - x^{-2}) \, dx$$

$$= \left[\tfrac{1}{3}x^3 - (-x^{-1}) \right]_{-4}^{-1}$$

$$= \left[\tfrac{1}{3}x^3 + \frac{1}{x} \right]_{-4}^{-1}$$

$$= \tfrac{1}{3}((-1)^3 - (-4)^3) + \left(\frac{1}{-1} - \frac{1}{-4} \right)$$

$$= \tfrac{1}{3}(-1 - (-64)) + \left(-1 + \tfrac{1}{4} \right)$$

$$= \tfrac{1}{3} \times 63 + \left(-\tfrac{3}{4} \right) = 21 - \tfrac{3}{4} = 20\tfrac{1}{4}$$

Notice the different ways of completing the calculation in Examples 5.5.1 and 5.5.2. In the first case the expression in the square brackets is worked out completely for $x = 3$ and $x = 1$ before subtracting, following exactly the procedure described in the text. In the second the subtraction is carried out for the two terms separately, and the two results are then put together to get the answer. The second method often leads to simpler arithmetic when the integral contains fractions, or when one (or both) of the limits of integration is negative. You can use whichever method you prefer.

Example 5.5.3
Find the area under $y = \sqrt{x}$ from $x = 1$ to $x = 4$, shown shaded in Fig. 5.11.

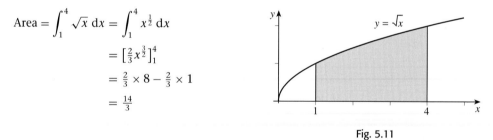

$$\text{Area} = \int_1^4 \sqrt{x} \, dx = \int_1^4 x^{\frac{1}{2}} \, dx$$

$$= \left[\tfrac{2}{3}x^{\frac{3}{2}} \right]_1^4$$

$$= \tfrac{2}{3} \times 8 - \tfrac{2}{3} \times 1$$

$$= \tfrac{14}{3}$$

Fig. 5.11

Exercise 5B

1 Evaluate the following definite integrals.

(a) $\int_1^2 3x^2 \, dx$ (b) $\int_2^5 8x \, dx$ (c) $\int_0^2 x^3 \, dx$

(d) $\int_{-1}^1 10x^4 \, dx$ (e) $\int_0^{\frac{1}{2}} \tfrac{1}{2}x \, dx$ (f) $\int_0^1 2 \, dx$

2 Evaluate the following definite integrals.

(a) $\int_0^2 (8x + 3) \, dx$ (b) $\int_2^4 (5x - 4) \, dx$ (c) $\int_{-2}^2 (6x^2 + 1) \, dx$

(d) $\int_0^1 (2x + 1)(x + 3) \, dx$ (e) $\int_{-3}^4 (6x^2 + 2x + 3) \, dx$ (f) $\int_{-3}^3 (6x^3 + 2x) \, dx$

3 Find the area under the curve $y = x^2$ from $x = 0$ to $x = 6$.

4 Find the area under the curve $y = 4x^3$ from $x = 1$ to $x = 2$.

5 Find the area under the curve $y = 12x^3$ from $x = 2$ to $x = 3$.

6 Find the area under the curve $y = 3x^2 + 2x$ from $x = 0$ to $x = 4$.

7 Find the area under the curve $y = 3x^2 - 2x$ from $x = -4$ to $x = 0$.

8 Find the area under the curve $y = x^4 + 5$ from $x = -1$ to $x = 1$.

9 The diagram shows the region under $y = 4x + 1$ between $x = 1$ and $x = 3$. Find the area of the shaded region by

(a) using the formula for the area of a trapezium,

(b) using integration.

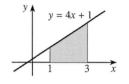

10 The diagram shows the region bounded by $y = \frac{1}{2}x - 3$, by $x = 14$ and the x-axis. Find the area of the shaded region by

(a) using the formula for the area of a triangle,

(b) using integration.

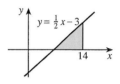

11 Find the area of the region shaded in each of the following diagrams.

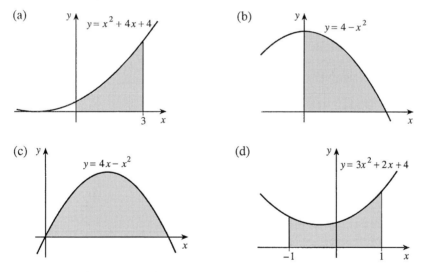

(a) $y = x^2 + 4x + 4$

(b) $y = 4 - x^2$

(c) $y = 4x - x^2$

(d) $y = 3x^2 + 2x + 4$

12 Evaluate the following definite integrals.

(a) $\displaystyle\int_0^8 12\sqrt[3]{x}\,dx$

(b) $\displaystyle\int_1^2 \frac{3}{x^2}\,dx$

(c) $\displaystyle\int_1^4 \frac{10}{\sqrt{x}}\,dx$

(d) $\displaystyle\int_1^2 \left(\frac{8}{x^3} + x^3\right)dx$

(e) $\displaystyle\int_4^9 \frac{2\sqrt{x} + 3}{\sqrt{x}}\,dx$

(f) $\displaystyle\int_1^8 \frac{1}{\sqrt[3]{x^2}}\,dx$

13 Find the area under the curve $y = \dfrac{6}{x^4}$ between $x = 1$ and $x = 2$.

14 Find the area under the curve $y = \sqrt[3]{x}$ between $x = 1$ and $x = 27$.

15 Find the area under the curve $y = \dfrac{5}{x^2}$ between $x = -3$ and $x = -1$.

16 Given that $\displaystyle\int_0^a 12x^2\,dx = 1372$, find the value of the constant a.

17 Given that $\displaystyle\int_0^9 p\sqrt{x}\,dx = 90$, find the value of the constant p.

18 Find the area of the shaded region in each of the following diagrams.

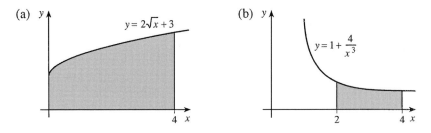

19 Find the area of the region between the curve $y = 9 + 15x - 6x^2$ and the x-axis.

5.6 Some properties of definite integrals

In definite integral notation the calculation in Example 5.3.2 of the area in Fig. 5.7 (reproduced here as Fig. 5.12) would be written

$$\int_0^2 (2x - x^2)\,dx = \left[x^2 - \tfrac{1}{3}x^3\right]_0^2 = \left(\tfrac{4}{3}\right) - (0) = \tfrac{4}{3}.$$

But how should you interpret the calculation

$$\int_0^3 (2x - x^2)\,dx = \left[x^2 - \tfrac{1}{3}x^3\right]_0^3 = (0) - (0) = 0?$$

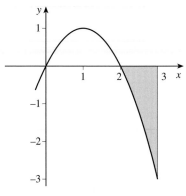

Fig. 5.12

Clearly the area between the graph and the x-axis between $x = 0$ and $x = 3$ is not zero as the value of the definite integral suggests.

You can find the clue by calculating the integral between $x = 2$ and $x = 3$:

$$\int_2^3 (2x - x^2)\,dx = \left[x^2 - \tfrac{1}{3}x^3\right]_2^3 = (0) - \left(\tfrac{4}{3}\right) = -\tfrac{4}{3}.$$

This shows that you need to be careful in identifying the definite integral as an area. In Fig. 5.12 the area of the shaded region is $\tfrac{4}{3}$, and the negative sign attached to the definite integral indicates that between $x = 2$ and $x = 3$ the graph lies below the x-axis.

The zero answer obtained for the integral from $x = 0$ to $x = 3$ is then explained by the fact that definite integrals are added exactly as you would expect:

$$\int_0^3 (2x - x^2)\,dx = \int_0^2 (2x - x^2)\,dx + \int_2^3 (2x - x^2)\,dx = \left(\tfrac{4}{3}\right) + \left(-\tfrac{4}{3}\right) = 0.$$

This is a special case of a general rule:

$$\int_a^b f(x)\,dx + \int_b^c f(x)\,dx = \int_a^c f(x)\,dx.$$

To prove this, let $I(x)$ denote the simplest integral of $f(x)$.

Then the sum of the integrals on the left side is equal to

$$\int_a^b f(x)\,dx + \int_b^c f(x)\,dx = \big[I(x)\big]_a^b + \big[I(x)\big]_b^c$$
$$= (I(b) - I(a)) + (I(c) - I(b))$$
$$= I(c) - I(a),$$

and the integral on the left side is

$$\int_a^c f(x)\,dx = \big[I(x)\big]_a^c = I(c) - I(a).$$

Example 5.6.1

Fig. 5.13 shows the graph of $y = x(x - 1)(x - 3)$, which crosses the x-axis at the points $(0, 0)$, $(1, 0)$ and $(3, 0)$. Find the areas of the regions labelled A and B between the curve and the x-axis.

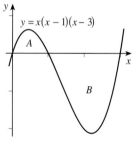

Fig. 5.13

To find the areas you have to calculate the definite integrals

$$\int_0^1 x(x - 1)(x - 3)\,dx = \int_0^1 (x^3 - 4x^2 + 3x)\,dx$$
$$= \left[\tfrac{1}{4}x^4 - \tfrac{4}{3}x^3 + \tfrac{3}{2}x^2\right]_0^1$$
$$= \tfrac{1}{4} - 1\tfrac{1}{3} + 1\tfrac{1}{2} = \tfrac{5}{12}$$

and

$$\int_1^3 x(x - 1)(x - 3)\,dx = \left[\tfrac{1}{4}x^4 - \tfrac{4}{3}x^3 + \tfrac{3}{2}x^2\right]_1^3$$
$$= \left(20\tfrac{1}{4} - 36 + 13\tfrac{1}{2}\right) - \left(\tfrac{1}{4} - 1\tfrac{1}{3} + 1\tfrac{1}{2}\right)$$
$$= -2\tfrac{2}{3}.$$

The minus sign in the value of the second integral shows that the region B lies below the x-axis.

Region A has area $\tfrac{5}{12}$, and region B has area $2\tfrac{2}{3}$.

Negative definite integrals can also arise when you interchange the bounds of integration. Since

$$\left[I(x)\right]_b^a = I(a) - I(b) = -(I(b) - I(a)) = -\left[I(x)\right]_a^b,$$

it follows that:

$$\int_b^a f(x)\,dx = -\int_a^b f(x)\,dx.$$

5.7   The area between a curve and the y-axis

When you find the area under a curve, the region whose area you are finding is bounded by parts of the x-axis and (possibly) two vertical lines with equations $x = a$ and $x = b$. The area is then given by $\int_a^b y\,dx$.

Sometimes you want to find the area of a region bounded by parts of the y-axis and (possibly) two horizontal lines with equations $y = c$ and $y = d$, as in Fig. 5.14. The method of calculating this is exactly the same, except that y and x are swapped round. The area is therefore given by $\int_c^d x\,dy$.

The only new feature is that, if you are given the equation of the curve in the form $y = f(x)$, you must rearrange it in the form $x = g(y)$ before finding the integral.

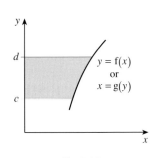

Fig. 5.14

Example 5.7.1

Find the area of the region bounded by parts of the y-axis, the lines $y = 1$ and $y = 8$ and the curve with equation $y = x\sqrt{x}$ (see Fig. 5.15).

The equation $y = x\sqrt{x}$ can be rewritten as $y^2 = x^3$, or as $x = y^{\frac{2}{3}}$ (for $y \geqslant 0$). So the area of the region is

$$\int_1^8 y^{\frac{2}{3}}\,dy = \left[\tfrac{3}{5}y^{\frac{5}{3}}\right]_1^8$$

$$= \tfrac{3}{5}\left(8^{\frac{5}{3}} - 1^{\frac{5}{3}}\right)$$

$$= \tfrac{3}{5}(32 - 1) = 18.6.$$

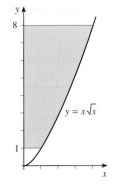

Fig. 5.15

Example 5.7.2

Fig 5.16 shows the part of the graph of $y^2 = 9 - x$ for which $x > 0$. Find the area between this curve and the y-axis.

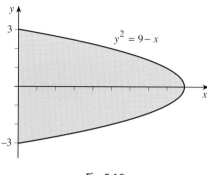

Fig. 5.16

When $x = 0$, $y^2 = 9$, so $y = -3$ or $+3$.

The equation of the curve can be rearranged as $x = 9 - y^2$. So the area is

$$\int_{-3}^{3} (9 - y^2)\,dy = \left[9y - \tfrac{1}{3}y^3\right]_{-3}^{3}$$
$$= 9(3 - (-3)) - \tfrac{1}{3}(27 - (-27)) = 9 \times 6 - \tfrac{1}{3} \times 54 = 54 - 18 = 36.$$

5.8 Infinite and improper integrals

All the regions whose areas you have found so far have been completely enclosed by lines or curves on all sides. This section shows how the idea of area can be applied to regions which extend indefinitely in the direction of one of the axes.

Example 5.8.1

Find the areas under the graph of $y = \dfrac{1}{x^2}$, in the intervals
(a) $x = 1$ to $x = s$, where $s > 1$,   (b) $x = r$ to $x = 1$, where $0 < r < 1$.

These areas are labelled (a), (b) in Fig. 5.17.

The function is x^{-2}, so the simplest integral is

$$-x^{-1} = -\frac{1}{x}.$$

The areas are therefore

(a) $\displaystyle\int_{1}^{s} \frac{1}{x^2}\,dx = \left[-\frac{1}{x}\right]_{1}^{s} = 1 - \frac{1}{s},$

(b) $\displaystyle\int_{r}^{1} \frac{1}{x^2}\,dx = \left[-\frac{1}{x}\right]_{r}^{1} = \frac{1}{r} - 1.$

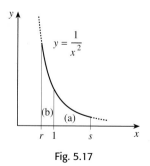

Fig. 5.17

The interesting feature of these results appears if you consider what happens in (a) if s becomes indefinitely large, and in (b) if r comes indefinitely close to 0.

Consider s first. By taking a large enough value for s, you can make $1 - \dfrac{1}{s}$ as close to 1 as you like, but it always remains less than 1. You can say that the integral (a) 'tends to 1 as s tends to infinity' (written '$\rightarrow 1$ as $s \rightarrow \infty$').

A shorthand for this is

$$\int_1^\infty \frac{1}{x^2}\,\mathrm{d}x = 1.$$

This is called an **infinite integral**.

Nothing comparable happens with the area in (b). As r approaches 0, the quantity $\dfrac{1}{r} - 1$ becomes very large. It can be made as large as you like by taking r close enough to 0. So you cannot give a meaning to the symbol

$$\int_0^1 \frac{1}{x^2}\,\mathrm{d}x.$$

Example 5.8.2

Find the areas under the graph of $y = \dfrac{1}{\sqrt{x}}$ in the intervals

(a) $x = 1$ to $x = s$, where $s > 1$,   (b) $x = r$ to $x = 1$, where $0 < r < 1$.

These areas are shown labelled (a) and (b) in Fig. 5.18.

The function is $x^{-\frac{1}{2}}$, so the simplest integral is

$$2x^{\frac{1}{2}} = 2\sqrt{x}.$$

The areas are therefore

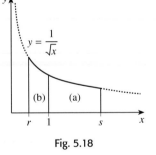

Fig. 5.18

(a) $\displaystyle\int_1^s \frac{1}{\sqrt{x}}\,\mathrm{d}x = \left[2\sqrt{x}\right]_1^s = 2\sqrt{s} - 2,$

(b) $\displaystyle\int_r^1 \frac{1}{\sqrt{x}}\,\mathrm{d}x = \left[2\sqrt{x}\right]_r^1 = 2 - 2\sqrt{r}.$

What happens if s becomes indefinitely large, and if r becomes indefinitely close to 0, is just the opposite to Example 5.8.1. The value of the expression $2\sqrt{s} - 2$ can be made as large as you like by taking a large enough value for s, so the integral (a) 'tends to infinity as s tends to infinity' (or '$\rightarrow \infty$ as $s \rightarrow \infty$').

Since 'infinity' is not a number, you cannot give a meaning to the symbol

$$\int_1^\infty \frac{1}{\sqrt{x}}\,\mathrm{d}x.$$

In the case of r, the situation is reversed. The expression $2 - 2\sqrt{r}$ tends to 2 as r tends to 0. So you can write

$$\int_0^1 \frac{1}{\sqrt{x}}\,dx = 2$$

even though the integrand $\dfrac{1}{\sqrt{x}}$ is not defined when $x = 0$. This is called an **improper integral**.

These results are summed up in Figs. 5.19 and 5.20. A value can be given to the areas of the shaded regions, even though they extend indefinitely far in the direction of one axis. But no value can be given to the areas left unshaded.

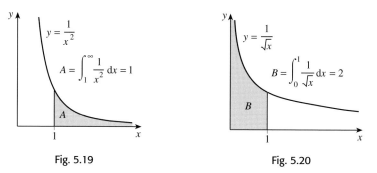

Fig. 5.19   Fig. 5.20

You can see from the graphs that, as you would expect, the cases where the integrals are defined correspond to regions in which the graph is very close to one of the axes. You can then say that the region has a finite area, even though it is unbounded.

Infinite and improper integrals can be defined formally using limit notation.

If $\displaystyle\int_a^s f(x)\,dx$ tends to a finite limit as $s \to \infty$, then

$\displaystyle\int_a^\infty f(x)\,dx = \lim_{s \to \infty} \int_a^s f(x)\,dx$. If $f(x) \to \infty$ but $\displaystyle\int_r^b f(x)\,dx$ tends to a finite

limit as $r \to a$ from above, then $\displaystyle\int_a^b f(x)\,dx = \lim_{r \to a} \int_r^b f(x)\,dx$.

Similar definitions can be given for other cases, such as infinite integrals of the form $\displaystyle\int_{-\infty}^b f(x)\,dx$ and improper integrals $\displaystyle\int_a^b f(x)\,dx$ when $f(x) \to \infty$ as $x \to b$ from below.

Example 5.8.3
Find the values of
(a) the infinite integral $\displaystyle\int_{10}^\infty \frac{1}{x^3}\,dx$,   (b) the improper integral $\displaystyle\int_0^8 \frac{1}{\sqrt[3]{x}}\,dx$.

(a) Begin by finding

$$\int_{10}^{s} \frac{1}{x^3}\,dx = \int_{10}^{s} x^{-3}\,dx = \left[-\tfrac{1}{2}x^{-2}\right]_{10}^{s} = \left[-\frac{1}{2x^2}\right]_{10}^{s} = -\frac{1}{2s^2} + \tfrac{1}{200}.$$

As $s \to \infty$, $\dfrac{1}{2s^2} \to 0$, so

$$\int_{10}^{\infty} \frac{1}{x^3}\,dx = \lim_{s\to\infty} \int_{10}^{s} \frac{1}{x^3}\,dx = \tfrac{1}{200}.$$

(b) Begin by finding

$$\int_{r}^{8} \frac{1}{\sqrt[3]{x}}\,dx = \int_{r}^{8} x^{-\frac{1}{3}}\,dx = \left[\tfrac{3}{2}x^{\frac{2}{3}}\right]_{r}^{8} = \tfrac{3}{2} \times 4 - \tfrac{3}{2}r^{\frac{2}{3}} = 6 - \tfrac{3}{2}\sqrt[3]{r^2}.$$

As $r \to 0$ from above, $\tfrac{3}{2}\sqrt[3]{r^2} \to 0$, so

$$\int_{0}^{8} \frac{1}{\sqrt[3]{x}}\,dx = \lim_{r\to 0} \int_{r}^{8} \frac{1}{\sqrt[3]{x}}\,dx = 6.$$

5.9   Calculating other areas

You sometimes want to find the area of a region bounded by the graphs of two functions f(x) and g(x), and by two lines $x = a$ and $x = b$, as in Fig. 5.21.

Although you could find this as the difference of the areas of two regions of the kind illustrated in Fig. 5.5, calculated as

$$\int_{a}^{b} f(x)\,dx - \int_{a}^{b} g(x)\,dx,$$

it is often simpler to find it as a single integral

$$\int_{a}^{b} (f(x) - g(x))\,dx.$$

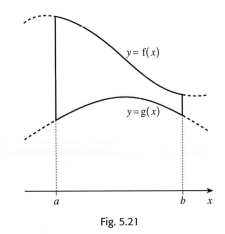

Fig. 5.21

Example 5.9.1
Fig. 5.22 shows the graph of $y = x^2$ and the chord joining the points $(-1, 1)$ and $(2, 4)$ on the curve. Find the area of the shaded region between the curve and the chord.

The first step is to find the equation of the chord. Since the gradient is

$$\frac{4-1}{2-(-1)} = \tfrac{3}{3} = 1,$$

its equation is

$$y - 1 = 1(x - (-1)), \quad \text{or more simply} \quad y = x + 2.$$

To find the area, use the formula $\displaystyle\int_a^b (f(x) - g(x))\, dx$
with $f(x) = x + 2$, $g(x) = x^2$, $a = -1$ and $b = 2$.

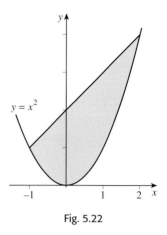

Fig. 5.22

$$\text{Area} = \int_{-1}^{2} (x + 2 - x^2)\, dx$$
$$= \left[\tfrac{1}{2}x^2 + 2x - \tfrac{1}{3}x^3 \right]_{-1}^{2}.$$

Because of the fractions, this is a calculation where it is simpler to carry out the subtractions term-by-term, as explained in Section 5.5. This gives the area as

$$\tfrac{1}{2}(2^2 - (-1)^2) + 2(2 - (-1)) - \tfrac{1}{3}(2^3 - (-1)^3)$$
$$= \tfrac{1}{2} \times 3 + 2 \times 3 - \tfrac{1}{3} \times 9$$
$$= 1\tfrac{1}{2} + 6 - 3 = 4\tfrac{1}{2}.$$

The area of the region between the curve and the chord is $4\tfrac{1}{2}$.

Notice that if you had used the formula with $f(x) = x^2$ and $g(x) = x + 2$ you would have got the answer $-4\tfrac{1}{2}$. This is because the curve lies below the chord in the interval $-1 < x < 2$. You should always try to choose the notation so that $f(x) > g(x)$ over the interval of values of x in which you are interested.

Example 5.9.2
Show that the graphs of $y = f(x)$ and $y = g(x)$, where $f(x) = x^3 - x^2 - 6x + 8$ and $g(x) = x^3 + 2x^2 - 1$, intersect at two points, and find the area of the region enclosed between the two curves.

The graphs intersect where the two values of y are equal, so that $f(x) = g(x)$. But before writing this as an equation for x, note that it can be written as $f(x) - g(x) = 0$.

Since you are going to need $f(x) - g(x)$ in the integral later, it will save work to begin by finding

$$f(x) - g(x) = (x^3 - x^2 - 6x + 8) - (x^3 + 2x^2 - 1)$$
$$= x^3 - x^2 - 6x + 8 - x^3 - 2x^2 + 1$$
$$= -3x^2 - 6x + 9$$
$$= -3(x^2 + 2x - 3)$$
$$= -3(x + 3)(x - 1).$$

The graphs intersect where this is 0, that is where $x = -3$ and $x = 1$. So there are two points of intersection, $(-3, -10)$ and $(1, 2)$.

Having got this far, you may find it helpful to display the two graphs on a graphic calculator in the interval between these values of x.

You can also use this expression for $f(x) - g(x)$ in factors to check that $f(x) > g(x)$. If $-3 < x < 1$, $x + 3$ is positive and $x - 1$ is negative, so that $f(x) - g(x) > 0$ as required.

All that remains is to calculate the area between the graphs as

$$
\begin{aligned}
\int_{-3}^{1} (f(x) - g(x))\, dx &= \int_{-3}^{1} (-3x^2 - 6x + 9)\, dx \\
&= \left[-x^3 - 3x^2 + 9x \right]_{-3}^{1} \\
&= (-1 - 3 + 9) - (27 - 27 - 27) \\
&= 5 - (-27) = 32.
\end{aligned}
$$

The area enclosed between the two graphs is 32.

> Notice that in this example, integrating $f(x) - g(x)$, rather than $f(x)$ and $g(x)$ separately, greatly reduces the amount of calculation.

Sometimes you need to find an area whose boundary includes part of a graph, but which is not the 'area under the graph' described in Section 5.3. Such areas can often be found by calculating the area under the graph and then adding or subtracting the area of some triangle or rectangle. Example 5.9.3 gives two typical calculations of this type.

Example 5.9.3
Fig. 5.23 shows the part of the graph $y = 3 + 2x - x^2$ which lies in the first quadrant. Calculate the areas of the regions labelled A and B.

In factor form and completed square form,

$$
\begin{aligned}
3 + 2x - x^2 &\equiv (3 - x)(1 + x) \\
&\equiv 4 - (x - 1)^2.
\end{aligned}
$$

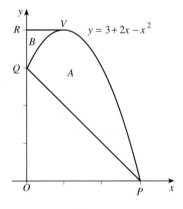

Fig. 5.23

Region A   Begin by finding the coordinates of P and Q, by putting $y = 0$ and $x = 0$ respectively. From the factor form, when $y = 0$, $x = 3$ (since $x > 0$). When $x = 0$, $y = 3$.

So P is $(3, 0)$ and Q is $(0, 3)$.

If you add the triangle OPQ to the region A you get the region under the graph from $x = 0$ to $x = 3$, whose area is

$$
\begin{aligned}
\int_{0}^{3} (3 + 2x - x^2)\, dx &= \left[3x + x^2 - \tfrac{1}{3}x^3 \right]_{0}^{3} \\
&= (9 + 9 - 9) - (0) = 9.
\end{aligned}
$$

The area of the triangle OPQ is $\tfrac{1}{2} \times 3 \times 3 = 4\tfrac{1}{2}$.

So the area of region A is $9 - 4\tfrac{1}{2} = 4\tfrac{1}{2}$.

Region B From the completed square form, the coordinates of the vertex V are $(1, 4)$.

Fig. 5.24 shows that, if you add the region B to the region under the graph from $x = 0$ to $x = 1$, you get the rectangle $ORVS$, of width 1 and height 4.

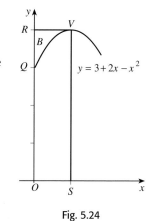

The area under the graph from $x = 0$ to $x = 1$ is

$$\int_0^1 (3 + 2x - x^2)\, dx = \left[3x + x^2 - \tfrac{1}{3}x^3\right]_0^1$$
$$= (3 + 1 - \tfrac{1}{3}) - (0) = 3\tfrac{2}{3}.$$

The area of the rectangle is $1 \times 4 = 4$.

So the area of region B is $4 - 3\tfrac{2}{3} = \tfrac{1}{3}$.

Fig. 5.24

In Example 5.9.3 the region B is bounded on one side by part of the y-axis, so you might expect to be able to calculate its area by the method described in Section 5.7. But this involves rearranging the equation to give x in terms of y. From the completed square form you can obtain

$$(x - 1)^2 = 4 - y.$$

This gives two values of x for each value of y less than 4. On the arc QV you want the smaller of these, so

$$x = 1 - \sqrt{4 - y}.$$

The area of region B is therefore

$$\int_3^4 \left(1 - \sqrt{4 - y}\right) dy.$$

Unfortunately you don't yet know how to integrate $\sqrt{4 - y}$. That is why it was necessary to use a different method.

Exercise 5C

1 Evaluate $\displaystyle\int_0^2 3x(x - 2)\, dx$ and comment on your answer.

2 Find the area of the region bounded by parts of the y-axis, the curve $y = x^3$ and the lines $y = 1$ and $y = 27$.

3 Find the area of the region bounded by parts of the y-axis, the curve $y = \sqrt{x}$ and the lines $y = 1$ and $y = 4$.

4 Sketch the curve $y^2 = x + 4$, and find the area enclosed between this graph and the y-axis. Comment on any special features of this calculation.

5 Find the total area of the region shaded in each of the following diagrams.

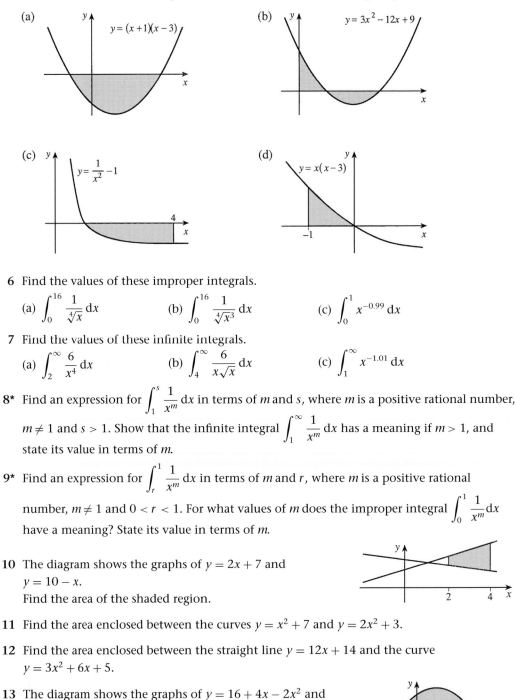

(a) $y = (x +1)(x - 3)$

(b) $y = 3x^2 - 12x + 9$

(c) $y = \dfrac{1}{x^2} - 1$

(d) $y = x(x - 3)$

6 Find the values of these improper integrals.

(a) $\displaystyle\int_0^{16} \frac{1}{\sqrt[4]{x}}\, dx$

(b) $\displaystyle\int_0^{16} \frac{1}{\sqrt[4]{x^3}}\, dx$

(c) $\displaystyle\int_0^{1} x^{-0.99}\, dx$

7 Find the values of these infinite integrals.

(a) $\displaystyle\int_2^{\infty} \frac{6}{x^4}\, dx$

(b) $\displaystyle\int_4^{\infty} \frac{6}{x\sqrt{x}}\, dx$

(c) $\displaystyle\int_1^{\infty} x^{-1.01}\, dx$

8* Find an expression for $\displaystyle\int_1^{s} \frac{1}{x^m}\, dx$ in terms of m and s, where m is a positive rational number, $m \neq 1$ and $s > 1$. Show that the infinite integral $\displaystyle\int_1^{\infty} \frac{1}{x^m}\, dx$ has a meaning if $m > 1$, and state its value in terms of m.

9* Find an expression for $\displaystyle\int_r^{1} \frac{1}{x^m}\, dx$ in terms of m and r, where m is a positive rational number, $m \neq 1$ and $0 < r < 1$. For what values of m does the improper integral $\displaystyle\int_0^{1} \frac{1}{x^m}\, dx$ have a meaning? State its value in terms of m.

10 The diagram shows the graphs of $y = 2x + 7$ and $y = 10 - x$.
Find the area of the shaded region.

11 Find the area enclosed between the curves $y = x^2 + 7$ and $y = 2x^2 + 3$.

12 Find the area enclosed between the straight line $y = 12x + 14$ and the curve $y = 3x^2 + 6x + 5$.

13 The diagram shows the graphs of $y = 16 + 4x - 2x^2$ and $y = x^2 - 2x - 8$. Find the area of the region, shaded in the diagram, between the curves.

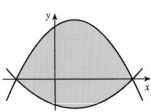

14 Find the area between the curves $y = (x - 4)(3x - 1)$ and $y = (4 - x)(1 + x)$.

15 The diagram shows the graph of $y = \sqrt{x}$. Given that the area of the shaded region is 72, find the value of the constant a.

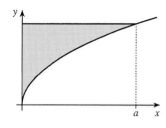

16 Parts of the graphs of $f(x) = 2x^3 + x^2 - 8x$ and $g(x) = 2x^3 - 3x - 4$ enclose a finite region. Find its area.

17 Find the area of the region shaded in each of the following diagrams.

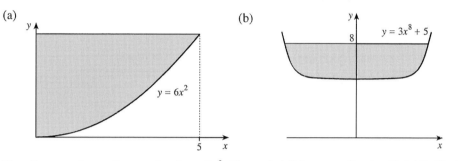

(a)

$y = 6x^2$

5

(b)

8

$y = 3x^8 + 5$

18 The diagram shows the graph of $y = 9x^2$. The point P has coordinates $(4, 144)$. Find the area of the shaded region.

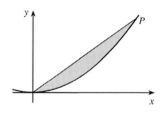

19 The diagram shows the graph of $y = \dfrac{1}{\sqrt{x}}$.

Show that the area of the shaded region is $3 - \dfrac{5\sqrt{3}}{3}$.

20 Find the area bounded by parts of the x-axis and the curves $y = \sqrt{x}$ and $y = 2\sqrt{x - 3}$.

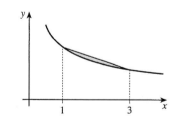

1   3

Miscellaneous exercise 5

1 A curve passes through $(2, 3)$ and is such that $\dfrac{\mathrm{d}y}{\mathrm{d}x} = \frac{1}{2}x^2 - \frac{1}{3}x + 1$. Find y in terms of x.

2 The diagram shows the graph of $y = 12 - 3x^2$. Determine the x-coordinate of each of the points where the curve crosses the x-axis. Find by integration the area of the region (shaded in the diagram) between the curve and the x-axis. (OCR)

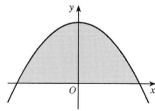

3 Find $\int 6\sqrt{x}\,dx$ and hence evaluate $\int_1^4 6\sqrt{x}\,dx$.   (OCR)

4 (a) Find $\int \left(\dfrac{1}{x^3} + x^3\right) dx$.   (b) Evaluate $\int_0^8 \dfrac{1}{\sqrt[3]{x}}\,dx$.   (OCR)

5 Find the area of the region enclosed between the curve $y = 12x^2 + 30x$ and the x-axis.

6 Find the value of the improper integral $\int_0^4 \dfrac{(x+2)^2}{\sqrt{x}}\,dx$.

7 Given that $\int_{-a}^a 15x^2\,dx = 3430$, find the value of the constant a.

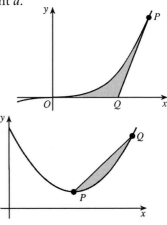

8 The diagram shows the curve $y = x^3$. The point P has coordinates $(3, 27)$ and PQ is the tangent to the curve at P. Find the area of the region enclosed between the curve, PQ and the x-axis.

9 The diagram shows the curve $y = (x-2)^2 + 1$ with minimum point P. The point Q on the curve is such that the gradient of PQ is 2. Find the area of the region, shaded in the diagram, between PQ and the curve.

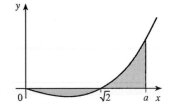

10 Evaluate $\int_0^2 x(x-1)(x-2)\,dx$ and explain your answer with reference to the graph of $y = x(x-1)(x-2)$.

11 (a) Find $\int x(x^2 - 2)\,dx$.

   (b) The diagram shows the graph of $y = x(x^2 - 2)$ for $x \geqslant 0$. The value of a is such that the two shaded regions have equal areas. Find the value of a.   (OCR)

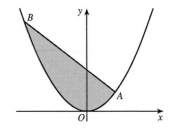

12 The diagram shows a sketch of the graph of $y = x^2$ and the normal to the curve at the point $A(1, 1)$.

   (a) Use differentiation to find the equation of the normal at A. Verify that the point B where the normal cuts the curve again has coordinates $\left(-\frac{3}{2}, \frac{9}{4}\right)$.

   (b) The region which is bounded by the curve and the normal is shaded in the diagram. Calculate its area, giving your answer as an exact fraction.   (OCR)

13 Given that $\int_1^p (8x^3 + 6x)\,dx = 39$, find two possible values of p. Use a graph to explain why there are two values.

14 Show that the area enclosed between the curves $y = 9 - x^2$ and $y = x^2 - 7$ is $\dfrac{128\sqrt{2}}{3}$.

15 Given that f(x) and g(x) are two functions such that $\int_0^4 f(x)\,dx = 17$ and $\int_0^4 g(x)\,dx = 11$, find, where possible, the value of each of the following.

(a) $\int_0^4 (f(x) - g(x))\,dx$ (b) $\int_0^4 (2f(x) + 3g(x))\,dx$ (c) $\int_0^2 f(x)\,dx$

(d) $\int_0^4 (f(x) + 2x + 3)\,dx$ (e) $\int_0^1 f(x)\,dx + \int_1^4 f(x)\,dx$ (f) $\int_4^0 g(x)\,dx$

(g)* $\int_1^5 f(x-1)\,dx$ (h)* $\int_{-4}^0 g(-t)\,dt$

16 The diagram shows the graph of $y = \sqrt[3]{x} - x^2$. Show by integration that the area of the region (shaded in the diagram) between the curve and the x-axis is $\frac{5}{12}$.   (OCR)

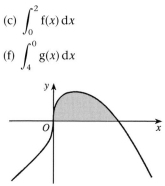

17 The diagram shows a sketch of the graph of the curve $y = x^3 - x$ together with the tangent to the curve at the point A(1, 0).

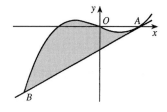

(a) Use differentiation to find the equation of the tangent to the curve at A, and verify that the point B where the tangent cuts the curve again has coordinates (−2, −6).

(b) Use integration to find the area of the region bounded by the curve and the tangent (shaded in the diagram), giving your answer as a fraction in its lowest terms.   (OCR)

18* The diagram shows part of the curve $y = x^n$, where $n > 1$.

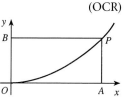

The point P on the curve has x-coordinate a. Show that the curve divides the rectangle OAPB into two regions whose areas are in the ratio $n : 1$.

19* Find the stationary points on the graph of $y = x^4 - 8x^2$. Use your answers to make a sketch of the graph. Show that the graphs of $y = x^4 - 8x^2$ and $y = x^2$ enclose two finite regions. Find the area of one of them.

20* Using the same axes, make sketches of the graphs of $y = x^3$ and $y = (x + 1)^3 - 1$. Then sketch on a larger scale the finite area enclosed between them.

Given that $(x + 1)^3 = x^3 + 3x^2 + 3x + 1$, find the area of the region.

21* A function f(x) is defined by $f(x) = \dfrac{6}{x^4} - \dfrac{2}{x^3}$ for $x > 0$.

(a) Find the values of $\int_2^3 f(x)\,dx$ and $\int_2^\infty f(x)\,dx$.

(b) Find the coordinates of (i) the point where the graph of $y = f(x)$ crosses the x-axis, (ii) the minimum point on the graph.

Use your answers to draw a sketch of the graph, and hence explain your answers to part (a).

Revision exercise 3

1 The height h centimetres of a bicycle pedal above the ground at time t seconds is given by the equation

$$h = 30 + 15 \cos 90t.$$

(a) Calculate the height of the pedal when $t = 1\frac{1}{3}$.

(b) Calculate the maximum and minimum heights of the pedal.

(c) Find the first two positive values of t for which the height of the pedal is 43 cm. Give your answers correct to 2 decimal places.

(d) How many revolutions does the pedal make in one minute?

2 Sketch the graphs of $y = 4 - x$ and $y = x^2 + 2x$, and calculate the coordinates of their points of intersection. Calculate the area of the finite region between the two graphs.

3 (a) Find the coordinates of the stationary points on the graph of $y = x^3 - 3x + 3$.

(b) Calculate the coordinates of the point for which $\dfrac{d^2 y}{dx^2} = 0$.

(c) Find the equation of the normal to the curve at the point where $x = -2$.

(d) Calculate the area enclosed between the curve, the x-axis and the lines $x = 0$ and $x = 2$.

4 Let n be a positive integer greater than 1. Sketch the graphs of $y = x^n$ and $y = x^{\frac{1}{n}}$ for $x \geqslant 0$ and find the area of the region between them.

5 A ladder is supported on a level floor by a strut of length 2.7 metres. The strut is attached to the ladder at a distance of 3 metres from the foot of the ladder. If the strut makes an angle of $10°$ with the vertical, what angle does the ladder make with the vertical?

6 A sequence of numbers $u_1, u_2, u_3, \ldots$ is defined by the equations $u_1 = 2$, $u_{r+1} = 3u_r + 2$ for $r = 1, 2, 3, \ldots$.

(a) Find the values of u_r for $r = 2, 3, 4, 5$ and 6.

(b) By adding 1 to each of your answers to part (a), suggest a formula for u_r.

7 Solve the following equations, giving values of θ in the interval $-180° \leqslant \theta \leqslant 180°$ correct to one decimal place.

(a) $3 \sin^2 \theta - 2 \cos^2 \theta = 1$ (b) $\cos \theta \tan \theta = -\frac{1}{2}$

(c) $3 + 4 \tan 2\theta = 5$ (d) $4 \cos^2 2\theta = 3$

8 (a) Solve the equation $\tan^2 2x = \frac{1}{3}$ giving all solutions in the interval $0° \leqslant x \leqslant 360°$.

(b) Prove that $\tan^2 \theta \equiv \dfrac{1}{\cos^2 \theta} - 1$.

(c) Write down the period of the graph of $y = \dfrac{3}{2 + \cos^2 2x}$, and also the coordinates of a maximum value of y.

9 A curve has an equation which satisfies $\dfrac{d^2 y}{dx^2} = 5$. The curve passes through the point $(0, 4)$ and the gradient of the tangent at this point is 3. Find y in terms of x.

10 Find the value of $\displaystyle\int_1^3 (x^3 - 6x^2 + 11x - 6)\, dx$. Interpret your result geometrically.

11 By drawing suitable sketch graphs, determine the number of roots of the equation

$$\cos x = \frac{10}{x}$$

which lie in the interval $-180° < x < 180°$.   (OCR, adapted)

12 The nth term of a series is $\frac{1}{2}(2n - 1)$. Write down the $(n + 1)$th term.
  (a) Prove that the series is an arithmetic progression.
  (b) Find, algebraically, the value of n for which the sum to n terms is 200.   (OCR)

13 (a) Determine the first three terms in the binomial expansion of $\left(x - \dfrac{1}{x}\right)^8$.

  (b) Write down the constant term in the binomial expansion of $\left(2x + \dfrac{3}{x}\right)^4$.   (OCR)

14 The tenth term of an arithmetic progression is 125 and the sum of the first ten terms is 260.
  (a) Show that the first term in the progression is -73.
  (b) Find the common difference.   (OCR)

15 The binomial expansion of $(1 + ax)^n$, where n is a positive integer, has six terms.
  (a) Write down the value of n.
  The coefficient of the x^3 term is $\frac{5}{4}$.
  (b) Find a.   (OCR)

16 A surveyor observes a vertical radio mast on a distant hill, and finds by measurement that the sight lines to the top and bottom of the mast make angles of $12°$ and $9°$ with the horizontal. She knows that the height of the mast is 180 metres. Find
  (a) the horizontal map distance of the surveyor from the mast,
  (b) the height of the foot of the mast above the surveyor's position.

17 If a sequence of numbers $u_1, u_2, u_3, \ldots$ is treated as a series, the sum of the first r terms $u_1 + u_2 + \cdots + u_r$ is denoted by S_r. You are given that $S_r = r^2(r + 1)$ for $r = 1, 2, 3, \ldots$.
  (a) Write down an expression for S_{r-1} in terms of r. Hence find an expression for u_r in terms of r.
  (b) Write down an expression for u_{r+1} in terms of r, and show that $u_{r+1} = u_r + 6r + 2$.
  (c) Give the value of u_1.
  (d) Check your answers by using the equations in parts (b) and (c) to find u_2 and u_3, and then calculate $S_2 = u_1 + u_2$ and $S_3 = u_1 + u_2 + u_3$. Do these agree with the values given by the formula $S_r = r^2(r + 1)$?

18 Find the coefficient of $\dfrac{1}{x^4}$ in the binomial expansion of $\left(1 + \dfrac{3}{x}\right)^6$.

19 An arithmetic progression has first term 3 and common difference 0.8. The sum of the first n terms of this arithmetic progression is 231. Find the value of n.

20 Two of the sides of a triangle have lengths 4 cm and 6 cm, and the angle between them is $120°$. Calculate the length of the third side, giving your answer in the form $m\sqrt{p}$, where m and p are integers, and p is prime.

21 It is given that $5 \sin 3\theta = 2 \cos 3\theta$.

    (a) Show that $\tan 3\theta = 0.4$.

    (b) Hence find the values of θ, in the interval $0° \leqslant \theta \leqslant 180°$, for which $5 \sin 3\theta = 2 \cos 3\theta$.
        Give your answers correct to 1 decimal place.   (OCR)

22 $1 + ax + bx^2$ are the first three terms of a binomial expansion for $(1 + cx)^n$. Write two equations involving n and c, and hence express n and c in terms of a and b.

    Prove that the next term of the expansion is $\dfrac{b}{3a}(4b - a^2)x^3$.

23 A tanker is steaming due north in a calm sea at a speed of 36 kilometres per hour when it sights an iceberg on a bearing of $052°$. Five minutes later the bearing of the iceberg is $061°$.

    (a) How far is the iceberg from the tanker when the second bearing is taken?

    (b) After a further five minutes a third bearing of the iceberg is taken. How far is the iceberg from the tanker then, and what is its bearing?

24 Find

    (a) $\displaystyle\int x(x + 1)\,dx,$ (b) $\displaystyle\int \dfrac{1}{x^2}\,dx.$ (OCR)

25 (a) Show that the equation $3 \sin 2\theta - \cos 2\theta = 0$ may be written as $\tan 2\theta = \tfrac{1}{3}$.

    (b) Hence solve the equation $3 \sin 2\theta - \cos 2\theta = 0$, giving all values of θ such that $0° \leqslant \theta \leqslant 360°$. Give your answers to the nearest $0.1°$.   (OCR)

26 The diagram shows the curve $y = 8 - 2x^2$, together with the straight line $y = 5 - x$.

    (a) Find the coordinates of the points where the curve and the line intersect.

    (b) Hence, or otherwise, solve the inequality
        $8 - 2x^2 < 5 - x$.

    (c) Show that the area of the shaded region enclosed by the line and the curve is $\tfrac{125}{24}$.   (OCR)

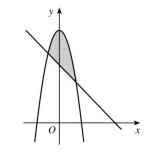

27 Find the exact value of $\cos 30° + 2 \sin 60°$.   (OCR)

28 The vertices of a field with the shape of a quadrilateral are A, B, C and D, in that order. The lengths of the sides BC, CD and DA are 60 m, 80 m and 100 m respectively. The angles BAD and BDA are $70°$ and $60°$ respectively.

Calculate

(a) the length BD,   (b) the angle BCD,   (c) the area of the field.

29 (a) Sketch the graph of $y = \sin x$, for values of x such that $0° \leqslant x \leqslant 720°$.

(b) Sketch, on the same diagram, the graph of $y = \sin \frac{1}{2}x$, for values of x such that $0° \leqslant x \leqslant 720°$.

(c) State the number of solutions to the equation $\sin x = \sin \frac{1}{2}x$ for values of x such that $0° \leqslant x \leqslant 720°$.

(d) Specify the transformation which transforms the complete graph of $y = \sin x$ (that is, the graph drawn for all values of x) to the complete graph of $y = \sin \frac{1}{2}x$.   (OCR)

30 (a) Express $2\cos^2 \theta - \sin^2 \theta - \sin \theta$ in the form $a\sin^2 \theta + b\sin \theta + c$, stating the values of the constants a, b and c.

(b) Hence solve the equation $2\cos^2 \theta - \sin^2 \theta - \sin \theta = 2$, giving all values of θ such that $0° \leqslant \theta \leqslant 360°$. Where appropriate, give your answers to the nearest 0.1.   (OCR)

31 The diagram shows the curve $y = 2x^2 - x^3$ and the tangent to the curve at the point $A(2, 0)$.

(a) Find $\dfrac{\mathrm{d}y}{\mathrm{d}x}$ and hence find the equation of the tangent at A.

(b) The tangent at A meets the curve again at the point B. Verify that the coordinates of B are $(-2, 16)$.

(c) Calculate the area of the shaded region between the straight line AB and the curve.   (OCR)

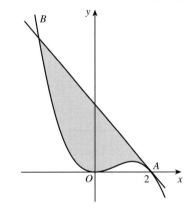

32 The gradient at the point (x, y) on a curve is given by $\dfrac{\mathrm{d}y}{\mathrm{d}x} = 5x^2 - 6x + 1$. The curve passes through $(0, 1)$.

(a) Find the equation of the curve.

(b) Find the x-coordinates of the stationary points on the curve and determine whether each stationary point is a maximum or a minimum.

(c) State the set of values of x for which the curve has a negative gradient.

(d) Find the x-coordinates of the points on the curve where the tangent to the curve has a positive gradient and also makes an angle of $45°$ with the x-axis. It may be assumed that the scales on the x-axis and the y-axis are equal.   (OCR)

33 In the diagram, BC represents the jib of a crane which is inclined at 60° to the horizontal. CA is a supporting wire hawser, where A is at the same level as B. The length of the jib is 20 m, and the distance AB is 10 m. The load D hangs 5 m below C.

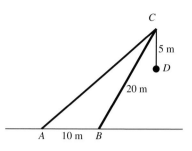

Calculate

(a) the height of D above the ground,

(b) the length of the wire hawser,

(c) the angle CAB.

34 Find the equation of the curve through $(0, 5)$ for which $\dfrac{dy}{dx} = -2x + 3$.   (OCR)

35 Solve the equation $\sin\theta = -\dfrac{\sqrt{3}}{2}$, giving all values of θ such that $0° \leqslant \theta \leqslant 360°$.   (OCR)

36 The diagram shows the curve $y = 3x^2 - 12x + 9$.

(a) Show that
$$\int_0^3 (3x^2 - 12x + 9)\,dx = 0.$$

(b) State what may be deduced from the result in part (a) about the areas labelled A and B.   (OCR)

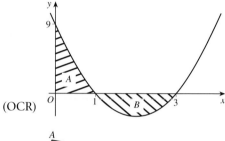

37 In the triangle ABC, $AB = 2\sqrt{2}$, $BC = 6\sqrt{2}$ and angle $ABC = 60°$.

(a) Find the length of AC, giving your answer in simplified surd form.

(b) Find the area of triangle ABC, giving your answer in simplified surd form.   (OCR)

38 (a) Expand $(2 + 3x)^4$ completely, simplifying the coefficients.

(b) Hence find the coefficient of x^2 in the expansion of $\left(1 - \frac{1}{2}x\right)^2(2 + 3x)^4$.   (OCR)

39 Find the equation of the tangent to the curve $y = (x^2 + 1)^5$ at the point $(-1, 32)$. Give your answer in the form $y = mx + c$.   (OCR)

40 The first term of an arithmetic progression is 14 and the 20th term is 25.4.

(a) Find the common difference.

(b) Find the sum of the first 500 terms.   (OCR)

41 (a) Find the first four terms in the expansion, in ascending powers of x, of $(1 + 3x)^8$.

(b) Show that, if terms involving x^4 and higher powers of x may be ignored,
$(1 - 3x)^8 + (1 + 3x)^8 = 2 + 504x^2$.

(c) Hence find the value of $1.000\,003^8 + 0.999\,997^8$ correct to 12 decimal places.   (OCR)

42 Find the sum of the first 400 positive integers.   (OCR)

43 Find $\displaystyle\int \left(x^3 + 2x + \frac{1}{x^2}\right) dx.$ (OCR)

44 (a) Express $3\cos^2\theta - 2\sin\theta$ in terms of $\sin\theta$.

(b) Hence solve the equation $3\cos^2\theta - 2\sin\theta = 2$, giving all values such that $0° \leqslant \theta \leqslant 360°$. Where appropriate, give your answers correct to 1 decimal place. (OCR)

45 *AE, BF, CG* and *DH* are vertical edges of the cuboid *ABCDEFGH*. The lengths of *AD, AB* and *AE* are 3 cm, 4 cm and 5 cm respectively. *A* and *H* are at opposite corners of one face, *A* and *F* are at opposite corners of another face and *A* and *C* are at opposite corners of a third face. Solve the triangle *CFH*.

46 (a) Sketch the graph of $y = \tan x$ for values of x such that $0° \leqslant x \leqslant 360°$.

(b) Sketch on a separate diagram the graph of $y = \tan(x - 90°)$ for values of x such that $0° \leqslant x \leqslant 360°$.

(c) Solve the equation $\tan(x - 90°) = 1$ for values of x such that $0° \leqslant x \leqslant 360°$. (OCR)

47 The diagram shows the curves $y = -3x^2 - 9x + 30$ and $y = x^2 + 3x - 10$.

(a) Verify that the graphs intersect at the points $A(-5, 0)$ and $B(2, 0)$.

(b) Show that the area of the shaded region is $\displaystyle\int_{-5}^{2}(-4x^2 - 12x + 40)\,dx$

(c) Hence or otherwise show that the area of the shaded region is $228\frac{2}{3}$. (OCR)

48 Find $\displaystyle\int \left(\frac{1}{x^2} - x\right) dx.$ (OCR)

49 (a) Show that $3\sin^2\theta + \cos^2\theta - \cos\theta\tan\theta - 1$ may be written as $2\sin^2\theta - \sin\theta$.

(b) Hence solve the equation $3\sin^2\theta + \cos^2\theta - \cos\theta\tan\theta - 1 = 0$, giving all values of θ such that $0° \leqslant \theta \leqslant 360°$. (OCR)

50 The diagram shows part of the curve $y = x^3 - 6x^2 + 12x - 8$. The points $P(1, k)$, $Q(2, 0)$ and $R(4, 8)$ lie on the curve. The points A, B and C have coordinates $(4, 0)$, $(0, k)$ and $(0, 8)$ respectively.

(a) Find the value of the constant k.

(b) Show that

$$\int_{2}^{4}(x^3 - 6x^2 + 12x - 8)\,dx = 4.$$

(c) Identify the region whose area is given by the integral in part (b).

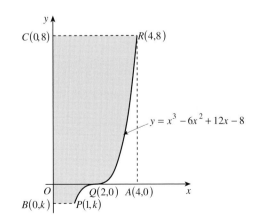

(d) Calculate the area of the shaded region *BPQRC*. (OCR)

51 It is given that $\dfrac{dy}{dx} = x^2 - 4 + \dfrac{4}{x^2}$, where $x > 0$.

    (a) Find $\dfrac{d^2 y}{dx^2}$.

    (b) Express y in terms of x, given that $y = 0$ when $x = 3$.   (OCR)

52 The diagram shows the curve $y = x^2 + 2$ and the straight line $y = 11$.

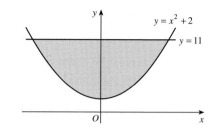

    (a) Find the x-coordinates of the points where the curve and the line intersect.

    (b) Calculate the area of the shaded region enclosed by the line $y = 11$ and the curve $y = x^2 + 2$.   (OCR)

53 (a) Given that the first three terms in the expansion of $(1 - 4x)^6$ are $1 + cx + dx^2$, find the values of the constants c and d.

    (b) Hence find the coefficient of x^2 in the expansion of $(2 - 3x - x^2)(1 - 4x)^6$.   (OCR)

6 Geometric sequences

This chapter introduces another type of sequence, in which the ratio of successive terms is constant. When you have completed it, you should

- recognise geometric sequences and be able to do calculations on them
- know and be able to obtain the formula for the sum of a geometric series
- know the condition for a geometric series to converge, and how to find its limiting sum.

6.1 Geometric sequences

In Chapter 2 you met arithmetic sequences, in which you get from one term to the next by adding a constant. A sequence in which you get from one term to the next by multiplying by a constant is called a **geometric sequence**.

Example 6.1.1
Show that the numbers 4, 12, 36, 108 form a geometric sequence. If the sequence is continued, find
(a) the next two terms, (b) the twentieth term.

Since

$$12 = 3 \times 4, \quad 36 = 3 \times 12, \quad 108 = 3 \times 36,$$

there is a constant multiplying factor of 3. So the numbers form a geometric sequence.

(a) The next term is $3 \times 108 = 324$, and the term after that is $3 \times 324 = 972$.

(b) To get from the first term to the twentieth you have to multiply by 3 nineteen times. So the twentieth term is 4×3^{19}. Correct to 4 significant figures, this is 4649 million.

Example 6.1.2
The first two terms of a geometric sequence are 4, 20 and the last term is 62 500. How many terms are there altogether?

To get from the first term to the second you must multiply by $\frac{20}{4} = 5$. To get from the first term to the last you must multiply by $\frac{62\,500}{4} = 15\,625$, which is 5^6.

So, going one step at a time, you start at the first term and then multiply by 5 six times. This means that 62 500 is the seventh term of the sequence.

A general definition for this kind of sequence is:

> A **geometric sequence**, or **geometric progression**, is a sequence defined by $u_1 = a$ and $u_{i+1} = ru_i$, where $r \neq 0$ or 1, and $i = 1, 2, 3, \ldots$.
>
> The constant r is called the **common ratio** of the sequence.

You should notice two points about this definition. First, since the letter r is conventionally used for the common ratio, a different letter, i, is used for the suffixes.

Secondly, the ratios 0 and 1 are excluded. If you put $r = 0$ in the definition you get the sequence $a, 0, 0, 0, \ldots$; if you put $r = 1$ you get $a, a, a, a, \ldots$. Neither is very interesting, and some of the properties of geometric sequences break down if $r = 0$ or 1. However, r can be negative; in that case the terms are alternately positive and negative.

It is easy to give a formula for the ith term. To get from u_1 to u_i you multiply by the common ratio $i - 1$ times, so $u_i = r^{i-1} \times u_1$, which gives $u_i = ar^{i-1}$.

> The ith term of a geometric sequence with first term a and common ratio r is ar^{i-1}.

Example 6.1.3
The first two terms of a geometric sequence are 10 and 11. Show that the first term greater than 1000 is the fiftieth.

The common ratio is $11 \div 10 = 1.1$. The ith term of the sequence is therefore $10 \times 1.1^{i-1}$.

Each term of the sequence is greater than the preceding term. You therefore have to show that the 49th term is less than 1000, and that the 50th term is greater than 1000.

The 49th term is $10 \times 1.1^{49-1} = 10 \times 1.1^{48} = 970.17\ldots$.

The 50th term is $10 \times 1.1^{50-1} = 10 \times 1.1^{49} = 1067.18\ldots$.

So the first term greater than 1000 is the fiftieth.

Example 6.1.4
Show that there are two geometric sequences whose first term is 5 and whose fifth term is 80. For each of these sequences, find the tenth term.

Since the first term is given, the sequence is determined by knowing the common ratio r. The fifth term is $5 \times r^{5-1} = 5 \times r^4$.

If $5 \times r^4 = 80, r^4 = 16$, so $r = \pm 2$.

The two sequences are $5, 10, 20, 40, 80, \ldots$ and $5, -10, 20, -40, 80, \ldots$.

The tenth term is $5 \times r^{10-1} = 5 \times r^9$.

So when $r = 2$, the tenth term is $5 \times 2^9 = 5 \times 512 = 2560$; when $r = -2$, the tenth term is $5 \times (-2)^9 = 5 \times (-512) = -2560$.

Exercise 6A

1 For each of the following geometric sequences find the common ratio and the next two terms.

(a) $3, 6, 12, \ldots$
(b) $2, 8, 32, \ldots$
(c) $32, 16, 8, \ldots$
(d) $2, -6, 18, -54, \ldots$
(e) $1.1, 1.21, 1.331, \ldots$
(f) $x^2, x, 1, \ldots$

2 Find an expression for the ith term of each of the following geometric sequences.

(a) $2, 6, 18, \ldots$
(b) $10, 5, 2.5, \ldots$
(c) $1, -2, 4, \ldots$
(d) $81, 27, 9, \ldots$
(e) $x, x^2, x^3, \ldots$
(f) $pq^2, q^3, p^{-1}q^4, \ldots$

3 Find the number of terms in each of these geometric progressions.

(a) $2, 4, 8, \ldots, 2048$
(b) $1, -3, 9, \ldots, 531\,441$
(c) $2, 6, 18, \ldots, 1458$
(d) $5, -10, 20, \ldots, -40\,960$
(e) $16, 12, 9, \ldots, 3.796\,875$
(f) $x^{-6}, x^{-2}, x^2, \ldots, x^{42}$

4 Find the common ratio and the first term in the geometric progressions where

(a) the 2nd term is 4 and the 5th term is 108,
(b) the 3rd term is 6 and the 7th term is 96,
(c) the 4th term is 19 683 and the 9th term is 81,
(d) the 3rd term is 8 and the 9th term is 64,

5 If x, y and z are the first three terms of a geometric sequence, show that x^2, y^2 and z^2 form another geometric sequence.

6* Different numbers x, y and z are the first three terms of a geometric progression with common ratio r, and also the first, second and fourth terms of an arithmetic progression.

(a) Find the value of r.
(b) Find which term of the arithmetic progression will next be equal to a term of the geometric progression.

7* Different numbers x, y and z are the first three terms of a geometric progression with common ratio r and also the first, second and fifth terms of an arithmetic progression.

(a) Find the value of r.
(b) Find which term of the arithmetic progression will next be equal to a term of the geometric progression.

6.2 Summing geometric series

Geometric sequences have many applications in finance, biology, mechanics and probability, and you often need to find the sum of all the terms. In this context it is usual to call the sequence a **geometric series**.

The method used in Chapter 2 to find the sum of an arithmetic series does not work for geometric series. You can see this by taking a simple geometric series like

$$1 + 2 + 4 + 8 + 16$$

and placing an upside-down copy next to it, as in Fig. 6.1.

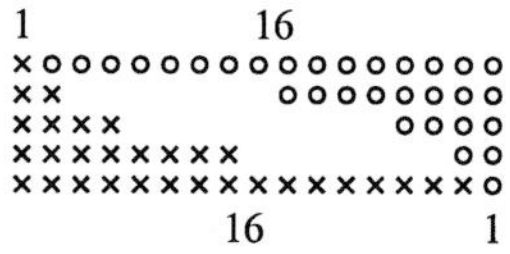

When you did this with arithmetic series the two sets of crosses and noughts made a perfect join (see Fig. 2.7), so they could easily be counted; but for the geometric series there is a gap in the middle.

Fig. 6.1

For geometric series a different method is used. If you multiply the equation

$$S = 1 + 2 + 4 + 8 + 16$$

by 2, then you get

$$2S = 2 + 4 + 8 + 16 + 32.$$

Notice that the right sides in these two equations have the terms $2 + 4 + 8 + 16$ in common. If you put all the other terms on the left sides, you get

$$S - 1 = 2 + 4 + 8 + 16$$

and $$2S - 32 = 2 + 4 + 8 + 16$$

so $$S - 1 = 2S - 32, \quad \text{giving} \quad S = 31.$$

You can use this method to find the sum of any geometric series. Let S be the sum of the first n terms of the series. Then

$$S = a + ar + ar^2 + \cdots + ar^{n-2} + ar^{n-1}.$$

If you multiply this equation by r, you get

$$Sr = ar + ar^2 + ar^3 + \cdots + ar^{n-1} + ar^n.$$

The right sides in these two equations have the terms $ar + ar^2 + \cdots + ar^{n-2} + ar^{n-1}$ in common; so

$$S - a = ar + ar^2 + \cdots + ar^{n-2} + ar^{n-1}$$

and $$Sr - ar^n = ar + ar^2 + \cdots + ar^{n-2} + ar^{n-1}.$$

Equating the left sides,

$$S - a = Sr - ar^n$$
$$S - Sr = a - ar^n$$
$$S(1 - r) = a(1 - r^n).$$

That is,

$$S = \frac{a(1 - r^n)}{1 - r}.$$

> The sum of the geometric series $a + ar + ar^2 + \cdots + ar^{n-1}$, with n terms, is
>
> $$\frac{a(1 - r^n)}{1 - r}.$$

Example 6.2.1

Find the sums of the geometric series having 9 terms with

(a) first term 6561, common ratio $\frac{1}{3}$;   (b) first term 1, common ratio 3;

(c) first term 1, common ratio –3.

(a) Setting $a = 6561$, $r = \frac{1}{3}$ and $n = 9$ in the formula gives the sum

$$\frac{6561\left(1 - \left(\frac{1}{3}\right)^9\right)}{1 - \frac{1}{3}} = \frac{6561 \times \left(1 - \frac{1}{19\,683}\right)}{\frac{2}{3}} = 6561 \times \frac{19\,682}{19\,683} \times \frac{3}{2} = 9841.$$

(b) Setting $a = 1$, $r = 3$ and $n = 9$ in the formula gives the sum

$$\frac{1(1 - 3^9)}{1 - 3} = \frac{1 - 19\,683}{-2} = \frac{-19\,682}{-2} = 9841.$$

> Can you see why the answers to parts (a) and (b) are the same?

(c) Setting $a = 1$, $r = -3$ and $n = 9$ in the formula gives the sum

$$\frac{1(1 - (-3)^9)}{1 - (-3)} = \frac{1 - (-19\,683)}{1 - (-3)} = \frac{1 + 19\,683}{1 + 3} = \frac{19\,684}{4} = 4921.$$

There are two points to notice in this example about the use of the formula for the sum.

- In part (c) it is used with a negative value of r. The algebraic argument used to produce the formula is equally valid whether r is positive or negative. The only value of r for which it breaks down is 1; but in the definition of a geometric sequence in Section 6.1 the value $r = 1$ is specifically excluded.

- In part (b), where r is greater than 1, both $1 - r^n$ and $1 - r$ are negative, so that when you apply the formula you get a fraction in which the top and the bottom are both negative. You could avoid the minus signs by noting that $1 - r^n = -(r^n - 1)$ and $1 - r = -(r - 1)$, so that

$$\frac{a(1 - r^n)}{1 - r} = \frac{-a(r^n - 1)}{-(r - 1)} = \frac{a(r^n - 1)}{r - 1}.$$

Some people like to use the formula in this alternative form when $r > 1$; it is one more result to remember, but you avoid the inconvenience of the minus signs. It's a matter of choice.

Example 6.2.2

A geometric series which begins $4 + 5 + \ldots$ has 15 terms. Find the sum, and compare it with the sum of the corresponding arithmetic series.

Since the first two terms are 4 and 5, the common ratio is $\frac{5}{4} = 1.25$. So the formula gives the sum of the geometric series as

$$\frac{4(1 - 1.25^{15})}{1 - 1.25} = \frac{4(1 - 28.42\ldots)}{-0.25}$$
$$= (-16) \times (-27.42\ldots)$$
$$= 438.7\ldots = 439 \text{ to the nearest integer.}$$

For the arithmetic series the common difference is 1. So the formula $S = \frac{1}{2}n(2a + (n-1)d)$ in Section 2.6 gives

$$S = \frac{1}{2} \times 15(2 \times 4 + 14 \times 1) = 165.$$

The sum of the geometric series is between $2\frac{1}{2}$ and 3 times as large as the sum of the arithmetic series.

Example 6.2.3

(a) The first and last terms of a geometric series are a and l, and the common ratio is r. Show that the sum of the series is $\dfrac{a - lr}{1 - r}$.

(b) Given that $5 + 15 + \cdots + 10\,935$ is a geometric series, find what proportion of the sum is contributed by the last term.

(a) From the sum formula

$$S = \frac{a(1 - r^n)}{1 - r} = \frac{a - ar^n}{1 - r} = \frac{a - r(ar^{n-1})}{1 - r}.$$

Since the last term $l = ar^{n-1}$,

$$S = \frac{a - rl}{1 - r}.$$

(b) The series has common ratio $\frac{15}{5} = 3$. Substituting $a = 5$, $r = 3$ and $l = 10\,935$ in the formula in part (a),

$$S = \frac{5 - 3 \times 10\,935}{1 - 3} = \frac{-32\,800}{-2} = 16\,400.$$

The proportion of this sum contributed by the last term is $\dfrac{10\,935}{16\,400} = 0.667\ldots$, which is just over $\frac{2}{3}$.

Example 6.2.4

A child lives 200 metres from school. He walks 60 metres in the first minute, and in each subsequent minute he walks 75% of the distance he walked in the previous minute. Show that he takes between 6 and 7 minutes to get to school.

The distances walked in the first, second, third, ..., nth minutes are $60\,\text{m}$, $60 \times 0.75\,\text{m}$, $60 \times 0.75^2\,\text{m}, \ldots, 60 \times 0.75^{n-1}\,\text{m}$. In the first n minutes the child walks S_n metres, where

$$S_n = 60 + 60 \times 0.75^1 + 60 \times 0.75^2 + \cdots + 60 \times 0.75^{n-1}$$
$$= \frac{60(1 - 0.75^n)}{1 - 0.75} = \frac{60(1 - 0.75^n)}{0.25} = 240(1 - 0.75^n).$$

From this formula you can calculate that

$$S_6 = 240(1 - 0.75^6) = 240(1 - 0.177...) = 197.2..., \text{ and}$$
$$S_7 = 240(1 - 0.75^7) = 240(1 - 0.133...) = 207.9....$$

So he has not reached school after 6 minutes, but (if he had gone on walking) he would have gone more than 200 m in 7 minutes. That is, he takes between 6 and 7 minutes to walk to school.

Example 6.2.5

Show that $\sum\limits_{i=1}^{10} 2 \times 3^i$ is the sum of a geometric progression, and find its value.

To interpret an expression in $\sum$ notation, it is usually enough to write out the first three terms and the last term. In this case,

$$\sum_{i=1}^{10} 2 \times 3^i = 2 \times 3^1 + 2 \times 3^2 + 2 \times 3^3 + \cdots + 2 \times 3^{10}$$
$$= 6 + 18 + 54 + \cdots + 2 \times 3^{10}.$$

To get from each term to the next you multiply by 3. So this is a geometric series with $a = 6$, $r = 3$ and $n = 10$.

Notice that 2×3^i is the same as $2 \times (3 \times 3^{i-1}) = 6 \times 3^{i-1}$. You will recognise this as the standard way of writing the ith term of a geometric sequence, ar^{i-1}, with $a = 6$ and $r = 3$.

The formula for the sum of a geometric series then gives

$$\sum_{i=1}^{10} 2 \times 3^i = \frac{6(1 - 3^{10})}{1 - 3} = \frac{-6(3^{10} - 1)}{-2} = 3(3^{10} - 1) = 177\,144.$$

Example 6.2.6
Find a simple expression for the sum $p^6 - p^5q + p^4q^2 - p^3q^3 + p^2q^4 - pq^5 + q^6$.

This is a geometric series of 7 terms, with first term p^6 and common ratio $-\dfrac{q}{p}$. Its sum is therefore

$$\frac{p^6(1-(-q/p)^7)}{1-(-q/p)} = \frac{p^6(1-(-q^7/p^7))}{1+q/p} = \frac{p^7(1+q^7/p^7)}{p(1+q/p)} = \frac{p^7+q^7}{p+q}.$$

Another way of writing the result of this example is

$$p^7 + q^7 = (p+q)(p^6 - p^5q + p^4q^2 - p^3q^3 + p^2q^4 - pq^5 + q^6).$$

You can use a similar method for any odd number n to express $p^n + q^n$ as the product of $p+q$ and another factor.

Exercise 6B

1 Find the sum, for the given number of terms, of each of the following geometric series. Give decimal answers correct to 4 places.

(a) $2 + 6 + 18 + \ldots$ 10 terms

(b) $2 - 6 + 18 - \ldots$ 10 terms

(c) $1 + \frac{1}{2} + \frac{1}{4} + \ldots$ 8 terms

(d) $1 - \frac{1}{2} + \frac{1}{4} - \ldots$ 8 terms

(e) $3 + 6 + 12 + \ldots$ 12 terms

(f) $12 - 4 + \frac{4}{3} - \ldots$ 10 terms

2 Find the sum of each of the following geometric series. Give numerical answers in parts (a) to (g) as rational numbers.

(a) $1 + 2 + 4 + \cdots + 1024$

(b) $1 - 2 + 4 - \cdots + 1024$

(c) $3 + 12 + 48 + \cdots + 196\,608$

(d) $1 + \frac{1}{2} + \frac{1}{4} + \cdots + \frac{1}{512}$

(e) $1 - \frac{1}{3} + \frac{1}{9} - \cdots - \frac{1}{19\,683}$

(f) $10 + 5 + 2.5 + \cdots + 0.156\,25$

(g) $\frac{1}{4} + \frac{1}{16} + \frac{1}{64} + \cdots + \frac{1}{1024}$

(h) $1 + \frac{1}{2} + \frac{1}{4} + \cdots + \frac{1}{2^n}$

(i) $16 + 4 + 1 + \cdots + \frac{1}{2^{2n}}$

(j) $81 - 27 + 9 - \cdots + \frac{1}{(-3)^n}$

3 Find the sum of each of the following geometric series. Give numerical answers as rational numbers.

(a) $\displaystyle\sum_{i=1}^{5} 3 \times 2^{i-1}$

(b) $\displaystyle\sum_{i=1}^{4} 2 \times (-2)^{i-1}$

(c) $\displaystyle\sum_{i=1}^{8} 16 \times \left(\tfrac{1}{2}\right)^{i-1}$

(d) $\displaystyle\sum_{i=1}^{7} 4^i$

4 A well-known story concerns the inventor of the game of chess. As a reward for inventing the game it is rumoured that he was asked to choose his own prize. He asked for 1 grain of rice to be placed on the first square of the board, 2 grains on the second square, 4 grains on the third square and so on in geometric progression until all 64 squares had been covered. Calculate the total number of grains of rice he would have received. Give your answer in standard form!

5   A problem similar to that of Question 4 is posed by the child who negotiates a pocket money deal of 1p on 1 February, 2p on 2 February, 4p on 3 February and so on for 28 days. How much should the child receive in total during February?

6   A firm sponsors a local orchestra for seven years. It agrees to give £2500 in the first year, and to increase its contribution by 20% each year. Show that the amounts contributed each year form a geometric sequence. How much does the firm give the orchestra altogether during the period of sponsorship?

7   An explorer sets out across the desert with 100 litres of water. He uses 6 litres on the first day. On subsequent days he rations himself to 95% of the amount he used the day before. Show that he has enough water to last for 34 days, but no more. How much will he then have left?

8   A competitor in a pie-eating contest eats one-third of his pie in the first minute. In each subsequent minute he eats three-quarters of the amount he ate in the previous minute. Find an expression for the amount of pie he has left to eat after n minutes. Show that he takes between 4 and 5 minutes to finish the pie.

9   Find expressions for the sum of n terms of the following series. Give your answer, in terms of n and x, in as simple a form as possible.

(a) $x + x^2 + x^3 + \cdots$ n terms   (b) $x - x^2 + x^3 - \cdots$ n terms

(c) $x + \frac{1}{x} + \frac{1}{x^3} + \cdots$ n terms   (d) $1 - \frac{1}{x^2} + \frac{1}{x^4} + \cdots$ n terms

10*   Consider the geometric progression

$$q^{n-1} + q^{n-2}p + q^{n-3}p^2 + \cdots + qp^{n-2} + p^{n-1}.$$

(a) Find the common ratio and the number of terms.

(b) Show that the sum of the series is equal to $\dfrac{q^n - p^n}{q - p}$.

(c) By considering the limit as $q \to p$ deduce expressions for $f'(p)$ in the cases
    (i) $f(x) = x^n$,   (ii) $f(x) = x^{-n}$,   for all positive integers n.

6.3   Convergent geometric series

Take any sequence, such as the sequence of triangle numbers $t_1 = 1, t_2 = 3, t_3 = 6, \ldots$ (see Section 2.2). Form a new sequence whose terms are the sums of successive triangle numbers:

$$S_1 = t_1 = 1, \quad S_2 = t_1 + t_2 = 1 + 3 = 4, \quad S_3 = t_1 + t_2 + t_3 = 1 + 3 + 6 = 10, \text{ and so on.}$$

This is called the sum sequence of the original sequence.

Notice that $S_2 = S_1 + t_2$, $S_3 = S_2 + t_3$, ... This property can be used to give a recursive definition for the sum sequence:

> For a given sequence u_i, the **sum sequence** $S_i = u_1 + \cdots + u_i$ is defined by
> $S_1 = u_1$ and $S_{i+1} = S_i + u_{i+1}$.

(If the original sequence begins with u_0 rather than u_1, the equation $S_1 = u_1$ in the definition is replaced by $S_0 = u_0$.)

Example 6.3.1

A sequence is given by the formula $u_n = n^3$ for $n = 1, 2, 3, \ldots$. Find the first five terms of its sum sequence.

The first five terms of the sequence u_n are

$$u_1 = 1, \quad u_2 = 8, \quad u_3 = 27, \quad u_4 = 64, \quad u_5 = 125,$$

so the first five terms of the sum sequence S_n are

$$S_1 = 1, \quad S_2 = 1 + 8 = 9, \quad S_3 = 9 + 27 = 36,$$
$$S_4 = 36 + 64 = 100, \quad S_5 = 100 + 125 = 225.$$

Geometric sequences have especially important sum sequences. Here are four examples, with different common ratios, each with first term $a = 1$:

(a) $r = 3$

u_i	1	3	9	27	81	243	729	...
S_i	1	4	13	40	121	364	1093	...

Table 6.1

(b) $r = 0.2$

u_i	1	0.2	0.04	0.008	0.001 6	0.000 32	0.000 064	...
S_i	1	1.2	1.24	1.248	1.249 6	1.249 92	1.249 984	...

Table 6.2

(c) $r = -0.2$

u_i	1	-0.2	0.04	-0.008	0.001 6	$-0.000 32$	0.000 064	...
S_i	1	0.8	0.84	0.832	0.833 6	0.833 28	0.833 344	...

Table 6.3

(d) $r = -3$

u_i	1	-3	9	-27	81	-243	729	$\ldots$
S_i	1	-2	7	-20	61	-182	547	$\ldots$

Table 6.4

The sum sequences for (b) and (c) are quite different from the others. You would guess that in (b) the values of S_i are getting close to 1.25, but never reach it. This can be proved, since the formula for the sum of the first n values of u_i gives, with $a = 1$ and $r = 0.2$,

$$\frac{1 - 0.2^n}{1 - 0.2} = \frac{1 - 0.2^n}{0.8} = 1.25(1 - 0.2^n).$$

Now you can make 0.2^n as small as you like by taking n large enough, and then the expression in brackets comes very close to 1, though it never equals 1. You can say that the sum tends to the limit 1.25 as n tends to infinity.

It seems that the sum in (c) tends to $0.833\,33\ldots$ (the recurring decimal for $\frac{5}{6}$) as n tends to infinity, but here the values are alternately above and below the limiting value. This is because the formula for the sum is

$$\frac{1 - (-0.2)^n}{1 - (-0.2)} = \frac{1 - (-0.2)^n}{1.2} = \tfrac{5}{6}(1 - (-0.2)^n).$$

In this formula the expression $(-0.2)^n$ is negative when n is odd, and positive when n is even. So $1 - (-0.2)^n$ alternates above and below 1.

The other two sequences, for which the sum formulae are

(a) $\tfrac{1}{2}(3^n - 1)$ and   (d) $\tfrac{1}{4}(1 - (-3)^n)$,

do not tend to a limit. The sum (a) can be made as large as you like by taking n large enough; it is said to **diverge to infinity** as n tends to infinity. The sum (d) can also be made as large as you like, but the values are alternately positive and negative: the sum sequence is said to **oscillate infinitely**.

It is the expression r^n in the sum formula $\dfrac{a(1 - r^n)}{1 - r}$ which determines whether or not the sum tends to a limit.

- If $r > 1$, then r^n increases indefinitely.

- If $r < -1$, the numerical value of r^n increases indefinitely, but r^n is negative when n is odd and positive when n is even.

- If $-1 < r < 1$, then r^n tends to 0 and the sum tends to the limiting value $\dfrac{a(1 - 0)}{1 - r} = \dfrac{a}{1 - r}$.

As long as $-1 < r < 1$, even if r is very close to 1, r^n becomes very small if n is large enough; for example, if $r = 0.9999$ and $n = 1\,000\,000$, then $r^n \approx 3.70 \times 10^{-44}$.

What happens if $r = -1$?

> If $-1 < r < 1$, the sum of the geometric series with first term a and common ratio r tends to the limit $S_\infty = \dfrac{a}{1-r}$ as the number of terms tends to infinity.
>
> The infinite geometric series is then said to be **convergent**.
>
> S_∞ is called the **sum to infinity** of the series.

Example 6.3.2
A geometric series begins $9 + 6 + 4 + \ldots$. Find an expression for the sum of the first n terms. Show that the series is convergent, and find the sum to infinity.

The series has common ratio $\dfrac{6}{9} = \dfrac{2}{3}$. Since $a = 9$, the sum of the first n terms is

$$\frac{9\left(1 - \left(\frac{2}{3}\right)^n\right)}{1 - \frac{2}{3}} = \frac{9}{\frac{1}{3}}\left(1 - \left(\tfrac{2}{3}\right)^n\right) = 27\left(1 - \left(\tfrac{2}{3}\right)^n\right).$$

Since the common ratio is between -1 and 1, the series is convergent. The sum to infinity is

$$\frac{9}{1 - \frac{2}{3}} = \frac{9}{\frac{1}{3}} = 27.$$

Example 6.3.3
The first term of a convergent geometric series is 20, and its sum to infinity is 15. Find the common ratio, and an expression for the sum of the first n terms.

If the common ratio is r,

$$\frac{20}{1-r} = 15.$$

So
$$20 = 15 - 15r,$$
$$15r = -5,$$
$$r = -\tfrac{1}{3}.$$

The sum of the first n terms is therefore

$$\frac{20\left(1 - \left(-\frac{1}{3}\right)^n\right)}{1 - \left(-\frac{1}{3}\right)} = \frac{20}{\frac{4}{3}}\left(1 - \left(-\tfrac{1}{3}\right)^n\right) = 15\left(1 - \left(-\tfrac{1}{3}\right)^n\right).$$

Example 6.3.4
Express the recurring decimal $0.296\,296\,296\ldots$ as a fraction.

The decimal can be written as

$$0.296 + 0.000\,296 + 0.000\,000\,296 + \ldots$$
$$= 0.296 + 0.296 \times 0.001 + 0.296 \times (0.001)^2 + \ldots,$$

which is a geometric series with $a = 0.296$ and $r = 0.001$. Since $-1 < r < 1$, the series is convergent with limiting sum $\dfrac{0.296}{1 - 0.001} = \dfrac{296}{999}$.

Since $296 = 8 \times 37$ and $999 = 27 \times 37$, this fraction in its simplest form is $\frac{8}{27}$.

Example 6.3.5

A beetle starts at a point O on the floor. It walks 1 m east, then $\frac{1}{2}$ m west, then $\frac{1}{4}$ m east, and so on, halving the distance at each change of direction. How far from O does it end up?

The final distance from O is $1 - \frac{1}{2} + \frac{1}{4} - \frac{1}{8} + \ldots$, which is a geometric series with common ratio $-\frac{1}{2}$. Since $-1 < -\frac{1}{2} < 1$, the series converges to a limit

$$\frac{1}{1 - \left(-\frac{1}{2}\right)} = \frac{1}{\frac{3}{2}} = \frac{2}{3}.$$

The beetle ends up $\frac{2}{3}$ m from O.

Notice that a point of trisection was obtained as the limit of a process of repeated halving.

6.4 Using sigma notation

Sigma notation can be used to represent a sum to infinity for a convergent series. The sum to infinity of a series with general term u_i is written as $\sum_{i=1}^{\infty} u_i$. In the case of a convergent geometric progression with common ratio r such that $-1 < r < 1$, the ith term is ar^{i-1}. So the sum to infinity is $\sum_{i=1}^{\infty} ar^{i-1}$.

$$\text{If} -1 < r < 1, \ \sum_{i=1}^{\infty} ar^{i-1} = \lim_{n \to \infty} \sum_{i=1}^{n} ar^{i-1} = \frac{a}{1-r}.$$

Example 6.4.1

The ith term of a geometric progression is $\left(\frac{1}{4}\right)^i$. Find the first term, the common ratio and $\sum_{i=1}^{\infty} \left(\frac{1}{4}\right)^i$.

The series begins

$$\left(\tfrac{1}{4}\right)^1 + \left(\tfrac{1}{4}\right)^2 + \left(\tfrac{1}{4}\right)^3 + \ldots = \tfrac{1}{4} + \tfrac{1}{16} + \tfrac{1}{64} + \ldots \ .$$

The first term is $\frac{1}{4}$, and the common ratio is $\frac{1}{16} \div \frac{1}{4} = \frac{1}{4}$.

Using the formula $\sum_{i=1}^{\infty} ar^{i-1} = \frac{a}{1-r}$ with $a = \frac{1}{4}$ and $r = \frac{1}{4}$,

$$\sum_{i=1}^{\infty} \left(\tfrac{1}{4}\right)^i = \frac{\frac{1}{4}}{1 - \frac{1}{4}} = \tfrac{1}{3}.$$

Exercise 6C

1 Find the sum to infinity of the following geometric series. Give your answers to parts (a) to (j) as whole numbers, fractions or exact decimals.

(a) $1 + \frac{1}{2} + \frac{1}{4} + \dots$

(b) $1 + \frac{1}{3} + \frac{1}{9} + \dots$

(c) $\frac{1}{5} + \frac{1}{25} + \frac{1}{125} + \dots$

(d) $0.1 + 0.01 + 0.001 + \dots$

(e) $1 - \frac{1}{3} + \frac{1}{9} - \dots$

(f) $0.2 - 0.04 + 0.008 - \dots$

(g) $\frac{3}{2} + \frac{3}{4} + \frac{3}{8} + \dots$

(h) $\frac{1}{2} - \frac{1}{4} + \frac{1}{8} - \dots$

(i) $10 - 5 + 2.5 - \dots$

(j) $50 + 10 + 2 + \dots$

(k) $x + x^2 + x^3 + \dots$, where $-1 < x < 1$

(l) $1 - x^2 + x^4 - \dots$, where $x^2 < 1$

(m) $1 + x^{-1} + x^{-2} + \dots$, where $x > 1$

(n) $x^2 - x + 1 - \dots$, where $x > 1$

2 Express each of the following recurring decimals as exact fractions.

(a) $0.363\,636\dots$

(b) $0.123\,123\,123\dots$

(c) $0.555\dots$

(d) $0.471\,471\,471\dots$

(e) $0.142\,857\,142\,857\,142\,857\dots$

(f) $0.285\,714\,285\,714\,285\,714\dots$

(g) $0.714\,285\,714\,285\,714\,285\dots$

(h) $0.857\,142\,857\,142\,857\,142\dots$

3 Find the common ratio of a geometric series which has a first term of 5 and a sum to infinity of 6.

4 Find the common ratio of a geometric series which has a first term of 11 and a sum to infinity of 6.

5 Find the first term of a geometric series which has a common ratio of $\frac{3}{4}$ and a sum to infinity of 12.

6 Find the first term of a geometric series which has a common ratio of $-\frac{3}{5}$ and a sum to infinity of 12.

7 Identify the general term u_i for the following geometric progressions. Also find $\sum_{i=1}^{10} u_i$ and, if the series is convergent, $\sum_{i=1}^{\infty} u_i$.

(a) $1 + \frac{1}{5} + \frac{1}{25} + \frac{1}{125} + \dots$

(b) $2 + 4 + 8 + 16 + \dots$

(c) $4 + 2 + 1 + \frac{1}{2} + \frac{1}{4} + \dots$

(d) $1 - \frac{1}{10} + \frac{1}{100} - \frac{1}{1000} + \dots$

8 In Example 6.3.5 a beetle starts at a point O on the floor. It walks 1 m east, then $\frac{1}{2}$ m west, then $\frac{1}{4}$ m east and so on. It finished $\frac{2}{3}$ m to the east of O. How far did it actually walk?

9 A beetle starts at a point O on the floor and walks 0.6 m east, then 0.36 m west, 0.216 m east and so on. Find its final position and how far it actually walks.

10 A 'supa-ball' is thrown upwards from ground level. It hits the ground after 2 seconds and continues to bounce. The time it is in the air for a particular bounce is always 0.8 of the time for the previous bounce. How long does it take for the ball to stop bouncing?

11 A 'supa-ball' is dropped from a height of 1 metre onto a level table. It always rises to a height equal to 0.9 of the height from which it was dropped. How far does it travel in total until it stops bouncing?

12 A frog sits at one end of a table which is 2 m long. In its first jump the frog goes a distance of 1 m along the table, with its second jump $\frac{1}{2}$ m, with its third jump $\frac{1}{4}$ m and so on.

   (a) What is the frog's final position?

   (b) After how many jumps will the frog be within 1 cm of the far end of the table?

Miscellaneous exercise 6

1 In a geometric progression, the fifth term is 100 and the seventh term is 400. Find the first term.

2 A geometric series has first term a and common ratio $\dfrac{1}{\sqrt{2}}$. Show that the sum to infinity of the series is $a(2 + \sqrt{2})$.

3 The nth term of a sequence is ar^{n-1}, where a and r are constants. The first term is 3 and the second term is $-\frac{3}{4}$. Find the values of a and r.

   Hence find $\displaystyle\sum_{i=1}^{N} ar^{n-1}$ and $\displaystyle\sum_{i=1}^{\infty} ar^{n-1}$.

4 Evaluate, correct to the nearest whole number,

   $$0.99 + 0.99^2 + 0.99^3 + \cdots + 0.99^{99}.$$

5 Find the sum of the infinite series $\dfrac{1}{10^3} + \dfrac{1}{10^6} + \dfrac{1}{10^9} + \ldots$, expressing your answer as a fraction in its lowest terms.

   Hence express the infinite recurring decimal 0.108 108 108... as a fraction in its lowest terms.

6 A geometric series has first term 1 and common ratio r. Given that the sum to infinity of the series is 5, find the value of r.

   Use a calculator to find, by trial, the least value of n for which the sum of the first n terms of the series exceeds 4.9.

7 In a geometric series, the first term is 12 and the fourth term is $-\frac{3}{2}$. Find the sum, S_n, of the first n terms of the series.

   Find the sum to infinity, S_∞, of the series. Find also, by trial, the least value of n for which the magnitude of the difference between S_n and S_∞ is less than 0.001.

8 A geometric series has non-zero first term a and common ratio r, where $0 < r < 1$. Given that $\displaystyle\sum_{i=1}^{8} ar^{n-1} = \frac{1}{2} \sum_{i=1}^{\infty} ar^{n-1}$, find the value of r, correct to 3 decimal places. Given also that the 17th term of the series is 10, find a.

9 A post is being driven into the ground by a mechanical hammer. The distance it is driven by the first blow is 8cm. Subsequently, the distance it is driven by each blow is $\frac{9}{10}$ of the distance it was driven by the previous blow. The post is to be driven a total distance of 70 cm into the ground. Show that at least 20 blows will be needed.

Explain why the post can never be driven a total distance of more than 80 cm into the ground.

10 At the beginning of 1990, an investor decided to invest £6000, believing that the value of the investment should increase, on average, by 6% each year. Show that, if this percentage rate of increase was in fact maintained for 10 years, the value of the investment will be about £10 745.

The investor added a further £6000 at the beginning of each year between 1991 and 1995 inclusive. Assuming that the 6% annual rate of increase continues to apply, show that the total value, in pounds, of the investment at the beginning of the year 2000 may be written as $6000(1.06^5 + 1.06^6 + \cdots + 1.06^{10})$ and evaluate this, correct to the nearest pound.

11 A person wants to borrow £100 000 to buy a house. He intends to pay back a fixed sum of £C at the end of each year, so that after 25 years he has completely paid off the debt. Assuming a steady interest rate of 4% per year, explain why

$$100\,000 = C\left(\frac{1}{1.04} + \frac{1}{1.04^2} + \frac{1}{1.04^3} + \cdots + \frac{1}{1.04^{25}}\right).$$

Calculate the value of C.

12 A person wants to buy a pension which will provide her with an income of £10 000 at the end of each of the next n years. Show that, with a steady interest rate of 5% per year, the pension should cost her

$$£10\,000\left(\frac{1}{1.05} + \frac{1}{1.05^2} + \frac{1}{1.05^3} + \cdots + \frac{1}{1.05^n}\right).$$

Find a simple formula for calculating this sum, and find its value when $n = 10, 20, 30, 40, 50$.

13 The sum of the infinite geometric series $1 + r + r^2 + \ldots$ is k times the sum of the series $1 - r + r^2 - \ldots$, where $k > 0$. Express r in terms of k.

14* A geometric series G has positive first term a, common ratio r and sum to infinity S. The sum to infinity of the even-numbered terms of G (the second, fourth, sixth, ... terms) is $-\frac{1}{2}S$. Find the value of r.

Given that the third term of G is 2, show that the sum to infinity of the odd-numbered terms of G (the first, third, fifth, ... terms) is $\frac{81}{4}$.

15* An infinite geometric series has first term a and sum to infinity b, where $b \neq 0$. Prove that a lies between 0 and $2b$.

16* Find the sum of the geometric series

$$(1 - x) + (x^3 - x^4) + (x^6 - x^7) + \cdots + (x^{3n} - x^{3n+1}).$$

Hence show that the sum of the infinite series $1 - x + x^3 - x^4 + x^6 - x^7 + \ldots$ is equal to $\dfrac{1}{1 + x + x^2}$, and state the values of x for which this is valid.

Use a similar method to find the sum of the infinite series $1 - x + x^5 - x^6 + x^{10} - x^{11} + \ldots$.

17 Find the sums of the infinite geometric series

(a) $\sin^2 x° + \sin^4 x° + \sin^6 x° + \sin^8 x° + \ldots$,

(b) $1 - \tan^2 x° + \tan^4 x° - \tan^6 x° + \tan^8 x° - \ldots$,

giving your answers in as simple a form as possible. For what values of x are your results valid?

18* Use the formula to sum the geometric series $1 + (1 + x) + (1 + x)^2 + \cdots + (1 + x)^6$ when $x \neq 0$. By considering the coefficients of x^2, deduce that

$$\binom{2}{2} + \binom{3}{2} + \binom{4}{2} + \binom{5}{2} + \binom{6}{2} = \binom{7}{3}.$$

Illustrate this result on a Pascal triangle.

Write down and prove a general result about binomial coefficients, of which this is a special case.

19* Make tables of values of $1 + x$, $1 + x + x^2$, $1 + x + x^2 + x^3$, $1 + x + x^2 + x^3 + x^4$ and $\dfrac{1}{1 - x}$ and use them to draw graphs of these functions of x for $-1.5 \leqslant x \leqslant 1.5$.

What do your graphs suggest about the possibility of using the polynomial

$1 + x + x^2 + x^3 + \cdots + x^n$ as an approximation to the function $\dfrac{1}{1 - x}$?

7 Exponentials and logarithms

In this chapter a new type of function is introduced which has many important applications. When you have completed it, you should

- know what is meant by an exponential function, and be familiar with the shape of exponential graphs
- know what is meant by a logarithm, and be able to switch between the exponential and the logarithmic form of an equation
- know the rules for logarithms, and how they can be proved from the rules for indices
- understand the idea of a logarithmic scale
- be able to solve equations and inequalities in which the unknown appears as an index.

7.1 Exponential functions

What are the next two numbers in the sequence which begins

$$1 \quad 1.2 \quad 1.44 \quad 1.728 \quad \ldots?$$

This looks like a geometric sequence, with first term 1 and common ratio 1.2. With this interpretation, the next two numbers would be $1.728 \times 1.2 = 2.0736$ and $2.0736 \times 1.2 = 2.488\,32$.

You could also write the sequence as

$$1.2^0 \quad 1.2^1 \quad 1.2^2 \quad 1.2^3 \quad \ldots$$

This suggests thinking of the sequence as a function

$$f(x) = 1.2^x$$

which is defined for values of x which are positive integers or zero. Its graph is shown in Fig. 7.1. It consists of a lot of isolated points, one for each positive integer and one for zero.

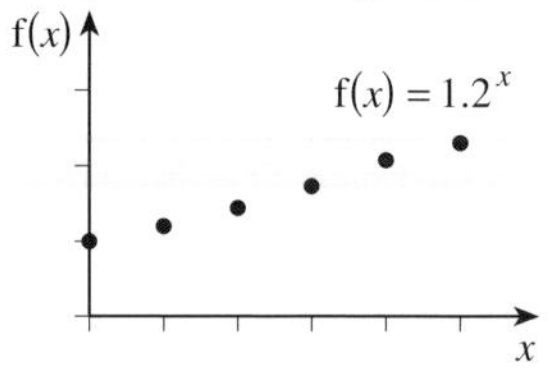

Fig. 7.1

But regarding 1.2^x as a function, there is no need to restrict x to being either an integer or positive. You know how to find 1.2^x for many other values of x. For example,

$$1.2^{\frac{1}{2}} = \sqrt{1.2} = 1.095\ldots, \qquad 1.2^{-1} = \frac{1}{1.2} = 0.833\ldots,$$

$$1.2^{0.8} = 1.2^{\frac{4}{5}} = \sqrt[5]{1.2^4} = 1.157\ldots, \qquad 1.2^{-3.5} = \frac{1}{1.2^{3.5}} = \frac{1}{1.2^3 \times \sqrt{1.2}} = 0.528\ldots, \text{ etc.}$$

In fact, the extension of index notation in C1 Chapter 7 provides a definition of 1.2^x where x is any rational number, positive or negative. If you fill in all these additional values you get the graph in Fig. 7.2.

The only values of x for which 1.2^x doesn't yet have a meaning are the irrational numbers, like π or $\sqrt{2}$. So far you don't have a definition for powers such as 1.2^π or $1.2^{\sqrt{2}}$. This means that the graph in Fig. 7.2 has gaps in it, though you can't see them! In fact you will find in C3 a way of defining expressions like b^x when x is any real number, which behave in just the same way as when x is rational. For the time being you can assume that this is true.

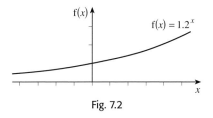

Fig. 7.2

The function 1.2^x is an example of an 'exponential function'. The reason for this name is that the variable x appears as an index, and 'exponent' is an alternative word for the index in an expression like b^x.

> An **exponential function** is a function of the form $f(x) = b^x$, where b is a positive real number and $b \neq 1$. The number b is called the **base**.

Notice the restrictions on the value of b in this definition. Negative numbers are excluded because, if $b < 0$, b^x has no meaning for some values of x; for example, $b^{\frac{1}{2}} = \sqrt{b}$ does not exist if $b < 0$. Zero is excluded for a similar reason; for example $b^{-1} = \dfrac{1}{b}$, and $\dfrac{1}{0}$ does not exist. The number 1 is also excluded, but for a different reason; since $1^x = 1$ for every value of x, the function 1^x is simply the constant number 1.

> Before reading on, use a graphic calculator to display some exponential functions with different bases. Choose an interval with both negative and positive values of x. Use some values of b greater than 1, and some between 0 and 1.

Fig. 7.3 shows the graphs of some typical exponential functions for different values of b. From these you will notice that they have a number of properties in common.

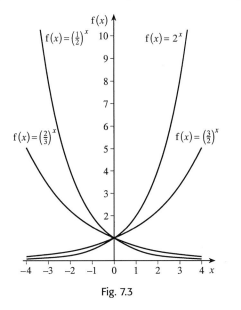

Fig. 7.3

- The point $(0, 1)$ lies on all the graphs, because $b^0 = 1$ for all positive numbers b.
- The graph of $y = b^x$ lies entirely above the x-axis.
- If $b > 1$ the graph of $y = b^x$ has positive gradient, so the function is increasing. If $0 < b < 1$ the graph has negative gradient, so the function is decreasing.
- The graph of $y = b^x$ bends upwards both for $b > 1$ and for $0 < b < 1$.
- If $b > 1$ the graph approaches the x-axis when x is negative and numerically large; with the notation introduced in Section 5.8, $b^x \to 0$ as $x \to -\infty$. If $0 < b < 1$, $b^x \to 0$ as $x \to +\infty$.
- The graph of $y = \left(\dfrac{1}{b}\right)^x$ is the reflection in the y-axis of the graph of $y = b^x$.

To prove the last statement, use the result in C1 Section 10.3 that replacing x by $-x$ in the equation of a graph produces a reflection in the y-axis. So the reflection in the y-axis of $y = b^x$ is $y = b^{-x}$. But, using the rules of indices in C1 Chapter 7,

$$b^{-x} = \frac{1}{b^x} = \left(\frac{1}{b}\right)^x.$$

So the reflection in the y-axis of $y = b^x$ is $y = \left(\dfrac{1}{b}\right)^x$.

The methods of transforming graphs in C1 Chapter 10 can be used to find other properties of exponential functions and their graphs. Some examples are suggested in Exercise 7A.

Exercise 7A

1　If $2^{-x} < 10^{-3}$, what can you say about 2^x?
　　Find the smallest integer x such that 2^{-x} is less than
　　(a) 10^{-3}, 　　　(b) 10^{-6}, 　　　(c) 10^{-12}.

2　If $3^x < 0.0005$, what can you say about 3^{-x}?

　　Find the largest integer x such that 3^x is less than
　　(a) 0.0005, 　　　(b) 2.5×10^{-7}, 　　(c) 10^{-7}.

3　(a) Use a graphic calculator to display, with the same axes, the graphs of $y = 1.1^x$ and $y = 1.21^x$.
　　(b) Show that $1.1^x \equiv 1.21^{\frac{1}{2}x}$. What does this tell you about the graphs in part (a)?

4　(a) Use a graphic calculator to display, with the same axes, the graphs of $y = 1.25^x$ and $y = 0.8^x$.
　　(b) Show that $1.25^x \equiv 0.8^{-x}$. What does this tell you about the graphs in part (a)?

5　Describe the transformation of the graph of $y = 2^x$ which will produce the graph of
　　(a) $y = 2^{x-3}$, 　　(b) $y = 2^{-x}$, 　　(c) $y = \left(\frac{1}{4}\right)^x$, 　　(d) $y = 2^x + 4$.

6　The graph of $y = 2^x$ is translated by 1 in the x-direction. What other transformation applied to the graph of $y = 2^x$ would produce the same effect?

7　The graph of $y = 3^x$ is translated by -2 in the x-direction. What other transformation applied to the graph of $y = 3^x$ would have the same effect?

8 What is the relation between the graphs of $y = a^x$ and $y = b^x$

    (a) if $b = a^2$,   (b) if $b = a^3$,   (c) if $b = \dfrac{1}{a}$?

9 (a) Explain why 3.141 59 and 3.1416 are rational numbers.

    (b) Use a calculator to find $1.2^{3.141\,59}$ and $1.2^{3.1416}$.

    (c) Given that π is between 3.141 59 and 3.1416, what does the answer to (b) suggest about the value of 1.2^{π}?

7.2 Logarithms

You have seen that, if $b > 1$, then $y = b^x$ increases over all values of x; if $0 < b < 1$ it decreases. This means that in either case, if y is any positive number, there can only be one number x such that $b^x = y$. This number is called the **logarithm to base b** of y. It is written $x = \log_b y$.

> If x is a real number and y is a positive real number, the statements
>
> $$b^x = y \quad \text{and} \quad x = \log_b y$$
>
> are equivalent.

In words, you can say that

    $\log_b y$ is the power to which b must be raised to give y.

Example 7.2.1

Find (a) $\log_3 81$,   (b) $\log_{81} 3$,   (c) $\log_3 \left(\dfrac{1}{81} \right)$,   (d) $\log_{\frac{1}{3}} 81$.

    (a) Since $81 = 3^4$, $\log_3 81 = 4$. The power to which 3 must be raised to give 81 is 4.

    (b) $3 = 81^{\frac{1}{4}}$, so $\log_{81} 3 = \frac{1}{4}$.

    (c) $\frac{1}{81} = 3^{-4}$, so $\log_3 \left(\dfrac{1}{81} \right) = -4$.

    (d) $81 = \dfrac{1}{\left(\frac{1}{3} \right)^4} = \left(\frac{1}{3} \right)^{-4}$, so $\log_{\frac{1}{3}} 81 = -4$.

It is important to notice that the logarithm exists only if y is positive, because (for any base b) the graph of $y = b^x$ lies entirely above the x-axis.

Some important results about logarithms follow from what you already know about indices. Here are some examples.

    Putting $x = 0$, since $b^0 = 1$, it follows that $0 = \log_b 1$.

    Putting $x = 1$ gives $b^1 = b$, so that $1 = \log_b b$.

    Putting $x = 2$ gives $b^2 = y$, so that $2 = \log_b b^2$.

More generally,

putting $x = n$ gives $b^n = y$, so that $n = \log_b b^n$.

For any base b,
$$\log_b 1 = 0, \quad \log_b b = 1 \quad \text{and} \quad \log_b b^n = n.$$

The result $\log_b b^n = n$ is not restricted to integer values of n; it is true when n is any real number. If in the box at the beginning of this section you substitute b^x for y in the second statement you get

$$x = \log_b b^x.$$

And if you substitute $\log_b y$ for x in the first statement you get

$$b^{\log_b y} = y.$$

Since these statements are true for any number x and for any positive number y they are in fact identities. What they say, in effect, is that the processes of 'raising to a power' and 'taking logarithms' cancel each other out. If you carry out one after the other, in either order, you get back to where you started.

For any base b,
$$\log_b b^x \equiv x \quad \text{and} \quad b^{\log_b y} \equiv y.$$

Try this with a calculator. The key labelled [log] calculates the logarithm to base 10. Choose a number, x, calculate 10^x, then press [log]. Or choose a number, y, press [log] and put the answer, x, in the memory; then calculate 10^x.

Exercise 7B

1 Write each of the following in the form $y = b^x$.

(a) $\log_2 8 = 3$ (b) $\log_3 81 = 4$ (c) $\log_5 0.04 = -2$

(d) $\log_7 x = 4$ (e) $\log_x 5 = t$ (f) $\log_p q = r$

2 Write each of the following in the form $x = \log_b y$.

(a) $2^3 = 8$ (b) $3^6 = 729$ (c) $4^{-3} = \frac{1}{64}$

(d) $a^8 = 20$ (e) $h^9 = g$ (f) $m^n = p$

3 Evaluate the following.

(a) $\log_2 16$ (b) $\log_4 16$ (c) $\log_7 \frac{1}{49}$

(d) $\log_4 1$ (e) $\log_5 5$ (f) $\log_{27} \frac{1}{3}$

(g) $\log_{16} 8$ (h) $\log_2 2\sqrt{2}$ (i) $\log_{\sqrt{2}} 8\sqrt{2}$

4 Find the value of y in each of the following.

(a) $\log_y 49 = 2$ (b) $\log_4 y = -3$ (c) $\log_3 81 = y$

(d) $\log_{10} y = -1$ (e) $\log_2 y = 2.5$ (f) $\log_y 1296 = 4$

(g) $\log_{\frac{1}{2}} y = 8$ (h) $\log_{\frac{1}{2}} 1024 = y$ (i) $\log_y 27 = -6$

5 If a is a positive number, express the following in their simplest form.

(a) $\log_a a^5$ (b) $\log_a \sqrt{a}$ (c) $\log_{\sqrt{a}} a$

(d) $\log_{a^3} a - \log_a \sqrt[3]{a}$ (e) $\log_{\sqrt{a}} a^4$ (f) $\log_a a^8 \div \log_a a^2$

7.3 Properties of logarithms

It was shown in C1 Section 7.1 that expressions involving indices can be simplified by applying a number of rules, such as the multiplication and division rules and the power-on-power rule. There are corresponding rules for logarithms.

The multiplication rule for indices states that $b^r \times b^s = b^{r+s}$. Using f(x) to denote the function b^x, this could be written as

$$\mathrm{f}(r) \times \mathrm{f}(s) = \mathrm{f}(r + s).$$

So this rule equates the *product* of values of the function for two values of x to the value of the function for their *sum*.

Logarithms do the opposite. The rule for logarithms equates the *sum* of values of the function $\log_b x$ for two values of x to the value of the function for their *product*. That is,

$$\log_b p + \log_b q = \log_b (p \times q).$$

This is the multiplication rule for logarithms. There is also a division rule and a power rule.

> Since these rules are true for logarithms to any base, the simpler symbol log will be written in place of $\log_b$ in this section where there is no ambiguity.

> For any positive real numbers p and q, any real number x, and logarithms to any base:
>
> The multiplication rule $\log(pq) = \log p + \log q$
>
> The division rule $\log\left(\dfrac{p}{q}\right) = \log p - \log q$
>
> The power rule $\log(p^x) = x \log p$

Example 7.3.1

If $\log 2 = r$ and $\log 3 = s$, express in terms of r and s
(a) $\log 16$,   (b) $\log 18$,   (c) $\log 13.5$.

(a) $\log 16 = \log 2^4 = 4 \log 2 = 4r$.

(b) $\log 18 = \log(2 \times 3^2) = \log 2 + \log 3^2 = \log 2 + 2 \log 3 = r + 2s$.

(c) $\log 13.5 = \log \dfrac{3^3}{2} = \log 3^3 - \log 2 = 3 \log 3 - \log 2 = 3s - r$.

Example 7.3.2

Find   (a) $\log_{10} 50 + \log_{10} 8000 - 2 \log_{10} 20$,   (b) $\log_{10} \sqrt{10}$.

(a) Use the power rule, then the multiplication and division rules.

$$2 \log_{10} 20 = \log_{10} 20^2 = \log_{10} 400,$$

so

$$\log_{10} 50 + \log_{10} 8000 - 2 \log_{10} 20 = \log_{10} 50 + \log_{10} 8000 - \log_{10} 400$$
$$= \log_{10} \left(\frac{50 \times 8000}{400} \right)$$
$$= \log_{10} 1000$$
$$= 3,$$

since $10^3 = 1000$.

(b) $\sqrt{10} = 10^{\frac{1}{2}}$,   so $\log_{10} \sqrt{10} = \frac{1}{2}$.

Example 7.3.3

Express $\log \left(\dfrac{p^3 q}{r^2} \right)$ in terms of $\log p$, $\log q$ and $\log r$.

$$\log \left(\frac{p^3 q}{r^2} \right) = \log(p^3) + \log q - \log(r^2)$$
$$= 3 \log p + \log q - 2 \log r.$$

Example 7.3.4

Express as a single logarithm   (a) $2 \log x - 3 \log y$,   (b) $\frac{1}{3} \log 64$.

(a) $2 \log x - 3 \log y = \log(x^2) - \log(y^3) = \log \left(\dfrac{x^2}{y^3} \right)$.

(b) $\frac{1}{3} \log 64 = \log 64^{\frac{1}{3}} = \log \sqrt[3]{64} = \log 4$.

A useful special case of the power rule is when x is a fraction $\dfrac{1}{n}$ where n is a positive integer.

Then $p^x = p^{\frac{1}{n}} = \sqrt[n]{p}$, so you get:

> **The *n*th root rule** $\log \sqrt[n]{p} = \dfrac{\log p}{n}$

Historically logarithms were important because for many years, before calculators and computers were available, they provided the most useful form of calculating aid. With a table of logarithms students would, for example, find the cube root of 100 by looking up the value of $\log 100$ and dividing it by 3. By the *n*th root rule, this gave $\log \sqrt[3]{100}$, and the cube root could then be obtained by using the logarithm table in reverse or from a table of the function 10^x.

You could simulate this process on your calculator by keying in $[100, \log, \div, 3, =, 10^x]$, giving successive displays 100, 2, 0.666 666 6... and the answer 4.641 588 83... . But of course you don't need to do this, since your calculator has a special key for working out roots directly.

The rules for logarithms can be proved directly from the definition of a logarithm and the rules for indices.

The multiplication and division rules

Denote $\log_b p$ by r and $\log_b q$ by s. Then, in exponential form, $p = b^r$ and $q = b^s$. So, using the multiplication and division rules for indices,

$$pq = b^r \times b^s = b^{r+s} \quad \text{and} \quad \frac{p}{q} = \frac{b^r}{b^s} = b^{r-s}.$$

Putting these back into logarithmic form gives

$$\log_b(pq) = r + s, \quad \text{which is} \quad \log_b p + \log_b q$$

and $\quad \log_b\left(\dfrac{p}{q}\right) = r - s, \quad \text{which is} \quad \log_b p - \log_b q.$

The power rule

Denote $\log_b p$ by r. Then $p = b^r$. So, using the power-on-power rule for indices,

$$p^x = (b^r)^x = b^{rx} = b^{xr}.$$

Putting this back into logarithmic form gives

$$\log_b(p^x) = xr, \text{ which is } x \log_b p.$$

7.4   Special bases

Although the base of a logarithm can be any real positive number except 1, only two bases are in common use. One is a number denoted by e, for which the logarithm has a number of special properties; these are explored in C3. Logarithms to base e are denoted by 'ln', and can be found using the [ln] key on your calculator.

The other base is 10, which is important because our system of writing numbers is based on powers of 10. On your calculator the key labelled [log] gives logarithms to base 10.

When logarithms were used to do calculations, students used tables which gave $\log_{10} x$ only for values of x between 1 and 10. So to find $\log 3456$, they would use the rules in Section 7.3 to write

$$\log 3456 = \log(3.456 \times 10^3) = \log 3.456 + \log 10^3 = \log 3.456 + 3.$$

The tables gave $\log 3.456$ as 0.5386 (correct to 4 decimal places), so $\log 3456$ is 3.5386. Notice that the number 3 before the decimal point is the same as the index when 3456 is written in standard form.

Logarithms to base 10 are sometimes useful in constructing logarithmic scales. As an example, suppose that you want to make a diagram to show the populations of countries which belong to the United Nations. In 1999 the largest of these was China, with about 1.2 billion people, and the smallest was San Marino, with 25 000. If you represented the population of China by a line of length 12 cm, then Nigeria would have length 1.1 cm, Malaysia just over 2 mm, and the line for San Marino would be only 0.0025 mm long!

Fig. 7.4 is an alternative way of showing the data.

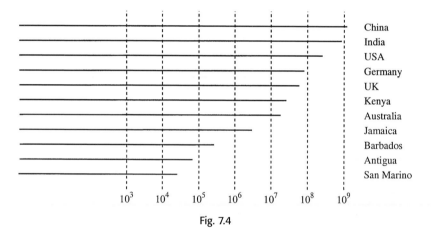

Fig. 7.4

Fig. 7.4 uses a logarithmic scale, in which a country with population P is shown by a line of length $\log P$ cm. China now has a length of just over 9 cm, and San Marino a length of between 4 and 5 cm. You have to understand the diagram in a different way; an extra centimetre in length implies a population 10 times as large, rather than 100 million larger. But the countries are still placed in the correct order, and the population of any country can be found as 10^x where x is the length of its line in centimetres.

Exercise 7C

1 Write each of the following in terms of $\log p$, $\log q$ and $\log r$. In parts (c), (h) and (i) the logarithms are to base 10; p, q and r are positive numbers.

(a) $\log pqr$

(b) $\log pq^2r^3$

(c) $\log 100pr^5$

(d) $\log\sqrt{\dfrac{p}{q^2r}}$

(e) $\log\dfrac{pq}{r^2}$

(f) $\log\dfrac{1}{pqr}$

(g) $\log\dfrac{p}{\sqrt{r}}$

(h) $\log\dfrac{qr^7p}{10}$

(i) $\log\sqrt{\dfrac{10p^{10}r}{q}}$

2 Express as a single logarithm, simplifying where possible. (All the logarithms have base 10, so, for example, an answer of $\log 100$ simplifies to 2.)

  (a) $2 \log 5 + \log 4$ (b) $2 \log 2 + \log 150 - \log 6000$

  (c) $3 \log 5 + 5 \log 3$ (d) $2 \log 4 - 4 \log 2$

  (e) $\log 24 - \frac{1}{2} \log 9 + \log 125$ (f) $3 \log 2 + 3 \log 5 - \log 10^6$

  (g) $\frac{1}{2} \log 16 + \frac{1}{3} \log 8$ (h) $\log 64 - 2 \log 4 + 5 \log 2 - \log 2^7$

3 If $\log 3 = p$, $\log 5 = q$ and $\log 10 = r$, express the following in terms of p, q and r. (All the logarithms have the same unspecified base.)

  (a) $\log 2$ (b) $\log 45$ (c) $\log \sqrt{90}$

  (d) $\log 0.2$ (e) $\log 750$ (f) $\log 60$

  (g) $\log \frac{1}{6}$ (h) $\log 4.05$ (i) $\log 0.15$

4 Show that the rule $\log_b b^x = x$ in Section 7.2 is a special case of the power rule $\log_b(p^x) = x \log_b p$.

5 Suppose that $\log_b c = r$ and $\log_c b = s$. Write these equations in their equivalent exponential forms, and use the rules for indices to show that $rs = 1$. Write this result as an identity connecting $\log_b c$ and $\log_c b$.

6* The acidity of a substance is measured by a quantity called pH. This is defined as the value of $-\log_{10} a_{H+}$, where a_{H+} is the hydrogen ion activity in the substance. The values of pH for a cola drink and for beer are approximately 2 and 5 respectively. What does this mean in terms of the relative levels of hydrogen ion activity in the two drinks?

7* The intensity of sound in decibels is equal to $10 \log_{10} \dfrac{P^2}{P_R^2}$, where P is the amplitude of the sound pressure wave and P_R is a reference pressure of 0.0002 microbars, which is chosen as the pressure of an undetectable sound. Write this formula in a simpler form.

  (a) An airport imposes a restriction of 110 decibels on aircraft taking off. To what pressure does this correspond?

  (b) A man and a woman are talking on the radio. The pressure on the listener's ear of the man's voice is double that of the woman's. What is the relationship between the sound intensity of their voices?

  (c) A new design of silencer reduces the noise of an engine by 10 decibels. What effect does this have on the amplitude of the sound pressure waves?

8* Earthquakes are recorded on a seismograph, which records surface waves whose amplitudes depend on the strength of the earthquake. The magnitude of an earthquake on the Richter scale is given by the formula $\log_{10}(k \times$ amplitude of the surface wave), where k is a constant.

  (a) Two earthquakes produce surface waves in the ratio 3:1. How do their magnitudes on the Richter scale compare?

  (b) Two earthquakes have magnitudes 6.9 and 7.5 on the Richter scale. How do the amplitudes of the recorded surface waves compare?

7.5   Equations and inequalities

You know that $\log_2 2 = 1$ and $\log_2 4 = 2$, but how can you find $\log_2 3$?

Suppose that $\log_2 3 = x$. Then from the definition,

$$2^x = 3.$$

So the problem is to solve an equation where the unknown appears in the index.

The trick is to use logarithms and to write the equation as

$$\log 2^x = \log 3.$$

This is often described as 'taking logarithms of both sides of the equation'. You can now use the power rule to write this as

$$x \log 2 = \log 3.$$

In this equation you can use logarithms to any base you like. In this section base 10 will be used. The log key on the calculator gives $\log 2 = 0.301...$ and $\log 3 = 0.477...$. So

$$x \times 0.301... = 0.477...,$$

which gives $x = \log_2 3 = \dfrac{0.477...}{0.301...} = 1.58$, correct to 3 significant figures.

This type of equation arises in various applications.

Example 7.5.1
In an area of heathland the number of rabbits increases by a factor of 2.5 every year. How many years will it take for the number of rabbits to be multiplied by 100?

After t years the number of rabbits will have been multiplied by 2.5^t. So the solution to the problem is given by the equation

$$2.5^t = 100.$$

Taking logarithms to base 10 of both sides of the equation,

$$\log 2.5^t = \log 100,$$

so $t \log 2.5 = \log 100,$

$$t = \frac{\log 100}{\log 2.5} = \frac{2}{0.3979...} = 5.025....$$

Assuming that the population increases continuously throughout the year, the number of rabbits will have multiplied by 100 after just over 5 years.

Example 7.5.2
Solve the equation $5^{3x-1} = 8$.

There is a choice of method. You can either take logarithms straight away, or begin by using the laws of indices to put the equation into the form $b^x = c$, which you know how to solve.

Method 1 Taking logarithms (to base 10) of both sides of the equation,

$$\log\left(5^{3x-1}\right) = \log 8.$$

Applying the power rule to the left side,

$$(3x - 1)\log 5 = \log 8$$

so

$$3x - 1 = \frac{\log 8}{\log 5} = \frac{0.903...}{0.698...} = 1.292...$$
$$3x = 1 + 1.292... = 2.292...$$
$$x = 2.292... \div 3 = 0.764, \text{ correct to 3 significant figures.}$$

If you use this method, you should keep as many figures at each stage as the calculator allows, only approximating to 3 significant figures at the end. In fact, you could if you prefer set out the solution as

$$3x = 1 + \frac{\log 8}{\log 5}$$
$$x = \left(1 + \frac{\log 8}{\log 5}\right) \div 3$$

and save all the calculation until the end.

Method 2 Begin by using the division and power-on-power laws for indices to give

$$5^{3x-1} = 5^{3x} \div 5^1 = (5^3)^x \div 5 = 125^x \div 5.$$

The equation can then be written as

$$125^x \div 5 = 8$$
$$125^x = 5 \times 8 = 40.$$

You have already met equations of this type. Taking logarithms (to base 10) of both sides and using the power law for logarithms,

$$x \log 125 = \log 40$$

so $$x = \frac{\log 40}{\log 125} = \frac{1.602...}{2.096...} = 0.764, \text{ correct to 3 significant figures.}$$

Some applications lead to the expression of the problem as an inequality rather than an equation. So instead of an argument of the form

$$p^x = c \quad \text{so} \quad \log p^x = \log c$$

you have

$$p^x > c \quad \text{so} \quad \log p^x > \log c \text{ (or similarly with } < \text{ in place of } >\text{)}.$$

For this to be valid it is necessary for the logarithm to be an increasing function: that is, for larger numbers to have larger logarithms. Is this true?

To answer this question, go back to the definition of a logarithm at the beginning of Section 7.2. This began with a positive number y, and it was stated that there is just one number x such that $b^x = y$. That number is called $\log_b y$. This is illustrated using the graph of $y = b^x$ in Fig. 7.5; the x-coordinate corresponding to each value of y is $\log_b y$. You can see that, as y gets larger the point P on the graph moves upwards and to the right, so $\log_b y$ also gets larger.

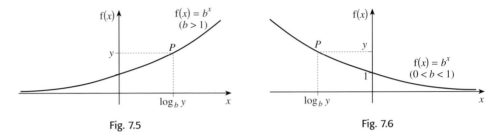

Fig. 7.5   Fig. 7.6

But this happens only because b is greater than 1. If $0 < b < 1$, you get a graph like Fig. 7.6. Now, as y gets larger, the point P moves upwards and to the left, so $\log_b y$ gets smaller.

What this implies for solving inequalities is that, if you take logarithms of both sides, then the inequality sign keeps the same direction provided that $b > 1$; but if $0 < b < 1$ you must reverse the direction of the inequality sign.

In practice, of course, nobody ever takes logarithms to a base less than 1. Both e and 10 are greater than 1. But it is still important to understand the theory on which the process is based.

> For logarithms to base $b > 1$, if $p > q$, then $\log p > \log q$.

Example 7.5.3
Iodine-131 is a radioactive isotope used in treatment of the thyroid gland. It decays so that, after t days, 1 unit of the isotope is reduced to 0.9174^t units. How many days does it take for the amount to fall to less than 0.1 units?

This requires solution of the inequality $0.9174^t < 0.1$. Since log is an increasing function, taking logarithms to base 10 gives

$$\log 0.9174^t < \log 0.1,$$

so $t \log 0.9174 < \log 0.1$.

Now beware! The value of $\log 0.9174$ is negative, so when you divide both sides by $\log 0.9174$ you must change the direction of the inequality:

$$t > \frac{\log 0.1}{\log 0.9174} = \frac{-1}{-0.0374\ldots} = 26.708\ldots\,.$$

The amount of iodine-131 will fall to less than 0.1 units after about 26.7 days.

Example 7.5.4

How many terms of the geometric series $1 + 1.01 + 1.01^2 + 1.01^3 + \dots$ must be taken to give a sum greater than 1 million?

The sum of n terms of the series is given by the formula (see Section 6.2)

$$\frac{1 - 1.01^n}{1 - 1.01} = \frac{1 - 1.01^n}{-0.01} = 100(1.01^n - 1).$$

The problem is to find the smallest value of n for which

$$100(1.01^n - 1) > 1\,000\,000,$$

which gives

$$1.01^n > 10\,001.$$

Taking logarithms to base 10 of both sides,

$$\log 1.01^n > \log 10\,001,$$

so

$$n \log 1.01 > \log 10\,001.$$

Since $\log 1.01$ is positive,

$$n > \frac{\log 10\,001}{\log 1.01} = \frac{4.000\dots}{0.004\,32\dots} = 925.6\dots\,.$$

The smallest integer n satisfying this inequality is 926.

Exercise 7D

1 Solve the following equations, giving those answers which are inexact correct to 3 significant figures.

(a) $3^x = 5$ (b) $7^x = 21$ (c) $6^{2x} = 60$

(d) $5^{2x-1} = 10$ (e) $4^{\frac{1}{2}x} = 12$ (f) $2^{x+1} = 3^x$

(g) $\left(\frac{1}{2}\right)^{3x+2} = 25$ (h) $2^x \times 2^{x+1} = 128$ (i) $\left(\frac{1}{4}\right)^{2x-1} = 7$

2 Solve the following inequalities, giving your answers correct to 3 significant figures.

(a) $3^x > 8$ (b) $5^x < 10$ (c) $7^{2x+5} \leqslant 24$

(d) $0.5^x < 0.001$ (e) $0.4^x < 0.0004$ (f) $0.2^x > 25$

(g) $4^x \times 4^{3-2x} \leqslant 1024$ (h) $0.8^{2x+5} \geqslant 4$ (i) $0.8^{1-3x} \geqslant 10$

3 Find the number of terms in the following geometric series. In parts (c) to (f) the last terms are not exact, but are correct to the number of significant figures given.

(a) $1 + 2 + 4 + \dots + 67\,108\,864$ (b) $4 + 12 + 36 + \dots + 57\,395\,628$

(c) $2 + 3 + 4.5 + \dots + 383\,502$ (d) $1 + 0.8 + 0.64 + \dots + 0.035\,18$

(e) $4 + 3 + 2.25 + \dots + 0.022\,55$ (f) $100 + 99 + 98.01 + \dots + 36.97$

4 Find which term in the following geometric sequences is the first one greater than the number stated. Calculate the value of this term, in standard form correct to 4 significant figures.

(a) $1, 1.1, 1.21, \ldots$; greater than 1000   (b) $2, 2.4, 2.88, \ldots$; greater than 10^{12}

(c) $4, 5, 6.25, \ldots$; greater than 5000   (d) $5, 7, 9.8, \ldots$; greater than 10^7

5 Find which term in the following geometric sequences is the first one less than the number stated. Calculate the value of this term, in standard form correct to 4 significant figures.

(a) $1, 0.9, 0.81, \ldots$; less than 10^{-3} (b) $5, 4, 3.2, \ldots$; less than 10^{-6}

(c) $0.4, 0.3, 0.225, \ldots$; less than 10^{-4}

6 How many terms of the geometric series $1 + 2 + 4 + 8 + \ldots$ must be taken for the sum to exceed 10^{11}?

7 How many terms of the geometric series $2 + 6 + 18 + 54 + \ldots$ must be taken for the sum to exceed 3 million?

8 How many terms of the geometric series $1 + \frac{1}{2} + \frac{1}{4} + \frac{1}{8} + \ldots$ must be taken for its sum to differ from 2 by less than 10^{-8}?

9 How many terms of the geometric series $2 + \frac{1}{3} + \frac{1}{18} + \frac{1}{108} + \ldots$ must be taken for its sum to differ from its sum to infinity by less than 10^{-5}?

10 A radioactive isotope decays so that after t days an amount 0.82^t units remains. How many days does it take for the amount to fall to less than 0.15 units?

11 To say that a radioactive isotope has a half-life of 6 days means that 1 unit of isotope is reduced to $\frac{1}{2}$ unit in 6 days. So if the daily decay rate is given by r, then $r^6 = 0.5$.

(a) For this isotope, find r.

(b) How long will it take for the amount to fall to 0.25 units?

(c) How long will it take for the amount to fall to 0.1 units?

12 Finding $\log_3 10$ is equivalent to solving the equation $x = \log_3 10$, which itself is equivalent to solving $3^x = 10$. Find the following logarithms by forming and solving the appropriate equations. Give your answers correct to 3 significant figures.

(a) $\log_4 12$ (b) $\log_7 100$ (c) $\log_8 2.75$

(d) $\log_{\frac{1}{2}} 250$ (e) $\log_3 \pi$ (f) $\log_{\frac{1}{4}} 0.04$

13* If $\log_{0.1} 2 = x$, show that $10^x = \frac{1}{2}$. Hence evaluate $\log_{0.1} 2$. Use a similar method to find $\log_{0.1} 3$, and verify that $\log_{0.1} 3 < \log_{0.1} 2$.

Miscellaneous exercise 7

1 Solve each of the following equations to find x in terms of a where $a > 0$ and $a \neq 100$. The logarithms are to base 10.

(a) $a^x = 10^{2x+1}$

(b) $2\log(2x) = 1 + \log a$ (OCR, adapted)

2 Solve the equation $3^{2x} = 4^{2-x}$, giving your answer to three significant figures.   (OCR)

3 Find y in terms of x for each of the following equations.

   (a) $3^y = 5^x$, expressing your answer in the form $y = cx$ and giving the exact value of the constant c.

   (b) $\ln(x^4) - \ln(x^2 y) + \ln(y^2) = 0$, expressing your answer in the form $y = kx^n$ and giving the values of the constants k and n.

4 Find the root of the equation $10^{2-2x} = 2 \times 10^{-x}$ giving your answer exactly in terms of logarithms.   (OCR, adapted)

5 Given the simultaneous equations

$$2^x = 3^y,$$
$$x + y = 1,$$

   show that $x = \dfrac{\log 3}{\log 6}$.   (OCR, adapted)

6 Express $\log(2\sqrt{10}) - \frac{1}{3}\log 0.8 - \log\left(\frac{10}{3}\right)$ in the form $c + \log d$ where c and d are rational numbers and the logarithms are to base 10.   (OCR, adapted)

7 An athlete plans a training schedule which involves running 20 km in the first week of training; in each subsequent week the distance is to be increased by 10% over the previous week. Write down an expression for the distance to be covered in the nth week according to this schedule, and find in which week the athlete would first cover more than 100 km.

8 Prove that $\log\left(\dfrac{p}{q}\right) + \log\left(\dfrac{q}{r}\right) + \log\left(\dfrac{r}{p}\right) = 0$.

9 If a, b and c are positive numbers in geometric progression, show that $\log a$, $\log b$ and $\log c$ are in arithmetic progression.

10 Express $\log_2(x + 2) - \log_2 x$ as a single logarithm.
   Hence solve the equation $\log_2(x + 2) - \log_2 x = 3$.

11 Solve the inequality $8^x > 10^{30}$.   (OCR)

12 (a) A curve has equation $y = 12 \times 4^x$. Find the value of x for which $y = 20\,000$.

   (b) The graph of $y = 12 \times 4^x$ is translated by one unit parallel to the positive x-axis. Given that the new graph has equation $y = cd^x$, write down the values of c and d.

   (c) The graph of $y = 12 \times 4^x$ is transformed by a stretch of scale factor 2 parallel to the x-axis followed by a stretch of scale factor $\frac{1}{3}$ parallel to the y-axis. Given that the new graph has equation $y = gh^x$, find the values of g and h.   (MEI)

13 Given that $\log_e p = 2600$, find the values of

   (a) $\log_e(pe^{10})$,   (b) $\log_e\left(\dfrac{1}{\sqrt{p}}\right)$.   (OCR, adapted)

14 (a) Solve the equation $\log_e\left(\frac{1}{2}x + 1\right) = 8$, giving your answer in terms of e.

   (b) Solve the equation $e^{\frac{1}{2}x+1} = 8$, giving your answer in terms of $\log_e 2$.   (OCR, adapted)

15* If $\log_r p = q$ and $\log_q r = p$ express p in terms of q and r, and r in terms of p and q. Hence prove that $\log_q p = pq$.

16* If $\log_b a = p$, $\log_c b = q$ and $\log_a c = r$, where a, b and c are positive numbers, express a in terms of b and p, b in terms of c and q, and c in terms of a and r. Deduce that $a^{pqr} = a$, and hence prove that $\log_b a \times \log_c b \times \log_a c = 1$.

8 Factors and remainders

This chapter is about factorising polynomials, and finding the remainder when division does not come out exactly. When you have completed it, you should

- understand and be able to use the factor and remainder theorems
- be able to use the method of equating coefficients
- understand the words 'quotient' and 'remainder' applied to the division of polynomials
- be able to find the quotient and the remainder when a quadratic or a cubic polynomial is divided by a linear polynomial.

8.1 Factorising quadratics

In C1 Section 4.3 you saw how to factorise quadratics. You saw that, when the coefficients get big, it can be quite a difficult and lengthy process.

Fortunately there is another method which is often quicker. It is based on the idea that, if a quadratic p(x) factorises as $(x - t)(x - u)$, where t and u are numbers, then p$(t) = (t - t)(t - u) = 0 \times (t - u) = 0$. So if $x - t$ is a factor of p(x), then p$(t) = 0$. (The letter p instead of f is used for functions in this chapter, since they are all polynomials.)

> Similar working also shows that if $x - u$ is a factor then p$(u) = 0$.

This is also true in reverse. That is, if p(t) is equal to 0, then $x - t$ is a factor of p(x). This is called the **factor theorem for quadratics**.

> Similarly, if p$(u) = 0$, then $x - u$ is a factor of p(x).

Consider the example p$(x) = 6x^2 - 7x - 10$. If this has a factor $x - t$, then t must divide exactly into 10, that is t must be one of ± 1, ± 2, ± 5 or ± 10. So try calculating

$$\text{p}(1) = 6 - 7 - 10 = -11, \ \text{p}(-1) = 6 + 7 - 10 = 3, \ \text{p}(2) = 24 - 14 - 10 = 0, \ldots$$

There is no need to go any further. Since p$(2) = 0$, $x - 2$ is a factor of p(x).

Once you have one factor, it is easy to write down the other, since $6x^2$ must split as $x \times 6x$, and -10 as $(-2) \times 5$. So

$$\text{p}(x) = (x - 2)(6x + 5)$$

and you can easily check that the middle term is $5x - 12x = -7x$.

> ### The **factor theorem for quadratics**
>
> If p$(x) = ax^2 + bx + c$, and if p$(t) = 0$, then $x - t$ is a factor of p(x).

In Exercise 8A Question 5 you will find an outline of a method of proving the statement in the box.

Example 8.1.1
Find the factors of $p(x) = 5x^2 + 11x - 12$.

The constant term -12 has a lot of factors, and you need to try in turn $\pm1, \pm2, \pm3,$ $\pm4, \pm6, \pm12$ until a number t is reached such that $p(t) = 0$. You can check that

$$p(1) = 4, p(-1) = -18, p(2) = 30, p(-2) = -14, p(3) = 66, p(-3) = 0, \ldots$$

The search can now stop. Since $p(-3) = 0$, $x - (-3)$ is a factor of $p(x)$; more simply, $x + 3$ is a factor.

To get the other factor, note that $5x^2 = x \times 5x$ and $-12 = 3 \times (-4)$.
So the other factor is $5x - 4$.

Finally, check the middle term in the product $(x + 3)(5x - 4)$, which is $-4x + 15x = 11x$, as expected.

So the factors of $p(x) = 5x^2 + 11x - 12$ are $(x + 3)(5x - 4)$.

The advantage of this method is that you don't have to juggle with both factors at the same time. The process is carried out in two steps:

> **Factorising a quadratic**
>
> **Step 1**   Use the factor theorem to find one factor.
>
> **Step 2**   Use the factor you have found to identify the second factor.

But all the examples used so far have been special, since they have all had one factor $x - t$ where t is an integer. What happens if none of the possible integer values of t give $p(t) = 0$?

Example 8.1.2
Factorise $6x^2 - 11x - 10$.

Let $p(x) = 6x^2 - 11x - 10$.

If you try evaluating $p(t)$ with $t = \pm1, \pm2, \pm5, \pm10$ you never get 0. This means that there cannot be factors with $6x^2$ split as $x \times 6x$. But it might split as $2x \times 3x$, so one factor might be one of $2x - 1$, $2x + 1$, $2x - 5$ or $2x + 5$. In that case you would get 0 if you put x equal to one of $\pm\frac{1}{2}$ or $\pm\frac{5}{2}$. So work out

$$p\left(\tfrac{1}{2}\right) = \tfrac{6}{4} - \tfrac{11}{2} - 10 = -14, \ p\left(-\tfrac{1}{2}\right) = \tfrac{6}{4} + \tfrac{11}{2} - 10 = -3,$$
$$p\left(\tfrac{5}{2}\right) = \tfrac{150}{4} - \tfrac{55}{2} - 10 = 0, \ldots \text{success!}$$

Since $p\left(\tfrac{5}{2}\right) = 0$, $2x - 5$ is a factor. This means that $6x^2$ splits as $2x \times 3x$, and -10 as $(-5) \times 2$, so the other factor is $3x + 2$.

As a check, multiply out $(2x - 5)(3x + 2)$, and make sure that the middle term is $4x - 15x = -11x$, as required.

Why were $2x - 2$, $2x + 2$, $2x - 10$, $2x + 10$ excluded from the list of possible factors?

The solution of this example is based on an extended version of the factor theorem:

The extended factor theorem for quadratics

If $p(x) = ax^2 + bx + c$, and if $p\left(\dfrac{t}{s}\right) = 0$, then $sx - t$ is a factor of $p(x)$.

Don't try to remember this as a formal statement. All you need to know is that you try possible values of s and t, where s divides exactly into a and t divides exactly into c. Then try $x = \dfrac{t}{s}$ to see if $p\left(\dfrac{t}{s}\right) = 0$. (It is easy to remember to put $x = \dfrac{t}{s}$ because this is the value of x that makes $sx - t$ equal to 0.)

8.2   Equating coefficients

There is another slightly different way of carrying out step 2, finding the second factor. It is not quite so quick for quadratics as the one described in the last section, but it has the advantage that it can be used for factorising polynomials whose degree is higher than 2, such as cubics and quartics. It is best explained by an example.

Example 8.2.1
Verify that one factor of $p(x) = 15x^2 + x - 6$ is $3x + 2$. Find the other factor.

To show that $3x + 2$ is a factor, calculate

$$p\left(-\tfrac{2}{3}\right) = 15 \times \tfrac{4}{9} - \tfrac{2}{3} - 6 = \tfrac{20}{3} - \tfrac{2}{3} - 6 = 0.$$

So, by the extended factor theorem, $3x + 2$ is a factor of $p(x)$.

Suppose that the other factor is $Ax + B$, where A and B are numbers that have to be found. Then

$$15x^2 + x - 6 = (3x + 2)(Ax + B).$$

Multiply out the brackets on the right. This gives

$$\begin{aligned}(3x + 2)(Ax + B) &= 3Ax^2 + 3Bx + 2Ax + 2B \\ &= 3Ax^2 + (3B + 2A)x + 2B.\end{aligned}$$

You want this to be the same as $15x^2 + x - 6$. This will happen if

$$3A = 15, \quad 3B + 2A = 1 \quad \text{and} \quad 2B = -6.$$

These equations are easy to solve. The first gives $A = 5$. Substituting 5 for A in the second equation gives $3B + 10 = 1$, so $B = -3$.

This leaves the third equation spare for use as a check. Since $2 \times (-3) = -6$, these values of A and B satisfy all three equations.

The other factor is therefore $5x - 3$.

To appreciate what is going on, you need to understand that when you write a quadratic in factors, for example

$$15x^2 + x - 6 = (3x + 2)(5x - 3),$$

what you are writing is an identity. That is, it is a statement which is true for all values of x.

You have already met identities in trigonometry, in Chapter 1. A distinction was made there between an equation such as $\cos\theta° + \sin\theta° = 1$, which is true only for certain values of θ (in this case, 0 and 90, $\pm$ any multiple of 360), and an identity such as $\cos^2\theta° + \sin^2\theta° \equiv 1$, which is true for all values of θ.

There is a similar distinction in algebra, between an equation such as $15x^2 + x - 6 = 0$, which is true for only some values of x (in this case $-\frac{2}{3}$ and $\frac{3}{5}$), and an identity such as $15x^2 + x - 6 \equiv (3x + 2)(5x - 3)$, which is true for all values of x.

> Notice the use of the symbol $\equiv$, to show that the statement is an identity rather than an equation.

The central part of the argument in Example 8.2.1 comes at the point where it is deduced from the identity

$$15x^2 + x - 6 \equiv 3Ax^2 + (3B + 2A)x + 2B$$

that the corresponding coefficients on the two sides are equal.

This is a particular example of a general result about quadratics:

> If $ax^2 + bx + c \equiv lx^2 + mx + n$, then $a = l$, $b = m$ and $c = n$.
>
> This is called **equating coefficients**.

You can prove this for yourself. It is Question 6 of Exercise 8A.

Example 8.2.2
For what value of c is $2x - 3$ a factor of $8x^2 + 2x + c$? Find the other factor in this case.

Let $p(x) = 8x^2 + 2x + c$.

Since $2x - 3$ is a factor of $p(x)$, $p\left(\frac{3}{2}\right) = 0$, so

$$8 \times \left(\tfrac{3}{2}\right)^2 + 2 \times \tfrac{3}{2} + c = 0,$$
$$c = -18 - 3 = -21.$$

To find the other factor, write

$$8x^2 + 2x - 21 = (2x - 3)(Ax + B)$$
$$\equiv 2Ax^2 + (2B - 3A)x - 3B.$$

Equating coefficients,

$$2A = 8, \quad 2B - 3A = 2 \quad \text{and} \quad -3B = -21.$$

From the first two equations, $A = 4$ and $2B - 12 = 2$, so $B = 7$. As a check, this satisfies the third equation.

The other factor is therefore $4x + 7$.

Exercise 8A

1 In this question you are given a quadratic p(x) and a linear expression f(x). Use the factor theorem to find whether or not f(x) is a factor of p(x). If it is, find the other factor.

(a) $3x^2 - 10x + 8, \quad x - 2$

(b) $2x^2 - x - 45, \quad x - 5$

(c) $4x^2 + 15x + 9, \quad x + 3$

(d) $3x^2 - 10x - 8, \quad x + 4$

(e) $6x^2 - 5x - 6, \quad 2x - 3$

(f) $6x^2 - 17x + 5, \quad 3x - 1$

(g) $8x^2 + 6x - 5, \quad 2x + 1$

(h) $15x^2 + 43x + 8, \quad 5x + 1$

2 In each of the following quadratic polynomials one factor is given. Use the method of equating coefficients to find the other factor.

(a) $x^2 + x - 12 \equiv (x + 4)(\quad)$

(b) $x^2 + 14x - 51 \equiv (x - 3)(\quad)$

(c) $3x^2 + 5x - 22 \equiv (x - 2)(\quad)$

(d) $35x^2 + 48x - 27 \equiv (5x + 9)(\quad)$

(e) $2x^2 - x - 15 \equiv (2x + 5)(\quad)$

(f) $14x^2 + 31x - 10 \equiv (2x + 5)(\quad)$

3 Use the factor theorem to find one factor of these quadratics. Then use the method of equating coefficients to find the other factor.

(a) $4x^2 + x - 5$

(b) $2x^2 - 5x - 3$

(c) $4x^2 + x - 3$

(d) $3x^2 + 10x + 8$

(e) $4x^2 - 8x - 5$

(f) $12x^2 - 19x + 4$

(g) $6x^2 + 13x + 6$

(h) $6x^2 + 13x - 15$

(i) $8x^2 + 2x - 3$

4 You are given a quadratic polynomial p(x) whose coefficients involve an unknown number k, and a linear polynomial f(x). Find the value(s) of k for which f(x) is a factor of p(x). Check your answer by finding the other factor.

(a) $x^2 + 5x + k, \quad x - 2$

(b) $2x^2 + kx + 9, \quad x + 3$

(c) $kx^2 + kx + 1, \quad 2x + 1$

(d) $6x^2 - x + k, \quad 3x - 2$

(e) $kx^2 + 2x + k^2, \quad x + 1$

(f) $3x^2 + kx - k, \quad x + 2$

5 Suppose that $p(x) = ax^2 + bx + c$, and that t is a number such that $p(t) = 0$. Explain why $c = -at^2 - bt$, and hence show that $p(x) = a(x^2 - t^2) + b(x - t)$. Deduce that $x - t$ is a factor of $p(x)$.

6 If $ax^2 + bx + c \equiv lx^2 + mx + n$, the values of the two quadratics are the same for all values of x. By applying this with $x = 0$, $x = -1$ and $x = 1$, deduce that $a = l$, $b = m$ and $c = n$.

8.3 Factorising cubics

There is nothing special about quadratics. All the methods so far described apply equally to polynomials of any degree. In this chapter, to keep the examples simple, none of the applications go beyond cubics; but you should have no difficulty in seeing how to extend them to quartics, quintics, and so on.

To factorise a cubic polynomial, the first step is to try to express it as a product of a linear expression and a quadratic. You can then examine the quadratic to see if that can be factorised further.

For a start, concentrate on finding the linear factor. Look at the highest degree term (for a cubic, the x^3 term) and the constant term, to decide how these might split. Then test the various possibilities, using the factor theorem just as for a quadratic.

Once you have found a linear factor, write the quadratic factor as $Ax^2 + Bx + C$ and use the method of equating coefficients to get equations for A, B and C. There will be four of these, one each for the x^3, x^2, x and constant terms. You can use the first three to find A, B and C, and the last one as a check.

> **Factorising a polynomial**
>
> **Step 1**   Use the factor theorem to find one factor.
>
> **Step 2**   Use the method of equating coefficients to find the second factor.

Example 8.3.1
Factorise $p(x) = x^3 + 7x^2 + 8x + 2$.

The x^3 term can only split as $x \times x^2$, and the constant term can split as 1×2 or 2×1, with both $+$ or both $-$ signs. So to find a linear factor $x - t$, work out $p(t)$ with $t = \pm 1$, ± 2 in turn.

$$p(1) = 1 + 7 + 8 + 2 = 18, \ p(-1) = -1 + 7 - 8 + 2 = 0, \ldots \text{stop!}$$

By the factor theorem, there is a linear factor $x - (-1)$, that is $x + 1$.

Now write

$$x^3 + 7x^2 + 8x + 2 \equiv (x + 1)(Ax^2 + Bx + C)$$

and multiply out the right side as

$$Ax^3 + (B + A)x^2 + (C + B)x + C.$$

Equating coefficients,

$$A = 1, B + A = 7, C + B = 8 \text{ and } C = 2.$$

So $A = 1$, $B = 7 - A = 6$, $C = 8 - B = 2$. Notice that the value of C agrees with that given by the fourth equation.

It follows that

$$x^3 + 7x^2 + 8x + 2 \equiv (x + 1)(x^2 + 6x + 2).$$

The quadratic $x^2 + 6x + 2$ does not split any further into factors with integer coefficients.

However, $x^2 + 6x + 2$ does factorise if you allow surds. The roots of $x^2 + 6x + 2 = 0$ are $-3 - \sqrt{7}$ and $-3 + \sqrt{7}$, showing that $x^2 + 6x + 2 \equiv (x + 3 + \sqrt{7})(x + 3 - \sqrt{7})$.

Example 8.3.2

Show that $3x - 2$ is a factor of $p(x) = 12x^3 + 40x^2 + 13x - 30$, and hence factorise $p(x)$ completely.

Using the extended factor theorem, note that the value of x which makes $3x - 2$ equal to 0 is $\frac{2}{3}$. So calculate

$$\begin{aligned}
p\left(\tfrac{2}{3}\right) &= 12\left(\tfrac{2}{3}\right)^3 + 40\left(\tfrac{2}{3}\right)^2 + 13\left(\tfrac{2}{3}\right) - 30 \\
&= \frac{12 \times 8}{27} + \frac{40 \times 4}{9} + \frac{13 \times 2}{3} - 30 \\
&= \tfrac{192}{9} + \tfrac{26}{3} - 30 = \tfrac{64}{3} + \tfrac{26}{3} - 30 \\
&= \tfrac{90}{3} - 30 = 0.
\end{aligned}$$

This proves that $3x - 2$ is a factor of $p(x)$.

To find the quadratic factor, write

$$12x^3 + 40x^2 + 13x - 30 \equiv (3x - 2)(Ax^2 + Bx + C)$$

and multiply out the right side to get

$$3Ax^3 + (3B - 2A)x^2 + (3C - 2B)x - 2C.$$

Equating the coefficients of this expression with those of the given cubic,

$$3A = 12, 3B - 2A = 40, 3C - 2B = 13 \text{ and } -2C = -30.$$

So $A = 4$, $B = \dfrac{40 + 8}{3} = 16$, $C = \dfrac{13 + 32}{3} = 15$. As a check, the value of C satisfies the fourth equation.

The first stage of the factorisation is therefore

$$12x^3 + 40x^2 + 13x - 30 \equiv (3x - 2)(4x^2 + 16x + 15).$$

It remains to investigate whether the quadratic factor can be split into two linear factors. You can do this by the methods described in Sections 8.1 and 8.2. It is left to you to show that this gives

$$4x^2 + 16x + 15 \equiv (2x + 3)(2x + 5).$$

The complete factorisation of the cubic is therefore

$$12x^3 + 40x^2 + 13x - 30 \equiv (3x - 2)(2x + 3)(2x + 5).$$

To sum up, the methods described in Sections 8.1 and 8.2 for quadratics can be extended to polynomials p(x) of any degree as follows.

The factor theorem

Let p(x) be a polynomial.

If p(t) = 0, then $x - t$ is a factor of p(x).

The extended factor theorem

If $\text{p}\left(\dfrac{t}{s}\right) = 0$, then $sx - t$ is a factor of p(x).

Equating coefficients

If $\text{p}(x) = ax^n + bx^{n-1} + cx^{n-2} + \cdots + k$ and
$\text{P}(x) = \alpha x^n + \beta x^{n-1} + \gamma x^{n-2} + \cdots + \kappa$ are two polynomials and if
p(x) $\equiv$ P(x), then $a = \alpha$, $b = \beta$, $c = \gamma$, ... $k = \kappa$.

Exercise 8B

1 In this question you are given a cubic polynomial p(x) and a linear polynomial f(x). Use the factor theorem to find whether or not f(x) is a factor of p(x). If it is, find the other factor; where possible, split this second factor into two linear factors.

(a) $x^3 + x + 2$, $x + 1$

(b) $4x^3 - 4x^2 - 21x - 9$, $x - 3$

(c) $2x^3 + 3x^2 - x + 6$, $x + 2$

(d) $x^3 - 5x + 2$, $x - 2$

(e) $2x^3 + 3x^2 + 3x + 1$, $2x + 1$

(f) $27x^3 + 27x^2 + 9x + 1$, $3x + 1$

(g) $9x^3 + 6x^2 - x - 6$, $3x - 2$

(h) $2x^3 - 5x^2 - 10x + 3$, $2x + 3$

2 The following polynomials are the product of three linear factors. Find them.

(a) $x^3 + 2x^2 - 5x - 6$

(b) $x^3 + x^2 - 16x + 20$

(c) $12x^3 + 4x^2 - 3x - 1$

(d) $8x^3 - 12x^2 + 6x - 1$

(e) $9x^3 + 27x^2 - x - 3$

(f) $x^3 - 6x - 4$

3 Use the factor theorem to factorise the following cubic polynomials p(x). In each case, write down the real roots of the equation p(x) = 0.

(a) $x^3 + 2x^2 - 11x - 12$

(b) $x^3 - 3x^2 - x + 3$

(c) $x^3 - 3x^2 - 13x + 15$

(d) $x^3 - 3x^2 - 9x - 5$

(e) $x^3 + 3x^2 - 4x - 12$

(f) $2x^3 + 7x^2 - 5x - 4$

(g) $3x^3 - x^2 - 12x + 4$

(h) $6x^3 + 7x^2 - x - 2$

(i) $x^3 + 2x^2 - 4x + 1$

4 In this question you are given a cubic polynomial p(x) involving an unknown constant k, and a linear polynomial f(x). Find the value(s) of k for which f(x) is a factor of p(x). In this case, factorise p(x) as completely as possible.

(a) $x^3 - 7x - k$, $x + 1$

(b) $4x^3 + kx - 6$, $x - 2$

(c) $kx^3 + x^2 + 25$, $2x + 5$

(d) $x^3 + 5x^2 + kx - k^2$, $x + 3$

5 Factorise the following.

(a) $x^3 - 8$

(b) $x^3 + 8$

(c) $x^3 - a^3$

(d) $x^3 + a^3$

8.4   Division of polynomials

What happens if $sx - t$ is not a factor of p(x)?

Example 8.4.1
A student trying to factorise p(x) = $x^3 - x + 6$ found that p(2) = 12 and p(−2) = 0, but mistakenly thought this meant that $x - 2$ (rather than $x + 2$) is a factor. What happened when he tried to find the other factor?

The student wrote

$$x^3 - x + 6 \equiv (x - 2)(Ax^2 + Bx + C)$$
$$\equiv Ax^3 + (B - 2A)x^2 + (C - 2B)x - 2C$$

and proceeded to equate coefficients:

$$A = 1, \quad B - 2A = 0, \quad C - 2B = -1, \quad -2C = 6.$$

He then found $A = 1$, $B = 2$, $C = 2 \times 2 - 1 = 3$, giving a quadratic $x^2 + 2x + 3$. But when he used the fourth equation as a check he found that it gave $-2 \times 3 = 6$. So he knew something was wrong!

In this example, to make the identity correct the student would have had to add 12 to the right side. That is, to make the original identity correct he needed to write

$$x^3 - x + 6 \equiv (x - 2)(Ax^2 + Bx + C) + R.$$

Then, when he equated coefficients, the last equation would have been $-2C + R = 6$; and since $C = 3$, R would be equal to $2C + 6 = 12$.

This would not, of course, put right his original mistake. But at least it would have stopped him writing the absurd equation $-2 \times 3 = 6$.

The number R in this calculation is called the 'remainder'. To see why, think of a similar situation with numbers rather than polynomials.

Suppose that 44 members of a club turn up on a Sunday morning to play football. Each football team needs 11 players. Then, since

$$44 = 11 \times 4$$

exactly 4 teams can be formed and everyone gets a game. This is because 11 is a factor of 44. The number 4 is called the 'quotient' when 44 is divided by 11. (This word comes from the Latin word *quot*, which means 'how many?'. In this case it is the answer to the question 'how many teams of 11 can be made with 44 people?'.)

But if 49 members turn up, only 44 can get a game and the remaining 5 are left out. The mathematics is expressed by the equation

$$49 = 11 \times 4 + 5.$$

The quotient when 49 is divided by 11 is still 4, since it is still the answer to the question 'how many teams?'. But there is also a remainder of 5.

Compare this with the situation in Example 8.4.1, where the correct identity is

$$x^3 - x + 6 \equiv (x - 2)(x^2 + 2x + 3) + 12.$$

This has the same structure as the equation with numbers, and the same language is used to describe it:

> The quotient when $x^3 - x + 6$ is divided by $x - 2$ is $x^2 + 2x + 3$, and there is a remainder of 12.

Example 8.4.2

(a) Use the factor theorem to show that $4x + 3$ is not a factor of $p(x) = 20x^3 - x^2 - 4x - 7$.

(b) Find the quotient and remainder when $20x^3 - x^2 - 4x - 7$ is divided by $4x + 3$.

(a) The value of x which makes $4x + 3$ equal to 0 is $-\frac{3}{4}$, so calculate

$$p\left(-\tfrac{3}{4}\right) = 20\left(-\tfrac{3}{4}\right)^3 - \left(-\tfrac{3}{4}\right)^2 - 4\left(-\tfrac{3}{4}\right) - 7$$
$$= -\frac{20 \times 27}{64} - \frac{9}{16} + \frac{4 \times 3}{4} - 7 = -\frac{135}{16} - \frac{9}{16} + 3 - 7$$
$$= -\frac{144}{16} + 3 - 7 = -9 + 3 - 7 = -13.$$

Since this is not zero, $4x + 3$ is not a factor of $p(x)$.

(b) Denote the quotient by $Ax^2 + Bx + C$ and the remainder by R. Then the problem is to find numbers A, B, C and R such that

$$20x^3 - x^2 - 4x - 7 \equiv (4x + 3)(Ax^2 + Bx + C) + R.$$

The right side when multiplied out is

$$4Ax^3 + (4B + 3A)x^2 + (4C + 3B)x + 3C + R.$$

Equating coefficients,

$$4A = 20, \quad 4B + 3A = -1, \quad 4C + 3B = -4, \quad 3C + R = -7.$$

So $A = 5$, $B = \dfrac{-1 - 3 \times 5}{4} = -4$, $C = \dfrac{-4 - 3 \times (-4)}{4} = 2$, $R = -7 - 3 \times 2 = -13$.

The quotient is $5x^2 - 4x + 2$, and the remainder is -13.

The processes described in this section can be summed up in a single statement, which holds when p(x) is a polynomial of any degree, not just for cubics.

> When a polynomial p(x) is divided by a linear polynomial $sx - t$, there is a **quotient** q(x) and a **remainder** R such that
>
> $$p(x) \equiv (sx - t)q(x) + R.$$
>
> The degree of the quotient is one less than the degree of p(x).

8.5 The remainder theorem

You probably noticed that in Example 8.4.2 the answer -13 found for the remainder in part (b) is the same as the value of $p\left(-\frac{3}{4}\right)$ found in part (a). The same was true in Example 8.4.1, where in the corrected calculation the remainder is 12, and $p(2) = 12$. This is no coincidence.

You are already used to calculating $p\left(\dfrac{t}{s}\right)$ when you try to find factors of p(x). If its value is 0, then $sx - t$ is a factor. It now seems that $p\left(\dfrac{t}{s}\right)$ also has significance if $sx - t$ is not a factor of p(x): it is the remainder when p(x) is divided by $sx - t$.

> The **remainder theorem**
> If a polynomial p(x) is divided by a linear polynomial $sx - t$,
> the remainder is $p\left(\dfrac{t}{s}\right)$.

This is very simple to prove. From the definition of quotient and remainder at the end of Section 8.4,

$$p(x) \equiv (sx - t)q(x) + R.$$

Since this is an identity, you can substitute any number you like for x. If you choose x so that $sx - t = 0$, that is $x = \dfrac{t}{s}$, you get

$$p\left(\frac{t}{s}\right) = \left(s \times \frac{t}{s} - t\right)q\left(\frac{t}{s}\right) + R = (t - t)q\left(\frac{t}{s}\right) + R = 0 \times q\left(\frac{t}{s}\right) + R.$$

Since $0 \times q\left(\dfrac{t}{s}\right) = 0$, it follows that $p\left(\dfrac{t}{s}\right) = R$.

Example 8.5.1

Find the remainders when $p(x) = 2x^3 + 3x^2 - x + 1$ is divided by
(a) $x - 3$, (b) $2x + 1$.

(a) The value of x which makes $x - 3$ equal to 0 is 3, so the remainder is

$$p(3) = 54 + 27 - 3 + 1 = 79.$$

(b) The value of x which makes $2x + 1$ equal to 0 is $-\frac{1}{2}$, so the remainder is

$$p\left(-\tfrac{1}{2}\right) = -\tfrac{1}{4} + \tfrac{3}{4} + \tfrac{1}{2} + 1 = 2.$$

The factor theorem now appears as just a special case of the remainder theorem. For if $p\left(\dfrac{t}{s}\right) = 0$, the remainder R is 0, so the division identity reduces to

$$p(x) \equiv (sx - t)q(x).$$

This means that $sx - t$ is a factor of $p(x)$.

Exercise 8C

1 In each of the following identities find the values of A, B and R.

(a) $x^2 - 2x + 7 \equiv (x + 3)(Ax + B) + R$ (b) $x^2 + 9x - 3 \equiv (x + 1)(Ax + B) + R$

(c) $15x^2 - 14x - 8 \equiv (5x + 2)(Ax + B) + R$ (d) $6x^2 + x - 5 \equiv (2x + 1)(Ax + B) + R$

(e) $12x^2 - 5x + 2 \equiv (3x - 2)(Ax + B) + R$ (f) $21x^2 - 11x + 6 \equiv (3x - 2)(Ax + B) + R$

2 In each of the following identities find the values of A, B, C and R.

(a) $x^3 - x^2 - x + 12 \equiv (x + 2)(Ax^2 + Bx + C) + R$

(b) $x^3 - 5x^2 + 10x + 10 \equiv (x - 3)(Ax^2 + Bx + C) + R$

(c) $2x^3 + x^2 - 3x + 4 \equiv (2x - 1)(Ax^2 + Bx + C) + R$

(d) $12x^3 + 11x^2 - 7x + 5 \equiv (3x + 2)(Ax^2 + Bx + C) + R$

(e) $4x^3 + 4x^2 - 37x + 5 \equiv (2x - 5)(Ax^2 + Bx + C) + R$

(f) $9x^3 + 12x^2 - 15x - 10 \equiv (3x + 4)(Ax^2 + Bx + C) + R$

3 Find the quotient and the remainder when

(a) $x^2 - 5x + 2$ is divided by $x - 3$, (b) $x^2 + 2x - 6$ is divided by $x + 1$,

(c) $2x^2 + 3x - 1$ is divided by $x - 2$, (d) $2x^2 + 3x + 1$ is divided by $2x - 1$,

(e) $6x^2 - x - 2$ is divided by $3x + 1$.

4 Find the quotient and the remainder when the first polynomial is divided by the second.

(a) $x^3 + 2x^2 - 3x + 1$ $x + 2$ (b) $x^3 - 3x^2 + 5x - 4$ $x - 5$

(c) $2x^3 + 4x - 5$ $x + 3$ (d) $5x^3 - 3x + 7$ $x - 4$

(e) $2x^3 - x^2 - 3x - 7$ $2x + 1$ (f) $6x^3 + 17x^2 - 17x + 5$ $3x - 2$

5 Find the remainder when the first polynomial is divided by the second.

(a) $x^3 - 5x^2 + 2x - 3$ $x - 1$ (b) $x^3 + x^2 - 6x + 5$ $x + 2$

(c) $2x^3 - 3x + 5$ $x - 3$ (d) $4x^3 - 5x^2 + 3x - 7$ $x + 4$

(e) $x^3 + 3x^2 - 2x + 1$ $2x - 1$ (f) $2x^3 + 5x^2 - 3x + 6$ $3x + 1$

(g) $x^4 - x^3 + 2x^2 - 7x - 2$ $x - 2$ (h) $3x^4 + x^2 - 7x + 6$ $x + 3$

6 When $x^3 + 2x^2 - px + 1$ is divided by $x - 1$, the remainder is 5. Find the value of p.

7 When $2x^3 + x^2 - 3x + q$ is divided by $x - 2$, the remainder is 12. Find the value of q.

8 When $x^3 + 2x^2 + px - 3$ is divided by $x + 1$, the remainder is the same as when it is divided by $x - 2$. Find the value of p.

9 When $x^3 + px^2 - x - 4$ is divided by $x - 1$, the remainder is the same as when it is divided by $x + 3$. Find the value of p.

10 When $3x^3 + 2x^2 + ax + b$ is divided by $x - 1$, the remainder is 5. When divided by $3x - 1$ the remainder is $-\frac{1}{3}$. Find the values of a and b.

11 When $x^3 + ax^2 + bx + 5$ is divided by $x - 2$, the remainder is 23. When divided by $x + 1$ the remainder is 11. Find the values of a and b.

12 When $x^3 + ax^2 + bx - 5$ is divided by $x - 1$, the remainder is -1. When divided by $x + 1$ the remainder is -5. Find the values of a and b.

13 When $2x^3 - x^2 + ax + b$ is divided by $x - 2$, the remainder is 25. When divided by $2x + 3$ the remainder is $-13\frac{1}{2}$. Find the values of a and b.

Miscellaneous exercise 8

1 It is given that

$$(x + a)(x^2 + bx + 2) \equiv x^3 - 2x^2 - x - 6$$

where a and b are constants. Find the value of a and the value of b.   (OCR)

2 Find the coordinates of the points where the graph of $y = 2x^3 + 3x^2 - 4x + 1$ cuts the x-axis.

3 Show that $(x - 1)$ is a factor of $6x^3 + 11x^2 - 5x - 12$, and find the other two linear factors of this expression.   (OCR)

4 The cubic polynomial $x^3 + ax^2 + bx - 8$, where a and b are constants, has factors $(x + 1)$ and $(x + 2)$. Find the values of a and b.   (OCR)

5 Find the value of a for which $(x - 2)$ is a factor of $3x^3 + ax^2 + x - 2$. Show that, for this value of a, the cubic equation $3x^3 + ax^2 + x - 2 = 0$ has only one real root.   (OCR)

6 Solve the equation $4x^3 + 8x^2 + x - 3 = 0$ given that one of the roots is an integer.   (OCR)

7 The cubic polynomial $x^3 - 2x^2 - 2x + 4$ has a factor $(x - a)$, where a is an integer.

   (a) Use the factor theorem to find the value of a.

   (b) Hence find exactly all three roots of the cubic equation $x^3 - 2x^2 - 2x + 4 = 0$.   (OCR)

8 The cubic polynomial $x^3 - 2x^2 - x - 6$ is denoted by f(x). Show that $(x - 3)$ is a factor of
   f(x). Factorise f(x). Hence find the number of real roots of the equation f(x) = 0, justifying
   your answer.

   Hence write down the number of points of intersection of the graphs with equations

   $$y = x^2 - 2x - 1 \quad \text{and} \quad y = \frac{6}{x},$$

   justifying your answer.   (OCR)

9 Given that $(2x + 1)$ is a factor of $2x^3 + ax^2 + 16x + 6$, show that $a = 9$.

   Find the real quadratic factor of $2x^3 + 9x^2 + 16x + 6$. By completing the square, or
   otherwise, show that this quadratic factor is positive for all real values of x.   (OCR)

10 Find the coordinates of the turning points on the curve with equation $y = 2x^4 - 7x^2 - 6x$.

11 The diagram shows the curve

   $$y = -x^3 + 2x^2 + ax - 10.$$

   The curve crosses the x-axis at $x = p$, $x = 2$ and
   $x = q$.

   (a) Show that $a = 5$.

   (b) Find the exact values of p and q.   (OCR)

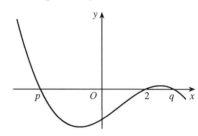

12 The polynomial $x^3 + 3x^2 + ax + b$ leaves a remainder of 3 when it is divided by $x + 1$
   and a remainder of 15 when it is divided by $x - 2$. Find the remainder when it is divided
   by $x + 3$.

13 Find the maximum and minimum points on the curve with equation $y = 3x^2 + 14x + \dfrac{8}{x}$.

14 Let p(x) = $4x^3 + 12x^2 + 5x - 6$.

   (a) Calculate p(2) and p(−2), and state what you can deduce from your answers.

   (b) Solve the equation $4x^3 + 12x^2 + 5x - 6 = 0$.

15 On the curve with equation $y = x^2(x - 4)$ the point P has coordinates $(1, -3)$.

   (a) Find the equation of the tangent to the curve at P and the coordinates of the point
       where the tangent meets the curve again.

   (b) Find the equation of the normal to the curve at P and the coordinates of the points
       where the normal meets the curve again.

16 The diagram shows the graph of $y = x^2 - 3$ and the part of the graph of $y = \dfrac{2}{x}$ for $x > 0$.

The two graphs intersect at C, and A and B are the points of intersection of $y = x^2 - 3$ with the x-axis. Write down the exact coordinates of A and B.

Show that the x-coordinate of C is given by the equation $x^3 - 3x - 2 = 0$.

Factorise $x^3 - 3x - 2$ completely.

Hence

(a) write down the x-coordinate of C,

(b) describe briefly the geometrical relationship between the graph of $y = x^2 - 3$ and the part of the graph of $y = \dfrac{2}{x}$ for which $x < 0$. (OCR)

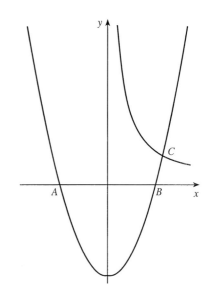

9 Radians

This chapter introduces radians, an alternative to degrees for measuring angles. When you have completed it, you should

- know how to convert from degrees to radians and vice versa
- be able to use the formula $r\theta$ for the length of a circular arc, and $\frac{1}{2}r^2\theta$ for the area of a circular sector
- know the graphs and symmetry properties of $\cos\theta$, $\sin\theta$ and $\tan\theta$ when θ is in radians
- be able to solve trigonometric equations with roots expressed in radians.

9.1 Radians

Suppose that you were meeting angles for the first time, and that you were asked to suggest a unit for measuring them. It seems highly unlikely that you would suggest the degree, which was invented by the Babylonians in ancient times. The full circle, or the right angle, both seem more natural units.

However, the unit used in modern mathematics is the radian, illustrated in Fig. 9.1. This is particularly useful in differentiating trigonometric functions, as you will see if you go on to module C4.

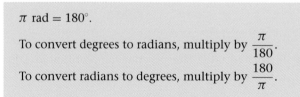

In a circle of radius 1 unit, radii joining the centre O to the ends of an arc of length 1 unit form an angle called **1 radian**. The abbreviation for radian is **rad**.

You can see immediately from this definition that there are 2π radians in $360°$. This leads to the following conversion rules for radians to degrees and vice versa:

Fig. 9.1

> π rad $= 180°$.
>
> To convert degrees to radians, multiply by $\dfrac{\pi}{180}$.
>
> To convert radians to degrees, multiply by $\dfrac{180}{\pi}$.

You could calculate that 1 radian is equal to $57.295...°$, but no one uses this conversion. It is simplest to remember that π rad $= 180°$, and to use this to convert between radians and degrees.

You can set your calculator to radian mode, and then work entirely in radians.

You might find on your calculator another unit for angle called the 'grad'; there are 100 grads to the right angle. Grads will not be used in this course.

Example 9.1.1
Convert $40°$ to radians, leaving your answer as a multiple of π.

Using the conversion factor $\dfrac{\pi}{180}$ in the box,

$$40° = 40 \times \frac{\pi}{180} \text{ rad} = \tfrac{2}{9}\pi \text{ rad}.$$

It is worthwhile learning a few common conversions, so that you can think in both radians and degrees. For example, you should know and recognise the following conversions:

$$180° = \pi \text{ rad}, \qquad 90° = \tfrac{1}{2}\pi \text{ rad}, \qquad 45° = \tfrac{1}{4}\pi \text{ rad},$$
$$30° = \tfrac{1}{6}\pi \text{ rad}, \qquad 60° = \tfrac{1}{3}\pi \text{ rad}, \qquad 360° = 2\pi \text{ rad}.$$

9.2 Formulae in degrees and radians

In Chapter 1 there were some identities established such as

$$\cos^2 \theta + \sin^2 \theta \equiv 1.$$

This identity holds for all angles, and it is not important that the units are degrees.

Similarly, the sine formula for a triangle

$$\frac{a}{\sin A} = \frac{b}{\sin B} = \frac{c}{\sin C}$$

is true whether the angles are in degrees or in radians.

However, in an identity such as

$$\cos(90° - \theta) \equiv \sin \theta,$$

the $90°$ makes it important that the angles are in degrees.

There is a similar identity in radians, but in this case the $90°$ is written in radians as $\tfrac{1}{2}\pi$. The equivalent identity then becomes

$$\cos\left(\tfrac{1}{2}\pi - \theta\right) \equiv \sin \theta.$$

More identities like this are given in Section 9.4.

It is conventionally assumed that, either the angles in $\cos\theta$ and $\sin\theta$ are in radians, or it doesn't matter in which units the angles are measured.

For example, later in this chapter the notation $\sin\frac{1}{2}\theta = \frac{4}{6} = 0.666...$, $\sin\theta$ and $\sin 1.459...$ will be used, without any specific indication that the angles are in radians. So when you see, for example, 'sin 12', you should read it as the sine of 12 radians. If it were the sine of 12° it would be written 'sin 12°'.

Example 9.2.1
Find   (a) $\sin\frac{1}{6}\pi$,   (b) $\cos\frac{5}{4}\pi$,   (c) $\sin 2$.

For parts (a) and (b), the best way to proceed is to recognise that $\frac{1}{6}\pi$ and $\frac{5}{4}\pi$ are angles which have exact sines and cosines.

(a) Knowing that $\frac{1}{6}\pi$ rad is 30°, $\sin\frac{1}{6}\pi = \frac{1}{2}$.

(b) Similarly, $\cos\frac{5}{4}\pi = \cos 225° = -\frac{1}{2}\sqrt{2}$.

(c) Use your calculator in radian mode to get $\sin 2 = 0.909$, correct to 3 significant figures.

9.3   Length of arc and area of sector

Fig. 9.2 shows a circle, centre O and radius r. An arc of this circle has been drawn with a thicker line, and the two radii at the ends of the arc have been drawn. These radii have an angle θ rad between them. This is described more briefly by saying that the arc **subtends** an angle θ rad at the centre of the circle. You can calculate the length of the circular arc by noticing that the length of the arc is the fraction $\dfrac{\theta}{2\pi}$ of the length $2\pi r$ of the circumference of the circle.

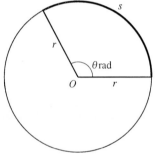

Fig. 9.2

Let s be the arc length. Then

$$s = \frac{\theta}{2\pi} \times 2\pi r = r\theta.$$

You can use a similar argument to calculate the area of a sector.

The circular sector, centre O and radius r, shown shaded in Fig. 9.3, has an angle θ rad at the centre.

The area of the circular sector is the fraction $\dfrac{\theta}{2\pi}$ of the area πr^2 of the full circle.

Let A be the required area. Then

$$A = \frac{\theta}{2\pi} \times \pi r^2 = \frac{1}{2}r^2\theta.$$

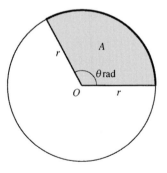

Fig. 9.3

> The length of a circular arc with radius r and angle θ rad is $s = r\theta$.
>
> The area of a circular sector with radius r and angle θ rad is $A = \frac{1}{2}r^2\theta$.

No units are given in the formulae above. The units are the appropriate units associated with the length; for instance, length in m and area in m^2.

Example 9.3.1

In Fig. 9.4, find the length of the arc AB and the area of the sector OAB.

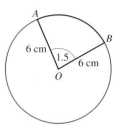

Using the formulae $s = r\theta$ and $A = \frac{1}{2}r^2\theta$ in the box,

length of the arc AB is 6×1.5 cm $= 9$ cm,
area of sector OAB is $\frac{1}{2} \times 6^2 \times 1.5$ cm$^2 = 27$ cm^2.

Fig. 9.4

Example 9.3.2

In Fig. 9.5, the area of the sector AOB is 18.4 m^2. Find the angle θ.

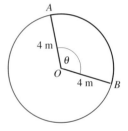

The area of the sector in m^2 is given by $\frac{1}{2} \times 4^2 \times \theta$, so

$$\frac{1}{2} \times 4^2 \times \theta = 18.4.$$

So $8\theta = 18.4$, giving $\theta = 2.3$.

The angle is 2.3 radians.

Fig. 9.5

Example 9.3.3

Find the perimeter and the area of the segment cut off by a chord PQ of length 8 cm from a circle centre O and radius 6 cm. Give your answers correct to 3 significant figures.

In problems of this type, it is helpful to start by thinking about the complete sector OPQ, rather than just the shaded segment of Fig. 9.6, over the page.

The perimeter of the segment consists of two parts, the straight part of length 8 cm, and the curved part; to calculate the length of the curved part you need to know the angle POQ.

Call this angle θ. As triangle POQ is isosceles, a perpendicular drawn from O to PQ bisects both PQ and angle POQ, shown in Fig. 9.7.

$$\sin \tfrac{1}{2}\theta = \tfrac{4}{6} = 0.666\ldots, \quad \text{so} \quad \tfrac{1}{2}\theta = 0.7297\ldots \quad \text{and} \quad \theta = 1.459\ldots.$$

Make sure that your calculator is in radian mode.

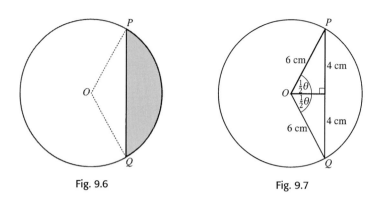

Fig. 9.6   Fig. 9.7

Then the perimeter d cm is given by $d = 8 + 6\theta = 16.756...$; the perimeter is 16.8 cm, correct to 3 significant figures.

To find the area of the segment, you need to find the area of the sector OPQ, and then subtract the area of the triangle OPQ. Using the formula $\frac{1}{2}bc\sin A$ for the area of a triangle, the area of the triangle POQ is given by $\frac{1}{2}r^2\sin\theta$. Thus the area in cm^2 of the shaded region is

$$\tfrac{1}{2}r^2(\theta - \sin\theta) = \tfrac{1}{2} \times 6^2 \times (1.459... - \sin 1.459...)$$
$$= 8.381... .$$

The area is 8.38 cm^2, correct to 3 significant figures.

> It is worthwhile using your calculator to store the value of θ to use in the calculations. If you round θ to 3 significant figures and use the rounded value, you are liable to introduce errors.

Example 9.3.4
A chord of a circle which subtends an angle of θ at the centre of the circle cuts off a segment equal in area to $\frac{1}{3}$ of the area of the whole circle.

(a) Show that $\theta - \sin\theta = \frac{2}{3}\pi$.

(b) Verify that $\theta = 2.61$, correct to 2 decimal places.

(a) Let r cm be the radius of the circle in Fig. 9.8. Using a method similar to the one in Example 9.3.3, the area of the segment is

$$\tfrac{1}{2}r^2(\theta - \sin\theta).$$

This is $\frac{1}{3}$ of the area of the whole circle if

$$\tfrac{1}{2}r^2(\theta - \sin\theta) = \tfrac{1}{3}\pi r^2.$$

Multiplying by 2 and dividing by r^2 you find

$$\theta - \sin\theta = \tfrac{2}{3}\pi.$$

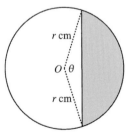

Fig. 9.8

(b) If you substitute $\theta = 2.61$ in the equation $f(\theta) \equiv \theta - \sin\theta$, you get
$f(2.61) = 2.103...$, which is very close to $\frac{2}{3}\pi = 2.094...$.

This suggests that θ is close to 2.61, but it is not enough to show that it is '2.61 correct to 2 decimal places'. To do that you need to show that θ lies between 2.605 and 2.615.

It is obvious from Fig. 9.5 that θ lies between 0 and π, and that the shaded area gets larger as θ increases. So you have to show that the area is too small when $\theta = 2.605$ and too large when $\theta = 2.615$.

$$f(2.605) = 2.605 - \sin 2.605 = 2.093..., \text{ and}$$
$$f(2.615) = 2.615 - \sin 2.615 = 2.112... .$$

The first of these is smaller, and the second larger, than $\frac{2}{3}\pi = 2.094...$.

It follows that the root of the equation is between 2.605 and 2.615; that is, the root is 2.61, correct to 2 decimal places.

Exercise 9A

1 Write each of the following angles in radians, leaving your answer as a multiple of π.

(a) $90°$ (b) $135°$ (c) $45°$ (d) $30°$ (e) $72°$ (f) $18°$

(g) $120°$ (h) $22\frac{1}{2}°$ (i) $720°$ (j) $600°$ (k) $270°$ (l) $1°$

2 Each of the following is an angle in radians. Without using a calculator change these to degrees.

(a) $\frac{1}{3}\pi$ (b) $\frac{1}{20}\pi$ (c) $\frac{1}{5}\pi$ (d) $\frac{1}{8}\pi$ (e) $\frac{1}{9}\pi$ (f) $\frac{2}{3}\pi$

(g) $\frac{5}{8}\pi$ (h) $\frac{3}{5}\pi$ (i) $\frac{1}{45}\pi$ (j) 6π (k) $-\frac{1}{2}\pi$ (l) $\frac{5}{18}\pi$

3 Without the use of a calculator write down the exact values of the following.

(a) $\sin\frac{1}{3}\pi$ (b) $\cos\frac{1}{4}\pi$ (c) $\tan\frac{1}{6}\pi$ (d) $\cos\frac{3}{2}\pi$

(e) $\sin\frac{7}{4}\pi$ (f) $\cos\frac{7}{6}\pi$ (g) $\tan\frac{5}{3}\pi$ (h) $\sin^2\frac{2}{3}\pi$

4 The following questions refer to the diagram, where
r = radius of circle (in cm),
s = arc length (in cm),
A = area of sector (in cm^2),
θ = angle subtended at centre (in radians).

(a) $r = 7$, $\theta = 1.2$. Find s and A.

(b) $r = 3.5$, $\theta = 2.1$. Find s and A.

(c) $s = 12$, $r = 8$. Find θ and A.   (d) $s = 14$, $\theta = 0.7$. Find r and A.

(e) $A = 30$, $r = 5$. Find θ and s.   (f) $A = 24$, $r = 6$. Find s.

(g) $A = 64$, $s = 16$. Find r and θ.   (h) $A = 30$, $s = 10$. Find θ.

5 Find the area of the shaded segment in each of the
   following cases.

   (a) $r = 5\,\text{cm}, \theta = \frac{1}{3}\pi$

   (b) $r = 3.1\,\text{cm}, \theta = \frac{2}{5}\pi$

   (c) $r = 28\,\text{cm}, \theta = \frac{5}{6}\pi$

   (d) $r = 6\,\text{cm}, s = 9\,\text{cm}$

   (e) $r = 9.5\,\text{cm}, s = 4\,\text{cm}$

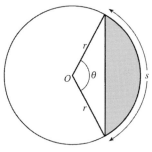

6 Find the area of the segment cut off by a chord of length $10\,\text{cm}$
   from a circle of radius $13\,\text{cm}$.

7 Find the perimeter of the segment cut off by a chord of length $14\,\text{cm}$ from a circle of
   radius $25\,\text{cm}$.

8 A chord of a circle which subtends an angle of θ at the centre cuts off a segment equal in
   area to $\frac{1}{4}$ of the area of the whole circle.

   (a) Show that $\theta - \sin\theta = \frac{1}{2}\pi$.

   (b) Verify that $\theta = 2.31$, correct to 2 decimal places.

9 Two circles of radii $5\,\text{cm}$ and $12\,\text{cm}$ are drawn,
   partly overlapping as shown in the diagram. Their
   centres are $13\,\text{cm}$ apart. Find the area common to
   the two circles.

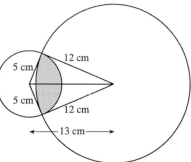

10 Two circles of radius $6\,\text{cm}$ and $4\,\text{cm}$ have their
    centres $7\,\text{cm}$ apart. Find the perimeter and area of
    the region common to both circles.

11* An eclipse of the Sun is said to be $x\%$ total when
     $x\%$ of the area of the Sun's disc is hidden behind
     the disc of the Moon.

     A child models this with two discs, each of radius
     r cm, as shown.

     Find the percentage total of the eclipse when the
     distance between the centres of the circles is $1.2r$.

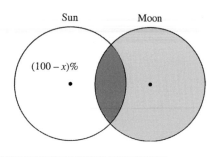

9.4 Graphs of the trigonometric functions

The graphs of $y = \cos\theta$, $y = \sin\theta$ and $y = \tan\theta$, when the angle is measured in radians, have a
similar shape to when the angle is measured in degrees, as drawn previously in Figs. 1.6, 1.8
and 1.9 in Sections 1.1 and 1.2. The only change is the scale along the θ-axis.

The graphs of $y = \cos\theta$, $y = \sin\theta$ and $y = \tan\theta$, with θ in radians, are shown in Figs. 9.9, 9.10
and 9.11 respectively. In each of these graphs the same scale is used on the two axes.

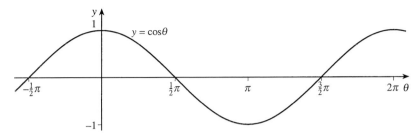

Fig. 9.9

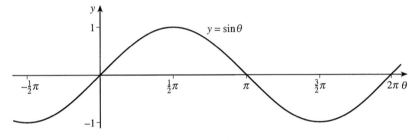

Fig. 9.10

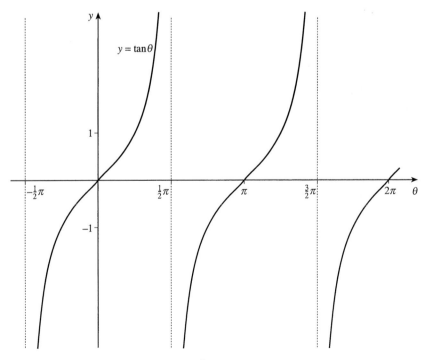

Fig. 9.11

If you were to draw the graphs in Sections 1.1 and 1.2 with the same scales in each direction, they would be very wide and flat compared with the graphs shown here.

In fact radians are almost always used when you need to find the gradients of the graphs of $y = \cos\theta$, $y = \sin\theta$ and $y = \tan\theta$.

These graphs also have symmetry properties similar to those that exist when the angle is measured in degrees.

> Periodic properties:
> $$\cos(\theta - 2\pi) = \cos\theta \quad \sin(\theta - 2\pi) = \sin\theta \quad \tan(\theta - \pi) = \tan\theta$$
> Odd/even properties:
> $$\cos(-\theta) = \cos\theta \quad \sin(-\theta) = -\sin\theta \quad \tan(-\theta) = -\tan\theta$$
> Translation properties:
> $$\cos(\theta - \pi) = -\cos\theta \quad \sin(\theta - \pi) = -\sin\theta$$
> Supplementary properties:
> $$\cos(\pi - \theta) = -\cos\theta \quad \sin(\pi - \theta) = \sin\theta \quad \tan(\pi - \theta) = -\tan\theta$$

Example 9.4.1
Express $\cos(\theta - \frac{1}{2}\pi)$ and $\sin(\theta - \frac{1}{2}\pi)$ in terms of $\cos\theta$ and $\sin\theta$.

The graph of $y = \cos(\theta - \frac{1}{2}\pi)$ has the shape of the graph of $y = \cos\theta$ translated by $\frac{1}{2}\pi$ to the right. You can see from Figs. 9.9 and 9.10 that this is the graph of $y = \sin\theta$. So $\cos(\theta - \frac{1}{2}\pi) \equiv \sin\theta$.

The graph of $y = \sin(\theta - \frac{1}{2}\pi)$ has the shape of the graph of $y = \sin\theta$ translated by $\frac{1}{2}\pi$ to the right. You can see that this is the graph of $y = \cos\theta$ upside down, that is reflected in the θ-axis. So $\sin(\theta - \frac{1}{2}\pi) \equiv -\cos\theta$.

Exercise 9B

1 Use the graphs of $y = \cos\theta$, $y = \sin\theta$ and $y = \tan\theta$ to draw sketches of
   (a) $y = \sin\frac{1}{2}\theta$,
   (b) $y = \cos 2\theta$,
   (c) $y = \tan(\theta - \frac{1}{4}\pi)$,
   (d) $y = 2\sin(\theta + \frac{1}{4}\pi)$.

2 Draw a sketch of the graph of $y = \sin\theta$, and a copy of the graph translated by $\frac{1}{2}\pi$ in the negative x-direction. Use your sketches, together with a sketch of $y = \cos\theta$ to show that $\sin(\theta - (-\frac{1}{2}\pi)) = \cos\theta$.

Use this property, and the symmetry properties of the sine and cosine functions in the box above, to establish the following results.
   (a) $\sin(\frac{1}{2}\pi - \theta) = \cos\theta$
   (b) $\sin(\frac{3}{2}\pi + \theta) = -\cos\theta$
   (c) $\cos(\frac{1}{2}\pi + \theta) = -\sin\theta$
   (d) $\sin(-\theta - \frac{1}{2}\pi) = -\cos\theta$

3 Use your calculator to draw, on the same axes, the graphs of $\tan(\theta - \tfrac{1}{2}\pi)$ and $y = \dfrac{1}{\tan\theta}$.

How do the graphs show that $\tan(\tfrac{1}{2}\pi - \theta) = \dfrac{1}{\tan\theta}$?

9.5 Solving trigonometric equations using radians

When you have a trigonometric equation to solve, you will sometimes want to find an angle in radians. The principles are similar to those that you used for working in degrees in Section 1.5, but, if you have your calculator in radian mode, the functions $\cos^{-1}$, $\sin^{-1}$ and $\tan^{-1}$ will now give you a value in radians.

You will need to remember that in radians the period of the functions $\cos\theta$ and $\sin\theta$ is 2π, and that the period of $\tan\theta$ is π.

Just as in Section 1.5, it is helpful to draw a sketch of what is going on. Your sketch need not be accurate but should be sufficiently good to pick up any obvious errors that you might make.

Example 9.5.1
Solve the equation $\cos\theta = -0.7$, giving all the roots in the interval $0 \leqslant \theta \leqslant 2\pi$, correct to 2 decimal places.

> **Step 1** $\cos^{-1}(-0.7) = 2.346...$. This gives one root in the interval $0 \leqslant \theta \leqslant 2\pi$.
>
> **Step 2**   Use the symmetry property $\cos(-\theta) = \cos\theta$ to show that $-2.346...$ is another root. Note that $-2.346...$ is not in the required interval.
>
> **Step 3**   Adding 2π (the period of $\cos\theta$) gives $-2.346... + 2\pi = 3.936...$, a root now in the required interval.

The roots of the equation $\cos\theta = -0.7$ in $0 \leqslant \theta \leqslant 2\pi$ are 2.35 and 3.94, correct to 2 decimal places.

Fig. 9.12 shows the graphs of $y = \cos\theta$ and $y = -0.7$. You can see that the roots of the equation $\cos\theta = -0.7$ are just smaller and just greater than π, which suggests that the algebra is correct.

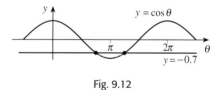

Fig. 9.12

Example 9.5.2
Solve the equation $\sin\theta = -0.2$, giving all the roots in the interval $-\pi \leqslant \theta \leqslant \pi$, correct to 2 decimal places.

> **Step 1** $\sin^{-1}(-0.2) = -0.201...$. This is one root in the interval $-\pi \leqslant \theta \leqslant \pi$.
>
> **Step 2**   Another root of the equation is $\pi - (-0.201...) = 3.342...$, but this is not in the required interval.

Step 3 Subtracting 2π gives $-2.940...$, the other root in the interval $-\pi \leqslant \theta \leqslant \pi$.

Therefore the roots of $\sin \theta = -0.2$ in $-\pi \leqslant \theta \leqslant \pi$ are -2.94 and -0.20, correct to 2 decimal places.

Fig. 9.13 shows the graphs of $y = \sin \theta$ and $y = -0.2$. You can see that the roots of the equation $\sin \theta = -0.2$ are both negative, as in the algebraic solution.

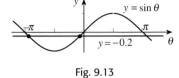

Fig. 9.13

Example 9.5.3

Solve the equation $\cos 3\theta = 0.3$, giving all the roots in the interval $-\pi \leqslant \theta \leqslant \pi$, correct to 2 decimal places.

Let $3\theta = \phi$, so that the equation becomes $\cos \phi = 0.3$. As θ lies in the interval $-\pi \leqslant \theta \leqslant \pi$, $\phi = 3\theta$ lies in the interval $-3\pi \leqslant \phi \leqslant 3\pi$ which is $-9.424... \leqslant \phi \leqslant 9.424...$.

The first part of the problem is to solve $\cos \phi = 0.3$ for $-9.424... \leqslant \phi \leqslant 9.424...$.

Step 1 $\cos^{-1} 0.3 = 1.266...$. This is one root in the interval $-9.424... \leqslant \phi \leqslant 9.424...$.

Step 2 Using the fact that the cosine function is even, another root is $-1.266...$.

Step 3 Adding 2π to and subtracting 2π from $1.266...$ gives $7.549...$ and $-5.017...$ as the other roots, while adding and subtracting 2π to $-1.266...$ gives $5.017...$ and $-7.549...$ which are also in the required interval.

Since $\theta = \frac{1}{3}\phi$, the roots of the original equation are -2.52, -1.67, -0.42, 0.42, 1.67, 2.52, correct to 2 decimal places.

Fig. 9.14 shows the graphs of $y = \cos 3\theta$, which is the graph of $y = \cos \theta$ stretched by the factor $\frac{1}{3}$ in the x-direction, and $y = 0.3$. You can see there are six roots symmetrically placed.

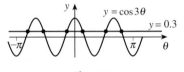

Fig. 9.14

Example 9.5.4

Solve the equation $\sin(x + 0.4) = 0.2$, giving all roots in the interval $0 \leqslant x \leqslant 2\pi$, correct to 2 decimal places.

Let $x + 0.4 = y$, so that the equation becomes $\sin y = 0.2$. As x lies in the interval $0 \leqslant x \leqslant 2\pi$, $y = x + 0.4$ lies in the interval $0.4 \leqslant y \leqslant 2\pi + 0.4$, or $0.4 \leqslant y \leqslant 6.68...$.

The first part of the problem is to solve $\sin y = 0.2$ for $0.4 \leqslant y \leqslant 6.68...$.

Step 1 $\sin^{-1} 0.2 = 0.201...$. However, $0.201...$ is not in the interval $0.4 \leqslant y \leqslant 6.68...$.

Step 2   Another solution of $\sin y = 0.2$ is $\pi - 0.201... = 2.94...$ and this is in the required interval.

Step 3   Using the fact that the period of the sine function is 2π, another root is $0.201... + 2\pi = 6.48...$.

Since $y = x + 0.4$, the roots of the original equation are $2.94... - 0.4$ and $6.48... - 0.4$ which are 2.54 and 6.08, correct to 2 decimal places.

Fig. 9.15 shows the graph of $y = \sin(x + 0.4)$, which is the graph of $y = \sin x$ translated by 0.4 in the negative x-direction, and $y = 0.2$. The values, 2.54 and 6.08, of the roots seem to be correct.

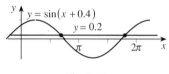

Fig. 9.15

Example 9.5.5
Solve the equation $\tan \theta = \cos \theta$, giving all the roots in the interval $0 \leqslant \theta \leqslant 2\pi$, correct to 2 decimal places.

If you have an equation like this it is usually a good idea to use the identity $\tan \theta \equiv \dfrac{\sin \theta}{\cos \theta}$ to replace $\tan \theta$. The equation then becomes $\dfrac{\sin \theta}{\cos \theta} = \cos \theta$, which, on multiplying both sides by $\cos \theta$, gives

$$\sin \theta = \cos^2 \theta.$$

As it stands you cannot solve this equation, but if you use the identity $\cos^2 \theta + \sin^2 \theta \equiv 1$ to replace $\cos^2 \theta$, you get the equation $\sin \theta = 1 - \sin^2 \theta$, which you can rewrite as

$$\sin^2 \theta + \sin \theta - 1 = 0.$$

This is a quadratic equation in $\sin \theta$, which you can solve using the quadratic formula in C1 Section 4.5:

$$\sin \theta = \frac{-1 \pm \sqrt{1^2 - 4 \times 1 \times (-1)}}{2},$$

giving $\sin \theta = 0.618...$ or $\sin \theta = -1.618...$.

One root is $\sin^{-1} 0.618... = 0.666...$. The other root of $\sin \theta = 0.618...$ in the interval, obtained from the symmetry of $\sin \theta$, is $\pi - 0.666... = 2.475...$.

The equation $\sin \theta = -1.618...$ has no roots, as $\sin \theta$ is always between -1 and 1.

So the required roots are 0.67 and 2.48, correct to 2 decimal places.

Exercise 9C

1 Find in radians correct to 2 decimal places, the two smallest positive values of θ for the following.

(a) $\sin\theta = 0.12$ (b) $\sin\theta = -0.86$ (c) $\sin\theta = 0.925$

(d) $\cos\theta = 0.81$ (e) $\cos\theta = -0.81$ (f) $\cos\theta = \sqrt{\frac{1}{3}}$

(g) $\tan\theta = 4.1$ (h) $\tan\theta = -0.35$ (i) $\tan\theta = 0.17$

2 Find all values of θ in the interval $-\pi \leqslant \theta \leqslant \pi$ which satisfy each of the following equations, giving your answers correct to 2 decimal places where appropriate.

(a) $\sin\theta = 0.84$ (b) $\cos\theta = 0.27$ (c) $\tan\theta = 1.9$

(d) $\sin\theta = -0.73$ (e) $\cos\theta = -0.15$ (f) $4\tan\theta + 5 = 0$

(g) $4\sin\theta = 3\cos\theta$ (h) $3\sin\theta = \dfrac{1}{\sin\theta}$ (i) $3\sin\theta = \tan\theta$

3 Find all the solutions in the interval $0 < x \leqslant 2\pi$ of each of the following equations.

(a) $\cos 2x = \frac{1}{4}$ (b) $\tan 3x = 3$ (c) $\sin 2x = -0.62$

(d) $\cos 4x = -\frac{1}{5}$ (e) $\tan 2x = 0.5$ (f) $\sin 3x = -0.45$

4 Find the roots in the interval $-\pi < t \leqslant \pi$ of each of the following equations.

(a) $\cos 3t = \frac{3}{4}$ (b) $\tan 2t = -2$ (c) $\sin 3t = -0.32$

(d) $\cos 2t = 0.264$ (e) $\tan 5t = 0.7$ (f) $\sin 2t = -0.42$

5 Find the roots (if there are any) in the interval $-\pi < \theta \leqslant \pi$ of the following equations.

(a) $\cos\frac{1}{2}\theta = \frac{1}{3}$ (b) $\tan\frac{2}{3}\theta = -5$ (c) $\sin\frac{1}{5}\theta = -\frac{1}{5}$

(d) $\cos\frac{1}{3}\theta = \frac{1}{2}$ (e) $\tan\frac{2}{3}\theta = 0.5$ (f) $\sin\frac{2}{5}\theta = -0.4$

6 Find the roots of the following equations which lie in the interval $0 \leqslant y \leqslant 2\pi$.

(a) $\sin(y + 0.1) = 0.4$ (b) $\cos(y - 0.2) = 0.6$ (c) $\tan(y - 0.5) = 0.4$

(d) $\sin(y - 1.5) = -0.3$ (e) $\cos(y + 1.2) = -0.7$ (f) $\tan(y + 4) = 2$

7 Find the roots (if there are any) in the interval $-\pi < \theta \leqslant \pi$ of the following equations.

(a) $\tan\theta = 2\cos\theta$ (b) $\sin^2\theta = 2\cos\theta$ (c) $\sin^2\theta = 2\cos^2\theta$

(d) $\sin^2\theta = 2\cos^2\theta - 1$ (e) $2\sin\theta = \tan\theta$ (f) $\tan^2\theta = 2\cos^2\theta$

8* Find in radians correct to 2 decimal places, the two smallest positive values of θ for which

(a) $\sin(\pi + \theta) = 0.3$,   (b) $\cos\left(\frac{1}{2}\pi - \theta\right) = -0.523$,   (c) $\tan\left(\frac{1}{2}\pi - \theta\right) = -4$,

(d) $\sin\left(2\theta + \frac{1}{3}\pi\right) = 0.123$,   (e) $\sin\left(\frac{1}{6}\pi - \theta\right) = 0.5$,   (f) $\cos\left(3\theta - \frac{2}{3}\pi\right) = 0$.

Miscellaneous exercise 9

1 The diagram shows a sector of a circle with centre O and radius 6 cm.

Angle $POQ = 0.6$ radians. Calculate the length of arc PQ and the area of sector POQ.   (OCR)

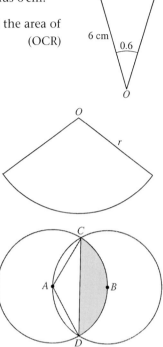

2 A sector OAB of a circle, of radius a and centre O, has $\angle AOB = \theta$ radians. Given that the area of the sector OAB is twice the square of the length of the arc AB, find θ.   (OCR)

3 The diagram shows a sector of a circle, with centre O and radius r. The length of the arc is equal to half the perimeter of the sector. Find the area of the sector in terms of r.   (OCR)

4 The diagram shows two circles, with centres A and B, intersecting at C and D in such a way that the centre of each lies on the circumference of the other. The radius of each circle is 1 unit. Write down the size of angle CAD and calculate the area of the shaded region (bounded by the arc CBD and the straight line CD). Hence show that the area of the region common to the interiors of the two circles is approximately 39% of the area of one circle.   (OCR)

5 In the diagram, ABC is an arc of a circle with centre O and radius 5 cm. The lines AD and CD are tangents to the circle at A and C respectively. Angle $AOC = \frac{2}{3}\pi$ radians.

Calculate the area of the region enclosed by AD, DC and the arc ABC, giving your answer correct to 2 significant figures.   (OCR)

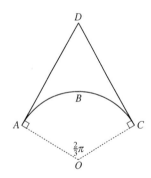

6 Find, either to 2 decimal places or an exact multiple of π, all values of x in the interval $-\pi < x \leqslant \pi$ satisfying

(a) $\sin x = -0.16$,   (b) $\cos x \, (1 + \sin x) = 0$,

(c) $(1 - \tan x) \sin x = 0$,   (d) $\sin 2x = 0.23$.

7 The diagram shows a circle with centre O and radius r, and a chord AB which subtends an angle θ radians at O. Express the area of the shaded segment bounded by the chord AB in terms of r and θ.

Given that the area of this segment is one-third of the area of triangle OAB, show that $3\theta - 4\sin\theta = 0$.

Find the positive value of θ satisfying $3\theta - 4\sin\theta = 0$ to within 0.1 radians, by tabulating values of $3\theta - 4\sin\theta$ and looking for a sign change, or otherwise.   (OCR)

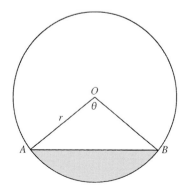

8 The diagram shows two circles, with centres A and B, which touch at C. The radius of each circle is r. The points D and E, one on each circle, are such that DE is parallel to the line ACB. Each of the angles DAC and EBC is θ radians, where $0 < \theta < \pi$. Express the length of DE in terms of r and θ.

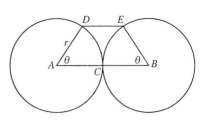

The length of DE is equal to the length of each of the minor arcs CD and CE.

(a) Show that $\theta + 2\cos\theta - 2 = 0$.

(b) Sketch the graph of $y = \cos\theta$ for $0 < \theta < \frac{1}{2}\pi$. By drawing on your graph a suitable straight line, the equation of which must be stated, show that the equation $\theta + 2\cos\theta - 2 = 0$ has exactly one root in the interval $0 < \theta < \frac{1}{2}\pi$.

Verify by calculation that θ lies between 1.10 and 1.11.   (OCR)

9 The diagram shows an arc ABC of a circle with centre O and radius r, and the chord AC. The length of the arc ABC is s, and angle $AOC = \theta$ rad. Express θ in terms of r and s, and deduce that the area of triangle AOC may be expressed as

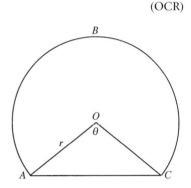

$$\tfrac{1}{2}r^2 \sin\left(2\pi - \frac{s}{r}\right).$$

Show, by a graphical argument based on a sketch of $y = \sin x$, or otherwise, that

$$\sin(2\pi - \alpha) = -\sin\alpha,$$

where α is any angle measured in radians.

Given that the area of triangle AOC is equal to one-fifth of the area of the major sector $OABC$, show that $\dfrac{s}{r} + 5\sin\left(\dfrac{s}{r}\right) = 0$.

10 Solve the equation $3\sin^2\theta + 4\cos\theta = 4$, giving all the roots, correct to 2 decimal places as appropriate, in the interval $0 \leqslant \theta \leqslant 2\pi$.

11 Solve the following equations giving any roots in terms of π in the interval $-2\pi \leqslant 0 \leqslant 2\pi$.

(a) $2\cos^2\theta + \sin^2\theta = 0$ (b) $2\cos^2\theta + \sin^2\theta = 1$ (c) $2\cos^2\theta + \sin^2\theta = 2$

10 The trapezium rule

This chapter is about approximating to integrals. When you have completed it, you should

- be able to use the trapezium rule to estimate the value of a definite integral
- be able to use a sketch, in some cases, to determine whether the trapezium rule approximation is an overestimate or an underestimate.

10.1 The need for approximation

There are times when it is not possible to evaluate a definite integral directly, using the standard method,

$$\int_a^b f(x)\,dx = \big[I(x)\big]_a^b = I(b) - I(a),$$

where $I(x)$ is the simplest function for which $\dfrac{d}{dx}I(x) = f(x)$.

Two examples which you cannot integrate are: $\displaystyle\int_0^1 \frac{1}{1+x^2}\,dx$, because you are not able to do it with your knowledge so far, and $\displaystyle\int_0^1 \sqrt{1+x^3}\,dx$, simply because it cannot be calculated exactly. You need to use another method to find approximate values of these integrals.

10.2 The trapezium rule: simple form

Suppose that you wish to find an estimate for the integral $\displaystyle\int_a^b f(x)\,dx$.

You know, from Section 5.5, that the value of the definite integral $\displaystyle\int_a^b f(x)\,dx$ can represent the shaded area in Fig. 10.1. The principle behind the trapezium rule is to approximate to this area by using the shaded trapezium in Fig. 10.2.

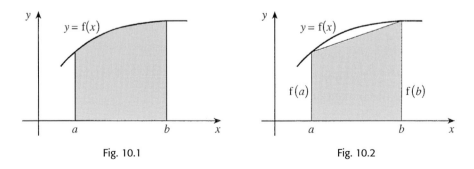

Fig. 10.1　　　　　　　　　　　　Fig. 10.2

The area of the shaded trapezium is given by

$$\text{area of trapezium} = \tfrac{1}{2} \times (\text{sum of parallel sides}) \times (\text{distance between them}),$$

so $$\text{area of trapezium} = \tfrac{1}{2} \times \{f(a) + f(b)\} \times (b - a).$$

So $$\int_a^b f(x)\, dx \approx \tfrac{1}{2}(b - a)\{f(a) + f(b)\}.$$

This is the simplest form of the **trapezium rule**.

> Notice that the symbol $\approx$, for 'is approximately equal to', is used rather than $=$ in stating the rule.

Example 10.2.1

Use the simplest form of the trapezium rule to find estimates for $\displaystyle\int_0^1 \frac{1}{1+x^2}\, dx$ and $\displaystyle\int_0^1 \sqrt{1+x^3}\, dx$.

$$\int_0^1 \frac{1}{1+x^2}\, dx \approx \tfrac{1}{2}(1 - 0)\left(\frac{1}{1+0^2} + \frac{1}{1+1^2} \right) = \tfrac{1}{2} \times 1 \times \left(1 + \tfrac{1}{2}\right) = 0.75.$$

$$\int_0^1 \sqrt{1+x^3}\, dx \approx \tfrac{1}{2}(1 - 0)\left(\sqrt{1+0^3} + \sqrt{1+1^3}\right) = \tfrac{1}{2} \times 1 \times \left(1 + \sqrt{2}\right) \approx 1.21.$$

10.3   The trapezium rule: general form

If you said that the simple form of the trapezium rule is not very accurate, especially over a large interval on the x-axis, you would be correct.

You can improve the accuracy by dividing the large interval from a to b into several smaller ones, and then using the trapezium rule on each interval. The amount of work sounds horrendous but, with good notation and organisation, it is not too bad.

Divide the interval from a to b into n equal intervals, each of width h, so that $nh = b - a$.

Call the x-coordinate of the left side of the first interval x_0, so $x_0 = a$, and then successively let $x_1 = x_0 + h$, $x_2 = x_0 + 2h$ and so on until $x_{n-1} = x_0 + (n-1)h$ and $x_n = x_0 + nh = b$.

To shorten the amount of writing, use the shorthand $y_0 = f(x_0)$, $y_1 = f(x_1)$ and so on, as in Fig. 10.3.

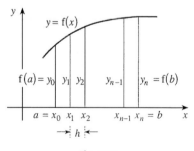

Fig. 10.3

Then, using the simple form of the trapezium rule on each interval of width h in turn, you find that

$$\int_a^b f(x)\,dx \approx \tfrac{1}{2}h(y_0 + y_1) + \tfrac{1}{2}h(y_1 + y_2) + \tfrac{1}{2}h(y_2 + y_3) + \cdots + \tfrac{1}{2}h(y_{n-1} + y_n)$$

$$= \tfrac{1}{2}h(y_0 + y_1 + y_1 + y_2 + y_2 + y_3 + \cdots + y_{n-2} + y_{n-1} + y_{n-1} + y_n)$$

$$= \tfrac{1}{2}h\{(y_0 + y_n) + 2(y_1 + y_2 + \cdots + y_{n-1})\}.$$

The trapezium rule with n intervals is sometimes called the trapezium rule with $n+1$ ordinates. (The term 'ordinate' means y-coordinate.)

> The **trapezium rule** with n intervals states that
>
> $$\int_a^b y\,dx \approx \tfrac{1}{2}h\{(y_0 + y_n) + 2(y_1 + y_2 + \cdots + y_{n-1})\},$$
>
> where $h = \dfrac{b-a}{n}, x_0 = a, x_r = a + rh$ for $r = 1, 2, \ldots, n-1,$
> $b = a + nh$, and y_r is the value of y at x_r.

Example 10.3.1

Use the trapezium rule with 5 intervals to estimate $\displaystyle\int_0^1 \frac{1}{1 + x^2}\,dx$, giving your answer correct to 3 decimal places.

It is convenient to use a tabular method to calculate $\{(y_0 + y_n) + 2(y_1 + y_2 + \cdots + y_{n-1})\}$. The values of y_n in the table are given correct to 5 decimal places.

n	x_n	y_n	Sums	Weight	Total
0	0	1			
5	1	0.5	1.5	$\times\, 1 =$	1.5
1	0.2	0.961 54			
2	0.4	0.862 07			
3	0.6	0.735 29			
4	0.8	0.609 76	3.168 66	$\times\, 2 =$	6.337 32
					7.837 32

The factor $\tfrac{1}{2}h$ is $\tfrac{1}{2} \times 0.2 = 0.1$. Therefore the approximation to the integral is $0.1 \times 7.837\,32 = 0.783\,732$. Thus the 5-interval approximation correct to 3 decimal places is 0.784.

The accurate value of $\displaystyle\int_0^1 \frac{1}{1 + x^2}\,dx$ is $\tfrac{1}{4}\pi$, which correct to 3 decimal places is 0.785, so you can see that the 5-interval version of the trapezium rule is a considerable improvement on the 1-interval version in Example 10.2.1.

How you organise the table to give the value of $\{(y_0 + y_n) + 2(y_1 + y_2 + \cdots + y_{n-1})\}$ is up to you, and may well depend on the kind of software or calculator that you have. It is important, however, that you make clear how you reach your answer.

10.4   Accuracy of the trapezium rule

It is not easy with the mathematics that you know at present to give a quantitative approach to the possible error involved with the trapezium rule.

However, in simple situations you can see whether the trapezium rule answer is too large or too small. If a graph is bending downwards over the whole interval from a to b, as in Fig. 10.4, then you can be certain that the trapezium rule will give you an underestimate of the true area. In Fig. 10.4 the approximation will underestimate by the area of the shaded region.

If on the other hand, a graph is bending upwards over the whole interval from a to b, as in Fig. 10.5, then you can be certain that the trapezium rule will give you an overestimate of the true area. In Fig. 10.5, where there are two trapezia, the approximation will overestimate by the area of the shaded region.

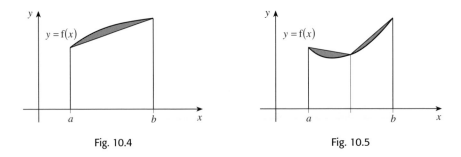

Fig. 10.4   Fig. 10.5

However, if the graph sometimes bends upwards and sometimes downwards over the interval from a to b, you cannot be sure whether your approximation to the integral is an overestimate or an underestimate.

Exercise 10

1 Use the simplest case of the trapezium rule (that is, 1 interval) to estimate the values of

(a) $\displaystyle\int_3^4 \sqrt{1+x}\,dx$,   (b) $\displaystyle\int_2^4 \frac{1}{x}\,dx$.

2 Use the trapezium rule with 3 intervals to estimate the value of $\displaystyle\int_0^3 \sqrt{1+x^2}\,dx$.

3 Use the trapezium rule with 3 ordinates (that is, 2 intervals) to estimate the value of
$$\int_1^3 \sqrt{1 + \sqrt{x}}\, dx.$$

4 Find approximations to the value of $\int_1^5 \frac{1}{x^2}\, dx$ by

(a) using the trapezium rule with 2 intervals,

(b) using the trapezium rule with 4 intervals.

(c) Evaluate the integral exactly and compare your answer with those found in parts (a) and (b).

5 The diagram shows the graph of $y = \frac{4}{\sqrt{x}}$.

Use the trapezium rule with 7 ordinates to find an approximation to the area of the shaded region, and explain why the trapezium rule overestimates the true value.

6 Use the trapezium rule with 5 intervals to estimate

the value of $\int_0^1 \left(\frac{1}{10}x^2 + 1\right) dx$. Draw the graph of

$y = \frac{1}{10}x^2 + 1$ and explain why the trapezium rule gives an overestimate of the true value of the integral.

7 Draw the graph of $y = x^3 + 8$ and use it to explain why use of the trapezium rule with 5 ordinates will give the exact value of $\int_{-2}^2 (x^3 + 8)\, dx$.

8 Find an approximation to $\int_1^2 \sqrt{x^2 + 4x}\, dx$ by using the trapezium rule with 4 intervals.

9 Find an approximation to $\int_0^4 \frac{x^2}{2^x}\, dx$ by using the trapezium rule with 8 intervals.

10 The diagram shows part of a circle with its centre at the origin. The curve has equation $y = \sqrt{25 - x^2}$.

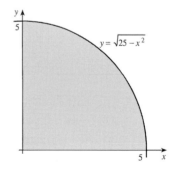

(a) Use the trapezium rule with 10 intervals to find an approximation to the area of the shaded region.

(b) Does the trapezium rule overestimate or underestimate the true area?

(c) Find the exact area of the shaded region.

(d) By comparing your answers to parts (a) and (c), obtain an estimate for π to 2 decimal places.

Miscellaneous exercise 10

1 Use the trapezium rule, with ordinates at $x = 1$, $x = 2$ and $x = 3$, to estimate the value of
$\int_1^3 \sqrt{40 - x^3}\, dx$.   (OCR)

2 The diagram shows the region R bounded by the curve
$y = \sqrt{1 + x^3}$, the axes and the line $x = 2$. Use the trapezium rule
with 4 intervals to obtain an approximation for the area of R,
showing your working and giving your answer to a suitable
degree of accuracy.

Explain, with the aid of a sketch, whether the approximation
is an overestimate or an underestimate.   (OCR)

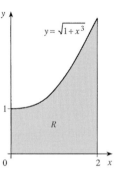

3 Use the trapezium rule with subdivisions at $x = 3$ and $x = 5$
to obtain an approximation to $\int_1^7 \dfrac{x^3}{1 + x^4}\, dx$, giving your answer
correct to 3 places of decimals.   (OCR)

4 Use the trapezium rule with 5 intervals to estimate the value of $\int_0^{0.5} \sqrt{1 + x^2}\, dx$, showing
your working. Give your answer correct to 2 decimal places.   (OCR)

5 The diagram shows the region R bounded by the axes, the
curve $y = (x^2 + 1)^{-\frac{3}{2}}$ and the line $x = 1$. Use the trapezium
rule, with ordinates at $x = 0$, $x = \frac{1}{2}$ and $x = 1$, to estimate
the value of

$$\int_0^1 (x^2 + 1)^{-\frac{3}{2}}\, dx$$

giving your answer correct to 2 significant figures. (OCR)

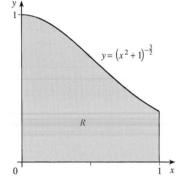

6 A certain function f is continuous and is such that

$\quad$ f(2.0) = 15, $\quad$ f(2.5) = 22, $\quad$ f(3.0) = 31,
$\quad$ f(3.5) = 28, $\quad$ f(4.0) = 27.

Use the trapezium rule to find an approximation to $\int_2^4 f(x)\, dx$.

7 The diagram shows a sketch of $y = \sqrt{2 + x^3}$ for values of
x between -0.5 and 0.5.
(a) Use the trapezium rule, with ordinates at $x = -0.5$,
$x = 0$ and $x = 0.5$ to find an approximate value for
$\int_{-0.5}^{0.5} \sqrt{2 + x^3}\, dx$.

(b) Explain briefly, with reference to the diagram, why
the trapezium rule can be expected to give a good
approximation to the value of the integral in this
case.   (OCR)

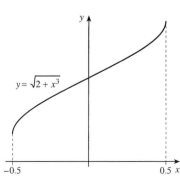

8 The speeds of an athlete on a training run were recorded at 30-second intervals:

Time after start (s)	0	30	60	90	120	150	180	210	240
Speed (m s^{-1})		3.0	4.6	4.8	5.1	5.4	5.2	4.9	4.6	3.8

The area under a speed–time graph represents the distance travelled. Use the trapezium rule to estimate the distance covered by the athlete, correct to the nearest 10 metres.

9 At a time t minutes after the start of a journey, the speed of a car travelling along a main road is v km h^{-1}. The table gives values of v every minute on the 10-minute journey.

t	0	1	2	3	4	5	6	7	8	9	10
v	0	31	46	42	54	57	73	70	68	48	0

Use the trapezium rule to estimate of the length of the 10-minute journey in kilometres.

10 A river is 18 metres wide in a certain region and its depth, d metres, at a point x metres from one side is given by the formula $d = \frac{1}{18}\sqrt{x(18 - x)(18 + x)}$.

(a) Produce a table showing the depths (correct to 3 decimal places where necessary) at $x = 0, 3, 6, 9, 12, 15$ and 18.

(b) Use the trapezium rule to estimate the cross-sectional area of the river in this region.

(c) Given that, in this region, the river is flowing at a uniform speed of 100 metres per minute, estimate the number of cubic metres of water passing per minute.   (OCR)

11 The left diagram shows the part of the curve $y = 2.5 - 2^{1-x^2}$ for which $-0.5 \leqslant x \leqslant 0.5$. The shaded region in the left diagram forms the cross-section of the straight concrete drainage channel shown in the right diagram. The units involved are metres.

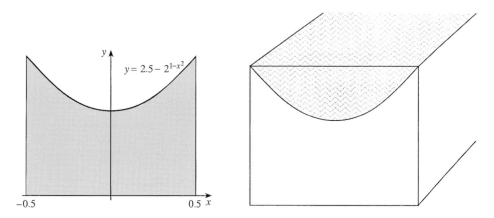

(a) Use the trapezium rule with 4 intervals to estimate the area of the shaded region.

(b) Estimate the volume of concrete in a 20-metre length of channel.

(c) Estimate the volume of water in the 20-metre length of channel when it is full.

(d) Of the estimates in parts (b) and (c), which is an overestimate and which is an underestimate?

12 The diagram shows the curve $y = 4^{-x}$. Taking subdivisions
    at $x = 0.25,\ 0.5,\ 0.75$, find an approximation to the shaded
    area.

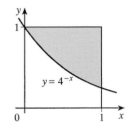

13 The integral $\displaystyle\int_{36}^{64} \sqrt{x}\,dx$ is denoted by I.

    (a) Find the exact value of I.

    (b) Use the trapezium rule with 2 intervals to find an estimate
        for I, giving your answer in terms of $\sqrt{2}$.

    Use your two answers to deduce that $\sqrt{2} \approx \frac{149}{105}$.

14* The trapezium rule, with 2 intervals of equal width, is to be used to find an approximate
    value for $\displaystyle\int_{1}^{2} \frac{1}{x^2}\,dx$. Explain, with the aid of a sketch, why the approximation will be
    greater than the exact value of the integral.

    Calculate the approximate value and the exact value, giving each answer correct to
    3 decimal places.

    Another approximation to $\displaystyle\int_{1}^{2} \frac{1}{x^2}\,dx$ is to be calculated by using two trapezia of unequal
    width; the ordinates are at $x = 1$, $x = h$ and $x = 2$. Find, in terms of h, the total area, T, of
    these two trapezia.

    Find the value of h for which T is a minimum, and find this minimum value of T, giving
    your answer correct to 3 decimal places.

15* (a) Calculate the exact value of the integral $\displaystyle\int_{0}^{1} x^2\,dx$.

    (b) Find the trapezium rule approximations to this integral using 1, 2, 4 and 8 intervals.
        Call these A_1, A_2, A_4 and A_8.

    (c) For each of your answers in part (b), calculate the error E_i, where

        $$E_i = \int_{0}^{1} x^2\,dx - A_i, \quad \text{for} \quad i = 1,\ 2,\ 4 \text{ and } 8.$$

    (d) Look at your results for part (c), and guess the relationship between the error E_n and
        the number n of intervals taken.

    (e) How many intervals would you need to approximate to the integral to within 10^{-6}?

Revision exercise 4

1 A teacher received a salary of £12 800 in his first full year of teaching. He models his future salary by assuming it to increase by a constant amount of £950 each year up to a maximum of £20 400.

   (a) How much will he earn in his fifth year of teaching?

   (b) In which year does he first receive the maximum salary?

   (c) Determine expressions for the total amount he will have received by the end of his nth year of teaching, stating clearly for which values of n each is valid.

   His twin sister chose accountancy as her profession. She started her career in the same year as he did. Her first year's salary was £13 500, and she can expect her salary to increase at a constant rate of 5% each year.

   (d) Select an appropriate mathematical model and use this to determine her annual salary in her nth year as an accountant.

   (e) Show that she earns less than he in their fourth year of working.

   (f) Which is the first year after that in which he earns less than she does? (OCR)

2 A geometric progression has first term 3 and common ratio 0.8. Find the sum of the first twelve terms of this geometric progression, giving your answer correct to two decimal places. Write down the sum to infinity of the geometric progression. (OCR)

3 Find the factors of the polynomial $x^3 - x^2 - 14x + 24$.

4 The diagram shows a sketch of the curve $y = 2x + \dfrac{1}{x}$ for positive values of x. Let R be the region bounded by the curve, the x-axis, and the lines $x = 1$ and $x = 4$. Use the trapezium rule, with intervals of width 0.5, to find an approximate value of the area of R, giving your answer to four significant figures.

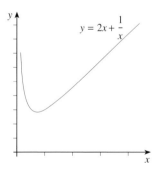

$$y = 2x + \frac{1}{x}$$

5 The polynomial P(x) is defined by: P(x) = $2x^3 - 7x^2 + 2x + 3$.

   (a) Show that $x + 2$ is not a factor of P(x).

   (b) Show that P(x) has a factor of $2x + 1$.

   (c) Express P(x) as the product of three linear factors. (OCR)

6 A region R is bounded by part of the curve with equation $y = \sqrt{64 - x^3}$, the positive x-axis and the positive y-axis. Use the trapezium rule with four intervals to approximate to the area of R, giving your answer to one decimal place.

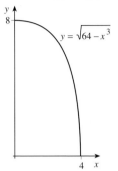

7 A polynomial $P(x)$ is the product of $(x^3 + ax^2 - x - 2)$ and $x - b$.
   (a) The coefficients of x^3 and x in $P(x)$ are zero. Find the values of a and b.
   (b) Hence factorise $P(x)$ completely and find the roots of the equation $P(x) = 0$.   (OCR)

8 The diagram shows a sector of a circle with centre C and radius 20 cm. The angle ACB is θ radians. Given that the length of the arc AB is 46 cm, find
   (a) the value of θ,
   (b) the area of the sector.   (OCR)

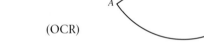

9 The first term of a sequence is 8 and the second term is 10.
   (a) Given that the terms of the sequence form an arithmetic progression, find the sum of the first 100 terms.
   (b) Given instead that the terms of the sequence form a geometric progression and that the sum of the first K terms is greater than 10^{15}, find the least possible value of K.   (OCR)

10 A geometric progression $u_1, u_2, u_3, \ldots$ is defined by
$$u_1 = 5, \qquad u_{n+1} = 0.6u_n.$$
   (a) Find u_4.
   (b) Find the sum to infinity of the terms of the geometric progression.   (OCR)

11 The diagram shows a sector of a circle with centre O and radius r cm. The arc AB subtends angle of $53°$ at O.
   (a) Express $53°$ in radians, correct to 3 decimal places.
   (b) Given that the length of the arc AB is 37 cm, find the value of r.

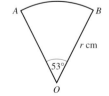

12 A geometric progression has first term 30 and common ratio 0.8. Find

    (a) the 20th term, giving your answer correct to 3 significant figures,

    (b) the sum of the first 20 terms, giving your answer correct to 3 significant figures,

    (c) the sum to infinity.

13 Find the smallest integer satisfying the inequality $2^n > 100^{643}$.   (OCR)

14 The polynomial $p(x)$, defined by $p(x) = (x + 2)^4 - 13x + a$, has $x - 1$ as a factor.

    (a) Find the value of the constant a.

    (b) Verify that the remainder when $p(x)$ is divided by $x + 1$ is -54.

    (c) Find the quotient when $p(x)$ is divided by $(x - 1)(x + 4)$.   (OCR)

15 Given that $x - 2$ is a factor of $ax^3 + ax^2 + ax - 42$, find the value of the constant a.   (OCR)

16 The diagram shows part of a circle with centre O and radius 15 cm. The major sector $OABC$ is shaded. The triangle AOC is equilateral. The reflex angle subtended at O by the major arc ABC is θ radians.

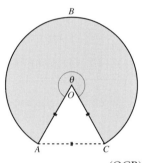

    (a) Find the value of θ.

    (b) Find the perimeter of the major sector $OABC$, giving your answer correct to 3 significant figures.

    (c) Find the area of the major sector $OABC$, giving your answer correct to 3 significant figures.   (OCR)

17 An arithmetic progression has first term 8 and common difference 1.2. The sum of the first n terms of the arithmetic progression is denoted by S_n.

A geometric progression has first term 8 and common ratio 1.2. The sum of the first 35 terms of the geometric progression is denoted by G.

Given that $S_n > G$, find the least possible value of n.   (OCR)

18 The first term of a geometric progression is 24 and the second term is 18. Find the sum to infinity.   (OCR)

19 A fitness programme includes a daily number of step-ups. The number of step-ups scheduled for Day 1 is 20 and the number on each successive day is to be 3 more than the previous day (23 on Day 2, 26 on Day 3, etc.).

The programme also includes a daily time to be spent jogging. The time, T_N minutes, to be spent jogging on Day N is given by the formula $T_N = 15 \times 1.05^{N-1}$.

    (a) Find the total number of step-ups scheduled to be completed during the first 30 days of the fitness programme.

    (b) Verify that the daily jogging time first exceeds 60 minutes on Day 30.

    (c) Find the total time to be spent jogging during the first 30 days of the fitness programme.   (OCR)

20 A coin is made by starting with an equilateral triangle ABC of side 2 cm. With centre A an arc of a circle is drawn joining B to C. Similar arcs join C to A and A to B.

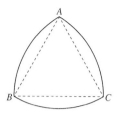

Find, exactly, the perimeter of the coin and the area of one of its faces.

21 The value of the definite integral $\displaystyle\int_0^{0.1} (1 + 3x^2)^{12}\, dx$ is denoted by I.

(a) Use the trapezium rule with 2 intervals, each of width 0.05, to find an approximation to I, giving your answer correct to 3 significant figures.

A second approximation to I is to be found, based on a binomial expansion.

(b) The first three terms in the expansion of $(1 + 3x^2)^{12}$ are $1 + ax^2 + bx^4$. Find the values of the constants a and b.

(c) Hence, by evaluating $\displaystyle\int_0^{0.1} \left(1 + ax^2 + bx^4\right) dx$, find this approximation to I, giving your answer correct to 4 decimal places.

22 It is given that $x - 2$ is a factor of $f(x)$, where $f(x) = 2x^3 - 7x^2 + x + a$. Find the value of a and factorise $f(x)$ completely.

Sketch the graph of $y = f(x)$. (You do not need to find the coordinates of the stationary points.)

Use the trapezium rule, with ordinates at $x = -1$, $x = 0$, $x = 1$ and $x = 2$ to find an approximation to $\displaystyle\int_{-1}^{2} f(x)\, dx$.

Find the exact value of the integral and show that the trapezium rule gives a value that is in error by about 11%.   (OCR)

23 Express $\log_b x + 2 \log_b y + 1$ as a single logarithm to base b.

24 When $£A$ is invested at compound interest at $100r\%$, the amount increases to $£A(1 + r)^n$ after n complete years.

(a) When $r = 0.05$, calculate the length of time required for an amount of money to double.

(b) How much money should be invested now at 5% interest in order to have £20 000 in 20 years time?

25 You are given that the area of the region between the curve with equation $y = \dfrac{1}{x}$ and the x-axis between $x = 1$ and $x = 2$ is 0.693, correct to 3 decimal places.

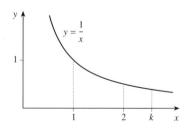

In the diagram, k is the number such that the area under the graph between $x = 2$ and $x = k$ is 1.

By approximating the area between $x = 2$ and $x = k$ by the area of a trapezium, find an approximation to the value of k.

Practice examination 1 for C2

Time 1 hour 30 minutes

Answer all the questions.
You are permitted to use a graphic calculator in this paper.

1 Find the expansion of $(2 - x)^5$ in powers of x, simplifying the coefficients. [4]

2 (i) Sketch the graph of $y = \cos x$, for $0 \leqslant x \leqslant \pi$. [1]

   (ii) Use the trapezium rule, with two intervals each of width $\frac{1}{6}\pi$, to find an approximate value for the area of the region bounded by the curve $y = \cos x$, the axes and the line $x = \frac{1}{3}\pi$. [3]

   (iii) State with a reason whether this approximation is an underestimate or an overestimate. [2]

3 (i) Express each of the following in terms of $\log_{10} x$:
   (a) $\log_{10}(x^2)$, [1]
   (b) $\log_{10}(10x^2)$. [2]

   (ii) Given that $\log_{10}(y + 1) = 2 - \log_{10} x$, express y in terms of x as simply as possible. [3]

4 (i) Use the factor theorem to show that $x + 2$ is a factor of $2x^3 + x^2 - 7x - 2$. [2]

   (ii) Find the quotient and remainder when $x^3 + 2$ is divided by $x + 2$. [5]

5 (i) Find $\int \left(\dfrac{1}{x^2} - \dfrac{1}{\sqrt{x}} \right) dx$. [4]

   (ii) A curve passes through the point $(1, 0)$ and is such that $\dfrac{dy}{dx} = \dfrac{1}{x^2} - \dfrac{1}{\sqrt{x}}$. Find the equation of the curve. [3]

6

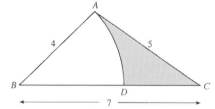

The diagram shows triangle ABC, in which $AB = 4$ cm, $BC = 7$ cm and $CA = 5$ cm.

(i) Calculate the size of angle B. [3]

The point D lies on BC, and the arc AD is part of a circle with centre B and radius 4 cm.

(ii) Calculate the perimeter and the area of the shaded region ADC. [6]

7 (i)   Show that the equation $3 \tan \theta = 2 \cos \theta$ may be written in the form

$2 \sin^2 \theta + 3 \sin \theta - 2 = 0$.   [3]

(ii)   Hence solve the equation $3 \tan \theta = 2 \cos \theta$, for $0 \leqslant x \leqslant 2\pi$.   [4]

(iii) Deduce the number of solutions of the equation $3 \tan \theta = 2 \cos \theta$ for which
$-5\pi \leqslant \theta \leqslant 5\pi$. Explain your reasoning clearly.   [2]

8

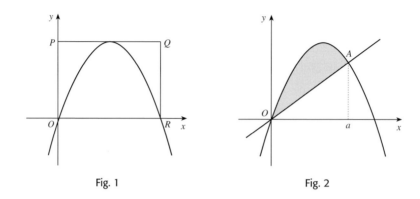

Fig. 1   Fig. 2

The curve with equation $y = x(6 - x)$ crosses the x-axis at the origin O and at the
point R. The rectangle OPQR is such that PQ is the tangent to the curve at its maximum
point (see Fig. 1).

(i)   Show that the area of the region between the curve and the x-axis is two-thirds of the
area of the rectangle OPQR.   [6]

A straight line through the origin meets the curve at the point A with x-coordinate a, as
shown in Fig. 2.

(ii) Find, in terms of a, the area of the shaded region between the curve and the line. Hence
find, correct to 3 significant figures, the value of a for which this area is half of the area
of the rectangle OPQR.   [6]

9 An arithmetic progression has first term a and common difference d.

(i)   Write down expressions, in terms of a and d, for the second and sixth terms of the
progression.   [2]

The first, second and sixth terms of this arithmetic progression are also the first three
terms of a geometric progression.

(ii) Prove that $d = 3a$.   [3]

(iii) Given that $a = 2$, find
(a) the sum of the first 15 terms of each progression,   [4]
(b) the least value of n for which the nth term of the geometric progression
exceeds 10^{50}.   [3]

Practice examination 2 for C2

Time 1 hour 30 minutes

Answer all the questions.
You are permitted to use a graphic calculator in this paper.

1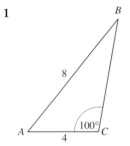

In triangle ABC, $AB = 8\,\text{cm}$, $AC = 4\,\text{cm}$ and angle $ACB = 100°$ (see diagram). Calculate

(i) the size of angle A,   [3]

(ii) the area of the triangle.   [2]

2 (i) Sketch the graph of $y = 2^x$, stating the coordinates of any intersections with
        the axes.   [2]

   (ii) The curve in part (i) is reflected in the y-axis. Show that the equation of the resulting
        graph can be written in the form $y = k^x$, and state the value of the constant k.   [3]

3 (i) Draw a sketch to illustrate the region whose area is given by $\displaystyle\int_2^8 \frac{1}{x^2}\,dx$, and evaluate
        this integral.   [5]

   (ii) State the value of $\displaystyle\int_2^\infty \frac{1}{x^2}\,dx$.   [1]

4 The gradient of a curve is given by $\dfrac{dy}{dx} = x^2 - 1$, and the curve passes through the point
   $(2, 1)$. Find the equation of the curve.   [6]

5 The polynomial $x^3 + Ax^2 + x + B$, where A and B are constants, is denoted by $f(x)$. When
   $f(x)$ is divided by $x - 1$ the remainder is 4, and when it is divided by $x + 2$ the remainder
   is -11. Show that $x + 1$ is a factor of $f(x)$.   [7]

6 (i) Express $\log_a 12 - \log_a 9 + \log_a 3 + 1$ as a single logarithm.   [4]

   (ii) Let $y = \log_2 x$ and $z = \log_8 x$.

       (a) Write down expressions for x in terms of y and x in terms of z.   [2]

       (b) Hence prove that $y = 3z$.   [2]

7 The height, h metres, of the water in a harbour t hours after noon is given by the formula
$h = 4 + 2\sin 30t$.

(i) Find the height at 5 p.m. [2]

(ii) State the greatest and least heights of the water. State also how many 'high tides' there
are in a 24-hour period, explaining your reasoning. [3]

(iii) A boat can enter the harbour provided that the height of the water is at least
3 metres. Find the times
(a) before midnight,
(b) after midnight,
between which the boat **cannot** enter the harbour. [6]

8 (i) A sequence $t_1, t_2, t_3, \ldots$ is defined by $t_n = 3n + 2$, for $n \geqslant 1$.

(a) Write down the values of t_1 and t_2. [2]

(b) Simplify $t_{n+1} - t_n$, and explain how the result shows that the sequence is an
arithmetic progression. [3]

(c) Find $\sum\limits_{r=1}^{1000} t_r$. [3]

(ii) A geometric progression has first term 2 and common ratio 1.05. Calculate the least
number of terms of this progression required for the sum of the terms to exceed the
value found in part (i)(c). [4]

9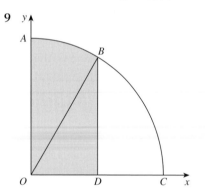

The diagram shows a quarter-circle ABC with centre O and radius 1 unit. D is the mid-point
of OC, and DB is parallel to OA.

(i) By considering separately the triangle OBD and the sector OAB, show that the area of
the shaded region $OABD$ is $\frac{1}{24}(2\pi + 3\sqrt{3})$. [6]

(ii) The equation of the circular arc ABC is $y = \sqrt{1 - x^2}$. Use the trapezium rule, with four
intervals, to calculate an estimate of the area of the shaded region, and show how this
leads to the approximation $\pi \approx 3.13$. [6]

Answers to C1

1 Coordinates, points and lines

Exercise 1A (page 5)

1 (a) 13   (b) 5   (c) 17   (d) 10
   (e) 5   (f) 5   (g) $\sqrt{50}$ (h) $\sqrt{52}$

5 5

6 (a) $DE = DG = \sqrt{10},\quad EF = FG = \sqrt{40}$
   (b) Kite

Exercise 1B (page 7)

1 (a) $(4, 13)$ (b) $(1, 8)$
   (c) $\left(-\frac{1}{2}, -4\frac{1}{2}\right)$ (d) $\left(-5\frac{1}{2}, 4\frac{1}{2}\right)$
   (e) $(2a, 3b)$ (f) $(a, -3b)$

2 $(2, 3)$

3 $(7, 10)$

4 $(-1, -3)$

6 A

7 $(4, -6)$

Exercise 1C (page 10)

1 (a) 2   (b) -3
   (c) $\frac{1}{2}$ (d) $-\frac{3}{4}$

2 $\frac{1}{2}, \frac{1}{2}$; points are collinear

3 No

4 $\frac{8}{5}$

5 7

6 (a) Gradients PQ and RS both
      -1, QR and SP both $\frac{3}{5}$
   (b) Parallelogram

7 (a) Gradients PQ and RS are both
      $-\frac{1}{3}$, QR is 4 and SP is $\frac{3}{4}$
   (b) Trapezium

Exercise 1D (page 12)

1 (a) $17a$ (b) $\sqrt{20}$
   (c) 23   (d) $9a$

3 (a) $(2p + 3, 2p - 3)$ (b) $(p + 4, -2)$
   (c) $(3p, 3q)$ (d) $(a + 3, b + 1)$

4 (a) -2 (b) -1
   (c) $(p - 3)/(q - 1)$ (d) 0

5 $\dfrac{y}{x - 3}, \dfrac{6 - y}{5 - x}$

6 5

7 (a) M is $\left(\frac{1}{2}, -1\frac{1}{2}\right)$, N is $\left(1\frac{1}{2}, 4\right)$

8 (a) $MN = 5$, $BC = 10$

9 (d) Rhombus

10 (d) Rectangle

12 (a) M is $(6, 1)$ (c) N is $\left(8, 5\frac{1}{2}\right)$

Exercise 1E (page 18)

1 (a) Yes   (b) No
   (c) Yes   (d) No
   (e) Yes   (f) No
   (g) Yes   (h) Yes

2 (a) $y = 5x - 7$ (b) $y = -3x + 1$
   (c) $2y = x + 8$ (d) $8y = -3x + 2$
   (e) $y = -3x$ (f) $y = 8$
   (g) $4y = -3x - 19$ (h) $2y = x + 3$
   (i) $8y = 3x + 1$ (j) $2y = -x + 11$
   (k) $y = -2x + 3$ (l) $y = 3x + 1$
   (m) $y = 7x - 4$ (n) $y = -x + 2$
   (o) $8y = -5x - 1$ (p) $5y = -3x + 9$
   (q) $y = 7x - 7d$ (r) $y = mx + 4$
   (s) $y = 3x + c$ (t) $y = mx - mc$

3 (a) $y = 3x + 1$ (b) $y = 2x - 3$
   (c) $2x + 3y - 12 = 0$ (d) $x - 3 = 0$
   (e) $3x - 5y - 45 = 0$ (f) $3x + y - 8 = 0$
   (g) $y = -3$ (h) $x + 3y - 2 = 0$
   (i) $5x + 3y + 14 = 0$ (j) $2x + 7y + 11 = 0$
   (k) $x + 3 = 0$ (l) $x + y + 1 = 0$
   (m) $y = 3x + 1$ (n) $5x + 3y + 13 = 0$
   (o) $3x + 5y = 0$ (p) $qx - py = 0$
   (q) $x + 3y - p - 3q = 0$ (r) $x - p = 0$
   (s) $x - y - p + q = 0$ (t) $qx + py - pq = 0$

4 (a) -2 (b) $\frac{3}{4}$
   (c) $-2\frac{1}{2}$ (d) 0
   (e) $1\frac{1}{2}$ (f) Undefined
   (g) -1 (h) 3
   (i) $-\frac{1}{2}$ (j) $2\frac{1}{3}$
   (k) m (l) $-p/q$

5 $x - 2y = -4$

6 $y = -2x + 5$

7 $3x + 8y - 19 = 0$

8 $x + y = 12$

9 $y - 7 = 0$

10 $y = mx - md$

11 (a) $(7, 3)$ (b) $(2, 7)$
(c) $\left(-\frac{1}{4}, -\frac{7}{8}\right)$ (d) $(-3, -1)$
(e) $(2, 4)$ (f) $(6, 5)$
(g) No intersection   (h) $(2, -1)$
(i) Same lines
(j) $(c/a(1 + 2b), 2c/(1 + 2b))$
(k) $((d - c)/2m, (c + d)/2)$
(l) $(1/(a - b), 1/(a - b))$

12 For example, $a = 0$, $b = 0$ and $c = 1$.

Exercise 1F (page 23)

1 (a) $-\frac{1}{2}$ (b) $\frac{1}{3}$ (c) $-1\frac{1}{3}$
(d) $1\frac{1}{5}$ (e) 1 (f) $-\frac{4}{7}$
(g) m (h) $-1/m$ (i) $-q/p$
(j) Undefined   (k) $1/m$ (l) $(c - b)/a$

2 (a) $x + 4y = 14$ (b) $y = 2x + 7$
(c) $x - 5y = 27$ (d) $x = 7$
(e) $3x - 2y = -11$ (f) $5x + 3y = 29$
(g) $y + 3 = 0$ (h) $x + 2y = 6$
(i) $x + my = 0$ (j) $x + my = a + mb$
(k) $nx + y = d + nc$ (l) $bx - ay = 2a - b$

3 $x + 3y = 13$, $(1, 4)$

4 $3x + 2y = 5$, $(3, -2)$

5 $x + 2y = 8$

6 (a) (i) $x = 8$ (ii) $x - 2y = 2$ (b) $(8, 3)$

Miscellaneous exercise 1 (page 23)

2 $(2, -1)$

3 (b) $(3.6, 0)$

4 (a) $3x - y = 9$ (b) $(3, 0)$ and $(5, 6)$

6 (a) $4x - 3y = 13$ (b) $(4, 1)$ (c) 5

7 Area $= 78$

8 $(0, 0)$, $(12, 12)$ and $(14, 4)$

9 $2x + 7y = 23$

10 $3x - 4y - 1 = 0$

11 $\left(3\frac{1}{2}, 4\right)$, $(4, 3)$

12 (a) $x + 3y = 9$ (b) $(0.9, 2.7)$ (c) $\sqrt{0.9}$

14 $3x + 5y - 4 = 0$, $\left(1\frac{1}{3}, 0\right)$

15 $\left(3\frac{1}{2}, -1\frac{1}{2}\right)$, -7, $x - 7y - 14 = 0$

16 (a) $(-3, 0)$, $(0, 1.5)$ (b) $x - 2y + 3 = 0$
(c) $(1.8, 2.4)$

17 $x - 2y - 8 = 0$, $(2, -3)$, $\sqrt{80}$

19 25

20 (a) $x + y = 1$ (b) $(2, -1)$, $(0, 1)$

21 $y = 2$, $3x + 4y = 18$, $y = 3x - 8$

22 $(-4, -16)$

23 $y = 5x - 6$

24 (a) $y = 4x - 5$ (b) $(3, 7)$ (c) $(4, 11)$

25 (a) $\frac{1}{2}$, -2, $-\frac{1}{3}$
(b) As gradient $AB \times$ gradient $BC = -1$, AB is perpendicular to BC, so triangle ABC is right-angled.

2   Surds

Exercise 2A (page 30)

1 (a) 3 (b) 10 (c) 16 (d) 4
(e) 8 (f) 6 (g) 15 (h) 30
(i) 72 (j) 60 (k) 28 (l) 27
(m) 5 (n) 48 (o) 256 (p) 5

2 (a) $3\sqrt{2}$ (b) $2\sqrt{5}$ (c) $2\sqrt{6}$
(d) $4\sqrt{2}$ (e) $2\sqrt{10}$ (f) $3\sqrt{5}$
(g) $4\sqrt{3}$ (h) $5\sqrt{2}$ (i) $3\sqrt{6}$
(j) $6\sqrt{2}$ (k) $3\sqrt{15}$ (l) $15\sqrt{3}$

3 (a) $5\sqrt{2}$ (b) $3\sqrt{3}$ (c) $\sqrt{5}$
(d) $2\sqrt{2}$ (e) 0 (f) $6\sqrt{3}$
(g) $6\sqrt{11}$ (h) $12\sqrt{2}$ (i) $13\sqrt{5}$
(j) $\sqrt{13}$ (k) $30\sqrt{5}$ (l) $6\sqrt{6} - \sqrt{3}$

4 (a) 2 (b) 3 (c) 2 (d) 5
(e) 5 (f) 3 (g) $\frac{1}{4}$ (h) $\frac{1}{2}$

5 (a) 1 (b) 7 (c) 4 (d) 7
(e) 46 (f) 5 (g) 107 (h) -3

6 (a) $\sqrt{3} + 1$ (b) $\sqrt{5} - 1$ (c) $\sqrt{6} + \sqrt{2}$
(d) $2 - \sqrt{3}$ (e) $3 + \sqrt{2}$ (f) $3 + \sqrt{6}$

Exercise 2B (page 34)

1 (a) $\frac{1}{3}\sqrt{3}$ (b) $\frac{1}{5}\sqrt{5}$
(c) $2\sqrt{2}$ (d) $\sqrt{6}$
(e) $\sqrt{11}$ (f) $\frac{1}{2}\sqrt{2}$
(g) $4\sqrt{3}$ (h) $2\sqrt{7}$
(i) $\sqrt{3}$ (j) $\frac{1}{3}\sqrt{3}$
(k) $\sqrt{15}$ (l) $\frac{4}{5}\sqrt{30}$
(m) $\frac{7}{6}\sqrt{6}$ (n) $\frac{2}{3}\sqrt{6}$
(o) $\frac{3}{2}\sqrt{6}$ (p) $\frac{1}{9}\sqrt{6}$

2 (a) $7\sqrt{3}$ (b) $4\sqrt{3}$ (c) $\sqrt{3}$
(d) $\sqrt{3}$ (e) $12\sqrt{3}$ (f) $-5\sqrt{3}$

3 (a) $20\sqrt{2}\,\text{cm}^2$ (b) $3\sqrt{10}\,\text{cm}$

4 (a) $x = 5\sqrt{2}$ (b) $y = -4\sqrt{2}$ (c) $z = 3\sqrt{2}$

5 (a) $2\sqrt[3]{3}$ (b) $4\sqrt[3]{3}$
(c) $3\sqrt[3]{3}$ (d) $5\sqrt[3]{3}$

6 (a) 10.198 039 027 2
   (b) 25.495 097 568 0
   (c) 2.549 509 756 8

7 (a) $4\sqrt{13}$ cm   (b) $5\sqrt{11}$ cm
   (c) $2\sqrt{15}$ cm   (d) $3\sqrt{5}$ cm

8 (a) $x = 3\sqrt{5}$, $y = 4$

9 (a) $\sqrt{2} + 1$ (b) $\frac{3+\sqrt{3}}{3}$
   (c) $\frac{4+\sqrt{2}}{7}$ (d) $\frac{6+\sqrt{2}}{17}$
   (e) $3 - 2\sqrt{2}$ (f) $3 + \sqrt{3}$
   (g) $\frac{5+3\sqrt{2}}{7}$ (h) $\frac{8+9\sqrt{2}}{14}$

10 $\frac{27-10\sqrt{2}}{23}$

11 $x = \sqrt{5} + 2$, $y = -\sqrt{5} - 1$

12 (a) $\left(1 - \frac{1}{2}\sqrt{2}\right)$ cm   (b) $\frac{1}{2}(\sqrt{3} - 1)$ cm
   (c) $\frac{1}{4}(3 - \sqrt{5})$ cm

Miscellaneous exercise 2 (page 35)

1 (a) $11 + \sqrt{2}$ (b) 29
   (c) $10 - 4\sqrt{5}$ (d) $128\sqrt{2}$

2 (a) $4\sqrt{3}$ (b) $\sqrt{7}$
   (c) $111\sqrt{10}$ (d) $3\sqrt[3]{2}$

3 (a) $\frac{3}{2}\sqrt{3}$ (b) $\frac{1}{25}\sqrt{5}$
   (c) $\frac{1}{3}\sqrt{2}$ (d) $\frac{2}{15}\sqrt{30}$

4 (a) $\sqrt{2}$ (b) $4\sqrt{5}$
   (c) $-2 + \frac{1}{2}\sqrt{2}$ (d) $4\sqrt{3}$

5 (a) $\sqrt{7} + \sqrt{3}$ (b) $\frac{15-3\sqrt{5}}{10}$
   (c) $\frac{11-6\sqrt{2}}{7}$ (d) $\frac{11\sqrt{7}-26}{9}$

6 $\frac{5}{7}\sqrt{7}$

7 $\sqrt{2} + 1$

9 (a) 14 cm^2

10 $2 + \sqrt{3}$

11 $x = 3\sqrt{2} + 4$, $y = 5\sqrt{2} - 7$

12 $2\sqrt{10}$, $(3, 0)$

13 $a(2 + \sqrt{2})$; $5(2 - \sqrt{2})$ m, $5(2 - \sqrt{2})$ m, $10(\sqrt{2} - 1)$ m

14 (a) $x + 2y = 8$ (c) $\sqrt{5}$ or $-\sqrt{5}$
   (d) $t = -\frac{1}{5}$, $\frac{8}{5}\sqrt{5}$

15 (c) They cannot be equal.

3   Some important graphs

Exercise 3A (page 40)

1 (a) 11   (b) 5   (c) -3 (d) 0
2 (a) 50   (b) 5   (c) 29   (d) 29

3 (a) 15   (b) $5\frac{1}{4}$ (c) 0   (d) 0
4 (a) 17   (b) 9   (d) 33
6 4
7 (a) and (c) are odd; (b) is even
8 $a = 5$, $b = -3$

Exercise 3B (page 41)

11 (c)
12 (a)

Exercise 3C (page 44)

1 (a) $(3, 14)$ (b) $(1, 3)$, $(4, 3)$
   (c) $(-4, 8)$, $(2, 8)$ (d) $(-3, -3)$, $\left(\frac{1}{2}, -3\right)$

2 (a) $(1, 2)$, $(3, 4)$,   (b) $(-4, -5)$, $(3, 9)$
   (c) $\left(-1\frac{1}{2}, 6\frac{1}{2}\right)$, $(2, 17)$ (d) $(-2, -7)$, $(2, 9)$
   (e) $\left(-\frac{1}{3}, 2\right)$, $\left(2\frac{1}{2}, -6\frac{1}{2}\right)$

3 (a) $(2, 6)$ (b) $(-3, -1)$
4 (a) $(0, 0)$, $(2, 2)$ (b) $(1, 0)$
5 (a) $(-4, 14)$ (b) $(-6, 24)$, $(-2, 12)$
6 (a) $(-1, 4)$, $(3, 8)$ (b) $(1, 6)$
7 (a) $(5, 51)$ (b) $(-2, 3)$ (c) $(0, 1)$
8 (a) $\left(-1, \frac{1}{2}\right)$, $\left(1, \frac{1}{2}\right)$ (b) $(1, 9)$, $(2, 18)$
   (c) $(-3, 1)$, $(-2, 3)$ (d) $(-1, -5)$, $(2, 19)$
   (e) $(-3, 65)$, $(2.4, 7.76)$ (f) $(0, 0)$, $(8, 80)$

Exercise 3D (page 48)

4 (a) $y = x^2 - 7x + 10$ (b) $y = x^2 + 17x + 70$
   (c) $y = x^2 + 2x - 15$ (d) $y = x^2 - 2x - 15$

6 (a) $y = 3x^2 - 18x + 15$
   (b) $y = 4x^2 - 20x - 56$
   (c) $y = -\frac{1}{2}x^2 - 4x - 6$
   (d) $y = -4x^2 - 4x + 24$
   (e) $y = 5x^2 + 15x - 350$

8 (a) A, B, G, H   (b) B, D, F   (c) F, G, H
   (d) D   (e) G   (f) I
   (g) B, E   (h) A, C, E

Miscellaneous exercise 3 (page 49)

1 (a) 45, $-\frac{1}{2}$, -39 (b) 2   (c) $\frac{2}{3}$ (d) 37
2 -1, 4
3 9
4 $\left(\frac{1}{2}, 1\frac{3}{4}\right)$, $(4, -7)$
5 $\left(-2\frac{1}{2}, -2\right)$, $(2, 7)$
6 $(1, -1)$
7 $(2, 0)$

9 $a = 2$, $b = -7$, $c = 6$

10 $\left(-\frac{3}{4}, 6\right)$

12 6

13 $(0, 108)$

14 $(3, 33)$

15 $c = 2$, $k = 14$, $(3, 2)$

16 2

17 $p = q = 13$

18 $(\sqrt{3}, -5\sqrt{3})$, $(-\sqrt{3}, 5\sqrt{3})$

20 (a) 2   (b) 0   (c) 1

4 Quadratics

Exercise 4A (page 57)

1 (a) $(x + 3)(x + 8)$ (b) $(l - 3)(l - 4)$
  (c) $(q - 5)(q - 7)$ (d) $(x - 2)(x + 3)$
  (e) $(x - 3)(x + 8)$ (f) $(n - 12)(n + 5)$
  (g) $(r - 1)(r - 16)$ (h) $(x - 3)(x - 11)$
  (i) $(x - 3)(x + 7)$

2 (a) $(x - 2)(3x - 2)$ (b) $(2x - 1)(2x - 5)$
  (c) $(3x + 1)(4x - 1)$ (d) $(x - 2)(3x + 2)$
  (e) $(x - 2)(8x + 1)$ (f) $(3x - 2)(2x + 3)$
  (g) $(2x - 5)(2x + 1)$ (h) $3(x - 3)(3x - 1)$
  (i) $2(3x - 4)(2x + 1)$

3 (a) $(x - 1)(x + 1)$ (b) $(2 - 5d)(2 + 5d)$
  (c) $4(5 - z)(5 + z)$ (d) $(1 - x)(1 + 3x)$
  (e) $(x + 1)(3x + 1)$ (f) $(x + 4)(3x - 2)$

4 (a) No factors   (b) $(x - 5)(x - 8)$
  (c) No factors   (d) No factors
  (e) $x(x + 14)$ (f) $(j - 10)(j + 6)$
  (g) No factors   (h) No factors
  (i) $(2x - 1)(x + 3)$

5 (a) $-5, 7$ (b) $-1, 3$ (c) $-9, 3$
  (d) $-\frac{2}{3}, \frac{3}{2}$ (e) $-\frac{2}{3}, \frac{3}{2}$ (f) $-\frac{3}{4}, \frac{2}{3}$

6 (a) $-4, 1$ (b) $-3, 3$ (c) $-\frac{1}{2}, 1$
  (d) $\frac{1}{2}, 2$ (e) 3   (f) $-\frac{1}{3}, \frac{1}{3}$

Exercise 4B (page 60)

1 (a) (i) $(2, 3)$ (ii) $x = 2$
  (b) (i) $(5, -4)$ (ii) $x = 5$
  (c) (i) $(-3, -7)$ (ii) $x = -3$
  (d) (i) $\left(\frac{3}{2}, 1\right)$ (ii) $x = \frac{3}{2}$
  (e) (i) $\left(-\frac{3}{5}, 2\right)$ (ii) $x = -\frac{3}{5}$
  (f) (i) $\left(-\frac{7}{3}, -4\right)$ (ii) $x = -\frac{7}{3}$
  (g) (i) $(3, c)$ (ii) $x = 3$
  (h) (i) (p, q) (ii) $x = p$
  (i) (i) $(-b/a, c)$ (ii) $x = -b/a$

2 (a) (i) -1 (ii) -2
  (b) (i) 2   (ii) 1
  (c) (i) 5   (ii) -3
  (d) (i) -7 (ii) $-\frac{1}{2}$
  (e) (i) 3   (ii) 4
  (f) (i) q (ii) $-p$
  (g) (i) $-q$ (ii) p
  (h) (i) r (ii) t
  (i) (i) c (ii) $-b/a$

3 (a) $3 \pm \sqrt{3}$ (b) $0, -4$
  (c) $-3 \pm \sqrt{10}/2$ (d) $(7 \pm 2\sqrt{2})/3$
  (e) $-p \pm \sqrt{q}$ (f) $-b \pm \sqrt{c}/a$

4 (a) $(x + 1)^2 + 1$ (b) $(x - 4)^2 - 19$
  (c) $\left(x + 1\frac{1}{2}\right)^2 - 9\frac{1}{4}$ (d) $(x - 3)^2 - 4$
  (e) $(x + 7)^2$ (f) $2(x + 3)^2 - 23$
  (g) $3(x - 2)^2 - 9$ (h) $11 - 4(x + 1)^2$
  (i) $2\left(x + 1\frac{1}{4}\right)^2 - 6\frac{1}{8}$

5 (a) $(x - 7)(x + 5)$ (b) $(x - 22)(x + 8)$
  (c) $(x + 24)(x - 18)$ (d) $(3x + 2)(2x - 3)$
  (e) $(2 + 7x)(7 - 2x)$ (f) $(4x + 3)(3x - 2)$

6 (a) 3 when $x = 2$ (b) $2\frac{3}{4}$ when $x = 1\frac{1}{2}$
  (c) 13 when $x = 3$ (d) $-1\frac{1}{8}$ when $x = 1\frac{1}{4}$
  (e) $-4\frac{1}{3}$ when $x = -\frac{1}{3}$ (f) $7\frac{1}{12}$ when $x = -1\frac{1}{6}$

7 (a) (i) $(2, 2)$ (ii) $x = 2$
  (b) (i) $(-3, -11)$ (ii) $x = -3$
  (c) (i) $(-5, 32)$ (ii) $x = -5$
  (d) (i) $\left(-1\frac{1}{2}, -1\frac{1}{4}\right)$ (ii) $x = -1\frac{1}{2}$
  (e) (i) $\left(1\frac{3}{4}, -4\frac{1}{8}\right)$ (ii) $x = 1\frac{3}{4}$
  (f) (i) $(2, -7)$ (ii) $x = 2$

Exercise 4C (page 65)

1 (a) $\frac{1}{2}\left(-3 \pm \sqrt{29}\right)$ (b) $2 \pm \sqrt{11}$
  (c) -3 (repeated)   (d) $\frac{1}{2}\left(-5 \pm \sqrt{17}\right)$
  (e) No solution   (f) $\frac{1}{6}\left(5 \pm \sqrt{97}\right)$
  (g) -3 and $-\frac{1}{2}$ (h) $\frac{1}{2}\left(-3 \pm \sqrt{41}\right)$
  (i) $\frac{1}{6}\left(2 \pm \sqrt{34}\right)$

2 (a) 2   (b) 1   (c) 0   (d) 0   (e) 2
  (f) 2   (g) 1   (h) 2   (i) 2   (j) 2

3 (a) $-\frac{9}{4}$ (b) $-\frac{25}{32}$ (c) 81
  (d) $\pm 2\sqrt{6}$ (e) $\pm 4\sqrt{6}$ (f) $p^2/4q$

4 (a) $k < \frac{9}{4}$ (b) $k = \frac{49}{4}$
  (c) $k > \frac{9}{20}$ (d) $k > -\frac{25}{12}$
  (e) $k = \frac{4}{3}$ (f) $k > \frac{25}{28}$
  (g) $k > 4$ or $k < -4$ (h) $-6 < k < 6$

5 (a) 2   (b) 0   (c) 1   (d) 0   (e) 2
  (f) 2   (g) 0   (h) 0   (i) 1

6 Intersects x-axis twice, bends upwards.

7 Intersects x-axis twice, bends downwards.

Exercise 4D (page 68)

1 (a) $x = 3$, $y = 4$ or $x = -4$, $y = -3$
   (b) $x = 3$, $y = 4$ or $x = 4$, $y = 3$
   (c) $x = 5$, $y = 2$ or $x = -1$, $y = -4$
   (d) $x = 3$, $y = -1$
   (e) $x = 0$, $y = 5$ or $x = 4$, $y = -3$
   (f) $x = 1$, $y = 0$ or $x = \frac{1}{2}$, $y = \frac{1}{2}$
   (g) $x = 0$, $y = 7$
   (h) $x = 3$, $y = -2$ or $x = \frac{1}{7}$, $y = -10\frac{4}{7}$

2 (a) $(2, 5)$ and $(1, 3)$
   (b) $(1, 5)$ and $(-2.2, -4.6)$
   (c) $(3, 4)$ and $(-1, -4)$
   (d) $(1, 1)$ and $\left(-4, 3\frac{1}{2}\right)$
   (e) $(4, 3)$
   (f) $(2, -1)$ and $\left(-\frac{7}{8}, 4\frac{3}{4}\right)$
   (g) $(5, -2)$ and $(27, 42)$
   (h) $\left(\frac{1}{2}, -1\right)$ and $\left(-1\frac{5}{8}, -1\frac{17}{20}\right)$

3 (a) 2   (b) 0   (c) 2
   (d) 1   (e) 0   (f) 1

4 (a) $\pm 1, \pm 2$ (b) $\pm 1, \pm 3$ (c) ± 2
   (d) $\pm\sqrt{6}$ (e) $-1, 2$ (f) $\sqrt[3]{3}, -\sqrt[3]{4}$

5 (a) 16   (b) 25, 9   (c) 49
   (d) 25   (e) 9   (f) 16

6 (a) $-2, 5$ (b) $-6, 1$ (c) $-3, \frac{1}{2}$
   (d) $-4, 3$ (e) 36   (f) 9

Miscellaneous exercise 4 (page 69)

1 $x = 3$, $y = -1$ or $x = -\frac{1}{3}$, $y = \frac{7}{3}$

2 $a = 5$, $b = -8$. Least value is -8 when $x = 5$.

3 $x = 2$, $y = -1$ or $x = -\frac{5}{4}$, $y = \frac{11}{2}$

4 8 and -8

5 (a) $2\sqrt{3}, 4\sqrt{3}$ (b) ± 1.86, ± 2.63

7 $(3x - 6)^2 + 16$. Takes values $\geqslant 16$.

8 $(-1.64, 6.63)$, $(0.24, -1.67)$

9 (a) $(3x + 2)^2 + 3$
   (b) $0 < \text{f}(x) \leqslant \frac{1}{3}$

10 ± 0.991 and ± 0.131

11 $a = 3$, $b = -\frac{5}{6}$, $c = -\frac{13}{12}$.
    Minimum is $\left(\frac{5}{6}, -\frac{13}{12}\right)$.

12 $(1, 6)$ and $(2, 3)$

13 (a) $\left(b/a, c - b^2/a\right)$ (b) $c = b(b + 1)/a$

14 (a) $kx^2 - x + 1 = 0$
    (b) (i) Line is tangent to curve.
         (ii) Line and curve do not intersect.

17 $£(12(x + y) + 15xy)$; $5z^2 + 8z - 4 = 0$;
    0.4

18 (a) -20
    (b) None; so the graph never crosses the x-axis and is either always positive or always negative. When $x = 0$, $2x^2 + 6x + 7 = 7$. As $7 > 0$, $2x^2 + 6x + 7$ is always positive.

19 $x = \frac{1}{2}$, $y = 3$ or $x = 3$, $y = 13$

20 (a) $4(x - 2)^2 - 8$ (b) $(2, -8)$
    (c) $2 - \sqrt{2}, 2 + \sqrt{2}$

21 (b) $x = -2$, $y = 2$ or $x = -1$, $y = 3$

22 (a) -8 (b) None

23 (a) $(x + 4)^2 + 2$ (b) $(-4, 2)$

24 (b) 4, 25

5 Differentiation

Exercise 5A (page 76)

1 (a) 4   (b) 1.2   (c) -2

2 (a) 5   (b) 9   (c) -3

3 (a) (i) 10   (ii) 24   (iii) -40
   (b) (i) 0.8   (ii) 3   (iii) -2
   (c) (i) 2   (ii) -4 (iii) 8

Exercise 5B (page 77)

1 (a) $20x$ (b) $2x$ (c) $6x - 4$

Exercise 5C (page 82)

1 (a) $2x$ (b) $2x - 1$ (c) $8x$
   (d) $6x - 2$ (e) -3 (f) $1 - 4x$
   (g) $4 - 6x$ (h) $\sqrt{2} - 2\sqrt{3}x$

2 (a) 3   (b) $-6x$ (c) 0
   (d) $2 + 6x$ (e) $-2x$ (f) $6 - 6x$
   (g) $2 - 4x$ (h) $4x + 1$

3 (a) 6   (b) 3   (c) -3
   (d) 8   (e) -8 (f) -6
   (g) 4   (h) -17

4 (a) $\frac{3}{4}$ (b) $\frac{1}{2}$ (c) $-\frac{3}{2}$
   (d) -1 (e) $\frac{3}{2}$ (f) $\frac{1}{2}$

5 (a) 3   (b) 0.75

7 (a) $3x^2 + 4x$ (b) $-6x^2 + 6x$
   (c) $3x^2 - 12x + 11$ (d) $6x^2 - 6x + 1$
   (e) $1 + 3x^2$ (f) $-4x^3$

8 (a) -10 (b) 6   (c) 58
   (d) -1 (e) 8   (f) -8

9 (a) $-2, 2$ (b) $-\frac{4}{3}, 2$ (c) $-5, 7$
   (d) 1   (e) $-1, -\frac{1}{3}$ (f) No values

Exercise 5D (page 85)

1 (a) $y = -2x - 1$ (b) $y = -x$
   (c) $y = 2x - 1$ (d) $y = 6x + 10$
   (e) $y = 1$ (f) $y = 0$

2 (a) $2y = x - 3$ (b) $4y = -x + 1$
   (c) $8y = -x - 58$ (d) $x = 0$
   (e) $2y = x + 9$ (f) $x = \frac{1}{2}$

3 $4y = 4x - 1$

4 $y = 0$

5 $y = -2x$

6 $12y = 12x - 17$

7 $x = 1$

8 $7y = -x + 64$

9 $y = 4x + 2$

10 $y = x + 2$

12 $y = -2x - 6$

13 $\left(\frac{1}{2}, -2\right)$

Exercise 5E (page 90)

1 $f'(p) = 3p^2$

2 $f'(p) = 8p^7$

Miscellaneous exercise 5 (page 90)

1 $y = 13x - 16$

2 (a) -9 (b) $a = -\frac{19}{3}, 3$

3 $80y = 32x - 51$

4 $9x - y = 16$

5 $(1, 0)$

6 $\left(-\frac{1}{3}, -4\frac{17}{27}\right), (2, 13)$

7 $x + 19y - 153 = 0$

8 13

9 $(2, 12)$

10 $k = 2$

11 -183

12 $\left(-\frac{1}{4}, \frac{1}{16}\right), \left(2\frac{1}{4}, 5\frac{1}{16}\right)$

6 Inequalities

Exercise 6A (page 94)

1 (a) $x > 14$ (b) $x < 4$ (c) $x \leqslant 2\frac{1}{2}$
   (d) $x \geqslant 7$ (e) $x > -4$ (f) $x \leqslant -3\frac{1}{5}$
   (g) $x < -3\frac{1}{2}$ (h) $x \leqslant -4$

2 (a) $x > 7$ (b) $x \leqslant 22$ (c) $x < -11\frac{1}{2}$
   (d) $x \leqslant 6$ (e) $x \geqslant -2\frac{3}{4}$ (f) $x > -2$
   (g) $x < 3\frac{1}{3}$ (h) $x \geqslant -4$

3 (a) $x \geqslant -4$ (b) $x \leqslant 4$ (c) $x > 9$
   (d) $x \geqslant -2$ (e) $x \geqslant \frac{1}{3}$ (f) $x < 1$
   (g) $x < 1\frac{2}{5}$ (h) $x > 2$

4 (a) $x > -7$ (b) $x \leqslant 2$ (c) $x < -6$
   (d) $x > 3$ (e) $x \geqslant 2\frac{3}{4}$ (f) $x < 19$
   (g) $x < 8\frac{1}{2}$ (h) $x \geqslant 9$

5 (a) $x \geqslant -9$ (b) $x \geqslant 4$ (c) $x > 6$
   (d) $x > 2\frac{1}{4}$ (e) $x \leqslant \frac{6}{7}$ (f) $x \geqslant -1$
   (g) $x < -\frac{3}{4}$ (h) $x > -3$ (i) $x \leqslant -\frac{1}{4}$

6 (a) $x > 5\frac{1}{2}$ (b) $x < -3$ (c) $x \geqslant -1\frac{5}{8}$
   (d) $x < -2$ (e) $x \leqslant 5$ (f) $x \leqslant 1\frac{7}{9}$
   (g) $x < -1\frac{2}{5}$ (h) $x \geqslant 4\frac{8}{13}$

Exercise 6B (page 99)

1 (a) $2 < x < 3$
   (b) $x < 4$ or $x > 7$
   (c) $1 < x < 3$
   (d) $x \leqslant -1$ or $x \geqslant 4$
   (e) $x < -3$ or $x > \frac{1}{2}$
   (f) $-2\frac{1}{2} \leqslant x \leqslant \frac{2}{3}$
   (g) $x \leqslant -2$ or $x \geqslant -1\frac{1}{4}$
   (h) $x < -3$ or $x > 1$
   (i) $x < 1\frac{1}{2}$ or $x > 5$
   (j) $-5 < x < 5$
   (k) $-1\frac{1}{3} < x < \frac{3}{4}$
   (l) $x \leqslant -\frac{2}{3}$ or $x \geqslant \frac{2}{3}$

2 (a) $3 < x < 6$
   (b) $x < 2$ or $x > 8$
   (c) $-5 \leqslant x \leqslant 2$
   (d) $x \leqslant -1$ or $x \geqslant 3$
   (e) $x < -1\frac{1}{2}$ or $x > 2$
   (f) $-5 \leqslant x \leqslant \frac{2}{3}$
   (g) $x \leqslant -3$ or $x \geqslant -\frac{4}{5}$
   (h) $x < -5$ or $x > 2$
   (i) $x < 2\frac{1}{2}$ or $x > 3$
   (j) $x \leqslant -\frac{1}{3}$ or $x \geqslant \frac{1}{3}$
   (k) $x < -1\frac{1}{3}$ or $x > \frac{2}{7}$
   (l) $x \leqslant -1\frac{2}{3}$ or $x \geqslant \frac{1}{3}$

3 (a) $x < -3$ or $x > -2$
   (b) $3 < x < 4$
   (c) $-3 \leqslant x \leqslant 5$
   (d) $x \leqslant -3$ or $x \geqslant 3$
   (e) $x \leqslant 1$ or $x \geqslant 1\frac{1}{2}$
   (f) $-\frac{2}{3} < x < 1\frac{1}{2}$
   (g) $x < \frac{1}{2}\left(-5 - \sqrt{17}\right)$ or $x > \frac{1}{2}\left(-5 + \sqrt{17}\right)$
   (h) $x < -\frac{1}{3}\sqrt{21}$ or $x > \frac{1}{3}\sqrt{21}$
   (i) True for no x

(j) True for all x

(k) $x < -\frac{3}{4}$ or $x > \frac{1}{3}$

(l) $\frac{1}{6}(7 - \sqrt{37}) \leqslant x \leqslant \frac{1}{6}(7 + \sqrt{37})$

Miscellaneous exercise 6 (page 100)

1 $-6 \leqslant x \leqslant 7$

2 $-4 < x < 2$

3 $-4 < x < 3$

4 $-1 < x < 0$ or $x > 1$

5 $-3 \leqslant x \leqslant 0$ or $x \geqslant 2$

6 (a) $k < 0$ or $k > 8$

(b) $-1\frac{1}{2} < k < 1\frac{1}{2}$ provided $k \neq 0$ (if $k = 0$ the equation is linear, and has just one root)

(c) $k < -2$ or $k > 2$

7 (a) $0 \leqslant k < 5$ (b) $k = 0$ (c) $-\frac{8}{25} < k < 0$

8 $k \leqslant 0$ or $k \geqslant \frac{4}{9}$

9 $x < -2$ or $x > \frac{2}{3}$

10 $-\frac{1}{2} < x < 0$ or $x > 2$

Revision exercise 1 (page 101)

1 (a) $a = 3, b = 11$ (b) $11, -3$ (c) $\frac{1}{11}$

2 25

3 (a) $12\sqrt{3}$ (b) 48

4 (a) 12.61   (b) 12.0601

(c) As you find the gradients of chords such as AX, with X getting closer to A, the gradients will get extremely close to the gradient of the tangent at A, which is 12.

5 $(x + 5)^2 + 13$;

(a) $13; -5$ (b) $x \leqslant -8$ or $x \geqslant -2$

6 $(2, 1)$; the line is a tangent to the curve.

7 (a) $x = -5, y = -8$ or $x = 4, y = 10$

(c) $-18\frac{1}{4}$

8 (a) $2x + y = 9$ (b) $x - 2y = 1 - 2k$ (c) $\frac{1}{2}$

9 $\left(-\frac{9}{4}, \frac{81}{16}\right)$

10 $x < -1$ or $x > 2$

11 (a) $\frac{3}{4}$ (b) $3y + 4x = 0$

12 (a) $2\sqrt{3}$ (b) $\frac{3}{2}$ (c) $2\sqrt{2}$

13 $x = 1, y = 1$ or $x = 4, y = -1$

14 $(-1, 7)$

15 (a) $(x - \sqrt{2})^2 + 2; a = -\sqrt{2}, b = 2$

(b) $x = \sqrt{2}$

16 $11\sqrt{2}$

17 (a) $2x + 3y = 7, \ 3x - 2y = 4$ (b) $(4, 4)$

18 (a) $x > \frac{4}{3}$ (b) $x > \frac{3}{2}$ (c) $x \leqslant 0$ or $x \geqslant 5$

19 $\pm 0.518, \pm 1.93$

20 $48x + 32y + 65 = 0$

21 $x + y = 5; 7$

22 $\frac{7}{10}\sqrt{2}$

23 $0, 5$

24 $k < -9$ or $k > 7$

25 (a) $(3, -1)$ (b) 5   (c) $2\sqrt{6} - 1$

26 (b) $k < 0$ and $k > \frac{3}{4}$ (c) $0, \frac{3}{4}$

27 (a) $\frac{1}{2} \leqslant x \leqslant 2$ (b) $-\frac{1}{2} < x < \frac{7}{2}$ (c) $x \geqslant 6.3$

28 $(-1, 6), x + y = 5$

7   Index notation

Exercise 7A (page 106)

1 (a) a^{12} (b) b^8 (c) c^4

(d) d^9 (e) e^{20} (f) $x^6 y^4$

(g) $15g^8$ (h) $3h^8$ (i) $72a^8$

(j) $p^7 q^{15}$ (k) $128x^7 y^{11}$ (l) $4c$

(m) $108m^{14} n^{10}$ (n) $7r^3 s$ (o) $2xy^2 z^3$

2 (a) 2^{26} (b) 2^{12} (c) 2^6 (d) 2^6

(e) 2^2 (f) 2^1 (g) 2^0 (h) 2^0

Exercise 7B (page 110)

1 (a) $\frac{1}{8}$ (b) $\frac{1}{16}$ (c) $\frac{1}{5}$

(d) $\frac{1}{9}$ (e) $\frac{1}{10\,000}$ (f) 1

(g) 2   (h) 27   (i) $\frac{2}{5}$

(j) $\frac{1}{128}$ (k) $\frac{27}{216}$ (l) $\frac{27}{64}$

2 (a) $\frac{1}{2}$ (b) $\frac{1}{512}$ (c) $\frac{1}{32}$

(d) 8   (e) $\frac{1}{8}$ (f) 8

3 (a) $\frac{1}{10}$ (b) $\frac{2}{5}$ (c) $\frac{2}{5}$

(d) $\frac{1}{10}$ (e) 10   (f) $\frac{2}{5}$

4 (a) a (b) b (c) c^{-6}

(d) 2   (e) e^{-9} (f) f^{-5}

(g) $3g^{-1}$ (h) $\frac{1}{9}h^{-4}$ (i) $\frac{1}{9}i^4$

(j) $8j^6$ (k) $8x^9 y^{-3}$ (l) $p^{-8} q^{-16} r^{-12}$

(m) $2m$ (n) $9n^{-9}$ (o) $8x$

(p) $\frac{25}{2}a^7 c^{-4}$ (q) $\frac{1}{64}q^6$ (r) $144x^{-2} y^4$

5 (a) $x = -2$ (b) $y = 0$ (c) $z = 4$

(d) $x = -2$ (e) $y = 120$ (f) $t = 0$

6 (a) $2.7 \times 10^{-5} \text{ m}^3$ (b) $5.4 \times 10^{-3} \text{ m}^2$

7 26.7 km h^{-1} (to 1 decimal place)

8 (a) $1.0 \times 10^{-3} \text{ m}^3$ (to 2 significant figures)

(b) 101.9 m (to 1 decimal place)

(c) $5.6 \times 10^{-3} \text{ m}$ (to 2 significant figures)

9 (a) 4.375×10^{-4} (b) 4.5×10^{-7}

10 $x = -3$

Exercise 7C (page 117)

1 (a) 5 (b) 2 (c) 6 (d) 2
(e) 3 (f) $\frac{1}{3}$ (g) $\frac{1}{2}$ (h) $\frac{1}{7}$
(i) $\frac{1}{10}$ (j) -3 (k) 16 (l) $\frac{1}{625}$

2 (a) 2 (b) $\frac{1}{16}$ (c) 16 (d) $\frac{1}{2}$
(e) 2 (f) $\frac{1}{2}$ (g) 16 (h) $\frac{1}{2}$

3 (a) 4 (b) 8 (c) $\frac{1}{27}$ (d) 81
(e) 4 (f) 8 (g) $\frac{1}{32}$ (h) 32
(i) $\frac{1}{1000}$ (j) 625 (k) $2\frac{1}{4}$ (l) $\frac{2}{3}$

4 (a) a^2 (b) $12b^{-1}$ (c) $12c^{\frac{3}{4}}$
(d) 1 (e) 2 (f) $5pq^2$

5 (a) 64 (b) 27 (c) 8 (d) 9
(e) $\frac{1}{4}$ (f) $\frac{1}{27}$ (g) 2 (h) 2

6 (a) 1.9 (to 1 decimal place)
(b) 2.2 m (to 1 decimal place)

7 6.5 cm (to 1 decimal place)

8 (a) $x = \frac{5}{2}$ (b) $y = -\frac{3}{2}$ (c) $z = \frac{1}{4}$ (d) $x = \frac{3}{2}$
(e) $y = \frac{4}{3}$ (f) $z = \frac{7}{3}$ (g) $t = \frac{6}{5}$ (h) $y = -\frac{7}{4}$

9 (a) 1, 4 (b) 9 (c) 1
(d) 0, 8 (e) 2 (f) 1, −27

10 (a) $x^{-\frac{1}{2}}$ (b) $4x^{\frac{1}{2}}$ (c) $2x^{\frac{1}{2}}$
(d) $3x^{\frac{5}{2}}$ (e) $x^{-\frac{2}{3}}$ (f) $6x^{-\frac{4}{3}}$

11 (a) $2\sqrt[3]{3}$ (b) $\sqrt[6]{2}$ (c) $\sqrt{6}$

12 (a) (i) 16 (iii) $-\frac{1}{4}$ (iv) 16
(ii), (v), (vi) No value
(c) q must be odd

Miscellaneous exercise 7 (page 118)

1 (a) 6 (b) $\frac{1}{16}$ (c) $\frac{1}{2}$ (d) $2\frac{10}{27}$

2 (a) $2p^{\frac{1}{8}}q^{-\frac{3}{2}}$ (b) $\frac{1}{10}b^{-3}$
(c) $2xy^2$ (d) $m^{-\frac{2}{3}}n^{\frac{1}{3}}$

3 $\dfrac{1}{3a^2}$

4 $a^{-\frac{2}{3}}$

5 −1 and 8

6 $x = \frac{8}{7}$

7 (a) 2.5×10^{179} (b) 1×10^{292}
(c) 2×10^{56} (d) 3×10^{-449}

8 (b) 1.5×10^{11} m (to 2 significant figures)

9 (a) $\frac{15}{4}\sqrt{2}$ (b) $\frac{13}{3} + \frac{40}{9}\sqrt{3}$

10 (a) 2^{71} (b) 2^{-399} (c) $2^{\frac{7}{3}}$
(d) 2^{99} (e) $2^{3.3}$

11 $x = -\frac{5}{6}$

12 (a) $S = 2^1 \times 3^1 \times V^{\frac{2}{3}}$
(b) $V = 2^{-\frac{3}{2}} \times 3^{-\frac{3}{2}} \times S^{\frac{3}{2}}$

13 1.5×10^{-10} joules

8 Graphs of nth power functions

Exercise 8A (page 125)

1 (a) $-2x^{-3}, -\dfrac{2}{x^3}$ (b) $-5x^{-6}, -\dfrac{5}{x^6}$
(c) $-9x^{-4}, -\dfrac{9}{x^4}$ (d) $4x^{-3}, \dfrac{4}{x^3}$
(e) $-x^{-5}, -\dfrac{1}{x^5}$ (f) $2x^{-7}, \dfrac{2}{x^7}$

2 (a) $-\dfrac{1}{4x^2}$ (b) $-\dfrac{6}{x^3}$ (c) 0
(d) $-\dfrac{3}{x^2} - \dfrac{1}{x^4}$ (e) $\dfrac{4-x}{x^3}$

3 (a) $y + 4x = 8$ (b) $y + 2x = 3$
(c) $y + 18x = 9$ (d) $y = 6$
(e) $y + x = 1$ (f) $2y - x = 2$

4 (a) $y = x - 1$ (b) $y = \frac{1}{2}x$
(c) $x = 2$ (d) $4y = x - 3$

5 (a) $(2, 4)$
(b) $(3, \frac{1}{3})$
(c) $(\sqrt{2}, \sqrt{2}), (-\sqrt{2}, -\sqrt{2})$
(d) $(\frac{1}{2}, 32), (-\frac{1}{2}, -32)$
(e) $(\frac{1}{3}, 243), (-\frac{1}{3}, -243)$
(f) $(2, 4), (-2, -4)$

6 (a) RQP (b) PQR (c) QPR (d) QRP

7 (a) $x > 10$
(b) $x < -50$ or $x > 50$
(c) $-\frac{1}{10}\sqrt{10} \leqslant x \leqslant \frac{1}{10}\sqrt{10}, x \neq 0$
(d) $x < -20$ or $x > 20$

Exercise 8B (page 129)

1 (a) $\frac{1}{3}x^{-\frac{2}{3}}$ (b) $\frac{5}{2}x^{\frac{3}{2}}$ (c) $2x^{-\frac{3}{5}}$
(d) $3x^{-\frac{8}{5}}$ (e) $-2x^{-\frac{3}{2}}$ (f) $3x^{-\frac{5}{2}}$

2 (a) $\dfrac{3}{4\sqrt[4]{x}}$ (b) $\dfrac{2}{\sqrt[3]{x^2}}$ (c) $-\dfrac{2}{\sqrt{x^3}}$
(d) $10\sqrt{x^3}$ (e) $-\dfrac{1}{6\sqrt[3]{x^4}}$ (f) $\dfrac{3x-1}{4\sqrt[4]{x^5}}$

3 (a) (i) 2, 2.008 298 8... (ii) 0.082 988...
(iii) $\frac{1}{12}$ (iv) $12y - x = 16$
(b) (i) 4, 4.033 264 2... (ii) 0.332 642...
(iii) $\frac{1}{3}$ (iv) $3y - x = 4$
(c) (i) 0.25, 0.247 938 1... (ii) −0.020 618...
(iii) $-\frac{1}{48}$ (iv) $48y + x = 20$
(d) (i) 0.0625, 0.061 473 3...
(ii) −0.010 266...
(iii) $-\frac{1}{96}$ (iv) $96y + x = 14$

4 (a) $6y = x + 9$ (b) $8y + x = 32$
(c) $y = 3x - 1$ (d) $y = 3$

5 (a) $(8, 4)$ (b) $(-1, -1), (1, 1)$

  (c) $\left(-8, \frac{3}{4}\right)$ (d) $(1, 4)$

6 $y = 2x + \frac{3}{8}$

7 The line $y = x$ bisects the angle between the axes.

Miscellaneous exercise 8 (page 130)

1 $y + 2x = 3$; $\left(\frac{9}{4}, -\frac{3}{2}\right)$

2 (a),(b) $2\sqrt{2}y = x + 3\sqrt{2}$

3 (a) $\dfrac{1}{p}$ (b) $-\dfrac{1}{p^2}$

  (c) $p^2 y + x = 2p$ (d) $(2p, 0), \left(0, \dfrac{2}{p}\right)$

  (e) 2

4 $y = 7x - 10, 7y + x = -20$; $y = \frac{1}{16}, x = 8$

5 (a) $\dfrac{1}{\sqrt{2x}}$ (b) $3\sqrt{x}, \frac{4}{3}\sqrt[3]{4x}$

6 (a) $-\frac{3}{2}x^{-\frac{5}{2}} + 2x^{-3}$ (b) $\frac{3}{2}x^{-\frac{5}{2}}$

  (c) $-3x^{-4} + 7x^{-\frac{9}{2}} - 4x^{-5}$ (d) $3x^{-\frac{5}{2}} - 3x^{-4}$

7 $\left(\frac{11}{20}, \frac{4}{5}\right)$

8 $\left(\frac{67}{32}, \frac{5}{8}\right)$

9 (b) $mn = -1$

9   Polynomials

Exercise 9 (page 135)

1 (a) 3   (b) 1   (c) 4

  (d) 0   (e) 1   (f) 0

2 (a) $4x^2 + 7x + 6$

  (b) $5x^3 + 3x^2 - 6x - 3$

  (c) $8x^4 - 3x^3 + 7x^2 - 3x + 1$

  (d) $2x^5 + 2x^4 - 5x^2 + 3$

  (e) $-x^3 - 2x^2 - 5x + 4$

3 (a) $2x^2 + x - 8$

  (b) $3x^3 + 7x^2 - 8x + 9$

  (c) $-2x^4 - x^3 + 7x^2 + 3x - 3$

  (d) $2x^5 - 2x^4 - 6x^3 + 5x^2 + 1$

  (e) $-x^3 - 6x^2 + 9x + 2$

4 (a) $2x^3 - 3x^2 + 9x - 2$

  (b) $3x^3 - 7x^2 + 16x - 13$

  (c) $x^3 - 4x^2 + 7x - 11$

  (d) $3x^3 - 8x^2 + 17x - 17$

5 (a) $6x^2 - 7x - 3$

  (b) $x^3 + x^2 - 7x + 2$

  (c) $2x^3 + 5x^2 - 3x - 9$

  (d) $12x^3 - 13x^2 + 9x - 2$

  (e) $x^4 + 2x^3 - 2x^2 + 2x - 3$

  (f) $8x^4 - 6x^3 - 15x^2 + 18x - 5$

  (g) $x^4 + 5x^3 + 5x^2 + 3x + 18$

  (h) $x^5 - 5x^4 + 3x^3 + 10x^2 - 8x + 5$

  (i) $6x^3 + 29x^2 - 7x - 10$

  (j) $6x^3 + 5x^2 - 13x - 12$

6 (a) $0, -1$ (b) $-11, -1$

  (c) $-3, -9$ (d) $25, -8$

  (e) $20, -21$ (f) $-16, 13$

  (g) $106, -81$ (h) $-5, 11$

7 (a) $4, 1$ (b) $2, -3$

  (c) $2, 1$ (d) $3, -2$

  (e) $1, 2$ (f) $2, -3$

Miscellaneous exercise 9 (page 136)

1 $4x^2 + 2, 2x^2 - 4x - 4,$

  $3x^4 - 4x^3 + 4x^2 + 8x - 3$

2 -25

3 (a) $-4x - 7, x^4 - 8x^3 + 13x^2 - 18x - 12$

  (b) $3, -\frac{4}{3}$

4 (a) 20   (b) -23

5 $30x^3 - 15x^2 - 20x + 5$

10   Transforming graphs

Exercise 10A (page 140)

2 (b) $(11, 3)$ (c) $y = \sqrt{x - 2}$

3 (a) $y = x^2 - 3x$

  (b) $y = x^2 + 3x + 4$

  (c) $y = x^2 - 3x + 4$

4 (a) $y = x^2 - x + 1$

  (b) $y = x^2 - 5x + 2$

  (c) $y = x^2 - x - 4$

5 (a) 3 units in the x-direction

  (b) 3 units in the x-direction then -3 units in the y-direction

6 If $y = x^2$ is translated by -4 units in the x-direction and -2 units in the y-direction, in either order, the equation becomes $y = x^2 + 8x + 14$.

7 $y = \dfrac{1}{x} - 2, y = \dfrac{1}{x + 1} - 2;$

  $\left(-\frac{1}{2}, 0\right), (0, -1); \left(\frac{1}{2}, 2\right), (1, 1)$

Exercise 10B (page 148)

2 (b) $(8, 4)$ (c) $y = \sqrt{2x}$

3 $y = (x + 1)^2$

4 9

5 $y = 4x^2, y = \frac{4}{9}x^2$

  (a) Use a factor of $\frac{3}{2}\sqrt{2}$.

  (b) Use a factor of $\frac{2}{9}$.

6 (a) y-axis   (b) x-axis

7 y-axis

8 Replacing x by $\dfrac{x}{c}$ in the equation of a graph produces a stretch of factor c in the x-direction.

9 (a) odd; $3x^2 + 3$, even
   (b) even; $14x$, odd
   (c) neither; $2x - 4$, neither
   (d) neither; $5x^4 + 9x^2$, even

The derivative of an even function is odd, and the derivative of an odd function is even.

Miscellaneous exercise 10 (page 149)

2 (a) 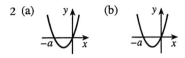 (b)

3 The curve remains the same.

4 $a = 6$, $b = -10$

5 $y = x - 4$, $y = 2x - 8$, $y = -2x + 8$

6 $y = -f(-x)$; $f(x)$ is an odd function.

7 (a)
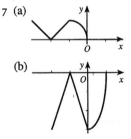

(b)

8 (a) Stretch, factor a in the y-direction
   (b) Translation a units in the y-direction
   (c) Translation $-a$ units in the x-direction
   (d) Stretch, factor $1/a$ in the x-direction

9 (a) The gradient at P' is the negative of the gradient at P. So $f'(-p) = -f'(p)$. The derivative of an even function is odd.

11 Investigating shapes of graphs

Exercise 11A (page 154)

1 (a) $(-1, -7)$ (b) $(3, 10)$
   (c) $(-3, 27)$, $(1, -5)$ (d) $(-2, 16)$, $(2, -16)$
   (e) $(0, 0)$, $(8, -256)$ (f) $(-1, 8)$, $(1, 0)$
   (g) $(-2, 0)$, $(0, 16)$, $(2, 0)$
   (h) $(-1, 0)$, $\left(-\frac{1}{3}, -\frac{4}{27}\right)$ (i) $(1, 1)$

2 (a) $(1, 4)$ (b) $\left(-\frac{1}{2}, -8\frac{1}{4}\right)$
   (c) $(-2, 9)$ (d) $(2, 0)$
   (e) $(0, 3)$ (f) $(-2, 2)$, $(0, -2)$
   (g) $\left(-\frac{2}{3}, \frac{4}{27}\right)$, $(0, 0)$ (h) $\left(-\frac{3}{4}, -\frac{27}{256}\right)$, $(0, 0)$
   (i) $(-2, -32)$, $(0, 0)$, $(5, -375)$

Exercise 11B (page 159)

1 (a) +, increasing   (b) –, decreasing
   (c) –, decreasing   (d) +, increasing
   (e) +, increasing   (f) +, increasing
   (g) –, decreasing   (h) –, decreasing

In questions 2–5 the gradient is positive/negative in the intervals excluding the end-points, but the function is increasing/decreasing in the intervals including the end-points.

2 (a) $2x - 5$, $x \geqslant \frac{5}{2}$ (b) $2x + 6$, $x \geqslant -3$
   (c) $-3 - 2x$, $x \leqslant -\frac{3}{2}$ (d) $6x - 5$, $x \geqslant \frac{5}{6}$
   (e) $10x + 3$, $x \geqslant -\frac{3}{10}$ (f) $-4 - 6x$, $x \leqslant -\frac{2}{3}$

3 (a) $2x + 4$, $x \leqslant -2$ (b) $2x - 3$, $x \leqslant \frac{3}{2}$
   (c) $-3 + 2x$, $x \leqslant \frac{3}{2}$ (d) $4x - 8$, $x \leqslant 2$
   (e) $7 - 4x$, $x \geqslant \frac{7}{4}$
   (f) $-5 - 14x$, $x \geqslant -\frac{5}{14}$

4 (a) $3x^2 - 12$, $x \leqslant -2$ and $x \geqslant 2$
   (b) $6x^2 - 18$, $x \leqslant -\sqrt{3}$ and $x \geqslant \sqrt{3}$
   (c) $6x^2 - 18x - 24$, $x \leqslant -1$ and $x \geqslant 4$
   (d) $3x^2 - 6x + 3$, all x
   (e) $4x^3 - 4x$, $-1 \leqslant x \leqslant 0$ and $x \geqslant 1$
   (f) $4x^3 + 12x^2$, $x \geqslant -3$
   (g) $3 - 3x^2$, $-1 \leqslant x \leqslant 1$
   (h) $10x^4 - 20x^3$, $x \leqslant 0$ and $x \geqslant 2$
   (i) $3(1 + x^2)$, all x

5 (a) $3x^2 - 27$, $-3 \leqslant x \leqslant 3$
   (b) $4x^3 + 8x$, $x \leqslant 0$
   (c) $3x^2 - 6x + 3$, none
   (d) $12 - 6x^2$, $x \leqslant -\sqrt{2}$ and $x \geqslant \sqrt{2}$
   (e) $6x^2 + 6x - 36$, $-3 \leqslant x \leqslant 2$
   (f) $12x^3 - 60x^2$, $x \leqslant 5$
   (g) $72x - 8x^3$, $-3 \leqslant x \leqslant 0$ and $x \geqslant 3$
   (h) $5x^4 - 5$, $-1 \leqslant x \leqslant 1$
   (i) $nx^{n-1} - n$; $x \leqslant 1$ if n is even
      $-1 \leqslant x \leqslant 1$ if n is odd

6 (a) (i) $(4, -12)$ (ii) minimum (iv) $y \geqslant -12$
   (b) (i) $(-2, -7)$ (ii) minimum (iv) $y \geqslant -7$
   (c) (i) $\left(-\frac{3}{5}, \frac{1}{5}\right)$ (ii) minimum (iv) $y \geqslant \frac{1}{5}$
   (d) (i) $(-3, 13)$ (ii) maximum (iv) $y \leqslant 13$
   (e) (i) $(-3, 0)$ (ii) minimum (iv) $y \geqslant 0$
   (f) (i) $\left(-\frac{1}{2}, 2\right)$ (ii) maximum (iv) $y \leqslant 2$

7 (a) $(-2, 21)$ maximum, $(2, -11)$ minimum
   (b) $(-4, -31)$ minimum, $(0, 1)$ maximum
   (c) $(-1, 7)$ maximum, $(2, -20)$ minimum
   (d) $(1, 2)$ maximum, $\left(1\frac{2}{3}, 1\frac{23}{27}\right)$ minimum
   (e) $(-1, 2)$ mimimum, $(0, 3)$ maximum, $(1, 2)$ minimum
   (f) $(1, 8)$ maximum

8 (a) $(-4, 213)$ maximum, $(3, -130)$ minimum
   (b) $(-3, 88)$ maximum, $(5, -168)$ minimum

(c) $(0, 0)$ minimum, $(1, 1)$ neither

(d) $(-2, 65)$ maximum, $(0, 1)$ neither, $(2, -63)$ minimum

(e) $\left(-\frac{1}{3}, -\frac{11}{27}\right)$ minimum, $\left(\frac{1}{2}, \frac{3}{4}\right)$ maximum

(f) $(-1, 0)$ neither

Exercise 11C (page 164)

1 $\left(2\frac{1}{2}, -6\frac{1}{4}\right); k > -6\frac{1}{4}$

2 $k > 1\frac{1}{3}$

3 (a) 2   (b) 3   (c) 4   (d) 0

4 (a) 3; one between $-\sqrt{3}$ and -1, one between -1 and 0, one greater than $\sqrt{3}$.

(b) 2; 1, and one less than $-\sqrt{3}$ (in fact, -2)

(c) 1; greater than $\sqrt{3}$.

5 If $f(x) = x^3 + 4x$, $f'(x) = 3x^2 + 4 > 0$, so y is an increasing function of x for all x.

6 (a) $(-6, 0)$ maximum, $(-2, -32)$ minimum

(c) (i) 2   (ii) 1   (iii) 3   (iv) 1

(d) $-32 < k < 0$; between -8 and -6, between -6 and -2, between -2 and 0

7 (a) $\left(-\frac{1}{2}, -\frac{3}{16}\right)$ minimum, $(0, 0)$ maximum, $(2, -8)$ minimum

(b) $(1 - \sqrt{3}, 0)$, $(0, 0)$, $(1 + \sqrt{3}, 0)$

(c) (i) 2   (ii) 2   (iii) 1

(d) (i) $k < -8$ (ii) $k = -8$

(iii) $-8 < k < -\frac{3}{16}$ and $k > 0$

(iv) $k = -\frac{3}{16}$ and $k = 0$ (v) $-\frac{3}{16} < k < 0$

(e) Between $-(\sqrt{3} - 1)$ and $-\frac{1}{2}$, between $-\frac{1}{2}$ and 0, between 0 and 2, between 2 and $1 + \sqrt{3}$

Exercise 11D (page 169)

3 (a) $+, +$ (b) $+, -$ (c) $+, 0$ (d) $-, +$

4 (a) 0   (b) -4 (c) $6x + 10$ (d) $30x^4$

5 (a) $(-1, -2)$ minimum, $(1, 2)$ maximum

(b) $(0, 0)$ maximum, $(2, -4)$ minimum

(c) $(0, 1)$ minimum

(d) $(-1, 11)$ maximum, $(2, -16)$ minimum

(e) $(2, 22)$ neither

6 (a) $(-1, -8)$ minimum, $(0, -3)$ maximum, $(2, -35)$ minimum

(b) none

(c) $\left(-\frac{4}{3}, -14\frac{2}{9}\right)$ minimum, $\left(\frac{4}{3}, 14\frac{2}{9}\right)$ maximum

(d) none

(e) $(0, 1)$ minimum

7 (a) $(-1, 0)$, $(0, 0)$, $(1, 0)$ (b) $3x^2 - 1$

(c) $6x$

8 (b) $3x^2 + 1$, $6x$ (c) $x > 0$

Exercise 11E (page 175)

1 (a) $(-1, -2)$ maximum, $(1, 2)$ minimum

(b) $(2, 3)$ minimum

(c) $(1, 1)$ maximum

(d) $(1, -3)$ minimum

(e) $\left(2, \frac{1}{4}\right)$ maximum

(f) $\left(-\frac{1}{2}, 3\right)$ minimum

(g) $(4, 3)$ minimum

(h) $\left(-3, -\frac{2}{9}\right)$ minimum, $\left(3, \frac{2}{9}\right)$ maximum

(i) $(-8, 16)$ maximum, $(8, -16)$ minimum

2 (a) $x \geqslant 2$ (b) $x \leqslant -1$, $x \geqslant 1$

(c) $x < 0$, $x > 0$

3 (a) $\left(2, -\frac{3}{8}\right)$ minimum

(b) $\left(4, \frac{1}{256}\right)$ maximum

(c) $(-1, 0)$ maximum, $(1, 4)$ minimum

(d) $(-2, 8)$ minimum, $(2, 8)$ minimum

(e) $(0, 0)$ minimum, $(4, 19.0\ldots)$ maximum

(f) $(1, 3)$ maximum

Miscellaneous exercise 11 (page 175)

1 $(-2, -4)$ maximum, $(2, 4)$ minimum; $x \leqslant -2$ and $x \geqslant 2$

2 (a) $(-1, -7)$, $(2, 20)$

(b) The graph crosses the x-axis 3 times.

(c) The graph has 3 intersections with the line $y = -5$.

(d) (i) $-7 < k < 20$ (ii) $k < -7$ and $k > 20$

3 $(-2, 4)$, $(2, -28)$; $-28 \leqslant k \leqslant 4$

4 $\left(-\frac{2}{3}, \frac{4}{27}\right)$, $(0, 0)$; $0 < k < \frac{4}{27}$

5 $\left(\frac{1}{3}, \frac{4}{27}\right)$, $(1, 0)$; $k < -\frac{2}{9}\sqrt{3}$ and $k > \frac{2}{9}\sqrt{3}$

6 (a) $15x^2 - 30x$

(b) $30x - 30$ (c) $0, 2$

(d) $x = 0$ maximum, $x = 2$ minimum

7 (a) $(-1, 0)$, $(2, -27)$

(b) $x = -1$ maximum, $x = 2$ minimum

(d) $k < -27$ and $k > 0$

8 $(-1, 5)$, $(0, 10)$, $(2, -22)$

(a) $5 < k < 10$

(b) $-22 < k < 5$ and $k > 10$

12 Applications of differentiation

Exercise 12A (page 181)

1 (a) Gradient of road

(b) Rate of increase of crowd inside the stadium

(c) Rate of change of magnetic force with respect to distance

(d) Acceleration of train

(e) Rate of increase of petrol consumption with respect to speed

2 (a) $\dfrac{dp}{dh}$, p in millibars, h in metres

(b) $\dfrac{d\theta}{dt}$, θ in degrees C, t in hours

(c) $\dfrac{dh}{dt}$, h in metres, t in hours

(d) $\dfrac{dW}{dt}$, W in kilograms, t in weeks

3 (a) $6t + 7$ (b) $1 - \dfrac{1}{2\sqrt{x}}$

(c) $1 - \dfrac{6}{y^3}$ (d) $2t - \dfrac{1}{2t\sqrt{t}}$

(e) $2t + 6$ (f) $12s^5 - 6s$

(g) 5 (h) $-\dfrac{2}{r^3} - 1$

4 (a) $\dfrac{dx}{dt} = c$

(b) $\dfrac{dA}{dt} = kA$; A stands for the amount deposited

(c) $\dfrac{dx}{dt} = f(\theta)$; x stands for diameter, θ for air temperature

5 (a) (i) 98 metres per minute
        (ii) 22 metres per minute
   (b) 60 metres per minute
   (c) 25 minutes

6 (a) 25 per km (b) 15 per km (c) 20 per km

7 (a) 19 200
   (b) (i) 50 per minute
        (ii) 102.5 per minute
   (c) 90 per minute

8 (a) $2\pi r$
   (b) $4\pi r^2$
        $\dfrac{dA}{dr}$ is the circumference of the circle,
        $\dfrac{dV}{dr}$ is the surface area of the sphere.

9 $-\dfrac{2C}{x^3}$

10 $-\dfrac{1.4k}{V^{2.4}}$

11 (a) $\dfrac{0.1}{\sqrt{l}}$
   (b) It will increase by 0.000 126 seconds

Exercise 12B (page 192)

1 (a) Rate of increase of inflation, positive

2 (a) Both positive, sudden change (drop in S), then $\dfrac{dS}{dt}$ is negative changing to positive with $\dfrac{d^2S}{dt^2}$ positive.

(b) Price rising sharply, sudden 'crash', price continues to drop but less quickly and then recovers to give steadier growth.

3 (b) +, −, −, +

4 (a) $\dfrac{dN}{dt} = -kN$, $k > 0$
   (c) +

5 $80\,\text{km h}^{-1}$

6 20 m

7 36

8 $4\sqrt{5}$

9 Greatest $V = 32\pi$ when $r = 4$, least $V = 0$ when $r = 0$ or $h = 0$

10 $x = 25$

11 (b) $1800\,\text{m}^2$

12 $0 < x < 20$, 7.36 cm

13 20 cm

14 (b) $38\,400\,\text{cm}^3$ (to 3 significant figures)

15 $2420\,\text{cm}^3$ (to 3 significant figures)

Miscellaneous exercise 12 (page 194)

1 (a) Velocity
   (b) (i) increasing   (ii) decreasing
   (c) 9, occurs when velocity is zero and direction of motion changes

2 (a) $\dfrac{dn}{dt} = kn$ (b) $\dfrac{d\theta}{dt} = -k\theta$

3 +, −, +

5 $(20 - 4t)\,\text{m s}^{-1}$, $-4\,\text{m s}^{-2}$; for $0 \leqslant t \leqslant 5$

6 50

7 (a) $9\sqrt{2}$ cm   (b) $40\frac{1}{2}\,\text{cm}^2$

8 (a) $P = 2x + 2r + \frac{1}{2}\pi r$, $A = \frac{1}{4}\pi r^2 + rx$
   (b) $x = \frac{1}{4}r(4 - \pi)$

9 (a) $1100 - 20x$
   (b) $£x(1100 - 20x)$
   (c) $£(24\,000 - 400x)$
      £37.50

13   Circles

Exercise 13A (page 199)

1 (a) $x^2 + y^2 = 9$
   (b) $(x - 2)^2 + y^2 = 25$
   (c) $(x - 1)^2 + (y - 4)^2 = 4$
   (d) $(x + 5)^2 + (y - 7)^2 = 1$
   (e) $(x - 6)^2 + (y + 2)^2 = 100$
   (f) $(x + 7)^2 + (y + 3)^2 = 100$

2 (a) $(3, 2)$, 5   (b) $(-4, -1)$, 3
  (c) $(6, 0)$, $2\sqrt{5}$ (d) $(2, 5)$, 7
  (e) $(-4, 1)$, $3\sqrt{2}$ (f) $\left(1, -\frac{1}{2}\right)$, $\frac{1}{2}$

3 (a) Centre $(0, 0)$, radius 4
  (b) Centre $(-3, -3)$, radius $3\sqrt{2}$, passes through the origin
  (c) Centre $(-2, 3)$, radius 2, touches the y-axis
  (d) Centre $(2, 3)$, radius 1
  (e) Centre $\left(1\frac{1}{2}, 5\right)$, passes through the origin
  (f) Centre $\left(1\frac{1}{2}, 2\frac{1}{2}\right)$, passes through the origin

4 $x^2 + y^2 - 4x + 10y + 9 = 0$

5 $x^2 + y^2 - 10x - 10y = 0$

6 (b) $\left(-\frac{5}{2}, \frac{3}{2}\right)$, $\frac{7}{2}\sqrt{2}$
  (c) $\left(-\frac{2}{3}, \frac{4}{3}\right)$, $\frac{4}{3}$
  (f) $(-1, -1)$, 32

Exercise 13B (page 205)

1 $x + 3y = 0$

2 $3x - 5y - 6 = 0$

3 $3x - y + 10 = 0$

4 $x + y - 3 = 0$

5 $4x - y = 0$

6 $2x + 3y = 0$

7 $(6, 1)$, $(8, 1)$

8 $(-10, -32)$, $(-10, 16)$

9 $(-3, -3)$, $(-1, 3)$

10 $(3, 1)$, $(5, -1)$

12 $(5, -3)$

13 $2\sqrt{5}$

14 (a) $3a$ (b) $2a$ (c) $y = -a$

15 -3, 17

16 $\frac{4}{3} \pm \frac{1}{3}\sqrt{7}$

Miscellaneous exercise 13 (page 206)

1 $\left(\frac{7}{2}, -\frac{1}{2}\right)$, $\frac{3}{2}\sqrt{2}$

2 88

3 on, inside, outside, on, inside

4 $\left(\frac{3}{2}, -\frac{5}{2}\right)$, $\frac{1}{6}\sqrt{30}$

5 $x^2 + y^2 - 6x + 4y - 39 = 0$

6 $(0, 3)$, 3; $\left(-\frac{9}{5}, \frac{3}{5}\right)$, $(3, 3)$

7 $3x + 2y + 3 = 0$

8 $x^2 + y^2 - 2x - 12y + 27 = 0$

9 $4\sqrt{10}$

10 ± 10

11 $-9 < k < 1$

12 (a) 3 units in the negative x-direction and 1 unit in the positive y-direction
  (b) $x^2 + y^2 - 17x + 3y + 59 = 0$
  (c) $x^2 + y^2 + 2x + 2y - 14 = 0$

13 10, 26

18 $x^2 + y^2 - 6x + 18y - 10 = 0$,
    $x^2 + y^2 - 6x - 14y - 42 = 0$

19 $x^2 + y^2 - 26x - 8y + 181 = 0$

Revision exercise 2 (page 208)

1 $8x^2$

2 (a) 1; $y = x + 16$
  (b) $23y - 22x = 360$
  (c) $(-8, 8)$

3 (a)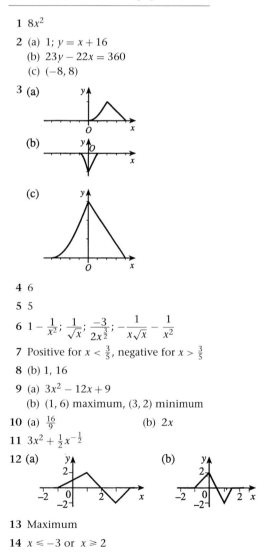
  (b)
  (c)

4 6

5 5

6 $1 - \frac{1}{x^2}$; $\frac{1}{\sqrt{x}}$; $\frac{-3}{2x^{\frac{3}{2}}}$; $\frac{1}{x\sqrt{x}} - \frac{1}{x^2}$

7 Positive for $x < \frac{3}{5}$, negative for $x > \frac{3}{5}$

8 (b) 1, 16

9 (a) $3x^2 - 12x + 9$
  (b) $(1, 6)$ maximum, $(3, 2)$ minimum

10 (a) $\frac{16}{9}$ (b) $2x$

11 $3x^2 + \frac{1}{2}x^{-\frac{1}{2}}$

12 (a)   (b)

13 Maximum

14 $x \leqslant -3$ or $x \geqslant 2$

15 $(7.8, 1.6)$

16 $\frac{1}{2}x^{-\frac{1}{2}} - \frac{1}{2}x^{-\frac{3}{2}}$; $1 - x^{-2}$

17 (a) 5   (b) $3x + 4y = 32$

18 x

19 (a) $6x^2 - 2x + \frac{3}{2}x^{\frac{1}{2}}$ (b) 91

20 (a) (i)

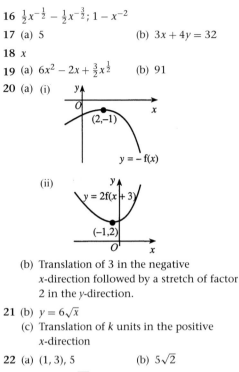

    (ii)

(b) Translation of 3 in the negative
   x-direction followed by a stretch of factor
   2 in the y-direction.

21 (b) $y = 6\sqrt{x}$
   (c) Translation of k units in the positive
   x-direction

22 (a) (1, 3), 5   (b) $5\sqrt{2}$

23 (a) (2, 3), $\sqrt{10}$
   (b) $x^2 + y^2 - 4x - 6y + 3 = 0$

24 Maximum at $(2, \frac{1}{4})$
   (a) $(2, 5\frac{1}{4})$ (b) $(3, \frac{1}{2})$

25 $(-1, -1)$, $(0, 0)$, $(1, 1)$

Practice examinations

Practice examination 1 for C1 (page 211)

1 $7 - 4\sqrt{3}$

2 $x < -\frac{3}{2}$ or $x > 0$

3 (i) (a) $x^3 - 16x$ (b) $3x^2 - 16$
   (ii) $-\frac{2}{x^3}$

4 (i) $(x - 2)^2 + 5$
   (ii) (a) (2, 5)   (b) $x = 2 \pm \sqrt{6}$

5 (ii) $(\frac{1}{2}, \frac{7}{2})$

6 (i)

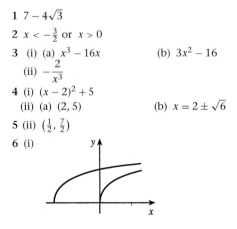

(a) (0, 0)
(b) $(-4, 0)$, $(0, 2)$
(ii) (4, 2)

7 (i) $x = 2$, $y = 1$ or $x = -5$, $y = 8$

9 (i) $(1, -2)$, 4
   (ii) Inside, since distance from the centre is $\sqrt{5}$
   which is less than 4
   (iii) $x + y = 1$

Practice examination 2 for C1 (page 213)

1 (i) 5   (ii) $\frac{1}{8}$ (iii) 4   (iv) 4

2 (i) $2 - \frac{1}{x^2}$ (ii) $\frac{2}{x^3}$

3 (i) $2(x + 2)^2 + 11$
   (ii) Least value 11, when $x = -2$

4 (i) 6.1, 6.05
   (ii) It approaches the gradient of the tangent
   at A, which is 6.

5 (ii) 1, 9

6 (i) (a)

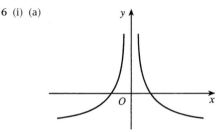

$(\pm 1, 0)$

(b)

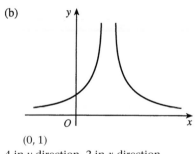

$(0, 1)$
(ii) 4 in y-direction, 2 in x-direction

7 (i) $y = 3x - 14$ (ii) (5, 1)   (iii) 30

8 (i) $y + 9x = 27$ (ii) (2, 4)

9 (i) $x^2 + y^2 - 8x + 7 = 0$
   (iii) $k = \pm\frac{3}{\sqrt{7}}$ (iv) 2

Answers to C2

1 Trigonometry

Exercise 1A (page 225)

1 (a) (i) 0.9063 (ii) 0.4226 (iii) 0.4663
  (b) (i) −0.5736 (ii) 0.8192 (iii) −1.4281
  (c) (i) −0.7071 (ii) −0.7071 (iii) 1.0000
  (d) (i) 0.8192 (ii) −0.5736 (iii) −0.7002
  (e) (i) −0.3420 (ii) 0.9397 (iii) −2.7475
  (f) (i) 0.3843 (ii) 0.9232 (iii) 2.4023
  (g) (i) −0.5721 (ii) 0.8202 (iii) −1.4335
  (h) (i) −0.9703 (ii) −0.2419 (iii) 0.2493

2 (a) max 3 at $x = 90°$, min 1 at $x = 270°$
  (b) max 11 at $x = 180°$, min 3 at $x = 360°$
  (c) max 13 at $x = 180°$, min −3 at $x = 90°$
  (d) max 4 at $x = 90°$, min 2 at $x = 270°$
  (e) max 10 at $x = 27\frac{1}{2}°$, min 8 at $x = 72\frac{1}{2}°$
  (f) max 30 at $x = 180°$, min 10 at $x = 360°$

3 (a) 160° (b) 320° (c) 240°
  (d) 50° (e) 220° (f) 340°
  (g) 40°, 140° (h) 30°, 330° (i) 70°, 250°
  (j) 80°, 100° (k) 160°, 200° (l) 100°, 280°

4 (a) $\frac{1}{2}\sqrt{2}$ (b) $-\frac{1}{2}$ (c) $-\frac{1}{2}$ (d) $\sqrt{3}$
  (e) $-\frac{1}{2}\sqrt{2}$ (f) $\frac{1}{2}\sqrt{3}$ (g) −1 (h) $-\frac{1}{2}\sqrt{3}$
  (i) $-\frac{1}{2}\sqrt{2}$ (j) 0 (k) 1 (l) $\frac{1}{2}\sqrt{2}$
  (m) $-\frac{1}{2}$ (n) −1 (o) $-\frac{1}{2}$ (p) 0

5 (a) 60° (b) 240° (c) 120° (d) 30°
  (e) 30° (f) 135° (g) 210° (h) 90°
  (i) 120° (j) 60° (k) 270° (l) 180°
  (m) 60° (n) 150° (o) 225° (p) 180°

7 $A = 5$, $B = 2.8$; 7.42 m

Exercise 1B (page 228)

2 reflection in the y-axis

Exercise 1C (page 234)

1 (a) 5.7°, 174.3° (b) 237.1°, 302.9°
  (c) 72.0°, 108.0° (d) 36.9°, 323.1°
  (e) 147.1°, 212.9° (f) 35.3°, 324.7°
  (g) 76.0°, 256.0° (h) 162.3°, 342.3°
  (i) 6.3°, 186.3° (j) 11.8°, 78.2°
  (k) 41.6°, 78.4° (l) 216.9°, 576.9°
  (m) 14.0°, 106.0° (n) 20.0°, 100.0°
  (o) 22.5°, 112.5°

2 (a) 53.1°, 126.9° (b) ±75.5°
  (c) −116.6°, 63.4° (d) −137.9°, −42.1°

  (e) ±96.9° (f) −36.9°, 143.1°
  (g) −128.7°, 51.3° (h) ±45°, ±135°
  (i) 0°, ±60°, ±180°

3 (a) 35.3°, 144.7°, 215.3°, 324.7°
  (b) 21.1°, 81.1°, 141.1°, 201.1°, 261.1°, 321.1°
  (c) 108.4°, 161.6°, 288.4°, 341.6°
  (d) 26.1°, 63.9°, 116.1°, 153.9°, 206.1°,
    243.9°, 296.1°, 333.9°
  (e) 10.9°, 100.9°, 190.9°, 280.9°
  (f) 68.3°, 111.7°, 188.3°, 231.7°, 308.3°,
    351.7°

4 (a) ±16.1°, ±103.9°, ±136.1°
  (b) −125.8°, −35.8°, 54.2°, 144.2°
  (c) −176.2°, −123.8°, −56.2°, −3.8°, 63.8°,
    116.2°
  (d) ±37.9°, ±142.1°
  (e) −172.3°, −136.3°, −100.3°, −64.3°,
    −28.3°, 7.7°, 43.7°, 79.7°, 115.7°, 151.7°
  (f) −78.5°, −11.5°, 101.5°, 168.5°

5 (a) ±96.4° (b) −107.3°, 162.7°
  (c) −56.0° (d) No roots in the interval
  (e) 35.4° (f) −43.6°

6 (a) 15°, 75°, 195°, 255°
  (b) 90°, 180°, 270°, 360°
  (c) 10°, 110°, 130°, 230°, 250°, 350°
  (d) 80°, 200°, 320°
  (e) 60°, 120°, 240°, 300°
  (f) 180°
  (g) none
  (h) 45°, 105°, 165°, 225°, 285°, 345°
  (i) none

7 (a) −170.8°, −9.2°
  (b) −90°, 90°
  (c) −180°, −135°, 0°, 45°, 180°
  (d) −173.4°, −96.6°, 6.6°, 83.4°
  (e) −155.8°, −24.2°, 24.2°, 155.8°
  (f) −180°, −150°, −30°, 0°, 180°

8 (a) 60°, 180° (b) 45°, 225° (c) 195°, 255°
  (d) 165°, 345° (e) 170°, 290° (f) 40°
  (g) 140°, 320° (h) 135°, 315° (i) 20°, 200°

9 (a) 50.8°, 359.2° (b) 165.5°, 310.5°
  (c) 1.6°, 181.6° (d) 268.1°, 341.9°
  (e) 86.6°, 355.4° (f) 92.4°, 272.4°

10 (a) 27°, 63°, 207°, 243°
  (b) 4°, 68°, 76°, 140°, 148°, 212°, 220°, 284°,
    292°, 356°
  (c) 20°, 80°, 140°, 200°, 260°, 320°

11 $0°$, $60°$, $120°$, $180°$

12 For example,

    (a) (i) $\sin 4\theta$ (ii) $\cos 4\theta$ (iii) $\tan 2\theta$

    (b) (i) $\sin 18\theta$ (ii) $\cos 18\theta$ (iii) $\tan 9\theta$

    (c) (i) $\sin \frac{15}{2}\theta$ (ii) $\cos \frac{15}{2}\theta$ (iii) $\tan \frac{15}{4}\theta$

    (d) (i) $\sin 3\theta$ (ii) $\cos 3\theta$ (iii) $\tan \frac{3}{2}\theta$

    (e) (i) $\sin \frac{1}{2}\theta$ (ii) $\cos \frac{1}{2}\theta$ (iii) $\tan \frac{1}{4}\theta$

    (f) (i) $\sin \frac{3}{5}\theta$ (ii) $\cos \frac{3}{5}\theta$ (iii) $\tan \frac{3}{10}\theta$

13 (a) $120°$ (b) $180°$ (c) $90°$

    (d) $540°$ (e) $720°$ (f) $720°$

    (g) $120°$ (h) $90°$ (i) $360°$

14 (a) 0.986

    (b) $A = 12$, $B = 6$, 6 hours 7 minutes

    (c) Days 202, 345

Exercise 1D (page 239)

1 (a) (i) 11 (ii) $\frac{4}{5}, \frac{3}{5}, \frac{4}{3}$

    (b) (i) 37.5 (ii) $\frac{15}{17}, \frac{8}{17}, \frac{15}{8}$

    (c) (i) $\sqrt{13}$ (ii) $\frac{3}{13}\sqrt{13}, \frac{2}{13}\sqrt{13}, \frac{3}{2}$

    (d) (i) 11 (ii) $\frac{5}{14}\sqrt{3}, \frac{11}{14}, \frac{5}{11}\sqrt{3}$

    (e) (i) $17\sqrt{5}$ (ii) $\frac{22}{85}\sqrt{5}, \frac{31}{85}\sqrt{5}, \frac{22}{31}$

    (f) (i) $12\sqrt{2}$ (ii) $\frac{1}{3}, \frac{2}{3}\sqrt{2}, \frac{1}{4}\sqrt{2}$

2 (a) $\cos^2 x$ (b) $\tan^2 x$ (c) $\tan^2 x$

3 (a) $-\frac{11}{14}$ (b) $\frac{20}{29}$ (c) $\pm\frac{1}{2}\sqrt{3}$

    (d) $0°, \pm78.5°$ (to 1 d.p.)

5 (a) $30°$, $150°$, $210°$, $330°$

    (b) $0°$, $180°$, $360°$

    (c) $0°$, $48.6°$, $131.4°$, $180°$, $360°$

    (d) $270°$

    (e) $0°$, $60°$, $300°$, $360°$

    (f) $60°$, $180°$, $300°$

    (g) $36.9°$, $143.1°$, $199.5°$, $340.5°$

    (h) $0°$, $51.0°$, $180°$, $309.0°$, $360°$

6 $-116.6°$, $-26.6°$, $63.4°$, $153.4°$

Miscellaneous exercise 1 (page 240)

1 (a) $360°$ (b) $90°$

2 (a) $\cos x°$ (b) $-\cos x°$

3 $(0°, 1)$, $(\pm180°, 0)$

4 (a) $21.8°$, $201.8°$

    (b) $11.8°$, $78.2°$, $191.8°$, $258.2°$

5 $24.1°$, $155.9°$

6 (a) Examples are $\tan x$, $\sin 2x$, $\cos 2x$

    (b) $10°$, $50°$, $130°$, $170°$

7 $30°$, $270°$

8 (a) $2\sin 2x$ (b) $105°$, $165°$, $285°$, $345°$

9 (a) $168.5°$ (b) $333.4°$ (c) $225°$ (d) $553.1°$

11 (a) $2, 0$; $180°, 90°$ (b) $9, 1$; $240°, 60°$

    (c) $49, 9$; $105°, 45°$ (d) $8, 5$; $90°, 180°$

    (e) $6, 3$; $180°, 360°$ (f) $60, 30$; $7\frac{1}{2}°, 52\frac{1}{2}°$

12 (a) $0°$, $180°$, $360°$ (b) $0°$, $30°$, $150°$, $180°$, $360°$

    (c) $67\frac{1}{2}°$, $157\frac{1}{2}°$, $247\frac{1}{2}°$, $337\frac{1}{2}°$

    (d) $30°$, $120°$, $210°$, $300°$

13 (a) $60°$ (b) $8.9°$, $68.9°$, $128.9°$

    (c) (i) $51.1°$ (ii) $21.1°$

14 (a) $4.8 \pm 1.2\sin 15t$ or $4.8 \pm 1.2\cos 15t$

    (b) $21\,500 \pm 6500\sin 36t$ or

      $21\,500 \pm 6500\cos 36t$

    (c) $12 \pm 10\sin t$ or $12 \pm 10\cos t$

15 (a) 0.1 cm, 0.0009 seconds

    (b) 0.0036 seconds

    (c) 278 (d) $0.002\,13$ seconds

16 (a) 110 cm and 90 cm   (b) 0.36 seconds

    (c) 0.72 seconds   (d) 0.468

17 (a) $k = \dfrac{360}{T}$ (b) $\dfrac{k}{360}$

18 (a) 7.2

    (b) (i) $N - C$ (ii) $N + C$, after 25 weeks

19 (a) 30 (b) 3.25 m   (c) 27

20 $A = 0.5$, $B = 4.5$, $\alpha = 1$, $\beta = 12$

2 Sequences

Exercise 2A (page 244)

1 (a) $7, 14, 21, 28, 35$

    (b) $13, 8, 3, -2, -7$

    (c) $4, 12, 36, 108, 324$

    (d) $6, 3, 1.5, 0.75, 0.375$

    (e) $2, 7, 22, 67, 202$

    (f) $1, 4, 19, 364, 132\,499$

2 (a) $u_1 = 2$, $u_{r+1} = u_r + 2$

    (b) $u_1 = 11$, $u_{r+1} = u_r - 2$

    (c) $u_1 = 2$, $u_{r+1} = u_r + 4$

    (d) $u_1 = 2$, $u_{r+1} = 3u_r$

    (e) $u_1 = \frac{1}{3}$, $u_{r+1} = \frac{1}{3}u_r$

    (f) $u_1 = \frac{1}{2}a$, $u_{r+1} = \frac{1}{2}u_r$

    (g) $u_1 = b - 2c$, $u_{r+1} = u_r + c$

    (h) $u_1 = 1$, $u_{r+1} = -u_r$

    (i) $u_1 = \dfrac{p}{q^3}$, $u_{r+1} = qu_r$

    (j) $u_1 = \dfrac{a^3}{b^2}$, $u_{r+1} = \dfrac{bu_r}{a}$

    (k) $u_1 = x^3$, $u_{r+1} = \dfrac{5u_r}{x}$

    (l) $u_1 = 1$, $u_{r+1} = (1 + x)u_r$

3 (a) 5, 7, 9, 11, 13; $u_1 = 5$, $u_{r+1} = u_r + 2$
  (b) 1, 4, 9, 16, 25; $u_1 = 1$, $u_{r+1} = u_r + 2r + 1$
  (c) 1, 3, 6, 10, 15; $u_1 = 1$, $u_{r+1} = u_r + r + 1$
  (d) 1, 5, 14, 30, 55; $u_1 = 1$, $u_{r+1} = u_r + (r+1)^2$
  (e) 6, 18, 54, 162, 486; $u_1 = 6$, $u_{r+1} = 3u_r$
  (f) 3, 15, 75, 375, 1875; $u_1 = 3$, $u_{r+1} = 5u_r$

4 (a) $u_r = 10 - r$ (b) $u_r = 2 \times 3^r$
  (c) $u_r = r^2 + 3$ (d) $u_r = 2r(r+1)$
  (e) $u_r = \dfrac{2r-1}{r+3}$ (f) $u_r = \dfrac{r^2+1}{2^r}$

Exercise 2B (page 249)

1 (a) 820   (b) 610   (c) 420   (d) 400

2 (a) 5040   (b) 6720   (c) 35

3 (a) $\dfrac{8!}{4!}$ (b) $\dfrac{12!}{8!}$ (c) $\dfrac{n!}{(n-3)!}$
  (d) $\dfrac{(n+1)!}{(n-2)!}$ (e) $\dfrac{(n+3)!}{(n-1)!}$ (f) $\dfrac{(n+6)!}{(n+3)!}$
  (g) 8!   (h) $n!$

4 (a) 12   (b) $22 \times 22!$
  (c) $n+1$ (d) $n \times n!$

5 (a) 1, 8, 28, 56, 70, 56, 28, 8, 1, 0, 0, ...
  (b) 1, 9, 36, 84, 126, 126, 84, 36, 9, 1, 0, ...

6 (a) $\dfrac{11!}{4! \times 7!}$ (b) $\dfrac{11!}{7! \times 4!}$ (c) $\dfrac{10!}{5! \times 5!}$
  (d) $\dfrac{12!}{3! \times 9!}$ (e) $\dfrac{12!}{9! \times 3!}$

8 $\dbinom{n}{r} + \dbinom{n}{r+1} = \dbinom{n+1}{r+1}$

10 (a) r (c) $1^3 = t_1{}^2 - t_0{}^2$, $2^3 = t_2{}^2 - t_1{}^2$,
  $3^3 = t_3{}^2 - t_2{}^2, \ldots, n^3 = t_n{}^2 - t_{n-1}^2$

11 The sum of the terms in the sequence is 2^n.

Exercise 2C (page 257)

1 (a), (d), (f), (h); 3, −2, q, x respectively

2 (a) 12, $2r$ (b) 32, $14 + 3r$
  (c) −10, $8 - 3r$ (d) 3.3, $0.9 + 0.4r$
  (e) $3\frac{1}{2}$, $\frac{1}{2} + \frac{1}{2}r$ (f) 43, $79 - 6r$
  (g) $x + 10$, $x - 2 + 2r$ (h) $1 + 4x$, $1 - 2x + xr$

3 (a) 14   (b) 88   (c) 36
  (d) 11   (e) 11   (f) 11
  (g) 16   (h) 28

4 (a) 610   (b) 795
  (c) −102   (d) $855\frac{1}{2}$
  (e) −1025   (f) 998 001
  (g) $3160a$ (h) $-15150p$

5 (a) 54, 3132   (b) 20, 920
  (c) 46, 6532   (d) 28, −910
  (e) 28, 1120   (f) 125, 42 875
  (g) 1000, 5 005 000   (h) 61, −988.2

6 (a) $a = 3$, $d = 4$ (b) $a = 2$, $d = 5$
  (c) $a = 1.4$, $d = 0.3$ (d) $a = 12$, $d = -2.5$
  (e) $a = 25$, $d = -3$ (f) $a = -7$, $d = 2$
  (g) $a = 3x$, $d = -x$ (h) $a = p+1$, $d = \frac{1}{2}p + 3$

7 (a) 20   (b) 12   (c) 16
  (d) 40   (e) 96   (f) 28

8 (a) 62   (b) 25

9 (a) £76   (b) £1272

10 (a) 5050   (b) 15 050   (c) $\frac{1}{2}n(3n+1)$

11 £1 626 000

Exercise 2D (page 263)

1 (a) $2 + 3$ (b) $2 + 2 + 2$
  (c) $1 + \frac{1}{2} + \frac{1}{3} + \frac{1}{4}$ (d) $1 + 4 + 9 + 16$
  (e) $5 + 7 + 9 + 11$ (f) $u_0 + u_1 + u_2$

2 (a) $\sum\limits_{r=2}^{4} r$ (b) $\sum\limits_{r=1}^{4} r^2$ (c) $\sum\limits_{r=3}^{7} r^3$
  (d) $\sum\limits_{r=1}^{3} \dfrac{1}{2r}$ (e) $\sum\limits_{r=1}^{4}(2r+1)$ (f) $\sum\limits_{r=1}^{5}(3r-1)$

3 (a) $0 + 1 + 2 + \cdots + n$
  (b) $2^2 + 3^2 + 4^2 + \cdots + (n-1)^2$
  (c) $\overbrace{3 + 3 + 3 + \cdots + 3}^{n-7 \text{ of these}}$
  (d) $\frac{1}{1} + \frac{1}{2} + \frac{1}{3} + \cdots + 1/(2n)$
  (e) $0^3 + 1^3 + 2^3 + \cdots + (2n-1)^3$
  (f) $u_1 + u_2 + u_3 + \cdots + u_{n-1}$

4 (a), (c) are true. (b) n (d) $2n + \sum\limits_{r=1}^{n} r^2$

5 (a) 1   (b) −1   (c) −1
  (d) 21   (e) $\frac{17}{60}$ (f) −1

6 (a) $\sum\limits_{r=1}^{101}(-1)^{r+1} r$ (b) $\sum\limits_{r=1}^{25}(-1)^r (2r)^2$
  (c) $\sum\limits_{r=1}^{49}(-1)^{r+1} \dfrac{1}{r}$

7 (a) $\sum\limits_{r=1}^{100}\left(r + \dfrac{1}{r}\right)$ (b) $\sum\limits_{r=0}^{n}\dbinom{n}{r} x^r$
  (c) $\sum\limits_{r=0}^{n}(r+1)x^r$ (d) $\sum\limits_{r=0}^{2n}(-1)^{r-1} r x^{r-1}$

8 $\sum\limits_{r=1}^{n}(a + (r-1)d) = \frac{1}{2}n(2a + (n-1)d)$

Miscellaneous exercise 2 (page 264)

1 1444

2 (a) (i) 1, 2, 5, 14, 41   (ii) 2, 5, 14, 41, 122
    (iii) 0, −1, −4, −13, −40
    (iv) $\frac{1}{2}, \frac{1}{2}, \frac{1}{2}, \frac{1}{2}, \frac{1}{2}$
  (b) (i) $b = \frac{1}{2}$ (ii) $b = \frac{3}{2}$
    (iii) $b = -\frac{1}{2}$ (iv) $b = 0$

3 (a) 3, 1, 3; alternately 1 and 3
  (b) All terms after the first are 2   (c) 2

4 (a) Alternately 0 and −1; 1, then alternately 0 and −1; gets increasingly large
(b) $\frac{1}{2}(1 \pm \sqrt{5})$

5 $n(2n+3)$

6 168

7 −750

8 $2n - \frac{1}{2}$

9 167 167; 111 445

10 40

11 (a) 991   (b) 50 045.5

12 (a) 18   (b) $2(2n + 1)$
(c) $a = 6$, $d = 4$, sum $= 2\,004\,000$

13 (a) $\frac{1}{2}n(3n + 1)$ (b) $n(n + 4)$ (c) $\frac{1}{2}n(7 - n)$

14 71 240

15 (a) 47, 12 years left over
(b) £345 450

16 $a = \dfrac{10\,000}{n} - 5(n - 1)$; 73

17 (a) 0, 1, 4, 9, 16; r^2 (b) 0, 1, 2, 3, 4; r
(c) 1, 2, 4, 8, 16; 2^r

3 The binomial theorem

Exercise 3A (page 270)

1 (a) $x^3 + 3x^2 + 3x + 1$
(b) $8x^3 + 12x^2 + 6x + 1$
(c) $64 + 48p + 12p^2 + p^3$
(d) $x^3 - 3x^2 + 3x - 1$
(e) $x^6 + 6x^4 + 12x^2 + 8$
(f) $1 - 15x^2 + 75x^4 - 125x^6$
(g) $x^6 + 3x^4y^3 + 3x^2y^6 + y^9$
(h) $27x^6 + 54x^4y^3 + 36x^2y^6 + 8y^9$
(i) $x^3 + 6x^2 + 12x + 8$
(j) $8p^3 + 36p^2q + 54pq^2 + 27q^3$
(k) $1 - 12x + 48x^2 - 64x^3$
(l) $1 - 3x^3 + 3x^6 - x^9$

2 (a) 12   (b) 150

3 (a) 240   (b) 54

4 (a) $1 + 10x + 40x^2 + 80x^3 + 80x^4 + 32x^5$
(b) $p^6 + 12p^5q + 60p^4q^2 + 160p^3q^3$
$+ 240p^2q^4 + 192pq^5 + 64q^6$
(c) $16m^4 - 96m^3n + 216m^2n^2$
$- 216mn^3 + 81n^4$
(d) $1 + 2x + \frac{3}{2}x^2 + \frac{1}{2}x^3 + \frac{3}{16}x^4$

5 (a) 270   (b) −1000

6 $1 + 3x + 9x^2 + 13x^3 + 18x^4 + 12x^5 + 8x^6$

7 $x^3 + 12x^2 + 48x + 64$;
$x^4 + 13x^3 + 60x^2 + 112x + 64$

8 $24x^4 + 124x^3 + 234x^2 + 189x + 54$

9 7

10 $x^{11} + 11x^{10}y + 55x^9y^2 + 165x^8y^3 + 330x^7y^4$
$+ 462x^6y^5 + 462x^5y^6 + 330x^4y^7 + 165x^3y^8$
$+ 55x^2y^9 + 11xy^{10} + y^{11}$

11 59 136

Exercise 3B (page 276)

1 (a) 35   (b) 28   (c) 126   (d) 715
(e) 15   (f) 45   (g) 11   (h) 1225

2 (a) 10   (b) −56   (c) 165   (d) −560

3 (a) 84   (b) −1512
(c) 4032   (d) $-\frac{99}{4}$

4 (a) 3003   (b) 192 192
(c) 560 431 872   (d) 48 048

5 (a) $1 + 13x + 78x^2 + 286x^3$
(b) $1 - 15x + 105x^2 - 455x^3$
(c) $1 + 30x + 405x^2 + 3240x^3$
(d) $128 - 2240x + 16\,800x^2 - 70\,000x^3$

6 (a) $1 + 22x + 231x^2$
(b) $1 - 30x + 435x^2$
(c) $1 - 72x + 2448x^2$
(d) $1 + 114x + 6156x^2$

7 $1 + 16x + 112x^2$; 1.17

8 $4096 + 122\,880x + 1\,689\,600x^2$; 4220.57

9 $1 + 32x + 480x^2 + 4480x^3$; 5920

10 $1 - 30x + 405x^2$; 234

11 7

12 $2 + 56x^2 + 140x^4 + 56x^6 + 2x^8$;
2.005 601 400 056 000 2

13 $a = 4$, $n = 9$

Miscellaneous exercise 3 (page 277)

1 $27 + 108x + 144x^2 + 64x^3$

2 (a) $1 + 40x + 720x^2$ (b) $1 - 32x + 480x^2$

3 (a) −48 384   (b) $\frac{875}{4}$

4 $2187 + 25\,515x + 127\,575x^2$; 2455

5 $256 + 256x + 112x^2 + 28x^3$; 258.571

6 $256 - 3072x + 16\,128x^2$; 253

7 $x^6 + 3x^3 + 3 + \dfrac{1}{x^3}$

8 $16x^4 - 96x + \dfrac{216}{x^2} - \dfrac{216}{x^5} + \dfrac{81}{x^8}$

9 $2x^6 + 15\dfrac{x^2}{2} + \dfrac{15}{8x^2} + \dfrac{1}{32x^6}$

10 48

11 20 000

12 495;   (a) 40 095   (b) 7920   (c) $\frac{495}{16}$

13 30

14 $1 + 40x + 760x^2$;

   (a) 1.0408   (b) 0.9230

15 $1024 - \dfrac{2560}{x^2} + \dfrac{2880}{x^4}$; 999

16 B, D

17 $\frac{7}{16}$

18 5376

19 $\frac{6435}{128}$

20 -2024

21 $1 + 12x + 70x^2$; 1.127

22 $270x^2 + 250$; $\pm \frac{4}{3}$

23 $\pm \frac{5}{6}$

24 (b) (i) 4 or 7   (ii) 3 or 13
           (iii) 7 or 13   (iv) 17 or 28

25 1.005 413 792 056 805

26 (a) $217 + 88\sqrt{6}$ (b) $698\sqrt{2} + 569\sqrt{3}$

27 (a) 568; 567 and 568   (b) 969 and 970

28 (a) $1 + 5\alpha t + 10\alpha^2 t^2$ (b) $1 - 8\beta t + 28\beta^2 t^2$
     $10\alpha^2 - 40\alpha\beta + 28\beta^2$

29 (b) (i) $a = 3, b = 6, c = 8$
       (ii) $a = 6, b = 4, c = 9$

31 $2n(n + 1)$

32 $a = -\frac{1}{6}, b = \frac{1}{2}, c = -\frac{1}{2}, d = \frac{1}{6}$

4 The sine and cosine rules

In this chapter, angles are given correct to 1 decimal place (unless they are exact), and lengths and areas correct to 3 significant figures.

Exercise 4A (page 284)

1 (a) 6 cm²   (b) 11.2 cm²
   (c) 1.93 m²   (d) 3.75 cm²
   (e) 5.03 cm²   (f) 0.311 m²

2 (a) 5.19 cm   (b) 4 cm
   (c) 1.60 m   (d) 9.53 cm
   (e) 43.5 cm   (f) 11.2 cm

3 (a) 33.7°   (b) 53.1°
   (c) 20.5°   (d) 56.3°
   (e) 11.6°   (f) 10.8°

4 (a) 146.3°   (b) 126.9°
   (c) 159.5°   (d) 123.7°
   (e) 168.4°   (f) 169.2°

Exercise 4B (page 287)

1 (a) 6.95 cm   (b) 32.9 cm
   (c) 3.14 cm   (d) 7.65 cm
   (e) 5.81 cm   (f) 8.18 cm

2 (a) $a = 12.4$ cm, $c = 12.5$ cm, 68.9 cm²
   (b) $p = 8.40$ cm, $r = 7.93$ cm, 29.4 cm²
   (c) $x = 14.8$ cm, $z = 13.4$ cm, 76.2 cm²
   (d) $l = 10.4$ cm, $n = 4.17$ cm, 17.7 cm²

3 (a) $A = 64.5°$, $C = 24.5°$
   (b) $Y = 59.5°$, $Z = 49.5°$

4 (a) $L = 92.1°$, $N = 74.9°$
   (b) $F = 111.8°$ $D = 28.2°$

5 (a) 119 m   (b) 102 m

6 (a) 80.0°   (b) 90.0°

7 The largest side must be opposite the largest angle, and B must be the largest angle.

8 (a) 5.64 cm   (b) 6.12 cm   (c) 21.5 cm²

Exercise 4C (page 293)

1 (a) 10.2 cm   (b) 16.3 cm
   (c) 5.91 cm   (d) 28.0 cm

2 (a) 69.5°   (b) 128.0°
   (c) 85.6°   (d) 90°

3 (a) 44.0°   (b) 43.8°
   (c) 24.1°   (d) 36.9°

4 34.2 cm²

Exercise 4D (page 296)

In the answers to this exercise unknown angles are given first, followed by unknown sides. They are given in alphabetical order, which may not be the same as the order in which you found them.

1 70°, 5.65 cm, 6.13 cm

2 42.4°, 57.6°, 4.79 cm

3 38.2°, 120°, 21.8°

4 33.1°, 36.9°, 17.2 cm

5 70°, 70°, 4.79 cm

Miscellaneous exercise 4 (page 296)

1 6.03 m

2 14.2 cm, 17.4 cm

3 9.45 cm

4 57.4°

5 35.4°, 48.2°, 96.4°, 31.3 cm^2

6 11.3 cm, 47.3°, 57.7°

7 59.9°

8 5.08 cm, 5.76 cm, 4.51 cm

9 25.7 cm^2

10 0.840 m

11 52.2 km

12 (a) 29.0°   (b) 11.6 m^2

13 (a) 139 m   (b) 55.0°   (c) 110 m

14 (a) 16.8°   (b) 17.4 cm^2

15 (a) 9.92 cm^2 (b) 1.32 cm

16 36.0 m

5 Integration

Exercise 5A (page 304)

1 (a) $x^4 + k$ (b) $x^6 + k$
   (c) $x^2 + k$ (d) $x^3 + x^5 + k$
   (e) $x^{10} - x^8 - x + k$ (f) $-x^7 + x^3 + x + k$

2 (a) $3x^3 - 2x^2 - 5x + k$
   (b) $4x^3 + 3x^2 + 4x + k$
   (c) $7x + k$
   (d) $4x^4 - 2x^3 + 5x^2 - 3x + k$
   (e) $\frac{1}{2}x^4 + \frac{5}{2}x^2 + k$
   (f) $\frac{1}{2}x^2 + \frac{2}{3}x^3 + k$
   (g) $\frac{2}{3}x^3 - \frac{3}{2}x^2 - 4x + k$
   (h) $x - x^2 - x^3 + k$

3 (a) $y = \frac{1}{5}x^5 + \frac{1}{3}x^3 + x + k$
   (b) $y = \frac{7}{2}x^2 - 3x + k$
   (c) $y = \frac{2}{3}x^3 + \frac{1}{2}x^2 - 8x + k$
   (d) $y = \frac{3}{2}x^4 - \frac{5}{3}x^3 + \frac{3}{2}x^2 + 2x + k$
   (e) $y = \frac{1}{6}x^4 + \frac{1}{6}x^3 + \frac{1}{6}x^2 + \frac{1}{6}x + k$
   (f) $y = \frac{1}{8}x^4 - \frac{1}{9}x^3 + \frac{1}{2}x^2 - \frac{1}{3}x + k$
   (g) $y = \frac{1}{2}x^2 - x^3 + x + k$
   (h) $y = \frac{1}{4}x^4 + \frac{1}{3}x^3 + \frac{1}{2}x^2 + x + k$

4 $4x^2 - 5x$

5 $y = 2x^3 - x - 19$

6 $y = \frac{1}{8}x^4 + \frac{1}{8}x^2 + x - 21$

7 $5x^3 - 3x^2 + 4x - 6$

9 $y = 4x\sqrt{x} - 7$

10 (a) $y = \frac{2}{3}x^{3/2} + k$ (b) $y = 12x^{1/3} + k$
    (c) $y = \frac{3}{4}x^{4/3} + k$
    (d) $y = \frac{4}{3}x\sqrt{x} - 4\sqrt{x} + k$
    (e) $y = \frac{15}{2}\sqrt[3]{x^2} + k$ (f) $y = -6\sqrt[3]{x} + k$

11 (a) $-x^{-1} + k$ (b) $-x^{-3} + k$
    (c) $-\dfrac{3}{x^2} + k$ (d) $2x^2 + \dfrac{3}{x} + k$
    (e) $-\dfrac{1}{2x^2} + \dfrac{1}{3x^3} + k$ (f) $-\dfrac{2}{x} - \frac{2}{3}x^3 + k$

12 $y = -\dfrac{4}{x} + 13$

13 $y = \sqrt{x} - 2$

14 $y = \frac{3}{4}x^{4/3} + 3x^{-2} + \frac{5}{4}$

15 (a) $y = x^3 + 3x^2 + k$
    (b) $y = 4x^3 + 2x^2 - 5x + k$
    (c) $y = 2x^2 - \dfrac{1}{x} + k$
    (d) $y = \frac{2}{3}x\sqrt{x} + 8\sqrt{x} + k$
    (e) $y = \frac{1}{2}x^2 + \frac{20}{3}x\sqrt{x} + 25x + k$
    (f) $y = x + 10\sqrt{x} + k$

16 (a) $\frac{1}{3}u^3 - \dfrac{1}{u} + k$
    (b) $\frac{1}{2}t^6 - \frac{1}{7}t^7 + k$
    (c) $p^4 + 4p^3 + 6p^2 + 4p + k$
    (d) $-\dfrac{2}{\sqrt{y}} + k$
    (e) $\frac{3}{7}z^{\frac{7}{3}} + \frac{12}{5}z^{\frac{5}{3}} + 6z + 12z^{\frac{1}{3}} - 3z^{-\frac{1}{3}} + k$
    (f) $v^2 \left(\frac{1}{2} + \frac{2}{5}\sqrt{v} \right) + k$

17 (a) 118 cm (to 3 s.f.)   (b) 27

18 17 months (to the nearest month)

19 192

Exercise 5B (page 312)

1 (a) 7   (b) 84   (c) 4
   (d) 4   (e) $\frac{1}{16}$ (f) 2

2 (a) 22   (b) 22   (c) 36
   (d) $7\frac{1}{6}$ (e) 210   (f) 0

3 72

4 15

5 195

6 80

7 80

8 $10\frac{2}{5}$

9 18

10 16

11 (a) 39   (b) $5\frac{1}{3}$
      (c) $10\frac{2}{3}$ (d) 10

12 (a) 144   (b) $1\frac{1}{2}$ (c) 20
      (d) $6\frac{3}{4}$ (e) 16   (f) 3

13 $1\frac{3}{4}$

14 60

15 $3\frac{1}{3}$

16 7

17 5

18 (a) $22\frac{2}{3}$ (b) $2\frac{3}{8}$

19 $42\frac{7}{8}$

Exercise 5C (page 323)

1 -4; the graph of $y = 3x(x - 2)$ lies below the x-axis for $0 < x < 2$.

2 60

3 21

4 $10\frac{2}{3}$; the negative value of $\int_{-2}^{2} x\,dy$ indicates that the region is on the left of the x-axis.

5 (a) $10\frac{2}{3}$ (b) 8   (c) $2\frac{1}{4}$ (d) $1\frac{5}{6}$

6 (a) $10\frac{2}{3}$ (b) 8   (c) 100

7 (a) $\frac{1}{4}$ (b) 6   (c) 100

8 $\dfrac{s^{1-m} - 1}{1 - m}$; $\dfrac{1}{m - 1}$

9 $\dfrac{1 - r^{1-m}}{1 - m}$; $m < 1$, $\dfrac{1}{1 - m}$

10 12

11 $10\frac{2}{3}$

12 32

13 108

14 $42\frac{2}{3}$

15 36

16 $4\frac{1}{2}$

17 (a) 500   (b) $5\frac{1}{3}$

18 96

20 4

Miscellaneous exercise 5 (page 325)

1 $y = \frac{1}{6}x^3 - \frac{1}{6}x^2 + x + \frac{1}{3}$

2 ± 2; 32

3 $4x\sqrt{x} + k$; 28

4 (a) $-\frac{1}{2}x^{-2} + \frac{1}{4}x^4 + k$ (b) 6

5 $31\frac{1}{4}$

6 $50\frac{2}{15}$

7 7

8 $6\frac{3}{4}$

9 $1\frac{1}{3}$

10 0; integrand is positive for $0 < x < 1$, negative for $1 < x < 2$.

11 (a) $\frac{1}{4}x^4 - x^2 + k$ (b) 2

12 (a) $y = -\frac{1}{2}x + \frac{3}{2}$ (b) $2\frac{29}{48}$

13 ± 2

15 (a) 6   (b) 67   (c) —   (d) 45
      (e) 17   (f) -11 (g) 17   (h) 11

17 (a) $y = 2x - 2$ (b) $6\frac{3}{4}$

19 $(0, 0)$, $(\pm 2, -16)$; 32.4

20 $\frac{1}{2}$

21 (a) $\frac{1}{27}$, 0
      (b) (i) $(3, 0)$ (ii) $\left(4, -\frac{1}{128}\right)$
      The minimum at $x = 4$ shows that the function takes both positive and negative values when $x > 2$.

Revision exercise 3 (page 328)

1 (a) 22.5 cm   (b) 45 cm, 15 cm
      (c) 0.33, 3.67   (d) 15

2 $(-4, 8)$, $(1, 3)$; $20\frac{5}{6}$

3 (a) $(-1, 5)$, $(1, 1)$ (b) $(0, 3)$
      (c) $9y + x = 7$ (d) 4

4 $\dfrac{n - 1}{n + 1}$

5 $27.6°$

6 (a) 8, 26, 80, 242, 728
      (b) $u_r = 3^r - 1$

7 (a) $\pm 50.8°$, $\pm 129.2°$ (b) $-150°$, $-30°$
      (c) $-166.7°$, $-76.7°$, $13.3°$, $103.3°$
      (d) $\pm 15°$, $\pm 75°$, $\pm 105°$, $\pm 165°$

8 (a) $15°$, $75°$, $105°$, $165°$, $195°$, $255°$, $285°$, $345°$
      (c) $90°$; for example, $(45°, 1.5)$

9 $y = \frac{5}{2}x^2 + 3x + 4$

10 0. Between $x = 1$ and $x = 3$, there is the same area above and below the x-axis.

11 Three roots

12 $\frac{1}{2}(2n + 1)$ (b) 20

13 (a) $x^8 - 8x^6 + 28x^4$ (b) 216

14 (b) 22

15 (a) 5   (b) $\frac{1}{2}$

16 (a) 3320 m   (b) 526 m

17 (a) $S_{r-1} = (r-1)^2 \, r$, $u_r = 3r^2 - r$
    (b) $u_{r+1} = 3r^2 + 5r + 2$
    (c) 2
    (d) $u_2 = 10$, $u_3 = 24$; $S_2 = 12 = 2^2 \, (2+1)$,
       $S_3 = 36 = 3^2(3+1)$

18 1215

19 21

20 $2\sqrt{19}$ cm

21 (b) $7.3°$, $67.3°$, $127.3°$

22 $a = nc$, $b = \frac{1}{2}n(n-1)c^2$;
$$n = \frac{a^2}{a^2 - 2b}, \; c = \frac{a^2 - 2b}{a}$$

23 (a) 15.1 km   (b) 13.9 km, 071.9°

24 (a) $\frac{1}{3}x^3 + \frac{1}{2}x^2 + k$ (b) $-\dfrac{1}{x} + k$

25 (b) $9.2°$, $99.2°$, $189.2°$, $279.2°$

26 (a) $(-1, 6)$, $(1\frac{1}{2}, 3\frac{1}{2})$ (b) $x < -1$ or $x > 1\frac{1}{2}$

27 $\frac{3}{2}\sqrt{3}$

28 (a) 123 m   (b) $121.7°$ (c) 7350 m^2

29 (c) 5
    (d) Stretch in the x-direction, factor 2

30 (a) $-3\sin^2\theta - \sin\theta + 2$, $a = -3$, $b = -1$, $c = 2$
    (b) $0°$, $180°$, $199.5°$, $340.5°$, $360°$

31 (a) $4x - 3x^2$, $4x + y = 8$
    (c) $21\frac{1}{3}$

32 (a) $y = \frac{5}{3}x^3 - 3x^2 + x + 1$
    (b) $\frac{1}{5}$ maximum, 1 minimum
    (c) $\frac{1}{5} < x < 1$
    (d) 0, $1\frac{1}{5}$

33 (a) 12.3 m   (b) 26.5 m   (c) $40.9°$

34 $y = -x^2 + 3x + 5$

35 $240°$, $300°$

36 (b) The areas marked A and B are equal in
      magnitude.

37 (a) $2\sqrt{14}$ (b) $6\sqrt{3}$

38 (a) $16 + 96x + 216x^2 + 216x^3 + 81x^4$
    (b) 124

39 $y = -160x - 128$

40 (a) 0.6   (b) 81 850

41 (a) $1 + 24x + 252x^2 + 1512x^3$
    (c) 2.000 000 000 504

42 80 200

43 $\frac{1}{4}x^4 + x^2 - \dfrac{1}{x} + k$

44 (a) $3 - 3\sin^2\theta - 2\sin\theta$
    (b) $19.5°$, $160.5°$, $270°$

45 $CF = 5.83$ cm, $FH = 5$ cm, $CH = 6.40$ cm;
    angle $C = 48.0°$, angle $F = 72.0°$,
    angle $H = 60.0°$

46 (c) $135°$, $315°$

48 $-\dfrac{1}{x} - \dfrac{1}{2}x^2 + k$

49 (b) $0°$, $30°$, $150°$, $180°$, $360°$

50 (a) -1
    (c) It is the area of the unshaded region
       bounded by the curve, the x-axis and the
       line $x = 4$.
    (d) $29\frac{1}{4}$

51 (a) $2x - \dfrac{8}{x^3}$ (b) $y = \frac{1}{3}x^3 - 4x - \dfrac{4}{x} + 4\frac{1}{3}$

52 (a) -3, 3 (b) 36

53 (a) -24, 240 (b) 551

6   Geometric sequences

Exercise 6A (page 337)

1 (a) 2; 24, 48   (b) 4; 128, 512
    (c) $\frac{1}{2}$; 4, 2   (d) -3; 162, -486
    (e) 1.1; 1.4641, 1.610 51   (f) $\dfrac{1}{x}$; $\dfrac{1}{x}$, $\dfrac{1}{x^2}$

2 (a) $2 \times 3^{i-1}$ (b) $10 \times \left(\frac{1}{2}\right)^{i-1}$ (c) $(-2)^{i-1}$
    (d) $81 \times \left(\frac{1}{3}\right)^{i-1}$ (e) x^i (f) $p^{2-i} \, q^{i+1}$

3 (a) 11   (b) 13   (c) 7
    (d) 14   (e) 6   (f) 13

4 (a) 3; $1\frac{1}{3}$ (b) 2; $1\frac{1}{2}$ or -2; $1\frac{1}{2}$
    (c) $\frac{1}{3}$; 531 441   (d) $\pm\sqrt{2}$; 4

6 (a) 2   (b) 8th

7 (a) 3   (b) 14th

Exercise 6B (page 342)

1 (a) 59 048   (b) $-29\,524$
    (c) 1.9922   (d) 0.6641
    (e) 12 285   (f) 8.9998

2 (a) 2047   (b) 683
    (c) 262 143   (d) $\dfrac{1023}{512}$
    (e) $\dfrac{14\,762}{19\,683}$ (f) 19.843 75
    (g) $\dfrac{341}{1024}$ (h) $2 - \left(\frac{1}{2}\right)^n$
    (i) $\frac{1}{3}\left(64 - \left(\frac{1}{4}\right)^n\right)$ (j) $\frac{1}{4}\left(243 + \left(-\frac{1}{3}\right)^n\right)$

3 (a) 93   (b) -10 (c) $31\frac{7}{8}$ (d) 21 844

4 $2^{64} - 1 \approx 1.84 \times 10^{19}$

5 £2 684 354.55

6 £32 289.76

7 0.979 litres

8 $\left(\frac{3}{4}\right)^{n-1} - \frac{1}{3}$

9 (a) $\dfrac{x(1-x^n)}{1-x}$ (b) $\dfrac{x(1-(-x)^n)}{1+x}$

   (c) $\dfrac{x^{2n}-1}{x^{2n-3}(x^2-1)}$ (d) $\dfrac{x^{2n}-(-1)^n}{x^{2n-2}(x^2+1)}$

10 (a) $\dfrac{p}{q}; n$ (c) (i) np^{n-1} (ii) $-np^{-(n+1)}$

Exercise 6C (page 348)

1 (a) 2   (b) $\frac{3}{2}$ (c) $\frac{1}{4}$ (d) $\frac{1}{9}$

   (e) $\frac{3}{4}$ (f) $\frac{1}{6}$ (g) 3   (h) $\frac{1}{3}$

   (i) $\frac{20}{3}$ (j) 62.5   (k) $\dfrac{x}{1-x}$ (l) $\dfrac{1}{1+x^2}$

   (m) $\dfrac{x}{x-1}$ (n) $\dfrac{x^3}{x+1}$

2 (a) $\frac{4}{11}$ (b) $\frac{41}{333}$ (c) $\frac{5}{9}$ (d) $\frac{157}{333}$

   (e) $\frac{1}{7}$ (f) $\frac{2}{7}$ (g) $\frac{5}{7}$ (h) $\frac{6}{7}$

3 $\frac{1}{6}$

4 $-\frac{5}{6}$

5 3

6 19.2

7 (a) $\left(\frac{1}{5}\right)^{i-1}, \dfrac{2\,441\,406}{1\,953\,125}, 1\frac{1}{4}$

   (b) 2^i, 2046, not convergent

   (c) $8 \times 2^{-i}, \dfrac{1023}{128}, 8$

   (d) $\left(-\frac{1}{10}\right)^{i-1}, \dfrac{909\,090\,909}{1\,000\,000\,000}, \dfrac{10}{11}$

8 2 m

9 0.375 m east of O, 1.5 m

10 10 seconds

11 19 m

12 (a) Edge of table   (b) 8

Miscellaneous exercise 6 (page 349)

1 $6\frac{1}{4}$

3 $a = 3, r = -\frac{1}{4}; 2.4\left(1-\left(-\frac{1}{4}\right)^N\right), 2.4$

4 62

5 $\frac{1}{999}; \frac{4}{37}$

6 $\frac{4}{5}; 18$

7 $8\left(1-\left(-\frac{1}{2}\right)^n\right); 8, 13$

8 $r = 0.917; a = 40$

9 The sum of the infinite series is only 80 cm.

10 £56 007

11 6401

12 £200 000 $\left(1 - \dfrac{1}{1.05^n}\right)$; £77 217, £124 622, £153 725, £171 591, £182 559

13 $r = \dfrac{k-1}{k+1}$

14 $r = -\frac{1}{3}$

16 $\dfrac{(1-x)(1-x^{3n+3})}{1-x^3}; -1 < x < 1;$

   $\dfrac{1}{1 + x + x^2 + x^3 + x^4}, -1 < x < 1$

17 (a) $\tan^2 x°, x \neq 90(2n+1)$, where n is an integer

   (b) $\cos^2 x°, (180n - 45) < x < (180n + 45)$, where n is an integer

18 $\dfrac{(1+x)^7 - 1}{x}$

$$\binom{r}{r} + \binom{r+1}{r} + \binom{r+2}{r} + \cdots + \binom{n}{r} = \binom{n+1}{r+1}$$

19 Possible if $-1 < x < 1$; within these bounds, the larger the value of n the better the approximation.

7 Exponentials and logarithms

Exercise 7A (page 354)

1 $2^x > 1000$ (a) 10   (b) 20   (c) 40

2 $3^{-x} > 2000$ (a) -7 (b) -14 (c) -15

3 (b) From 1.21^x to 1.1^x is a stretch of factor 2.

4 (b) They are reflections of each other in the y-axis.

5 (a) Translation of 3 in the positive x-direction, or a stretch in the y-direction with factor $\frac{1}{8}$

   (b) Reflection in the y-axis

   (c) Reflection in the y-axis and a stretch in the x-direction of factor $\frac{1}{2}$, in either order

   (d) Translation of 4 in the y-direction

6 A stretch of factor $\frac{1}{2}$ in the y-direction

7 A stretch of factor 9 in the y-direction

8 (a) From b^x to a^x is a stretch of factor 2.
 (b) From b^x to a^x is a stretch of factor 3.
 (c) They are reflections of each other in the y-axis.

9 (a) $3.14159 = \frac{314159}{100000}$, $3.1416 = \frac{31416}{10000}$
 (b) $1.773188\ldots$, $1.773192\ldots$
 (c) $1.2^\pi = 1.77319$, correct to 5 decimal places.

Exercise 7B (page 356)

1 (a) $8 = 2^3$ (b) $81 = 3^4$
 (c) $0.04 = 5^{-2}$ (d) $x = 7^4$
 (e) $5 = x^t$ (f) $q = p^r$

2 (a) $3 = \log_2 8$ (b) $6 = \log_3 729$
 (c) $-3 = \log_4 \frac{1}{64}$ (d) $8 = \log_a 20$
 (e) $9 = \log_h g$ (f) $n = \log_m p$

3 (a) 4 (b) 2 (c) -2
 (d) 0 (e) 1 (f) $-\frac{1}{3}$
 (g) $\frac{3}{4}$ (h) $\frac{3}{2}$ (i) 7

4 (a) 7 (b) $\frac{1}{64}$ (c) 4
 (d) $\frac{1}{10}$ (e) $4\sqrt{2}$ (f) 6
 (g) $\frac{1}{256}$ (h) -10 (i) $\frac{1}{3}\sqrt{3}$

5 (a) 5 (b) $\frac{1}{2}$ (c) 2
 (d) 0 (e) 8 (f) 4

Exercise 7C (page 360)

1 (a) $\log p + \log q + \log r$
 (b) $\log p + 2\log q + 3\log r$
 (c) $2 + \log p + 5\log r$
 (d) $\frac{1}{2}(\log p - 2\log q - \log r)$
 (e) $\log p + \log q - 2\log r$
 (f) $-(\log p + \log q + \log r)$
 (g) $\log p - \frac{1}{2}\log r$
 (h) $\log p + \log q + 7\log r - 1$
 (i) $\frac{1}{2}(1 + 10\log p - \log q + \log r)$

2 (a) 2 (b) -1 (c) $\log 30\,375$ (d) 0
 (e) 3 (f) -3 (g) $\log 8$ (h) 0

3 (a) $r - q$ (b) $2p + q$ (c) $p + \frac{1}{2}r$
 (d) $-q$ (e) $p + 2q + r$ (f) $p - q + 2r$
 (g) $q - p - r$ (h) $4p + q - 2r$ (i) $p + q - 2r$

5 $c = b^r$, $b = c^s$; $\log_b c \times \log_c b = 1$

6 The hydrogen ion activity of cola is about 1000 times that of beer.

7 $20\log_{10}(5000P)$ (a) 63.2 microbars
 (b) The man's sound intensity is 6.02 decibels more than the woman's.
 (c) The amplitude is reduced by a factor of 0.316

8 (a) The magnitudes differ by 0.477.
 (b) The ratio of the amplitudes is 3.98.

Exercise 7D (page 365)

1 (a) 1.46 (b) 1.56 (c) 1.14
 (d) 1.22 (e) 3.58 (f) 1.71
 (g) -2.21 (h) 3 (i) -0.202

2 (a) $x > 1.89$ (b) $x < 1.43$ (c) $x \leqslant -1.68$
 (d) $x > 9.97$ (e) $x > 8.54$ (f) $x < -2$
 (g) $x \geqslant -2$ (h) $x \leqslant -5.61$ (i) $x \geqslant 3.77$

3 (a) 27 (b) 16 (c) 31
 (d) 16 (e) 19 (f) 100

4 (a) 74, 1.051×10^3 (b) 149, 1.047×10^{12}
 (c) 33, 5.049×10^3 (d) 45, 1.345×10^7

5 (a) 67, 9.550×10^{-4} (b) 71, 8.228×10^{-7}
 (c) 30, 9.524×10^{-5}

6 37

7 14

8 28

9 7

10 9.56

11 (a) 0.891 (b) 12 days (c) 19.9 days

12 (a) 1.79 (b) 2.37 (c) 0.486
 (d) -7.97 (e) 1.04 (f) 2.32

13 -0.301, -0.477

Miscellaneous exercise 7 (page 366)

1 (a) $\dfrac{1}{\log a - 2}$ (b) $\sqrt{\dfrac{5a}{2}}$

2 0.774

3 (a) $y = \dfrac{\log 5}{\log 3}x$; $c = \dfrac{\log 5}{\log 3}$
 (b) $y = x^{-2}$; $k = 1$, $n = -2$

4 $2 - \log 2$

6 $\log 3 - \frac{1}{6}$

7 $20 \times 1.1^{n-1}$; 18

10 $\log_2 \dfrac{x+2}{x}$, $\frac{2}{7}$

11 $x > 33.2$

12 (a) 5.35 (b) 3, 4 (c) 4, 2

13 (a) 2610 (b) -1300

14 (a) $x = 2(e^8 - 1)$ (b) $x = 6\log_e 2 - 2$

15 $p = r^q$, $r = q^p$

16 $a = b^p$, $b = c^q$, $c = a^r$

8   Factors and remainders

Exercise 8A (page 373)

1 (a) yes, $3x - 4$ (b) yes, $2x + 9$
  (c) yes, $4x + 3$ (d) no
  (e) yes, $3x + 2$ (f) yes, $2x - 5$
  (g) no   (h) yes, $3x + 8$

2 (a) $x - 3$ (b) $x + 17$
  (c) $3x + 11$ (d) $7x - 3$
  (e) $x - 3$ (f) $7x - 2$

3 (a) $x - 1, 4x + 5$ (b) $x - 3, 2x + 1$
  (c) $x + 1, 4x - 3$ (d) $x + 2, 3x + 4$
  (e) $2x + 1, 2x - 5$ (f) $4x - 1, 3x - 4$
  (g) $2x + 3, 3x + 2$ (h) $x + 3, 6x - 5$
  (i) $2x - 1, 4x + 3$

4 (a) $-14, x + 7$ (b) $9, 2x + 3$
  (c) $4, 2x + 1$ (d) $-2, 2x + 1$
  (e) $1, x + 1$ or $-2, -2x + 4$ (f) $4, 3x - 2$

Exercise 8B (page 376)

1 (a) yes, $x^2 - x + 2$
  (b) yes, $4x^2 + 8x + 3 \equiv (2x + 1)(2x + 3)$
  (c) no
  (d) yes, $x^2 + 2x - 1 \equiv (x + 1 + \sqrt{2})(x + 1 - \sqrt{2})$
  (e) yes, $x^2 + x + 1$
  (f) yes, $9x^2 + 6x + 1 \equiv (3x + 1)^2$
  (g) no
  (h) yes, $x^2 - 4x + 1 \equiv (x - 2 + \sqrt{3})(x - 2 - \sqrt{3})$

2 (a) $x + 1, x - 2, x + 3$
  (b) $x - 2, x - 2, x + 5$
  (c) $2x - 1, 2x + 1, 3x + 1$
  (d) $2x - 1, 2x - 1, 2x - 1$
  (e) $x + 3, 3x - 1, 3x + 1$
  (f) $x + 2, x - 1 + \sqrt{3}, x - 1 - \sqrt{3}$

3 (a) $(x + 1)(x - 3)(x + 4)$ $-4, -1, 3$
  (b) $(x - 1)(x - 3)(x + 1)$ $-1, 1, 3$
  (c) $(x - 1)(x - 5)(x + 3)$ $-3, 1, 5$
  (d) $(x + 1)^2(x - 5)$ $-1, 5$
  (e) $(x - 2)(x + 2)(x + 3)$ $-3, -2, 2$
  (f) $(2x + 1)(x - 1)(x + 4)$ $-4, -\frac{1}{2}, 1$
  (g) $(3x - 1)(x - 2)(x + 2)$ $-2, \frac{1}{3}, 2$
  (h) $(x + 1)(2x - 1)(3x + 2)$ $-1, -\frac{2}{3}, \frac{1}{2}$
  (i) $(x - 1)(x^2 + 3x - 1)$ $1, \frac{1}{2}(\pm\sqrt{13} - 3)$

4 (a) $6, (x + 1)(x + 2)(x - 3)$
  (b) $-13, (x - 2)(2x + 1)(2x + 3)$
  (c) $2, (2x + 5)(x^2 - 2x + 5)$
  (d) $3, (x + 3)^2(x - 1)$ or
    $-6, (x + 3)(x + 1 + \sqrt{13})(x + 1 - \sqrt{13})$

5 (a) $(x - 2)(x^2 + 2x + 4)$
  (b) $(x + 2)(x^2 - 2x + 4)$
  (c) $(x - a)(x^2 + ax + a^2)$
  (d) $(x + a)(x^2 - ax + a^2)$

Exercise 8C (page 380)

1 (a) $1, -5, 22$ (b) $1, 8, -11$
  (c) $3, -4, 0$ (d) $3, -1, -4$
  (e) $4, 1, 4$ (f) $7, 1, 8$

2 (a) $1, -3, 5, 2$ (b) $1, -2, 4, 22$
  (c) $1, 1, -1, 3$ (d) $4, 1, -3, 11$
  (e) $2, 7, -1, 0$ (f) $3, 0, -5, 10$

3 (a) $x - 2, -4$ (b) $x + 1, -7$
  (c) $2x + 7, 13$ (d) $x + 2, 3$
  (e) $2x - 1, -1$

4 (a) $x^2 - 3, 7$
  (b) $x^2 + 2x + 15, 71$
  (c) $2x^2 - 6x + 22, -71$
  (d) $5x^2 + 20x + 77, 315$
  (e) $x^2 - x - 1, -6$
  (f) $2x^2 + 7x - 1, 3$

5 (a) -5 (b) 13 (c) 50 (d) -355
  (e) $\frac{7}{8}$ (f) $7\frac{13}{27}$ (g) 0 (h) 279

6 -1

7 -2

8 -5

9 3

10 $1, -1$

11 $4, -3$

12 $2, 1$

13 $5, 3$

Miscellaneous exercise 8 (page 381)

1 $a = -3, b = 1$

2 $(\frac{1}{2}, 0), (\sqrt{2} - 1, 0), (-\sqrt{2} - 1, 0)$

3 $3x + 4, 2x + 3$

4 $a = -1, b = -10$

5 -6

6 $-1, \frac{1}{2}, -\frac{3}{2}$

7 (a) 2
  (b) $2, \sqrt{2}, -\sqrt{2}$

8 $(x - 3)(x^2 + x + 2)$; one root only as the discriminant of the quadratic is negative; one point only, as the equation for the intersections is the given cubic.

9 $x^2 + 4x + 6 \equiv (x + 2)^2 + 2$

10 $(-1, 1), \left(-\frac{1}{2}, 1\frac{3}{8}\right), \left(1\frac{1}{2}, -14\frac{5}{8}\right)$

11 (b) $p = -\sqrt{5}, q = \sqrt{5}$

12 5

13 $(-2, -20)$ minimum, $(-1, -19)$ maximum, $\left(\frac{2}{3}, 22\frac{2}{3}\right)$ minimum

14 (a) 84, 0; the remainder when p(x) is divided by $x - 2$ is 84; $x + 2$ is a factor of p(x).
(b) $-2, -1\frac{1}{2}, \frac{1}{2}$

15 (a) $y + 5x = 2, (2, -8)$
(b) $5y - x = -16,$
$\left(\frac{3}{2} \pm \frac{1}{10}\sqrt{545}, -\frac{29}{10} \pm \frac{1}{50}\sqrt{545}\right)$

16 $A(-\sqrt{3}, 0), B(\sqrt{3}, 0); (x - 2)(x + 1)^2$
(a) 2
(b) They touch at $(-1, -2)$.

9   Radians

Exercise 9A (page 389)

1 (a) $\frac{1}{2}\pi$ (b) $\frac{3}{4}\pi$ (c) $\frac{1}{4}\pi$ (d) $\frac{1}{6}\pi$
(e) $\frac{2}{5}\pi$ (f) $\frac{1}{10}\pi$ (g) $\frac{2}{3}\pi$ (h) $\frac{1}{8}\pi$
(i) 4π (j) $\frac{10}{3}\pi$ (k) $\frac{3}{2}\pi$ (l) $\frac{1}{180}\pi$

2 (a) $60°$ (b) $9°$ (c) $36°$ (d) $22\frac{1}{2}°$
(e) $20°$ (f) $120°$ (g) $112\frac{1}{2}°$ (h) $108°$
(i) $4°$ (j) $1080°$ (k) $-90°$ (l) $50°$

3 (a) $\frac{1}{2}\sqrt{3}$ (b) $\frac{1}{2}\sqrt{2}$ (c) $\frac{1}{3}\sqrt{3}$ (d) 0
(e) $-\frac{1}{2}\sqrt{2}$ (f) $-\frac{1}{2}\sqrt{3}$ (g) $-\sqrt{3}$ (h) $\frac{3}{4}$

4 (a) $s = 8.4, A = 29.4$
(b) $s = 7.35, A = 12.9$
(c) $\theta = 1.5, A = 48$ (d) $r = 20, A = 140$
(e) $\theta = 2.4, s = 12$ (f) $s = 8$
(g) $r = 8, \theta = 2$ (h) $\theta = \frac{5}{3}$

5 (a) 2.26 cm^2 (b) 1.47 cm^2
(c) 830 cm^2 (d) 9.05 cm^2
(e) 0.556 cm^2

6 6.72 cm^2

7 28.2 cm

9 26.3 cm^2

10 15.5 cm, 14.3 cm^2

11 28.5%

Exercise 9B (page 392)

3 By noticing that the reflection of the graph of $\tan(\theta - \frac{1}{2}\pi)$ in the y-axis, that is, the graph of $y = -\tan(\theta - \frac{1}{2}\pi)$, or $y = \tan(\frac{1}{2}\pi - \theta)$, is the same as the graph of $y = \dfrac{1}{\tan\theta}$

Exercise 9C (page 396)

1 (a) 0.12, 3.02 (b) 4.18, 5.25
(c) 1.18, 1.96 (d) 0.63, 5.66
(e) 2.51, 3.77 (f) 0.96, 5.33
(g) 1.33, 4.47 (h) 2.80, 5.95
(i) 0.17, 3.31

2 (a) 1.00, 2.14 (b) $-1.30, 1.30$
(c) $-2.06, 1.09$ (d) $-2.32, -0.82$
(e) $-1.72, 1.72$ (f) $-0.90, 2.25$
(g) $-2.50, 0.64$
(h) $-2.53, -0.62, 0.62, 2.53$
(i) $-\pi, -1.23, 0, 1.23, \pi$

3 (a) 0.66, 2.48, 3.80, 5.62
(b) 0.42, 1.46, 2.51, 3.56, 4.61, 5.65
(c) 1.91, 2.81, 5.05, 5.95
(d) 0.44, 1.13, 2.01, 2.70, 3.58, 4.27, 5.16, 5.84
(e) 0.23, 1.80, 3.37, 4.94
(f) 1.20, 1.94, 3.30, 4.03, 5.39, 6.13

4 (a) $-2.34, -1.85, -0.24, 0.24, 1.85, 2.34$
(b) $-2.12, -0.55, 1.02, 2.59$
(c) $-3.03, -2.20, -0.94, -0.11, 1.16, 1.99$
(d) $-2.49, -0.65, 0.65, 2.49$
(e) $-3.02, -2.39, -1.76, -1.13, -0.51, 0.12,$
$0.75, 1.38, 2.01, 2.64$
(f) $-1.35, -0.22, 1.79, 2.92$

5 (a) $-2.46, 2.46$ (b) $-2.06, 2.65$
(c) -1.01 (d) π
(e) 0.70 (f) -1.03

6 (a) 0.31, 2.63 (b) 1.13, 5.56
(c) 0.88, 4.02 (d) 1.20, 4.95
(e) 1.15, 2.74 (f) 0.25, 3.39

7 (a) 0.90, 2.25 (b) $-1.14, 1.14$
(c) $-2.19, -0.96, 0.96, 2.19$
(d) $-2.53, -0.62, 0.62, 2.53$
(e) $-\frac{1}{3}\pi, 0, \frac{1}{3}\pi, \pi$
(f) $-\frac{3}{4}\pi, -\frac{1}{4}\pi, \frac{1}{4}\pi, \frac{3}{4}\pi$

8 (a) 3.45, 5.98 (b) 3.69, 5.73
(c) 2.90, 6.04 (d) 0.99, 2.68
(e) 4.19, 6.28 (f) 0.17, 1.22

Miscellaneous exercise 9 (page 397)

1 3.6 cm, 10.8 cm^2

2 $\frac{1}{4}$

3 r^2

4 $\frac{2}{3}\pi, \frac{1}{3}\pi - \frac{1}{4}\sqrt{3}$

5 17 cm^2

6 (a) $-2.98, -0.16$ (b) $-\frac{1}{2}\pi, \frac{1}{2}\pi$
(c) $-\frac{3}{4}\pi, 0, \frac{1}{4}\pi, \pi$
(d) $-3.03, -1.69, 0.12, 1.45$

7 $\frac{1}{2}r^2(\theta - \sin\theta)$, $1.2 < \theta < 1.3$

8 $DE = 2r - 2r\cos\theta$

   (b) $y = 1 - \frac{1}{2}\theta$

9 $\theta = 2\pi - \dfrac{s}{r}$

10 0, 1.23, 5.05, 2π

11 (a) No roots
   (b) $-\frac{3}{2}\pi$, $-\frac{1}{2}\pi$, $\frac{1}{2}\pi$, $\frac{3}{2}\pi$
   (c) -2π, $-\pi$, 0, π, 2π

10 The trapezium rule

Exercise 10 (page 402)

1 (a) 2.12   (b) 0.75

2 5.73

3 3.09

4 (a) 1.26   (b) 0.94   (c) 0.8

5 8.04; the curve always lies beneath the approximating trapezia.

6 1.034; the curve always lies beneath the approximating trapezia.

7 The overestimates of the trapezium rule between 0 and 1, and 1 and 2 are exactly compensated by the underestimates between 0 and −1, and −1 and −2.

8 2.86

9 3.14

10 (a) 19.40   (b) Underestimates   (c) 6.25π
   (d) 3.10

Miscellaneous exercise 10 (page 404)

1 10.6

2 3.28; overestimate

3 1.701

4 0.52

5 0.70

6 51

7 (a) 1.41; the overestimate between 0 and 0.5 looks to be roughly balanced by the underestimate between 0 and −0.5.

8 1140 m

9 8.15 km

10 (a) 0, 1.708, 2.309, 2.598, 2.582, 2.141, 0
   (b) 34.0 m^2 (c) 3400 m^3

11 (a) 0.622 m^2 (b) 12.4 m^3 (c) 3.9 m^3
   (d) (b) overestimate, (c) underestimate

12 0.55

13 (a) $\frac{592}{3}$ (b) $98 + 70\sqrt{2}$

14 0.535, 0.5;
   $T = \frac{3}{8}h - \frac{1}{4} + \frac{1}{2}h^{-2}$;
   $h = 2 \times 3^{-\frac{1}{3}}$, or 1.39;
   $T = \frac{3}{8} \times 3^{\frac{2}{3}} - \frac{1}{4} \approx 0.530$

15 (a) $\frac{1}{3}$ (b) $\frac{1}{2}$, $\frac{3}{8}$, $\frac{11}{32}$, $\frac{43}{128}$
   (c) $-\frac{1}{6}$, $-\frac{1}{24}$, $-\frac{1}{96}$, $-\frac{1}{384}$
   (d) $E_n = -\dfrac{1}{6n^2}$ (e) 409, or more

Revision exercise 4 (page 407)

1 (a) £16 600   (b) Year 9
   (c) £$(475n^2 + 12\,325n)$ for $1 \leqslant n \leqslant 9$:
       £$(20\,400n - 34\,200)$ for $n > 9$
   (d) £13 500 × 1.05^{n-1}
   (f) Year 10

2 13.97, 15

3 $(x + 4)(x - 2)(x - 3)$

4 16.41

5 (c) $(2x + 1)(x - 1)(x - 3)$

6 25.5

7 (a) $a = b = 2$
   (b) $(x - 1)(x + 1)(x - 2)(x + 2)$; ± 1, ± 2

8 (a) 2.3   (b) 460 cm^2

9 (a) 10 700   (b) 140

10 (a) 1.08   (b) 12.5

11 (a) 0.925   (b) 40.0

12 (a) 0.432   (b) 148   (c) 150

13 4272

14 (a) −68   (c) $x^2 + 5x + 13$

15 3

16 (a) $\frac{5}{3}\pi$ (b) 109 cm   (c) 589 cm^2

17 193

18 96

19 (a) 1905   (c) 997 minutes

20 2π cm, $2(2\pi - \sqrt{3})$ cm^2

21 (a) 0.115   (b) 36, 594   (c) 0.1132

22 $a = 10$, $(x + 1)(x - 2)(2x - 5)$; 16; 18

23 $\log_b(xy^2b)$

24 (a) 15 years   (b) £7537.79

25 2.706

Practice examinations

Practice examination 1 for C2 (page 411)

1 $32 - 80x + 80x^2 - 40x^3 + 10x^4 - x^5$

2 (i)
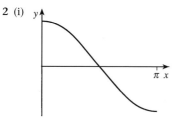

(ii) 0.846

(iii) Underestimate, as trapezia lie under the curve

3 (i) (a) $2\log_{10}x$ (b) $1 + 2\log_{10}x$

(ii) $y = \dfrac{100}{x} - 1$

4 (ii) $x^2 - 2x + 4, -6$

5 (i) $-\dfrac{1}{x} - 2\sqrt{x} + k$

(ii) $y = -\dfrac{1}{x} - 2\sqrt{x} + 3$

6 (i) 0.775 radians or 44.4°

(ii) 11.1 cm, 3.60 cm^2

7 (ii) $\frac{1}{6}\pi, \frac{5}{6}\pi$

(iii) 10, as the interval covers 5 periods of 2π each containing 2 roots

8 (ii) $\frac{1}{6}a^3$, 5.45

9 (i) $a + d, a + 5d$

(ii) (a) 660, 7.16×10^8 (b) 84

Practice examination 2 for C2 (page 413)

1 (i) 50.5°

(ii) 12.3 cm^2

2 (i)
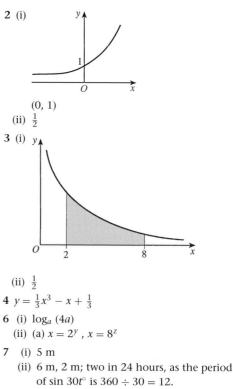

(0, 1)

(ii) $\frac{1}{2}$

3 (i)

(ii) $\frac{1}{2}$

4 $y = \frac{1}{3}x^3 - x + \frac{1}{3}$

6 (i) $\log_a(4a)$

(ii) (a) $x = 2^y$, $x = 8^z$

7 (i) 5 m

(ii) 6 m, 2 m; two in 24 hours, as the period of $\sin 30t°$ is $360 \div 30 = 12$.

(iii) (a) Between 7 p.m. and 11 p.m.,

(b) Between 7 a.m. and 11 a.m.

8 (i) (a) 5, 8

(b) 3; constant difference between consecutive terms

(c) 1 503 500

(ii) 216

9 (ii) 0.4776

Index

The page numbers refer to the first mention of each term, or the blue box if there is one.